MOOSEWOOD RESTAURANT DAILY SPECIAL

MOOSEWOOD RESTAURANT DAILY SPECIAL

More Than 275
Recipes for Soups, Stews,
Salads & Extras

THE
MOOSEWOOD COLLECTIVE

CLARKSON POTTER/PUBLISHERS
NEW YORK

Published by Clarkson Potter/Publishers
201 East 50th Street, New York, New York 10022
Member of the Crown Publishing Group

Random House, Inc. New York, Toronto, London, Sydney, Auckland
www.randomhouse.com

CLARKSON POTTER, POTTER, and colophon are
registered trademarks of Random House, Inc.

Printed in the United States of America

BOOK DESIGN BY SHERI G. LEE | JOYFUNSTUDIO
ILLUSTRATIONS BY ANDREA WISNEWSKI
Illustration on page 105 copyright © 1998 by Ellen Blonder.
Used by permission.

Library of Congress Cataloging-in-Publication Data
Moosewood Restaurant Daily Special
by the Moosewood Collective. — 1st ed.
    Includes index.
    1. Soups. 2. Salads. 3. Moosewood Restaurant.
I. Moosewood Collective.   TX757.M68   1999
641.8'13 — dc21   99-13543

ISBN 0-609-60166-0 (hardcover)
ISBN 0-609-80242-9 (paperback)

10   9   8   7   6   5   4   3   2   1

First Edition

Acknowledgments

We want to give very special acknowledgment to Judy Barringer, one of the original soupmakers in our salad days, and to Kris Miller and Therese Tischler, all founding mothers of Moosewood Restaurant. Their idealism, generosity, love of interesting food, appreciation of people, and flair for good cooking became the cornerstones of Moosewood's identity. Their friendship and support have sustained us for more than twenty-five years.

Our agents, Elise and Arnold Goodman, continue to be our trusted advocates and advisors. They've been our staunch supporters for fourteen years, providing guidance with good humor and great savvy.

We have nothing but admiration and gratitude for our editor, Pam Krauss. We rely on her good taste in prose as well as food. Somehow, she is able to help weave together the strands of our many voices, trimming and tightening them into a colorful, sturdy fabric: not a small feat. She tests our recipes at home and enthusiastically serves them to loved ones and colleagues. We love hearing her report, "They all asked for the recipe!" Thanks are also due to our book designer, Sheri Lee, and the other staff at Clarkson Potter whose work provides the finishing touches for our book.

To our helpful and adventurous friends and family, thank you for tasting, testing, and telling us what's what. If a recipe didn't please you, we didn't include it.

Illustrator Andrea Wisnewski is a rare find. When she sent her portfolio, we knew immediately that we were looking at a very unusual and distinctive sampler. We were struck by the dynamic, yet wonderfully graceful lines of her intricate, intriguing art, and we're thrilled with her work on this book.

We dedicate this book to our customers, so many of whom have ordered our Daily Specials and our Soup & Salad Plates over the last twenty-five years. Their demand for excitement, variety, and excellence encourages us to make each day's menu special.

Contents

Recipes by Chapter

Moosewood Restaurant is located in the cosmopolitan little city of Ithaca, in the beautiful Finger Lakes Region of central New York State, known for its vineyards, wineries, and dramatic gorges. Established in 1973, Moosewood has served natural foods with a vegetarian emphasis from a variety of international, ethnic, and regional cuisines for more than twenty-five years now. Moosewood is owned by the nineteen members of the Moosewood Collective and is staffed and operated by Collective members along with a dedicated and gifted crew of employees. Over the last few years, the restaurant has more than doubled in size, and although it looks less rustic than it did in the '70s, our approach to food is the same. We serve generous portions at moderate prices and see ourselves as part of an important movement toward cultivating more healthful diets based on the creative use of the freshest high-quality ingredients and natural whole foods. So at Moosewood, the focus is on preserving the integrity of the basic ingredients and paying careful attention to all aspects of preparation. We use lavish, exciting seasonings and make simple but beautiful presentations. And one of the main ways we do all of this is with the ever-changing Daily Specials that grace our restaurant's blackboard each day. At most restaurants, the daily special is a sandwich or a main dish offered in addition to the fixed menu. What's unique about Moosewood's menu is that it changes every day; the only selection that's *always* on the menu is

the Daily Special—a cup or bowl of soup, a salad, and a thick slice of bread.

And it's the most inexpensive meal we offer. We have loyal customers who have ordered the Daily Special as their "usual" for twenty years. This may sound monotonous, but it's not, because the choice of soups is continuously changing, and our customers can vary their salads with different dressings and toppings.

There are two other ways that soup, salad, and bread make a meal at Moosewood. Throughout all of the warm months and on many brisk, chilly days as well, we offer the Daily Special Salad Combo Plate, which is either one main dish salad or a combination of smaller salads, served with soup. Moosewood also serves main dish stews much like a number of the chunky, robust soups in this book with a house salad and bread. Whether it's the soup or the salad that is the main course, no one leaves hungry. ✳

Both at Moosewood where we decided the Daily Special each morning — and in our homes — juxtaposing one dish with another is an abiding delight of cooking. Resourceful mixing and matching mutually enhances each dish in a meal. That spicy little carrot salad looks so bright and beautiful next to the bowl of deep green spinach soup. It seems sweeter, colder, and crisper because the soup is earthy, smooth, and thick. The bread seems more fragrant and wholesome. Imaginatively and harmoniously combining dishes to make a meal provides constant variety and interest. So even if one dish is a reliable and beloved old standby, your menu today can be fresh and new. Although none of the dishes may be difficult to make or a showoff on its own, the whole meal can be exceptional. We all need something special daily. ✳

Moosewood Restaurant Daily Special is our latest effort to share the food we truly love and enjoy making. At Moosewood, soup, salad, and bread are a trio with tradition. Nothing else is needed for a satisfying and complete lunch or supper. A big salad and a cup of soup has become the meal of choice for many working people. A salad heaped in a plastic container and soup in a Thermos make the perfect portable meal. And for families that may not always be able to sit down together to eat, a pot of warm soup on the stove or a salad or two chilling in the fridge gives everyone equal access to wholesome, full-flavored meals without resorting to prepared foods. ✳

Soups soothe and comfort; salads stimulate and refresh. Their contrasting tastes, textures, and temperatures can serve as delightful counterpoints for each other. For example, we would serve hot and spicy Choklay's Tibetan Lentil Soup with cool and refreshing East Indian Fruit Salad. A rich substantial soup, such as Vegetable Pistou or Creamy Onion & Fontina Soup, is perfectly complemented by a light, green salad with a tonic sharpness such as Five-Herb Salad. Silky smooth and slightly sweet, Yellow Pepper Purée is a natural with another dish of Tuscan origin, Bean & Radicchio Salad, but it also goes nicely with crisp and chewy Bulghur Grape Salad, or with earthy Wilted Spinach & Portabella Mushrooms. That same Wilted Spinach & Portabella Mushroom salad is really wonderful with Jamaican Tomato Soup. ✳

When the Daily Special Salad Combo Plate is a combination of two or three salads, we usually choose a particular ethnic or regional theme such as Mediterranean, Caribbean, or East Asian, or a seasonal theme such as springtime or autumn harvest. And it's this kind of thinking we encourage you to apply to every meal you prepare. You'll find some of the pairings we like best at the bottom of each recipe, but the possibilities are truly endless. We hope to inspire you to make soups and salads central to your way of eating. Together, they can provide fortifying nutrition in meals that are practical and economical. According to our calculations, this book could give you at least a year of great home cooking without revisiting the same menu twice (although you may want to). You could eat soup and salad every day and stay fit and energetic.

Often, however, when cooking at home, most of us don't have time to prepare more than one soup, one salad, and a couple of accompaniments. So, we plan to have leftovers that can round out a menu or serve as the basis for additions and improvisations. For suggestions on making the most of leftovers see Transforming Leftovers, pages 8–9, which also gives pragmatic ways to incorporate bountiful seasonal produce and other ingredients you may have on hand into your meals. *

At the end of each recipe you'll find menu ideas for creating Daily Specials of your own. These options will help you plan meals with nutritional balance, contrasts in texture, pleasing visual presentation, and compatible flavors. *

Our recipes are reliable and easy to follow. They have been thoroughly tested in our own homes, prepared in quantity at Moosewood, and sampled and evaluated by our customers. Some of these dishes are delicate and light, some are fancy and elegant, many are hearty and filling, and most we think of as sturdy workhorses, recipes you'll use again and again. *

We have paid special attention to creating a broad variety of dishes that are lower in fat—more than 50 percent of the recipes included qualify, in fact—and we've included a page of tips for how to reduce the fat content in the foods you love to cook. You will find a nutritional analysis for each recipe. We believe that it's beneficial to have reliable information about food content and its nutritional breakdown. The feedback from our readers is that this information is useful and reassuring. We also know that time constraints plague many of our readers and that quick and easy recipes are especially appreciated. Fortunately, soups and salads are well within the realm of what's possible to accomplish for very busy people.

Beginning cooks can get a great start cooking at home with soups and salads. These recipes are somewhat forgiving; few require fancy techniques, exact measurement, or precise timing. You can even experiment with some different ingredients and proportions and still have a success. This is why our newest cooks begin their training in the Moosewood kitchen with tried-and-true soup and salad recipes.

At Moosewood, we are forever inventing new dishes to keep ourselves and our customers engaged. As always, our study of ethnic cuisines has been an inexhaustible source of inspiration. We have reinterpreted many of these dishes to make them vegetarian or more healthful or a little simpler to execute.

A few recipes require unusual ingredients that you might not keep in your pantry, but most have been adapted for ingredients that are easy to obtain. Transforming traditional dishes in these ways, while retaining their distinctive ethnic or regional character, is our forte and our passion. ✳

The recipes in this book are organized into three sections: Soups, Salads, and Accompaniments (a section devoted to breads, dressings, croutons, and garnishes such as edible flowers). There is an extensive Glossary of Ingredients & Techniques that provides practical information and intriguing lore about the ingredients we use and recommend, as well as basic tips on how to cook dried beans and grains, and other handy techniques. And on pages 388–395 we've sorted recipes into lists to help you find exactly the kind of recipe you're looking for, including brunch and buffet fare, low-fat, low-carbohydrate, quick and easy, vegan, and children's favorites. ✳

We love to eat, and we hate to be bored by food. The Daily Special is at the heart of Moosewood's cuisine. It's the most fundamental meal on our menu, and it has yielded some of our best cooking. It has challenged us to be creative, and we hope the results will inspire you. A pot of homemade soup has an almost uncanny power to communicate abundance, security, and well-being. Eating well is a central part of living well. Preparing food at home and sharing it with others provides opportunities for learning and teaching, creativity, sharing culture, and bringing people closer together. Sometimes, amid all of the distractions of our workaday existence, a little thing—a bowl of soup, say—comes into sharp focus. We experience a moment of pure awareness and feel grateful for the simple goodness of it. It's rare that we make a perfect dish, one that can't be improved, but what a piece of luck that we enjoy trying. It's one of the long-term pleasures of the kitchen. Just put on a pot of soup, make a salad, and break bread. The rewards are immediate and sustaining. ✳

About the Recipes

In most of our recipes, the ingredients list gives the quantity of prepared vegetables in cups. Particularly for less common vegetables, we add in parentheses the estimated number of whole vegetables needed to yield this amount. In some cases, when the exact amount of a vegetable isn't crucial, we simply call for "1 vegetable" and we mean a middle-of-the-road, medium-sized one. ✳

Peeling is mostly determined by the eventual function of the fruit or vegetable, your aesthetic judgment, and whether or not the vegetable was grown organically. We always peel sweet potatoes, parsnips, beets, and carrots. Fruit, potatoes, eggplant, and cucumbers are peeled or not on a case-by-case basis.

When we call for potatoes, we mean any non-baking potato unless otherwise specified. When we use whole canned tomatoes, we often use a knife to cut them right in the can before adding them to soup pot. If the tomatoes have tough skins, we usually squeeze them into the pot by hand and discard the skins. A convenient product that can always be used in place of chopped canned whole tomatoes is "fresh cut" canned tomatoes (also called diced tomatoes). ✳

If the amount of a fresh herb is in the ingredients list followed by its dried equivalent in parentheses, this indicates that either is fine, although we prefer the fresh herb if it is available. When only the fresh herb is listed, we do not recommend using its dried counterpart. If you prefer to use a fresh herb where we have listed only dried, use about 3 to 4 times the dried amount and add the fresh herb near the end of the cooking process. ✳

CBORD Group, Inc., of Ithaca, New York, prepared the data for the nutritional bars that follow each recipe. When a recipe suggests a range of servings, the analysis applies to the largest number of servings listed. Overall, the serving sizes in this cookbook are considered generous when compared with usual industry standards. ✳

When several choices appear in the original ingredients list, the nutritional calculations are based on the first choice that appears. The nutritional analysis does not take into account optional ingredients or garnishes for which no quantity is specified. No nutritional analysis was done for recipe variations. ✳

Tips for Lowering Fat

When you want to minimize the fat content in your diet, soups and salads are a good place to start. Low-fat cooking is not the primary focus of this book, but each recipe comes with nutritional data and we have listed the low-fat dishes on page 390–391. We don't recommend that you try to make a low-fat version of an unabashedly rich dish such as Welsh Rarebit Soup, but discreetly reducing the fat in most dishes is not difficult, and the flavor should be comparable to that of the original recipes. *

A lower-fat cooking technique can make a big difference in a soup's fat content. As we discovered in *Moosewood Restaurant Low-Fat Favorites,* sautéing the vegetables in as little as a teaspoon or two of oil, rather than the more usual 2 or 3 tablespoons, works as long as you reduce the heat and take a bit more time to allow the vegetables to release their own liquid. Sprinkling the vegetables with a little salt will hasten the release of juices. Cooking spray can reduce the amount of oil you use, but keep in mind that the equivalent of 1 teaspoon of oil is sprayed on in only about 5 seconds. We recommend using a mono-unsaturated spray oil, such as canola or olive oil. Sautéing in a small amount of fat is easier in nonstick pans. Although fats do carry flavor, for an even larger reduction in fat, you can omit the oil and cook the vegetables in a small amount of liquid such as vegetable stock, wine, or tomato juice. *

Increasing the amount of aromatic herbs or vegetables, such as onions or mushrooms, will boost the flavor in a low-fat soup. Sometimes a spoonful or two of miso added at the end of cooking does the trick. Although most of our soups can be made with water, using stock deepens the flavor without adding fat, and it enriches the soup with all of those water-soluble vitamins. *

To lower the fat in a creamy dairy soup, replace the milk or cream with thick and flavorful buttermilk or slightly sweet evaporated skim milk. Most reduced-fat cheeses don't melt well, and we don't recommend their use in soups. Neufchâtel is an exception and often just a tablespoon of this low-fat cream cheese can give a whole pot of soup a smooth creamy texture. Garnish the finished soup with nonfat sour cream or yogurt cheese. *

It is also possible to create creamy-seeming soups without milk products; sometimes soy milk or rice milk can be substituted. Soy milk has an overall fat content similar to low-fat milk, but its fat is unsaturated. Rice milk is often quite sweet, so it works best in soups that feature sweet vegetables such as carrots, onions, or sweet potatoes. *

Puréed soups that are thickened with potatoes, rice, oats, or bread rather than a roux are lower in fat. The technique used in Creamy Herbed Carrot Soup or Cream of Spinach Soup can be adapted for other vegetables. Oats added to a soup before puréeing can provide a surprisingly creamy texture, as in Creamless Broccoli Soup. Or whirl raw rice in a blender until powdered and add it to simmering soup to thicken it and boost it nutritionally. ✳

Salads can be a little more resistant to fat-trimming than soups, but sometimes you can alter the proportions of a salad recipe a bit without drastically changing its character. Reduce the higher-fat ingredients and add a little more of the lower-fat ingredients with strong flavors or interesting textures. When you do use a high-fat ingredient, be sure to get the most out of it. Sharp cheeses rather than mild and toasted nuts rather than raw provide more richness per gram of fat. ✳

Most of the fat in salads is in the dressing, but there are some good ways to improve the numbers. In this book, we offer several low-fat dressings that are as delicious as their full-fat counterparts. Experiment with other dressing recipes to reduce fat. Replace some of the oil with flavorful stock or fruit juice. In place of a stronger vinegar such as wine or cider vinegar, substitute some orange juice, apple juice, or a mild vinegar such as rice vinegar or balsamic vinegar, and the dressing will require less oil to offset the acidity. When you reduce the oil in a dressing, you may wish to add flavor in other ways: sometimes you can increase the herbs and other seasonings or add a dash of soy sauce for saltiness or mirin for sweetness. Grated ginger, minced scallions, citrus zest, and garlic can provide additional accents. ✳

Maybe the best way to lower the amount of fat you consume from dressings is simply to limit how much you use. It's easy to trim the amount of dressing called for in many salad recipes without a sense of deprivation. Serve the dressing for tossed green salads on the side in small individual cups. Then dip the tip of your fork into the dressing before spearing each bite of salad, and you'll find that the dressing taste is immediate. When you've finished your salad, you'll notice that you've consumed less dressing than if the leaves were coated. ✳

Transforming Leftovers

Having leftovers isn't such a bad thing. In fact, anticipating leftovers can be a creative part of meal planning: a sensible saving of labor and time. Often at Moosewood, we deliberately make more than we need of a particular element of a dish—extra beans, grains, sauce, or dressing that we plan to use to augment future meals. At home, leftover soup can be altered enough that it's quite different the second time around, and leftover salads can be paired with something freshly made to make a combo plate. Stews, thick gumbos, and chunky bean soups can be served the next day over rice, polenta, or other grains. *

Sometimes we freeze leftover soups until much later, when they won't even seem like leftovers. When there isn't quite enough soup left to make a meal, you may be able to "stretch" it by adding stock, milk, juice, or maybe puréed canned tomatoes. Soups containing grains or pasta, which tend to thicken with time, are especially easy to stretch this way. Most often we stretch a brothy soup by adding grain, beans, cheese, tofu, vegetables, or greens to bulk it up and modify it. For example, add black beans or briefly sautéed mushrooms and some chunky salsa to Butternut Squash Soup with Sizzled Sage. You can always add greens to a bean soup, giving it a nutritional boost in the process. Rice, barley, quinoa, or pasta can stretch a smooth soup. *

Consider serving leftover minestrone in the Italian way called *ribollita,* or "reboiled": soak slices of dense bread in the soup until the bread nearly dissolves and the soup thickens enough to hold up a wooden spoon. Then sprinkle it with grated cheese and bake it. You'll sing the praises of leftovers. *

Many smooth, puréed soups are good bases for creative variations. Transform a leftover soup like Creamy Herbed Potato into vegetable chowder by adding diced carrots and red peppers and some frozen peas and corn; or add puréed steamed broccoli to the soup. Two smooth, thick soups can be served side by side in the same bowl: Peach Soup and Raspberry Soup look lovely lightly swirled together. *

Sometimes a new topping or garnish is enough to spruce up a leftover soup. Take Yellow Pepper Purée, for example. The recipe calls for Parmesan cheese and croutons—and those are good, but on day two it will taste delicious and different topped with slivers of roasted red peppers and chickpeas. Or ignore this soup's Italian origin and push it toward the Caribbean or Southeast Asia by changing the spices. Or think of what it would be like with fresh cilantro, a squeeze of fresh lime juice, and a few crumbled tortilla chips. Try Oaxacan Potato Soup topped with chopped fresh tomatoes and avocado cubes, or serve Parsnip Pear Soup topped with crumbled blue cheese and Pumpernickel Croutons. Our section on accompaniments may give you ideas for new soup garnishes. *

Leftover salads don't lend themselves as readily as soups to quick changes, but they do adapt nicely to new surroundings. Seafood salads and fruit salads should be eaten in a day or two, but most bean, grain, pasta, and marinated vegetable salads keep very well in the refrigerator for several days. *

To create another meal from a leftover grain, bean, or vegetable salad, serve it on greens or as part of a chef's salad or combo plate. A salad such as Lentil, Rice & Fruit Salad or Balkan Roasted Vegetable Salad served on greens with a wedge of cheese and bread is a luncheon feast. Balinese Rice Salad is great on its own, but it's also wonderful in combination with a crisp slaw and Baked Seasoned Tofu. Leftover side-dish salads served together can become the main dish. Imagine a colorful grouping of Bean & Radicchio Salad, one of the Simple Tomato Salads, and Tunisian Carrot Salad or Syrian Beet Salad. *

When you know you're making more than you will immediately use of a composed salad, assemble the amount you want to serve and refrigerate the extras, wrapped separately, for later use. The vegetables you served with Roasted Garlic Aioli yesterday may be perfect served today with Gado Gado. Dress individual portions of a leafy salad, and the leftover greens will stay dry and crisp for tomorrow, when you can use a different dressing or topping: a green salad with Low-fat Tomato Basil Dressing and Fried Shallots is quite unlike the same salad with Best Blue Cheese Dressing and edible flowers. *

Some salads can serve as fillings. Stuff Turkish Roasted Eggplant Salad or Nepalese Egg Salad into pita for an easy sandwich. Wrap a cheese omelette around a few spears of Asparagus Vinaigrette. Stuff a tomato with Curried Potato Salad or serve leftover Melba Vinaigrette in a wedge of honeydew melon. As the risotto cooks, chop up the leftover Wilted Spinach & Portabella Mushrooms to add at the end. *

Making a soup or salad can be so easy if you work with what you have on hand. A leftover sauce could become the base of a delicious soup. Sauté a handful of green beans, a couple of carrots, and half a dozen mushrooms; stir them into the sauce and you've got soup! If you have leftover black beans, add some frozen corn, a jar of salsa, and some orange juice or water; heat it up and get out the soup bowls. Wondering what to do with plain leftover rice? If it's sticky, add it to a brothy vegetable soup, and if it's not, make rice salad. Keeping pantry items such as canned artichoke hearts, pimientos, and chickpeas on hand can help you transform the leftovers you find in the refrigerator into delightful meals. *

When we make a big pot of homemade soup, it's the goal of many of us to get at least a couple of meals from it. We're glad to see last night's delicious salad in our lunch bag. With all the time we save by serving a leftover, maybe there's time to make some fresh warm bread. *

Soups

Every day, Moosewood cooks pick up the kitchen phone to answer the "what's on the menu?" calls. "Hi. What kind of soup do you have today?" is most common. This seems to matter even more to our customers than what's for dessert. In the morning sometimes we hear, "Have you started making the soup yet? Maybe you could make my favorite?" and in the evening it's, "Hello, I've been thinking all day about the soup I had at noon. Do you have the recipe for that one?"

Soups have fed us since people have had pots to cook them in. It's no surprise that the words "soup," "sup," "sop," and "supper" all have the same etymology. Everyone seems to love good soup, which for many represents basic nourishment and the comfort of home. No wonder soup is the heart of Moosewood's Daily Special 365 days a year.

Soup is a wonderful meal at the close of day. It's also good for lunch or a snack. Some soups can be breakfast. Soup can be served as an appetizer, a first course, a one-dish meal, or even dessert. Soups are welcome any time of year and for all occasions, from the fanciest ceremonial dinner to supper at home in pajamas. The variety of soups is enormous. Ranging from familiar old favorites to exciting new discoveries, soups can be hot, cold, delicate, substantial, smooth, chunky, simple, complex, sweet, sour, bitter, bland, fiery, soothing, and stimulating. Soups can be inexpensive, easy to make, and healthful. There are quick last-minute soups and fine make-ahead soups. Every day is a good day for soup.

When we match a soup with a salad and bread for a Daily Special, we consider a number of factors: taste, of course, but also texture, temperature, and color. We usually look for contrasting characteristics in a soup and salad pair, such as a smooth yellow soup with a multicolored chunky salad. If time is a consideration, you may want to take into account the ease of preparation of the dishes in your meal. For instance, with a more time-consuming soup, select a quickly thrown together salad. At Moosewood, sometimes we couple a soup and salad from the same ethnic family. Other times, we mix cuisines for a seasonal theme. Trying different combinations is all part of the fun.

Most soups are fairly simple to make following a general model. Usually we begin by sautéing ingredients that form the base common to many recipes—onions, garlic, carrots, celery, perhaps spices or chiles. Then we add slow-cooking vegetables such as root vegetables, and a liquid such as water, stock, or juice. Next we add watery vegetables like tomatoes or squash. Leafy greens, delicate vegetables such as peas or asparagus tips, and fresh herbs are added at the end so that they remain vibrant. With this basic pattern in mind, you can improvise soups based on what looks good at the market or what happens to be in your refrigerator.

Even if you follow a recipe faithfully, one batch of the same soup is rarely an exact replica of the last. Maybe the garlic is a little more pungent or the tomatoes are sweeter than before. A different brand of pasta or another kind of miso can make a difference. The intensity of herbs and spices depends upon their growing conditions and time of harvest and upon their freshness when you add them to the soup. Sample what you are cooking and make adjustments to please your own taste, perhaps adding more salt or pepper, another pinch of your favorite herb, or a dash of lemon juice, wine, or soy sauce.

Look for ways to save time here and there. Rather than washing, peeling, and chopping all of the ingredients before you begin cooking, you may have time while the early ingredients cook to prepare the next ones to go into the pot. Make soup for today and stock for later at the same time; they probably contain many common ingredients and a simmering pot of stock requires very little attention. Or start today's soup while the stock simmers, and when the stock is ready, strain it directly into the soup.

Most soups reheat very well, and some are even better after the flavors have mingled during an overnight rest in the refrigerator. Reheat soups containing milk or eggs slowly and gently to prevent curdling. If a soup has thickened too much, thin it with a little water, stock, juice, or milk. When a brothy soup contains rice or pasta, we often cook the rice or pasta separately and add it at the end. Chilling often mutes flavors, so wait to adjust the seasonings until after the soup has been reheated. To keep soup piping hot at the table, warm the soup bowls in a 200° oven before serving the soup.

Stocks

Every night at Moosewood, toward the end of the evening meal, one of the cooks puts a huge pot of water and vegetables on the stove. Besides onions, potatoes, and celery, we might add a few things saved from the food preparations of the day—snipped ends of green beans, parsley and mushroom stems perhaps, maybe an apple or the leftover chopped scallions. After simmering for about 45 minutes, the vegetables have released their flavor, color, and nutrients, and the stock is done. The late-night pot washer strains the stock and refrigerates it. In the morning, the lunch cooks make delicious soups with this flavorful liquid.

Well, that sounds wonderful, you're thinking, but Moosewood has a professional kitchen with a well-oiled routine. What home kitchen has bushels of vegetables in the refrigerator and pot washers to finish up the work? We're here to persuade you, based on experience in our own homes, that making stock may take some extra time, but it's a relaxed activity and not at all difficult.

The majority of our soup recipes can be made with plain water, but many taste even better made with stock, and stock is essential to the flavor of some brothy soups. Organic vegetables are best for stock. It is not necessary to peel organic potatoes, sweet potatoes, or carrots. But if they're not organically grown, it is wise to peel them because some herbicides and pesticides are absorbed by the skin and scrubbing doesn't remove the residue. Don't worry about neatly chopping the vegetables; they'll be discarded when the stock is done. Avoid vegetables whose strong flavors can dominate or make a stock bitter: artichokes, asparagus, bell peppers, eggplant, and the whole *Brassica* family (broccoli, cabbage, cauliflower, Brussels sprouts, bok choy, turnips, rutabaga, and mustard greens). Because the color of beets bleeds into the water, use them only if you plan to make a beet soup. Be cautious about adding tomatoes to stock that will be used in a soup made with milk because the acidity may curdle the soup.

Vegetable stock keeps in the refrigerator for 3 to 4 days; store it in glass or plastic containers with tight-fitting lids. When we make stock at home, we usually make a double batch so that we can sock away half of it in the freezer for the rainy day when we've got to have soup right away. Freeze stock in widemouthed containers for easy removal and be sure to leave headroom because the liquid will expand as it freezes. Do not refreeze thawed stock.

At the restaurant, we never use bouillon cubes or powders or canned vegetable broth, but many of us keep them in our pantries at home. Read the labels carefully because many of these products contain sugars, fat, MSG and other additives, and too much sodium. Our favorite brands of canned vegetable broth are Pritikin Fat-Free, Hain Healthy Naturals, and Westbrae Natural. The bouillon cubes or broth powders we recommend are Morga and Frontier Herbs and Spices. Keep in mind that each of these products has a distinctive flavor that will become the underlying flavor of your soup. A stock you make yourself is fresher, better tasting, and probably more nutritious and lower in sodium; it can also be tailored to suit your soup.

We have six different recipes for stock in this book. Basic Light Vegetable Stock is our standard; it's simple to put together with everyday ingredients you probably have on hand. Dark Vegetable Stock, fortified with lentils and mushrooms, has an earthy, full-bodied appeal. The titles say it all with Garlic Stock and Mock Chicken Stock; both have great body and character. Asian Soup Stock complements Asian-style soups. Roasted Vegetable Stock is rich, deep, and hearty with concentrated flavor. In our soup recipes, we often recommend a particular stock; if none is specified, Basic Light Vegetable Stock will work fine.

Any of our stock recipes can be modified: mix and match the ingredients a bit. You can always add more garlic. For a sweeter stock, add more carrots and onions. If you like the effect of the lentils in Dark Vegetable Stock, try adding lentils to a different stock recipe. If you're going to make a fresh corn soup, add the corncobs to the stock for a stronger corn taste. Pea pods in the stock will make for an intensified pea soup. You can use leftover roasted vegetables or cooking water from beans or potatoes. Add dried mushrooms, sun-dried tomatoes, wine, konbu, miso, ginger root, or a few drops of dark sesame oil for more flavor.

Homemade Stocks

Basic Light Vegetable Stock

This is our standard vegetable stock and would work in any recipe that calls for stock. It is light in color and mild in flavor. Simple to prepare, it uses ingredients that most cooks have on hand. Many stock recipes call for mushrooms, but in this light stock they are optional; the stock will be flavorful either way, though stock made with mushrooms will be a slightly darker light amber.

YIELDS ABOUT 8 CUPS
TOTAL TIME: 1 HOUR, 10 MINUTES

PER 8-OUNCE SERVING: 24 CALORIES, 0.5 G PROTEIN, 0.1 G FAT, 5.6 G CARBO-HYDRATES, 0 G SATURATED FATTY ACIDS, 0 MG CHOLESTEROL, 154 MG SODIUM, 0.6 G TOTAL DIETARY FIBER

10 cups water
2 medium onions, quartered
2 medium sweet potatoes or 4 medium carrots, peeled
3 garlic cloves, unpeeled and smashed
2 large potatoes, thickly sliced
2 celery stalks, coarsely chopped
2 fresh parsley sprigs
1 bay leaf
½ teaspoon salt
6 peppercorns
4 allspice berries
1 cup mushroom stems (optional)

Wash the vegetables well, removing any soil or sand. Combine all of the ingredients in a large soup pot and cover with a tight-fitting lid. On high heat, bring the stock to a boil and then lower the heat and simmer for about 45 minutes. When the vegetables are quite soft and have lost their bright colors, the stock is done.

Strain the stock through a large colander or sieve, pressing out as much liquid as possible. Discard or compost the vegetable solids. Use the stock right away, or refrigerate it in a sealed container for up to 4 days, or freeze it for up to 6 months.

Asian Soup Stock

This delicately flavored broth needs only some tender young bok choy or snow peas, sliced seasoned tofu, and a splash of soy sauce to become a delightful, soothing, and light soup.

YIELDS ABOUT 8 CUPS
TOTAL TIME: 1¼ HOURS

PER 8-OUNCE SERVING: 24 CALORIES, 0.6 G PROTEIN, 0.1 G FAT, 5.5 G CARBO-HYDRATES, 0 G SATURATED FATTY ACIDS, 0 MG CHOLESTEROL, 170 MG SODIUM, 1.1 G TOTAL DIETARY FIBER

10 cups water
2 leeks, 2 large onions, or 2 bunches scallions, chopped
4 or 5 large carrots, peeled and sliced
4 celery stalks with leaves, chopped
10 garlic cloves, unpeeled and smashed
¼ teaspoon whole black peppercorns or Sichuan peppercorns
6 whole cloves
3-inch piece of fresh ginger root, sliced (about 1½ ounces)
4 or 5 dried shiitake (optional)
2 large parsley sprigs
½ teaspoon salt

Combine all of the ingredients in a large soup pot, cover, and bring to a boil. Lower the heat and simmer for 45 minutes to 1 hour. Strain the stock and use it right away, or refrigerate it in a covered container for up to 4 days, or freeze it for up to 6 months.

Dark Vegetable Stock

Traditionally, a dark stock is a standard meat stock made from beef bone marrow and leftover scraps, ends, peels, stems, cores, and skins of vegetables. This is a vegetarian version, sweetened with carrots, onions, and sweet potatoes, and given earthy substance with mushrooms and lentils. Use this stock as a base for hearty bean, lentil, and vegetable soups.

YIELDS ABOUT 8 CUPS
TOTAL TIME: 1½ HOURS

PER 8-OUNCE SERVING: 32 CALORIES, 0 G PROTEIN, 1.6 G FAT, 2.4 G CARBOHYDRATES, 0.8 G SATURATED FATTY ACIDS, 0 MG CHOLESTEROL, 160 MG SODIUM, 0.8 G TOTAL DIETARY FIBER

1 tablespoon canola or other vegetable oil
1 large onion, chopped
4 unpeeled garlic cloves, smashed with the broad side of a knife
10 cups water
2 carrots, peeled and chopped
1 large sweeto potato or potato, scrubbed and coarsely chopped
2 celery stalks with leaves, chopped
8 large button mushrooms or 1 portabella mushroom, chopped
1 cup coarsely chopped fresh parsley
2 bay leaves
¼ teaspoon whole black peppercorns
½ teaspoon salt
6 whole cloves
½ cup lentils, rinsed (optional)

In a large soup pot, heat the vegetable oil. Add the onions and garlic and sauté until lightly browned, 8 to 10 minutes. Add all of the remaining ingredients, cover, and bring to a boil. Lower the heat and simmer for about 50 minutes, until all of the vegetables are very soft. Strain the stock through a sieve or colander. Use the stock right away, or refrigerate it in a sealed container for up to 4 days, or freeze it for up to 6 months.

Garlic Stock

A basic stock with lots of . . . you guessed it: garlic!

YIELDS ABOUT 8 CUPS
TOTAL TIME: 1½ HOURS

PER 8-OUNCE SERVING: 16 CALORIES, 0.8 G PROTEIN, 0 G FAT, 4 G CARBOHY-DRATES, 0 G SATURATED FATTY ACIDS, 0 MG CHOLESTEROL, 160 MG SODIUM, 0.8 G TOTAL DIETARY FIBER

3 whole heads of garlic
10 cups water
2 or 3 bay leaves
8 whole black peppercorns
½ teaspoon salt
2 potatoes, scrubbed and coarsely chopped
2 or 3 celery stalks, coarsely chopped
2 medium carrots, peeled and coarsely chopped
¼ teaspoon dried thyme or 4 fresh thyme sprigs
4 fresh parsley sprigs

Remove the loose, papery outer skins of the heads of garlic and break them apart into cloves. (There is no need to peel the cloves.) Combine all of the ingredients in a large pot and bring to a boil. Cover, lower the heat, and simmer for 1 hour. Strain the stock and use it right away, or refrigerate it in a sealed container for up to 4 days, or freeze it for up to 6 months.

Mock Chicken Stock

This is powerful medicine. It only takes 20 minutes to throw it together in a big pot because all of the vegetables are rough-chopped. The remainder of the time is stove-top simmering. If this stock is eaten as a soup broth or with just a few added ingredients, its full flavor will come out upon simply seasoning with salt to taste.

Turmeric gives this stock a yellowish tinge, which becomes more evident the longer a soup sits.

YIELDS ABOUT 8 CUPS
TOTAL TIME: ABOUT 1½ HOURS

PER 8-OUNCE SERVING: 40 CALORIES, 0.8 G PROTEIN, 0 G FAT, 8.8 G CARBOHY-DRATES, 0 G SATURATED FATTY ACIDS, 0 MG CHOLESTEROL, 176 MG SODIUM, 1.6 G TOTAL DIETARY FIBER

14 cups water
7 cups chopped onions
4 cups chopped celery
4 cups peeled and chopped carrots
4 potatoes, scrubbed and chopped
2 heads of garlic, broken apart*
5 bay leaves
1½ teaspoons dried thyme
1½ teaspoons turmeric
½ teaspoon salt
½ bunch of fresh parsley

There is no need to peel the garlic cloves.

Put the water into a large stockpot on high heat. Add the vegetables to the pot, then stir in the garlic, bay leaves, thyme, turmeric, salt, and parsley. Bring to a boil and cook, uncovered, for 15 minutes. Then cover the pot, reduce the heat to low, and simmer for 1 hour. Set aside to cool and then strain. Use the stock right away, or refrigerate it in a sealed container for up to 4 days, or freeze it for up to 6 months.

Roasted Vegetable Stock

This rich, delicious stock is well worth the extra trouble of roasting and then simmering the ingredients. If you make the stock a day in advance, its flavor will deepen by the next day.

YIELDS ABOUT 8 CUPS
PREPARATION TIME: 15 MINUTES
COOKING TIME: 1½ HOURS

PER 8-OUNCE SERVING: 24 CALORIES, 0 G PROTEIN, 1.6 G FAT, 2.4 G CARBOHYDRATES, 0.8 G SATURATED FATTY ACIDS, 0 MG CHOLESTEROL, 160 MG SODIUM, 0.8 G TOTAL DIETARY FIBER

1 cup peeled and sliced carrots
1 cup chopped onions
1 cup chopped celery
1 cup scrubbed and coarsely chopped sweet potatoes
1 cup fresh or canned chopped tomatoes
5 garlic cloves, minced or pressed
1 tablespoon canola or other vegetable oil
½ teaspoon whole black peppercorns
½ teaspoon salt
10½ cups water

Preheat the oven to 400°.
   Combine all of the ingredients except the water in a nonreactive 9 × 12-inch baking pan and toss well to lightly coat with the oil. Bake, uncovered, for 30 to 45 minutes, stirring occasionally, until the vegetables are tender and browned.

   Transfer the roasted vegetables to a large nonreactive soup pot. Add ½ cup of the water to the baking pan, stir to deglaze the juices, and add them to the soup pot. Add the remaining 10 cups of water, cover, and bring to a boil; then lower the heat and simmer for 30 minutes. Strain. Use the stock right away, or refrigerate it in a sealed container for up to 4 days, or freeze it for up to 6 months.

VEGETABLE SOUPS

Vegetables in splendid variety and abundance are the heart of Moosewood's cuisine. We look forward to the arrival each morning of Dan, the diligent produce man, the conscientious and friendly owner of Fall Creek Produce in Newfield, New York, who faithfully delivers the goods to us "no mind the wind and weather." We take a moment from chopping mounds of vegetables in our busy kitchen to poke through the boxes to see if he brought some slender, crisp asparagus or to admire some particularly glorious tomatoes. As we're cooking, **we take great pleasure in the beauty of the colors, shapes, and feel of vegetables.** Each vegetable is unique and has its own particular aesthetic and nutritional gifts. And it is this more than anything that is likely to suggest to that day's menu planner a new and intriguing soup or salad for the Daily Special.

❋ Vegetables are packed with phytonutrients, vitamins, minerals, proteins, fiber, and antioxidants, and soup is a good way to get more of them into your diet. You won't have to "strive for five" as you gobble up a bunch of different vegetables in a delicious soup. All that good stuff is in the pot. ❋ Vegetable soups are important in every cuisine. In this section, we have recipes from Spain, Russia, Jamaica, Greece, Japan, Morocco, Mexico, India, Southeast Asia, and various regions of the United States. Some of the recipes are vegetarian renditions of soups that customarily contain meat. Our Mushroom Noodle Goulash is rich and delectable, just fine without the beef. Our Mock Chicken Noodle Soup, which includes fried wheat gluten, a Chinese canned product, is an interesting variation, and as a comforting remedy much like chicken soup. ❋ Some of these soups are familiar ones, rendered here with a twist. You may have had pumpkin soup before, but not quite like this—a lovely purée topped with a swirl of

Tunisian spices. Our French onion soup uses roasted onions and a Dark Vegetable Stock made with lentils and mushrooms. ✳ A few of these soups are recent discoveries on their way to becoming Moosewood favorites. Japanese miso soups are usually thin and brothy, but Ozoni is a hearty miso-based stew of potatoes, daikon radish, mizuna, and hijiki seaweed. It's popular for its great taste and its extremely low-fat profile. ✳ Sometimes the idea for a soup springs from the imagination of a talented Moosewood cook. With a sunny picture in her head of yellow and orange vegetables, Linda developed Golden Summer Soup. Infatuated with the sage in her garden, Susan came up with Butternut Squash Soup with Sizzled Sage. ✳ There are a number of chunky could-have-been-called-stew soups in this section. With all the component parts mingled into a whole, stews are one-pot meals. Still, you can't throw just anything into the pot. In our recipes, ingredient combinations are carefully chosen for taste, texture, and color, and the best cooking sequence is described. Most vegetarian stews are happily not long-simmering affairs, but are done rather quickly. And as a bonus, all you need for a Daily Special is a quick little side salad. ✳ You'll find some year-round soups here. Classic Tomato Garlic Soup and Roasted Red Pepper Coconut Soup, made with common pantry and freezer ingredients, are good anytime. We often pair these soups with a salad made of the freshest vegetables or fruits of the season. But sometimes it's the soup that celebrates the season. A stew of tiny onions, asparagus, peas, and new potatoes heralds the spring. Fall is the time for mushrooms and butternut squash. A soup of root vegetables or cabbage hits the spot on a cold winter day. Vegetable soups can mark the pattern of the year and add variety and spice to your life. ✳

Albondigas Soup

This delicious and flavorful soup is a popular classic in Spanish-speaking countries and Hispanic communities in the United States. Albondigas are tasty little spherical dumplings that are cooked in a simple, vegetable soup with a delightful saffron broth. For a Daily Special, we might pair this homey soup with a salad more flamboyant in color and texture.

To separate eggs, crack a cold egg on the rim of a bowl and gently break the shell in two, keeping the yolk in one half of the shell. Let the white drain off into the bowl by slipping the yolk from one half shell to the other.

SERVES 6 TO 8
YIELDS 12 CUPS
TOTAL TIME: 1 HOUR

PER 12-OUNCE SERVING: 250 CALORIES, 7.5 G PROTEIN, 6.9 G FAT, 39.9 G CARBO-HYDRATES, 1.8 G SATURATED FATTY ACIDS, 1057 MG SODIUM, 3.5 G TOTAL DIETARY FIBER

BROTH

2 tablespoons canola or other vegetable oil
1 cup chopped onions
4 garlic cloves, minced or pressed
1 cup peeled and chopped carrots
2 celery stalks, diced
4 cups thinly sliced potatoes
8 cups boiling water
1 teaspoon crumbled saffron threads
1 teaspoon paprika
2 teaspoons salt
2 tablespoons chopped fresh cilantro

ALBONDIGAS

1 small onion, chopped
2 garlic cloves, minced or pressed
2 cups fresh bread crumbs*
3 tablespoons chopped fresh parsley
½ teaspoon salt
2 eggs, separated*
a handful of unbleached white flour

*If using store-bought or dry-toasted bread crumbs, use 3 eggs.

In a large soup pot, heat the oil and sauté the onions and garlic on medium heat until the onions are translucent, about 10 minutes. Add the carrots, celery, potatoes, boiling water, saffron, paprika, salt, and cilantro. Cover and simmer for about 30 minutes.

While the broth simmers, combine the onions, garlic, bread crumbs, parsley, salt, and egg yolks in a food processor and whirl for about 5 minutes to form a very smooth paste. Scrape this dough into a bowl.

Beat the egg whites until stiff. Gently fold them by thirds into the dough. Dust a plate with flour. With a teaspoon, scoop up little balls of dough about the size of quarters, and with your fingers or another spoon, push them onto the plate. Carefully drop the whole batch of albondigas into the simmering soup. They will first sink and then float to the top. About 5 minutes after they rise, the soup is ready.

DAILY SPECIAL

MENU IDEAS Andean Quinoa & Corn Salad (page 189) ✻ **Florida Salad with Ginger Dressing (page 263)** ✻ **Golden Tomato Avocado Salad (page 268)** ✻ **Tropical Fruit & Shrimp Salad (page 312)** ✻ **tossed green salad with Low-fat Tomato Basil Dressing (page 321)**

Artichoke Heart Soup

From the Iberian peninsula to the Fertile Crescent, artichoke soups grace the table in countless varieties, adding zest and distinctive flavor to meals. If you already have vegetable stock on hand, this light, tangy soup is ready in just half an hour—elegant and simple. When creating a Daily Special combo, choose one or two salads of Mediterranean origin.

SERVES 4 TO 6
YIELDS 12 CUPS
TOTAL TIME: 30 MINUTES

PER 16-OUNCE SERVING: 144 CALORIES, 6.6 G PROTEIN, 2.9 G FAT, 25.8 G CARBO-HYDRATES, 0.4 G SATURATED FATTY ACIDS, 0 MG CHOLESTEROL, 730 MG SODIUM, 8.2 G TOTAL DIETARY FIBER

1 tablespoon olive oil
1 cup thinly sliced onions
3 garlic cloves, minced or pressed
2 celery stalks with leaves
5 artichoke hearts (14-ounce can, drained)*
1 cup chopped tomatoes
2 cups fresh, frozen, or canned peas
8 cups Garlic Stock (page 19) or other vegetable stock
1 tablespoon fresh lemon juice
1 to 2 tablespoons chopped fresh basil (½ teaspoon dried)
1 teaspoon salt
¼ teaspoon freshly ground black pepper

grated Parmesan or Pecorino Romano cheese (optional)
chopped fresh parsley (optional)

A 9-ounce frozen package will also work fine. Thaw the artichoke hearts or run the package under warm water to separate and soften them before slicing.

Warm the oil in a large nonreactive soup pot and sauté the onions and garlic on medium heat for about 5 minutes, until lightly browned, stirring occasionally. Meanwhile, thinly slice the celery to make about 1 cup and cut the artichoke hearts into eighths. When the onions are golden brown, add the artichoke hearts and celery and cook for 5 minutes, continuing to stir.

Stir in the tomatoes and peas and gently simmer for about 5 more minutes. Add the stock, lemon juice, basil, salt, and pepper, increase the heat to medium-high, and cook for about 10 minutes.

If you wish, serve topped with grated cheese and chopped parsley.

DAILY SPECIAL

MENU IDEAS **Greek Pasta Salad (page 214)** ✳ **Orzo & Pesto Stuffed Tomatoes (page 223)** ✳ **North African Roasted Cauliflower (page 279)** ✳ **North African Couscous Salad (page 222)** ✳ **Asparagus Vinaigrette (page 248) with Filo Croutons (page 342)** ✳ **French Barley Salad (page 210)**

Butternut Squash Soup with Sizzled Sage

The burnished gold of this elegant but easily prepared soup can bring warmth and brightness to a winter holiday party or a crisp autumn evening. The tantalizing aroma and light crunch of the tender, delicate sage leaves provides the perfect garnish for the sweet and creamy texture of butternut squash.

SERVES 4 TO 6
YIELDS 10 CUPS
PREPARATION TIME: 30 MINUTES
BAKING TIME: 55 TO 60 MINUTES

PER 11.5-OUNCE SERVING: 245 CALO-RIES, 2.4 G PROTEIN, 11.5 G FAT, 22.2 G CARBOHYDRATES, 2.4 G SATURATED FATTY ACIDS, 3 MG CHOLESTEROL, 420 MG SODIUM, 1.2 G TOTAL DIETARY FIBER

¼ cup olive oil
2 or 3 small butternut squash (about 3 pounds)
6 unpeeled garlic cloves
2 large Spanish onions, peeled and quartered
¼ cup water
3 cups apple juice or vegetable stock*
½ teaspoon dried thyme
¼ teaspoon ground or freshly grated nutmeg
1 teaspoon salt, or more to taste
ground black pepper to taste
2 teaspoons butter
20 fresh sage leaves, sliced on the diagonal

* *If you like, replace the apple juice or stock with a combination of 2 cups of apple cider and 1 cup of water (see Note).*

Preheat the oven to 400°. Brush the bottom of a large baking pan with about 2 tablespoons of the olive oil and set aside.

Cut the squash through the stem ends into halves, prick the skin in several places with a knife, and scoop out the seeds with a spoon. Brush the cut surfaces with about a tablespoon of the olive oil. Nest the garlic inside the squash cavities and place the squash halves in the pan cut side down. Add the onions to the pan and brush with the remaining olive oil.

Pour the water into the bottom of the pan, cover with aluminum foil, and bake for 50 minutes. Uncover and bake for 5 to 10 minutes more, until the squash is tender and the onions are soft. When the squash is cool enough to handle, scoop out the flesh. Squeeze the garlic cloves out of their skins and discard the skins.

In batches in a blender, combine the baked vegetables, apple juice or stock, thyme, nutmeg, salt, and pepper and purée until smooth. Pour the soup into a pot and heat gently.

In a small skillet, melt the butter and sauté the sage leaves until dark and curled. Garnish each bowl of soup with the sage leaves.

Note Using only apple juice or cider yields a thicker, sweeter soup. Using veg-etable stock or replacing part of the juice or cider with water yields a thinner, more savory soup. If the soup becomes too thick, add more water or stock and adjust the seasonings.

DAILY SPECIAL

MENU IDEAS **Solstice Salad (page 227)** ✳ **Artichoke Heart & Bulghur Salat (page 190)** ✳ **Fattoush (page 209)** ✳ **Fennel Salad with Blue Cheese (page 260)** ✳ **Bulghur Grape Salad (page 200)**

Caribbean Sweet Potato Coconut Soup

With the tropical flavors of ginger, coconut, and rum, this golden soup is silky smooth and piquant. It's delicious either unadorned or topped with toasted coconut, crunchy croutons, scallions, or cilantro.

SERVES 4 TO 6
YIELDS 8 CUPS
TOTAL TIME: 50 MINUTES

PER 12-OUNCE SERVING: 272 CALORIES, 4.4 G PROTEIN, 8.8 G FAT, 42.8 G CARBO-HYDRATES, 4.2 G SATURATED FATTY ACIDS, 0 MG CHOLESTEROL, 311 MG SODIUM, 4.2 G TOTAL DIETARY FIBER

2 cups chopped onions
⅔ cup chopped celery
1 tablespoon canola or other vegetable oil
1 tablespoon grated fresh ginger root
1 teaspoon curry powder
¼ teaspoon ground nutmeg
2 bay leaves
½ teaspoon salt
3 cups water or Basic Light Vegetable Stock (page 16)
4 cups peeled and cubed sweet potatoes
½ teaspoon freshly grated lemon or orange peel
2 tablespoons dark rum
1 cup pineapple or orange juice
1¾ cups reduced-fat coconut milk (14-ounce can)
2 tablespoons fresh lemon or lime juice, or to taste

chopped cilantro or scallions (optional)
toasted unsweetened coconut flakes* (optional)

* To toast shredded coconut, spread it on an unoiled baking sheet and toast at 350° in a standard oven or a toaster oven for 2 to 3 minutes, until lightly golden.

In a soup pot, sauté the onions and celery in the oil until the onions are translucent, about 10 minutes. Cover the pot and stir often to prevent sticking.

Add the ginger, curry, nutmeg, bay leaves, and salt and sauté for another minute, stirring constantly. Add the water or stock, sweet pota-toes, grated citrus peel, and rum. Cover and bring to a boil. Reduce the heat and simmer until the vegetables are tender, 15 to 20 minutes.

Remove and discard the bay leaves. Pour the pineapple or orange juice and the coconut milk into the soup pot. Purée the soup in a blender in batches until smooth (see Note). Reheat gently, if necessary. Stir in the lemon or lime juice.

If desired, garnish with cilantro or scallions and/or toasted coconut.

Note If you prefer a brothier soup, add up to ½ cup more water or stock.

MENU IDEAS **Alabama Hot Slaw (page 245)** ✳ **Golden Tomato Avocado Salad (page 268)** ✳ **Kale Salad (page 272)** ✳ **Tropical Fruit & Shrimp Salad (page 312)** ✳ **Spinach with Cilantro Cashew Dressing (page 289)** ✳ **Southern Wheat-free Cornbread (page 335)** ✳ **Pineapple Passion (page 265)**

Classic Tomato Garlic Soup

This soup is a Moosewood classic. The recipe has been slowly evolving for twenty-five years while Tomato Garlic Soup, in all its incarnations, remains a perennial customer favorite.

We love it, too — it's fast, it's easy, *and* it's versatile. Add a pinch of saffron and some cooked rice or a few tortellini. Replace the Parmesan cheese with a spoonful of pesto. Add chickpeas and feta cheese. Or try our Mexican variation below. They're all good!

SERVES 6 TO 8
YIELDS 8 CUPS
TOTAL TIME: 30 TO 35 MINUTES

PER 8-OUNCE SERVING: 190 CALORIES, 3.9 G PROTEIN, 9.6 G FAT, 22.7 G CARBO-HYDRATES, 2.5 G SATURATED FATTY ACIDS, 6 MG CHOLESTEROL, 810 MG SODIUM, 1.6 G TOTAL DIETARY FIBER

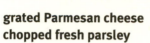

2 tablespoons olive oil
4 to 6 garlic cloves, minced or pressed
1 tablespoon paprika
6 cups tomato juice (46-ounce can)*
1 cup water or Basic Light Vegetable Stock (page 16)
¼ cup dry sherry

HERBED CROUTONS
4 cups small bread cubes
1½ tablespoons olive oil
1½ tablespoons butter
pinch of dried thyme
pinch of dried marjoram

grated Parmesan cheese
chopped fresh parsley

* Or two undrained 28-ounce cans of tomatoes puréed until smooth.

Preheat the oven to 350°.
In a nonreactive soup pot, warm the olive oil. Add the garlic and sauté, stirring constantly, until sizzling and golden, 1 to 2 minutes. Sprinkle in the paprika and cook for about 30 seconds more; be careful not to scorch the paprika or the soup will have a bitter flavor. Add the tomato juice, water or stock, and sherry. Cover the pot and bring the soup to a boil; then reduce the heat and simmer for 10 to 15 minutes.

While the soup simmers, make the croutons. Spread the bread cubes on an unoiled baking sheet and bake until crisp and dry, 10 to 15 minutes. In a very small saucepan or in the microwave, heat the olive oil, butter, thyme, and marjoram until the butter has melted. Pour the herbed butter over the toasted bread cubes and toss to coat well. Let the croutons cool and crisp up on the baking sheet.

Serve topped with croutons, Parmesan, and parsley.

Variation For Mexican Sopa de Tortilla, omit the paprika and sherry and add 1 seeded and minced fresh chile, ½ cup minced onions, ½ cup minced green bell peppers, 1 teaspoon ground cumin, and 1 teaspoon ground coriander. Sauté the chile, onions, bell peppers, and garlic for about 5 minutes. Add the spices and liquids and proceed as above. Serve topped with grated Monterey Jack cheese, crushed tortilla chips, and chopped fresh cilantro.

DAILY SPECIAL

MENU IDEAS **Wilted Spinach & Portabella Mushrooms (page 239)** ✳ **Roasted Garlic Aioli Salad (page 225)** ✳ **Pinzimonio (page 280)** ✳ **Farfalle e Fagiole Salad (page 208)** ✳ **Three-Bean Pasta Salad (page 232)**

Creamless Broccoli Soup

Yes, this soup takes the cream out of "creamy," but we promise you'll never miss a drop of it. The secret ingredient in this silky, rich, and robust vegan soup is—oatmeal! Who would ever guess?

For a Daily Special, we would complement this pale green, mildly seasoned soup with a colorful and more assertively seasoned salad. If you'd like to pair this soup with a vegan salad, see page 394.

SERVES 4 TO 6
YIELDS 7½ CUPS
TOTAL TIME: 50 MINUTES

PER 10-OUNCE SERVING: 109 CALORIES, 5.8 G PROTEIN, 3.4 G FAT, 16.8 G CARBO-HYDRATES, 0.8 G SATURATED FATTY ACIDS, 0 MG CHOLESTEROL, 239 MG SODIUM, 5.4 G TOTAL DIETARY FIBER

1 tablespoon canola or other vegetable oil
2 cups chopped onions
¼ cup diced celery
2 garlic cloves, minced or pressed
½ teaspoon salt
2 large broccoli stalks
4½ cups water or vegetable stock
⅓ cup quick-cooking oatmeal*
1 tablespoon fresh lemon juice
1 tablespoon chopped fresh dill (1 teaspoon dried)
½ teaspoon ground black pepper

fresh dill sprigs, paper-thin lemon slices, or minced fresh chives

*Or use a scant ½ cup of old-fashioned rolled oats, whirled in a blender for about 15 seconds.

In a soup pot, combine the oil, onions, celery, garlic, and salt and cook, covered, on medium heat for 10 minutes, stirring often. Meanwhile, rinse the broccoli, cut into 4 to 5 cups of florets, and peel and chop the stems to make about 2 cups. Reserve 1 cup of the florets.

When the onions are translucent, add 4 cups of the water or stock and all of the broccoli except for the reserved florets. Cover and bring to a boil; then lower the heat and simmer for 5 minutes. Add the oats and simmer gently for about 10 minutes, stirring often, until the broccoli is tender and the soup begins to thicken. Remove from the heat, and then stir in the lemon juice, dill, and pepper. Working in batches, purée the soup in a blender until smooth.

Bring the remaining ½ cup water to a boil in a small saucepan. Add the reserved broccoli florets and cook, covered, until they are bright green and crisp-tender, 3 to 5 minutes. Stir the florets and their cooking water into the soup.

Serve garnished with dill sprigs, lemon slices, or minced chives.

MENU IDEAS **Curried Rice Salad (page 205)** ✳ **Curried Potato Salad (page 255)** ✳ **Fattoush (page 209)** ✳ **Orzo & Pesto Stuffed Tomatoes (page 223)** ✳ **Composed Beet Salad (page 254)** ✳ **French Pasta Salad (page 211)**

Curried Cauliflower Soup

Cauliflower and potatoes are a heavenly couple when curried. Try this beautiful golden soup flecked with the deep green of fresh cilantro. The addition of basmati rice both enhances the curry spices and adds an interesting flavor of its own.

This soup goes well with salads of Indian origin but is also good in a meal with flavors of the Caribbean, southern Africa, and southern United States.

SERVES 4 TO 6
YIELDS ABOUT 7½ CUPS
PREPARATION TIME: 10 MINUTES
COOKING TIME: 30 MINUTES

PER 11-OUNCE SERVING: 145 CALORIES, 3.2 G PROTEIN, 5.5 G FAT, 22.5 G CARBOHYDRATES, 1.3 G SATURATED FATTY ACIDS, 0 MG CHOLESTEROL, 468 MG SODIUM, 3.4 G TOTAL DIETARY FIBER

2 tablespoons canola or other vegetable oil
1½ cups chopped onions
1 tablespoon minced fresh chiles, seeds removed for a milder "hot"
1 tablespoon grated fresh ginger root
dash of salt
1 teaspoon turmeric
1 teaspoon ground cumin
1 teaspoon ground coriander
½ teaspoon ground cinnamon
2 cups cubed white or red potatoes
4 cups cauliflower florets (about 1 medium head)
4 cups water or vegetable stock
1 teaspoon salt
¼ cup raw white basmati rice
1 tablespoon fresh lemon juice
1 teaspoon sugar
2 to 3 tablespoons chopped fresh cilantro
salt and ground black pepper to taste

plain nonfat yogurt (optional)

In a soup pot, heat the oil on low heat. Add the onions, chiles, and ginger and sprinkle with a dash of salt. Cover and cook, stirring occasionally, for about 10 minutes, or until the onions are translucent.

Add the turmeric, cumin, coriander, and cinnamon and cook for 1 to 2 minutes, stirring constantly to keep the spices from burning. Add the potatoes, cauliflower, water or stock, and salt, and then cover and bring to a boil. Meanwhile, rinse the rice. When the water boils, add the rice to the pot, cover, and simmer until the vegetables and rice are tender, about 15 minutes.

In a blender, purée about 2 cups of the soup and return it to the pot. Stir in the lemon juice, sugar, and cilantro. Add salt and pepper to taste.

Serve topped with a dollop of yogurt, if desired.

MENU IDEAS **Indian Green Beans & Red Peppers (page 270)** * **Spinach with Cilantro Cashew Dressing (page 289)** * **East Indian Fruit Salad (page 258)** * **Louisiana Black-eyed Pea Salad (page 221)**

Eastern European Vegetable Stew

With so many sweet root vegetables and greens, this Eastern European–style soup has it all. It's hearty, healthful, quite pretty, and absolutely delectable — one of our best.

SERVES 6 TO 8
YIELDS 12 CUPS
PREPARATION TIME: 30 MINUTES
COOKING TIME: 30 MINUTES

PER 12.5-OUNCE SERVING: 113 CALORIES, 2.2 G PROTEIN, 3.9 G FAT, 19 G CARBOHYDRATES, 1 G SATURATED FATTY ACIDS, 0 MG CHOLESTEROL, 695 MG SODIUM, 2.3 G TOTAL DIETARY FIBER

2 tablespoons vegetable oil or olive oil
2 cups chopped onions
3 garlic cloves, minced or pressed
1 cup peeled and diced potatoes
1 cup peeled and diced carrots
1 cup peeled and diced parsnips
2 cups peeled and diced turnips and/or rutabaga
2 cups peeled and diced beets
6 cups water
2 teaspoons salt
2 bay leaves
1 tablespoon minced fresh thyme and/or dill (1 teaspoon dried)
¼ cup cider vinegar
5 cups rinsed and chopped beet greens, Swiss chard, or spinach
salt and ground black pepper to taste

½ cup sour cream or plain nonfat yogurt (optional)

In a large soup pot, heat the oil and add the onions and garlic. Cover and sauté on medium heat for about 7 minutes, stirring frequently, until the onions are soft. Add the potatoes, carrots, parsnips, turnips and/or rutabaga, beets, water, salt, bay leaves, and herbs. Cover and bring to a boil; then cook on medium-low heat for 15 minutes.

Add the vinegar and greens. Gently simmer for 5 to 10 minutes, until the greens are tender. Add salt and pepper to taste. Find and discard the bay leaves.

Serve garnished with a dollop of sour cream or yogurt, if you like.

DAILY SPECIAL

MENU IDEAS **Lobio (page 274)** ✳ **Celeriac Remoulade (page 253)** ✳ **Broiled Tofu & Sugar Snap Peas (page 199)** ✳ **tossed green salad with Zesty Feta Garlic Dressing (page 326) or Best Blue Cheese Dressing (page 318)** ✳ **Pumpernickel Croutons (page 349)** ✳ **Herbed Cheese Quick Bread (page 332)**

Faux Pho

At Moosewood, we find it amusing to refer to this soup as "faux pho." Traditional Vietnamese pho is very rich with beef stock, so our meatless soup is lighter. But the cooking shallots and lemongrass evoke the smells and flavors of pho. After simmering the dumplings, the broth is rich and "meaty."

The ages-old dumpling-making technique does take some time, particularly the first time, but it's fun to roll those little balls around in the rice flour once you see how it works. Children often enjoy helping, and once made, the dumplings freeze well (see Note).

We like to feature the soft, smooth little dumplings in the soup, so we serve it without garnishes. Everyone loves biting into dumplings and getting an instant burst of flavor. But if you'd like a little crunch, top with mung bean sprouts or scallions.

SERVES 6
YIELDS 7 CUPS BROTH,
** ABOUT 24 DUMPLINGS**
TOTAL TIME: 1¹/₂ HOURS

PER 12-OUNCE SERVING: 234 CALORIES, 4.8 G PROTEIN, 3.2 G FAT, 47.8 G CARBO-HYDRATES, 0.8 G SATURATED FATTY ACIDS, 0 MG CHOLESTEROL, 611 MG SODIUM, 2.9 G TOTAL DIETARY FIBER

1 tablespoon canola or other vegetable oil
3 or 4 shallots, minced (about 1 cup)
5 or 6 large garlic cloves, minced or pressed
4 scallions, thinly sliced
1 teaspoon salt, more to taste
1 fresh lemongrass stalk, minced*
1 teaspoon whole Sichuan peppercorns
1 star anise
8 cups water
8 to 10 small dried shiitake, rinsed
1 small sweet potato (about ¼ pound)
2 cups glutinous rice flour (page 376)
1 to 2 tablespoons soy sauce

Peel off at least two layers of the tough outer leaves of the lemongrass and slice off the top and the root end. Mince only 3 to 4 inches of the tender lower stalk.

In a soup pot on medium-high heat, warm the oil until almost smoking. Add the shallots, garlic, scallions, and salt and stir-fry until the shallots begin to turn golden, about 5 minutes. Remove 2 tablespoons of the shallot mixture and set aside in a medium bowl.

Add the lemongrass, peppercorns, and star anise to the soup pot and stir-fry on medium-high heat for 2 to 3 minutes, until fragrant. Add the water and shiitake, cover, and bring to a boil. Meanwhile, peel the sweet potato, cut it into 3 or 4 large pieces, and add it to the broth. Simmer for 20 minutes, or until the sweet potatoes are soft.

While the broth simmers, sprinkle a dinner plate with some of the rice flour and put the rest in a cake pan or other deep, flat-bottomed container. Find your most shallow, rounded strainer and a bowl large enough to hold the strainer. Fill the bowl ³/₄ full of water and set aside.

When the sweet potatoes are soft, strain the broth, reserving the potato chunks and shiitake. Slice off and discard the shiitake stems and mince the caps. Add the minced shiitake, potatoes, and 1 tablespoon of the soy sauce to the reserved shallot mixture and mash well. Add more soy sauce to taste.

Form this dumpling mixture into about two dozen 1-inch balls. Place 5 or 6 balls into the cake pan of rice flour and shake and swirl the pan for a few seconds—the balls will roll around and become evenly coated with rice flour. Transfer the coated balls to the strainer and dunk them very briefly in the bowl of water. Shake off the excess water, gently toss them back into the rice flour, and coat again (see Note). Repeat the dunking and coating procedure 5 more times and set the finished dumplings aside on the floured dinner plate. Repeat the process until all of the balls are coated (see Note).

Transfer the broth back to the soup pot, add salt to taste, and return it to a boil. Add all of the dumplings and cook for about 8 minutes. To serve, ladle broth and 3 or 4 dumplings into each bowl.

Note If the dumplings clump together or flatten when you toss them all together, you may need to transfer them one by one from the strainer to the cake pan.

Coated, uncooked dumplings can be frozen and stored for up to 3 months: freeze them on a tray until hard; then transfer to a freezer bag. To use, ease the frozen dumplings into simmering soup and cook until thoroughly heated.

If you have leftover soup, refrigerate the dumplings and the broth separately. To rewarm, bring the broth to a simmer and then add the dumplings. Serve when the dumplings are heated through.

DAILY SPECIAL

MENU IDEAS **Asian Beet & Tofu Salad (page 192)** ✳ **Broiled Tofu & Sugar Snap Peas (page 199)** ✳ **Florida Salad with Ginger Dressing (page 263)** ✳ **Thai Tossed Salad (page 292)** ✳ **Asian Spinach & Orange Salad (page 246)** ✳ **Spicy Cucumber Salad (page 288)**

Flemish Farm Soup

The foundation of this soup is based on the same technique used to make French onion soup: sauté the onions for a long time until they're reduced and browned, then add the other vegetables and light stock. The soup is rich and brothy with a few sliced carrots and potatoes for texture.

The grilled crouton, speckled with caraway and topped with cheese, adds distinctive flavor and is a surefire guarantee that this soup is no mere appetizer, but a meal in itself. If you don't have time to make the caraway cheese croutons, offer a hearty rye or pumpernickel bread.

SERVES 4
YIELDS 7 CUPS
PREPARATION TIME: 20 MINUTES
COOKING TIME: 55 MINUTES

PER 18-OUNCE SERVING: 377 CALORIES, 9.2 G PROTEIN, 19.4 G FAT, 43.5 G CARBOHYDRATES, 4.7 G SATURATED FATTY ACIDS, 16 MG CHOLESTEROL, 1141 MG SODIUM, 4.9 G TOTAL DIETARY FIBER

3 cups thinly sliced onions
1 teaspoon salt
1 tablespoon olive oil
3 garlic cloves, minced or pressed
1 cup peeled and thinly sliced carrots
1 cup peeled and thinly sliced potatoes
6 cups Basic Light Vegetable Stock (page 16)
¼ cup loosely packed chopped fresh parsley
2 tablespoons chopped fresh dill (2 teaspoons dried)
freshly ground black pepper to taste

GIANT CROUTONS
3 tablespoons butter or olive oil
¼ teaspoon caraway seeds
4 slices of French bread, cut on the diagonal
4 slices of Gouda or Edam cheese

In a heavy soup pot on medium-low heat, cook the onions and salt in the olive oil for about 30 minutes, until thoroughly limp and brown. Keep the soup pot covered so the juices will not evaporate, and stir frequently to prevent the onions from sticking.

Add the garlic and continue to cook for another 1 or 2 minutes. Add the carrots, potatoes, and stock and simmer for 15 to 20 minutes. Stir in the parsley, dill, and pepper. Cover and simmer on very low heat while you prepare the croutons.

Preheat the broiler.

In a small skillet on low heat, warm the butter or olive oil. Stir in the caraway seeds, sauté for a few seconds, and remove from the heat. Brush the 4 bread slices with the melted caraway butter or olive oil and top each with a slice of cheese. Broil for a few minutes, checking frequently to prevent any black, charred, and disappointing mishaps. When the cheese has melted and the edges of the bread are lightly browned, remove from the broiler.

Serve the steaming soup in large bowls, each topped with a cheese crouton.

DAILY SPECIAL

MENU IDEAS **Honey Mustard Green Beans Vinaigrette (page 269)** ✳ **Celeriac Remoulade (page 253)** ✳ **Bean & Radicchio Salad (page 249)** ✳ **Summer Millet Salad (page 290)**

French Roasted Onion Soup

Onion soups require a good rich stock for the best flavor. Our Dark Vegetable Stock is a perfect choice and can be made while the onions for the soup are roasting. The sweet, smoky flavor of caramelized onions and garlic lend our soup its special distinction.

This beautiful, deep caramel brown soup is appealing next to a colorful salad and makes a very satisfying meal.

SERVES 4 TO 6
YIELDS 10 CUPS
ROASTING TIME: 45 TO 50 MINUTES
SIMMERING TIME: 30 MINUTES

PER 13.5-OUNCE SERVING: 181 CALORIES, 3.2 G PROTEIN, 7.5 G FAT, 22.2 G CARBOHYDRATES, 1.3 G SATURATED FATTY ACIDS, 0 MG CHOLESTEROL, 912 MG SODIUM, 3.3 G TOTAL DIETARY FIBER

4 or 5 large Spanish onions, cut lengthwise into thin slices (about 8 cups)
8 garlic cloves, minced or pressed
1 teaspoon salt
2 tablespoons olive oil
4 bay leaves
1 teaspoon dried thyme
¾ to 1 cup dry white wine
8 cups Dark Vegetable Stock (page 18)
2 tablespoons soy sauce
salt and ground black pepper to taste

Herbed Croutons (page 30)
grated Gruyère, Swiss, or Parmesan cheese

Preheat the oven to 375°.
In two shallow, nonreactive baking pans large enough to accommodate all of the onions in a single layer, combine the onions, garlic, salt, oil, bay leaves, and thyme. Roast for 45 to 50 minutes, stirring every 15 minutes, until the onions have softened and lightly browned. Remove from the oven, add the wine to the baking pans, and stir well with a wooden spoon to deglaze.

Transfer the roasted mixture to a soup pot. Add the stock and soy sauce, cover, and bring to a boil; then lower the heat and gently simmer for 30 minutes. Find and discard the bay leaves and add salt and pepper to taste.

Serve with croutons and grated cheese.

MENU IDEAS Pinzimonio (page 280) ✳ **Asparagus Vinaigrette (page 248)** ✳ **Celeriac Remoulade (page 253)** ✳ **Orzo & Pesto Stuffed Tomatoes (page 223)** ✳ **Five-Herb Salad (page 262)**

Golden Summer Soup

In August we get an early glimpse of autumn color when we create this soup from the abundant yellow summer squash and corn that fill our gardens here in the Finger Lakes Region of New York. However, its lightly sweet, inviting flavor is enjoyable any time of the year.

SERVES 6 TO 8
YIELDS 10 CUPS
TOTAL TIME: 45 MINUTES

PER 11-OUNCE SERVING: 158 CALORIES, 3.1 G PROTEIN, 4.5 G FAT, 29.1 G CARBO-HYDRATES, 1.1 G SATURATED FATTY ACIDS, 0 MG CHOLESTEROL, 621 MG SODIUM, 4.1 G TOTAL DIETARY FIBER

1½ cups chopped onions
2 tablespoons canola or other vegetable oil
1 cup peeled and diced carrots
2½ cups peeled and diced sweet potatoes
6 cups water
4 cups diced yellow summer squash
2 cups fresh or frozen corn kernels
½ teaspoon turmeric
4 teaspoons fresh lemon juice
2 teaspoons salt
1 tablespoon chopped fresh sage (1 teaspoon dried)
freshly ground black pepper to taste

grated Monterey Jack cheese or reduced-fat sour cream
chopped fresh parsley or snipped fresh chives

In a soup pot, sauté the onions in the oil on medium-high heat for 2 minutes. Add the carrots and about 1¾ cups of the sweet potatoes, stir well, and cook for 1 to 2 minutes. Add 3 cups of the water, cover, and bring to a boil; then lower the heat and simmer for about 10 minutes, until the potatoes are soft. Purée the mixture in a blender or food processor until smooth and set aside.

Meanwhile, bring the remaining 3 cups of water to a boil. Carefully add the rest of the sweet potatoes and simmer for 5 minutes. Ease in the summer squash, corn, turmeric, lemon juice, and salt, cover, and simmer for 10 minutes. Stir in the sage and the reserved purée. Add pepper to taste.

Gently reheat, if necessary. Top with grated cheese or a dollop of sour cream and sprinkle with parsley or chives.

DAILY SPECIAL

MENU IDEAS **French Barley Salad (page 210)** ✳ **Arugula & Warm Mozzarella Salad (page 191)** ✳ **Simple Tomato Salads (page 286)** ✳ **Honey Mustard Green Beans Vinaigrette (page 269)** ✳ **Three-Bean Pasta Salad (page 232)**

Grecian Isle Stew

This stew-like soup is lusty with bold flavors. While the eggplant is draining, you have time to prepare the rest of the ingredients. Serve the finished stew piping hot with some crusty bread, a glass of wine, and a video of Melina Mercouri in *Never on Sunday*.

If you add a little salad or two, your Daily Special meal can become an epic feast for epicureans.

SERVES 4 TO 6
YIELDS 10 CUPS
PREPARATION TIME: 25 MINUTES
COOKING TIME: 45 MINUTES

PER 12-OUNCE SERVING: 207 CALORIES, 4 G PROTEIN, 8.9 G FAT, 28.6 G CARBOHY-DRATES, 1.2 G SATURATED FATTY ACIDS, 0 MG CHOLESTEROL, 785 MG SODIUM, 5.4 G TOTAL DIETARY FIBER

1 medium eggplant, peeled and cubed
1 teaspoon salt
2 tablespoons olive oil
2 cups chopped onions
6 garlic cloves, minced or pressed
2 cups diced potatoes
½ teaspoon dried oregano
¼ to ½ teaspoon red pepper flakes
3 cups water
1 cup cut green beans (1-inch pieces)
2 cups chopped red and/or green bell peppers
2 cups chopped fresh or undrained canned tomatoes (14-ounce can)
½ cup dry red wine
¼ cup coarsely chopped pitted kalamata olives (about 12 large)*
½ cup chopped fresh parsley
1 tablespoon fresh lemon juice
1 tablespoon drained capers
1 tablespoon minced fresh dill
salt and ground black pepper to taste

grated feta or Kasseri cheese, or plain nonfat yogurt (optional)

* *To pit, slice lengthwise all the way around each olive and twist the halves apart, or place the flat side of a broad-bladed knife on the olive and whack it sharply with the heel of your other hand to break open the olive.*

To remove any bitterness, place the cubed eggplant in a colander, sprinkle it with salt, and cover it with a plate weighted down with a heavy can. Set the colander in a bowl or the sink; allow the eggplant to drain for 15 to 20 minutes. Rinse well and set aside to drain again.

Warm the olive oil in a heavy, nonreactive soup pot. Add the onions and garlic and sauté on medium-high heat until the onions are translucent, about 10 minutes. Add the eggplant and cook for 5 minutes, stirring often. Add the potatoes, oregano, red pepper flakes, and water; cover and simmer for 5 minutes. Add the green beans, bell peppers, tomatoes, and wine. Cover and simmer for 15 to 20 minutes, or until the vegetables are tender. Add the olives, parsley, lemon juice, capers, and dill and heat thoroughly. Add salt and pepper to taste.

If desired, top each serving with cheese or yogurt.

MENU IDEAS **Arugula & Warm Mozzarella Salad (page 191)** ✳ **Caesar Salad (page 201)** ✳ **Mediterranean Orange & Olive Salad (page 276)** ✳ **Greek Chickpea Salad (page 277)** ✳ **tossed green salad with Low-fat Tomato Basil Dressing (page 321)**

Indian Roasted Eggplant Soup

The simple procedure of roasting eggplants, bell peppers, and tomatoes concentrates the sweetness of the vegetables. Add to this the slightly smoky flavor, the Indian influence of the spices and coconut, and the creamy smooth mouth feel and you have a velvety, complex, and novel soup, sure to intrigue and delight everyone.

To round out a meal, we would probably choose a salad with a grain or other protein to accompany this soup.

SERVES 6 TO 8
YIELDS 9 CUPS
PREPARATION TIME: 25 MINUTES
ROASTING TIME: 45 MINUTES

PER 11-OUNCE SERVING: 175 CALORIES, 2.9 G PROTEIN, 13.3 G FAT, 13.5 G CARBOHYDRATES, 3.8 G SATURATED FATTY ACIDS, 0 MG CHOLESTEROL, 335 MG SODIUM, 3.6 G TOTAL DIETARY FIBER

¼ cup olive oil, more or less as desired
2 medium eggplants (about 2 pounds)
2 red bell peppers (about ¾ pound)
3 tomatoes (about 1 pound)
sprinkling of salt and ground black pepper

SPICE MIXTURE
2 teaspoons olive oil
½ teaspoon black mustard seeds
1 teaspoon cumin seeds
1 teaspoon ground coriander
¼ teaspoon ground cinnamon
⅛ teaspoon ground cardamom
¼ teaspoon cayenne or red pepper flakes

1¾ cups reduced-fat coconut milk (14-ounce can)
1 teaspoon salt
1½ to 3 cups water

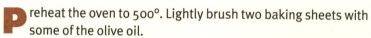

Preheat the oven to 500°. Lightly brush two baking sheets with some of the olive oil.

Halve the eggplants and bell peppers lengthwise. Stem the tomatoes and halve them crosswise. Place all of the vegetable halves cut side up on the baking sheets. Brush the vegetables with the remaining olive oil and sprinkle them with salt and pepper. Roast for about 45 minutes, until dark brown and soft or, for a smoky flavor, even slightly charred. Remove from the oven and set aside to cool.

Meanwhile, in a small skillet on medium heat, warm 2 teaspoons of olive oil. Add the black mustard and cumin seeds and simmer until they begin to pop. Reduce the heat to low and add the coriander, cinnamon, cardamom, and cayenne or red pepper flakes. Stirring constantly, heat for 2 to 3 minutes, until fragrant, taking care not to burn the spices. Remove from the heat and set aside.

When the roasted vegetables are cool enough to handle, remove their skins. In batches in a blender, purée the vegetables with the coconut milk, salt, and enough water to make the soup the thickness you like. Place the purée in a nonreactive soup pot and gently heat. Stir in half of the reserved spice mixture and then add more to taste.

DAILY SPECIAL

MENU IDEAS **Persian Rice & Pistachio Salad (page 224)** ✳ **Curried Rice Salad (page 205)** ✳ **Curried Scallop & Noodle Salad (page 300)** ✳ **Indonesian Tahu Goreng (page 218)** ✳ **Nepalese Egg Salad sandwiches (page 278)**

Jamaican Tomato Soup

This zesty Moosewood favorite combines tomatoes with an unusual mélange of orange and lemon juices, basil, cilantro, and grated orange peel. Depending on the season, use fresh or canned tomatoes—or a combination of both as we do here. In the summer, make a splash by topping with bright, peppery nasturtium blossoms, which are fun to eat.

YIELDS 7½ CUPS
PREPARATION TIME:
 20 TO 25 MINUTES
COOKING TIME: 30 MINUTES

PER 10-OUNCE SERVING: 149 CALORIES, 3.3 G PROTEIN, 5.6 G FAT, 24.1 G CARBO-HYDRATES, 0.7 G SATURATED FATTY ACIDS, 0 MG CHOLESTEROL, 358 MG SODIUM, 1.8 G TOTAL DIETARY FIBER

2 tablespoons olive oil
1 cup chopped onions
3 cups chopped fresh tomatoes
3 cups undrained canned tomatoes, chopped (28-ounce can)
¼ cup chopped fresh basil
1 teaspoon sugar
3 tablespoons fresh lemon juice
1 tablespoon freshly grated orange peel
2 cups orange juice
3 tablespoons chopped fresh cilantro
3 tablespoons chopped fresh parsley
½ teaspoon salt
ground black pepper to taste

chopped fresh basil, parsley, or scallions
Curried Croutons (page 339)
nasturtium blossoms (page 340) (optional)

Heat the olive oil in a nonreactive soup pot for a few seconds, then add the onions and sauté on medium heat for about 10 minutes, stirring frequently, until translucent. Add the fresh and canned tomatoes, the basil, sugar, lemon juice, and orange peel, and bring to a boil. Lower the heat, cover, and simmer for 10 minutes.

In a blender, combine the orange juice, cilantro, parsley, salt, and pepper and purée until thoroughly mixed. Ladle about 2 cups of the cooked, seasoned tomatoes from the soup pot, add them to the mixture in the blender, and purée until smooth. Stir the purée back into the soup and heat gently for 10 minutes.

Serve hot, topped with chopped basil, parsley, or scallions and with Curried Croutons. Decorate with nasturtium blossoms, if desired.

Variation Purée all of the cooked tomatoes in batches in a blender to make a completely smooth soup, chill for at least 40 minutes, and serve cold.

MENU IDEAS **Caribbean Rice Salad (page 202)** ✳ **Florida Salad with Ginger Dressing (page 263)** ✳ **Gado Gado (page 212)** ✳ **Curried Tofu Salad (page 256)** ✳ **Avocado Melon Mélange (page 264)**

Mole de Olla Rodriguez

Jenny Wang adapted this from a stew made by Licha Rodriguez of Cuernavaca, Mexico. It must be carefully and respectfully prepared to be true to the Señora's spirit, and the mole sauce should be made from scratch, not left to a store-bought preparation.

This is a tasty stew, created with widely available late summer and early fall vegetables. If you can find them, include epazote, a fresh green herb, and chayote, a type of squash, to give this stew an authentic touch of Mexico. The chayote can replace some or all of the zucchini in the recipe and epazote can be added to taste near the end of cooking.

SERVES 4 TO 6
YIELDS ABOUT 8 CUPS
TOTAL TIME: 55 MINUTES

PER 10-OUNCE SERVING: 156 CALORIES, 4.5 G PROTEIN, 3.5 G FAT, 31.4 G CARBO-HYDRATES, 0.8 G SATURATED FATTY ACIDS, 0 MG CHOLESTEROL, 442 MG SODIUM, 6.8 G TOTAL DIETARY FIBER

MOLE SAUCE
2 or 3 garlic cloves
½ Spanish onion, sliced into thick rings
3 dried guajillo or New Mexico chiles*
1 cup water

STEW BASE
1 tablespoon canola or other vegetable oil
½ Spanish onion, diced
3 garlic cloves, minced
1 teaspoon salt
1 large potato, diced
1 quart water
½ pound green beans, trimmed and cut into 1-inch pieces (about 2 cups)
1 medium zucchini or yellow summer squash, diced
3 cups corn kernels (preferably fresh, cobs reserved)**
salt to taste

grated Monterey Jack cheese
crumbled tortilla chips

Guajillo chiles are 4 to 5 inches long, smooth, and shiny. They range in color from dark red to orange. New Mexico chiles are a reasonable substitute and may be easier to find. Look in the produce section near the fresh chiles or in the Mexican section of the grocery store.

Be careful when handling chiles: if you touch your eyes, nose, or lips, it can cause a burning sensation. Washing your hands will remove the oil residues that cause this.

**If using frozen or canned corn, add it with the potatoes. Cooking it longer will provide some of the extra flavor that the corn cobs from fresh corn would impart.*

To make the mole sauce, roast the garlic cloves, onion rings, and dried chiles in a dry, heavy skillet on medium heat. Place the garlic and onions to one side of the pan, turning them every couple of minutes, until they have browned and softened somewhat, about 15 minutes.

At the same time in the other half of the skillet, toast the dried chiles one at a time for about 45 seconds each. To heat them evenly, use tongs or a spatula to press down and turn often, until fragrant, pliant, and swollen. Take care not to burn them. When the toasted chiles have cooled enough to handle, remove the stems and ribs and shake out the seeds.

Transfer the softened garlic and onions to a small saucepan, add the seeded chiles, cover with the water, and bring to a boil. Cook for 2 to 3 minutes, remove from the heat, and set aside.

For the stew base, warm the oil in a soup pot on medium heat. Add the diced onions, garlic, and salt and sauté until the onions begin to soften, about 5 minutes. Increase the heat to high, add the potatoes, and sauté for another 5 minutes. Add the water and, if you have them, the reserved corn cobs and bring to a boil. Add the green beans, cover, and cook until the potatoes and green beans are barely tender, about 10 minutes.

Meanwhile, drain the roasted onions, garlic, and chiles and reserve the liquid. Purée them in a blender, adding just enough reserved liquid to keep things moving. Strain the puréed mole sauce through a sieve, pressing on the solids with the back of a spoon and adding more of the reserved liquid if that helps. Discard the solids and set the strained mole aside.

Add the zucchini and fresh corn kernels to the stew and cook for another 5 minutes, or until all of the vegetables are tender. Remove the corn cobs, if using, and discard. In case the mole sauce is *very* spicy, stir in half of it to start; then add salt and more mole to taste.

Serve each bowl of stew topped with grated Monterey Jack cheese and tortilla chips.

DAILY SPECIAL ❧ MENU IDEAS **Avocado Seitan Salad (page 194)** ✳ **Mexican Shrimp & Spinach Salad (page 301)** ✳ **Florida Salad with Ginger Dressing (page 263)** ✳ **Mexican Chickpea Salad (page 277)** ✳ **Southern Wheat-free Cornbread (page 335)**

Mock Chicken Noodle Soup

Every once in a while at Moosewood, we come across a food product new to us, and it's fun to figure out how to use it. Fried gluten is just such a discovery. It is tasty, convenient, and high in protein, and we think it's perfect as mock chicken.

Any egg noodles from extra-wide to very fine will work nicely in this homey brew. Use whichever you like best or remember most fondly from the chicken noodle soups of childhood.

SERVES 8 TO 10
YIELDS 11 CUPS
PREPARATION TIME: 30 MINUTES
COOKING TIME: 30 MINUTES

PER 9-OUNCE SERVING: 217 CALORIES, 8 G PROTEIN, 7.1 G FAT, 31.2 G CARBOHYDRATES, 1.4 G SATURATED FATTY ACIDS, 24 MG CHOLESTEROL, 712 MG SODIUM, 2.8 G TOTAL DIETARY FIBER

2 cups diced onions
1 cup diced celery
2 bay leaves
3 tablespoons canola or other vegetable oil
1 cup peeled and diced carrots
1 teaspoon pressed or minced garlic
¼ teaspoon dried dill
¼ teaspoon dried thyme
1½ teaspoons salt
½ teaspoon ground black pepper
6- to 10-ounce can fried gluten*
6 cups Mock Chicken Stock (page 20)
1 cup water or additional stock
½ cup chopped fresh parsley
8 to 10 ounces egg noodles

* *Try Golden Leaf Vegetarian Mock Chicken Meat or shop in Asian or natural food stores for another kind that strikes your fancy.*

In a covered soup pot, sauté the onions, celery, and bay leaves in the oil on medium heat for 10 minutes, stirring occasionally. Add the carrots, garlic, dill, thyme, salt, and pepper and continue to sauté for 10 minutes.

While the vegetables cook, drain, rinse, and dice the fried gluten. Add the gluten pieces, Mock Chicken Stock, water, and parsley to the soup pot. Cover and simmer for at least 10 minutes.

Just before serving the soup, cook the noodles until al dente in a large pot of boiling water. Drain the noodles well. Place a serving of noodles into each individual soup bowl and ladle on the piping hot soup (see Note).

Note If you don't expect to have leftovers, it's fine to just stir all of the noodles into the pot of soup and serve. Otherwise, it's best to apportion the noodles to order and save leftover soup without any noodles in it, because if the noodles sit in the soup, they'll absorb the broth and make the soup too thick.

DAILY SPECIAL

MENU IDEAS **Tomato Flowers (page 236)** ✳ **East Indian Fruit Salad (page 258)** ✳ **Solstice Salad (page 227)** ✳ **Honey Mustard Green Beans Vinaigrette (page 269)** ✳ **Celeriac Remoulade (page 253)** ✳ **Balkan Roasted Vegetable Salad (page 196)**

Moroccan Root Vegetable Stew

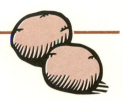

Root vegetables have an appealing heartiness, are low in calories, have virtually no fat, and are a good source of vitamin C, fiber, and potassium. Their great flavor adds a sweet under-current to the spiciness of this dish.

For uniform cooking and aesthetic appeal, it's best to chop the celery, carrots, turnips, and rutabaga about the same size and to cube the potatoes just a bit larger.

This stew makes a fine meal when accompanied by a simple salad and some pita bread—we would often choose a salad from the Mediterranean region.

SERVES 4 TO 6
YIELDS 8 TO 9 CUPS
PREPARATION TIME: 35 MINUTES
SIMMERING TIME: 20 MINUTES

PER 12-OUNCE SERVING: 149 CALORIES, 2.7 G PROTEIN, 4.1 G FAT, 27.6 G CARBO-HYDRATES, 1 G SATURATED FATTY ACIDS, 0 MG CHOLESTEROL, 448 MG SODIUM, 4 G TOTAL DIETARY FIBER

1½ tablespoons canola or other vegetable oil
2 cups chopped onions
3 garlic cloves, minced or pressed
2 cups peeled and diced carrots
½ cup diced celery, stalks and leaves
1½ teaspoons ground cumin
1 teaspoon paprika
½ teaspoon ground coriander
1 teaspoon salt
⅛ teaspoon ground black pepper
pinch of cayenne
4 cups water or vegetable stock
1 cup peeled and cubed sweet potatoes
1 cup peeled and diced turnips
1 cup cubed potatoes
1½ cups peeled and diced rutabaga (optional, see Note)
2 bay leaves
¼ cup currants
3 tablespoons fresh lemon juice
¼ cup chopped fresh cilantro

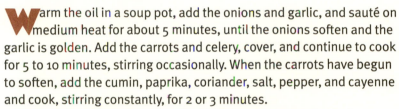

Warm the oil in a soup pot, add the onions and garlic, and sauté on medium heat for about 5 minutes, until the onions soften and the garlic is golden. Add the carrots and celery, cover, and continue to cook for 5 to 10 minutes, stirring occasionally. When the carrots have begun to soften, add the cumin, paprika, coriander, salt, pepper, and cayenne and cook, stirring constantly, for 2 or 3 minutes.

Pour in the water or stock and add the sweet potatoes, turnips, potatoes, and rutabaga, if using. Cover and bring to a boil. Reduce the heat to low, add the bay leaves and currants, cover, and simmer for 20 minutes. Discard the bay leaves. For a thicker stew, purée 2 cups of the stew in a blender or food processor and stir it back into the soup pot.

Just before serving, stir in the lemon juice and cilantro.

Note Rutabaga adds a nice touch to the stew, but it seems to absorb the spices and make the final flavor quite mild. So, if you use rutabaga, we suggest increasing the spices: add ½ teaspoon of cumin, ½ teaspoon of paprika, ¼ teaspoon of coriander, and ¼ teaspoon of salt.

DAILY SPECIAL

MENU IDEAS **Persian Rice & Pistachio Salad (page 224)** ✳ **Mediterranean Orange & Olive Salad (page 276)** ✳ **Yemiser Salata (page 295)** ✳ **Lobio (page 274)** ✳ **Fattoush (page 209)** ✳ **Fig & Endive Salad (page 261)** ✳ **Fennel & Arugula Salad with Grapefruit (page 259)**

Mushroom Noodle Goulash

This is a wild Hungarian gypsy of a soup, teeming with earthy riches and romantic flourishes. It's savory and hearty on its own, but when combined with a salad and dark bread, it's a very special meal. For a festive touch, garnish with sour cream or yogurt topped with a dusting of bright red paprika.

As this soup sits, the noodles soak up liquid. For an encore presentation, when you reheat the soup, add more water and/or tomato juice as needed.

SERVES 6 TO 8
YIELDS 12 CUPS WITHOUT NOODLES
PREPARATION TIME: 25 MINUTES
SIMMERING TIME: 25 MINUTES

PER 12-OUNCE SERVING: 161 CALORIES, 5.2 G PROTEIN, 4.9 G FAT, 24.8 G CARBO-HYDRATES, 1.2 G SATURATED FATTY ACIDS, 18 MG CHOLESTEROL, 267 MG SODIUM, 2.5 G TOTAL DIETARY FIBER

½ ounce dried porcini mushrooms
¼ cup sherry or mirin
2 tablespoons canola or other vegetable oil
1 onion, chopped (about 1 cup)
2 garlic cloves, minced or pressed
1 tablespoon paprika
1 large carrot, peeled and chopped (about 1 cup)
1 red bell pepper, seeded and chopped (about 1 cup)
1 tablespoon soy sauce
12 ounces mushrooms, coarsely chopped
1 large portabella mushroom, cut into large chunks
3 cups undrained canned crushed tomatoes (28-ounce can)
4 cups water
2 tablespoons chopped fresh dill
2 dashes of cayenne, Tabasco, or other hot pepper sauce
6 ounces fine egg noodles
salt and ground black pepper to taste

sour cream or plain nonfat yogurt (optional)

In a small bowl, cover the dried porcini with ½ cup boiling water and the sherry. Set aside to soak for 25 minutes.

Meanwhile, in a nonreactive soup pot, warm the oil and sauté the onions and garlic for 3 or 4 minutes on medium heat. Sprinkle with the paprika and continue to sauté until the onions soften, about 5 minutes. Add the carrots, cover, and cook for a few minutes. Stir in the bell peppers and soy sauce and sauté for 3 more minutes.

Add the mushrooms and portabellas. Remove the porcini from the soaking liquid, thinly slice, and add to the sautéing vegetables. Strain and add the soaking liquid. Sauté until the mushrooms have wilted. Add the tomatoes and water, stir well, and bring to a low boil. Cover, reduce the heat, and simmer for 20 minutes. Remove from the heat and stir in the dill and cayenne or Tabasco.

When the soup has almost finished simmering, bring a large pot of salted water to a boil. Cook the egg noodles for about 3 minutes, drain in a colander, and stir into the soup. Add salt and pepper to taste. If you like, garnish with sour cream or yogurt.

DAILY SPECIAL

MENU IDEAS **Composed Beet Salad (page 254)** ✳ **Fig & Endive Salad (page 261)** ✳ **Celeriac Remoulade (page 253)** ✳ **Fennel Salad with Blue Cheese (page 260)** ✳ **Five-Herb Salad (page 262)** ✳ **Pumpernickel Croutons (page 349)**

Navarin of Spring Vegetables

Fresh tender vegetables just cooked in a delicate broth make for an extremely light and elegant dish. In France, this pretty springtime stew is a delectable change after heavier winter fare. While the growing season is shorter in upstate New York, we're blessed with supermarkets that might carry beautiful baby vegetables in November, so we can serve Navarin well beyond spring. Goat Cheese Toasts are the perfect accompaniment.

SERVES 6
YIELDS ABOUT 10 CUPS
PREPARATION TIME: 25 MINUTES
SIMMERING TIME:
20 TO 25 MINUTES

PER 13-OUNCE SERVING: 195 CALORIES, 8.2 G PROTEIN, 0.9 G FAT, 42.6 G CARBO-HYDRATES, 0.2 G SATURATED FATTY ACIDS, 0 MG CHOLESTEROL, 383 MG SODIUM, 8.5 G TOTAL DIETARY FIBER

6 cups Basic Light Vegetable Stock (page 16),
   Garlic Stock (page 19), or canned vegetable broth*
½ cup dry white wine (optional)
4 garlic cloves, minced or pressed
1 large bay leaf
12 to 18 new potatoes, scrubbed, peeled if you wish, and cut in half
   or into bite-sized cubes (about 3 cups)
18 baby carrots, peeled (1 scant cup)
3 small turnips, peeled and each cut into 8 wedges (about 1½ cups)
12 to 18 small boiling onions or 24 pearl onions, peeled
   (about 3 cups)
½ pound asparagus, trimmed and cut into 2-inch lengths
5 artichoke hearts, drained and cut into quarters (14-ounce can)
1 teaspoon dried thyme
1 teaspoon dried tarragon
1 cup fresh or frozen green peas
1 tablespoon light miso
salt and ground black pepper to taste

Goat Cheese Toasts (page 344)

* We recommend Pritikin and Hain brands of canned vegetable broths.

In a soup pot, bring the stock and, if using, the white wine to a boil and add the garlic, bay leaf, potatoes, carrots, turnips, and onions. Lower the heat, cover, and simmer for about 15 minutes, until the vegetables are nearly tender.

Add the asparagus, artichoke hearts, thyme, tarragon, and peas and cook for another 5 minutes. Remove and discard the bay leaf. Add the miso and stir until dissolved. Add salt and pepper to taste.

Ladle immediately into shallow bowls, top each with a Goat Cheese Toast, and serve hot.

DAILY SPECIAL

MENU IDEAS **Five-Herb Salad (page 262)** ✳ **Fresh Pear & Blue Cheese Salad (page 266)** ✳ **tossed green salad topped with our Versatile Vinaigrette (page 325)** ✳ **Focaccia (page 330)**

Ozoni

Ozoni, the soup served in Japan to celebrate the new year, is simple to prepare, healthful, and heartier than most miso soups. We've created a version that includes one of our favorite greens, mizuna.

Musky sesame oil and the briny essences of tamari and *hijiki,* a type of seaweed, are some of the exotic flavors that enrich this nourishing soup. Fresh soybeans are a treasure worth shopping for and adding to the soup but, alas, they're only available seasonally. You can buy them frozen in the pods in most Asian grocery stores.

Accompany Ozoni with a salad, perhaps one made with tofu, to create a harmonious Daily Special.

SERVES 4 TO 6
YIELDS 8 CUPS
TOTAL TIME: 30 MINUTES

PER 11-OUNCE SERVING: 111 CALORIES, 4.3 G PROTEIN, 2 G FAT, 20.8 G CARBOHYDRATES, 0.3 G SATURATED FATTY ACIDS, 0 MG CHOLESTEROL, 643 MG SODIUM, 2.8 G TOTAL DIETARY FIBER

6 cups water
½ cup thinly sliced onions, cut into half moons
1 cup peeled and sliced daikon radish, cut into ¼-inch-thick half moons
2 medium yellow or white potatoes, peeled and cut into large chunks
1 teaspoon soy sauce
⅓ to ½ cup white or barley miso
1 teaspoon dark sesame oil
1 tablespoon dried crumbled hijiki (page 377)
1½ cups coarsely chopped mizuna (about 2 ounces)*

1 sheet of toasted nori (page 377), cut crosswise into thin 2-inch-long strips
fresh unroasted soybeans (optional)**

If you can't find mizuna, substitute shredded fresh spinach.
**Fresh soybeans are similar in size and texture to fresh baby limas and are available seasonally at farmers' markets, Asian groceries, and some well-stocked produce markets. The best time to find them is during their harvesting time from midsummer to late summer.*

In a soup pot, bring the water, onions, daikon, potatoes, and soy sauce to a boil. Lower the heat, cover, and simmer for about 10 minutes. Stir together the miso and ¼ cup of the hot soup stock until the miso dissolves, then stir it back into the soup. Add the sesame oil and simmer for about 5 more minutes.

Just before serving, add the hijiki and mizuna to the soup. When the mizuna has wilted, serve the soup topped with the toasted nori and, if you like, fresh soybeans.

Note You can purchase toasted nori or, to make your own, just wave a sheet of untoasted nori briefly over a flame until it stiffens slightly.

MENU IDEAS **Asian Beet & Tofu Salad (page 192)** ✳ **Broiled Tofu & Sugar Snap Peas (page 199)** ✳ **Vietnamese Cellophane Noodle Salad (page 238)** ✳ **"Japanese" Tofu Salad (page 271)** ✳ **Thai Rice & Mushroom Salad (page 234)**

Parsnip Pear Soup

Smooth texture plus sweet and savory flavors make this a lovely first course for a holiday meal. As a bonus, it's very simple and easy to prepare. We think the proportions are just right, with the parsnip and pear flavors most dominant. Try it garnished with crisp croutons made from pumpernickel or rye for a superb contrast.

SERVES 4 TO 6
YIELDS ABOUT 8 CUPS
TOTAL TIME: 50 MINUTES

PER 10-OUNCE SERVING: 101 CALORIES, 1.4 G PROTEIN, 2 G FAT, 21.2 G CARBOHYDRATES, 0.5 G SATURATED FATTY ACIDS, 0 MG CHOLESTEROL, 422 MG SODIUM, 4 G TOTAL DIETARY FIBER

2 teaspoons canola or other vegetable oil
1½ cups chopped onions
1½ cups peeled and chopped carrots
1½ cups peeled and chopped parsnips
1½ cups peeled, cored, and chopped pears (preferably Bosc)
1 teaspoon salt
1½ teaspoons brown sugar, packed
½ teaspoon ground cinnamon
¼ teaspoon ground allspice
4½ cups water

In a soup pot, warm the oil. Add the onions, carrots, parsnips, pears, and salt and sauté on medium heat for about 10 minutes, until the onions are translucent. Add the brown sugar, cinnamon, allspice, and water. Cover and bring to a boil; then lower the heat and simmer for 20 minutes.

In batches in a blender, purée the soup. Reheat and serve.

DAILY SPECIAL

MENU IDEAS **Solstice Salad (page 227)** ✳ **Wilted Spinach & Portabella Mushrooms (page 239)** ✳ **Lentil, Rice & Fruit Salad (page 220)** ✳ **Arugula & Warm Mozzarella Salad (page 191)** ✳ **Eastern European Kasha & Mushrooms (page 206)** ✳ **Mussel Salad (page 304)**

Pepperpot

Such interesting flavor combos are found in the cuisines of the Deep South and the Caribbean: cinnamon, thyme, molasses, chiles, mustard greens, sweet bell peppers . . . what could be bad? Look for a refreshing salad with the same general geographic identity as hot and sweet Pepperpot. Use a milder foil like biscuits to sop up the last drop of stew.

If desired, enrich the stew with cooked shrimp or rice for heartier fare. Or top it with grated Monterey Jack cheese, as we sometimes do at Moosewood.

SERVES 4 TO 6
YIELDS 8 CUPS
TOTAL TIME: 1 HOUR

PER 10-OUNCE SERVING: 111 CALORIES, 2.2 G PROTEIN, 5.1 G FAT, 15.9 G CARBOHYDRATES, 0.7 G SATURATED FATTY ACIDS, 0 MG CHOLESTEROL, 519 MG SODIUM, 2 G TOTAL DIETARY FIBER

2 tablespoons olive oil
1 cup chopped onions
3 garlic cloves, minced or pressed
1 small fresh chile, minced, seeds removed for a milder "hot"
1 cup diced celery
1 teaspoon dried thyme
½ teaspoon ground cinnamon
1 teaspoon salt
1 cup diced red bell peppers
1 cup diced green bell peppers
1 cup cubed potatoes (½-inch cubes)
4 cups water or vegetable stock
1½ cups undrained canned tomatoes, chopped (14½-ounce can)
¼ teaspoon ground black pepper
1 tablespoon unsulphured molasses
4 cups chopped mustard greens, loosely packed
salt to taste

In a nonreactive soup pot on medium heat, warm the oil. Add the onions, garlic, chiles, celery, thyme, cinnamon, and salt. Sauté, stirring often, for about 10 minutes or until the onions are translucent. Add the bell peppers and potatoes, reduce the heat to low, cover, and cook for 7 to 10 minutes, stirring often, until the bell peppers are just tender.

Add the water or stock, the tomatoes with their juice, the black pepper, and the molasses. Cover and cook for about 10 minutes or until all of the vegetables are tender. Add the mustard greens, cover, and cook for 3 to 4 minutes, until just wilted. Add salt to taste.

DAILY SPECIAL

MENU IDEAS Florida Salad with Ginger Dressing (page 263) ✳ **Fennel & Arugula Salad with Grapefruit (page 259)** ✳ **Southern Red Rice & Pecan Salad (page 228)** ✳ **Alabama Hot Slaw (page 245)** ✳ **Kiwi, Orange & Baby Greens (page 273)** ✳ **Featherlight Blue Mountain Biscuits (page 327)**

Potato & Escarole Soup

This traditional Italian soup is a welcome appetizer or main dish any season of the year. The sweetness of the Garlic Stock perfectly balances the bitter escarole, and the potatoes add body to this light but filling soup. Our Tony Del Plato's mama made this soup regularly, especially when escarole was on sale. Choose one or two of the easy Mediterranean salads suggested below for a thoroughly enjoyable meal.

SERVES 6
YIELDS 12 CUPS
PREPARATION TIME: 25 MINUTES
SIMMERING TIME:
  15 TO 20 MINUTES

PER 15-OUNCE SERVING: 232 CALORIES, 12.4 G PROTEIN, 8.7 G FAT, 27.2 G CARBO-HYDRATES, 4.6 G SATURATED FATTY ACIDS, 18 MG CHOLESTEROL, 1041 MG SODIUM, 3.7 G TOTAL DIETARY FIBER

2 teaspoons olive oil
2 cups chopped onions
1 teaspoon salt
1 teaspoon ground fennel seeds
1 head of escarole, rinsed and chopped (about 4 cups, packed)
2½ cups peeled and cubed potatoes
8 cups Garlic Stock (page 19)
¼ teaspoon ground black pepper, or to taste

1 cup grated Pecorino Romano or Parmesan cheese

Warm the oil in a soup pot on low heat. Add the onions, sprinkle with the salt, and cook until caramelized (see Note), about 20 minutes. Stir frequently and add a little stock or water, if necessary, to prevent sticking.

Add the fennel and escarole, cover, and cook until the escarole has wilted, 5 to 10 minutes. Stir occasionally, if needed. Add the potatoes and stock and bring to a boil. Cover, reduce the heat, and simmer until the potatoes are tender, 15 to 20 minutes. Add the pepper.

Serve topped with grated cheese.

Note Onions are caramelized when their sugars are released and the onions become very soft and browned.

DAILY SPECIAL

MENU IDEAS **Bean & Radicchio Salad (page 249)** ✳ **Mediterranean Orange & Olive Salad (page 276)** ✳ **Pinzimonio (page 280)** ✳ **Simple Tomato Salads (page 286)**

Roasted Red Pepper Coconut Soup

The gorgeous carmine color of this sweet and hot soup matches in intensity the earthy aroma of roasted red peppers—and with already roasted peppers, it couldn't be easier to make. At Moosewood we like the soup fairly spicy, so if you prefer mild "hotness," reduce the red pepper flakes to taste.

Select a salad for a Daily Special from the cuisine of hot places. A rice salad can temper the heat of the soup. This is a good soup to make ahead of time. After puréeing, just refrigerate it in a covered container until ready to heat. Leftover soup will keep well for over a week.

SERVES 6 TO 8
YIELDS 9½ CUPS
TOTAL TIME: 35 MINUTES WITH ALREADY ROASTED PEPPERS, 60 MINUTES IF ROASTING FRESH BELL PEPPERS

PER 10-OUNCE SERVING: 130 CALORIES, 2.9 G PROTEIN, 8.4 G FAT, 12.6 G CARBO-HYDRATES, 3.6 G SATURATED FATTY ACIDS, 0 MG CHOLESTEROL, 377 MG SODIUM, 1.6 G TOTAL DIETARY FIBER

6 red bell peppers, roasted (pages 374–375), or
two 13-ounce cans roasted sweet red peppers
2 tablespoons canola or other vegetable oil
2 cups chopped onions
2 garlic cloves, peeled and left whole
1 teaspoon red pepper flakes or ¼ teaspoon cayenne, more to taste
1 teaspoon salt
2 cups undrained canned tomatoes (16-ounce can)
1¾ cups reduced-fat coconut milk (14-ounce can)
2 cups water

If you've roasted fresh red peppers, set them aside in a tightly covered bowl to cool and then stem, seed, and peel them. If you're using canned roasted red peppers, rinse them well in a colander and set aside to drain.

In a covered nonreactive soup pot on medium heat, warm the oil. Add the onions, garlic, red pepper flakes, and salt and sauté for about 15 minutes, until the onions are very soft and translucent. Remove the pot from the heat and add the tomatoes, coconut milk, water, and roasted red peppers.

In batches in a blender, purée the soup until smooth. Return it to the soup pot and cook on medium heat until hot. Serve immediately.

MENU IDEAS **Balinese Rice Salad (page 195)** ∗ **Caribbean Rice Salad (page 202)** ∗ **Curried Rice Salad (page 205)** ∗ **Thai Noodle Salad (page 233)** ∗ **Thai Rice & Mushroom Salad (page 234)** ∗ **East Indian Fruit Salad (page 258)** ∗ **Spinach with Cilantro Cashew Dressing (page 289) and Spiced Paneer (page 351)**

Shchi

In Ambrose Bierce's *Devil's Dictionary*, cabbage is defined as "a familiar kitchen-garden vegetable about as large and wise as a man's head." This traditional Russian cabbage soup is earthy, sweet, and sour—one of the most delicious and satisfying soups we know. Surely it originated with someone very wise in the ways of cabbage.

SERVES 4 TO 6
YIELDS 12 CUPS
PREPARATION TIME: 35 MINUTES
COOKING TIME: 30 MINUTES

PER 16-OUNCE SERVING: 236 CALORIES, 4.3 G PROTEIN, 8 G FAT, 41.4 G CARBOHYDRATES, 1.9 G SATURATED FATTY ACIDS, 0 MG CHOLESTEROL, 1003 MG SODIUM, 5.6 G TOTAL DIETARY FIBER

1 large onion, coarsely chopped
2 large garlic cloves, minced or pressed
2 tablespoons canola or other vegetable oil
3 medium carrots, peeled and diced
2 medium turnips, peeled and diced
1 tablespoon dried dill
1 red bell pepper, seeded and diced
10 pitted prunes, diced
½ cup raisins
4 cups shredded green cabbage
8 cups Dark Vegetable Stock (page 18)
3 cups undrained whole tomatoes (28-ounce can)*
1 tablespoon honey
1 tablespoon cider vinegar
1½ teaspoons salt
½ tablespoon ground black pepper

sour cream or plain nonfat yogurt (optional)

* If you prefer, 2 to 2½ cups of chopped fresh tomatoes and ½ to 1 cup of tomato juice—to equal 3 cups total—can replace the canned tomatoes in the recipe.

In a large nonreactive soup pot, sauté the onions and garlic in the oil on medium-high heat for about 5 minutes, until the onions soften. Add the carrots and turnips and sauté for 5 minutes. Add the dill, bell peppers, prunes, and raisins and cook until the peppers soften. Add the cabbage, sprinkle with salt, and continue to cook for 5 minutes.

Stir in the stock and the juice from the can of tomatoes. With a knife, roughly chop the tomatoes right in the can and add them to the soup. Bring to a boil; then add the honey, vinegar, salt, and pepper and stir thoroughly. Lower the heat, cover, and simmer for 30 to 40 minutes.

Serve each bowl topped with a dollop of sour cream or yogurt, if you wish.

DAILY SPECIAL

MENU IDEAS **Eastern European Kasha & Mushrooms (page 206)** * **Three-Bean Pasta Salad (page 232)** * **Lobio (page 274)** * **Harvest Rice Salad (page 215)** * **Turkish Roasted Eggplant Salad (page 294)** * **Herbed Cheese Quick Bread (page 332)** * **Pears Parmesan (page 265)**

Spiced Mexican Squash Stew

This unusual and authentic Mexican stew is so pretty — gold, red, green, and yellow — and just hot enough. The sweetness of butternut squash and cinnamon is accentuated by tangy tomatoes and a fresh jalapeño. A cool dollop of sour cream or some grated Monterey Jack cheese will smooth out the spiciness. For those who prefer an extra little kick, try garnishing the stew with Jalapeño Cream and some Fried Shallots (page 343). With a multicolored salad alongside, it's a fiesta meal.

SERVES 6 TO 8
YIELDS ABOUT 10 CUPS
TOTAL TIME: 45 MINUTES

PER 10-OUNCE SERVING: 120 CALORIES, 3.1 G PROTEIN, 3.6 G FAT, 22.5 G CARBO-HYDRATES, 0.5 G SATURATED FATTY ACIDS, 0 MG CHOLESTEROL, 188 MG SODIUM, 2.6 G TOTAL DIETARY FIBER

1½ tablespoons olive oil or vegetable oil
2 cups chopped onions
6 garlic cloves, minced or pressed
½ teaspoon salt
1 butternut squash
½ small fresh jalapeño or other chile, minced
    (seeds removed for a milder "hot")
½ teaspoon ground cinnamon
2 teaspoons ground cumin
3 cups water
2 cups chopped fresh tomatoes or undrained canned tomatoes
    (15-ounce can)
2 cups chopped red and/or green bell peppers
2 cups fresh or frozen corn kernels (10-ounce package, frozen)
salt and ground black pepper to taste

sour cream, Jalapeño Cream (page 345), or grated
    Monterey Jack cheese

Place the oil, onions, garlic, and salt in a nonreactive soup pot. Cover and cook on medium heat for about 10 minutes, stirring often, until the onions are translucent.

Meanwhile, halve and peel the squash, scoop out and discard the seeds, and dice into ½-inch cubes (see Note). Add the squash, jalapeño, cinnamon, cumin, and water to the soup pot and simmer for 5 to 10 minutes. Add the tomatoes and bell peppers and cook for 10 to 15 minutes or until all of the vegetables are tender. Stir in the corn and return to a simmer. Add salt and pepper to taste.

Serve each bowl topped with a dollop of sour cream or Jalapeño Cream or a sprinkling of grated cheese.

Note If the cubed squash is 5 cups or more, you may need an additional ½ to ¾ cup of water.

DAILY SPECIAL

MENU IDEAS **Mexican Shrimp & Spinach Salad (page 301)** ✳ **Three-Bean Pasta Salad (page 232)** ✳ **Mexican Chickpea Salad (page 277)** ✳ **Avocado Seitan Salad (page 194)** ✳ **Southern Wheat-free Cornbread (page 335)**

Spicy Carrot Peanut Soup

In the cuisines of Africa and Southeast Asia, peanuts and peanut butter are a staple ingredient in sauces and condiments. Here, peanut butter is the background that offsets the spices, garlic, and sour and salty flavors in this rich and aromatic soup. Use any gourmet or commercial peanut butter or roast and grind your own peanuts into a paste.

This thick soup when served with a crisp salad makes an interesting meal.

SERVES 6 TO 8
YIELDS ABOUT 8 CUPS
PREPARATION TIME: 20 MINUTES
COOKING TIME: 35 MINUTES

PER 9-OUNCE SERVING: 95 CALORIES, 2.6 G PROTEIN, 3.8 G FAT, 14.2 G CARBO-HYDRATES, 0.8 G SATURATED FATTY ACIDS, 0 MG CHOLESTEROL, 691 MG SODIUM, 4 G TOTAL DIETARY FIBER

1 tablespoon canola or other vegetable oil
1 large onion, thinly sliced (about 2 cups)
2 pounds carrots, peeled and thinly sliced (about 6 cups)
1 celery stalk, thinly sliced
1 teaspoon salt
1 teaspoon Chinese chili paste*
6 cups water
2 tablespoons peanut butter (see Note)
3 tablespoons soy sauce
2 tablespoons fresh lime juice

a few fresh lime wedges

* Or use 1 fresh stemmed and chopped fresh chile and 2 minced garlic cloves.

In a soup pot on medium heat, warm the oil and add the onions, carrots, celery, salt, and chili paste. Sauté on high heat for 5 minutes, stirring often. Add the water, cover, and bring to a boil. Lower the heat and simmer until the carrots are soft, about 25 minutes.

Stir in the peanut butter, soy sauce, and lime juice. In a blender, purée the soup in batches. Reheat, if necessary.

Serve with lime wedges.

Note If you wish, replace the peanut butter with freshly ground peanuts. Grind ½ cup unsalted roasted peanuts in a blender or small food processor and add them to the soup just before puréeing it.

Variation Try serving the soup cold. It's not your usual chilled soup candidate, but we like it!

DAILY SPECIAL

MENU IDEAS **Thai Rice & Mushroom Salad (page 234)** ✳ **Curried Tofu Salad (page 256)** ✳ **Asian Spinach & Orange Salad (page 246)** ✳ **Asparagus & Snow Pea Salad (page 247)** ✳ **tossed green salad with Moosewood Ginger Miso Dressing (page 323)** ✳ **Seafood & Chermoulla Couscous Salad (page 306)**

Tunisian Pumpkin Soup

Each country of North Africa has its own signature spice mixture. In Tunisia, it is called *tabil*. Tabil is primarily a mix of coriander, caraway, hot pepper, and garlic — all dried and finely ground. We have borrowed this blend of spices and added a few ingredients of our own to create a spice swirl for our pumpkin soup. The soup tastes great on its own, but the swirl will send you spinning into ecstasy.

If parsnips are not available, use a total of 1 cup of carrots in the recipe instead. Try replacing the pumpkin with 2 cups of baked winter squash.

SERVES 4
YIELDS 6½ CUPS
TOTAL TIME: 50 MINUTES

PER 13-OUNCE SERVING: 284 CALORIES, 3.8 G PROTEIN, 15.2 G FAT, 27.9 G CARBO-HYDRATES, 2.2 G SATURATED FATTY ACIDS, 0 MG CHOLESTEROL, 1445 MG SODIUM, 3.5 G TOTAL DIETARY FIBER

2 cups chopped onions
2 tablespoons olive oil
½ cup peeled and sliced carrots
½ cup peeled and sliced parsnips
1½ teaspoons salt
2½ cups water or Basic Light Vegetable Stock (page 16)
1¼ cups unsweetened apple juice
½ cup tomato juice
1 teaspoon ground cumin
½ teaspoon ground nutmeg
½ teaspoon ground cinnamon
½ teaspoon paprika
1¾ cups cooked pumpkin (15-ounce can)

SPICE SWIRL
2 tablespoons olive oil
1 teaspoon minced or pressed garlic
4 teaspoons ground coriander
1 teaspoon ground caraway seeds
¼ teaspoon cayenne
2 tablespoons fresh lemon juice
2 tablespoons minced fresh cilantro
⅛ teaspoon salt

In a soup pot, sauté the onions in the oil until they become translu-cent, about 10 minutes. Stir in the carrots, parsnips, and salt and continue to sauté for about 5 minutes. Add the water or stock, apple and tomato juices, cumin, nutmeg, cinnamon, and paprika. Cover the pot and bring to a boil; then reduce the heat and simmer until the veg-etables are tender. Stir in the pumpkin. In a blender, purée the soup until smooth. Gently reheat, if necessary.

To make the swirl, heat the oil in a small skillet and sauté the garlic on medium heat for 1 minute. Add the coriander, caraway, and cayenne and continue to cook, stirring constantly. When the mixture begins to bubble, 2 to 3 minutes, remove it from the heat and transfer to a small bowl. Stir in the lemon juice, cilantro, and salt.

Ladle the soup into bowls and top each with some spice swirl.

MENU IDEAS **North African Couscous Salad (page 222)** ✳ **Yemiser Salata (page 295)** ✳ **North African Roasted Cauliflower (page 279)** ✳ **Artichoke Heart & Bulghur Salat (page 190)** ✳ **French Barley Salad (page 210)** ✳ **Fresh Fruit Combinations (page 264)** ✳ **Curried Croutons (page 339)**

DAILY SPECIAL

Westphalian Vegetable Stew

This hearty stew is highlighted by the naturally sweet flavors of root vegetables, pears, and wine. A topping of smoked cheese will lend an authentic flavor to our vegetarian version of this stew, which is traditionally made with ham.

SERVES 4 TO 6
YIELDS 7 TO 8 CUPS
TOTAL TIME: 1 HOUR

PER 11-OUNCE SERVING: 172 CALORIES, 3 G PROTEIN, 4.5 G FAT, 29.6 G CARBOHYDRATES, 2.5 G SATURATED FATTY ACIDS, 10 MG CHOLESTEROL, 485 MG SODIUM, 5.1 G TOTAL DIETARY FIBER

2 tablespoons butter
2½ cups chopped leeks, white and tender green parts
½ teaspoon dried thyme
1 teaspoon ground fennel seeds
2 bay leaves
2 garlic cloves, minced or pressed
½ cup dry white wine
1 cup peeled and chopped carrots
2 cups chopped potatoes
1 cup peeled and chopped parsnips or turnips
4 cups water or vegetable stock
1 teaspoon salt
1½ cups cut green beans
1 cup peeled and chopped pears, such as Bartlett or Bosc
1 tablespoon cider vinegar
2 teaspoons Dijon mustard
ground black pepper to taste

grated smoked Cheddar or similar cheese
    (optional)

Melt the butter in a nonreactive soup pot and add the leeks, thyme, fennel, bay leaves, and garlic. Sauté on medium heat for 5 minutes, stirring often. Add the wine, increase the heat, and cook for about 5 minutes to reduce the liquid.

Add the carrots, potatoes, parsnips or turnips, water or stock, and salt. Cover and bring to a boil; then add the green beans and pears, lower to a simmer, and cook for 15 minutes, or until the vegetables are tender. Add the vinegar, mustard, and pepper and cook for 3 more minutes. Remove and discard the bay leaves.

Serve topped with a sprinkling of smoked cheese, if you like.

Variation Add 1 cup of diced seasoned seitan (page 377) when you add the vinegar and mustard, and cook until the seitan is heated through.

MENU IDEAS **Solstice Salad (page 227)** ✳ **Wilted Spinach & Portabella Mushrooms (page 239)** ✳ **Butternut Squash with Spicy Cranberry Sauce (page 252)** ✳ **Fruit with Cranberry Currant Dressing (page 267)** ✳ **Alabama Hot Slaw (page 245)** ✳ **Popovers (page 334)** ✳ **Featherlight Blue Mountain Biscuits (page 327)**

Yellow Pepper Purée

This beautiful golden soup is a signature dish of Fabio Picchi, chef owner of the famous Florentine restaurant Cibreo. In our version, the peppers are roasted. This allows the easiest removal of the skins, which is necessary for the best taste and texture and which mellows and sweetens the peppers. The result is uniquely silky and flavorful. Shop for large bright yellow peppers, heavy for their size, with shiny, tight skins.

Salty Parmesan cheese and vivid green parsley pesto offset the soup perfectly. This is a wonderful first course for an Italian dinner and a versatile, accommodating partner in a Daily Special. It goes well with salads from many cuisines.

SERVES 6 TO 8
YIELDS 10 CUPS
TOTAL TIME: 1 HOUR

PER 12-OUNCE SERVING: 118 CALORIES, 2.7 G PROTEIN, 2.2 G FAT, 23.9 G CARBO-HYDRATES, 0.3 G SATURATED FATTY ACIDS, 0 MG CHOLESTEROL, 341 MG SODIUM, 4 G TOTAL DIETARY FIBER

6 large yellow bell peppers
1 tablespoon olive oil
4 cups chopped onions
1 cup peeled and chopped carrots
½ cup diced celery
4 cups water
3 cups peeled and finely chopped potatoes, such as Yukon Gold
1 teaspoon salt
2 bay leaves
salt and ground black pepper to taste

freshly grated Parmesan cheese
Herbed Croutons (page 30), or toasted bread spread with Parsley Pesto (page 348) or Rich Dairyless Hazelnut Pesto (page 101)

Preheat the oven to 500°.

Meanwhile, lightly oil a baking pan. Halve and seed the peppers and place them cut side down on the baking pan. Bake for 25 to 30 minutes, until the skins begin to wrinkle and the peppers become a deeper gold.

While the peppers roast, warm the olive oil in a soup pot and sauté the onions, carrots, and celery for about 10 minutes, until the onions are translucent but not browned. Add the water, potatoes, salt, and bay leaves, cover, and bring to a boil; then reduce the heat and simmer until the potatoes are tender, 20 to 25 minutes.

When the peppers are roasted, place them in a covered bowl. When cool enough to handle, slip off their skins and add the peppers to the soup pot.

When the potatoes are tender, remove the bay leaves. In batches, purée the soup in a blender or food processor until smooth and thick. Add salt and pepper to taste. Reheat gently, if needed.

Serve topped with grated Parmesan cheese and either croutons or pesto toasts.

DAILY SPECIAL

MENU IDEAS **Lobio (page 274)** ✳ **Bean & Radicchio Salad (page 249)** ✳ **Orzo & Pesto Stuffed Tomatoes (page 223)** ✳ **Asparagus & Fennel Pasta Salad (page 193)** ✳ **Pinzimonio (page 280)** ✳ **Artichoke Heart & Bulghur Salat (page 190)**

Zucchini & Rice Soup

If you have cooked rice and Garlic Stock on hand, this soup is a snap to prepare. If not, you can cook the rice in a separate pot while you prepare the soup—minus the rice. By the time the soup is prepared, the rice will be tender and ready to stir in. The rice adds body and rounds out the texture of this simple and flavorful soup: we offer a range, so make the soup as thick as you like.

Zucchini & Rice Soup can also be puréed and served as a luscious, smooth soup. Either way, it's perfect for a light lunch or full-course meal when paired with a sharper-tasting salad.

SERVES 4 TO 6
YIELDS 9 TO 10 CUPS
TOTAL TIME: 30 MINUTES

PER 12.5-OUNCE SERVING: 126 CALO-RIES, 4.6 G PROTEIN, 3.8 G FAT, 19.4 G CARBOHYDRATES, 1.4 G SATURATED FATTY ACIDS, 4 MG CHOLESTEROL, 296 MG SODIUM, 1.8 G TOTAL DIETARY FIBER

2 cups chopped onions
2 teaspoons extra-virgin olive oil
2 cups chopped zucchini
6 cups Garlic Stock (page 19)
1 to 1½ cups cooked brown rice
2 tablespoons chopped fresh basil (2 teaspoons dried)*
salt and ground black pepper to taste

¼ cup grated Parmesan or Pecorino Romano cheese
chopped fresh parsley (optional)

If using dried basil, add it to the pot with the zucchini. Sautéing the dried herb will enhance the final flavor of the soup.

In a soup pot, sauté the onions in the oil on medium-high heat until golden brown, about 8 minutes. Add the zucchini and sauté until just tender, about 4 minutes. Add the stock and cooked rice, cover, and bring to a simmer. Add the fresh basil and salt and pepper to taste. Cover and gently simmer for 10 minutes.

Serve topped with grated cheese and, if desired, a sprinkling of chopped parsley.

MENU IDEAS **Caesar Salad (page 201)** ✳ **Bean & Radicchio Salad (page 249)** ✳ **Pinzimonio (page 280)** ✳ **Simple Tomato Salads (page 286)** ✳ **Orzo & Pesto Stuffed Tomatoes (page 223)** ✳ **Strawberries with a Touch of Tart (page 265)**

BEAN & GRAIN SOUPS

There are more than 1,000 varieties of beans, and it is believed that they have been cultivated for 8,000 years. Grains have been cultivated for more than 10,000 years. In many languages, the word for grain is the same as the word for food. Grains and beans have been primary to our survival and today are the base of the widely recognized USDA food pyramid. It would be hard to overstate their nutritional benefits or their importance in vegetarian diets. ✱ **Beans and grains are the staples of cuisines the world over and are certainly one of the fundamental building blocks of Moosewood's cuisine.**

In this section of the book, we have grouped together soup recipes that feature familiar grains like rice and barley, as well as newly rediscovered ancient grains like quinoa, millet, and spelt. We have also included soups with pasta, cornmeal, and bread. Our bean soups use ten different kinds of beans, as well as peanuts and tofu. ✱ Earthy peasant-style foods have lately gained respect, prestige, and even an aura of glamour. We see this in grocery stores and supermarkets by the explosion of items new to most Americans. Humble beans have been called "poor man's meat," and yet today we find (and sometimes pay a premium for) obscure but fashionable varieties of beans, dubbed "designer beans." Grains new to most American palates, like quinoa and farro, are showing up on the shelves. ✱ Beans and grains are relatively inexpensive and have a long shelf life, so by keeping a diverse selection on hand, you'll be rewarded with a freer creative hand and you'll tend to eat more good soup. Beans and grains are versatile. The creamy richness of beans and the nutty-flavored starch of grains are both ideal backgrounds for sharp greens, sweet root vegetables, savory herbs, pungent spices, mellow garlic, and the acidity of tomatoes. ✱ Most of the recipes in this section are substantial whole-meal soups, wonderfully thick and robust, laden with wholesome ingredients. The word minestrone translates as "big soup." We've included four minestrone recipes (based on the seasons), as well as many other big soups with beans, lentils, or split peas reinforced with vegetables. Tofu, which is made from soybeans, usually has the starring role in Asian soups. Rice, barley, corn, and other grains are used to provide strength and character in these soups, and half a dozen of them feature pasta. ✳ Bean soups are almost always prepared with water rather than stock. The bean-cooking water is an important part of a bean soup and the lack of it is one disadvantage of using canned beans. When time is a consideration, lentils and split peas, which require no soaking and have a shorter cooking time, are never a problem. And don't hesitate to use canned beans. They can be satisfactory and convenient substitutes for cooking dried beans from scratch — certainly better than no bean soup at all. Chickpeas, especially, hold up well to the canning process. ✳ When a soup recipe calls for an abundance of ingredients, you can often alter the ingredients a bit based on what's available and your own preference. If you have a somewhat different mix of summer vegetables on hand than the ones called for in Summer Minestrone, create your own adaptation. You won't go too far wrong substituting one type of greens for another or one variety of bean for another either. ✳ Most bean and grain soups can be the centerpiece of a pleasing meal. You need only a small, contrasting side salad for a well-balanced Daily Special. The more lavish the soup, the simpler the accompaniments should be. Serve big, hearty bean and grain soups with a little salad of crisp greens or tomato slices, or maybe with a piece of bread, a bit of cheese, or some fruit. What a feast! ✳

Asian Bean Curd Soup

This tasty soup is brothy yet hearty and can be spiced up or down to taste. Sichuan peppercorns, star anise, sesame oil, and dried shiitake are widely available and keep well in the pantry. The shopping list for the vegetables and tofu is short and simple. Without a doubt, this will beat your average Chinese take-out soup every time.

Carrots, celery, and onions are used in both the broth and the soup, so prepare the total amount needed and then set aside the broth vegetables in one bowl and the soup vegetables in another. Small, thin slices look best and produce a more flavorful broth. Quarter the carrots lengthwise and cut them into nickle-thick slices. Quarter the onion from stem to root and thinly slice the wedges crosswise.

SERVES 6
YIELDS 8 CUPS
TOTAL TIME: 1¼ HOURS

PER 11-OUNCE SERVING: 121 CALORIES, 6.3 G PROTEIN, 5.6 G FAT, 14.5 G CARBOHYDRATES, 1.1 G SATURATED FATTY ACIDS, 0 MG CHOLESTEROL, 705 MG SODIUM, 3.3 G TOTAL DIETARY FIBER

BROTH

½ teaspoon Sichuan peppercorns
1 whole star anise
1 or 2 whole dried chile peppers or ½ teaspoon crushed red pepper flakes
1 teaspoon salt
1 tablespoon canola or other vegetable oil
4 large garlic cloves, pressed or smashed
2 cups peeled and diced carrots
2 cups thinly sliced celery
2½ cups thinly sliced onions
6 cups water

SOUP

½ cup dried shiitake (about 8 to 12)
½ cup hot water
1 cake of regular or silken tofu (10 to 12 ounces)
½ cup peeled and diced carrots
½ cup thinly sliced celery
¼ cup thinly sliced onions
½ teaspoon dark sesame oil
2 tablespoons soy sauce
2 tablespoons thinly sliced scallions
1 cup fresh spinach leaves chiffonade

Chinese chili paste (optional)
soy sauce (optional)

For the broth, dry-roast the Sichuan peppercorns, star anise, chile peppers or red pepper flakes, and salt in a soup pot on medium heat until the peppercorns start to pop and the mixture becomes fragrant, 1 to 2 minutes (see Note). Add the oil to the soup pot and stir in the garlic, carrots, celery, and onions. Stir-fry for 5 minutes, or until the vegetables start to release their juices. Add the water, increase the heat to high, cover, and bring to a boil; then reduce the heat and simmer for 30 minutes.

Meanwhile, place the shiitake and hot water in a small bowl. Cover the bowl and set aside for 10 to 15 minutes. While the shiitake soak, cut the tofu into bite-sized cubes and set aside. When the shiitake are softened, lift them out, and then strain the soaking liquid through a fine sieve into the simmering broth. Cut the shiitake into halves or quarters, trimming and discarding any hard stems, and set aside.

When the broth has simmered for 30 minutes, strain it into another soup pot and return it to a simmer. Discard the vegetables from the broth. Add the reserved shiitake and the raw carrots, celery, and onions. When the vegetables are just tender, 5 to 10 minutes, add the tofu. Remove the soup from the heat and stir in the sesame oil and soy sauce. Divide the scallions and spinach among individual soup bowls and ladle the hot soup on top.

Serve hot, passing chili paste and/or a cruet of soy sauce, if desired.

Note Dry-roasting the dried chile pepper(s) or red pepper flakes can temporarily inflame the air and make it difficult to breathe, so take a deep breath before you begin and be prepared.

 DAILY SPECIAL

MENU IDEAS **Balinese Rice Salad (page 195)** ✳ **Classic Sichuan Noodles (page 204)** ✳ **Asparagus & Snow Pea Salad (page 247)** ✳ **Bean Sprout Salad (page 250)** ✳ **Asian Spinach & Orange Salad (page 246)** ✳ **tossed green salad with Moosewood Ginger Miso Dressing (page 323)** ✳ **Asian Pear & Grapefruit on Greens (page 264)**

Algerian Tomato Soup with Vermicelli

This spicy, vibrant tomato soup with aromatic North African spices features interesting textures of pasta and celery. The pasta will absorb the broth as it sits, so serve it immediately for the best results. If you want to prepare the soup ahead, omit the vermicelli; then reheat the soup to a boil just before serving, add the vermicelli, and cook until tender.

You probably won't want tomatoes or pasta in your salad choice for a Daily Special, but that's about the only caveat.

SERVES 4 TO 8
YIELDS 8 CUPS
PREPARATION TIME: 15 MINUTES
COOKING TIME: 25 MINUTES

PER 8-OUNCE SERVING: 104 CALORIES, 2.7 G PROTEIN, 4.1 G FAT, 15.8 G CARBO-HYDRATES, 0.5 G SATURATED FATTY ACIDS, 0 MG CHOLESTEROL, 359 MG SODIUM, 1.7 G TOTAL DIETARY FIBER

2 tablespoons olive oil
2 cups diced onions
3 garlic cloves, minced or pressed
⅛ teaspoon cayenne
1 teaspoon ground coriander
1 teaspoon ground cumin
½ teaspoon curry powder
½ teaspoon ground cinnamon
¾ teaspoon salt
1 tablespoon freshly grated orange peel
3 cups undrained canned tomatoes, chopped (28-ounce can)
3 cups water or vegetable stock
2 cups diced red bell peppers
2 cups thinly sliced celery
½ cup vermicelli, broken into ½-inch pieces
2 teaspoons fresh lemon juice

Heat the olive oil in a nonreactive soup pot, add the onions and garlic, and sauté on medium heat for about 10 minutes, until the onions are translucent. Add the cayenne, coriander, cumin, curry powder, cinnamon, salt, and orange peel and sauté for 2 minutes, stirring constantly. Add the tomatoes and water or stock, cover, and bring to a boil.

Add the peppers and celery, return the mixture to a boil, and cook for 5 minutes. Add the vermicelli and simmer, uncovered, for about 5 more minutes, until the pasta is al dente and the vegetables are tender. Stir in the lemon juice and serve.

DAILY SPECIAL

MENU IDEAS **Bulghur Grape Salad (page 200)** ✳ **Mediterranean Orange & Olive Salad (page 276)** ✳ **Arugula & Warm Mozzarella Salad (page 191)** ✳ **Yemiser Salata (page 295)** ✳ **Tunisian Carrot Salad (page 293)** ✳ **Curried Potato Salad (page 255)** ✳ **Turkish Roasted Eggplant Salad (page 294)**

Autumn Minestrone

When a dark chilly afternoon in October portends a killing frost, gather the last of the garden's bounty and make a steaming pot of soup for dinner. This recipe makes a generous amount that will feed a family for more than one satisfying meal.

SERVES 6 TO 8
YIELDS 12 CUPS
TOTAL TIME: 45 MINUTES

PER 12-OUNCE SERVING: 137 CALORIES, 3.9 G PROTEIN, 3.9 G FAT, 23 G CARBOHYDRATES, 1 G SATURATED FATTY ACIDS, 0 MG CHOLESTEROL, 744 MG SODIUM, 4.2 G TOTAL DIETARY FIBER

2 tablespoons canola or other vegetable oil
1 cup chopped onions
2 garlic cloves, minced or pressed
2½ cups peeled and cubed winter squash*
2 celery stalks, diced
½ cup peeled and diced carrots
2½ cups cubed potatoes
1 teaspoon dried oregano
2 teaspoons salt
½ teaspoon ground black pepper
6 cups water
4 cups chopped kale
1½ cups cooked or canned cannellini beans
    (15-ounce can, drained)

* We recomend a firm, rich winter squash, such as acorn, delicata, or buttercup.

Warm the oil in a large soup pot on medium heat. Add the onions and garlic, and sauté for 5 minutes. Add the squash, celery, carrots, potatoes, oregano, salt, pepper, and water and cook for 10 minutes or until the potatoes are almost done. Add the kale and beans and simmer for another 5 to 7 minutes, until the kale is tender and the beans are hot.

    Serve immediately.

MENU IDEAS **Arugula & Warm Mozzarella Salad (page 191)** ✳ **Caesar Salad (page 201)** ✳ **Fennel Salad with Blue Cheese (page 260)** ✳ **Roasted Red Pepper & Cauliflower Salad (page 226)** ✳ **Anadama Bread (page 328)** ✳ **Popovers (page 334)**

Azuki Bean Soup

The azuki bean, also called aduki or adzuki, is a low-fat bean that originated in Japan, where it holds an honored place and is often served on holidays. Azuki beans are frequently made into a traditional sweetened paste used in many Japanese desserts. Here we take the savory route with this warming, nutritious soup. For a Daily Special, accompany this soup with an Asian-style salad and fresh fruit.

SERVES 4 TO 6
YIELDS 7 CUPS
TOTAL TIME: 45 MINUTES

PER 10-OUNCE SERVING: 245 CALORIES, 4.6 G PROTEIN, 3.4 G FAT, 50.2 G CARBO-HYDRATES, 0.9 G SATURATED FATTY ACIDS, 0 MG CHOLESTEROL, 701 MG SODIUM, 2.5 G TOTAL DIETARY FIBER

½ ounce dried shiitake
1 cup boiling water
4 teaspoons canola or other vegetable oil
1 cup chopped onions or red onions
2 garlic cloves, minced or pressed
1 tablespoon grated fresh ginger root
¾ teaspoon salt
2 small carrots
1 celery stalk
3 cups water or Basic Light Vegetable Stock (page 16)
1½ cups cooked azuki beans (15-ounce can, undrained)*
2 cups thinly sliced bok choy, celery cabbage, or Chinese cabbage
1 tablespoon soy sauce
ground black pepper to taste

thinly sliced scallions

½ cup dried azuki beans cooked in 1½ to 2 cups water for about an hour until tender will yield 1½ cups cooked.

Place the shiitake in a small heatproof bowl, pour the boiling water over them, cover, and set aside.

Heat the oil in a soup pot. Add the onions, garlic, ginger root, and salt and sauté until the onions are translucent, about 10 minutes.

While the onions cook, peel the carrots, slice them in half lengthwise, and then cut them crosswise into ¼-inch half moons to yield about 1 cup. Thinly slice the celery to make about ½ cup. Remove the softened shiitake from the water, reserving the soaking liquid. Slice off and discard any tough stems and thinly slice the caps. Add the carrots, celery, and shiitake to the soup pot and sauté for 2 to 3 minutes.

Strain the shiitake-soaking liquid and add it to the soup pot with the water or stock. Bring to a boil, reduce the heat, and simmer for 5 to 10 minutes, until the carrots are just tender. Stir in the azuki beans, their liquid, and the bok choy or cabbage. Return to a simmer and cook until the beans are heated through and the cabbage has wilted. Add the soy sauce and pepper.

Serve topped with a sprinkling of scallions.

DAILY SPECIAL

MENU IDEAS **Asian Beet & Tofu Salad (page 192)** ✳ **"Japanese" Tofu Salad (page 271)** ✳ **Teriyaki Fish & Soba Noodle Salad (page 310)** ✳ **Hijiki Rice Salad (page 216)** ✳ **Pilwun's Daikon Salad (page 282) with Broiled Tofu & Sugar Snap Peas (page 199)** ✳ **Seaweed Salad (page 285)** ✳ **Pineapple Passion (page 265)**

Baked Bean Soup

New England baked beans were the inspiration for this soup. It's got that great hearty mustard, molasses, and tomato zing, and it's quick to prepare once the beans are cooked. This soup has wide appeal and kids love its sweet and spicy flavor. If you use paprika and cayenne in place of the chili powder, use the larger amount of mustard.

This soup might become a favorite weekend night supper. Try it with baked apples, corn on the cob, and a tossed green salad laced with a few bitter greens such as escarole and radicchio and topped with our Low-fat Honey Dijon Vinaigrette (also available on some supermarket shelves).

SERVES 4 TO 6
YIELDS 6 CUPS
TOTAL TIME (WITH COOKED BEANS):
   40 MINUTES

PER 9-OUNCE SERVING: 170 CALORIES, 7.1 G PROTEIN, 3.3 G FAT, 30 G CARBOHYDRATES, 0.4 G SATURATED FATTY ACIDS, 0 MG CHOLESTEROL, 316 MG SODIUM, 1.9 G TOTAL DIETARY FIBER

2 cups chopped onions
1 tablespoon olive oil
½ cup diced celery
1 cup peeled and diced carrots
1 tablespoon chili powder*
2 to 3 teaspoons Dijon or German-style mustard
2 cups water
1½ cups undrained canned stewed tomatoes (14½-ounce can)
1⅔ cups cooked white beans**
2 teaspoons cider vinegar
2 tablespoons unsulphured molasses
1 tablespoon soy sauce
salt and ground black pepper to taste

* *The chili powder can be replaced with 1½ teaspoons paprika plus ⅛ teaspoon cayenne. Without the chili powder, the flavor will be less smoky and the color burnt orange rather than brick red. Both ways are delicious.*

** *⅔ cup dried navy (pea) beans brought to a boil with 3 cups of water and then simmered for 1¾ hours yields 1⅔ cups cooked beans. A 15½-ounce can of cannellini or Great Northern beans, rinsed and drained, also works fine.*

In a soup pot on medium-high heat, sauté the onions in the oil for about 10 minutes, stirring frequently, until the onions are translucent. Add the celery, carrots, and chili powder and continue to cook until the vegetables are tender, about 5 minutes. Stir in the mustard, water, tomatoes, beans, vinegar, molasses, and soy sauce. Cover and bring to a boil. Then lower the heat and gently simmer for about 15 minutes. Add salt and pepper to taste.

Variation For a thicker soup, purée about a cup of the vegetables and beans in a blender or food processor with just enough broth to keep things moving. Stir the puréed mixture back into the soup.

DAILY SPECIAL

MENU IDEAS **Celeriac Remoulade** (page 253) * **Alabama Hot Slaw** (page 245) * **Fresh Pear & Blue Cheese Salad** (page 266) * **Southern Wheat-free Cornbread** (page 335) * **Featherlight Blue Mountain Biscuits** (page 327) * **Herbed Cheese Quick Bread** (page 332)

Black Bean & Chipotle Soup

How surprising—the wonderful smoky flavor of even a tiny chipotle pepper can pervade a thick, hearty bean soup loaded with vegetables. It's the perfect counterpoint to the mellow black beans.

The best sidekick for this soup in a Daily Special is a bright-tasting salad with the bite of bitter greens or the acidity of tomatoes or citrus.

SERVES 4 TO 6
YIELDS 8 CUPS
PREPARATION TIME:
 25 TO 35 MINUTES
SIMMERING TIME: 20 MINUTES

PER 12.5-OUNCE SERVING: 312 CALORIES, 12.5 G PROTEIN, 10.8 G FAT, 44.7 G CARBOHYDRATES, 1.5 G SATURATED FATTY ACIDS, 0 MG CHOLESTEROL, 56 MG SODIUM, 13.3 G TOTAL DIETARY FIBER

¼ cup olive oil
2 cups chopped onions
4 garlic cloves, minced or pressed
2 cups peeled and diced carrots
1½ teaspoons ground cumin
1 cup chopped celery
1 cup chopped green bell peppers
3 cups cooked black beans (two 15-ounce cans, undrained)*
½ dried chipotle pepper or 1 canned chipotle pepper in
 adobo sauce**
2 cups chopped fresh or undrained canned tomatoes (14-ounce can)
½ cup orange juice
½ cup water

sour cream or Jalapeño Cream (page 345) (optional)
chopped fresh cilantro (optional)

 * 1 cup dried black beans will yield about 3 cups cooked.
** These spicy hot, smoky peppers are available in the produce sections of well-stocked supermarkets. If using dried chipotle, remove it before serving. If using canned chipotle, choose one that can be packed into a teaspoon measure. It will disintegrate as the soup cooks. We recommend La Torre brand canned chipotles in adobo sauce, which is a thick, spicy tomato purée (see Note, page 99).

Warm the oil in a nonreactive soup pot. Sauté the onions and garlic in the oil for about 10 minutes, stirring frequently, until the onions are translucent. Add the carrots and cumin and cook on medium heat, stirring often, for a few minutes. Add the celery and bell peppers, lower the heat, cover, and cook for about 10 minutes. Add the beans, chipotle, tomatoes, orange juice, and water and simmer, covered, for 20 minutes (see Notes). If you're not using canned beans, add ½ cup of bean-cooking liquid or additional water.

If desired, garnish each serving with a dollop of sour cream or Jalapeño Cream and a sprinkling of cilantro.

Notes To save time, prepare the carrots, celery, and bell peppers while the onions cook. Just remember to stir the onions in between chopping!

If using fresh tomatoes, you may want to simmer the soup for an additional 5 minutes.

MENU IDEAS **Tomato Flowers (page 236)** ✳ **Five-Herb Salad (page 262)** ✳ **Florida Salad with Ginger Dressing (page 263)** ✳ **Kiwi, Orange & Baby Greens (page 273)** ✳ **Southern Wheat-free Cornbread (page 335)**

Broccoli & Pasta Soup

This simple, nutritious one-pot-meal-of-a-soup is best when the broccoli florets are cooked to a crisp-tender vivid green. Add the pasta just before serving so it won't have a chance to absorb too much of the broth.

SERVES 4 TO 6
YIELDS 9 CUPS
TOTAL TIME: 40 MINUTES

PER 13-OUNCE SERVING: 336 CALORIES, 18.7 G PROTEIN, 10.4 G FAT, 42 G CARBO-HYDRATES, 4.8 G SATURATED FATTY ACIDS, 18 MG CHOLESTEROL, 555 MG SODIUM, 5.9 G TOTAL DIETARY FIBER

3 to 5 garlic cloves, minced or pressed
2 cups finely chopped onions
1 tablespoon olive oil
¼ cup dry white wine or water
⅛ teaspoon red pepper flakes
8 cups chopped broccoli, florets and peeled stems (about 2 heads)
5 cups water or vegetable stock
¼ teaspoon salt, more to taste
½ pound short chunky pasta, such as orecchiette, tubetti, or
    small shells

1 cup freshly grated Pecorino or Parmesan cheese

Bring a covered pot of water to a boil for cooking the pasta. Meanwhile, combine the garlic, onions, and oil in a soup pot and sauté on medium heat for 8 to 10 minutes, stirring regularly, until the onions start to caramelize. Add the wine or water and stir well. Cook until the liquid evaporates, 4 to 5 minutes. Add the red pepper flakes, broccoli, water or stock, and the salt. Cover and cook for 7 to 9 minutes, or until the broccoli is tender.

When the pasta water boils, add the pasta and cook until al dente, 8 to 10 minutes. Drain and set aside.

When the broccoli is tender, purée about ⅓ of the soup mixture in a blender until smooth and return it to the soup pot. Stir in the cooked pasta. Add a little water or stock if you prefer a thinner soup.

Top with the grated cheese and serve immediately.

MENU IDEAS **Mediterranean Orange & Olive Salad (page 276)** ✳ **Balkan Roasted Vegetable Salad (page 196)** ✳ **Mussel Salad (page 304)** ✳ **Kiwi, Orange & Baby Greens (page 273)**

Broccoli Rabe & Rice Soup

The hint of bitterness in broccoli rabe is just what is needed to set this otherwise mild soup deliciously on edge. We like to use arborio rice because of the creamy texture it adds to the soup. Pecorino Romano cheese, a chunk of bread, and a glass of red table wine can round out this hearty and flavorful "zuppa"—which makes a good, tasty leftover as well.

SERVES 4 TO 6
YIELDS 12 CUPS
TOTAL TIME: 50 MINUTES

PER 16-OUNCE SERVING: 150 CALORIES, 4.7 G PROTEIN, 3 G FAT, 28.4 G CARBOHYDRATES, 0.4 G SATURATED FATTY ACIDS, 0 MG CHOLESTEROL, 295 MG SODIUM, 5.4 G TOTAL DIETARY FIBER

2 cups thinly sliced onions
1 tablespoon olive oil
1 bunch of broccoli rabe, thoroughly rinsed and chopped*
1 cup peeled and diced carrots
4 celery stalks with leaves, chopped (about 2 cups)
½ cup raw arborio rice or other white rice
8 cups Garlic Stock (page 19)
1 bay leaf
salt and ground black pepper to taste

grated Pecorino Romano or Parmesan cheese

*Broccoli rabe is also known as rapini greens. After rinsing, slice off and discard the bottom ½ inch of each stem and any tough, hollow stems. Then chop into small, bite-sized pieces.

In a large soup pot, sauté the onions in the oil on medium-high heat until they begin to soften, about 5 minutes. Add the broccoli rabe, carrots, and celery. Cover and cook for another 5 minutes, stirring occasionally, until the vegetables are just tender.

Stir in the rice and continue to toss it with the vegetables for a few minutes, until the surfaces of the rice kernels start to become gummy. Add the stock and bay leaf and cover and simmer on low heat for 20 minutes or more, until the rice is tender. Add salt and pepper to taste. Remove and discard the bay leaf.

Serve with grated cheese sprinkled on each serving.

MENU IDEAS **Solstice Salad (page 227)** * **Tomatoes Capriccio (page 286)** * **Fig & Endive Salad (page 261)** * **Mediterranean Orange & Olive Salad (page 276)**

Choklay's Tibetan Lentil Soup

This recipe is a specialty of one of our cooks, Choklay Lhamo. Lentils, carrots, and potatoes are seasoned with onions, cumin, coriander, and a green chile to make a simple, hearty, unusually spiced soup that is really satisfying.

A Tibetan by birth, Choklay ran her own successful restaurant in India before coming to Moosewood. She came to Ithaca through the Tibetan Resettlement Program, as have several of our co-workers. Her great Tibetan dishes are featured on our Sunday night ethnic menus and at the many celebrations and events to which the Tibetan community here welcomes Ithacan friends and visitors from all over the world.

SERVES 6
YIELDS 10 CUPS
TOTAL TIME: 45 MINUTES

PER 14-OUNCE SERVING: 269 CALORIES, 16.2 G PROTEIN, 3.4 G FAT, 46.8 G CARBO-HYDRATES, 0.7 G SATURATED FATTY ACIDS, 0 MG CHOLESTEROL, 786 MG SODIUM, 15.7 G TOTAL DIETARY FIBER

1½ cups dried lentils, rinsed
6 cups water
1 tablespoon canola or other vegetable oil
1½ cups chopped onions
2 garlic cloves, minced or pressed
1 fresh chile, seeded and finely minced
1 carrot, peeled and diced into ½-inch cubes
1 potato, diced into ½-inch cubes
2 teaspoons ground coriander
1 teaspoon ground cumin
3 cups undrained canned tomatoes
　(28-ounce can)
1 tablespoon chopped fresh cilantro
1½ teaspoons salt

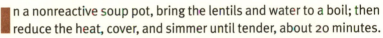

In a nonreactive soup pot, bring the lentils and water to a boil; then reduce the heat, cover, and simmer until tender, about 20 minutes.

Meanwhile, heat the oil in a medium saucepan and sauté the onions, garlic, and chile for 5 minutes. Add the carrots, potatoes, coriander, and cumin and sauté for another minute, stirring to prevent sticking. Remove from the heat and set aside.

When the lentils are tender, coarsely chop the tomatoes right in the can and stir them into the soup pot. Add the chopped cilantro, salt, and the sautéed vegetables. Cover and simmer for 10 to 12 minutes, until all of the vegetables are tender.

MENU IDEAS **Curried Rice Salad (page 205)** ✳ **East Indian Fruit Salad (page 258)** ✳ **Nepalese Egg Salad (page 278)** ✳ **Indian Green Beans & Red Peppers (page 270)** ✳ **Turkish Roasted Eggplant Salad (page 294)** ✳ **Balinese Rice Salad (page 195)** ✳ **Indonesian Tahu Goreng (page 218)** ✳ **Asian Pear & Grapefruit on Greens (page 264)**

East African Groundnut Soup

Groundnuts (peanuts) are a staple throughout East Africa, West Africa, and southern Africa. Across the continent, there must be hundreds of versions of groundnut soups and stews—maybe even one for each cook.

The curry spices in this peanut soup make it a departure from the peanut soups, stews, and sauces we've previously developed. The Asian influence on African cooking is particularly strong in eastern and South Africa, but curry scents waft out of the pots of West Africa as well.

For a companion salad to this thick rich soup, think contrasts: a light fruity salad or one with crisp greens.

SERVES 6 TO 8
YIELDS 13 CUPS
PREPARATION AND SAUTÉ TIME:
  30 MINUTES
SIMMERING TIME:
  40 TO 45 MINUTES

PER 13.5-OUNCE SERVING: 244 CALO-RIES, 7.2 G PROTEIN, 10 G FAT, 34.5 G CARBOHYDRATES, 2 G SATURATED FATTY ACIDS, 0 MG CHOLESTEROL, 488 MG SODIUM, 2.6 G TOTAL DIETARY FIBER

3 cups chopped onions
3 celery stalks, diced (about 1 cup)
1 tablespoon canola or other vegetable oil
2 green and/or red bell peppers, diced (about 2 cups)
⅛ to ¼ teaspoon cayenne
2 tablespoons garam masala or other curry powder
1 cup raw brown rice
3 cups canned "fresh cut" diced tomatoes in juice (28-ounce can)*
6 cups water
1 teaspoon salt**
½ cup peanut butter**
1 to 2 tablespoons sugar**
2 tablespoons fresh lime juice

chopped fresh cilantro (optional)
chopped scallions (optional)

* *Canned diced tomatoes, sometimes called "fresh cut," are more convenient than whole tomatoes when you want chopped tomatoes. As a bonus, the tomato pieces are firmer and hold their shape better in soups and stews. Several major brands, such as Hunt and Del Monte, as well as lesser-known brands produce fresh cut diced tomatoes. Look for diced tomatoes packed in juice, not purée.*
** *Although most supermarkets stock natural unhomogenized peanut butters without sweeteners or stabilizers, many commercial peanut butters do have salt and sugar added to them. Be sure to check the label. You may want to use less salt and/or sugar depending on the type of peanut butter you use.*

In a large nonreactive soup pot, sauté the onions and celery in the oil for about 10 minutes on medium-high heat, until the onions are soft and translucent. Add the bell peppers and sauté for 5 more minutes. Stir in the cayenne and garam masala or curry powder. Add the rice, tomatoes, water, and salt and stir well. Cover and bring to a boil; then reduce the heat and simmer for about 40 minutes, until the rice is tender.

Whisk in the peanut butter, sugar, and lime juice. Top each serving with chopped cilantro and scallions, if you like.

DAILY SPECIAL

MENU IDEAS **Florida Salad with Ginger Dressing (page 263)** ✳ **Kiwi, Orange & Baby Greens (page 273)** ✳ **Alabama Hot Slaw (page 245)** ✳ **Kale Salad (page 272)**

Ecuadorian Quinoa & Vegetable Soup

Quinoa, an ancient grain whose recorded use dates back to the Incan empire, has been rediscovered in recent years as another delicious option in the grain family. Quinoa has a mild, nutty flavor and crunchy texture, is rich in vitamins, minerals, and amino acids, and cooks in about 15 minutes. Here, it thickens a soup made of other crops indigenous to the Americas: potatoes, squash, peppers, and tomatoes.

SERVES 4 TO 6
YIELDS ABOUT 7½ CUPS
PREPARATION TIME:
  20 MINUTES
SIMMERING TIME:
  25 TO 30 MINUTES

PER 10.5-OUNCE SERVING: 150 CALO-RIES, 3.6 G PROTEIN, 5.9 G FAT, 22.8 G CARBOHYDRATES, 0.8 G SATURATED FATTY ACIDS, 0 MG CHOLESTEROL, 408 MG SODIUM, 3 G TOTAL DIETARY FIBER

½ cup raw quinoa
2 tablespoons olive oil
2 cups chopped onions
1 teaspoon salt
1 cup diced potatoes
1 cup chopped red or green bell peppers
1 teaspoon ground coriander
1 teaspoon ground cumin
1 teaspoon dried oregano
½ teaspoon ground black pepper
3 cups water or vegetable stock
1½ cups chopped fresh or undrained canned tomatoes
    (14½-ounce can)
1 cup diced zucchini or yellow squash
1 tablespoon fresh lemon juice

chopped scallions, chopped fresh cilantro, crumbled tortilla chips, and/or grated Cheddar or Monterey Jack cheese (optional)

Thoroughly rinse the quinoa in a fine-mesh strainer under cold running water. Set aside to drain.

Warm the oil in a nonreactive soup pot, add the onions and salt, cover, and cook on medium heat for 5 minutes, stirring occasionally. Add the drained quinoa, potatoes, bell peppers, coriander, cumin, oregano, black pepper, water or stock, and tomatoes. Cover and bring to a boil; then reduce the heat and simmer gently for 10 minutes. Add the zucchini, cover, and simmer for 15 to 20 minutes, or until all of the vegetables are tender.

Stir in the lemon juice. If desired, serve with a sprinkling of scallions, cilantro, tortilla chips, and/or grated cheese.

MENU IDEAS Avocado Seitan Salad (page 194) ✳ Mexican Shrimp & Spinach Salad (page 301) ✳ Florida Salad with Ginger Dressing (page 263) ✳ Mexican Chickpea Salad (page 277)

Egyptian Red Lentil Soup

We developed this simple-to-prepare soup for a "North African night" at Moosewood, based on the descriptions of red lentil soups enjoyed in Egypt by Moosewood workers Robin Wichman and Tricia Hackett. Ancient Egyptians believed that lentils promote generosity, enlightenment, and the capacity to forgive. While we don't know about all that, we *do* know that this lentil soup is surely restorative and a delight to the senses.

Red lentils turn a rich golden color when cooked—which may come as a surprise the first time you use them. This soup will be a greenish-gold once the fresh cilantro is blended in.

SERVES 6 TO 8
YIELDS 8½ CUPS
TOTAL TIME: 50 TO 55 MINUTES

PER 8-OUNCE SERVING: 140 CALORIES, 7.6 G PROTEIN, 2.3 G FAT, 23.8 G CARBOHYDRATES, 0.5 G SATURATED FATTY ACIDS, 0 MG CHOLESTEROL, 326 MG SODIUM, 8.1 G TOTAL DIETARY FIBER

5 cups water
1 cup dried red lentils
2 cups chopped onions
2 cups chopped potatoes
8 large garlic cloves, peeled and left whole
1 tablespoon canola or other vegetable oil
2 teaspoons ground cumin
½ teaspoon turmeric
1 teaspoon salt
⅓ cup chopped fresh cilantro
3 tablespoons fresh lemon juice
salt and ground black pepper to taste

Combine the water, lentils, onions, potatoes, and garlic in a soup pot, cover, and bring to a boil. Reduce the heat and simmer until everything is tender, 15 to 20 minutes. Remove from the heat.

In a small saucepan on low heat, warm the oil until it is hot but not smoking. Add the cumin, turmeric, and salt and cook, stirring constantly for 2 to 3 minutes, until the cumin is fragrant. Take care not to scorch the spices. Set aside for about a minute or the oil may splatter when added to the soup. Stir the slightly cooled spices into the soup and add the cilantro.

Working in small batches, purée the soup in a blender until smooth. Add the lemon juice. Return the soup to the pot and reheat gently. Add salt and pepper to taste.

MENU IDEAS **Artichoke Heart & Bulghur Salat (page 190)** ✳ **Fattoush (page 209)** ✳ **Persian Rice & Pistachio Salad (page 224)** ✳ **Tunisian Carrot Salad (page 293)** ✳ **Balkan Roasted Vegetable Salad (page 196)**

Everyday Split Pea Soup

This is *the* vegetarian split pea soup for those of us who remember with longing those bowls of thick, ham bone-flavored soup that our grandmothers used to make. Here, mushrooms add texture and the miso gives a rich flavor, yet the soup's virtually fat-free!

We've made this soup with several types of dried mushrooms. Chanterelles have a particularly nice flavor, texture, and color with split peas. Dried portabellas also have a good flavor and are usually reasonably priced. We've even made split pea soup with shiitake. A mix is nice, too.

Split pea soup tastes great left over, but reheat it gently—miso should never be heated to boiling.

SERVES 8
YIELDS 13 CUPS
PREPARATION TIME: 25 MINUTES
COOKING TIME: 1 HOUR

PER 13-OUNCE SERVING: 273 CALORIES, 16.5 G PROTEIN, 1.4 G FAT, 51.1 G CARBO-HYDRATES, 0.2 G SATURATED FATTY ACIDS, 0 MG CHOLESTEROL, 642 MG SODIUM, 17.3 G TOTAL DIETARY FIBER

½ ounce dried mushrooms, softened in 1 cup boiling water*
2 cups dried split peas (about 1 pound)
8 cups water
3 bay leaves
1 teaspoon dried marjoram
2 cups chopped onions
1½ cups peeled and diced carrots
1½ cups chopped celery (include some leafy tops)
2 cups diced potatoes
¼ to ⅓ cup light miso
1 teaspoon salt
⅛ teaspoon ground black pepper

* You can find ½-ounce bags of dried mushrooms in the produce sections of many supermarkets. To soften, place the dried mushrooms in a heatproof bowl, cover with the boiling water, and set aside for about 20 minutes.

In a large covered soup pot on high heat, combine the split peas, water, bay leaves, marjoram, onions, carrots, celery, and potatoes. When the soup begins to boil, stir well, reduce the heat to a simmer, cover, and continue to cook.

Meanwhile, remove the mushrooms from the soaking liquid and discard any hard stems. Slice or chop the softened mushrooms and add them to the soup. Strain the soaking liquid to remove any sediment or dirt and add the clear liquid to the soup pot.

After the soup has simmered for about 30 minutes, stir it well. Maintain on low heat with occasional stirring or place the pot on a heat diffuser to prevent sticking and cook for another 20 minutes, until the split peas are very soft and the soup becomes "creamy" when stirred. Discard the bay leaves. Stir in ¼ cup of the miso, the salt, and pepper. Add more miso to taste and serve.

Note If you plan to serve the soup later, set it aside to cool a bit and then refrigerate it. Reheat gently before serving, stirring often to prevent scorching.

MENU IDEAS **Alabama Hot Slaw (page 245)** ✳ **Syrian Beet Salad (page 291)** ✳ **fresh baby spinach with Moosewood House Dressing (page 324) and Filo Croutons (page 342)** ✳ **Anadama Bread (page 328)** ✳ **Our Special Gluten-free Bread (page 333)** ✳ **Pears Parmesan (page 265)**

Farinata

With origins in the rustic mountainous regions of Northern Italy, *farinata* is a robust vegetable soup thickened with cornmeal. It has long been a staple in Italy and seems to inspire passionate loyalty to treasured family recipes in some Italian-American communities. This version has aromatic rosemary as well as kale and tomatoes. Combine it with a delicate salad and some bread for a beautiful meal. *Mangia.*

SERVES 4 TO 6
YIELDS 8 CUPS
TOTAL TIME: 40 MINUTES

PER 12-OUNCE SERVING: 115 CALORIES, 3.4 G PROTEIN, 3 G FAT, 19.9 G CARBOHYDRATES, 0.4 G SATURATED FATTY ACIDS, 0 MG CHOLESTEROL, 610 MG SODIUM, 2.9 G TOTAL DIETARY FIBER

1 tablespoon olive oil
2 cups chopped onions
1 tablespoon chopped fresh rosemary (1 teaspoon dried)
1 cup diced celery
1 cup peeled and chopped carrots
1 teaspoon salt
3 cups undrained chopped canned tomatoes (28-ounce can)
3½ cups water
4 cups rinsed and chopped kale
¼ to ⅓ cup fine cornmeal (see Note)
salt and ground black pepper to taste

grated Parmesan or Pecorino Romano cheese (optional)

Warm the olive oil in a nonreactive soup pot. Add the onions and rosemary and sauté on medium-high heat for 5 minutes, stirring frequently. Add the celery, carrots, and salt and continue to sauté for 5 minutes. Add the tomatoes and 3 cups of the water, cover, and bring to a boil; then lower the heat to a simmer and cook for 10 minutes.

Add the kale and simmer for about 10 minutes longer, until all of the vegetables are tender. In a bowl, whisk together the cornmeal and the remaining ½ cup of water until smooth and lump-free. Add it to the soup in a slow stream while stirring briskly. Simmer for 5 minutes. Add salt and pepper to taste.

Serve with grated cheese, if you wish.

Note Use more or less cornmeal to make a thicker or thinner soup.

DAILY SPECIAL

MENU IDEAS **Mediterranean Orange & Olive Salad (page 276)** ✳ **Arugula & Warm Mozzarella Salad (page 191)** ✳ **Bean & Radicchio Salad (page 249)** ✳ **Wilted Spinach & Portabella Mushrooms (page 239)** ✳ **Composed Beet Salad (page 254)** ✳ **Focaccia (page 330)**

Fassoulada

This hearty bean and vegetable soup from the Greek countryside can be made year-round, but it's especially good when fresh thyme and Swiss chard are available.

Fresh thyme has a delicate taste and fragrance and can be used more liberally than its dried counterpart.

SERVES 6 TO 8
YIELDS 10 TO 11 CUPS
TOTAL TIME: 45 MINUTES

PER 13-OUNCE SERVING: 202 CALORIES, 8.3 G PROTEIN, 4.2 G FAT, 34.9 G CARBO-HYDRATES, 0.6 G SATURATED FATTY ACIDS, 0 MG CHOLESTEROL, 581 MG SODIUM, 6.3 G TOTAL DIETARY FIBER

2 tablespoons olive oil
1 large onion, chopped (about 2 cups)
4 garlic cloves, minced or pressed
1 large red potato, diced (about 2 cups)
2 tablespoons minced fresh thyme (1½ teaspoons dried)
6 cups Basic Light Vegetable Stock (page 16), water, or reserved bean-cooking liquid*
2½ to 3 cups drained canned navy beans, pea beans, cannellini, or other white beans (two 15½-ounce cans)*
1 green bell pepper, seeded and diced (about 1 cup)
1 red bell pepper, seeded and diced (about 1 cup)
¼ cup tomato paste
5 to 6 cups rinsed, stemmed, and chopped Swiss chard or spinach
½ cup chopped fresh parsley
3 tablespoons fresh lemon juice
salt and ground black pepper to taste

chopped fresh parsley
crumbled feta cheese (optional)

*If you prefer freshly cooked beans, sort 1 cup of dried beans, cover them with water, and soak overnight or for at least 5 hours. Drain the soaked beans, cover with 10 cups of fresh water, and bring to a boil. Reduce the heat and simmer for 1½ hours or until tender. Add more water during cooking, if needed. Drain, reserving 6 cups of the bean water to use in the soup.

In a soup pot, warm the olive oil. Add the onions and garlic and sauté on medium-low heat until the onions are translucent but not brown, about 10 minutes. Add the potatoes and half of the thyme and continue to cook for 5 minutes. Add the stock, water, or bean-cooking liquid, cover, and simmer until the potatoes are tender, 5 to 10 minutes.

Stir in the beans, bell peppers, and tomato paste. Add the Swiss chard or spinach, the parsley, and the remaining thyme and heat for about 3 minutes or until the greens are wilted and tender. Stir in the lemon juice and add salt and black pepper to taste.

Top each serving with parsley and crumbled feta, if desired.

DAILY SPECIAL

MENU IDEAS **Orzo & Pesto Stuffed Tomatoes (page 223)** ✳ **Fennel & Arugula Salad with Grapefruit (page 259)** ✳ **Fennel Salad with Blue Cheese (page 260)** ✳ **Syrian Beet Salad (page 291)** ✳ **Greek Pasta Salad (page 214)**

Green & White Gumbo

This meatless gumbo is an excellent, full-bodied stew with authentic New Orleans taste and texture, designed in the tradition of the French *"gumbo aux herbes"* — full of zesty herbs and vitamin-rich greens. Here, black-eyed peas and rice lend flavor, protein, and heartiness.

Use any combination of greens. We're fond of spinach, kale, and Swiss chard in equal amounts, but other possibilities could be collards, watercress, and mustard, beet, or turnip greens. To save time, you can prepare the greens while the stew simmers.

Pass Tabasco or another hot pepper sauce at the table for those who like it like that. Add a couple of salads and it's a Creole banquet.

SERVES 4 TO 6
YIELDS 9 CUPS
PREPARATION TIME: 20 MINUTES
COOKING TIME: 35 MINUTES

PER 12-OUNCE SERVING: 245 CALORIES, 6.5 G PROTEIN, 10.6 G FAT, 33.5 G CARBOHYDRATES, 2.7 G SATURATED FATTY ACIDS, 0 MG CHOLESTEROL, 612 MG SODIUM, 5 G TOTAL DIETARY FIBER

¼ **cup canola or other vegetable oil**
⅓ **cup all-purpose flour**
3 cups chopped onions
1 teaspoon salt
¼ **cup sliced scallions, cut on the diagonal**
3 garlic cloves, minced or pressed
3 bay leaves
½ **teaspoon dried thyme**
⅛ **teaspoon cayenne**
½ **cup diced celery**
½ **cup stemmed and halved green beans**
4 cups water or vegetable stock
½ **cup fresh or frozen corn kernels**
1 cup cooked black-eyed peas (15-ounce can, drained)
1 cup cooked brown rice
1 cup frozen cut okra
4 cups chopped mixed fresh greens (spinach, kale, Swiss chard)
¼ **cup chopped fresh parsley**
salt and ground black pepper to taste

In a soup pot on medium-high heat, warm the oil. Add the flour and whisk or stir well with a wooden spoon to make a smooth paste. Cook, stirring vigilantly, for about 5 minutes, then lower the heat and cook for another 3 to 5 minutes, still stirring, until the roux has become a golden brown (almost copper) color.

Add the onions and salt and cook on medium heat for about 5 minutes, stirring frequently, until the onions are just soft. Add the scallions, garlic, bay leaves, thyme, cayenne, celery, and green beans. Cover and cook until the celery and green beans are tender, about 5 minutes. Stir in the water or stock and bring to a boil. Add the corn, black-eyed peas, rice, and okra, cover, and lower the heat to gently simmer for 10 minutes. Stir in the greens and parsley and continue to simmer for about 5 minutes. Remove the bay leaves, add salt and pepper to taste, and serve.

Note Since this stew has quite a few ingredients, making a double batch may be a good plan. The gumbo freezes very well stored in a plastic container with an airtight lid. Just defrost it and gently reheat, stirring occasionally.

DAILY SPECIAL

MENU IDEAS **Farm-style Tomato Salad (page 286)** ✳ **Tropical Fruit & Shrimp Salad (page 312)** ✳ **Spicy Cucumber Salad (page 288)** ✳ **tossed green salad with Moosewood Ginger Miso Dressing (page 323)** ✳ **Popovers (page 334)** ✳ **Southern Wheat-free Cornbread (page 335)**

Indian Tomato Rice Soup

The fragrance of basmati rice pervades this simple tomato rice soup, which is flecked with cilantro. Seasoned with ground cumin and coriander, the soup's mild flavor becomes very hot with the addition of delicious Spiced Paneer cheese.

SERVES 4
YIELDS 6 CUPS
TOTAL TIME: 50 MINUTES

PER 12-OUNCE SERVING: 201 CALORIES, 3.7 G PROTEIN, 7.9 G FAT, 30.6 G CARBO-HYDRATES, 2 G SATURATED FATTY ACIDS, 0 MG CHOLESTEROL, 513 MG SODIUM, 3 G TOTAL DIETARY FIBER

2 tablespoons canola or other vegetable oil
2 cups finely chopped onions
3 garlic cloves, minced or pressed
½ teaspoon salt
1 teaspoon ground cumin
1 teaspoon ground coriander
⅓ cup raw white basmati rice, rinsed and drained
4 cups water or Basic Light Vegetable Stock (page 16)
2 cups finely chopped tomatoes
2 tablespoons chopped fresh cilantro
salt and ground black pepper to taste

Spiced Paneer (page 351)

Warm the oil in a medium nonreactive saucepan. Add the onions, garlic, and salt and sauté on medium heat for about 10 minutes, until the onions are translucent, stirring often. Add the cumin and coriander and sauté for a minute, stirring constantly. Add the rice and water or vegetable stock. Cover and bring to a boil; then reduce the heat, cover, and cook until the rice is tender, about 25 minutes.

Stir in the chopped tomatoes, cover, and cook on low heat for about 5 minutes, until the tomatoes are tender. Add the cilantro and salt and pepper to taste.

Serve topped with Spiced Paneer.

MENU IDEAS **Indian Green Beans & Red Peppers (page 270)** ✳ **Curried Tofu Salad (page 256)** ✳ **East Indian Fruit Salad (page 258)** ✳ **Gado Gado (page 212)** ✳ **Tropical Fruit & Shrimp Salad (page 312)** ✳ **Asian Pear & Grapefruit on Greens (page 264)**

Italian Green, White & Red Soup

Simple and very satisfying, this brightly colored soup is quite popular with adults and is a children's favorite, despite all that good, healthful spinach.

SERVES 4 TO 6
YIELDS 9 CUPS
TOTAL TIME: 30 MINUTES

PER 12-OUNCE SERVING: 272 CALORIES, 14.7 G PROTEIN, 12.4 G FAT, 26.9 G CARBOHYDRATES, 5.1 G SATURATED FATTY ACIDS, 18 MG CHOLESTEROL, 625 MG SODIUM, 2.7 G TOTAL DIETARY FIBER

¼ pound vermicelli pasta, broken into 2-inch lengths
generous pinch of salt
5 garlic cloves, minced or pressed
2 tablespoons olive oil
4 cups Mock Chicken Stock (page 20)
2 cups chopped tomatoes
10 ounces spinach, rinsed, stemmed, and chopped
   (about 6 loosely packed cups)
1 cup chopped fresh basil, loosely packed

freshly grated Parmesan cheese

Bring a large pot of water to a boil, add the vermicelli and salt, stir, partially cover the pot, and cook until al dente, about 5 minutes. Drain well in a colander and set aside.

In a nonreactive soup pot, sauté the garlic in the olive oil on medium heat for 1 to 2 minutes, until it just turns golden. Pour in the stock, cover, and bring to a simmer. Add the tomatoes, cover, and simmer for 5 minutes. Add the spinach, basil, and cooked pasta and heat briefly for 1 to 2 minutes, until the spinach is just wilted and still bright green.

Top each serving with a generous amount of grated Parmesan and serve immediately.

MENU IDEAS **Mediterranean Orange & Olive Salad (page 276)** ∗ **Bean & Radicchio Salad (page 249)** ∗ **Marinated Mushrooms (page 347)** ∗ **Fennel Salad with Blue Cheese (page 260)** ∗ **Focaccia (page 330)**

Korean Pine Nut Porridge

This is Moosewood cook Jenny Wang's adaptation of an exquisite pine nut porridge she and Penny Goldin had as part of an elegant seven-course vegetarian meal at Hangawi, a Korean restaurant in New York City. Defying Western classification, it is reminiscent of a rich hot breakfast cereal, but has a texture similar to vichyssoise. The simplicity of the flavor of pine nuts and ginger makes this something you'll want to try at least once in your life.

SERVES 4
YIELDS 4 CUPS
TOTAL TIME: 30 MINUTES

PER 9-OUNCE SERVING: 183 CALORIES, 5.6 G PROTEIN, 10.3 G FAT, 21.5 G CARBO-HYDRATES, 1.6 G SATURATED FATTY ACIDS, 0 MG CHOLESTEROL, 151 MG SODIUM, 1.2 G TOTAL DIETARY FIBER

½ cup pine nuts
1 piece of crystallized ginger the size of a quarter (page 364)
4 cups water
½ cup white rice flour (page 376)
¼ teaspoon salt, more to taste
2 tablespoons sugar, more to taste

fan of thin strawberry slices* or thin kiwi slices

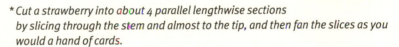

Cut a strawberry into about 4 parallel lengthwise sections by slicing through the stem and almost to the tip, and then fan the slices as you would a hand of cards.

In a dry skillet on the stove or in a 350° oven, toast the pine nuts until golden and fragrant, stirring occasionally to brown them evenly. Combine the pine nuts, crystallized ginger, and 1 cup of the water in a blender and purée. Strain the milky liquid through a fine sieve, pressing on the solids. Discard the solids and set aside the liquid.

In a small soup pot, whisk together the remaining water and the rice flour. Cook on medium heat, stirring often, until the mixture thickens. Add the reserved pine nut liquid, salt, and sugar and heat thoroughly.

Serve topped with a floating fruit garnish and offer additional salt and sugar at the table.

MENU IDEAS **Broiled Tofu & Sugar Snap Peas (page 199)** ✳ **Spicy Pineapple Tofu Salad (page 230)** ✳ **Asian Spinach & Orange Salad (page 246)** ✳ **Asparagus & Snow Pea Salad (page 247)** ✳ **Asian Beet & Tofu Salad (page 192)** ✳ **"Japanese" Tofu Salad (page 271)** ✳ **Mango Salsa Salad (page 265)** ✳ **Oranges, Hot & Sweet (page 265)**

Liberian Black-eyed Pea Soup

Black-eyed peas are a favorite ingredient in all of the regions of West Africa. There, traditional soups are rather plain, so to add corn, greens, and/or okra to this soup would be considered quite "fancy" by most West Africans. And if you add the quantity of cayenne that most West Africans would, this soup would be considered insanely fiery by the majority of North Americans!

Try varying the combination of vegetables a bit, playing with the quantities of the optional ingredients, or doubling the amount of greens. Reduce the water and you'll have a stew, delicious served on polenta or grits.

Top each bowl with chopped scallions, more chopped cilantro, or grated Cheddar or smoked cheese.

SERVES 6 TO 8
YIELDS ABOUT 10 CUPS
TOTAL TIME: 1 HOUR

PER 10-OUNCE SERVING: 152 CALORIES, 7.3 G PROTEIN, 4.2 G FAT, 23.3 G CARBOHYDRATES, 1 G SATURATED FATTY ACIDS, 0 MG CHOLESTEROL, 148 MG SODIUM, 3.5 G TOTAL DIETARY FIBER

1 cup dried black-eyed peas
2 garlic cloves, peeled
6 cups water
2 cups chopped onions
1 cup diced celery
2 tablespoons canola or other vegetable oil
pinch of cayenne, more to taste
2 teaspoons ground allspice
pinch of dried thyme
1 green or red bell pepper, seeded and chopped
1 cup fresh or frozen corn kernels (optional)
1 cup sliced fresh or frozen okra (optional)
2 cups chopped fresh collards, kale, chard, or spinach (optional)
3 cups canned diced tomatoes in juice (28-ounce can)*
1 to 2 tablespoons chopped fresh cilantro (optional)
salt and ground black pepper to taste

* Canned diced tomatoes, sometimes called "fresh cut," are more convenient than whole tomatoes when you want chopped tomatoes. As a bonus, the tomato pieces are firmer and hold their shape better in soups and stews. Several major brands, such as Hunt and Del Monte, as well as lesser-known brands produce fresh cut diced tomatoes. Look for diced tomatoes packed in juice, not purée.

In a covered saucepan, bring the black-eyed peas, garlic cloves, and 4 cups of the water to a boil. Reduce the heat and simmer until tender, about 45 minutes.

Meanwhile, in a nonreactive soup pot, sauté the onions and celery in the oil on medium heat for about 10 minutes, until the onions are translucent. Stir in the cayenne, allspice, and thyme and cook for 1 to 2 minutes, stirring frequently. Add the bell peppers, stir well, cover, and cook for 3 to 4 minutes. Stir in the corn, okra, tomatoes, and the remaining 2 cups of water. Cover and bring just to a boil; then add the greens, gently simmer until tender, and remove from the heat until the black-eyed peas are ready.

When the black-eyed peas are tender, remove the garlic cloves or mash them with a fork against the side of the pan. Add the black-eyed peas and their cooking liquid to the soup pot. Stir in the cilantro, if using, and add salt and black pepper to taste.

DAILY SPECIAL

MENU IDEAS **Florida Salad with Ginger Dressing (page 263)** * **East Indian Fruit Salad (page 258)** * **Alabama Hot Slaw (page 245)** * **Oranges Exotic (page 265)**

Mexican Butter Bean Soup

The inspiration for this soup came from our own *Habas Verdes con Queso* (*New Recipes from Moosewood Restaurant*, page 130), a popular white chili we've served at the restaurant for over twenty years. This spin-off shares the bright, hot taste and creamy consistency of our original *Habas*, and the corn kernels add textural distinction to our new soup version.

Serve with a light and colorful salad and cornbread for an out-of-the-ordinary Mexican meal.

SERVES 6 TO 8
YIELDS 10 CUPS
TOTAL TIME: 50 TO 60 MINUTES

PER 10-OUNCE SERVING: 203 CALORIES, 7.9 G PROTEIN, 9.8 G FAT, 23.7 G CARBO-HYDRATES, 5 G SATURATED FATTY ACIDS, 22 MG CHOLESTEROL, 366 MG SODIUM, 4.9 G TOTAL DIETARY FIBER

2 cups chopped onions
2 garlic cloves, minced or pressed
1 tablespoon canola or other vegetable oil
1 tablespoon ground coriander
1 tablespoon ground cumin
⅛ teaspoon cayenne, or to taste
⅛ teaspoon dried thyme
1 red bell pepper, seeded and diced
3 cups water or Basic Light Vegetable Stock (page 16)
2 cups cooked butter beans (two 15-ounce cans, drained)
2 cups fresh or undrained canned chopped tomatoes (15-ounce can)
1 cup fresh or frozen corn kernels
4 ounces Neufchâtel or cream cheese, cut into small chunks
½ cup grated Monterey Jack cheese
¼ cup chopped fresh cilantro
salt and ground black pepper to taste

chopped fresh parsley
sliced black olives

In a covered soup pot on medium heat, sauté the onions and garlic in the oil, stirring occasionally, until the onions are very soft, about 15 minutes. Stir in the coriander, cumin, cayenne, and thyme. Add the bell peppers, cover, and cook for 2 to 3 minutes.

Meanwhile, combine about a cup of the water or stock with half of the butter beans in a blender and purée until smooth. Add the purée to the soup pot with the remaining water or stock. Stir well so that no spices are left sticking to the bottom of the pot. Add the tomatoes and remaining butter beans, cover, and bring to a simmer. Add the corn, Neufchâtel or cream cheese, and the Monterey Jack and return to a simmer, stirring frequently, until the corn is hot and the cheese has melted. Stir in the cilantro and add salt and pepper to taste.

Serve topped with parsley and sliced black olives.

DAILY SPECIAL

MENU IDEAS **Golden Tomato Avocado Salad (page 268)** ✳ **Simple Tomato Salads (page 286)** ✳ **Southern Wheat-free Cornbread (page 335)** ✳ **Avocado Melon Mélange (page 264)**

Matzo Ball Soup

Our Moosewood vegetarian version of matzo ball soup is marvelously satisfying and tasty—nonvegetarians may even prefer it to the traditional chicken soup. It will undoubtedly please everyone around a seder table.

At first the recipe may look time-consuming, but it really has three simple parts and any of them can be done in advance. If the matzo ball dough and Mock Chicken Stock are prepared ahead, the soup broth can be made during the 35 minutes that the matzo balls cook. Or with matzo ball dough and the finished soup broth ready and refrigerated, you'll spend only 10 minutes forming the balls and preparing the "extras"—while the matzo balls simmer and the broth reheats, you can just relax and inhale the aromas.

SERVES 6 TO 8
YIELDS 8 TO 9 CUPS SOUP,
 25 TO 30 MATZO BALLS
TOTAL TIME: 1½ HOURS

PER 10.5-OUNCE SERVING: 262 CALORIES, 7.5 G PROTEIN, 14.9 G FAT, 25.2 G CARBOHYDRATES, 3.9 G SATURATED FATTY ACIDS, 132 MG CHOLESTEROL, 1298 MG SODIUM, 2.5 G TOTAL DIETARY FIBER

MATZO BALLS
4 eggs, lightly beaten
3 tablespoons canola or other vegetable oil
2 tablespoons water
1½ teaspoons salt
1 cup matzo meal

SOUP BROTH
3 tablespoons canola or other vegetable oil
2 cups chopped onions
2 garlic cloves, pressed or minced
2 teaspoons salt
¼ to ½ teaspoon dried thyme
½ teaspoon dried dill
¼ teaspoon ground black pepper
4 cups Mock Chicken Stock (page 20)
4 cups water

MATZO BALL COOKING LIQUID
4 cups Mock Chicken Stock (page 20)
6 cups water

EXTRAS
5 scallions, minced
¼ cup chopped fresh parsley
1 teaspoon dark sesame oil
1 to 3 teaspoons soy sauce, or to taste

Whisk together all of the matzo ball ingredients, adding the matzo meal last. Refrigerate the dough for at least 30 minutes or overnight.

Meanwhile, warm the oil in a soup pot. Add the onions, garlic, salt, thyme, dill, and pepper. Cover and sauté on medium-high heat, stirring frequently, until the onions are golden brown, 10 to 15 minutes. Add the stock and water and bring to a boil; then lower the heat and simmer for about 10 minutes.

Bring the ingredients for the matzo ball cooking liquid to a simmer in a large pot. For light, feathery matzo balls, do not "form" balls by rolling or shaping them. Instead, scoop up some chilled matzo ball dough with a flatware teaspoon. Use your finger to carefully push the roughly shaped spoonful of dough into the simmering broth. Repeat until all of the dough is used. Cover the pot and simmer for 35 to 40 minutes, until the balls are firm, tender, and heated through.

To serve, sprinkle some chopped scallions and parsley and a few drops of sesame oil and soy sauce in the bottom of individual soup bowls. With a slotted spoon, remove the matzo balls from their cooking liquid and place a few in each bowl. Ladle in the hot soup broth and serve immediately.

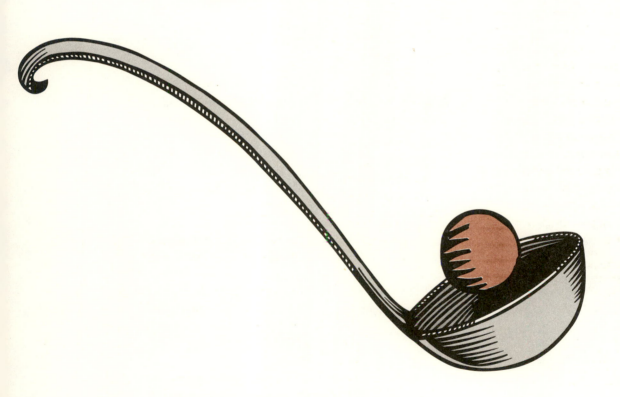

DAILY SPECIAL **MENU IDEAS** **Five-Herb Salad (page 262)** ∗ **Speltberry & Fruit Salad (page 229)** ∗ **Solstice Salad (page 227)** ∗ **Fig & Endive Salad (page 261)** ∗ **Eastern European Kasha & Mushrooms (page 206)** ∗ **Lobio (page 274)** ∗ **Brussels Sprouts & Carrot Salad (page 251)**

Middle Eastern Chickpea Soup

Here is a thick, exotically spiced soup with luscious bits of onion and fresh tomato. The secret to achieving a smooth consistency is to blend very well-cooked chickpeas and potatoes to create a rich, dairyless purée.

Try serving the soup with toasted pita wedges and an interesting assortment of olives. This is a great leftover: it keeps for up to a week and is just as good when reheated.

This recipe calls for cooked chickpeas. Sahadi brand canned chickpeas are a good, natural product without preservatives. If you begin with dried chickpeas, follow the cooking instructions on page 354 and cook until quite tender.

SERVES 4 TO 8
YIELDS 8 TO 9 CUPS
PREPARATION TIME: 10 MINUTES,
 IF USING COOKED CHICKPEAS
COOKING TIME: 30 MINUTES

PER 10-OUNCE SERVING: 242 CALORIES, 7.9 G PROTEIN, 5.5 G FAT, 42.3 G CARBOHYDRATES, 0.7 G SATURATED FATTY ACIDS, 0 MG CHOLESTEROL, 1019 MG SODIUM, 7.1 G TOTAL DIETARY FIBER

1 large red potato, diced (about 2 cups)
4 cups water
3 to 4 cups reserved potato-cooking liquid or vegetable stock
4 cups cooked chickpeas (two 15-ounce cans, drained and rinsed)
1 tablespoon minced fresh mint
2 tablespoons olive oil
1 large onion, chopped (about 2 cups)
3 garlic cloves, minced or pressed
2 teaspoons salt
1 tablespoon ground cumin
1 tablespoon ground coriander
1 teaspoon turmeric
⅛ to ¼ teaspoon cayenne
ground black pepper to taste
2 cups diced tomatoes

chopped fresh parsley
lemon wedges

Boil the potatoes in the water until very soft and then drain, reserving the cooking liquid. In a blender, combine the potatoes with about 1 cup of the cooking liquid or stock and purée; then transfer to a soup pot. Combine the chickpeas, mint, and about 2 cups of the cooking liquid and/or stock and blend until very smooth. Add the chickpea purée to the soup pot and heat gently, stirring frequently.

Meanwhile, in a skillet, heat the oil and sauté the onions, garlic, salt, cumin, coriander, turmeric, cayenne, and black pepper until the onions are translucent, about 10 minutes. Stir the sautéed onions into the soup. If the soup is too thick, add more cooking liquid, water, or stock. When the soup is hot, stir in the diced tomatoes and cook for a few more minutes. Add more salt and black pepper to taste.

Serve topped with parsley and offer lemon wedges on the side.

Variations Stir 2 cups of chopped fresh spinach leaves or Swiss chard into the hot soup. Top it with Fried Shallots (page 343) for a crunchy contrast.

MENU IDEAS **Fattoush (page 209)** * **Artichoke Heart & Bulghur Salat (page 190)** * **Roasted Green Tomato & Feta Salad (page 283)** * **Tunisian Carrot Salad (page 293)** * **mixed baby greens with Zesty Feta Garlic Dressing (page 326)** * **Filo Croutons (page 342)** * **Goat Cheese Toasts (page 344)**

Miso Noodle Soup

Here is a soup that's packed with wholesome nutrition and great taste. Miso, used to make a common Japanese broth, is a soft, fermented soybean paste that is traditionally hailed as beneficial for the circulatory and digestive systems. Konbu, a type of seaweed and staple of Japanese broths, is high in calcium, iodine, and the vitamins A, B₂, and C. In Japan, miso soup might be served at any meal—including breakfast!

SERVES 4 TO 6
YIELDS 8 CUPS WITHOUT NOODLES
TOTAL TIME: 40 MINUTES

PER 11-OUNCE SERVING: 233 CALORIES, 8.9 G PROTEIN, 5.9 G FAT, 39.9 G CARBO-HYDRATES, 1.4 G SATURATED FATTY ACIDS, 0 MG CHOLESTEROL, 899 MG SODIUM, 4.2 G TOTAL DIETARY FIBER

4 quarts water
2 pieces konbu (about 6-inch lengths, ¼ ounce) (page 377)
½ teaspoon salt
8 ounces udon noodles (page 386)
2 cups thinly sliced onions
2 garlic cloves, thinly sliced
2 tablespoons canola or other vegetable oil
2 cups peeled and thinly sliced carrots, cut on the diagonal
2 teaspoons grated fresh ginger root
4 cups vegetable stock or water
2 cups rinsed and finely chopped bok choy, mustard greens, or spinach
⅓ cup light or dark miso
1 tablespoon soy sauce, more to taste

4 scallions, thinly sliced on the diagonal

Combine 1 quart of the water and the konbu in a covered saucepan and bring to a boil; then lower the heat and simmer for 15 minutes. Remove the konbu and either discard it or save it for use in another dish. Reserve the liquid, or *dashi*.

While the konbu cooks, place the remaining 3 quarts of water and the salt in a large pot and bring to a boil. Add the udon noodles, cover, and cook at a simmer for 7 to 10 minutes, until al dente. Drain and rinse the noodles with cold water to remove excess starch. Set aside.

Meanwhile, in a soup pot on low heat, cook the onions and garlic in the oil for 3 minutes. Add the carrots and ginger root and sauté for 5 minutes, stirring occasionally. Add the stock or water, cover, and bring to a boil. Reduce the heat and simmer for 5 minutes. Add the chopped greens—bok choy or mustard greens should be added for the last 3 minutes of simmering; spinach for only the last minute.

Whisk the miso into the reserved konbu *dashi* until it is free of lumps and mostly dissolved. Add the soy sauce and stir the *dashi* mixture into the soup. Gently reheat, if necessary, but don't allow the soup to boil.

To serve, evenly divide the noodles among the soup bowls and top with the hot broth and vegetables. Garnish with sliced scallions.

MENU IDEAS **Broiled Tofu & Sugar Snap Peas (page 199)** ✳ **Asian Beet & Tofu Salad (page 192)** ✳ **"Japanese" Tofu Salad (page 271)** ✳ **Seaweed Salad (page 285)** ✳ **Pilwun's Daikon Salad (page 282)**

Risi e Bisi

Famous as the first dish served on St. Mark's Day each April in Venice, *risi e bisi* is one of the most beloved foods of Italy. This very thick soup is almost a risotto, thanks to the characteristic starchiness of arborio rice. It is best made with newly picked peas, but frozen baby peas, or *petit pois,* are also delectable.

It's a good idea to reserve some stock in case you have leftover soup, because the rice will continue to absorb liquid as it sits. Just thin the leftover soup with stock before reheating.

For a nice meal, choose a salad to serve with Risi e Bisi, keeping the springtime theme in mind. Serve with a crusty bread and a dry white wine.

SERVES 4 TO 6
YIELDS 9½ CUPS
TOTAL TIME: 50 MINUTES

PER 11-OUNCE SERVING: 364 CALORIES, 16.6 G PROTEIN, 12 G FAT, 49.2 G CARBOHYDRATES, 5.9 G SATURATED FATTY ACIDS, 23 MG CHOLESTEROL, 1156 MG SODIUM, 8.1 G TOTAL DIETARY FIBER

1 tablespoon butter
1 tablespoon extra-virgin olive oil
1 large onion, chopped (about 2 cups)
8 cups Mock Chicken Stock (page 20)
1 teaspoon salt
1 cup raw arborio rice
2 cups baby peas or frozen petit pois (see Note)
2 tablespoons chopped fresh parsley
1 cup grated Parmesan cheese
salt and ground black pepper to taste

Warm the butter and olive oil in a soup pot until the butter melts. Add the onions and sauté on medium-high heat for about 10 minutes, until golden. Add the stock and salt and bring to a boil. Stir in the rice, lower the heat to a simmer, cover, and cook for 20 to 25 minutes, until the rice is tender.

Add the peas and cook for 2 to 3 minutes. Stir in the parsley and ½ cup of the Parmesan cheese. Add salt and pepper to taste.

Serve immediately, topped with the remaining Parmesan.

Note If you have pea pods from shelling fresh peas, simmer them in the stock to heighten the sweet pea flavor. Remove the pods before adding the stock to the soup.

DAILY SPECIAL **MENU IDEAS Asparagus Vinaigrette (page 248)** ✳ **Arugula & Warm Mozzarella Salad (page 191)** ✳ **Tomatoes Capriccio (page 286)** ✳ **Five-Herb Salad (page 262)** ✳ **Pinzimonio (page 280)** ✳ **Focaccia (page 330)**

Southeast Asian Rice & Tofu Soup

This is a wonderful soup, brightly colored and exotically flavored. It provides a prime opportunity to discover the subtle charms of lemongrass, if you're not already enamored. If you like, trim the lemongrass before making the stock of your choice and add the lemongrass trimmings to your stock ingredients.

The soup is at its prettiest when served immediately, garnished with a thin circle of lime and a few cilantro sprigs. Later, the rice absorbs broth and the soup thickens considerably.

SERVES 4 TO 6
YIELDS 8 TO 9 CUPS
TOTAL TIME: 1 HOUR

PER 12-OUNCE SERVING: 141 CALORIES, 5.4 G PROTEIN, 4.5 G FAT, 21.4 G CARBO-HYDRATES, 0.9 G SATURATED FATTY ACIDS, 0 MG CHOLESTEROL, 560 MG SODIUM, 2.5 G TOTAL DIETARY FIBER

SPICE PASTE

3 fresh lemongrass stalks
1 x 1½-inch piece of fresh ginger root
1 fresh chile, seeds removed for a milder "hot"
3 garlic cloves, chopped
½ cup chopped onions or shallots
½ teaspoon turmeric
½ teaspoon ground coriander
½ teaspoon salt

1 cup thinly sliced onions (2-inch lengths)
1 tablespoon canola, peanut, or other vegetable oil
⅓ cup raw white rice, such as basmati (page 375)
6 cups Basic Light Vegetable Stock (page 16)
½ cup cut green beans (½-inch pieces)
1 cup thinly sliced red bell pepper strips (½-inch lengths)
8 ounces tofu, cut into small cubes*
2 tablespoons fresh lime juice
2 tablespoons chopped fresh cilantro
½ teaspoon salt
1 cup reduced-fat or regular coconut milk (optional)

* *If you'd like the tofu to have a chewier texture, pat it dry with a towel and then sauté it in a little oil before adding it to the soup.*

Trim the root ends and the tops of the lemongrass, leaving a 5- to 6-inch stalk. Remove any tough outer layers and chop the inner stem into very small pieces. Peel the ginger root and thinly slice it. Combine all of the spice paste ingredients in a food processor or high-powered blender and purée until quite smooth. If necessary, add about a tablespoon of water to facilitate blending. Set aside.

In a soup pot, sauté the onions in the oil on medium heat until translucent, about 10 minutes. Add the spice paste and cook, stirring constantly, for 1 to 2 minutes. Stir in the rice and the stock and bring to a boil; reduce the heat, cover, and simmer for 10 minutes.

Add the green beans and cook for about 3 minutes. Add the bell peppers, tofu, lime juice, cilantro, and salt, and simmer for 5 to 10 minutes, until the vegetables are tender but still brightly colored. Add the coconut milk, if using.

DAILY SPECIAL

MENU IDEAS **Asian Spinach & Orange Salad (page 246)** * **Bean Sprout Salad (page 250)** *
Marinated Broccoli & Carrots (page 275) * **Scallion Pancakes (page 350)**

Spicy Tofu & Greens Soup

This is a healthy, stimulating soup. The hot pepper and ginger provide a permeating warmth, and the tofu and greens are nourishing and satisfying. Take a few liberties with flavoring and ingredients: vary the hot pepper and ginger according to your internal thermometer.

For an impressive meal, use the time while the stock simmers and the tofu bakes to make one or two of the salads suggested below.

SERVES 4 TO 6
YIELDS ABOUT 8 CUPS
TOTAL TIME: 1¼ HOURS

PER 12-OUNCE SERVING: 133 CALORIES, 7.7 G PROTEIN, 5.5 G FAT, 15.9 G CARBO-HYDRATES, 1.1 G SATURATED FATTY ACIDS, 0 MG CHOLESTEROL, 865 MG SODIUM, 4.2 G TOTAL DIETARY FIBER

STOCK

2 cups peeled and sliced carrots
2 cups thinly sliced onions
1 cup coarsely chopped fresh parsley
8 garlic cloves, sliced
8 thin slices of fresh ginger root (about the size of a quarter)
1 to 2 dried chiles, sliced in half*
8 cups water

1 cake of firm tofu (about 12 ounces)
1 tablespoon grated fresh ginger root
4 garlic cloves, minced or pressed
1 to 2 dried chiles, sliced in half*
1 tablespoon canola or peanut oil
⅜ cup soy sauce
⅓ cup julienned carrots or red bell peppers
2 cups shredded greens, such as bok choy, mustard greens, kale, Chinese cabbage, spinach, and/or pea shoots
a few drops of dark sesame oil
2 scallions, thinly sliced

* Or use ⅛ to ¼ teaspoon of crushed red pepper flakes.

Preheat the oven to 375°.

Place the stock ingredients in a large soup pot, cover, and bring to a boil on medium heat. Lower the heat and simmer for 45 minutes.

Meanwhile, slice the tofu into small, bite-sized cubes and set aside in a baking dish. Combine the ginger, garlic, chiles, oil, and 2 tablespoons of the soy sauce in a heavy skillet, sauté for a few seconds, and then add to the tofu. Gently toss the tofu until evenly coated. Bake for 25 minutes, stirring twice to roast evenly. Remove the chile halves.

Strain the stock into another soup pot. Add the baked tofu and the carrots or peppers and simmer for 3 to 4 minutes. Stir in the shredded greens. When the soup returns to a simmer, remove from the heat and add the sesame oil and the remaining ¼ cup of soy sauce.

Serve immediately, scattering freshly sliced scallions into each bowl.

Variation Try 1½ to 2 tablespoons of Chinese chili paste (page 359) in place of the garlic and dried chiles.

MENU IDEAS **Marinated Broccoli & Carrots (page 275)** ✳ **Scallion Pancakes (page 350)** ✳ **Spicy Cucumber Salad (page 288)** ✳ **Pilwun's Daikon Salad (page 282)** ✳ **Balinese Rice Salad (page 195)**

Spring Minestrone

In this soup, the various green hues of spring and summer vegetables shine through the clear broth. To add a delicious tang, serve each portion with a wedge of lemon.

Serve a big bowl of Spring Minestrone with a crusty bread and an exquisite salad for an attractive light meal.

SERVES 4 TO 6
YIELDS 9 TO 10 CUPS
TOTAL TIME: 45 MINUTES

PER 12-OUNCE SERVING: 138 CALORIES, 5 G PROTEIN, 2.9 G FAT, 24.8 G CARBOHY-DRATES, 0.4 G SATURATED FATTY ACIDS, 0 MG CHOLESTEROL, 537 MG SODIUM, 6.2 G TOTAL DIETARY FIBER

1 tablespoon olive oil
1 cup chopped onions
1 garlic clove, minced or pressed
2 leeks, washed and chopped (white and tender green parts only)
2 celery stalks, diced (about 1 cup)
¼ teaspoon dried oregano
1 teaspoon ground fennel seeds
½ teaspoon salt
¼ teaspoon ground black pepper
4 cups Basic Light Vegetable Stock (page 16)
1 small zucchini, cubed (about 1 cup)
1½ cups cooked cannellini or other white beans (15-ounce can, drained and rinsed)
2 cups shredded greens, such as Swiss chard, kale, spinach, or beet greens
1 cup fresh or frozen green peas (optional)
1 cup cut asparagus (2-inch pieces) (optional)
a splash of fresh lemon juice or cider vinegar to taste

grated Parmesan cheese (optional)

Combine the oil, onions, and garlic in a nonreactive soup pot and sauté for about 5 minutes, until the onions soften. Stir in the leeks and sauté for 2 or 3 minutes. Add the celery, oregano, fennel, salt, and pepper and continue to sauté for another 5 minutes, stirring occasionally.

Stir in the stock and bring to a boil. Reduce the heat, add the zucchini, and simmer for about 5 minutes. Add the white beans and return to a gentle simmer. Stir in the greens and, if using, the peas and/or asparagus and simmer until tender, about 10 minutes. Just before serving, add the lemon juice or vinegar.

Top each serving with Parmesan, if you wish, and serve immediately, while the greens are at their best and brightest.

MENU IDEAS **Fig & Endive Salad (page 261)** ＊ **Tomatoes Capriccio (page 286)** ＊ **tossed green salad with Low-fat Tomato Basil Dressing (page 321)** ＊ **Focaccia (page 330)**

Summer Minestrone

Summertime is when vegetables are clearly in their glory—juicy, aromatic, tender, and full of flavor. It's the perfect season for this colorful minestrone, bursting with carrots, zucchini, tomatoes, and corn. Pick the youngest, most tender vegetables you can find and feel free to experiment with other vegetable combinations. Summer Minestrone inspires improvisation.

The recipe calls for either navy beans or Roman beans *(habichuelas romanas)*, their larger counterparts. Both work well, and just 1½ cups of cooked beans adds body to the soup without altering its light, brothy character.

SERVES 6 TO 8
YIELDS 11 CUPS
PREPARATION TIME: 25 MINUTES
COOKING TIME: 35 MINUTES

PER 10.5-OUNCE SERVING: 117 CALORIES, 5.3 G PROTEIN, 1.9 G FAT, 21.8 G CARBOHYDRATES, 0.3 G SATURATED FATTY ACIDS, 0 MG CHOLESTEROL, 469 MG SODIUM, 2.6 G TOTAL DIETARY FIBER

2 teaspoons olive oil
2 onions, chopped (about 2 cups)
3 garlic cloves, minced or pressed
1½ teaspoons salt
2 carrots, peeled and chopped (about 2 cups)
¼ pound green beans, stemmed and cut into 1-inch pieces (about 1¼ cups)
2 cups diced zucchini
2 large tomatoes, diced (about 2½ cups)
½ cup fresh or frozen corn kernels
¼ cup chopped fresh basil (1 tablespoon dried)
2 tablespoons minced fresh marjoram (2 teaspoons dried)
4 cups water or vegetable stock
1½ cups cooked navy beans or Roman beans (16-ounce can, drained)*
2 tablespoons fresh lemon juice
¼ cup chopped fresh parsley

grated Parmesan or Asiago cheese (optional)

*½ cup of dried beans will make about 1½ cups of cooked drained beans. If you prefer home-cooked beans to canned ones, see page 354 for cooking instructions.

In a soup pot on medium-high heat, combine the oil, onions, garlic, and salt and sauté for about 10 minutes, stirring frequently. If using dried basil and marjoram, stir them in. Lower the heat to medium and add the carrots and green beans, cover, and cook for 10 minutes, stirring occasionally to prevent sticking.

Add the zucchini, tomatoes, and corn, cover, and cook for 5 minutes. If using fresh basil and marjoram, stir them in and cook for 2 minutes. Add the water or stock and the navy or Roman beans, bring to a boil, lower the heat, and gently simmer for 10 minutes. Stir in the lemon juice and parsley.

Serve hot with grated cheese sprinkled on top, if you like.

MENU IDEAS **Arugula & Warm Mozzarella Salad (page 191)** ✳ **Orzo & Pesto Stuffed Tomatoes (page 223)** ✳ **Mediterranean Orange & Olive Salad (page 276)** ✳ **Summer Millet Salad (page 290)** ✳ **Focaccia (page 330)**

Texts Two-Bean Soup

Yahoo! Fire up the stove and feed the cowpokes. This hearty, spicy soup is very popular at Moosewood—it can pretty near cause a stampede.

For an even more substantial soup, add 1 cup of fresh or frozen corn kernels, and/or 1 cup of fresh or frozen sliced okra at the same time that you add the cooked beans.

SERVES 4 TO 6
YIELDS ABOUT 8 CUPS
TOTAL TIME: 1 HOUR, USING COOKED BEANS

PER 10-OUNCE SERVING: 173 CALORIES, 7.5 G PROTEIN, 4.6 G FAT, 27.3 G CARBO-HYDRATES, 0.6 G SATURATED FATTY ACIDS, 0 MG CHOLESTEROL, 443 MG SODIUM, 6.6 G TOTAL DIETARY FIBER

2 cups chopped onions
6 garlic cloves, minced or pressed
2 tablespoons olive oil
½ teaspoon salt
1 cup diced celery
2 cups chopped red and green bell peppers
1 small fresh chile, minced, seeds removed for a milder "hot"
1 teaspoon dried oregano
½ teaspoon dried thyme
2 teaspoons ground cumin
½ teaspoon ground black pepper
2 cups water
1½ cups undrained canned tomatoes, chopped (14½-ounce can)
1½ cups cooked black-eyed peas (15½-ounce can, drained, or 10-ounce frozen package)
1½ cups cooked pinto, red kidney, or black beans (15½-ounce can, drained)
¼ cup barbecue sauce*
salt to taste

crushed tortilla chips
grated jalapeño Monterey Jack cheese, Jalapeño Cream (page 345), or sour cream (optional)

Regular, low-fat, and nonfat barbecue sauces are all commercially available. We recommend ones without additives, such as Dave's, Annie's, or Ralph's brands. If you'd like to make your own, see Moosewood Restaurant Low-Fat Favorites, page 355.

In a nonreactive soup pot, combine the onions and garlic with the oil and salt. Cover and cook on medium heat for 8 to 10 minutes, until the onions are soft and translucent, stirring occasionally. Add the celery, bell peppers, chile, oregano, thyme, cumin, and black pepper, and sauté for 10 minutes, stirring often.

Add the water and tomatoes, cover, and simmer until the vegetables are tender, 10 to 15 minutes. Add the black-eyed peas, your choice of beans, and the barbecue sauce. Mix well, cover, and simmer gently for 10 minutes. Add salt to taste.

Just before serving, garnish with tortilla chips and, if desired, top with grated cheese, Jalapeño Cream, or sour cream.

MENU IDEAS Andean Quinoa & Corn Salad (page 189) ✳ **Dave's Mom's Best Slaw (page 257)** ✳ **Fennel Salad with Blue Cheese (page 260)** ✳ **Kale Salad (page 272)** ✳ **Southern Wheat-free Cornbread (page 335)**

Tomato Rasam

Rasams are spicy brothy soups from South India considered healthful and easily digestible. In India, every household has a favorite rasam recipe, so the variations are nearly endless. Traditionally, a rasam would be served at the end of a large meal, but we like it paired with a mildly flavored substantial salad.

This is a good soup for cooks who enjoy experimenting with spices and unusual ingredients. Extra rasam powder can be stored in a jar, so the next time you make this soup, you'll already be halfway there; it's also useful for other curried dishes. Note that the flavor of the rasam powder will diminish after a few months.

SERVES 4 TO 6
YIELDS ABOUT 6 CUPS
PREPARATION TIME: 15 MINUTES
COOKING TIME: ABOUT 45 MINUTES

PER 8-OUNCE SERVING: 114 CALORIES, 4.5 G PROTEIN, 4.8 G FAT, 17.4 G CARBO-HYDRATES, 0.9 G SATURATED FATTY ACIDS, 0 MG CHOLESTEROL, 221 MG SODIUM, 3.5 G TOTAL DIETARY FIBER

TOOR DAHL
¼ cup dried split pigeon peas*
1½ cups water
pinch of turmeric

RASAM POWDER
⅛ cup dried split pigeon peas*
¼ cup coriander seeds
1 tablespoon whole black peppercorns
⅛ to ¼ cup dried red chiles
½ tablespoon cumin seeds
¼ teaspoon turmeric

3 tomatoes, chopped (about 3 cups)
4 cups water
½ teaspoon salt
2 tablespoons minced onions
2 garlic cloves, minced or pressed
1 teaspoon tamarind concentrate (page 385) (optional)
1 tablespoon canola or other vegetable oil
2 teaspoons black mustard seeds
2 teaspoons cumin seeds

chopped fresh cilantro
4 to 6 lime wedges

*Available in Indian grocery stores and in the ethnic section of some well-stocked supermarkets, sometimes labeled "toor dal" or "toovar dal." If unavailable, red lentils or "red gram dal" can be used.

Place the pigeon peas in a sieve and rinse well. In a small pot, combine them with the water and turmeric. Bring to a simmer, cover, and cook on low heat for about 45 minutes, until most of the water has been absorbed and the peas are soft.

Meanwhile, make the rasam powder. Roast the pigeon peas, coriander seeds, peppercorns, chiles, and cumin seeds in a small, heavy dry skillet on low heat. When the spices are fragrant and begin to turn brown, transfer the mixture to a small bowl. Allow to cool for a few minutes; then whirl in small batches in a spice grinder until finely ground. Stir in the turmeric and set aside.

When the pigeon peas have simmered for about 25 minutes, in another nonreactive soup pot, combine the tomatoes, water, salt, onions, garlic, 1 tablespoon of the rasam powder, and the tamarind, if using. Cover and bring to a boil; then lower the heat and simmer for about 15 minutes, until the tomatoes and onions are soft.

Meanwhile, heat the oil in a small, heavy skillet on low heat. Add the mustard and cumin seeds and sizzle them just until the mustard seeds begin to pop. Stir the spices and oil into the soup pot and add the cooked pigeon peas.

Serve hot topped with cilantro and accompanied by lime wedges.

Variation For Buttermilk Rasam, omit the tamarind and lime wedges and, just before serving, stir in 1 cup of buttermilk and reheat gently.

 MENU IDEAS **Curried Rice Salad (page 205)** ✳ **Nepalese Egg Salad (page 278)** ✳ **Balinese Rice Salad (page 195)** ✳ **Curried Potato Salad (page 255)** ✳ **Spinach with Cilantro Cashew Dressing (page 289)** ✳ **Spiced Paneer (page 351)** ✳ **Curried Scallop & Noodle Salad (page 300)**

Tomato & Kale Soup with Barley

This bright, light soup is a departure from classic, heartier barley soups. While the barley cooks and the sun-dried tomatoes soak, you have time to prepare all of the rest of the ingredients. Although the garnish of feta cheese is optional, we highly recommend it—tomatoes and feta are a perfect pair.

SERVES 4 TO 6
YIELDS 8 CUPS
TOTAL TIME: 45 MINUTES

PER 11-OUNCE SERVING: 150 CALORIES, 5.5 G PROTEIN, 3.4 G FAT, 27.6 G CARBO-HYDRATES, 0.7 G SATURATED FATTY ACIDS, 0 MG CHOLESTEROL, 914 MG SODIUM, 4.8 G TOTAL DIETARY FIBER

⅓ cup pearled barley (page 354)
1 bay leaf
5 cups water
7 sun-dried tomatoes, not packed in oil
½ cup hot water
1 tablespoon canola or other vegetable oil
1 cup chopped onions
2 garlic cloves, minced or pressed
3 cups undrained canned tomatoes, chopped (28-ounce can)
2 teaspoons minced fresh dill (1 teaspoon dried)
pinch of cayenne
1 teaspoon salt
2 cups loosely packed rinsed, stemmed, and chopped kale
ground black pepper to taste

fresh dill sprigs
crumbled feta cheese (optional)

Combine the barley, bay leaf, and water in a nonreactive soup pot. Cover and bring to a boil; then lower the heat and simmer for about 25 minutes, until the barley is tender. Meanwhile, place the sun-dried tomatoes in a small heatproof bowl, cover with the hot water, and let stand until softened, about 20 minutes.

While the sun-dried tomatoes soak, warm the oil in a small skillet. Add the onions and garlic and sauté for about 10 minutes, until the onions are translucent. Remove from the heat.

When the barley is cooked, remove the bay leaf and stir in the sautéed onions and garlic, canned tomatoes, dill, cayenne, and salt. Drain the sun-dried tomatoes, reserving the soaking liquid. Dice and add them with their soaking liquid to the soup pot. Cover and bring to a boil. Add the kale, reduce the heat, and simmer for 3 to 5 minutes. Season to taste with pepper.

Garnish each bowl with a fresh dill sprig and top with crumbled feta cheese, if you wish.

DAILY SPECIAL

MENU IDEAS Marinated Mushrooms (page 347) ✳ **Fresh Pear & Blue Cheese Salad (page 266)** ✳ **Fig & Endive Salad (page 261)** ✳ **Louisiana Black-eyed Pea Salad (page 221)** ✳ **tossed green salad with Zesty Feta Garlic Dressing (page 326)** ✳ **Focaccia (page 330)** ✳ **Popovers (page 334)**

Tortilla Soup

This classic Mexican soup is a spicy, piquant broth brimming with colorful vegetables and vibrant flavors. We've lightened the traditional recipe by using our Mock Chicken Stock and by baking the tortilla chips instead of frying them.

SERVES 6 TO 8
YIELDS 12 CUPS
PREPARATION TIME: 20 MINUTES
COOKING AND BAKING TIME:
  35 MINUTES

PER 12-OUNCE SERVING: 210 CALORIES, 6.2 G PROTEIN, 4.4 G FAT, 41.6 G CARBO-HYDRATES, 0.4 G SATURATED FATTY ACIDS, 0 MG CHOLESTEROL, 244 MG SODIUM, 4.8 G TOTAL DIETARY FIBER

1 tablespoon olive oil
1 large onion, diced (about 2 cups)
1 jalapeño, seeded and minced
1 canned chipotle pepper, diced*
2 tomatillos, husked, seeded, and diced
1 red bell pepper, seeded and diced
1 medium zucchini, diced (about 1 cup)
1 tablespoon ground coriander
1 tablespoon ground cumin
1 teaspoon dried oregano
8 cups Mock Chicken Stock (page 20)
¼ to ⅓ cup fresh lime juice
1 teaspoon adobo sauce from chipotle jar*
1 tablespoon chopped fresh cilantro, or more to taste
3 cups fresh or frozen corn kernels
8 corn tortillas (6-inch), cut into ½ x 2-inch strips

avocado cubes (optional)
grated Monterey Jack cheese (optional)

* Chipotle peppers in a spicy adobo sauce are available in small jars or cans in Latin American groceries and the ethnic section of many supermarkets. The peppers add a delicious smoky flavor and the adobo adds body. Adobo sauce contains tomatoes, vinegar, onions, sugar, and spices. We recommend La Torre brand, a product of Mexico, distributed by Intermex Products, PO Box 170062, Arlington, Texas 76003 (214-660-2071).

Preheat the oven to 400°.
  In a nonreactive soup pot, warm the oil and sauté the onions, jalapeños, chipotle, tomatillos, bell peppers, and zucchini for 5 to 10 minutes, stirring frequently, until softened. Add the coriander, cumin, and oregano and sauté for about 3 more minutes. Stir in the stock, lime juice, and adobo sauce and bring to a simmer. Add the cilantro and corn and continue to simmer gently for 10 minutes.

  Meanwhile, bake the tortilla strips on an unoiled baking sheet for 15 to 20 minutes, until crisp.

  To serve, place the tortilla strips in individual serving bowls and ladle the soup on top. Garnish with avocado cubes and grated cheese, if desired.

MENU IDEAS **Avocado Seitan Salad (page 194)** ✳ **Caribbean Rice Salad (page 202)** ✳ **Golden Tomato Avocado Salad (page 268)** ✳ **Tropical Fruit & Shrimp Salad (page 312)**

Tuscan Bean Soup

Slice a juicy tomato or two. Put out a good crusty loaf of bread and some fruity green olive oil. Then bring in steaming bowls of this thick and nourishing bean soup, flavored with sage and garlic, for an irresistible repast.

In a Daily Special, the dense, earthy quality of Tuscan Bean Soup is best offset by a light, crisp salad. Fresh garlic bread or slices of a dark loaf are wonderful alongside. Fresh fruit is the perfect dessert.

Made with canned beans, this is a tasty quick-and-easy soup. Made with freshly cooked beans, the results are superior: beans firm to the eye and tender to the teeth.

SERVES 6 TO 8
YIELDS 8½ CUPS
TOTAL TIME: 30 MINUTES

PER 9.5-OUNCE SERVING: 293 CALORIES, 15.3 G PROTEIN, 3.1 G FAT, 53.3 G CARBO-HYDRATES, 0.6 G SATURATED FATTY ACIDS, 0 MG CHOLESTEROL, 105 MG SODIUM, 16.6 G TOTAL DIETARY FIBER

2 cups diced onions
1 cup peeled and diced carrots
4 garlic cloves, minced or pressed
1 tablespoon olive oil
15 large fresh sage leaves
6 cups cooked pinto, Roman, or small red or white beans (three 15- or 16-ounce cans, undrained)*
3 to 4 cups Basic Light Vegetable Stock (page 16), Garlic Stock (page 19), bean-cooking liquid, or water
salt and ground black pepper to taste

* *2 cups of dried beans will yield about 6 cups cooked. See page 354 for cooking instructions. Anasazi beans, grown in the southwestern United States, resemble small pinto beans, have good flavor, and are another nice choice for this soup.*

In a soup pot, sauté the onions, carrots, and garlic in the olive oil on medium-low heat until the onions are translucent and the carrots are tender, about 10 minutes. Stack the sage leaves and cut them crosswise into thin strips. Stir the sage into the vegetables. Add the cooked beans and 3 cups of the stock, bean-cooking liquid, or water. Continue to cook on medium heat, stirring occasionally, until the soup is hot and simmering, 5 to 10 minutes.

Carefully ladle about 3 cups of the soup into a blender and purée until smooth. Stir the purée back into the soup. If you wish, add more stock or water for a less thick consistency. Add salt and pepper to taste.

Gently reheat the soup and serve hot.

Variations Drizzle some extra-virgin olive oil onto each serving or top with sautéed mushroom slices or croutons. Or, when stirring in the beans and cooking liquid, add cooked grains, such as wheat-berries (page 387) or spelt, or cooked greens, such as escarole or mustard greens.

MENU IDEAS **Five-Herb Salad (page 262)** * **Fresh Pear & Blue Cheese Salad (page 266)** * **Fig & Endive Salad (page 261)** * **Fennel & Arugula Salad with Grapefruit (page 259)** * **Focaccia (page 330)**

Vegetable Pistou

Pistou is the French word for pesto, a sumptuous paste of basil, nuts, garlic, olive oil, and aged cheese. It's also the namesake of the classic Provençal soup that has pesto as its essential ingredient. We've developed a delicious basil pesto using toasted hazelnuts, garlic, a snappy bit of fresh lemon juice, and, unlike most versions, no cheese!

Traditional pistou recipes share three things in common: they all have pesto, the vegetables are simmered without sautéing first, and the dried beans are cooked separately and added near the end of cooking. Moosewood's dairyless version is faithful to these traditional methods, but we add the tomatoes and zucchini late in the cooking. To save time, prepare the pesto while the soup simmers.

SERVES 4 TO 6
YIELDS ¾ CUP PESTO, 9 CUPS SOUP
PREPARATION TIME: 30 MINUTES
COOKING TIME: 30 TO 35 MINUTES

PER 14-OUNCE SERVING: 327 CALORIES, 10.5 G PROTEIN, 12.9 G FAT, 45.4 G CARBOHYDRATES, 1.5 G SATURATED FATTY ACIDS, 0 MG CHOLESTEROL, 828 MG SODIUM, 3.7 G TOTAL DIETARY FIBER

RICH DAIRYLESS HAZELNUT PESTO
1½ cups rinsed packed fresh basil leaves
3 garlic cloves, minced or pressed
⅓ cup whole hazelnuts, toasted*
3 tablespoons olive oil
2 to 3 teaspoons fresh lemon juice
½ teaspoon salt

1 cup cut green beans or yellow wax beans (about ¼ pound)
1 cup diced potatoes (unpeeled, if you prefer)
1½ cups chopped onions
1 cup peeled and chopped carrots
½ cup diced celery
3 bay leaves
½ teaspoon dried marjoram
4 garlic cloves, minced or pressed
1½ teaspoons salt
¼ teaspoon ground black pepper
6 cups water or vegetable stock
1½ cups chopped tomatoes
½ cup quartered and sliced zucchini
½ cup stelline (little pasta stars) or baby shells (about ¼ pound)
1½ cups drained cooked navy beans, cannellini, or cranberry beans

* Toast a single layer of hazelnuts on an unoiled tray for about 10 minutes in a 325° oven, until lightly browned and fragrant. Then rub the hazelnuts briskly with a clean towel to remove most of the skins. If using a blender rather than a food processor to make the pesto, coarsely chop the toasted hazelnuts.

Combine all of the pesto ingredients in a food processor or blender and purée until smooth. Set aside.

In a large soup pot, combine the green or yellow beans, potatoes, onions, carrots, celery, bay leaves, marjoram, garlic, salt, pepper, and water or stock. Cover and bring to a boil; then lower the heat and simmer for about 20 minutes. Stir in the tomatoes, zucchini, and pasta, cover, and cook for 5 minutes. Add the navy beans, cover, and very gently simmer for 5 to 10 minutes, until the pasta is al dente and all of the vegetables are tender. Remove and discard the bay leaves.

Stir the pesto into the soup and serve.

MENU IDEAS Fig & Endive Salad (page 261) ✳ **Fresh Pear & Blue Cheese Salad (page 266)** ✳ **Mediterranean Orange & Olive Salad (page 276)** ✳ **Fennel & Arugula Salad with Grapefruit (page 259)** ✳ **Popovers (page 334)** ✳ **Pears Parmesan (page 265)**

Wild Rice & Asparagus Soup

Hearty and warming, this is a soothing soup for a rainy spring day. We usually match this earthy soup with a salad that is slightly sweet. This soup is at its most attractive served immediately.

SERVES 4 TO 6
YIELDS 7 CUPS
TOTAL TIME: 1¼ HOURS

PER 8.5-OUNCE SERVING: 103 CALORIES, 4.1 G PROTEIN, 2.3 G FAT, 18.1 G CARBO-HYDRATES, 0.3 G SATURATED FATTY ACIDS, 0 MG CHOLESTEROL, 409 MG SODIUM, 1.8 G TOTAL DIETARY FIBER

RICE

½ cup raw wild rice, rinsed
½ teaspoon salt
1 bay leaf
3 cups water

SOUP

2 cups chopped onions or leeks
2 garlic cloves, minced or pressed
½ cup diced celery
1 tablespoon olive oil
1 pound asparagus
5 cups Garlic Stock (page 19) or
    Roasted Vegetable Stock (page 21)
¼ teaspoon dried thyme
¼ teaspoon dried tarragon
½ teaspoon salt
1 cup diced red bell peppers
2 tablespoons dry sherry
ground black pepper to taste

grated Parmesan cheese

In a small pot, combine all of the rice ingredients, cover, and bring to a boil; then reduce the heat and simmer until tender, about 45 minutes. Drain any remaining liquid.

When the rice has cooked for about 30 minutes, combine the onions, garlic, and celery in a soup pot and sauté them in the oil on medium heat until the onions are translucent, about 10 minutes.

Meanwhile, rinse the asparagus thoroughly, snap off and discard the tough stem ends, and slice off and reserve the tips. Cut the spears into 1-inch pieces and add them to the soup pot along with the stock, thyme, tarragon, and salt. Bring to a boil; then lower the heat and simmer for 5 minutes. Add the bell peppers, sherry, cooked rice, and reserved asparagus tips and simmer for another 5 to 10 minutes. Add black pepper to taste.

Serve garnished with a little grated Parmesan cheese.

DAILY SPECIAL

MENU IDEAS **Apple Pear variation of Celeriac Remoulade (page 253)** ✳ **Composed Beet Salad (page 254)** ✳ **Fresh Pear & Blue Cheese Salad (page 266)** ✳ **Wilted Spinach & Portabella Mushrooms (page 239)** ✳ **Roasted Garlic Aioli Salad (page 225)** ✳ **Arugula & Warm Mozzarella Salad (page 191)**

Wild Rice & Mushroom Soup

Think of lakes in Ontario, Canada, where wild rice grows in shallow coves, dried pungent leaves scent the air, and swallows dip and dive over the still water. You wander back to your cabin where a steaming, hearty soup waits.

This is an assertive soup with strong flavors: wild rice, mushrooms, and rosemary. Using one of our Moosewood stocks to cook the rice will give the soup a fuller dimension, but if there isn't time to make stock, water will work fine. While the rice cooks, you have time to prepare the other ingredients.

SERVES 4 TO 6
YIELDS 8 CUPS
TOTAL TIME: 45 MINUTES

PER 10.5-OUNCE SERVING: 161 CALORIES, 3.8 G PROTEIN, 6.1 G FAT, 23.6 G CARBOHYDRATES, 1.5 G SATURATED FATTY ACIDS, 0 MG CHOLESTEROL, 1321 MG SODIUM, 3.7 G TOTAL DIETARY FIBER

1 cup raw wild rice
3 cups Dark Vegetable Stock (page 18), Roasted Vegetable Stock (page 21), or water
2 tablespoons canola or other vegetable oil
2 leeks, rinsed and chopped (about 2 cups) (page 366)
1 cup peeled and chopped carrots
1 cup diced celery
½ teaspoon dried rosemary
½ teaspoon dried thyme
2 bay leaves
2 teaspoons salt
4 ounces fresh wild mushrooms, rinsed, tough stem ends removed, and chopped (2 cups)*
4 dried shiitake, broken into little pieces, stems discarded
4 cups water
3 tablespoons soy sauce
¼ cup dry sherry
ground black pepper to taste

* Chanterelles, white pompoms, and oyster mushrooms are good choices.

In a heavy pot with a tight-fitting lid, bring the rice and 3 cups of stock or water to a boil. Reduce the heat, cover, and simmer until the rice is tender, about 45 minutes.

Meanwhile, heat the oil in a soup pot and sauté the leeks for 5 minutes. Add the carrots, celery, rosemary, thyme, bay leaves, salt, fresh mushrooms, and shiitake and sauté for another 5 minutes. Stir in the water, soy sauce, and sherry and simmer for 10 minutes. Remove and discard the bay leaves.

When the rice is cooked, stir it into the soup. Add pepper to taste and serve hot.

DAILY SPECIAL

MENU IDEAS **Caesar Salad (page 201)** * **Fresh Pear & Blue Cheese Salad (page 266)** * **Composed Beet Salad (page 254)** * **Celeriac Remoulade (page 253)** * **Spicy Pineapple Tofu Salad (page 230)** * **Spicy Cucumber Salad (page 288)** * **watercress and baby greens with Moosewood Ginger Miso Dressing (page 323) and Baked Seasoned Tofu (page 336)**

Wonton Soup

This is a tasty, time-honored soup, good as an appetizer or a meal. Cook the wontons in boiling water until tender; then place a few in individual bowls, ladle on the hot broth, and top with chopped scallions and a drop of dark sesame oil. Delicious!

The wontons are a bit of work, but once they're done, the soup is a snap. This recipe makes enough wontons for two batches of soup, so we suggest you freeze the leftover wontons for later use. Wontons also make a good side dish: boil until tender, drain, place in a serving bowl, and drizzle with soy sauce and sesame oil. Or eat them as a pan-fried appetizer or snack: stir-fry cooked wontons in a little oil until crisp and serve with a dipping sauce of soy sauce and lemon juice or vinegar.

SERVES 4 TO 6
YIELDS 7½ CUPS BROTH,
  ABOUT 50 WONTONS
PREPARATION TIME: 1 HOUR
COOKING TIME: 30 MINUTES

PER 13-OUNCE SERVING: 385 CALORIES, 15.9 G PROTEIN, 13.8 G FAT, 51.8 G CAR-BOHYDRATES, 2.8 G SATURATED FATTY ACIDS, 49 MG CHOLESTEROL, 959 MG SODIUM, 4.4 G TOTAL DIETARY FIBER

BROTH

2 tablespoons canola or other vegetable oil
2 cups minced onions
3 garlic cloves, minced or pressed
½ teaspoon salt
6 cups Mock Chicken Stock (page 20) or Garlic Stock (page 19)
1 teaspoon soy sauce

WONTONS

1 cake of tofu (12 to 16 ounces), frozen and thawed (page 385)
10 ounces fresh spinach
1 tablespoon grated fresh ginger root
1 tablespoon peanut oil
1 tablespoon soy sauce
1 tablespoon peanut butter
3 tablespoons finely chopped scallions
½ to 1 teaspoon Chinese chili paste (page 359)
1 tablespoon cornstarch
1 egg
12-ounce package wonton wrappers (about 50 wrappers)

chopped scallions
a few drops of dark sesame oil

To make the broth, warm the oil in a covered soup pot on medium-low heat. Add the onions, garlic, and salt and gently sauté for about 15 minutes, until very soft and golden but not browned. Add the stock and soy sauce, cover, bring to a low simmer, cook for 10 minutes, and remove from the heat.

Meanwhile, for the wontons, squeeze the thawed tofu to remove as much water as possible. Cut it into pieces, place it in the bowl of a food processor, process until crumbled, and transfer to a large bowl. Rinse the spinach. In a covered saucepan, steam the damp spinach until wilted but still bright green. Drain well, pressing out as much liquid as possible, and then finely chop it and add it to the bowl.

Add the ginger, peanut oil, soy sauce, peanut butter, scallions, chili paste, and cornstarch and stir well. Taste the filling and add more chili paste and/or soy sauce to taste. Add the egg and mix well. Set aside half of the filling in the refrigerator to use later for frozen wontons (see Note).

Prepare a dry work surface and have nearby the other half of the filling, a stack of about 25 wrappers covered with a damp cloth, a small bowl of water, a baking sheet dusted with cornstarch, and a clean dry cloth.

Orient a wrapper on the dry surface with one of the corners pointing toward you. Mound a teaspoon of filling just below the center of the wrapper. Fold the bottom corner up over the filling and tuck the tip of the corner under the filling. Continue to roll up the wrapper like a jelly roll, but only roll it up ⅔ of the way, leaving the triangular top corner of the wrapper exposed.

With your fingers, very gently flatten the sides of the roll by pressing out any air trapped next to the filling. Dip a finger in the water to moisten the outer edges on each side of the roll; press to seal. Curve the two flattened sides of the roll down beneath the filled center of the roll. Moisten the right-hand side, cross it over the left side, and pinch firmly together to seal. The finished wonton resembles (this is a long shot) a miniature head in a bonnet. As you finish the wontons, place them on the baking sheet not touching each other and cover with the dry cloth.

For one batch of soup, assemble 16 or 17 wontons and then bring a large pot of water to a boil. Continue to make another 8 or 9 wontons while the water heats. When it boils, ease in the wontons and return to a simmer. The finished wontons will float to the top. Drain. Reheat the broth, if necessary. Place warm wontons in the bottom of individual bowls, ladle in hot broth, and top each bowl of soup with a sprinkling of chopped scallions and a drop or two of dark sesame oil.

Note Covered with plastic wrap, the filling will keep for 2 to 3 hours, so you can enjoy your meal and then finish assembling wontons. Place the baking sheet of uncooked filled wontons in the freezer until the wontons are frozen solid; then transfer them to a plastic bag or container. Frozen wontons will keep for several weeks. Cook them, without defrosting, in boiling water.

Uncooked wontons do not store well in the refrigerator.

MENU IDEAS **Asparagus & Snow Pea Salad (page 247)** ∗ **Bean Sprout Salad (page 250)** ∗ **Pilwun's Daikon Salad (page 282)** ∗ **Spicy Cucumber Salad (page 288)** ∗ **tossed green salad with Moosewood Ginger Miso Dressing (page 323)**

Winter Minestrone

Bursting with a multitude of naturally sweet root vegetables and bolstered by red and/or white beans, this hefty soup makes a meal for 6 to 8 people—and you may have leftovers. It is, as with many soups, thicker and even more delicious the second day. Add ½ to 1 cup of water before reheating, if you want a brothier soup.

SERVES 6 TO 8
YIELDS 12 CUPS
PREPARATION TIME: 25 MINUTES
SIMMERING TIME:
  30 TO 40 MINUTES

PER 11.25-OUNCE SERVING: 178 CALORIES, 6.7 G PROTEIN, 4.2 G FAT, 30.5 G CARBOHYDRATES, 0 .6 G SATURATED FATTY ACIDS, 0 MG CHOLESTEROL, 445 MG SODIUM, 2.7 G TOTAL DIETARY FIBER

1½ cups chopped onions
5 or 6 garlic cloves, minced or pressed
1 cup diced celery
2 tablespoons olive oil
1 teaspoon salt
1 cup peeled and diced carrots
1 cup peeled and diced parsnips
1 cup chopped fennel bulb
1½ cups peeled and cubed sweet potatoes
2 teaspoons ground fennel seeds
2 teaspoons dried oregano
⅛ to ¼ teaspoon dried red pepper flakes
1 teaspoon freshly ground dried rosemary or 1 fresh rosemary sprig
3 cups canned tomatoes in juice, chopped or puréed
2 to 3 cups water
½ cup dry red wine (optional)
1½ cups cooked drained kidney beans (15-ounce can)*
¾ cup chopped fresh parsley

freshly grated Parmesan cheese (optional)

White and red kidneys are both fine, and if you prefer to substitute another type of bean, go right ahead.

In a large nonreactive soup pot, sauté the onions, garlic, and celery in the oil on low heat for 10 minutes. Stir in the salt, carrots, parsnips, and chopped fennel, and then cover and continue to cook for 10 minutes, stirring frequently. Add the sweet potatoes, ground fennel, oregano, red pepper flakes, and rosemary and simmer for about 5 minutes. (If the vegetables stick or begin to brown, add a splash of water.)

Add the tomatoes, water, and, if using, the wine. Cover and simmer for 20 to 30 minutes. Add the beans and parsley and cook for another 10 minutes.

Serve plain or topped with grated Parmesan cheese.

MENU IDEAS **Five-Herb Salad (page 262)** ✳ **Kiwi, Orange & Baby Greens (page 273)** ✳ **Mediterranean Orange & Olive Salad (page 276)** ✳ **Solstice Salad (page 227)** ✳ **Focaccia (page 330)** ✳ **Parsley Pesto (page 348)** ✳ **Our Special Gluten-free Bread (page 333)**

Ybor City Garbanzo Soup

Ybor City is an old Cuban neighborhood in Tampa, Florida, and was once the cigar-making capital of the United States. Moosewood sisters Susan Harville and Nancy Lazarus have memories of going there as children to the beautiful Columbia Restaurant to feast on garbanzo bean soup and yellow rice or Cuban sandwiches. It was always a glamorous and exciting time.

Our garbanzo bean soup is vegetarian and much lower in fat than traditional Ybor City versions, yet it still retains the unique flavor of foods from that colorful community. We suggest a salad with fruit as the ideal partner in a Daily Special.

SERVES 6
YIELDS 9 CUPS
PREPARATION TIME: 25 MINUTES
COOKING TIME: 35 MINUTES

PER 12-OUNCE SERVING: 216 CALORIES, 5.4 G PROTEIN, 5.8 G FAT, 37.3 G CARBO-HYDRATES, 1.3 G SATURATED FATTY ACIDS, 0 MG CHOLESTEROL, 586 MG SODIUM, 5.3 G TOTAL DIETARY FIBER

2 tablespoons canola or other vegetable oil
2 cups finely chopped onions
2 celery stalks, finely chopped
2 garlic cloves, minced or pressed
1 teaspoon ground cumin
1 teaspoon ground fennel seeds
pinch of thyme
½ teaspoon paprika
1 teaspoon salt
½ teaspoon ground black pepper
dash of cayenne (optional)
1 red bell pepper, seeded and chopped into 1-inch pieces
4 cups water
4 cups cubed potatoes (about 1-inch)
1½ cups drained cooked garbanzo beans* (15-ounce can)
generous pinch of saffron
2 tablespoons very hot water
1 tablespoon white vinegar or fresh lemon juice

* Also called chickpeas.

Combine the oil, onions, and celery in a soup pot and sauté on medium heat, stirring occasionally, until the onions are very soft and beginning to brown, about 15 minutes.

Stir in the garlic, cumin, fennel, thyme, paprika, salt, black pepper, and cayenne, if using. Add the bell peppers and cook, stirring constantly, for 2 minutes. Add the water and the potatoes, cover, and bring to a boil. Then lower the heat and simmer until the potatoes are tender, about 20 minutes.

When the potatoes are tender, add the garbanzo beans. Put the saffron threads in a cup and cover with the hot water. With the back of a spoon, crush the saffron against the side of the cup for about a minute. Add the saffron and water to the soup. Swirl some of the soup broth around the inside of the cup to get every precious bit of saffron out of the cup and into the soup. Stir in the vinegar or lemon juice.

Serve immediately.

MENU IDEAS **Florida Salad with Ginger Dressing (page 263)** ✳ **East Indian Fruit Salad (page 258)** ✳ **Mediterranean Orange & Olive Salad (page 276)** ✳ **Golden Tomato Avocado Salad (page 268)**

CREAMY DAIRY SOUPS

Creamy dairy soups are among the most popular soups at Moosewood Restaurant. Some creamy soups have a certain elegance and refinement, and others could be described as soothing and satisfying "comfort food." * Many of these soups are built on one or maybe two vegetables and are at least partially puréed to give them a thick, smooth texture: all of the separate flavors may be blended into one, but the character of the dominant vegetable remains the core of the soup. A soup like Cream of Asparagus eloquently expresses the pale green essence of that vegetable, like a poem to springtime. Other soups, such as Santa Fe Chowder, are not smooth purées but instead are chunky with pieces of vegetables in a creamy base. * In this section of creamy soups, some are surprisingly lean, like Creamy Herbed Carrot Soup, a savory purée that is thickened with sweet potatoes and can be made with soy milk. A few other soups are unequivocally extravagant with cheese. Both Celery Roquefort Soup and Creamy Onion & Fontina Soup are interesting and sumptuous pairings of a vegetable and cheese. Some puréed soups are made with a traditional roux, which produces a smooth satiny soup such as Creamy Tomato. Others are thickened by puréeing the main vegetable with potatoes, as in Curried Zucchini and Cream of Spinach. We find that often just a couple of tablespoons of Neufchâtel or cream cheese can give a soup the smooth "mouth feel" we associate with heavy cream. * Three of the soups in this chapter are enriched with eggs. Artichoke Avgolemono is a vegetable-rich version of the Greek lemon, egg, and rice soup. At the end, eggs are stirred into Chinese Velvet Corn Soup and Tomato Egg Drop Soup to form silky threads suspended in the soup. * For some puréed soups, we suggest garnishes that add a different color or texture or accent a flavor. Good garnishes for purées include croutons, snipped fresh herbs, chopped fresh tomatoes, dollops of yogurt or sour cream, and crisp Fried Shallots. Roasting a few chopped turnips and stirring them into the finished soup brings out the true nature of Back to Your Roots Soup. ✳ In general, when we serve a creamy dairy soup with a salad to create a Daily Special Soup & Salad Plate, we consider contrasts in flavors, colors, and textures. For example, a rich cheese soup such as Cauliflower, Cheese & Tomato Soup is best with an astringent, brisk green salad such as Five-Herb Salad. On the other hand, a simple soup with a strong single vegetable note is nicely paired with a more complex salad of grains, beans, or fish. Smooth Cream of Mushroom Soup is a wonderful prelude to a textural and multiflavored mélange such as Balinese Rice Salad. Creamy Tomato Soup is the perfect contrast and comple-ment for Tropical Fruit & Shrimp Salad. Sometimes, it seems best to keep the Daily Special duo in the same regional family or related to the same ethnic cui-sine. Subtle Chinese Velvet Corn Soup goes well with crisp Sichuan-style Spicy Cucumber Salad. ✳ At the grocery store, you can purchase creamy potato soup in a 15-ounce can, but it's so easy to make a whole big potful yourself. The canned potato soup is a poor substitute for savory Creamy Herbed Potato Soup, tasty Creamy Potato Cabbage Soup, or zesty Roasted Chile & Potato Soup. You can find canned or (horrors!) even powdered cheese soups, but they just don't hold a candle to our Welsh Rarebit Soup, a robust blend of sharp Cheddar, tangy mus-tard, and beer topped with chunks of fresh tomato and crisp Pumpernickel Crou-tons. ✳ Homemade soup is always the winner when it comes to matters of taste. **It's a simple formula—wholesome, fresh ingredients com-bined with care result in creamy, delicious nourishment. ✳**

Artichoke Avgolemono

Rich and velvety, this soup is a vegetarian adaptation of the classic Greek avgolemono. We've added artichokes and savory vegetables to the customary ingredients of eggs, lemon juice, and rice — an interesting twist on an old favorite.

SERVES 4 TO 6
YIELDS 8 TO 9 CUPS
TOTAL TIME: 55 MINUTES

PER 12-OUNCE SERVING: 161 CALORIES, 7.4 G PROTEIN, 5.8 G FAT, 21.9 G CARBO-HYDRATES, 1.3 G SATURATED FATTY ACIDS, 132 MG CHOLESTEROL, 606 MG SODIUM, 4.9 G TOTAL DIETARY FIBER

2 cups chopped leeks (page 366)
1 cup peeled and chopped carrots
1 cup diced celery
2 garlic cloves, minced or pressed
1 teaspoon salt
1 tablespoon olive oil
¼ cup raw white rice
6 cups vegetable stock*
2 bay leaves
2 teaspoons chopped fresh tarragon (1 teaspoon dried)
5 artichoke hearts, quartered (14-ounce can, drained)**
3 large eggs
¼ cup fresh lemon juice
salt and ground black pepper to taste

* *We recommend using either Garlic Stock (page 19) or Mock Chicken Stock (page 20) for the fullest, most authentic flavor.*
** *Sometimes a canned artichoke heart has a few bristly leaves in the center; if so, remove and discard those leaves for a smoother soup.*

In a soup pot on medium-low heat, sauté the leeks, carrots, celery, garlic, and salt in the oil for 10 minutes, stirring occasionally. Add the rice, vegetable stock, bay leaves, and tarragon. Cover and bring to a boil; then reduce the heat and simmer for 20 minutes, or until the rice and vegetables are tender. Add the artichoke hearts and continue to cook for 2 to 3 minutes. Turn off the heat and remove and discard the bay leaves.

In a large bowl, whisk together the eggs and lemon juice until blended, and then whisk in about a cup of the hot soup. While stirring the soup, gradually pour in the egg mixture. Reheat gently, stirring constantly until the soup thickens: the heat must be low and even or the eggs may "scramble" instead of adding body to the broth. When the soup is smooth and thickened, add salt and pepper to taste.

Variation For a creamy version, purée the soup in batches in a blender or food processor until smooth. Reheat gently and serve at once.

DAILY SPECIAL

MENU IDEAS **Greek Chickpea Salad (page 277)** ✳ **Seafood & Chermoulla Couscous Salad (page 306)** ✳ **Roasted Red Pepper & Cauliflower Salad (page 226)** ✳ **Roasted Green Tomato & Feta Salad (page 283)**

Back to Your Roots Soup

Like so many folks, we, too, have wondered, "What can you do with a turnip?" and "Aren't parsnips just a little weird?" Well, we think we've created a very tasty soup with these enduring, if perplexing, vegetables—and in the process, we've really come to appreciate those little roots.

Serve this smooth, thick, mildly sweet purée with a more assertively flavored salad, whether sweet or sharp, and they will enhance one another.

SERVES 6 TO 8
YIELDS 9 CUPS
TOTAL TIME: 1 HOUR

PER 11-OUNCE SERVING: 146 CALORIES, 2.8 G PROTEIN, 5 G FAT, 24.3 G CARBOHYDRATES, 1.1 G SATURATED FATTY ACIDS, 3 MG CHOLESTEROL, 627 MG SODIUM, 2.6 G TOTAL DIETARY FIBER

4 cups thinly sliced leeks, white parts and tender greens (about 4 medium leeks)
1 large garlic clove, minced or pressed
2 tablespoons olive oil
5½ cups peeled and chopped turnips (2½ pounds)
2 cups peeled and thinly sliced parsnips (½ pound)
1 tablespoon chopped fresh tarragon (1 teaspoon dried)
2 teaspoons ground fennel seeds
5 cups water or Basic Light Vegetable Stock (page 16)
1½ teaspoons salt
¼ cup sour cream
1 teaspoon fresh lemon juice
salt and ground black pepper to taste

croutons

In a soup pot, sauté the leeks and garlic in the olive oil for about 5 minutes, until the leeks are bright green and aromatic. Stir frequently to prevent sticking and browning. Add the turnips, parsnips, tarragon, and fennel and sauté for another 3 to 4 minutes.

Pour in the water or stock and add the salt. Cover and bring to a boil; then reduce the heat and simmer until the vegetables are soft, about 10 minutes. Remove from the heat and stir in the sour cream.

In a food processor or in batches in a blender, purée the soup until smooth and return it to the soup pot. Stir in the lemon juice. Add salt and pepper to taste.

Serve garnished with croutons.

Variation For a more pronounced turnip flavor, reserve 1½ cups of the chopped turnips, sprinkle them with salt, toss them with 2 teaspoons of oil in a baking pan, and roast them at 500° in a preheated oven until tender, 10 to 15 minutes. Stir the roasted turnips into the finished soup and gently reheat, if needed.

MENU IDEAS **Bulghur Grape Salad (page 200)** ✳ **Five-Herb Salad (page 262)** ✳ **Asian Beet & Tofu Salad (page 192)** ✳ **Fresh Pear & Blue Cheese Salad (page 266)**

Cauliflower, Cheese & Tomato Soup

In the sixteenth century, cauliflower and potatoes made their way to Europe from Asia and South America on the ships of European explorers. Cooks introduced these vegetables to their regional cheeses and herbs and, as a result, created wonderfully tasty dishes that have become classics.

We've used Cheddar cheese (which originated in Somerset, England) and added a twist—tomatoes—for a sprightly fresh flavor and beautiful salmony color. Serve this thick, invigorating soup on a cold winter night.

SERVES 4 TO 6
YIELDS 9 TO 10 CUPS
TOTAL TIME: 1 HOUR

PER 12-OUNCE SERVING: 312 CALORIES, 12.2 G PROTEIN, 18.9 G FAT, 26.1 G CAR-BOHYDRATES, 9.3 G SATURATED FATTY ACIDS, 43 MG CHOLESTEROL, 283 MG SODIUM, 4.9 G TOTAL DIETARY FIBER

2 tablespoons olive oil
2 cups chopped onions
4 garlic cloves, minced or pressed
1 cup peeled and diced carrots
⅓ cup diced celery
2½ cups diced potatoes
4 cups chopped cauliflower
1 teaspoon dried oregano
2 cups water
2 cups chopped fresh or canned tomatoes (28-ounce can, drained)
1½ cups grated sharp Cheddar cheese
2 tablespoons chopped fresh basil
½ teaspoon ground black pepper
¼ cup Neufchâtel or cream cheese (2 ounces)
½ cup milk
salt to taste

Warm the olive oil in a nonreactive soup pot, add the onions, cover, and cook on medium heat for 8 to 10 minutes, until the onions are translucent; stir often. Add the garlic, carrots, and celery and continue to cook for 5 minutes. Add the potatoes, cauliflower, oregano, and water, cover, and bring to a boil. Reduce the heat to very low, cover, and simmer for 10 to 15 minutes, until all of the vegetables are tender. Add the tomatoes, cover, and cook for about 5 more minutes.

In a blender or food processor, purée about 3½ cups of the soup with the Cheddar cheese, basil, pepper, Neufchâtel, and milk until smooth. Return the puréed mixture to the pot, add salt to taste, gently reheat the soup, and serve.

MENU IDEAS Wilted Spinach & Portabella Mushrooms (page 239) ✳ **Fruit with Cranberry Currant Dressing (page 267)** ✳ **Fresh Pear & Blue Cheese Salad (page 266)** ✳ **Five-Herb Salad (page 262)** ✳ **Focaccia (page 330)** ✳ **Pumpernickel Croutons (page 349)** ✳ **Seafood Paella Salad (page 308)**

Celery Roquefort Soup

Rich, creamy, and subtle, with the flavors of blue cheese and celery, this is an excellent soup for a simple meal with a crusty bread and slices of fresh apples or pears. Or for a well-balanced Daily Special, choose a salad with fresh sharp flavors to serve as a counterpoint to this luxurious soup.

SERVES 4 TO 6
YIELDS ABOUT 6 CUPS
TOTAL TIME: 40 MINUTES

PER 8-OUNCE SERVING: 297 CALORIES, 10 G PROTEIN, 25.3 G FAT, 8.5 G CARBO-HYDRATES, 16 G SATURATED FATTY ACIDS, 77 MG CHOLESTEROL, 513 MG SODIUM, 0.9 G TOTAL DIETARY FIBER

2 tablespoons butter
1 cup diced onions
2 cups diced celery
1 cup water
2 cups milk
4 ounces Roquefort or blue cheese
8 ounces Neufchâtel or cream cheese
salt and ground black pepper to taste

In a soup pot, melt the butter on medium heat. Add the onions and celery, cover, and cook, stirring frequently, until soft but not browned, 10 to 15 minutes. Add the water, cover, and bring to a simmer.

In a blender, combine the milk, Roquefort or blue cheese, and the Neufchâtel or cream cheese and purée until very smooth. Stir the purée into the soup and add salt and pepper to taste.

Reheat gently and serve hot.

MENU IDEAS **Roasted Potato & Tomato Salad (page 284)** ✳ **Five-Herb Salad (page 262)** ✳ **Florida Salad with Ginger Dressing (page 263)** ✳ **Fruit with Cranberry Currant Dressing (page 267)** ✳ **Bulghur Grape Salad (page 200)** ✳ **Fresh Pear & Blue Cheese Salad (page 266) without the blue cheese!**

Chinese Velvet Corn Soup

Creamy, simple, and rich, this soup can be made quickly and easily anytime. The Sichuan peppercorns and sherry add depth and enhance the sweetness of the corn. Ribbons of egg white add texture and delicacy to the already ethereal quality of this lovely soup. It's the perfect lead-in to an Asian main dish salad.

SERVES 4
YIELDS 6½ CUPS
TOTAL TIME: 40 MINUTES

PER 12-OUNCE SERVING: 206 CALORIES, 5.5 G PROTEIN, 5.7 G FAT, 37.3 G CARBO-HYDRATES, 1.2 G SATURATED FATTY ACIDS, 0 MG CHOLESTEROL, 929 MG SODIUM, 4 G TOTAL DIETARY FIBER

1 tablespoon canola or other vegetable oil
2 cups chopped onions
¼ teaspoon ground Sichuan peppercorns
1½ teaspoons salt
3 cups fresh or frozen corn kernels
4 cups water
1 teaspoon sugar
2 tablespoons dry sherry
1½ teaspoons rice vinegar
1 egg white
1 tablespoon cornstarch dissolved in 1 tablespoon water
½ teaspoon dark sesame oil

minced scallions

In a soup pot, heat the oil on medium-high heat and add the chopped onions, ground Sichuan peppercorns, and salt. Sauté until soft and translucent, about 10 minutes. Add 2 cups of the corn and sauté for 5 minutes. Add the water, sugar, sherry, and rice vinegar, cover the pot, and bring to a boil; then reduce the heat and simmer for 10 minutes.

Carefully purée the hot soup in a blender in batches. Return it to the soup pot, add the remaining cup of corn, and reheat very gently. Meanwhile, beat the egg white in a small bowl until frothy. Pour it into the pot in a thin stream while stirring the soup slowly. Add the dissolved cornstarch and the sesame oil and continue to stir until slightly thickened.

Serve hot, garnished with scallions.

Variation Before starting the soup, marinate ½ pound of peeled uncooked shrimp in 1 tablespoon of dry sherry and 1 tablespoon of minced garlic. Just before serving, add the marinated shrimp to the soup and poach it until just cooked through, about 5 minutes.

DAILY SPECIAL

MENU IDEAS **Balinese Rice Salad (page 195)** * **Classic Sichuan Noodles (page 204)** * **Thai Rice & Mushroom Salad (page 234)** * **Vietnamese Cellophane Noodle Salad (page 238)** * **Asian Beet & Tofu Salad (page 192)** * **Broiled Tofu & Sugar Snap Peas (page 199)**

Corn Chowder

A creamy, sunny-hued classic that you can make at any time of the year, Corn Chowder is a friendly, comforting soup especially popular with young folks and sweet corn lovers of any age. We tend to match this soup with all-American summer garden salads for combo meals, but it also works in a Mexican, Italian, or Caribbean menu.

SERVES 4 TO 6
YIELDS 8 CUPS
TOTAL TIME: 45 TO 50 MINUTES

PER 12-OUNCE SERVING: 238 CALORIES, 7.2 G PROTEIN, 6.5 G FAT, 42.8 G CARBO-HYDRATES, 2.6 G SATURATED FATTY ACIDS, 11 MG CHOLESTEROL, 94 MG SODIUM, 4.4 G TOTAL DIETARY FIBER

1 cup chopped onions
1 tablespoon canola or other vegetable oil
2½ cups diced potatoes
½ cup diced celery
scant ½ teaspoon dried dill
¼ teaspoon dried thyme
1 bay leaf
3 cups water or vegetable stock (see Note)
1 cup diced red and/or yellow bell peppers
4 cups fresh, frozen, or canned corn kernels (see Note)
1 tablespoon chopped fresh basil (optional)
2 cups milk
salt and ground black pepper to taste

fresh dill or parsley sprigs or a few fresh basil leaves

In a soup pot on medium heat, sauté the onions in the oil for about 10 minutes, until translucent, stirring often. Add the potatoes, celery, dill, thyme, bay leaf, and water or stock. Cover and simmer gently for about 5 minutes, until the potatoes begin to soften. Add the bell peppers and corn and cook for 5 minutes. Stir in the basil, if using. Remove and discard the bay leaf.

Ladle 2 cups of the soup into a blender and add the milk. Whirl until smooth and return the puréed mixture to the soup pot. Add salt and pepper to taste. Gently reheat.

Serve with a few fresh dill or parsley sprigs or decorate with some fresh basil leaves.

Note If you're using fresh corn, use the cobs to make this lovely stock: Place the corn cobs, 1 chopped potato, 1 chopped celery stalk, 3 peeled whole garlic cloves, a pinch of salt, and 10 cups of water in a large soup pot. Bring to a boil, then lower the heat, cover, and simmer gently for an hour. Strain through a colander. Yields about 6 cups of stock.

DAILY SPECIAL

MENU IDEAS Caesar Salad (page 201) ✳ **Tomato Flowers (page 236)** ✳ **Alabama Hot Slaw (page 245)** ✳ **Farm-style Tomato Salad (page 286)** ✳ **Honey Mustard Green Beans Vinaigrette (page 269)** ✳ **Louisiana Black-eyed Pea Salad (page 221)**

Cream of Asparagus Soup

This potage uses a basic roux in the classic French tradition and culminates with a velvety, rich purée of lovely spring green. Use the first tender asparagus of the season and an already elegant soup becomes superb. Pair with any of our menu suggestions and you can create an enjoyable spring meal.

SERVES 4 TO 6
YIELDS 7 CUPS
PREPARATION TIME: 20 MINUTES
COOKING TIME: 30 MINUTES

PER 10-OUNCE SERVING: 187 CALORIES, 5.7 G PROTEIN, 13.2 G FAT, 13.3 G CARBO-HYDRATES, 7.2 G SATURATED FATTY ACIDS, 31 MG CHOLESTEROL, 348 MG SODIUM, 0.5 G TOTAL DIETARY FIBER

1 cup chopped onions
½ teaspoon salt
1 teaspoon dried tarragon*
1 tablespoon canola or other vegetable oil
2 pounds fresh asparagus
2¼ cups water
¼ cup butter
¼ cup unbleached white flour
2 cups hot (not boiling) milk
1 teaspoon fresh lemon juice (optional)
salt and ground black pepper to taste

Herbed Croutons (page 30)
minced fresh chives

* 1 tablespoon of minced fresh tarragon can replace the dried amount. Add the fresh herb to the soup just before puréeing it.

In a soup pot, sauté the onions, salt, and tarragon in the oil on medium heat, stirring often, until the onions are translucent, about 10 minutes.

While the onions cook, prepare the asparagus. Snap off the tough stem ends and discard. Rinse the spears to remove any sand or grit. Snap off the tips and slice them on the diagonal into ¼-inch pieces; set aside. Chop the spears.

Add the chopped spears and 2 cups of the water to the soup pot. Cover, bring to a boil, reduce the heat, and simmer until the asparagus is bright green and tender, 8 to 10 minutes. Set aside.

Steam the asparagus tips in the remaining ¼ cup of water for 3 to 4 minutes, until tender but still bright green. Drain and set aside.

Melt the butter on low heat and whisk in the flour to make a roux. Cook on low heat, stirring constantly for 3 to 4 minutes. Whisk in the hot milk and stir until thickened, about 5 minutes. Combine the roux with the sautéed onions and cooked asparagus spears in a blender and purée until smooth. Add lemon juice, if desired, and salt and pepper to taste. Stir in the reserved asparagus tips and gently reheat.

Serve garnished with croutons or minced chives.

MENU IDEAS **Arugula & Warm Mozzarella Salad (page 191)** * **Wilted Spinach & Portabella Mushrooms (page 239)** * **Bulghur Grape Salad (page 200)** * **Fresh Pear & Blue Cheese Salad (page 266)** * **Popovers (page 334)**

Cream of Mushroom Soup

Don't worry—this is nothing like the condensed mushroom soup your mother may have stirred into weekly noodle casseroles to feed the hungry brood. No indeed, this is a lush soup, redolent with savory mushrooms browned in butter and garlic, rich with sherry and cream.

Pressed garlic often produces a sharper bite, so here we recommend slicing the garlic for a mellower flavor that lends depth to the subtle earthiness of the mushrooms.

SERVES 6
YIELDS 8 CUPS
PREPARATION TIME: 15 MINUTES
COOKING TIME: 25 MINUTES

PER 10-OUNCE SERVING: 223 CALORIES, 3.6 G PROTEIN, 18.3 G FAT, 12.9 G CARBO-HYDRATES, 11.2 G SATURATED FATTY ACIDS, 62 MG CHOLESTEROL, 452 MG SODIUM, 2.3 G TOTAL DIETARY FIBER

2 tablespoons butter
1 tablespoon thinly sliced garlic
1 cup diced onions
1½ pounds mushrooms, rinsed and sliced
1 teaspoon salt
1 tablespoon fresh lemon juice
5 tablespoons unbleached white flour
4 cups water
1 cup heavy cream
1 tablespoon dry sherry
1 teaspoon finely chopped fresh thyme (¼ teaspoon dried)*
freshly ground black pepper to taste

If using dried thyme, sauté it with the onions and garlic rather than adding it at the end to ensure a more even and mellow flavor.

In a soup pot on medium heat, melt the butter. Add the garlic and sauté just until golden. Add the onions and sauté until soft, about 5 minutes. Add the mushrooms, salt, and lemon juice and continue to cook, stirring frequently, until the mushrooms are soft and have released liquid, about 7 minutes.

Sprinkle in the flour a little at a time, stirring briskly to prevent lumps. Add the water, cream, and sherry and stir well. Bring to a boil; then reduce the heat and cook for about 5 minutes, until thickened. Add the fresh thyme and pepper to taste.

MENU IDEAS Balkan Roasted Vegetable Salad (page 196) ✳ **Harvest Rice Salad (page 215)** ✳ **Composed Beet Salad (page 254)** ✳ **Lentil, Rice & Fruit Salad (page 220)** ✳ **Brussels Sprouts & Carrot Salad (page 251)** ✳ **French Barley Salad (page 210)**

Cream of Spinach Soup

The beautiful delicate green of this soup mimics the indescribably fresh color of early spring in the northeastern United States. Here in Ithaca, spinach is one of the first vegetables to grace our gardens and makes a welcome appearance in the local farmers' market in late April or May. While spring is the perfect time to make this soup, it can be enjoyed year-round and can even be served chilled during the hot days of summer.

SERVES 4 TO 6
YIELDS 7 CUPS
TOTAL TIME: 25 MINUTES

PER 10-OUNCE SERVING: 180 CALORIES, 4.7 G PROTEIN, 9 G FAT, 21.7 G CARBOHYDRATES, 3.8 G SATURATED FATTY ACIDS, 13 MG CHOLESTEROL, 114 MG SODIUM, 2.8 G TOTAL DIETARY FIBER

2 tablespoons canola or
  other vegetable oil
1 tablespoon butter
2 cups coarsely chopped onions
½ cup chopped celery
dash of salt
3 cups chopped potatoes
2½ cups water or vegetable stock
10 ounces fresh spinach, rinsed
1½ cups milk*
¼ teaspoon freshly grated nutmeg
salt and ground black pepper to taste

Herbed Croutons (page 30)

* *For a richer, creamier soup, replace ½ cup of the milk with ½ cup of half-and-half.*

In a soup pot, warm the oil and butter. Add the onions and celery, sprinkle with salt, cover, and cook on low heat for about 10 minutes, stirring occasionally, until the onions are soft and translucent. Add the potatoes and the water or stock, cover, and cook on medium heat about 10 minutes, until the potatoes are soft.

Stir in the spinach, cover, and set aside off the heat for 2 minutes, until the spinach is wilted but still bright green. Purée the soup in batches in a blender or food processor until smooth, gradually adding the milk. Stir in the nutmeg and add salt and pepper to taste. Gently reheat.

Serve topped with croutons, if desired.

DAILY SPECIAL

MENU IDEAS **Goat Cheese Toasts (page 344)** ✳ **Bulghur Grape Salad (page 200)** ✳ **Lentil, Rice & Fruit Salad (page 220)** ✳ **Fattoush (page 209)** ✳ **Lemon Rice & Seafood Salad (page 302)**

Creamy Herbed Carrot Soup

Sweet potatoes add a creamy texture and enhance the natural sweetness of carrots in this lovely soup — what a delicious way to get a double dose of beta-carotene! Because the vegetables in this soup are all so sweet, we recommend a salad with a bit of a bite for a Daily Special.

SERVES 4 TO 6
YIELDS 8 CUPS
TOTAL TIME: 45 MINUTES

PER 10-OUNCE SERVING: 172 CALORIES, 4.7 G PROTEIN, 5.5 G FAT, 27.3 G CARBO-HYDRATES, 2.4 G SATURATED FATTY ACIDS, 11 MG CHOLESTEROL, 198 MG SODIUM, 4.1 G TOTAL DIETARY FIBER

1½ cups chopped onions
1 tablespoon canola or other vegetable oil
1 celery stalk, chopped
2 garlic cloves, minced or pressed
1 bay leaf
3 cups peeled and chopped carrots
1½ cups peeled and chopped sweet potatoes
3 cups water or Basic Light Vegetable Stock (page 16)
½ teaspoon dried thyme
½ teaspoon dried dill
2 cups milk or plain soy or rice milk
salt and ground black pepper to taste
2 to 3 teaspoons fresh lemon juice (optional)

minced fresh chives or parsley
fresh dill sprigs
Herbed Croutons (page 30)

In a soup pot, sauté the onions in the oil for about 5 minutes. Add the celery, garlic, and bay leaf and sauté, stirring occasionally, until the onions are translucent, about 5 minutes. Add the carrots, sweet potatoes, water or stock, thyme, and dill. Bring to a boil and then reduce the heat, cover, and simmer until the vegetables are soft, about 20 minutes. Remove the bay leaf.

Working in batches in a blender, purée the soup with the milk, soy milk, or rice milk. Add salt, pepper, and lemon juice to taste. Return the soup to the pot and gently reheat.

Serve topped with chives or parsley, dill sprigs, and croutons.

MENU IDEAS **Arugula & Warm Mozzarella Salad (page 191)** ✳ **Broccoli Pine Nut Pasta Salad (page 198)** ✳ **Asparagus & Fennel Pasta Salad (page 193)** ✳ **Bean & Radicchio Salad (page 249)** ✳ **Herbed Cheese Quick Bread (page 332)**

Creamy Herbed Potato Soup

One potato, two potato, three potato, four. Anytime you eat this, you'll want more. This soup fits easily into any menu. It goes with everything and everyone loves it.

SERVES 4 TO 6
YIELDS ABOUT 8 CUPS
TOTAL TIME: 35 MINUTES

PER 10-OUNCE SERVING: 134 CALORIES, 3.2 G PROTEIN, 5.4 G FAT, 19.2 G CARBO-HYDRATES, 3.3 G SATURATED FATTY ACIDS, 16 MG CHOLESTEROL, 480 MG SODIUM, 2 G TOTAL DIETARY FIBER

1½ cups chopped onions
1½ cups chopped celery
1 teaspoon salt
2 tablespoons butter
3 cups cubed red potatoes*
3 cups water
1 tablespoon chopped fresh dill (1 teaspoon dried)
1½ teaspoons chopped fresh marjoram (½ teaspoon dried)
1 cup milk
2 to 4 tablespoons Neufchâtel or cream cheese (optional)

*If you don't peel the potatoes, the finished soup will have tiny flecks of red in it.

In a soup pot, sauté the onions, celery, and salt in the butter for 5 minutes on medium-high heat. Add the potatoes, water, dill, and marjoram, cover, and bring to a boil. Reduce the heat and simmer until the potatoes are soft, about 10 minutes.

In a blender in batches, purée the vegetable mixture with the milk and, if using, the Neufchâtel or cream cheese. Return the soup to the pot and gently reheat.

DAILY SPECIAL ❧

MENU IDEAS **Eastern European Kasha & Mushrooms (page 206)** ✳ **Loblo (page 274)** ✳ **Roasted Green Tomato & Feta Salad (page 283)** ✳ **Asian Beet & Tofu Salad (page 192)** ✳ **Kale Salad (page 272)** ✳ **Asparagus Vinaigrette (page 248)**

Creamy Onion & Fontina Soup

In some ways this unassuming tasty soup seems as familiar as a grilled cheese sandwich, yet in other ways it has the simple elegance of haute cuisine at its best. Although traditionally the onions would be sautéed in one saucepan and the roux made in another, here you simply add the flour to the caramelized onions to make the roux and then add the rest of the ingredients—a one-pot affair that saves time on cleanup.

If you prefer a perfectly smooth soup, purée the finished soup and gently reheat, if needed. For added flair, serve topped with garlicky croutons.

SERVES 4 TO 6
YIELDS ABOUT 6½ CUPS
TOTAL TIME: 45 MINUTES

PER 9-OUNCE SERVING: 306 CALORIES, 13.8 G PROTEIN, 18.5 G FAT, 20.9 G CARBOHYDRATES, 10.4 G SATURATED FATTY ACIDS, 57 MG CHOLESTEROL, 750 MG SODIUM, 1.8 G TOTAL DIETARY FIBER

1 tablespoon canola or other vegetable oil
1 tablespoon butter
5 cups thinly sliced onions
1 teaspoon salt
½ teaspoon dried thyme
¼ teaspoon freshly grated nutmeg
⅛ teaspoon ground black pepper
rounded ⅓ cup sifted unbleached white flour
2½ cups milk*
2½ cups water
¼ cup dry white wine
2 teaspoons Dijon mustard
2 cups grated Fontina cheese, packed (about 7 ounces)

dash of freshly grated nutmeg
chopped fresh parsley

* Brought to room temperature or warmed in a microwave.

Warm the oil and melt the butter in a soup pot. Add the onions and salt and sauté, uncovered, on medium-high heat for about 10 minutes, stirring often, until the onions are translucent. Add the thyme, nutmeg, and black pepper and continue to sauté until the onions are lightly browned, 5 to 10 minutes.

Lower the heat and while stirring constantly, gradually add the flour to make a thick roux the consistency of paste. Gently cook for 1 minute, stirring constantly. Add 1 cup of the milk and stir well to make a smooth, thick sauce. Whisk in the remaining 1½ cups of milk and the water, and increase the heat to medium. Stir until smooth and beginning to thicken, about 5 minutes.

Add the wine, mustard, and grated cheese. Cover and cook on low heat for 5 minutes, stirring occasionally, until the cheese has melted and the soup is hot.

Top each serving with a dash of nutmeg and a sprinkling of parsley.

DAILY SPECIAL

MENU IDEAS Asparagus Vinaigrette (page 248) ✳ **North African Roasted Cauliflower (page 279)** ✳ **Wilted Spinach & Portabella Mushrooms (page 239)** ✳ **Five-Herb Salad (page 262)** ✳ **Chef Salad à la Moosewood (page 203)** ✳ **Herbed Croutons (page 30)** ✳ **Our Special Gluten-free Bread (page 333)**

Creamy Potato Cabbage Soup

Sweet cabbage and creamy potatoes in a humble, warm-hearted soup offer cozy comfort for those who live in cold, damp climates where these vegetables happily thrive. The caraway and dill add appetizing flavor and fragrance.

SERVES 4
YIELDS 5½ CUPS
TOTAL TIME: 45 MINUTES

PER 11-OUNCE SERVING: 266 CALORIES, 5.1 G PROTEIN, 17.6 G FAT, 24.4 G CARBO-HYDRATES, 8.1 G SATURATED FATTY ACIDS, 31 MG CHOLESTEROL, 439 MG SODIUM, 4.7 G TOTAL DIETARY FIBER

2 tablespoons canola or other vegetable oil
2 cups coarsely chopped onions
1 teaspoon ground caraway seeds
½ teaspoon salt
4 cups coarsely chopped green cabbage
2 cups sliced white or red potatoes
3 cups water or vegetable stock
1 teaspoon dried dill
4 ounces Neufchâtel or cream cheese
salt and ground black pepper to taste

Warm the oil in a soup pot on medium heat, add the onions and sprinkle with the caraway and about half of the salt. Cover and cook, stirring occasionally, for about 10 minutes, until the onions are translucent. Add the cabbage and the remaining salt, cover, and continue to cook, stirring occasionally, until the cabbage begins to wilt. Add the potatoes and water, cover, and bring to a boil; then reduce the heat and simmer until all of the vegetables are tender.

In a blender in batches, purée the vegetable mixture, dill, and Neufchâtel or cream cheese until smooth. Return the soup to the pot and gently reheat. Add salt and pepper to taste. Add a little more water if the soup is too thick.

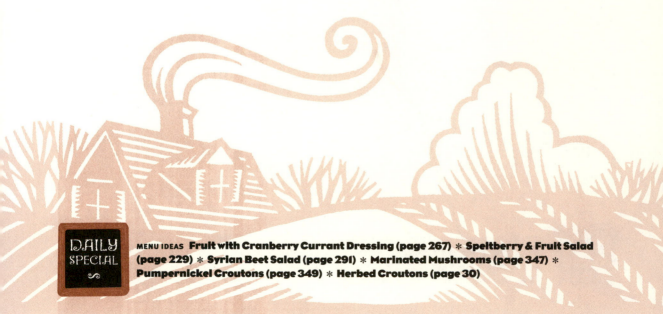

DAILY SPECIAL

MENU IDEAS **Fruit with Cranberry Currant Dressing (page 267)** * **Speltberry & Fruit Salad (page 229)** * **Syrian Beet Salad (page 291)** * **Marinated Mushrooms (page 347)** * **Pumpernickel Croutons (page 349)** * **Herbed Croutons (page 30)**

Creamy Tomato Soup

This rich, elegant tomato soup is satiny smooth and sleek. Basil leaves and chopped tomatoes give it a summer garden freshness even in midwinter. Serve it as the first course of a formal dinner or as the main dish for lunch. For a Daily Special, just select a salad without tomatoes and it's likely to be a good match.

Heat the soup gradually and don't let it come to a full boil or it may curdle. Garnished with croutons or fried shallots and a dollop of sour cream, it's an appetizing and captivating sight.

SERVES 6 TO 8
YIELDS 9 CUPS
TOTAL TIME: 70 MINUTES

PER 9.25-OUNCE SERVING: 147 CALORIES, 3.4 G PROTEIN, 10 G FAT, 12.6 G CARBOHYDRATES, 5.2 G SATURATED FATTY ACIDS, 25 MG CHOLESTEROL, 751 MG SODIUM, 1.1 G TOTAL DIETARY FIBER

1 tablespoon olive oil
1 tablespoon butter
1 cup diced onions
4 to 6 garlic cloves, minced or pressed
¾ cup diced celery, stalks and leaves
1 teaspoon salt
½ teaspoon dried oregano
⅛ to ¼ teaspoon red pepper flakes or cayenne to taste
1 cup water
4 cups tomato juice
½ teaspoon sugar
2 cups half-and-half
3 tablespoons unbleached white flour dissolved in ¼ cup water
2 tomatoes, chopped
¼ cup chopped fresh basil

Pumpernickel Croutons (page 349) or Fried Shallots (page 343)
sour cream (optional)

Warm the olive oil and butter in a nonreactive soup pot. Stir in the onions, garlic, and celery, cover, and sauté on medium heat for 15 minutes. Add the salt, oregano, and red pepper flakes, and cook for another 3 to 4 minutes. Add the water, tomato juice, and sugar, cover, and gently simmer for 20 to 25 minutes, stirring occasionally.

When the vegetables have simmered for about 20 minutes, carefully heat the half-and-half in a saucepan until hot but not boiling.

Meanwhile, strain the simmered vegetables and broth through a sieve or food mill: discard the vegetables and return the broth to the soup pot. Stir the flour mixture until smooth and whisk it into the broth. Cook on medium heat, stirring continuously until thickened, about 5 minutes; then gradually whisk in the hot half-and-half. Add the chopped tomatoes and basil, and heat the soup to just below the boiling point.

Serve immediately in warm bowls topped with croutons or fried shallots and, if desired, a luxurious little dab of sour cream.

MENU IDEAS **Asparagus & Fennel Pasta Salad (page 193)** ✳ **Honey Mustard Green Beans Vinaigrette (page 269)** ✳ **Bulghur Grape Salad (page 200)** ✳ **Bean & Radicchio Salad (page 249)** ✳ **Artichoke Heart & Bulghur Salat (page 190)** ✳ **French Barley Salad (page 210)** ✳ **Herbed Cheese Quick Bread (page 332)**

Curried Zucchini Soup

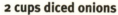

In this vividly hued soup, the mild flavor of zucchini is enlivened with the spark of curry and ginger. A splash of vinegar adds tang and gusto. The soup is very good served hot or cold and makes a wonderful leftover.

SERVES 4 TO 6
YIELDS ABOUT 8½ CUPS
TOTAL TIME: 50 MINUTES
CHILLING TIME (OPTIONAL):
AT LEAST 30 MINUTES

PER 12-OUNCE SERVING: 149 CALORIES, 5 G PROTEIN, 4.5 G FAT, 23.7 G CARBOHYDRATES, 1.8 G SATURATED FATTY ACIDS, 7 MG CHOLESTEROL, 605 MG SODIUM, 3.3 G TOTAL DIETARY FIBER

2 cups diced onions
1 tablespoon canola or other
    vegetable oil
3 garlic cloves, minced or pressed
1 teaspoon grated fresh ginger root
2 teaspoons curry powder
2½ cups water or Basic Light Vegetable Stock (page 16)
2 cups cubed potatoes
5 cups sliced zucchini, cut into ¼-inch-thick half circles*
1 to 1½ teaspoons salt
2 tablespoons chopped fresh cilantro (optional)
1 cup milk
¾ cup plain yogurt
1 tablespoon cider vinegar

plain yogurt
chopped fresh cilantro, scallions, or chives

If you have large zucchini, cut them in half lengthwise, seed them, cut the halves lengthwise again, and then slice crosswise into ¼-inch-thick pieces.

In a covered soup pot on medium heat, sauté the onions in the oil until translucent, about 10 minutes. Add the garlic, ginger root, and curry powder and sauté for 1 minute, stirring constantly. Add the water or stock, potatoes, zucchini, and salt. Cover the pot and bring to a boil; then reduce the heat and simmer for 10 minutes.

Add the cilantro, if using, and continue to simmer until the vegetables are very tender, another 5 to 10 minutes. Stir in the milk and yogurt and remove from the heat; stir in the vinegar. In batches in a blender, purée the soup until smooth.

Reheat gently, or refrigerate for at least 30 minutes if you prefer a chilled soup. Serve topped with a dollop of yogurt and a smidgen of cilantro, scallions, or chives.

DAILY SPECIAL

MENU IDEAS **Kiwi, Orange & Baby Greens (page 273)** * **North African Couscous Salad (page 222)** * **Persian Rice & Pistachio Salad (page 224)** * **Speltberry & Fruit Salad (page 229)** * **Tomato Flowers (page 236)** * **Mexican Shrimp & Spinach Salad (page 301)**

Hungarian Green Bean Soup

When the garden trellis is brimming with wildly tangled bean vines, or when the farmers' market has bushels of plump green beans that cannot be passed by, let these legumes move from their usual supporting role as side dish into the limelight—as the star ingredient in this delicate soup.

SERVES 6 TO 8
YIELDS 10 CUPS
PREPARATION TIME: 25 MINUTES
COOKING TIME: 30 MINUTES

PER 10-OUNCE SERVING: 141 CALORIES, 3.9 G PROTEIN, 5.7 G FAT, 18.1 G CARBO-HYDRATES, 2.7 G SATURATED FATTY ACIDS, 12 MG CHOLESTEROL, 186 MG SODIUM, 3.5 G TOTAL DIETARY FIBER

1 tablespoon canola or other vegetable oil
2 cups chopped onions
3 garlic cloves, minced or pressed
1 cup peeled and chopped carrots
1 cup chopped celery
½ teaspoon dried marjoram
1 bay leaf
1 tablespoon sweet Hungarian paprika
2 cups chopped potatoes
4½ cups water
½ cup dry white wine
1 tablespoon soy sauce
2½ cups stemmed and cut green beans
   (1-inch pieces)
2 ounces Neufchâtel or cream cheese
1 cup milk
1 tablespoon minced fresh dill (1 teaspoon dried)
salt and ground black pepper to taste

plain nonfat yogurt or sour cream (optional)

Warm the oil in a soup pot. Sauté the onions and garlic in the oil until the onions are translucent, about 7 minutes. Add the carrots and celery and cook for 5 minutes, stirring often. Add the marjoram, bay leaf, paprika, potatoes, and water. Cover, bring to a simmer, and cook for 5 minutes. Add the wine, soy sauce, and green beans and simmer on low heat for 10 to 15 minutes, until the vegetables are tender.

In a blender, combine 2 cups of the soup with the Neufchâtel or cream cheese and the milk and purée until smooth.

Return the puréed mixture to the pot. Stir in the dill and add salt and pepper to taste. Garnish each serving with a dollop of yogurt or sour cream.

DAILY SPECIAL

MENU IDEAS **Fresh Pear & Blue Cheese Salad (page 266)** ✳ **Wilted Spinach & Portabella Mushrooms (page 239)** ✳ **Marinated Mushrooms (page 347)** ✳ **Roasted Green Tomato & Feta Salad (page 283)** ✳ **Filo Croutons (page 342)**

Oaxacan Potato Soup

The interesting cuisine of Oaxaca (wä-hä'-ka), Mexico, is typically a contradictory combination of extremes, both mild and piquant. This creamy soup is a good example. The comforting combination of potatoes, peas, and carrots is given a surprising kick with the hot and tangy flavors of mustard, pickled jalapeños, and green olives. Use either plain green olives or those stuffed with pimientos. Choose a salad that complements the Mexican theme for a knockout combo plate.

SERVES 6 TO 8
YIELDS 10 CUPS
TOTAL TIME: 50 MINUTES

PER 10-OUNCE SERVING: 179 CALORIES, 4 G PROTEIN, 7.3 G FAT, 25.8 G CARBOHY-DRATES, 3.2 G SATURATED FATTY ACIDS, 13 MG CHOLESTEROL, 850 MG SODIUM, 4.3 G TOTAL DIETARY FIBER

2 cups finely chopped onions
2 tablespoons butter
5 cups peeled and chopped potatoes
4 cups water
1 teaspoon salt
2 teaspoons prepared yellow mustard
1 cup peeled and diced carrots (pea-sized cubes)
1 cup fresh or frozen green peas
½ cup chopped pitted green olives
¼ cup chopped pickled jalapeños or banana peppers
½ cup sour cream
¼ teaspoon ground black pepper

chopped scallions or red onions

In a soup pot on medium heat, sauté the onions in the butter for about 7 minutes, until soft but not browned. Add the potatoes, water, salt, and mustard. Cover and bring to a boil on high heat. Cook until the potatoes are just soft, about 10 minutes.

Remove the soup pot from the heat and coarsely mash the potatoes in the soup pot with a potato masher. Use slow, steady pressure to avoid splashing the hot cooking liquid. Return the soup pot to the heat, add the carrots, cover, and simmer for 5 minutes. Add the peas, olives, and pickled peppers and simmer for 5 to 10 minutes, just until the peas are tender.

In a small mixing bowl, combine the sour cream, black pepper, and a couple of ladlefuls of the soup broth. Pour the hot sour cream mixture back into the soup pot and stir well.

Serve garnished with chopped scallions or red onions.

MENU IDEAS **Tostada Salad (page 237)** ✳ **Kiwi, Orange & Baby Greens (page 273)** ✳ **Tomato Flowers (page 236)** ✳ **Golden Tomato Avocado Salad (page 268)** ✳ **Mexican Shrimp & Spinach Salad (page 301)**

Persian Yogurt Rice Soup

After some experimentation, we discovered that beating an egg into yogurt before adding it to a soup prevents curdling and produces a beautiful velvety texture.

This is a lovely, unusual soup with many interesting spices. Be prudent with your cayenne: if it's fresh and hot, even ⅛ teaspoon may be too much.

SERVES 4
YIELDS 4 TO 5 CUPS
PREPARATION TIME: 30 MINUTES
SIMMERING TIME: 25 MINUTES

PER 9.5-OUNCE SERVING: 145 CALORIES, 6.1 G PROTEIN, 5.4 G FAT, 18.3 G CARBO-HYDRATES, 1.1 G SATURATED FATTY ACIDS, 67 MG CHOLESTEROL, 441 MG SODIUM, 1.7 G TOTAL DIETARY FIBER

1 tablespoon olive oil
1 cup finely chopped onions
3 or 4 garlic cloves, minced or pressed
½ teaspoon salt
½ cup peeled and diced carrots
¼ teaspoon ground cardamom
½ teaspoon ground coriander
⅛ teaspoon cayenne, or to taste
¼ cup raw white basmati rice, rinsed
    and drained (see Note)
3 cups water or vegetable stock
4 cups stemmed chopped spinach,
    loosely packed
1 egg
⅔ cup plain nonfat yogurt
2 tablespoons chopped fresh cilantro
salt and ground black pepper to taste

Warm the oil in a nonreactive soup pot. Add the onions, garlic, and salt and sauté on medium heat for about 10 minutes, until the onions are translucent, stirring frequently. Add the carrots and sauté for about 5 minutes. Stir in the cardamom, coriander, and cayenne and sauté for another minute, stirring constantly.

Add the rice and the water or vegetable stock. Cover and bring to a boil; then reduce the heat and simmer until the rice is tender, about 25 minutes (see Note). When the rice is tender, add the spinach to the soup and stir well. In a bowl, thoroughly beat together the egg and yogurt and gradually whisk the mixture into the soup. Stir in the cilantro and gently reheat, being careful the soup doesn't boil. Add salt and pepper to taste.

Note If you prefer to use brown basmati rice, simmer it on very low heat in a pot with a tight-fitting lid for about 45 minutes, until the rice is tender.

MENU IDEAS **Cado Cado (page 212)** ✳ **Indonesian Tahu Goreng (page 218)** ✳ **Roasted Red Pepper & Cauliflower Salad (page 226)** ✳ **Solstice Salad (page 227)** ✳ **Syrian Beet Salad (page 291)** ✳ **Spinach with Cilantro Cashew Dressing (page 289)** ✳ **Scallion Pancakes (page 350)**

Potage Celeste

This lovely pale green purée was originally developed by Celeste Tischler, a cook at Moosewood in the 1970s. Over the years it has changed as it passed from one cook to another. Here, in one of its many incarnations, we add rice, a classic French touch, for texture and substance. However, if you prefer, you can savor the unadorned smoothness of this soup on its own without the rice.

SERVES 4 TO 6
YIELDS 8 CUPS
PREPARATION TIME: 20 MINUTES
COOKING TIME: 30 MINUTES

PER 11.5-OUNCE SERVING: 186 CALO-RIES, 4.3 G PROTEIN, 5.8 G FAT, 31 G CAR-BOHYDRATES, 2.6 G SATURATED FATTY ACIDS, 11 MG CHOLESTEROL, 922 MG SODIUM, 3.9 G TOTAL DIETARY FIBER

2 cups chopped leeks, white and tender green parts
1 tablespoon canola or other vegetable oil
3 cups diced celery (include some leaves, if possible)
2 teaspoons salt
1 teaspoon dried tarragon
1 medium carrot, peeled and cut into a few chunks
3 cups peeled and chopped potatoes
1 cup peeled and chopped apples
2 bay leaves
1 large peeled garlic clove
4 cups water
1 cup milk
2 tablespoons Neufchâtel or cream cheese
1 teaspoon freshly grated lemon peel
½ cup cooked white or brown rice
salt and ground black pepper to taste

In a soup pot, sauté the leeks in the oil until aromatic, about 5 minutes. Stir frequently to prevent scorching. Add the celery, salt, and tarragon and sauté for 5 more minutes. Add the carrots, potatoes, apples, bay leaves, garlic, and water. Bring the vegetables to a rapid boil; then lower the heat and simmer until the carrots and potatoes are tender, about 20 minutes.

With a slotted spoon or a pair of tongs, remove the chunks of carrot. Add the milk and the Neufchâtel or cream cheese to the soup pot. In batches in a blender, purée the soup (including the bay leaves and garlic clove) and strain each puréed batch through a sieve into a second pot. Stir in the grated lemon peel and the rice, season with salt and pepper to taste, and gently reheat until piping hot.

MENU IDEAS **Balkan Roasted Vegetable Salad (page 196)** * **Harvest Rice Salad (page 215)** * **Fresh Pear & Blue Cheese Salad (page 266)** * **French Pasta Salad (page 211)** * **Caesar Salad (page 201)** * **Focaccia (page 330)** * **Herbed Cheese Quick Bread (page 332)**

Roasted Chile & Potato Soup

The term "sparky" is part of our collective vocabulary at Moosewood, used to indicate to our waiters that a particular dish may be a bit too spicy for some of our customers. In this soup, roasted bell peppers and chiles provide a smoky accent and enough hotness to warrant the designation "sparky." Chiles vary greatly in intensity. If the "hot" disappoints you, add a little Tabasco sauce or cayenne.

A thick, creamy white soup like this goes best with a brightly colored salad.

SERVES 4
YIELDS 5 TO 6 CUPS
PREPARATION TIME: 50 MINUTES
SIMMERING TIME: 15 MINUTES

PER 11-OUNCE SERVING: 251 CALORIES, 4.7 G PROTEIN, 17.5 G FAT, 21.1 G CARBO-HYDRATES, 8.1 G SATURATED FATTY ACIDS, 31 MG CHOLESTEROL, 688 MG SODIUM, 2.5 G TOTAL DIETARY FIBER

1 red, green, or yellow bell pepper
1 fresh green chile
2 cups chopped onions
2 tablespoons canola or other vegetable oil
2 teaspoons ground cumin
1 teaspoon ground coriander
1 teaspoon salt
3 cups diced potatoes
3 cups water
2 tablespoons fresh lemon juice
2 tablespoons chopped fresh cilantro
½ cup Neufchâtel or cream cheese, at room temperature

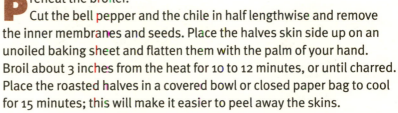

Preheat the broiler.
Cut the bell pepper and the chile in half lengthwise and remove the inner membranes and seeds. Place the halves skin side up on an unoiled baking sheet and flatten them with the palm of your hand. Broil about 3 inches from the heat for 10 to 12 minutes, or until charred. Place the roasted halves in a covered bowl or closed paper bag to cool for 15 minutes; this will make it easier to peel away the skins.

In a soup pot, sauté the onions in the oil on medium heat, stirring occasionally, for about 10 minutes. Meanwhile, peel and discard the roasted bell pepper and chile skins. Scrape and rinse away any blackened residue and dice the flesh.

When the onions are translucent, add the diced roasted peppers and chiles, the cumin, coriander, and salt and continue to cook for 2 or 3 minutes, stirring often. Stir in the potatoes and water, cover, and bring to a boil; then lower the heat and simmer for about 15 minutes, until the potatoes are tender.

Remove from the heat and stir in the lemon juice and cilantro. In a blender or food processor, combine half of the soup mixture with the Neufchâtel or cream cheese and purée until smooth. Stir the purée back into the soup.

Note To save time, prepare the onions, potatoes, lemon juice, and cilantro while the bell pepper and chile are roasting.

DAILY SPECIAL

MENU IDEAS **Tunisian Carrot Salad (page 293)** ✳ **Tomato Flowers (page 236)** ✳ **Kale Salad (page 272)** ✳ **Florida Salad with Ginger Dressing (page 263)**

Santa Fe Chowder

Sara Robbins' Santa Fe Chowder is one of our most popular soups, inspired by a recipe from Ithaca chef Jay Solomon's old Clinton Hall Cafe. Sara combined the southwestern flavors of cumin, chile, and coriander and mellowed them a bit with Cheddar and creamy Neufchâtel. But make no mistake about it—this is still a spicy little sopa. We like to serve it decorated with tortilla chips.

Cilantro is completely optional here. Sara's no fan so she leaves it out, but the soup is excellent both ways.

SERVES 6 TO 8
YIELDS 8½ CUPS
PREPARATION TIME: 15 MINUTES
COOKING TIME: 35 MINUTES

PER 9-OUNCE SERVING: 224 CALORIES, 6.1 G PROTEIN, 10.1 G FAT, 29.5 G CARBO-HYDRATES, 4.7 G SATURATED FATTY ACIDS, 19 MG CHOLESTEROL, 249 MG SODIUM, 3.5 G TOTAL DIETARY FIBER

2 tablespoons minced fresh green chile
1 cup chopped onions
1½ teaspoons ground cumin
1 teaspoon ground coriander
½ teaspoon dried oregano
½ teaspoon salt
2 tablespoons canola or other vegetable oil
½ cup peeled and diced carrots
2 cups peeled and diced sweet potatoes
2 cups diced potatoes
3 cups water
1 cup diced red and/or green bell peppers
1 cup chopped tomatoes
1 cup fresh or frozen corn kernels
1 cup diced zucchini or yellow squash
2 ounces Neufchâtel or cream cheese
½ cup grated sharp Cheddar cheese
1 cup milk

minced fresh cilantro (optional)
Jalapeño Cream (page 345) (optional)

In a soup pot, combine the chiles, onions, cumin, coriander, oregano, salt, and oil and sauté for about 10 minutes on medium heat, stirring occasionally, until the onions are translucent.

Add the carrots, sweet potatoes, potatoes, and water. Bring to a boil, then lower the heat, cover, and simmer for 10 minutes. Stir in the bell peppers, tomatoes, corn, and zucchini, cover, and cook on medium-high heat until the vegetables are tender, about 15 minutes. Ladle 3 cups of vegetables from the soup into a blender or food processor, add the Neufchâtel, Cheddar, and milk, and purée until smooth. Stir the purée back into the soup and gently reheat, if necessary.

Add minced cilantro and a dollop of Jalapeño Cream to each serving, if you wish.

MENU IDEAS Marinated Chickpeas or White Beans (page 346) ✳ **Tostada Salad (page 237)** ✳ **tossed green salad with either Moosewood House Dressing (page 324) or our Versatile Vinaigrette (page 325)** ✳ **Our Special Gluten-free Bread (page 333)** ✳ **Three-Bean Pasta Salad (page 232)**

Tomato Egg Drop Soup

Here's a simple and satisfying soup that we've been making at Moosewood for over twenty years. It will complement most Asian salads and is light enough to use as the introduction to the most complex of meals as well.

SERVES 4
YIELDS 6 CUPS
TOTAL TIME: 30 MINUTES

PER 12-OUNCE SERVING: 137 CALORIES, 3.9 G PROTEIN, 6.7 G FAT, 15.2 G CARBO-HYDRATES, 1.6 G SATURATED FATTY ACIDS, 66 MG CHOLESTEROL, 669 MG SODIUM, 2.1 G TOTAL DIETARY FIBER

1¼ cups thinly sliced onions
1 tablespoon canola or other vegetable oil
2 teaspoons grated fresh ginger root
4 cups Asian Soup Stock (page 17), Garlic Stock (page 19), or Basic Light Vegetable Stock (page 16)
2 tablespoons dry sherry or rice wine
2 tablespoons soy sauce
1 tablespoon rice vinegar
1 tomato, diced (about 1 cup)
1 tablespoon cornstarch
2 tablespoons cold water
1 teaspoon dark sesame oil
salt and ground black or white pepper to taste
1 large egg, lightly beaten

thinly sliced scallions
dark sesame oil

In a covered nonreactive soup pot, sauté the onions in the oil until softened, 7 or 8 minutes. Add the ginger root and sauté, stirring constantly, for another minute. Stir in the stock, sherry or rice wine, soy sauce, and vinegar. Bring to a boil; then lower the heat and simmer for 2 or 3 minutes. Stir in the tomatoes.

In a small bowl, dissolve the cornstarch in the cold water. Add the mixture to the simmering soup and stir for about 2 minutes, until the soup is slightly thickened. Add the sesame oil and salt and pepper to taste.

With the soup at a low simmer, drizzle the beaten egg into the center of the pot in a thin stream while stirring *gently* in a clockwise direction. The egg will form thin threads upon contact with the hot liquid. Be careful not to overstir.

Remove the pot from the heat and serve the soup at once, garnished with sliced scallions and a few drops of sesame oil.

DAILY SPECIAL

MENU IDEAS **Asian Beet & Tofu Salad (page 192)** ✳ **Balinese Rice Salad (page 195)** ✳ **Broiled Tofu & Sugar Snap Peas (page 199)** ✳ **Classic Sichuan Noodles (page 204)** ✳ **Indonesian Tahu Goreng (page 218)** ✳ **Spicy Cucumber Salad (page 288)**

Very Creamy Vegetable Chowder

This is a crowd-pleasing Moosewood standard. There is nothing more appealing and satisfying than sweet, fresh vegetables in a smooth, saucy Cheddar and cream cheese base: it's food that makes you feel safe and sound and well cared for.

This soup is sweet and mild and filled with enough vegetables for one meal, so serve it with a peppery little salad for contrast.

SERVES 8 TO 10
YIELDS 11 CUPS
TOTAL TIME: 50 MINUTES

PER 8.25-OUNCE SERVING: 174 CALORIES, 6.6 G PROTEIN, 10.2 G FAT, 15.2 G CARBOHYDRATES, 5.8 G SATURATED FATTY ACIDS, 28 MG CHOLESTEROL, 549 MG SODIUM, 2.5 G TOTAL DIETARY FIBER

2 cups chopped onions
1 tablespoon butter
1 tablespoon canola or other vegetable oil
2 celery stalks, diced
1 cup peeled and diced carrots
1½ cups diced potatoes
3 cups water or Basic Light Vegetable Stock (page 16)
½ teaspoon dried thyme
1 bay leaf
1½ teaspoons salt
½ teaspoon ground black pepper
½ cup green beans, cut into 1-inch pieces
½ cup diced red bell peppers
1 cup diced zucchini
½ cup fresh or frozen green peas
2 tablespoons chopped fresh parsley
2 cups milk
1 cup grated Cheddar cheese
2 ounces Neufchâtel or cream cheese

In a large soup pot on medium heat, sauté the onions in the butter and oil for 3 to 4 minutes. Stir in the celery, cover, and cook until just soft, stirring occasionally. Add the carrots, potatoes, water or stock, thyme, bay leaf, salt, and pepper and bring to a boil; then reduce the heat, cover, and simmer until the vegetables are just tender, about 5 minutes. With a strainer or slotted spoon, remove about 1½ cups of the cooked vegetables and set aside in a blender or food processor.

Add the green beans, bell peppers, and zucchini to the soup pot and cook until the green beans are tender, about 5 minutes. Stir in the peas and parsley, simmer for 2 more minutes, and then remove from the heat. Discard the bay leaf.

Purée the reserved vegetables with the milk and cheeses to make a smooth sauce. Stir the sauce into the soup and gently reheat. Serve hot.

Variation   Simplify the soup by omitting either the green beans or the peas. It's still teeming with vegetables.

DAILY SPECIAL

MENU IDEAS **Garlicky Tomato Salad (page 287)** ∗ **Five-Herb Salad (page 262)** ∗ **tossed green salad with Low-fat Tomato Basil Dressing (page 321)** ∗ **Anadama Bread (page 328)** ∗ **Popovers (page 334)**

Welsh Rarebit Soup

Thick, rich, and smooth, this soup has all the tangy, wonderful flavors of classic Welsh rarebit. Use any mustard you like and your favorite amber-colored beer —dark beer is too bitter and makes the color of the soup a bit murky.

Save the leftover potato-cooking water to use as stock. Stored in a sealed container in the refrigerator or freezer, it will keep for up to 3 weeks.

In a Daily Special meal, this full-flavored cheese soup should be coupled with an equally assertive salad. The bread should be dense and dark.

SERVES 6 TO 8
YIELDS 11 CUPS
PREPARATION TIME: 30 MINUTES
COOKING TIME: 20 MINUTES

PER 12-OUNCE SERVING: 399 CALORIES, 17.2 G PROTEIN, 26 G FAT, 22.8 G CARBO-HYDRATES, 15 G SATURATED FATTY ACIDS, 69 MG CHOLESTEROL, 737 MG SODIUM, 2.1 G TOTAL DIETARY FIBER

8 cups water
1 teaspoon salt
5 cups chopped potatoes
6 garlic cloves
2 tablespoons butter
2 tablespoons canola or other vegetable oil
2 cups chopped onions
1 cup diced celery
2 bay leaves
pinch of cayenne
12 ounces beer*
2 teaspoons Dijon mustard
2 teaspoons Worcestershire sauce (page 387)
1 cup 2% milk
1 pound sharp Cheddar cheese, grated

chopped tomatoes
Pumpernickel Croutons (page 349)
chopped fresh chives (optional)

* Use an ale or other light beer, not a dark beer such as stout or porter.

In a large pot, bring the water and salt to a boil. Add the potatoes and garlic, cover, and simmer until the potatoes are very tender, about 20 minutes.

While the potatoes cook, warm the butter and oil in a soup pot. Add the onions, celery, bay leaves, and cayenne and sauté on medium heat, stirring frequently, until the vegetables are very tender but not browned, about 10 minutes. Remove and discard the bay leaves. Stir in the beer, mustard, and Worcestershire sauce and simmer for a couple of minutes.

Drain the potatoes, reserving their cooking liquid. Add all of the potatoes, 2 cups of the potato-cooking liquid, the milk, and the grated cheese to the soup pot and stir well. In batches in a blender, purée the soup until velvety smooth. Return to the soup pot and gently reheat, if needed. If the soup is too thick, add enough potato-cooking liquid to reach the consistency you want.

Serve topped with chopped tomatoes and croutons and, if you wish, sprinkle with chives.

DAILY SPECIAL

MENU IDEAS **Wilted Spinach & Portabella Mushrooms (page 239)** * **Brussels Sprouts & Carrot Salad (page 251)** * **Fruit with Cranberry Currant Dressing (page 267)** * **Speltberry & Fruit Salad (page 229)** * **Solstice Salad (page 227)** * **Louisiana Black-eyed Pea Salad (page 221)**

CHILLED SOUPS

During the summer months, when the sun is blinding, sidewalks are scorched, and it's hot, steaming hot, the thought of *eating* something steaming hot is altogether unappealing. In fact, who wants to eat at all? In the dog days of summer, icy cold soups make their way into the Daily Special frequently, because **chilled soup is refreshing and can revive appetites dulled by hot weather.** ✻ The ingredients in cold soups are often chosen for their appetite-stimulating qualities. We think first of fresh, ripe summer fruits: consider juicy, sweet peaches or berries blended with citrus and creamy yogurt or buttermilk into a smooth, restorative nectar, or bits of luscious, colorful melons suspended in a cool potion. A tangy cold soup with crisp, raw vegetables invigorates as it extinguishes the fire. Pleasantly tart or even pickly flavors can revive a wilted hunger. Ginger, mint, fennel, and chiles offer little jolts of flavor in an icy liquid. ✻ Chilled soups are perfect do-ahead meals. As the soup cools in the refrigerator, you can sit back and chill out. While you're creeping through a sweltering traffic jam, you can anticipate the relief of a cool, delicious meal waiting at home. Chilled soups are often very light and low in fat—making them doubly appreciated when it's hot outside. ✻ Chilled soups go great with salads in a hot-weather Daily Special. After Fast & Fresh Tomato Soup, you'll be ready to tackle French Barley Salad. Let your guests sip Mango Soup in frosty glasses while you put the finishing touches on Curried Rice Salad or Thai Noodle Salad. Everyone feels restored and perfectly content after a cool soup and salad meal. ✻ While chilled soups are a lovely way to ease into a meal in sultry summer, they are also good at other times of year. The contrast between a cold soup and a hot rest of the meal can be quite pleasing. Many chilled soups, such as Fennel Vichyssoise or Gingered Carrot Soup, are elegant first courses for a dinner party. Cold soups go especially well with the spicy foods of the Caribbean, Mexico, and Southeast Asia. A soup like Chlodnik, a piquant mixture of crisp vegetables in buttermilk, can be a main dish, especially served as we suggest with hot buttered potatoes. Gingered Plum Soup, Peach Soup, and other fruity soups make wonderful desserts. ✽ Some chilled soups are smooth purées that can be sipped from a cup as easily as eaten with a spoon, making them a fine snack and even a nice breakfast. Strawberry Soup or Raspberry Soup and a muffin will give your day a delicious, uplifting start. ✽ Many of these blender concoctions can be made in minutes, a special boon in the summer kitchen. When you're *really* in a hurry for a chilled soup, add ice cubes to the mixture as you whirl it in the blender. Yogurt is a frequent ingredient; choose a cultured yogurt free of sugars and gelatin or other thickeners. Because chilling mutes flavors slightly, taste cold soups just before serving. You may want to add more herbs or a dash of salt, pepper, or lemon juice. ✽ When you're looking for a chilled soup recipe, don't limit yourself to the soups in this section. Many other hot soups in this book are also good served cold, and several in this section are excellent when hot. (Usually we make a suggestion on the recipe if we like a soup both ways.) Many puréed vegetable soups, tomato soups, potato soups, and cream-of-something soups are excellent chilled. Even a bean soup could be served cold with a dollop of yogurt, salsa, or chopped tomatoes. We think the rule should be: If you like it hot, you might like it cold. ✽

August Melon Soup

Quick, easy-to-make, fat-free, and nutritious, this pretty soup is cool and fresh tasting, a luscious celebration of melon and wonderful for a summer dinner party or brunch. It can be served as a refreshing counterpoint to something piquant and a bit hot: a Chinese, Thai, or Caribbean grain salad would be a good choice. Or offer it as an inviting starter or as a naturally sweet dessert. Serving the soup in chilled cups is a nice touch.

The flavors of perfectly ripe melons make all the difference in such a simple soup. Choosing the most flavorful cantaloupe can be tricky—almost a matter of luck: look for one that feels heavy for its size, has a slight give at the stem end, has a golden hue under the netting on the skin, and smells sweetly fragrant.

SERVES 4
YIELDS 8 CUPS
PREPARATION TIME: 25 MINUTES
CHILLING TIME: 30 MINUTES

PER 9.75-OUNCE SERVING: 101 CALORIES, 1.7 G PROTEIN, 0.4 G FAT, 25.3 G CARBOHYDRATES, 0 G SATURATED FATTY ACIDS, 0 MG CHOLESTEROL, 67 MG SODIUM, 1.6 G TOTAL DIETARY FIBER

1 large honeydew melon, peeled, seeded, and chopped (about 6 cups)
2 tablespoons fresh lemon juice
¾ cup orange juice
pinch of salt
1 cantaloupe, peeled, seeded, and cut into ½-inch cubes (3 to 4 cups)
1 tablespoon chopped fresh mint
½ teaspoon freshly grated nutmeg (optional)
¼ cup rum or Midori liqueur (optional)

In batches in a blender, purée the honeydew melon with the lemon juice, orange juice, and salt. Pour into a bowl and stir in the cantaloupe cubes and the mint. If you wish, add the nutmeg and/or rum or melon liqueur. Cover and refrigerate for 30 minutes.

Serve cold.

Variation Replace some of the cantaloupe cubes with bright red Sugar Baby or golden Yellow Doll watermelon cubes.

MENU IDEAS **Caribbean Rice Salad (page 202)** ✳ **Classic Sichuan Noodles (page 204)** ✳ **Thai Noodle Salad (page 233)** ✳ **Seafood & Chermoulla Couscous Salad (page 306)** ✳ **one of the Fresh Fruit Combinations (page 264)** ✳ **Spicy Pineapple Tofu Salad (page 230)**

Avocado Tomatillo Soup

Tomatillos are a great home garden crop because they are prolific and have few pest problems. On the other hand, if you have a good crop, after making some Mexican-style tomatillo sauce, you may wonder what you are going to do with them all.

This soup is divine. It is hearty yet elegant, with a velvety texture and unusual smoky flavor. The tang of tomatillos is beautifully balanced by the richness of avocado. A cup of this soup followed by a light Mexican or Caribbean main dish salad makes a luxurious Daily Special.

SERVES 4 TO 6
YIELDS ABOUT 6 CUPS
PREPARATION TIME: 30 MINUTES
CHILLING TIME: 30 MINUTES

PER 9-OUNCE SERVING: 153 CALORIES, 3 G PROTEIN, 11.4 G FAT, 13.9 G CARBOHYDRATES, 1.8 G SATURATED FATTY ACIDS, 0 MG CHOLESTEROL, 221 MG SODIUM, 5.8 G TOTAL DIETARY FIBER

1 to 2 fresh green chiles
1 quart fresh tomatillos (about 1½ pounds), husked and rinsed
2 ripe Hass avocados*
4 teaspoons fresh lime juice
2 scallions, chopped
2 tablespoons chopped fresh cilantro
3 cups cold water
½ teaspoon salt
⅛ teaspoon ground black pepper

A ripe avocado is somewhat fragrant and yields slightly to thumb pressure. When perfectly ripe, the soft flesh can be easily separated from the peel. Dark, discolored spots are a sign of bruising and/or overripeness.

Preheat the broiler. Place the chiles and the tomatillos (stem side down) on an unoiled, nonreactive, heatproof baking pan and broil near the heat source for about 10 minutes. Turn them over with tongs and broil for 5 minutes more. The tomatillos will intensify in color and may scorch slightly—when removed from the broiler, they should collapse or wilt.

Meanwhile, slice each avocado lengthwise around its center, gently twist the halves apart, and remove the pit. Scoop the avocado flesh into a large bowl. Sprinkle on the lime juice and toss to coat well.

Remove the baking pan from the broiler and set aside the chiles for the moment. Transfer the tomatillos and all of their juices to a separate bowl to cool. Return the chiles to the baking pan, broil for 5 minutes longer, and then set aside.

When cool, add the tomatillo juices to the avocados. Turn each tomatillo inside out through its stem scar and use a spoon to scrape the flesh into the bowl of avocados. Discard the skins. Remove and discard the stems and any tough seeds from the chiles (see Note). Add the stemmed chiles, scallions, cilantro, water, salt, and pepper to the bowl.

In a blender, purée everything in batches until very smooth and thick. If needed, stop the blender once or twice to scrape down the sides. Add up to 1 cup of water if you prefer the soup less thick.

Refrigerate at least 30 minutes before serving.

Note If desired, remove all of the chile seeds for a milder hot.

MENU IDEAS **Andean Quinoa & Corn Salad (page 189)** ✳ **Mexican Chickpea Salad (page 277)** ✳ **Mexican Shrimp & Spinach Salad (page 301)** ✳ **Tropical Fruit & Shrimp Salad (page 312)** ✳ **Southern Wheat-free Cornbread (page 335)**

Cherry Almond Soup

Cherries and almonds share a close botanical relationship and are used in many cuisines. This quick, vegan recipe develops their kinship into a highly enjoyable, delicately flavored soup. Using frozen cherries creates an instantly cold refresher for a hot-weather meal.

The menu suggestions we've made for Daily Special combos are wide-ranging, and this soup also pairs well with Japanese, Scandinavian, or Russian-style salads. It is excellent as dessert, too.

It's important to find a good-quality vegan almond milk. We like one made by Pacific Foods that uses almonds, malt, and brown rice sweetener and is available at natural food stores.

SERVES 4 TO 6
YIELDS 6 CUPS
TOTAL TIME: 10 MINUTES

PER 9-OUNCE SERVING: 132 CALORIES, 2.2 G PROTEIN, 1.5 G FAT, 29.4 G CARBOHYDRATES, 0.1 G SATURATED FATTY ACIDS, 0 MG CHOLESTEROL, 52 MG SODIUM, 1.1 G TOTAL DIETARY FIBER

6 cups pitted frozen sweet cherries (2 pounds)
3 cups almond milk
¼ cup pure maple syrup, or to taste
½ teaspoon freshly grated nutmeg
½ teaspoon pure almond extract

fresh mint sprigs (optional)

Slice 1 cup of the cherries into halves and set aside. Combine the rest of the cherries, the almond milk, maple syrup, nutmeg, and almond extract and purée in batches in a blender until smooth. Stir in the reserved cherries.

Serve at once or chill. Garnish with fresh mint, if you like.

MENU IDEAS **Arugula & Warm Mozzarella Salad (page 191)** * **Eastern European Kasha & Mushrooms (page 206)** * **Asparagus & Fennel Pasta Salad (page 193)** * **North African Couscous Salad (page 222)**

Cherry Berry Beet Soup

Here is a bright, lively, and unusual borscht with sweet cherries and berry juices. It requires no cooking if canned beets are used. Its deep burgundy color is even more magnificent when garnished with dill sprigs and paper-thin rounds of lemon or orange, or topped by a spoonful of sour cream or yogurt and a few berries.

SERVES 4 TO 6
YIELDS 8 CUPS
TOTAL TIME: 15 MINUTES
CHILLING TIME: AT LEAST 1 HOUR

PER 11.5-OUNCE SERVING: 136 CALO-RIES, 3.9 G PROTEIN, 0.5 G FAT, 32 G CAR-BOHYDRATES, 0.1 G SATURATED FATTY ACIDS, 0 MG CHOLESTEROL, 516 MG SODIUM, 4.1 G TOTAL DIETARY FIBER

4 cups peeled, diced, cooked beets*
2 cups reserved beet cooking liquid*
1 pound pitted frozen sweet cherries (about 2 cups)
⅓ cup fresh orange juice
3 tablespoons frozen or bottled cranberry-raspberry juice concentrate
¼ cup minced red onions
½ teaspoon salt
1 tablespoon chopped fresh dill

* Three 15-ounce cans of whole beets will yield 4 cups diced and provide 2 cups of beet liquid—exactly right for this recipe. Two bunches of fresh beets, about 1½ pounds without their green tops, will yield about 4 cups diced. Cook them in ample simmering water to cover until tender, about 35 minutes.

Place the diced beets in a large bowl and set aside. In a blender, combine the reserved beet-cooking liquid with the cherries, orange juice, cranberry-raspberry concentrate, red onions, and salt and purée until very smooth. Stir the purée into the bowl of beets and add the chopped dill. Chill the soup for at least an hour before serving.

MENU IDEAS **Eastern Euopean Kasha & Mushrooms (page 206)** ✻ **Harvest Rice Salad (page 215)** ✻ **Lobio (page 274)** ✻ **Balkan Roasted Vegetable Salad (page 196)** ✻ **Pumpernickel Croutons (page 349)**

Chlodnik

Sometimes as the late afternoon sun slants across the beach in Florida where he lives now, Wynelle's father, Milt Stein, feels nostalgic for the flavors from his Russian immigrant background. Nothing satisfies that longing better than this thoroughly refreshing soup. So don't be a *nudnik,* enjoy some Chlodnik.

P.S. We also love it with hot buttered potatoes and a thick slice of dark rye bread. Add one of the suggested salads and you have a complete and delectable meal.

SERVES 4 TO 6
YIELDS 6 CUPS
PREPARATION TIME: 20 MINUTES
CHILLING TIME: 20 MINUTES

PER 11-OUNCE SERVING: 163 CALORIES, 12 G PROTEIN, 4.7 G FAT, 17 G CARBOHYDRATES, 1.8 G SATURATED FATTY ACIDS, 130 MG CHOLESTEROL, 405 MG SODIUM, 1.1 G TOTAL DIETARY FIBER

1 cup fat-free sour cream
¼ cup chilled sauerkraut
¼ cup chilled sauerkraut juice
1 tablespoon sugar
2 tablespoons minced fresh chives or scallions
2 tablespoons minced fresh dill (2 teaspoons dried)
6 radishes, sliced paper thin (about ⅓ cup)
1 turnip, peeled and coarsely grated (about 1 cup)
1 medium cucumber, peeled, seeded, and diced (about 1½ cups)
1 quart buttermilk
salt and ground black pepper to taste

3 hard-boiled eggs, peeled and quartered

In a large, nonreactive bowl, whisk together the sour cream, sauerkraut, sauerkraut juice, sugar, chives, and dill. Stir in the radishes, turnip, cucumber, and buttermilk. Add salt and pepper to taste. Chill for at least 20 minutes.

Serve in chilled bowls and top with hard-boiled eggs.

DAILY SPECIAL

MENU IDEAS **Fruit with Cranberry Currant Dressing (page 267)** ✳ **Loblo (page 274)** ✳ **Wilted Spinach & Portabella Mushrooms (page 239)** ✳ **Brussels Sprouts & Carrot Salad (page 251)** ✳ **Composed Beet Salad (page 254)**

Creamy Orange Soup

Very quick to prepare, this delightful soup might remind you of a creamsicle. It is a refreshing beginning, ending, or accompaniment for a spicy Indian, Southeast Asian, or Mexican meal.

SERVES 4
YIELDS 4 CUPS
TOTAL TIME: 10 TO 15 MINUTES

PER 8-OUNCE SERVING: 161 CALORIES, 6 G PROTEIN, 6 G FAT, 22.2 G CARBOHY-DRATES, 2.3 G SATURATED FATTY ACIDS, 9 MG CHOLESTEROL, 72 MG SODIUM, 1.6 G TOTAL DIETARY FIBER

2 navel oranges, peeled and chopped (see Note)
1 cup orange juice
1 cup milk
1 cup plain nonfat yogurt
2 tablespoons fresh lemon juice
2 teaspoons coarsely chopped fresh mint
1 teaspoon honey
1 tablespoon canola or other vegetable oil
1 teaspoon cider vinegar

a few fresh mint leaves

In a blender, purée all of the ingredients until smooth. If the orange is not completely pulverized, strain the mixture through a sieve (see Note).

Garnish each serving with a fresh mint leaf.

Note If you section the oranges, it will not be necessary to strain the soup. To section an orange, slice off the ends, place it cut side down on the working surface, and slice down the curved sides with broad strokes all the way around the outside, positioning the knife just deep enough to remove the peel and the white pith. Holding the peeled orange over a bowl to catch the dripping juices, slip a paring knife between the membrane and one of the sides of an orange section. Cut in toward the center of the orange and then cut back out the other side with a V-like motion; the orange section will fall into the bowl. Repeat the process around the entire orange and then squeeze the juice from the membrane into the bowl.

MENU IDEAS **Indonesian Tahu Goreng (page 218)** ✳ **Curried Tofu Salad (page 256)** ✳ **Mexican Shrimp & Spinach Salad (page 301)** ✳ **Indian Green Beans & Red Peppers (page 270)** ✳ **Balinese Rice Salad (page 195).**

Creamy Yogurt Barley Soup

Barley is a widely grown, nutritious grain used in the cuisines of many countries — Ethiopia, Chile, the British Isles, and Greece, to name just a few. Barley's natural affinity for yogurt is most often celebrated in recipes from around the Mediterranean Sea. Our choice here is a creamy soup in the Greek tradition. It is good warm or chilled, and is enhanced by the textures of barley, toasted walnuts, and fresh mint.

SERVES 4
YIELDS ABOUT 5 CUPS
TOTAL TIME: 20 TO 25 MINUTES
  WITH COOKED BARLEY
COOKING TIME FOR BARLEY:
  45 TO 60 MINUTES

PER 10-OUNCE SERVING: 333 CALORIES, 10.8 G PROTEIN, 16.5 G FAT, 38.5 G CARBOHYDRATES, 1.9 G SATURATED FATTY ACIDS, 2 MG CHOLESTEROL, 131 MG SODIUM, 6.3 G TOTAL DIETARY FIBER

½ cup raw hulled barley (page 354)
2 cups water
2 tablespoons olive oil
2 cups chopped onions
2 large garlic cloves, minced or pressed
2 celery stalks, minced (about 1 cup)
dash of salt
1½ cups plain nonfat or low-fat yogurt
½ cup coarsely chopped walnuts, toasted*
½ cup water or vegetable stock
2 tablespoons chopped fresh mint (2 teaspoons dried)
salt and ground black pepper to taste

* Toast the walnuts in a single layer on an unoiled baking sheet at 350° for about 5 minutes, until fragrant and golden brown.

Rinse the barley and place it in a medium saucepan with 2 cups of water. Bring to a boil, cover, and simmer on low heat until the barley is tender, about 1 hour. Most of the water should be absorbed — if necessary, add more to prevent sticking. Set aside to cool.

While the barley cooks, warm the oil in a large skillet. Add the onions, garlic, and celery and sprinkle with salt. Cover and cook, stirring occasionally, until the onions are translucent and the celery is soft, 10 to 15 minutes.

In a blender, combine the cooked onion mixture with ½ cup of the yogurt and purée until smooth. Transfer to a serving bowl or nonreactive soup pot and set aside. Purée the walnuts with the remaining 1 cup of yogurt until smooth and stir into the onion mixture. Add the cooked barley, the water or stock, the mint, and salt and pepper to taste.

Serve warm, at room temperature, or chilled.

Note Barley continues to absorb liquid as it sits, so if the soup is not served right away it may be necessary to add more water or stock.

DAILY SPECIAL

MENU IDEAS **Balkan Roasted Vegetable Salad (page 196)** ✳ **Chef Salad à la Moosewood (page 203)** ✳ **Solstice Salad (page 227)** ✳ **East Indian Fruit Salad (page 258)** ✳ **Tunisian Carrot Salad (page 293)**

Cucumber Yogurt Soup

This classic Greek soup is the perfect balm for a beastly hot day; there's nothing more refreshing. For a Daily Special, serve it with wedges of warm pita bread and a hearty salad—not necessarily a Greek one: Think Russian, North African, Indian, Scandinavian, or New England.

SERVES 6
YIELDS 6 CUPS
TOTAL TIME: 25 MINUTES

PER 7-OUNCE SERVING: 95 CALORIES, 5 G PROTEIN, 3.7 G FAT, 11.4 G CARBOHYDRATES, 1.4 G SATURATED FATTY ACIDS, 5 MG CHOLESTEROL, 356 MG SODIUM, 0.9 G TOTAL DIETARY FIBER

5 cucumbers, peeled
2 cups plain low-fat yogurt
1 garlic clove, minced or pressed
¼ cup coarsely chopped fresh chives
1 tablespoon chopped fresh dill
2 tablespoon chopped fresh mint (2 teaspoons dried)
1 tablespoon canola or other vegetable oil
2 teaspoons fresh lemon juice
2 teaspoons honey
¾ teaspoon salt
¼ teaspoon ground black pepper

Coarsely chop 4 of the cucumbers to make about 5 cups. Combine them in a medium bowl with the yogurt, garlic, chives, dill, mint, oil, lemon juice, honey, salt, and pepper. Working in batches, purée in a blender until smooth. Seed and dice the remaining cucumber and add to the soup.

Serve at once or refrigerate and serve chilled.

MENU IDEAS **Roasted Red Pepper & Cauliflower Salad (page 226)** ✳ **Balkan Roasted Vegetable Salad (page 196)** ✳ **Eastern European Kasha & Mushrooms (page 206)** ✳ **Yemiser Salata (page 295)** ✳ **North African Roasted Cauliflower (page 279)** ✳ **North African Couscous Salad (page 222)**

Fast & Fresh Tomato Soup

In the fullness of late summer when tomatoes are at their ripest we're always looking for ways to get them on the menu. Combine them with fragrant fresh basil and an excellent-quality olive oil for an invigorating cold soup. It's great on a hot day: only the garlic is cooked and then it's a breeze to prepare the soup in a blender.

SERVES 4 TO 6
YIELDS 8 CUPS
PREPARATION TIME: 20 MINUTES
CHILLING TIME: 1 HOUR

PER 11.5-OUNCE SERVING: 139 CALORIES, 3.1 G PROTEIN, 8 G FAT, 17.1 G CARBOHYDRATES, 1.1 G SATURATED FATTY ACIDS, 0 MG CHOLESTEROL, 828 MG SODIUM, 2.5 G TOTAL DIETARY FIBER

8 tomatoes (about 3 pounds)
3 tablespoons extra-virgin olive oil
4 garlic cloves, minced or pressed
3 tablespoons chopped fresh basil
1 tablespoon red wine vinegar
1 teaspoon salt
3 cups chilled tomato juice

chopped fresh basil
cubed fresh mozzarella (optional)
minced red onions (optional)

Coarsely chop 6 of the tomatoes. Place them in a blender with 2 tablespoons of the olive oil and purée until smooth. In a small skillet, warm the remaining tablespoon of olive oil and briefly sauté the garlic on medium heat until just golden, taking care not to scorch it.

Add the sautéed garlic, the basil, vinegar, and salt to the blender and purée until thoroughly mixed. Pour the purée into a large nonreactive bowl or soup pot. Stir in the tomato juice. Chop the remaining tomatoes into bite-sized pieces and stir them into the soup. Chill for about an hour.

Serve each bowl of soup topped with basil. If you like, sprinkle in a few small cubes of fresh mozzarella and some minced red onions.

MENU IDEAS French Pasta Salad (page 211) ∗ **Greek Pasta Salad (page 214)** ∗ **French Barley Salad (page 210)** ∗ **Caesar Salad (page 201)** ∗ **Bean Purée with Seven Savories (page 197)** ∗ **Focaccia (page 330)** ∗ **Polenta Croutons (page 174)**

Fennel Vichyssoise

Classic Vichyssoise is a thick and creamy rich potato leek soup. Here is a reduced-fat version made even more elegant with the addition of the fresh, sweet anise flavor of aromatic fennel.

Serve it as the first course at a dinner party or accompany it with a flavorful salad for a relaxed midday meal.

SERVES 4 TO 6
YIELDS 9 CUPS
PREPARATION TIME: 20 MINUTES
COOKING TIME: 25 MINUTES
CHILLING TIME (OPTIONAL):
ABOUT 30 MINUTES

PER 12-OUNCE SERVING: 157 CALORIES, 5.9 G PROTEIN, 4 G FAT, 25.3 G CARBOHYDRATES, 1.6 G SATURATED FATTY ACIDS, 9 MG CHOLESTEROL, 581 MG SODIUM, 1.8 G TOTAL DIETARY FIBER

3 cups chopped potatoes
3 cups water or vegetable stock
1 tablespoon fresh lemon juice
1½ cups chopped leeks, white parts only
2 teaspoons olive oil
4 garlic cloves, minced or pressed
2¼ cups chopped fresh fennel bulbs (1 or 2 large bulbs, 2½ pounds whole plants with fronds)
½ cup peeled and chopped parsnips (optional)
1 tablespoon dry white wine or water
1 to 1½ teaspoons salt
⅛ teaspoon ground black pepper
½ teaspoon ground fennel seeds
½ cup minced fresh parsley
3 cups 2% milk

minced fresh chives

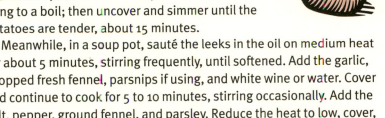

Combine the potatoes, water or stock, and lemon juice in a medium pot. Cover and bring to a boil; then uncover and simmer until the potatoes are tender, about 15 minutes.

Meanwhile, in a soup pot, sauté the leeks in the oil on medium heat for about 5 minutes, stirring frequently, until softened. Add the garlic, chopped fresh fennel, parsnips if using, and white wine or water. Cover and continue to cook for 5 to 10 minutes, stirring occasionally. Add the salt, pepper, ground fennel, and parsley. Reduce the heat to low, cover, and cook until the vegetables are very tender, about 5 minutes. Add the potatoes to the soup pot.

In batches in a blender or food processor, purée the soup with the milk until smooth and creamy. Serve hot, at room temperature, or chilled. Top each serving with a sprinkling of minced chives.

DAILY SPECIAL

MENU IDEAS **Fattoush (page 209)** ✳ **Bean & Radicchio Salad (page 249)** ✳ **Bulghur Grape Salad (page 200)** ✳ **Focaccia (page 330)** ✳ **Cherries Royale (page 265)**

Fragrant Lemongrass Fruit Soup

Lemongrass grows in tall, pale green, fibrous stalks. It's available in Asian groceries and some large supermarkets. If you want to take advantage of its lovely, lemony scent, trim away the dry outer leaves and use only the fresh bulb and shoots underneath.

The light "lemongrass cream," infused with the delicate, evanescent flavors of lemongrass and spices, makes a beautifully festive soup when sprinkled with chopped fruits, such as mango, peaches, or strawberries. Serve it for brunch, a snack, or a light dessert. When creating a Daily Special, try serving it *after* a savory salad.

SERVES 4 TO 6
YIELDS 3 CUPS LEMONGRASS CREAM (WITHOUT FRUIT)
PREPARATION TIME: 10 MINUTES
COOKING TIME: ABOUT 30 MINUTES
CHILLING TIME: 8 TO 24 HOURS

PER 8-OUNCE SERVING: 170 CALORIES, 5.6 G PROTEIN, 5.9 G FAT, 25.7 G CARBOHYDRATES, 3.5 G SATURATED FATTY ACIDS, 22 MG CHOLESTEROL, 78 MG SODIUM, 1.9 G TOTAL DIETARY FIBER

LEMONGRASS CREAM
1 quart whole milk
1 teaspoon cardamom seeds
2 cinnamon sticks
20 whole allspice berries
1 cup thinly sliced fresh lemongrass (2 or 3 stalks) (page 366)
¼ cup sugar

FRUIT
2 to 2½ cups finely diced fresh fruit, such as mangoes, pears, peaches, strawberries, and/or plums

Combine the milk, cardamom, cinnamon, and allspice in a nonreactive saucepan and slowly bring to a low simmer, uncovered, on low heat, stirring occasionally. Add the lemongrass and sugar and simmer for 3 minutes, stirring constantly. Cover and set aside to cool at room temperature for about 30 minutes; then refrigerate for at least 8 hours or up to 24 hours. Strain through a sieve.

When ready to serve, add the fruit and ladle the soup into small decorative bowls.

Variation Try with tropical fruits such as guava and persimmon. Kama brand is well known for its quality canned tropical fruits.

DAILY SPECIAL

MENU IDEAS **Vietnamese Shrimp & Noodle Salad (page 313)** ✳ **Thai Tossed Salad (page 292)** ✳ **Vietnamese Cellophane Noodle Salad (page 238)** ✳ **Indonesian Tahu Goreng (page 218)** ✳ **Curried Rice Salad (page 205)**

Gingered Carrot Soup

Simply prepared and brightly flavored, this smooth and spicy soup is good hot or cold. The choice of juice makes a striking difference in the overall flavor of the soup and which version tastes best is clearly a matter of individual preference. With orange juice, the soup is lighter tasting and especially good chilled. With apple juice, cider, or apple apricot juice, it has a more savory flavor.

Serve it as a first course or as an after-dinner dessert soup or beverage.

SERVES 4 TO 6
YIELDS 6 CUPS
PREPARATION TIME: 15 MINUTES
COOKING TIME: 35 MINUTES
CHILLING TIME (OPTIONAL):
   45 MINUTES

PER 9-OUNCE SERVING: 105 CALORIES, 1.9 G PROTEIN, 2 G FAT, 21 G CARBOHYDRATES, 0.5 G SATURATED FATTY ACIDS, 0 MG CHOLESTEROL, 131 MG SODIUM, 2.3 G TOTAL DIETARY FIBER

2 cups chopped onions
2 teaspoons canola or other vegetable oil
2 cups peeled and diced carrots
1 tablespoon grated fresh ginger root (see Note)
¼ teaspoon salt
¼ teaspoon ground black pepper
3 cups water
3 cups orange juice or unsweetened apple juice or cider*

sprinkling of freshly grated nutmeg

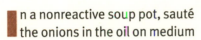

* If planning to serve this soup warm, bring the juice to room temperature before blending.

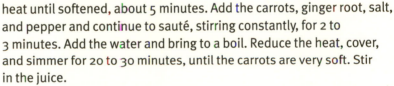

In a nonreactive soup pot, sauté the onions in the oil on medium heat until softened, about 5 minutes. Add the carrots, ginger root, salt, and pepper and continue to sauté, stirring constantly, for 2 to 3 minutes. Add the water and bring to a boil. Reduce the heat, cover, and simmer for 20 to 30 minutes, until the carrots are very soft. Stir in the juice.

In batches in a blender, purée the soup until smooth and velvety. Serve warm or chilled with a dash of fresh nutmeg.

Note You can vary the amount of grated ginger. We like the punch of a full tablespoon, but you may want to try less at first. If so, sauté 2 teaspoons of ginger with the onions. If, after all, you'd like more ginger, thoroughly blend in a little grated raw ginger to taste or add a few drops of fresh ginger juice.

Variation Replace the apple juice or cider with apple apricot juice.

MENU IDEAS **Tropical Fruit & Shrimp Salad (page 312)** ✳ **Harvest Rice Salad (page 215)** ✳ **Indonesian Tahu Goreng (page 218)** ✳ **Thai Rice & Mushroom Salad (page 234)** ✳ **French Pasta Salad (page 211)**

Gingered Plum Soup

This exquisite jewel-like soup features the magical combo of fresh ginger and deep purple plums. In late summer, serve it as a sweet and tart prelude to an outdoor meal. In winter, offer it as a beautiful dessert soup. Add to its elegance and deliciousness by topping with a dollop of yogurt and touch of chopped fresh mint leaves.

SERVES 6 TO 8
YIELDS ABOUT 8 CUPS
TOTAL TIME: 25 MINUTES
CHILLING TIME (OPTIONAL): 1 HOUR

PER 9-OUNCE SERVING: 123 CALORIES, 1.5 G PROTEIN, 1.1 G FAT, 29.6 G CARBO-HYDRATES, 0.1 G SATURATED FATTY ACIDS, 0 MG CHOLESTEROL, 22 MG SODIUM, 2.8 G TOTAL DIETARY FIBER

12 purple Santa Rosa plums, pitted and quartered (about 8 cups)
2 cups water
1 teaspoon grated fresh ginger root
1 tablespoon freshly grated orange peel
2 to 5 tablespoons sugar, to taste*
pinch of salt

nonfat plain or vanilla yogurt
chopped fresh mint leaves

The amount of sugar will depend upon the sweetness of the plums, which can vary quite a bit, and your personal preference.

In a medium nonreactive saucepan, bring the plums, water, ginger, orange peel, sugar, and salt to a simmer. Cover and cook for 10 minutes.

Remove from the heat and either strain the mixture through a food mill, whirl it in a food processor until very smooth, or purée in a blender and strain through a sieve or screened ladle.

Serve warm or chill for at least an hour and serve cold. Top with a spoonful of yogurt and sprinkle with fresh mint.

DAILY SPECIAL

MENU IDEAS **"Japanese" Tofu Salad (page 271) with Spicy Cucumber Salad (page 288)** ✳ **Classic Sichuan Noodles (page 204) with Marinated Broccoli & Carrots (page 275) and Baked Seasoned Tofu (page 336)**

Golden Gazpacho

This chilled summer soup is most unusual and complex in flavor and texture. It combines smooth, ripe mango, tender tomatoes, and crisp cucumber. The sweetness of the fruit is offset by the piquant zing of lime juice, scallions, and chiles.

Yellow and orange tomatoes are not widely available except in the midsummer to fall season, so take advantage of them when they appear. They are tasty and sweet, bursting with the full-bodied flavor of ripe tomatoes without the acidic bite.

Prepare the soup with cold ingredients, if possible, to save chilling time.

Serve with a Caribbean or tropical rice dish or simply with garlic bread.

SERVES 6
YIELDS 11 CUPS
PREPARATION TIME: 45 MINUTES
CHILLING TIME:
AT LEAST 30 MINUTES

PER 12-OUNCE SERVING: 149 CALORIES, 2.5 G PROTEIN, 5.5 G FAT, 25.7 G CARBO-HYDRATES, 0.7 G SATURATED FATTY ACIDS, 0 MG CHOLESTEROL, 170 MG SODIUM, 3.3 G TOTAL DIETARY FIBER

3 yellow or orange tomatoes
1 cup Basic Light Vegetable Stock (page 16)
½ fresh chile, finely minced, seeds and membrane removed
½ cup fresh lime juice with pulp
½ teaspoon turmeric
¼ teaspoon salt
2 cups orange juice
1 ripe mango, diced (about 1¾ cups)*
¼ ripe cantaloupe, diced (about 2 cups)
1 yellow bell pepper, diced (1 to 1½ cups)
1 cucumber, peeled, seeded, and diced (1½ cups)
2 tablespoons extra-virgin olive oil
½ cup finely sliced scallions
1 tablespoon minced fresh cilantro (optional)
salt and ground black pepper to taste

a few fresh cilantro leaves
sliced scallions
lime wedges

Mangoes have large pits and the pulp is slippery. A shallow slice from end to end along each of the two broad, flat sides works best. Score the mango flesh of each slice into cubes and pare them away from the skin. Peel the rest of the skin around the pit, then carefully cut the remaining tender pulp away from the pit and dice it.

Peel and chop one of the tomatoes. In a blender, purée the tomato, stock, chile, lime juice, turmeric, salt, orange juice, ¾ cup of the diced mango, and ¾ cup of the diced cantaloupe for about 30 seconds, or until smooth but not frothy. Pour the mixture into a nonreactive soup pot or soup tureen.

Dice the remaining tomatoes and stir them into the soup with the rest of the mango and cantaloupe. Add the bell peppers, cucumbers, olive oil, and scallions, and the cilantro, if using. Season with salt and black pepper to taste. Cover and chill for at least 30 minutes.

Serve the gazpacho cold and garnished with cilantro or scallions. For extra zing, serve with a wedge of lime.

MENU IDEAS Curried Rice Salad (page 205) * **North African Couscous Salad (page 222)** *
Thai Rice & Mushroom Salad (page 234) * **Curried Tofu Salad (page 256)**

Mango Soup

Is it a thick, creamy soup or a luscious beverage? The answer may depend on how thirsty you are and the time of day. Those of us who love our fruit puréed into a smoothie may be tempted to drink this delightful concoction from a glass.

All of the ingredients are blended and require no cooking. We recommend Mango Soup as a first course before a spicy curry or as a dessert soup with a crumbly cookie. Serve it in a handsome soup plate and savor it slowly with a spoon — or toss it in a Thermos bottle and take it on a picnic with a stack of paper cups!

SERVES 4 TO 6
YIELDS 5½ CUPS
TOTAL TIME: 25 MINUTES

PER 7-OUNCE SERVING: 116 CALORIES, 1.4 G PROTEIN, 0.4 G FAT, 26.6 G CARBO-HYDRATES, 0.1 G SATURATED FATTY ACIDS, 0 MG CHOLESTEROL, 11 MG SODIUM, 1.7 G TOTAL DIETARY FIBER

2 large or 3 medium ripe mangoes, peeled and cut into chunks (page 367)
⅓ cup fresh lime juice
1 cup fresh orange juice (about 4 oranges)
¼ cup regular or nonfat vanilla yogurt
1 cup unsweetened apple apricot juice*
2 tablespoons pure maple syrup
pinch of freshly grated nutmeg

If apple apricot juice is unavailable, use unsweetened apple juice instead.

In a blender, combine all of the ingredients and purée until smooth. Serve at once or chill.

MENU IDEAS **Balinese Rice Salad (page 195)** ✳ **Curried Rice Salad (page 205)** ✳ **Indonesian Tahu Goreng (page 218)** ✳ **Spicy Pineapple Tofu Salad (page 230)** ✳ **Tostada Salad (page 237)**

Minted Pea Soup

This is the quintessential "cool" soup. It is smooth, cold, *and* contains mint, which actually cools the mouth with its menthol. This is ancient, intuitive wisdom to those living in hot climates or accustomed to spicy hot foods, and mint abounds in the foods of Southeast Asia, the Middle East, India, the Mediterranean, and the southern United States.

We use peppermint here, but you can experiment with others, such as spearmint, apple mint, orange mint, and ginger mint, that may be available to you.

SERVES 4 TO 6
YIELDS 6 CUPS
PREPARATION TIME: 30 MINUTES
SIMMERING TIME: 30 MINUTES
CHILLING TIME: 1 HOUR

PER 9-OUNCE SERVING: 143 CALORIES, 5.3 G PROTEIN, 4.1 G FAT, 22.4 G CARBO-HYDRATES, 1.5 G SATURATED FATTY ACIDS, 5 MG CHOLESTEROL, 507 MG SODIUM, 5.2 G TOTAL DIETARY FIBER

1 tablespoon canola or other vegetable oil
1 cup chopped onions
1 cup peeled and chopped potatoes
1 medium carrot, peeled and cut lengthwise into quarters
1 cup peeled and chopped apples
2 garlic cloves, peeled and left whole
2 bay leaves
½ teaspoon dried tarragon
1 teaspoon salt
2½ cups water
1 parsley sprig (optional)
2 cups fresh or frozen green peas
2 green leaf lettuce leaves
1 cup milk
1 to 2 teaspoons fresh lemon juice, to taste
1 heaping tablespoon minced fresh peppermint (1 teaspoon dried)
salt and ground black pepper to taste

chopped fresh mint (optional)
Filo Croutons (page 342) or Herbed Croutons (page 30)

Heat the oil briefly in a soup pot. Add the onions and sauté on medium heat, stirring frequently, until the onions are translucent, about 7 minutes. Add the potatoes, carrots, apples, garlic, bay leaves, tarragon, salt, water, and the parsley, if using. Cover and bring to a boil; then reduce the heat and simmer for about 20 minutes.

When all of the vegetables are just tender, stir in the peas and lay the lettuce leaves on top of the vegetables (see Note). Cover and return to a simmer for another 10 minutes.

Remove the pot from the heat. Find and discard the bay leaves. For the most velvety texture and brilliant green color, remove the carrot pieces with a slotted spoon or tongs before puréeing the soup. In a blender in batches, purée the rest of the soup with the milk. Then stir in the lemon juice and fresh peppermint. Add salt and pepper to taste.

Refrigerate for about an hour and serve chilled. If desired, garnish each serving with fresh mint and/or croutons.

Note If using dried peppermint, add it with the peas and lettuce.

DAILY SPECIAL

MENU IDEAS Artichoke Heart & Bulghur Salat (page 190) ✳ **Thai Tossed Salad (page 292)** ✳ **Indian Green Beans & Red Peppers (page 270)** ✳ **Popovers (page 334)**

Peach Soup

What could be better than this luscious, versatile fruit soup accompanied by a cold, savory main dish salad for a summer brunch? Or try it as an elegant dessert accompanied by almond cookies or biscotti. For the best flavor, use fresh, very ripe peaches and add peach, orange, or almond liqueur for a special touch. For a delicious and artful effect, swirl blueberry or raspberry sauce into the soup just before serving.

On a sizzling day in August, freeze the peaches and then blend them with the other ingredients for a peaches 'n' cream "slushy." If you have gorgeous fresh peaches, you may not want to drink anything else.

SERVES 4 TO 6
YIELDS 4 CUPS
TOTAL TIME: 10 MINUTES

PER 5.75-OUNCE SERVING: 69 CALORIES, 0.8 G PROTEIN, 0.2 G FAT, 17.4 G CARBO-HYDRATES, 0 G SATURATED FATTY ACIDS, 0 MG CHOLESTEROL, 0 MG SODIUM, 1.8 G TOTAL DIETARY FIBER

2½ to 3 cups sliced fresh or thawed frozen peaches*
2 tablespoons sugar, more to taste
2 tablespoons plain nonfat yogurt or sour cream (optional)
1 cup water
1 cup orange juice
generous dash of cinnamon

* *4 medium fresh peeled peaches (about 1½ pounds) or one 16-ounce bag of frozen peaches.*

In a blender, purée all of the ingredients until smooth. Serve at once or refrigerate until ready to serve.

MENU IDEAS **Orzo & Pesto Stuffed Tomatoes (page 223)** * **Broccoli Pine Nut Pasta Salad (page 198)** * **Farfalle e Fagiole Salad (page 208)** * **North African Couscous Salad (page 222)** * **Mussel Salad (page 304)**

Raspberry Soup

This little concoction has a bright flavor and luscious color. Serve it as a refreshing first course, between courses, or as a dessert soup—or drink it as a smoothie for a snack. We also make this soup with fresh or frozen blackberries, which darkens the color and adds a deliciously musky undertone. Adjust the sweetness and orange rind to suit your taste.

SERVES 4
YIELDS 4½ CUPS
PREPARATION TIME: 15 MINUTES
CHILLING TIME (OPTIONAL):
  15 MINUTES

PER 8.5-OUNCE SERVING: 140 CALORIES, 4.7 G PROTEIN, 1.5 G FAT, 28.1 G CARBO-HYDRATES, 0.7 G SATURATED FATTY ACIDS, 4 MG CHOLESTEROL, 121 MG SODIUM, 4.3 G TOTAL DIETARY FIBER

1 pint fresh raspberries (12 ounces)*
2 cups buttermilk
½ teaspoon freshly grated orange peel
1 cup fresh orange juice
¼ teaspoon freshly grated nutmeg
¼ cup pure maple syrup

*Or use a 16-ounce package of unsweetened whole frozen raspberries not in syrup. If you can only find frozen raspberries in syrup, blend the soup without any maple syrup. If it's too sweet, add more buttermilk or a tablespoon of fresh lemon or lime juice. Otherwise, add maple syrup to taste.

Combine all of the ingredients in a blender and purée until smooth. Remove the irritating little raspberry seeds by straining through a sieve, stirring with a spoon to keep the liquid flowing through.
Serve at once or refrigerate until ready to serve.

MENU IDEAS **French Barley Salad (page 210)** ✳ **French Pasta Salad (page 211)** ✳ **Asparagus & Fennel Pasta Salad (page 193)** ✳ **Roasted Garlic Aioli Salad (page 225)** ✳ **Summer Millet Salad (page 290)** ✳ **for breakfast with Anadama Bread (page 328)**

Scandinavian Dried Fruit Soup

This lovely, light soup is naturally sweet. It can be served as a starter course or an elegant dessert.

SERVES 6
YIELDS ABOUT 6½ CUPS
PREPARATION TIME: 5 MINUTES
COOKING TIME: 15 TO 20 MINUTES
COOLING TIME: 2 HOURS

PER 8-OUNCE SERVING: 243 CALORIES, 2.2 G PROTEIN, 0.4 G FAT, 63.3 G CARBO-HYDRATES, 0 G SATURATED FATTY ACIDS, 0 MG CHOLESTEROL, 16 MG SODIUM, 3.9 G TOTAL DIETARY FIBER

2 cups dried fruit, such as peaches, apricots, cherries, pears, and raisins*
4 cups bottled peach juice**
1 whole cinnamon stick
1 tablespoon freshly grated orange peel
1 tablespoon freshly grated lemon peel
3 tablespoons cornstarch dissolved in 3 tablespoons water
2 cups water

vanilla yogurt, sweetened sour cream, or whipped cream

 * *Choose four or more different kinds for best flavor.*
** *We recommend After the Fall brand "Georgia Peach" juice blend. All of the "peach" juices with which we are familiar are actually juice blends.*

Chop the dried fruit into bite-sized pieces. Combine 2 cups of the peach juice, the cinnamon stick, orange peel, lemon peel, and the chopped fruit in a nonreactive saucepan. Bring to a boil, then reduce the heat and simmer for 10 to 15 minutes.

Stir the dissolved cornstarch into the simmering fruit. Cook gently, stirring frequently, until thickened and glossy. Remove from the heat. Stir in the remaining peach juice and the water. Refrigerate at least 2 hours until well chilled. If you like, purée the soup in batches in a blender for a smooth, creamy texture.

Serve topped with a dollop of vanilla yogurt, sour cream, or whipped cream.

MENU IDEAS **Eastern European Kasha & Mushrooms (page 206)** ✳ **Composed Beet Salad (page 254)** ✳ **Balkan Roasted Vegetable Salad (page 196)** ✳ **Lobio (page 274)** ✳ **Lentil, Rice & Fruit Salad (page 220)** ✳ **Mussel Salad (page 304)**

Strawberry Soup

It is hard to imagine anything better on a hot summer's day than this light, rosy, chilled strawberry soup. The simplicity of this recipe allows the flavor of the strawberries to step forward. It takes only minutes to prepare, requires very few ingredients, and can be made with either fresh or frozen berries. The amount of sugar required is a matter of personal preference and will also depend upon the sweetness of the berries.

SERVES 4
YIELDS 4 CUPS
TOTAL TIME: 10 MINUTES

PER 9.5-OUNCE SERVING: 182 CALORIES, 3 G PROTEIN, 1.2 G FAT, 34.7 G CARBOHY-DRATES, 0.4 G SATURATED FATTY ACIDS, 2 MG CHOLESTEROL, 62 MG SODIUM, 3.9 G TOTAL DIETARY FIBER

4 cups stemmed and quartered fresh or frozen strawberries*
¼ cup orange juice
¼ cup Cointreau or other orange-flavored liqueur**
1 cup buttermilk
¼ cup sugar, or to taste

* *2 pints of fresh strawberries (about 20 ounces before stemming) or a 16-ounce package of frozen strawberries will yield 4 cups prepared.*
** *We prefer this soup with the Cointreau, but you can replace it with ¼ cup of orange juice, if you wish.*

In a blender or food processor, combine the strawberries, orange juice, Cointreau, and buttermilk and pureé until smooth. Add sugar to taste.

Serve at once or refrigerate.

MENU IDEAS Artichoke Heart & Bulghur Salat (page 190) * **French Barley Salad (page 210)** * **Asparagus & Fennel Pasta Salad (page 193)** * **Summer Millet Salad (page 290)** * **Speltberry & Fruit Salad (page 229)**

SEAFOOD SOUPS

Fish and seafood are appreciated by people the world over and lend their versatility to the seasonings and aesthetics of many different cuisines. Here are recipes inspired by the cuisines of northern and southern Europe, New England, Louisiana, Southeast Asia, and the Caribbean. **Whether briny or delicate in taste and chewy or tender in texture, seafood makes soups delicious, substantial, and nourishing.** Seafood soups can have a sturdy home-spun character, or they can be quite luxurious, even extravagant. ✳ Seafood soups express essence of place—the different climates and geography, the different ways people have found to season food from the sea with the finest ingredients provided by the land. Ranging from comfortable, plain-spoken New England chowders to lusty, aromatic Portuguese Mussel Stew, from the tangy and sweet zing of Southeast Asian Tamarind Pineapple Fish Soup to the colorful and spice-rich Caribbean Shrimp & Vegetable Soup, each is a unique blend of seafood, plant foods, seasonings, and the romance associated with a certain place. ✳ In small portions, seafood soups can serve as the festive beginning of a lavish meal, but more often these are perfect main dish soups. A soup like Louisiana-style Catfish Gumbo, loaded with vegetables and big chunks of meaty catfish, is pretty much all you need for a zydeco party—maybe add a crisp slaw or some Kale Salad. Richly flavorful and fragrant, Hot & Sour Shrimp Soup can anchor a Southeast Asian feast, accompanied by Thai Tossed Salad and sweet, juicy Pineapple Passion. After a big bowl of beautiful Venetian Seafood Stew with its mussels, clams, shrimp, and savory Polenta Croutons, you'll feel quite serene as you finish the

wine and nibble a piece of fruit. ✳ Most of our fish and seafood recipes suggest several types of fish, and we recommend that you buy whatever is freshest at your market. Fresh fish is firm and resilient to the touch and has a pleasant marine fragrance. When it's available, try fish caught in or near your region, although fish from other regions that has been flash frozen immediately after being harvested (labeled "previously frozen" in the display case) sometimes stays fresher than never-frozen fish that has been kept on ice during transport and at the market. When a particular species is most abundant, the catches must be shipped immediately to market. The happy result: the freshest fish is often featured at the lowest price.
✳ Refrigerate these perishable foods immediately and cook them within 1 or 2 days of purchase. Fish bought fresh and carefully wrapped, and stored for a few days in your own freezer can survive the freezing process better than commercially packaged frozen fillets, which sometimes have freezer burn. Thaw frozen fish for 24 hours in the refrigerator or for 1 or 2 hours in a sealed plastic bag in a sink full of cool water. Before cooking thawed fish, pat it dry with a paper towel to absorb the moisture it has released. ✳ Generally, deep-sea fish are higher in fat than fish caught in rivers and lakes, but they also contain omega-3 polyunsaturated fatty acids, which may lower blood cholesterol and triglycerides. Including fish in your diet may help prevent heart disease, arteriosclerosis, arthritis, and psoriasis by reducing the buildup of blood clots and plaque in blood vessels. Eating fish and seafood can be a helpful, high-protein way to bridge moving from a meat-based diet toward a lighter diet with an emphasis on vegetables and grains. ✳

Bourride

Bourride is a savory fish soup from Provence, distinguished by the addition of aioli—a vibrant, garlic-infused mayonnaise that imparts a rich flavor, heady aroma, and velvety smoothness. It is an economical kin of bouillabaisse made without shellfish and saffron. With green beans, bell peppers, and potatoes, our version has more vegetables than a classic bourride, but it faithfully retains the traditional accompaniment of crisp French bread rounds spread with aioli. *C'est magnifique!*

SERVES 4
YIELDS 12 CUPS
TOTAL TIME: 50 MINUTES

PER 22-OUNCE SERVING: 609 CALORIES, 45.9 G PROTEIN, 28.2 G FAT, 45.1 G CARBOHYDRATES, 4.2 G SATURATED FATTY ACIDS, 180 MG CHOLESTEROL, 927 MG SODIUM, 4.7 G TOTAL DIETARY FIBER

2 pounds fish steaks or fillets (mahimahi, salmon, or sea bass)
2 eight-ounce bottles clam juice
2 cups water
3 cups sliced potatoes
2 bay leaves
½ teaspoon dried thyme (1 teaspoon fresh)
½ teaspoon ground fennel seeds
2 cups stemmed and halved green beans
1 fresh fennel bulb, sliced (about 1½ cups)
1 cup sliced red bell peppers

AIOLI
1 cup prepared mayonnaise
1 tablespoon cider vinegar
1 teaspoon Dijon mustard
2 tablespoons extra-virgin olive oil
3 large garlic cloves, minced or pressed

1 tablespoon fresh lemon juice
2 tablespoons chopped fresh parsley
salt and freshly ground black pepper to taste

toasted ½-inch-thick rounds of French or Italian bread

Rinse the fish, cut in half, and set aside in the refrigerator. Combine the clam juice, water, potatoes, bay leaves, thyme, and ground fennel in a large soup pot. Cover, bring to a boil, reduce the heat, and simmer for 5 minutes. Add the green beans, sliced fresh fennel, and bell peppers, and cook for about 10 minutes, until the vegetables are tender. Remove and discard the bay leaves.

Combine all of the aioli ingredients in a small bowl and set aside.

A few minutes before serving, sprinkle the fish with the lemon juice, parsley, salt, and pepper. Lower the fish into the simmering soup and poach for 4 minutes per ½-inch thickness of fish. The fish is cooked when the flesh has just turned opaque and flakes easily with a fork.

If necessary, remove the fish and slice into servings. Distribute the fish among heated bowls, ladle on the soup, and swirl a heaping tablespoon of the aioli into each bowl. Accompany with toasted bread slathered with aioli. Offer extra aioli at the table.

DAILY SPECIAL

MENU IDEAS **Fig & Endive Salad (page 261)** ✳ **Five-Herb Salad (page 262)** ✳ **Mediterranean Orange & Olive Salad (page 276)** ✳ **greens with Low-fat Tomato Basil Dressing (page 321)**

Caribbean Shrimp & Vegetable Soup

Prepare a feast for the senses. This rich, aromatic seafood soup features the dazzling colors of the Caribbean and exhilarating tropical flavors of lime, coconut, chile, and cilantro to tingle your palate as well. Serve with a multicolored salad and Anadama Bread (with its molasses-flavored hint of the tropics) for an exciting Daily Special.

Using peeled and deveined shrimp makes it a quick dish to assemble. Unpeeled shrimp take a little longer to prepare, but the shells can be used to enhance the flavor of the stock.

SERVES 6
YIELDS 8 CUPS
TOTAL TIME: 30 MINUTES

PER 12.5-OUNCE SERVING: 178 CALORIES, 12.2 G PROTEIN, 6.6 G FAT, 18.3 G CARBOHYDRATES, 2.8 G SATURATED FATTY ACIDS, 89 MG CHOLESTEROL, 248 MG SODIUM, 2.3 G TOTAL DIETARY FIBER

1 cup chopped onions
2 garlic cloves, minced or pressed
1 minced fresh green chile
2 teaspoons grated fresh ginger root
1 tablespoon canola or other vegetable oil
¼ teaspoon turmeric
½ teaspoon dried thyme
4 cups Basic Light Vegetable Stock (page 16)*
1 cup peeled and diced sweet potatoes
1 cup chopped tomatoes
1 cup diced red and/or yellow bell peppers
10 to 12 ounces fresh or frozen small peeled shrimp*
1 tablespoon chopped fresh cilantro
1 to 2 tablespoons fresh lime juice
1 cup reduced-fat or regular coconut milk (page 360)
salt and ground black pepper to taste

a few fresh cilantro sprigs

For added richness, use unshelled shrimp and include the shells when preparing the stock. About 1 pound of unshelled shrimp will equal the amount of shelled shrimp in the recipe.

Combine the onions, garlic, chile, ginger root, and oil in a soup pot, cover, and sauté on medium heat for about 5 minutes, until the onions begin to soften. Add the turmeric and thyme and continue to sauté for about 5 minutes, stirring occasionally, until the onions are translucent.

Add the stock and sweet potatoes, cover, and bring to a boil. Lower the heat, cover, and simmer for 3 to 4 minutes, until the potatoes are just tender. Add the tomatoes and bell peppers and cook for another 3 to 4 minutes. Add the shrimp, cilantro, lime juice, and coconut milk and simmer until the shrimp just turn pink. Season to taste with salt and pepper. Top with fresh cilantro sprigs.

DAILY SPECIAL

MENU IDEAS Avocado Melon Mélange (page 264) ✳ **Kale Salad (page 272)** ✳ **Florida Salad with Ginger Dressing (page 263)** ✳ **Solstice Salad (page 227)** ✳ **Anadama Bread (page 328)**

Catfish Gumbo

Catfish became popular at Moosewood when one of our most creative menu planners, Joan Adler, began designing Southern combo plates. In this recipe, we simmer tender chunks of catfish with the traditional Louisiana ingredients of okra, bell pepper, tomato, thyme, bay leaf, and a generous pinch of cayenne for a steamy gumbo certain to add a Cajun spark to any dull evening. Serve it as a first course or main course with a wedge of lemon and some golden brown garlic bread, if you like.

SERVES 6
YIELDS 7 CUPS
PREPARATION TIME: 30 MINUTES
COOKING TIME: 30 MINUTES

PER 10-OUNCE SERVING: 180 CALORIES, 8 G PROTEIN, 8.4 G FAT, 19.4 G CARBOHYDRATES, 2.1 G SATURATED FATTY ACIDS, 19 MG CHOLESTEROL, 229 MG SODIUM, 2.7 G TOTAL DIETARY FIBER

8-ounce catfish fillet

3 tablespoons canola or other vegetable oil
1 cup chopped onions
2 garlic cloves, minced or pressed
2 tablespoons unbleached white flour
3 cups water or Basic Light Vegetable Stock (page 16)
1 cup peeled and diced carrots
1 cup chopped potatoes
1 celery stalk, finely chopped
1 cup chopped fresh or frozen okra
½ cup chopped green or red bell peppers
1½ cups undrained canned tomatoes, chopped (14-ounce can)
½ teaspoon dried thyme
½ teaspoon dried oregano
2 bay leaves
pinch of cayenne
1 tablespoon fresh lemon juice
salt and ground black pepper to taste

Rinse the catfish, cut it into bite-sized chunks, and set it aside in the refrigerator.

Combine the oil, onions, and garlic in a soup pot on medium heat and sauté for about 10 minutes, until the onions are translucent. Reduce the heat to low, whisk in the flour, and cook for 2 to 3 minutes, stirring constantly to prevent sticking.

Gradually stir in the water or stock and cook on medium heat, stirring occasionally, until thickened. Add the carrots, potatoes, and celery, cover, and cook for about 5 minutes. Add the okra, bell peppers, tomatoes, thyme, oregano, bay leaves, and cayenne and simmer until the carrots and potatoes are tender, about 5 minutes. Add the chunks of catfish and the lemon juice and simmer for another 5 minutes. Add salt and black pepper to taste. Remove and discard the bay leaves before serving.

DAILY SPECIAL

MENU IDEAS Southern Red Rice & Pecan Salad (page 228) ✳ **Alabama Hot Slaw (page 245)** ✳ **Honey Mustard Green Beans Vinaigrette (page 269)** ✳ **Featherlight Blue Mountain Biscuits (page 327)**

Classic Clam Chowder

This is the kind of soup often referred to as honest: simple, likeable, and one that may taste even a little better the next day. It's a good choice for large gatherings.

SERVES 6
YIELDS 9 CUPS
TOTAL TIME: 50 MINUTES

PER 12-OUNCE SERVING: 349 CALORIES, 20 G PROTEIN, 16.1 G FAT, 31.6 G CARBOHYDRATES, 8.5 G SATURATED FATTY ACIDS, 77 MG CHOLESTEROL, 615 MG SODIUM, 2.7 G TOTAL DIETARY FIBER

5 cups water
1 teaspoon salt
4 cups cubed potatoes (½-inch cubes)
5 tablespoons butter
1 tablespoon canola or other vegetable oil
2 cups diced onions
1 cup diced celery
1 tablespoon dry white wine (optional)
1 teaspoon dried dill (1 tablespoon fresh)
2 cups bottled clam juice
2 cups whole milk
3 tablespoons unbleached white flour
**1½ cups undrained canned chopped clams
   (two 6-ounce cans)**
salt and ground black pepper to taste

chopped fresh parsley
a few lemon wedges

In a soup pot, combine the water and salt, cover, and bring it to a boil. Add the potatoes, cover, and cook for 7 to 10 minutes, until still firm and just tender.

Meanwhile, in another saucepan, combine 1 tablespoon of the butter with the vegetable oil and heat on medium-high heat until the butter melts. Add the onions and sauté for 3 to 4 minutes, until they begin to soften. Add the celery, white wine, if using, and dill, and cook, stirring occasionally, until the vegetables are soft, about 5 minutes.

Drain the cooked potatoes, transfer them to a large bowl, and gently toss with 1 tablespoon of the butter. Add the sautéed onions and celery, cover the bowl, and set aside.

In a small saucepan, warm the clam juice and milk on medium heat. Meanwhile, melt the remaining 3 tablespoons of butter on low heat in the soup pot. Stir in the flour and cook for 3 minutes to make a roux, whisking constantly to avoid scorching. Gradually add the hot clam juice mixture; whisk for several minutes until thickened.

Stir in the chopped clams and return to a simmer. Add the bowl of reserved vegetables and season to taste with salt and pepper. Garnish with parsley and serve with lemon wedges.

MENU IDEAS Butternut Squash with Spicy Cranberry Sauce (page 252) ✳ **Honey Mustard Green Beans Vinaigrette (page 269)** ✳ **Popovers (page 334)** ✳ **Anadama Bread (page 328)**

Hot & Sour Shrimp Soup

This highly fragrant, delicate soup is our simplified version of a traditional favorite. As Thai cooking becomes more popular in this country, fresh lemongrass and Thai basil have become easier to find in supermarkets. Fresh lemongrass keeps well for a few weeks, wrapped in plastic and refrigerated. Thai basil has a more anise-like flavor than its Italian relative. If you have a garden, this is worth growing.

Shelling shrimp is well worth the effort for the authentic fresh flavor the shrimp shells add to this lively soup. However, if only shelled uncooked shrimp are available, use 7 cups of Mock Chicken Stock (page 20) in place of the water called for in the recipe.

SERVES 4 TO 6
YIELDS ABOUT 9 CUPS
PREPARATION TIME: 20 MINUTES
COOKING TIME: 25 MINUTES

PER 12-OUNCE SERVING: 128 CALORIES, 13.6 G PROTEIN, 3.4 G FAT, 11.8 G CARBO-HYDRATES, 0.8 G SATURATED FATTY ACIDS, 108 MG CHOLESTEROL, 587 MG SODIUM, 2.2 G TOTAL DIETARY FIBER

1 pound shrimp, peeled and shells reserved (see headnote)

STOCK
1 tablespoon canola or other vegetable oil
½ cup chopped onions
7 cups water
6 quarter-sized slices of fresh ginger root
½ teaspoon turmeric
2 whole garlic cloves, peeled
2 fresh lemongrass stalks (page 366)

1½ cups peeled and julienned carrots
1 minced fresh chile, seeds removed for a milder "hot"
1 cup thinly sliced red bell peppers
2 to 3 tablespoons fish sauce (page 363)
1 can drained straw mushrooms (page 370)
3 to 5 tablespoons fresh lime juice
2 teaspoons sugar
3 tablespoons chopped fresh Thai basil or basil

chopped scallions (optional)

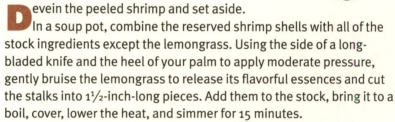

Devein the peeled shrimp and set aside.
In a soup pot, combine the reserved shrimp shells with all of the stock ingredients except the lemongrass. Using the side of a long-bladed knife and the heel of your palm to apply moderate pressure, gently bruise the lemongrass to release its flavorful essences and cut the stalks into 1½-inch-long pieces. Add them to the stock, bring it to a boil, cover, lower the heat, and simmer for 15 minutes.

Strain the stock, discarding the solids, and return the stock to the soup pot. Add the carrots, chile, and peppers and simmer for 10 minutes. Add the fish sauce, straw mushrooms, lime juice, sugar, and shrimp and cook briefly, until the shrimp have turned pink, 3 to 5 minutes depending upon the size of the shrimp. Stir in the basil and remove from the heat.

Serve at once, topping each serving with scallions, if desired.

Variation Cook some plain, wide rice noodles in a separate pot, drain them, and ladle the soup over them in individual serving bowls. Pass extra chopped chiles and basil, fish sauce, and fresh lime juice at the table so everyone can adjust the seasonings to taste.

DAILY SPECIAL

MENU IDEAS **Thai Tossed Salad (page 292)** ✴ **Bean Sprout Salad (page 250)** ✴ **Scallion Pancakes (page 350)** ✴ **Pineapple Passion (page 265)**

Portuguese Mussel Stew

This recipe was inspired by the childhood experiences of Moosewood cook Penny Goldin. Penny grew up in Fall River, Massachusetts, with many friends and neighbors of Portuguese descent who apparently know their seafood.

The crusty bread suggested as an accompaniment soaks up the flavors of this rich broth so well that we recommend incorporating it as an additional ingredient. Try ladling the stew directly over a slice of toasted bread or dunk pieces into your steaming bowl.

SERVES 6 TO 8
YIELDS 11 CUPS
TOTAL TIME: 50 MINUTES

PER 10-OUNCE SERVING: 156 CALORIES, 6.2 G PROTEIN, 8.4 G FAT, 13.6 G CARBO-HYDRATES, 1.2 G SATURATED FATTY ACIDS, 11 MG CHOLESTEROL, 229 MG SODIUM, 2 G TOTAL DIETARY FIBER

¼ cup olive oil
4 bay leaves
2 cups finely chopped onions
¾ cup diced celery
1 tablespoon minced or pressed garlic
1 cup diced red and/or green bell peppers
½ cup dry sherry
¼ teaspoon ground black pepper
4 cups chopped tomatoes
2 cups bottled or canned clam juice*
3 tablespoons fresh lemon juice
1 cup water
¼ teaspoon crumbled saffron threads
2 pounds fresh mussels, rinsed and cleaned**
2 tablespoons chopped fresh parsley
salt and ground black pepper to taste

lemon wedges
crusty bread, such as a French baguette

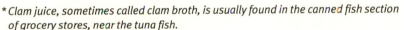

Clam juice, sometimes called clam broth, is usually found in the canned fish section of grocery stores, near the tuna fish.
**Most supermarket seafood sections carry prepackaged 2-pound bags of cultivated mussels that are cleaner and easier to sort than wild mussels. Discard any that are open or broken and rinse the rest with cold water. Place the mussels in a bowl, cover with cold water, and keep in the refrigerator until just before serving. Drain before adding them to the stew.*

In a large soup pot on medium-low heat, warm the oil. Increase the heat and sauté the bay leaves and onions, stirring frequently to prevent sticking, for 4 or 5 minutes. Add the celery and garlic, reduce the heat, cover, and cook until tender, about 10 minutes.

Add the bell peppers, sherry, and black pepper. Cover and simmer for about 10 minutes. Stir in the tomatoes, clam juice, lemon juice, water, and saffron and bring to a boil. As soon as the stew boils, add the mussels, cover the pot, and steam the mussels until their shells open, 3 to 5 minutes. Add the parsley and salt and pepper to taste. Remove and discard the bay leaves and any unopened mussels.

Serve immediately, with lemon wedges and bread.

DAILY SPECIAL

MENU IDEAS **Mediterranean Orange & Olive Salad (page 276)** ✳ **Kiwi, Orange & Baby Greens (page 273)** ✳ **Wilted Spinach & Portabella Mushrooms (page 239)** ✳ **Celeriac Remoulade (page 253)** ✳ **Kale Salad (page 272)**

San Juan Shrimp & Rice Soup

Inspired by a shrimp and rice entrée served at a lovely restaurant in Woodstock, New York, Moosewood cook Neil Minnis transformed the dish into a soup with the proper measure of culinary ingenuity. We hope you'll agree with us — it's a knock-out soup. For a fantastic combo plate, choose a Caribbean-style salad with fried *plátanos* (plantains) on the side.

SERVES 6 TO 8
YIELDS 11 CUPS
TOTAL TIME: 50 MINUTES

PER 11.5-OUNCE SERVING: 184 CALORIES, 14.4 G PROTEIN, 6.1 G FAT, 19.6 G CARBOHYDRATES, 0.9 G SATURATED FATTY ACIDS, 97 MG CHOLESTEROL, 1002 MG SODIUM, 4.6 G TOTAL DIETARY FIBER

2 teaspoons annatto seeds (page 352)
2 tablespoons canola or other vegetable oil
2 cups diced onions
2 garlic cloves, minced or pressed
⅓ cup raw white rice, such as basmati
7 cups water
1 pound shrimp, peeled and deveined* (see Note)
5 or 6 artichoke hearts, cut into quarters (14½-ounce can)
2 cups diced tomatoes
¼ cup chopped Spanish olives
2 tablespoons fresh lemon juice
2 teaspoons salt
¼ teaspoon ground black pepper
½ cup fresh or frozen green peas
¼ cup chopped fresh cilantro

a few fresh cilantro sprigs
chopped Spanish olives (optional)

* *1 pound of firm fish fillets, cut into bite-sized pieces, can be substituted for shrimp. Swordfish, mahimahi, or halibut are all good choices.*

In a very small saucepan or skillet, combine the annatto seeds and oil. Cook on medium-low heat, stirring frequently to prevent scorching, until the oil becomes bright reddish orange in color. Remove from the heat, strain the oil through a small sieve, and discard the seeds.

In a large, nonreactive soup pot, sauté the onions and garlic in the annatto oil on medium heat until soft. Add the rice and water. Cover and bring to a boil; then reduce the heat and simmer for 10 minutes. Stir in the shrimp, artichoke hearts, tomatoes, olives, lemon juice, salt, and pepper and simmer until the shrimp has just turned pink, about 5 minutes. Add the peas and cilantro and remove from the heat. Let sit for a couple of minutes.

Serve garnished with cilantro sprigs and, if you like, olives.

Note If you buy unshelled shrimp, you can make a tasty stock to replace the water in the recipe. Combine 1 cup of chopped onions, 4 whole peeled garlic cloves, ½ cup of chopped celery, the shells from the shrimp, and 8 cups of water in a soup pot. Cover and bring to a boil; then reduce the heat and simmer, covered, for about 15 minutes. Strain the stock and discard the solids.

DAILY SPECIAL

MENU IDEAS Spicy Pineapple Tofu Salad (page 230) ✳ **Kale Salad (page 272)** ✳ **Apricot Berry Sweet Talk (page 264)** ✳ **Melon & Mint (page 265)** ✳ **Popovers (page 334)**

Scandinavian Salmon Soup

Scandinavian Salmon Soup is a beautiful, elegant, satisfying creation, worthy of a place in Norse legends. Maybe Leif Eriksson would have had second thoughts about leaving Iceland if there'd been a bowl of this waiting for him at home! It's nice with sourdough bread and a glass of Chardonnay.

Note that the recipe calls for salmon fillet, not salmon steak, which, though very delicious, is quite bony. Salmon fillets are virtually boneless and work wonderfully in this soup.

SERVES 4 TO 6
YIELDS 8 CUPS
TOTAL TIME: 1 HOUR

PER 11-OUNCE SERVING: 290 CALORIES, 20.2 G PROTEIN, 12 G FAT, 22.3 G CARBO-HYDRATES, 3.3 G SATURATED FATTY ACIDS, 63 MG CHOLESTEROL, 509 MG SODIUM, 2.4 G TOTAL DIETARY FIBER

1-pound salmon fillet

COURT BOUILLON
4 cups water
½ cup dry white wine
1 bay leaf
1 small celery stalk
3 to 4 leek leaves (the green parts)
6 to 10 peppercorns
4 fresh parsley sprigs

2 cups chopped leeks, white and tender green parts
½ cup chopped celery
1 tablespoon canola or other vegetable oil
3 cups diced potatoes (½-inch cubes)
1 tablespoon capers (page 357)
1 to 2 tablespoons prepared white horseradish
1 teaspoon salt
½ cup sour cream
freshly ground black pepper to taste

Rinse and dry the salmon and set it aside. In a soup pot, combine all of the court bouillon ingredients, cover, and bring to a boil. Reduce the heat, add the salmon, cover, and simmer until the salmon is firm and flaky, about 10 minutes. Remove the salmon with a slotted spoon or Chinese strainer. When cool enough to handle, peel the skin from the salmon if necessary and, using the side of a fork, cut the fillet into bite-sized pieces and set aside. Strain the poaching liquid and return it to the soup pot.

In a saucepan, sauté the leeks and celery in the oil for about 10 minutes, until soft; then transfer them to the soup pot. Stir in the potatoes, capers, horseradish, and salt and bring to a boil. Reduce the heat, cover, and simmer for 10 to 15 minutes, until the potatoes are tender. Remove from the heat.

In a blender or food processor, combine half of the cooked vegetable mixture with the sour cream and purée until smooth. Stir the purée back into the soup and add the flaked salmon. Gently reheat.

Just before serving, add freshly ground black pepper to taste.

DAILY SPECIAL

MENU IDEAS **Caesar Salad (page 201)** ✳ **tossed salad with Marinated Mushrooms (page 347) and Zesty Feta Garlic Dressing (page 326)** ✳ **Honey Mustard Green Beans Vinaigrette (page 269)** ✳ **Brussels Sprouts & Carrot Salad (page 251)**

Sopa de Camarones

Treat yourself to the wonderful tropical tastes of fresh avocados and shrimp with this simple and elegant soup. Serve it chilled or hot, in colorful, wide-rimmed, shallow soup bowls and garnish it with a delicate sprinkling of fresh cilantro leaves and thin slivers of lemon.

SERVES 4 TO 6
YIELDS 6 CUPS
TOTAL TIME: 20 MINUTES
CHILLING TIME (OPTIONAL):
  ABOUT 1 HOUR

PER 8.5-OUNCE SERVING: 197 CALORIES, 15.9 G PROTEIN, 11.8 G FAT, 9.3 G CARBO-HYDRATES, 1.9 G SATURATED FATTY ACIDS, 130 MG CHOLESTEROL, 558 MG SODIUM, 4.9 G TOTAL DIETARY FIBER

2 cups water
1 pound medium shrimp, peeled and deveined
2 ripe Hass avocados, pitted and peeled*
2 tomatoes, chopped
1 to 2 fresh chiles, minced, seeds removed for a milder "hot"
⅓ cup fresh lemon juice
¼ cup chopped fresh cilantro
1 teaspoon salt

thinly sliced fresh lemon rounds
fresh cilantro leaves (optional)

A ripe avocado is somewhat fragrant and yields slightly to thumb pressure. To pit and peel, slice each avocado lengthwise around its center, gently twist the halves apart, and remove the pit. Use a spoon to scoop the avocado flesh away from the skin and into the blender.

In a covered saucepan, bring the water to a boil. Carefully ease in the shrimp and cook for about 5 minutes, until just pink. Take care not to overcook it. Drain well, reserving the cooking liquid.

In a blender or food processor, combine the avocados, tomatoes, chile(s), lemon juice, cilantro, salt, and reserved shrimp broth and purée until smooth. Transfer the soup to a nonreactive soup pot and stir in the cooked shrimp.

Gently reheat to serve hot. Or refrigerate for at least an hour and serve cold. Float a very thin slice of fresh lemon on each serving and, if you wish, top with a few cilantro leaves.

MENU IDEAS Louisiana Black-eyed Pea Salad (page 221) ✳ **Andean Quinoa & Corn Salad (page 189)** ✳ **Caribbean Rice Salad (page 202)** ✳ **Summer Fruit Fest (page 265)** ✳ **Southern Wheat-free Cornbread (page 335)**

Tamarind Pineapple Fish Soup

Hot and sweet and sour, this easy-to-make soup will make your kitchen smell oh-so-good. Use red or yellow bell peppers and chiles for the best broth color. Hot or mild fresh chiles are both good. Our first choice is Thai peppers or long red peppers, but serranos and jalapeños are fine. If fresh chiles are unavailable, use ½ to 1 teaspoon of red pepper flakes or 1 to 2 tablespoons of Chinese chili paste.

If you prefer a vegetarian version, replace the fish with cubed or julienned seasoned tofu or regular firm tofu. To serve Vietnamese style, ladle the soup over rice noodles, shredded lettuce, and bean sprouts or cucumbers and garnish with sprinklings of cilantro, mint, and scallions.

SERVES 4 TO 6
YIELDS 7 CUPS WITHOUT FISH,
ABOUT 9 CUPS WITH FISH
TOTAL TIME: ABOUT 1 HOUR

PER 12-OUNCE SERVING: 188 CALORIES, 16.6 G PROTEIN, 5.5 G FAT, 19 G CARBO-HYDRATES, 1.3 G SATURATED FATTY ACIDS, 54 MG CHOLESTEROL, 332 MG SODIUM, 1.4 G TOTAL DIETARY FIBER

CHILI PASTE

3 or 4 fresh chiles, stemmed, seeded, and chopped
1 red, yellow, or green bell pepper, chopped
1 red onion, chopped (about 2 cups)
3 fresh lemongrass stalks (about 4 inches of the tender lower stalk), minced
3 garlic cloves, minced or pressed
1 tablespoon grated fresh ginger root
1 cup water

1 tablespoon canola or other vegetable oil
4 cups water
2 teaspoons tamarind concentrate*
2 cups unsweetened crushed pineapple, undrained (20-ounce can)
2 tablespoons soy sauce
1 pound firm fish fillets, such as sea bass, red snapper, or mahimahi, cut into 2-inch chunks
¼ cup whole or chopped fresh cilantro leaves
¼ cup fresh basil chiffonade
½ cup mung sprouts and/or peeled, seeded, and diced cucumbers

Tamarind concentrate is available in jars in the Indian or Asian section of most supermarkets and in Asian groceries. To use tamarind pulp instead, soak 2 tablespoons in a cup of the hot soup broth for 15 minutes. Stir and mash with a fork, then strain through a sieve, pressing the pulp with a spoon to extract the liquid.

In a food processor or blender, whirl all of the chili paste ingredients until very smooth (see Note). In a nonreactive soup pot, warm the oil. Add the chili paste carefully to avoid splattering. Increase the heat to high and cook, stirring frequently, for 10 minutes. Add the water, cover, and simmer for at least 20 minutes.

In a small bowl, add a ladleful of the chili paste broth to the tamarind concentrate and stir to dissolve. Stir the dissolved tamarind back into the soup pot. Add the pineapple and soy sauce. Add the fish and simmer for 5 to 10 minutes, until the fish is tender and cooked.

To serve, divide the cilantro, basil, and mung sprouts and/or cucumbers among individual bowls and ladle the soup on top.

Note If some lemongrass pieces are not well puréed, just strain the soup through a colander to remove them before you add the tamarind.

DAILY SPECIAL

MENU IDEAS **Pilwun's Daikon Salad (page 282)** ✳ **Asparagus & Snow Pea Salad (page 247)** ✳ **Balinese Rice Salad (page 195)** ✳ **Indonesian Tahu Goreng (page 218)**

Venetian Seafood Stew

On a trip to Italy, Tony Del Plato rediscovered the fun of eating clams and mussels out of the shells. With fresh seafood, this Italian bouillabaisse can be the primary ingredient of a very good time.

Served in large, shallow bowls and topped with open shells and golden nuggets of polenta, this stew makes an elegant centerpiece. Accompany with a small, bright salad and Italian opera. *Buonissimo!*

SERVES 6
YIELDS 14 CUPS, INCLUDING SHELLS
TOTAL TIME: 1¼ HOURS

PER 18-OUNCE SERVING: 283 CALORIES, 11.6 G PROTEIN, 5.9 G FAT, 47.3 G CARBO-HYDRATES, 0.8 G SATURATED FATTY ACIDS, 14 MG CHOLESTEROL, 660 MG SODIUM, 4.9 G TOTAL DIETARY FIBER

POLENTA CROUTONS (SEE NOTE)

3 cups water
1½ cups cornmeal
½ teaspoon ground fennel seeds
1 teaspoon salt
2 teaspoons olive oil
ground black pepper to taste
1 garlic clove, minced or pressed

STEW

20 fresh mussels (about 1 pound)*
1 dozen Little Neck or Maine Mahogany clams (about 1 pound)*
3 cups chopped onions
2 or 3 garlic cloves, minced or pressed (about 1 tablespoon)
1 tablespoon olive oil
1 teaspoon ground fennel seeds
2 cups diagonally sliced celery
2 cups coarsely chopped red or green bell peppers
3 cups undrained canned tomatoes, chopped (28-ounce can)
4 cups water, clam juice, or a combination
¼ teaspoon crumbled saffron (optional)
6 large shrimp, rinsed (about ⅓ pound)(optional)
3 tablespoons fresh lemon juice
salt and ground black pepper to taste

fresh parsley sprigs
lemon wedges

Most supermarket seafood sections carry prepackaged 2-pound bags of rinsed and cleaned mussels that are convenient and easier to sort than loose mussels. An undrained 10-ounce can of clams can replace the fresh amount listed.

Preheat the oven to 450°.
Bring the water for the polenta croutons to a boil in a heavy non-reactive pot. Gradually pour in the cornmeal in a thin steady stream, stirring constantly until blended. Lower the heat and simmer for about 10 minutes, stirring often. Mix in the fennel, salt, 1 teaspoon of the olive oil, and black pepper to taste. Pour the polenta into an oiled 8-inch square baking pan and spread it with the back of a large spoon to a thickness of 1 to 1½ inches. Set aside for about 20 minutes to cool and firm up, then brush with the remaining teaspoon of oil and spread on the minced garlic.

Meanwhile, for the stew, discard any fresh mussels and clams that are open or cracked. Rinse the rest well and scrub, if necessary. Place the mussels and clams in a large bowl, cover with cold water, and refrigerate.

Combine the onions, garlic, and oil in a large soup pot and sauté on medium heat until the onions soften, about 5 minutes. Add the fennel and celery and cook for 10 minutes, stirring occasionally, until tender. Add the bell peppers, tomatoes, and water and/or clam juice, cover, bring to a simmer, and continue to cook on low heat for at least 15 minutes.

Cut the cooled polenta into small cubes with a sharp, damp knife. With a spatula, transfer them to a baking sheet and then separate them, leaving about ½ inch between them. Bake for 15 minutes or until golden and crusty. Turn off the oven, but don't remove the croutons, which will crisp further.

Add the saffron, if you wish, to the simmering stew. Drain the mussels and clams and add them to the stew. Cook for about 10 minutes, until the clams and mussels open up; discard any that do not open. If using shrimp, stir them in right before serving and cook just until they turn pink, 2 to 3 minutes. Add the lemon juice, salt, and pepper.

Serve immediately with parsley sprigs and lemon wedges and top each serving with several polenta croutons.

Note If you make the croutons ahead of time, warm them before serving in a 350° oven for 5 to 10 minutes.

DAILY SPECIAL

MENU IDEAS **Kiwi, Orange & Baby Greens (page 273)** ✳ **Mediterranean Orange & Olive Salad (page 276)** ✳ **Wilted Spinach & Portabella Mushrooms (page 239)** ✳ **tossed green salad with Low-fat Honey Dijon Vinaigrette (page 320)**

Salads

What comes to mind when you think of salad? Do you see a bowl brimming with bright green frilly leaves, ribbons of purple cabbage, rings of red pepper and white onion, disks of cucumber, and wedges of tomato? Or maybe you picture a hefty bowl of perfectly cooked potato salad, golden with hard-boiled eggs, seasoned with Vidalia onions, and spiked with Worcestershire and hot pepper sauce. If it isn't one of these classic American salads you envision, maybe it's a bowl of marinated broccoli or asparagus, or a platter of sliced ripe tomatoes, black olives, and fresh mozzarella or feta, dressed with olive oil, vinegar, and garlic?

At Moosewood, we sell tons of salad. Hearty main dish salads are the centerpieces of our Daily Special Salad Plates. We serve our customers a green salad before the entrée, and side salads often provide a light, refreshing contrast to rich entrées. Several salads can be combined for a substantial combo plate. Sometimes we include a fruit salad on our daily dessert menu. Whether eating out or eating at home, all of these beautiful, bright, crisp, and tender vegetables and fruits spell life and health.

To say that salad has become a broadly defined category is an understatement. The enormous variety of dishes we call salads almost defies a common definition. But that's okay because we know what we mean when we say salad: just about anything that's not something else. Usually it's served cold or at room temperature, but it might be warm. It's probably dressed with tart and tangy flavors, but it might be sweet. It's likely to contain some raw or cooked fruits and/or vegetables and herbs. The only limits are within the imagination.

In the United States, there are so many regional and ethnic cuisines that we have access to an astonishing multiplicity of foods. Salads reflect that wonderful diversity. Most of us at Moosewood didn't grow up eating mangoes, sprouts, fresh mozzarella, baked marinated tofu, seasoned seitan, shiitake, or mesclun, but they're all part of our food culture today. Over the years, Moosewood's cooks and menu planners have enjoyed exploring international cuisine. Our interest is sparked in part by our search for alternatives to meat-based cooking, but mostly by our culinary curiosity. Our love of traditional ethnic dishes has inspired us to create many lighter, more healthful meatless adaptations and has resulted in an eclectic use of ingredients and seasonings. Our salad repertoire has flourished under this multicultural cross-pollination, as has the rest of our menu.

Salads can make a filling, high-protein meal that still leaves you light on your feet. Bolster leftover salads with one of our Simple Tomato Salads or Fresh Fruit Combinations; you'll have a combo plate. And while you fix it, the leftover soup from your freezer can be heating gently. This is a simple no-nonsense way to eat.

Our salads are grouped in three sections: Main Dish Salads, Simple Vegetable & Side Dish Salads, and Seafood Salads. Look in the Accompaniments section for Moosewood's most-asked-for salad dressings, inventive toppings to enhance salads, a few great breads, and the rundown on edible flowers.

Many salads can and should be assembled ahead of time, but even the most carefully prepared dish may need more dressing and seasoning just before being served because beans, grains, pasta, and potatoes absorb moisture and flavors while they sit. These salads should be stored in the refrigerator, yet they taste better at room temperature. Be aware that some olive oil dressings congeal when chilled but liquefy at room temperature, so chilled pasta salad may appear to have absorbed all of its dressing. When a salad has been refrigerated, bring it close to room temperature and then adjust the dressing and seasonings before serving.

Salad is stimulating, refreshing food, the essence of a sensible, healthful diet. When we eat a good, fresh salad we can feel its benefits almost immediately. Often the prettiest course on the menu, even the simplest salad can lend a gracious, aesthetic touch to the dining table and add as much color and natural beauty as a floral centerpiece. Salad can show up at the beginning, middle, or end of a meal. It can awaken the appetite as a first course, complement other small dishes or a savory main dish, serve as an invigorating main course itself, or bring delight as a dessert.

Greens Galore

If we were so inclined, we could certainly put up a sign at Moosewood proclaiming OVER 2½ MILLION SALADS SOLD. Green salads offer the perfect counterpoint to cooked fare and are fresh, crisp, and welcome in any season. We feel so strongly about salads that every entrée that isn't a main dish salad is accompanied by a fresh, leafy green salad and one of our signature dressings. ✱ A simple green salad relies upon the integrity of its ingredients. We prepare our own mix of greens from a variety of lettuces and other vegetables. Most supermarkets now carry mixed greens such as mesclun, field greens, spring mix, or baby lettuces sold loose by weight. The best mixes are a combination of multicolored, multishaped greens that range from mild to sharp in flavor and crisp to tender in texture. Fresh herb sprigs and the occasional edible flower are sometimes included. If you purchase premixed, prebagged salad blends, be sure the contents are appropriately colored and not wilted, limp, or dry. ✱ Because some greens do not ship well, have a short shelf life, or are less well known, supermarkets limit their selection. Farmers' markets, however, can offer an extensive range of fresh and specialty salad greens. Better yet, even a small but sunny garden plot can yield an impressive harvest of salad fare. Most greens such as lettuces, arugula, and spinach grow best in cool weather and will hold into cold weather. They can precede or follow hot-weather favorites such as tomatoes, cucumbers, and bell peppers. ✱ A discreet amount of fresh herb sprigs or snipped or torn leaves will contribute flavor to a salad without overwhelming it. Use tender young leaves of parsley, chervil, chives, dill, tarragon, mint, or basil. Herbed salads are best with simple dressings like a drizzle of a good-tasting olive oil and splash of vinegar. ✱ Regional differences may affect availability, but we've noticed in our travels that consumer interest and savvy marketing have generated an expanded definition of what now constitutes a green salad—good-bye iceberg lettuce with two cucumber slices, one wedge of pale red tomato, and a single red onion ring. On the following pages is an informative list of typical salad greens.

LETTUCES

A complete and varied salad can be composed of several types of this basic green. Or use it as the foundation upon which to build more complex salads.

Butterhead, also called **Boston** or **Bibb,** has the most tender, mild, pale green or yellow inner leaves—a nice contrast to crisper and sharper greens.

Crisphead or **Iceberg,** once the standard, is something of a has-been, but the mild-flavored crisp leaves are good mixers. Some newer varieties with shaded red leaves are pretty but harder to come by.

Looseleaf encompasses many varieties under its heading. Its colors range from chartreuse to deep green, red to maroon. Leaf shapes vary from lobed oakleaf lettuces to lightly curled or savoyed, to some with deeply frizzled edges. Texture varies with type, although most are moderately crisp.

Romaine has large, crisp leaves with a juicy central rib. The distinguishing feature of this lettuce is certainly its crunch. It is good in sandwiches.

ASIAN GREENS

A multitude of mustard family greens make tangy and attractive additions to salads when small, immature plants or leaves are used. Mature greens are best utilized in cooking. Asian greens keep well and don't turn brown as quickly as lettuces. The use of some of the following greens in commercial mesclun mixes has provided exposure to a wider audience. When composing your own mix, look for these in well-stocked supermarkets or Asian groceries.

Mizuna is a mild-tasting Japanese green with elegant, feathery foliage.

Tatsoi is a type of bok choy with small, oval, deep green leaves and tender white stems. The plant grows in handsome rosettes.

Chinese cabbage has a mild flavor and crunchy texture, which characterize both the oval Napa type and the tall Michihli.

OTHER GREENS

Many of these greens are good both raw and cooked. Some of us prefer to briefly blanch the more bitter varieties in boiling water to soften their edge.

Arugula has an unusual flavor that combines elements of hot pepper and toasted sesame seeds. This mustard family member is a wildflower in Italy and also known as rocket or rucola. Spiciness varies from bunch to bunch, but definitely increases with the age of the plant. For a milder taste, look for arugula with 3- to 4-inch leaves.

Beet greens add bright color to salads; use only the very youngest and most tender leaves.

Cabbage, especially finely shredded red cabbage, adds color and crunch. Savoy types have attractively curled and wavy leaves. Shredded green cabbage is classic in slaws of all kinds as well as in many Southeast Asian salads.

Corn salad has small tender leaves with a delicate floral flavor that hints at perfume. This mild green is sometimes referred to as Mâche or lamb's lettuce. Corn salad will nicely mellow a salad with sharper greens such as radicchio or arugula.

Endive, both the curly-leafed (or frisée) and the wavy-leafed types (or escarole), add crunch, visual interest, and a mildly bitter flavor to salads. Frisée is the more attractive of the two, with its very pale and deeply cut, frilled, narrow leaves. With both of these greens, uncooked tender inner leaves are best for salads. Use the outer leaves, briefly cooked, for other dishes.

Radicchio is a member of the chicory family and has brilliantly colored small heads of reddish-purple leaves with creamy white ribs. The more or less bitter leaves, which vary from plant to plant, add character and "bite" to salads. Radicchio combines nicely with sweeter fare, such as pears, fresh fennel bulb, or mildly flavored greens.

Spinach has distinctively flavored, dark green, flat or crinkled leaves that provide color contrast to paler greens. This familiar, easily obtained vegetable is preferred raw by many. It is adaptable to all kinds of leafy salads.

Watercress, a mustard relative, has small deep green leaves that are nicely peppery and will perk up mixed salads. The fragile leaves should be used as soon after purchase as possible.

Wild greens are worth learning about. Doubtless our pre-supermarket ancestors had good knowledge of which greens could be eaten in their locales. Today, market gardeners grow "wild" greens year-round in glass houses to supply trendy restaurants with something different. When many of us at Moosewood moved to the countryside near Ithaca, we read Euell Gibbons' *Stalking the Wild Asparagus* and learned about eating dandelion, purslane, pigweed, sorrel, fiddlehead ferns, and other tasty and nutritious wildings. Harvesting directly from nature is certainly a worthwhile pursuit, but be sure you can identify the species you want, purchase a reliable plant guide, and avoid roadsides or other locations that may have been sprayed with herbicides or pesticides.

COMBINING GREENS

There are lots of ways to combine greens and make an appealing salad. Here are a few of our favorite combos paired with a suggested dressing. Look for our line of bottled Moosewood salad dressings at your favorite supermarket.

Butterhead lettuce, curly endive, parsley, and red cabbage
with **Moosewood House Dressing** (page 324).

Chinese cabbage, mizuna, watercress, and spinach
with **Moosewood Ginger Miso Dressing** (page 323).

Baby lettuces, arugula, corn salad, and beet greens
with **Versatile Vinaigrette** (page 325).

Romaine and red leaf lettuces, radicchio, and spinach
with **Low-fat Tomato Basil Dressing** (page 321).

CLEANING GREENS

Store unwashed greens in the refrigerator in perforated plastic bags after removing twist-ties and rubber bands, which can bruise the leaves. When ready to use, remove bruised or decayed leaves and any surviving bits of wildlife from the garden that may be lodged in the leaves.

We do not recommend rinsing greens under a running faucet, which can easily bruise the leaves without removing clinging grit. A thorough soaking in very cold water in a sink or large pot is the best way to remove dirt. While the greens soak, dirt sinks to the bottom and the leaves rehydrate. Remove the greens. If you notice a lot of dirt in the drained sink or pot bottom, or if the greens were quite sandy, it's best to give a second soaking: gritty greens will ruin any salad.

Gently lift the greens from the sink and dry them in small batches in a salad spinner. Very tender baby greens or other fragile types can be placed on kitchen towels and gently patted dry. Drying greens well, wrapping them loosely in paper towels, and storing in sealed plastic bags (or other containers that limit air contact) will help to delay deterioration. Refrigerate until ready to use.

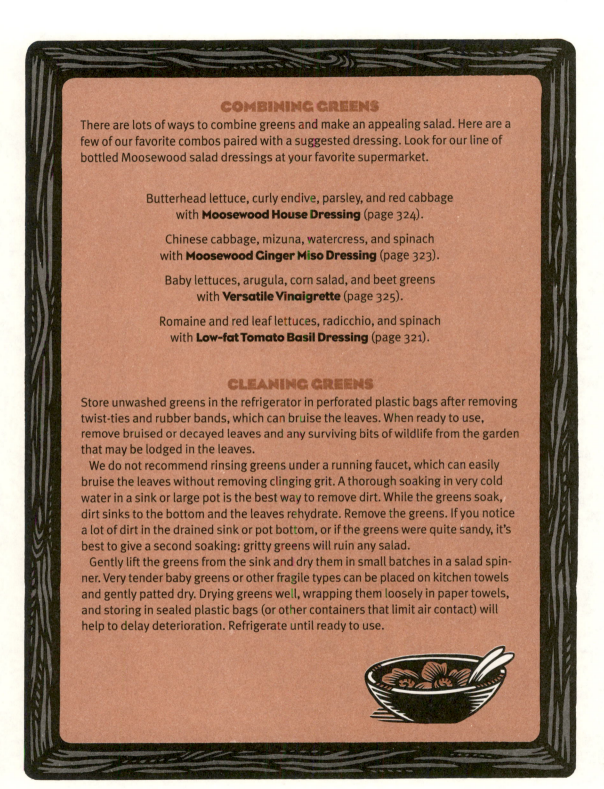

MAIN DISH SALADS

At Moosewood, one of the things we do best is main dish salads, which have held the status of entrées on our menu since the restaurant began. They are the foundation of the Daily Special Soup & Salad Plate. In addition to vegetables or fruit, most of our main course salads contain beans and grains or pasta and are topped with toasted nuts, grated cheese, seasoned tofu, or tempeh. Typically, we arrange generous portions on beds of tender greens, garnish them with fresh herbs and fruit, and serve them with a soup from our ever-changing menu. Our innovative salad plates are beautiful to the eye, deliciously well seasoned, and best of all, healthful and energizing. In colder months, the salad plate is a light, yet satisfying meal, especially popular with our business lunch crowd. In the summertime, there is nothing more refreshing than to be outdoors on our patio, dining on this simple but magnificent fare. ✳ What makes a salad a main dish rather than a side dish? To be honest, it's largely portion size and substance. The salad must be hearty enough to be the main event of your meal; if it is, you've got a main dish salad. A smaller portion of the same salad might serve perfectly well as an appetizer, a side dish, or as part of a combo plate. The recipes in this section yield main dish portions and most provide some protein and the kind of nutrition we expect from a main dish. What makes them salads? Well, most are served chilled or at room temperature and they're seasoned with tangy herbed or spiced marinades and dressings. Here you will find pasta salads and a host of grain salads from rice, bulghur, and barley to couscous, kasha, quinoa, and corn embellished with pita, pine nuts, peanuts, and pecans. The Seafood Salads section contains several additional main course salads for those who eat fish. ✳ Like all our offerings, main dish salads at Moosewood reflect the influence of international cuisine. We've created or adapted a variety of dishes in particular ethnic styles, drawing from North Africa, Latin America, Asia, the Mediterranean, and the Caribbean, as well as the United States. Among our all-time favorites from Asia are sweet, refreshing Balinese Rice Salad and light, fragrant Thai Noodle Salad, both very popular at the restaurant. Classic Sichuan Noodles makes the most of peanut butter, vinegar, and hot red pepper. Hijiki Rice Salad is both healthful and good looking. Gado Gado, an Indonesian dish of cooked and raw vegetables, has a fabulous and versatile spicy peanut sauce. ✳ We've developed several recipes with Middle Eastern origins, including Persian Rice & Pistachio Salad, North African Couscous Salad, and Fattoush, a zingy salad of fresh tomatoes and toasted pita bread. There are also several Mediterranean-style dishes, like Arugula & Warm Mozzarella Salad, Orzo & Pesto Stuffed Tomatoes, and Roasted Garlic Aioli Salad. ✳ Some of the dishes in this section, such as Broiled Tofu & Sugar Snap Peas and Avocado Seitan Salad, include soy or wheat gluten to provide protein. Others feature legumes: Farfalle e Fagiole Salad and Bean Purée with Seven Savories served family style. We especially enjoy our unusual grain salads, such as Andean Quinoa & Corn Salad and French Barley Salad. If you love nuts, try Southern Red Rice & Pecan Salad; the combination of rice and nuts provides protein, hearty flavor, and crunch. ✳ If you're just venturing into fixing big salads as a main course, start with something familiar, like Caesar Salad or Chef Salad à la Moosewood. **Main course salads are a wonderful opportunity for experimentation.** While adventurous cooks should find the recipes in this section diverse enough to be exciting, we also hope to inspire your creativity. One of the best things about preparing a main dish salad is that the risk of failure is low. Start with a basic tossed salad of mixed greens and your favorite salad veggies, then bolster it with additions like hard-boiled eggs, spiced tofu, marinated artichoke hearts, fresh shrimp, crisp sprouts, or crumbled or shredded cheese. A salad is a good way to use up left-over rice, bulghur, cooked beans, potatoes, or pasta: toss in some celery, peppers, onions or scallions, and a simple herbed vinaigrette dressing and you're in business. This is a smart, economical way to eat well, and it can also be a canvas for self-expression and true artistry. ✱ When your salad contains starches, choosing the right type of dressing is important. We tend to use vinaigrettes and spiced or fruity marinades on salads with beans, pasta, rice and other grains, and fruit. Herbed or garlicky mayonnaise, thick-chunky-creamy dressings, and substantial, spicy sauces are usually reserved for salads with assertive greens, potatoes, long noodles, seafood, or steamed vegetables. ✱ Moosewood's Daily Special Soup & Salad Plates are often liberally topped with something crunchy, chewy, or savory, such as toasted nuts or the Fried Shallots, Curried Croutons, or Baked Seasoned Tofu in our Accompaniments section. Our salad plates are also usually served with a thick slice of bread or whole grain crackers and cheese. A few of these extras can make your main dish salad an especially handsome meal. ✱

Andean Quinoa & Corn Salad

Quinoa is a high-protein South American grain with a chewy, satisfying texture and a nutty flavor similar to bulghur. It cooks very quickly and retains its consistency well. Here it is the basis of a tangy salad that makes great summer fare. We often pair it with a soup of potatoes, another gift of the Andes.

While the quinoa cooks, you can prepare all of the remaining ingredients. If the salad isn't served for several hours, it may be necessary to adjust the seasonings with additional lemon juice, cumin, and cilantro to taste.

SERVES 4 TO 6
PREPARATION AND COOKING TIME:
 30 MINUTES
CHILLING TIME: 15 MINUTES

PER 10-OUNCE SERVING: 172 CALORIES, 3.6 G PROTEIN, 8.3 G FAT, 24.8 G CARBO-HYDRATES, 1.1 G SATURATED FATTY ACIDS, 0 MG CHOLESTEROL, 441 MG SODIUM, 3.2 G TOTAL DIETARY FIBER

GRAIN MIXTURE
1 cup raw quinoa
1 tablespoon olive oil
1 teaspoon paprika
2 cups water
1 teaspoon salt

1 cup water
2 cups fresh or frozen corn kernels
2 tablespoons olive oil or other vegetable oil
1 large onion, finely chopped (about 2 cups)
2 garlic cloves, minced or pressed
1 teaspoon ground cumin
1 teaspoon ground coriander
2 red and/or green bell peppers, seeded and diced
1 fresh chile, stemmed, seeded, and minced
2 tablespoons minced fresh cilantro, more to taste
1 large tomato, chopped
2 tablespoons minced fresh parsley
¼ cup fresh lemon juice
salt and ground black pepper to taste

In a sieve, rinse the quinoa under running water and set aside to drain. Heat the oil in a saucepan, add the paprika, and stir constantly for about 1 minute. Add the quinoa, water, and salt, cover, and bring to a boil. Then lower the heat and simmer for 15 to 20 minutes, or until the water is absorbed and the quinoa is tender but still chewy.

Meanwhile, bring the water to a boil in a separate pot. Add the corn and cook until tender, drain well, and set aside in the refrigerator. Heat the oil and sauté the onions, garlic, cumin, and coriander until the onions are translucent, about 10 minutes. Stir in the bell peppers, chile, and cilantro, and sauté for another 3 to 5 minutes.

In a large serving bowl, combine the cooked quinoa and the sautéed vegetables and chill for 15 minutes. Stir in the corn, tomatoes, parsley, lemon juice, salt, and black pepper. Add more chopped cilantro, if desired, and serve immediately or refrigerate for later.

DAILY SPECIAL

MENU IDEAS **Black Bean & Chipotle Soup (page 70)** ✳ **Tortilla Soup (page 99)** ✳ **Creamy Herbed Potato Soup (page 122)** ✳ **Roasted Chile & Potato Soup (page 131)** ✳ **Golden Gazpacho (page 153)** ✳ **Avocado Melon Mélange (page 264)**

Artichoke Heart & Bulghur Salat

The Fertile Crescent has been called the cradle of civilization and has certainly inspired some great food. This lively, refreshing salad can be served as a main dish, a side dish, or at a picnic, when a tired, humdrum potato or macaroni salad just won't do.

SERVES 4
TOTAL TIME: 40 MINUTES

PER 13.5-OUNCE SERVING: 519 CALORIES, 18.4 G PROTEIN, 18.6 G FAT, 78.7 G CARBOHYDRATES, 4.9 G SATURATED FATTY ACIDS, 17 MG CHOLESTEROL, 710 MG SODIUM, 22.4 G TOTAL DIETARY FIBER

2 cups raw bulghur (medium-grain)
1¾ cups boiling water
½ teaspoon salt
2 teaspoons plus 3 tablespoons olive oil
2 large garlic cloves, minced or pressed
10 ounces fresh spinach, rinsed and large stems removed
2 tablespoons fresh lemon juice
1 tablespoon minced fresh mint leaves (2 teaspoons dried)
½ teaspoon dried oregano, more to taste
1½ cups artichoke hearts, cut into eighths (14-ounce can, drained)
⅔ cup grated feta cheese
salt and ground black pepper to taste

sliced roasted red peppers
chickpeas
grated feta cheese
chopped tomatoes

Combine the bulghur, water, and salt in a large heatproof bowl (see Note). Cover tightly and set aside for 30 minutes, until the water has been absorbed and the bulghur is soft but still chewy. If it's too chewy, add a splash of boiling water and let it sit for another few minutes.

Meanwhile, warm 2 teaspoons of the olive oil in a large skillet and briefly sauté the garlic until lightly golden. Add the still-damp spinach, cover, and cook on medium heat until the spinach has just wilted. Drain it well and, when cool enough to handle, chop it finely.

When the bulghur is ready, add the spinach, lemon juice, the remaining olive oil, the mint, oregano, artichoke hearts, and feta and toss well. Add salt and pepper to taste. Dress up the salad with any or all of the garnishes listed: sliced roasted red peppers, chickpeas, grated feta cheese, and/or chopped fresh tomatoes.

Serve at room temperature or chilled.

Note We have observed that a heavy, ceramic bowl, by virtue of some magic (perhaps heat retention-mass ratios?), produces the best bulghur.

DAILY SPECIAL ❧

MENU IDEAS **Tomatoes Capriccio (page 286)** ✳ **Algerian Tomato Soup with Vermicelli (page 66)** ✳ **chilled Cucumber Yogurt Soup (page 147)** ✳ **Mediterranean Orange & Olive Salad (page 276)** ✳ **Greek Chickpea Salad (page 277)**

Arugula & Warm Mozzarella Salad

The four components of this composed salad mix, match, and meld in a wonderful way. The tomatoes provide natural sweetness, the arugula gives bite and depth, the parsley-pine nut dressing is tart and assertive, and the warm mozzarella is oh-so-rich. The technique of breading and warming the mozzarella may be new to you, but don't worry; it's fast and easy, and the result is beautiful.

SERVES 4
TOTAL TIME: 20 TO 25 MINUTES

PER 6-OUNCE SERVING: 308 CALORIES, 11.7 G PROTEIN, 24.9 G FAT, 12.1 G CARBOHYDRATES, 6.4 G SATURATED FATTY ACIDS, 22 MG CHOLESTEROL, 700 MG SODIUM, 1.7 G TOTAL DIETARY FIBER

DRESSING

2 tablespoons pine nuts
¼ cup chopped fresh parsley, packed
1 or 2 garlic cloves, peeled
½ teaspoon salt
¼ cup olive oil
2 tablespoons fresh lemon juice
2 tablespoons water

2 cups arugula (about 2½ ounces)
2 small tomatoes
¼ cup bread crumbs
¼ teaspoon salt
2 egg-shaped balls of fresh mozzarella (about ⅓ pound)
1 teaspoon olive oil

Toast the pine nuts in a single layer on an unoiled baking sheet in a conventional or toaster oven at 350° until lightly browned and fragrant, about 3 to 5 minutes.

In a blender, whirl the parsley, garlic, salt, olive oil, lemon juice, water, and toasted pine nuts until smooth and emulsified. Pour into a cruet or small pitcher.

Wash and dry the arugula and lay the leaves on a large platter or on individual salad plates. Cut the tomatoes into wedges and arrange them on the arugula. Mix together the bread crumbs and salt in a large bowl. Cut the fresh mozzarella into ½-inch cubes. Place the cubes in the bowl with the bread crumbs and toss to coat well.

Heat a heavy iron skillet until almost smoking. Remove the hot skillet from the heat, add the teaspoon of olive oil, and swirl to coat the bottom of the pan. Add the breaded mozzarella cubes and shake the pan to heat them evenly. The trick is to warm them until they become soft and to stop before they become rubbery. Have a bowl nearby so you can scoop them out at just the right moment. You should be able to see or feel the cubes get soft, but if milky-colored whey seeps out, you're overheating them.

Arrange the warm mozzarella cubes on the bed of arugula and tomatoes and pass the dressing separately.

MENU IDEAS **French Roasted Onion Soup (page 37)** ✳ **Navarin of Spring Vegetables (page 47)** ✳ **Creamy Herbed Carrot Soup (page 121)** ✳ **chilled Fennel Vichyssoise (page 149)** ✳ **chilled Peach Soup (page 156)** ✳ **Focaccia (page 330)**

Asian Beet & Tofu Salad

Moosewood cook Maureen Vivino created this dish when serving as *tenzo* (cook) at a 7-day *sesshin* (Zen practice retreat). Lots of participants said they loved the lunch with the shocking pink tofu. If this salad is composed in the concentric groupings we recommend, you will be rewarded with a display of bright green, burgundy, and ivory; mix it up and the tofu will turn beet red!

SERVES 6
TOTAL TIME: 55 TO 60 MINUTES

PER 7.25-OUNCE SERVING: 100 CALO-RIES, 8.9 G PROTEIN, 3.8 G FAT, 10.7 G CARBOHYDRATES, 0.6 G SATURATED FATTY ACIDS, 0 MG CHOLESTEROL, 777 MG SODIUM, 2.9 G TOTAL DIETARY FIBER

4 fresh beets, roots and stems removed (about 3-inch diameter)
1 cake of tofu (about 16 ounces)
10 ounces spinach, rinsed and stemmed

MARINADE
⅓ cup soy sauce
½ cup fresh lemon juice
3 garlic cloves, minced or pressed
1 tablespoon grated fresh ginger root
¼ cup chopped scallions

1 scallion, sliced on the extreme diagonal
1 tablespoon grated daikon (optional)

In a covered saucepan, simmer the beets in boiling water to cover for 25 to 35 minutes, until tender and easily pierced with a knife. Meanwhile, place the tofu between two plates, weight the top plate with a heavy object, and press for 20 minutes.

In a saucepan, bring about ½ inch of water to a boil. Add the spinach, cover, and steam for 3 to 4 minutes, until just wilted but still bright green. Place the spinach in a colander and set aside to drain and cool. Press to remove some liquid and coarsely chop (see Note).

While the spinach cools, whisk together the marinade ingredients and pour into a large shallow bowl. Cut the pressed tofu into ¾-inch cubes and add it to the bowl. Stir to coat evenly and set aside for about 10 minutes.

When the beets are tender, drain and rinse with cold water until they can be handled comfortably. Remove the skins by gently squeezing the beets under cold running water. Quarter each beet and cut into ¼-inch-thick slices.

Set aside the tofu, leaving the marinade in the bowl. Add the beet slices to the marinade, stir well, and set aside for 10 minutes. Transfer the beets from the marinade to the serving dish. Add the chopped spinach to the marinade and toss lightly, then arrange it around the beets. Mound the tofu in the center and top with the sliced scallions. If you like, garnish with the grated daikon, which will add a peppery, radish accent.

Note If you're a spinach lover, try the steamed spinach leaves whole rather than chopped.

MENU IDEAS **Chinese Velvet Corn Soup (page 116)** ✳ **Miso Noodle Soup (page 89)** ✳ **Scallion Pancakes (page 350)** ✳ **Bean Sprout Salad (page 250)** ✳ **Seaweed Salad (page 285)**

Asparagus & Fennel Pasta Salad

This sophisticated pasta salad is crisp and fresh, with an unexpected combination of flavors. Fresh fennel, a light green bulb with celery-like stalks and feathery leaves, adds a sweet and licoricey note. Roasting the fennel mellows it, making a delicate background for the more pronounced accents of tomatoes, Greek olives, and feta cheese.

To save time, preheat the oven and begin to boil the water for the pasta before you begin to prepare the ingredients: prepare the vegetables for roasting first, and while they roast, prepare the rest.

SERVES 4 TO 6
TOTAL TIME: 1 HOUR

PER 12-OUNCE SERVING: 365 CALORIES, 11.4 G PROTEIN, 17.6 G FAT, 43.2 G CARBOHYDRATES, 4.6 G SATURATED FATTY ACIDS, 17 MG CHOLESTEROL, 617 MG SODIUM, 3 G TOTAL DIETARY FIBER

ROASTED VEGETABLES
1 fresh fennel bulb, cored and thinly sliced*
2 cups thinly sliced onions
1 pound asparagus, stemmed and cut into ¾-inch pieces
2 tablespoons olive oil

DRESSING
2 tablespoons olive oil
2 tablespoons fresh lemon juice
1 teaspoon minced or pressed garlic
¼ teaspoon Dijon mustard
¼ teaspoon salt
⅛ teaspoon ground black pepper

8 ounces penne (tubular pasta)
2 cups diced tomatoes
12 kalamata olives, pitted and thinly sliced**
1 cup chopped fresh parsley
1 cup grated feta cheese

* Remove the stalks and fronds from the fennel bulb and slice the bulb crosswise into thin circles. Remove and discard the innermost round core sections, and cut larger pieces from the outer layers into 2-inch lengths.
** To pit, slice lengthwise around each olive and twist the halves apart. Or whack each olive sharply to break it open.

Preheat the oven to 400°. Lightly oil an 8 × 15-inch baking pan and begin to bring 2 quarts of water to a boil.

Place the fennel, onions, and asparagus on the baking pan, drizzle with the olive oil, sprinkle with salt, and toss to evenly coat. Roast uncovered for 20 minutes, stirring about every 7 minutes. The vegetables should be crisp-tender and the asparagus still bright green.

While the vegetables roast, whisk all of the dressing ingredients and set aside. When the water boils, cook the pasta until al dente, about 7 minutes.

While the pasta cooks, combine the tomatoes, olives, and parsley in a large serving bowl. Mix in the roasted vegetables. Drain the pasta, add it to the bowl, pour on the dressing, and toss well. Stir in the feta or sprinkle it on top. Serve warm or at room temperature.

MENU IDEAS **chilled Cucumber Yogurt Soup (page 147)** ✳ **chilled Minted Pea Soup (page 155)** ✳ **Middle Eastern Chickpea Soup (page 88)** ✳ **Creamy Herbed Carrot Soup (page 121)** ✳ **Sopa de Camarones (page 172)** ✳ **Oaxacan Potato Soup (page 128)** ✳ **Strawberries with a Touch of Tart (page 265)**

Avocado Seitan Salad

The zip of chile, the zest of lime, and the added zing of cilantro create a delectable lip-smacking dressing for the cool combination of creamy avocado chunks mixed with crisp cucumbers and ripe tomatoes. Seitan and cheese cubes make the salad a substantial main dish. It has a lot of color and texture, so we usually match it in a Daily Special with a strong, single note soup.

SERVES 4 TO 6
TOTAL TIME: 30 MINUTES

PER 9-OUNCE SERVING: 328 CALORIES, 3.5 G PROTEIN, 30.4 G FAT, 14.9 G CARBO-HYDRATES, 6.7 G SATURATED FATTY ACIDS, 0 MG CHOLESTEROL, 302 MG SODIUM, 6 G TOTAL DIETARY FIBER

1 fresh chile, seeded and chopped
3 tablespoons fresh lime juice
2 tablespoons chopped fresh cilantro
½ teaspoon salt
½ cup canola or other vegetable oil
2 avocados, preferably Hass
2 cucumbers, peeled, seeded, and cut into crescents
1 small red onion, thinly sliced
2 small tomatoes, cut into chunks
1 cup cubed seasoned seitan (4 ounces)*
6 cups loosely packed mixed salad greens (about ¼ pound)

Monterey Jack cheese, cut into ½-inch cubes (optional)
chopped black olives (optional)

* *Seasoned or flavored seitan is available in natural food stores and in most well-stocked supermarkets.*

Combine the chile, lime juice, cilantro, salt, and oil in a blender, purée until smooth, and set aside.

Halve each avocado, twist to separate the halves, and remove the pit. Score the flesh into chunks and, with a spoon, scoop the chunks away from the peel and into a bowl. Add the cucumbers, red onions, tomatoes, and seitan. Pour the dressing over the vegetables and toss lightly until well coated.

Rinse the salad greens and spin or pat dry. Arrange them on a large platter or in a shallow serving bowl. Mound the vegetables on the greens and, if you wish, top with the cheese cubes and olives.

MENU IDEAS **Caribbean Sweet Potato Coconut Soup (page 29)** ✳ **Oaxacan Potato Soup (page 128)** ✳ **Sante Fe Chowder (page 132)** ✳ **Roasted Chile & Potato Soup (page 131)** ✳ **chilled Mango Soup (page 154)** ✳ **Jamaican Tomato Soup (page 41)** ✳ **Southern Wheat-free Cornbread (page 335)**

Balinese Rice Salad

With complex flavors that are savory, salty, sweet, and tangy, this exotic, tropical salad can be made quickly with leftover rice and served as a main course or side dish that is perfect for a last-minute picnic or an easy summer supper.

SERVES 6
TOTAL TIME: 20 MINUTES
CHILLING TIME (OPTIONAL):
   30 MINUTES

PER 12-OUNCE SERVING: 389 CALORIES, 8.9 G PROTEIN, 11.6 G FAT, 67.6 G CARBO-HYDRATES, 2.3 G SATURATED FATTY ACIDS, 0 MG CHOLESTEROL, 705 MG SODIUM, 3.3 G TOTAL DIETARY FIBER

DRESSING
½ cup prepared mango chutney*
2 tablespoons cider vinegar
2 tablespoons canola or other vegetable oil
2 tablespoons unsweetened pineapple or orange juice
1 large garlic clove, minced or pressed
1 tablespoon soy sauce
1 teaspoon salt
pinch of cayenne

4 cups cooked brown rice, cooled to room temperature
1 cup fresh or unsweetened canned pineapple chunks
2 scallions, sliced on the diagonal
2 celery stalks, thinly sliced on the diagonal
1 red, yellow, or green bell pepper, seeded and chopped
½ cup raisins
2 cups mung bean sprouts (½ pound)
1 cup drained baby corn (15-ounce can)
½ cup toasted peanuts or cashews**

*A brand we recommend is Patak's Major Grey Mango Chutney.
**Toast nuts in a single layer on an unoiled baking tray in a conventional or toaster oven at 350° for about 5 minutes, until fragrant and golden.

In a blender or food processor, purée all of the dressing ingredients until smooth.

In a large serving bowl, combine the rice, pineapple, scallions, celery, peppers, and raisins. Add the dressing and toss well. Gently mix in the sprouts and baby corn or scatter them on top, if you prefer. Garnish with the nuts.

Serve at room temperature or chill for about 30 minutes.

Note If you want to whisk together the dressing by hand, first finely chop any large pieces of mango in the chutney.

MENU IDEAS **Asian Bean Curd Soup (page 64)** ✳ **Baked Seasoned Tofu (page 336)** ✳ **Spicy Tofu & Greens Soup (page 92)** ✳ **chilled Fragrant Lemongrass Fruit Soup (page 150)** ✳ **Creamy Tomato Soup (page 125)** ✳ **Cream of Spinach Soup (page 120)**

Balkan Roasted Vegetable Salad

Roasting vegetables brings out their sweetness and intensifies their flavors. Here, eggplant, bell peppers, onions, and mushrooms sizzle together in a tangy marinade. The mushrooms release just enough of their juices to keep the eggplant from sticking to the pan and, by the end of the baking, most of the liquid will have evaporated.

Serve this salad warm, at room temperature, or chilled. It will keep for over a week when well wrapped and refrigerated. You may wish to make a double batch and serve it several times, varying the temperature and accompaniments. It is a good appetizer when paired with Focaccia (page 330) or toasted pita bread.

SERVES 4 TO 6
PREPARATION TIME: 20 MINUTES
BAKING TIME: 35 TO 40 MINUTES
CHILLING TIME (OPTIONAL):
  20 MINUTES

PER 9.25-OUNCE SERVING: 198 CALORIES, 3.6 G PROTEIN, 15.1 G FAT, 15 G CARBOHYDRATES, 3.2 G SATURATED FATTY ACIDS, 8 MG CHOLESTEROL, 314 MG SODIUM, 3.6 G TOTAL DIETARY FIBER

MARINADE

½ cup red wine vinegar
2 tablespoons fresh lemon juice
⅓ cup olive oil
¼ cup chopped fresh basil
1 to 1½ teaspoons ground fennel seeds
½ teaspoon dried oregano
½ teaspoon salt
¼ teaspoon ground black pepper

VEGETABLES

1 large eggplant, cut into ½-inch cubes*
1 red and 1 green bell pepper, seeded and cut into bite-sized pieces
1 cup chopped onions
2 cups mushrooms, trimmed and cut in half (large ones quartered)
2 tomatoes
1 cucumber

½ cup grated feta cheese

*If the eggplant is ripe and its skin not tough or bitter, there's no need to peel it for this recipe. To cube the eggplant, slice off and discard the ends, cut the eggplant crosswise into ½-inch slices, then stack and hold several slices together as you cut through them crosswise and lengthwise to make the cubes.

Preheat the oven to 500°.
Combine the marinade ingredients by whirling briefly in a blender or food processor, or by whisking them in a bowl. Set aside. On a large baking pan with raised sides, spread out the eggplant cubes and sprinkle lightly with salt. Add the bell peppers, onions, and mushrooms and drizzle with about ⅔ of the marinade. Right on the baking tray, toss the vegetables with the marinade until evenly coated. Bake for 35 to 40 minutes, until tender and slightly browned.

While the vegetables roast, dice the tomatoes and peel, seed, and dice the cucumber. Place them in a serving bowl and drizzle with the remaining marinade. With a slotted spatula, transfer the roasted vegetables to the bowl and toss well.

Serve immediately, or at room temperature or chilled. Top each portion with grated feta.

MENU IDEAS **Artichoke Avgolemono (page 112)** ✳ **chilled Minted Pea Soup (page 155)** ✳ **Hungarian Green Bean Soup (page 127)** ✳ **Grecian Isle Stew (page 39)** ✳ **Fassoulada (page 79)** ✳ **Fig & Endive Salad (page 261)**

Bean Purée with Seven Savories

A smooth, creamy purée of butter beans is the perfect foil for seven different savory garnishes. Just dip wedges of pita into the purée and scoop up a taste of sautéed spinach and garlic, chopped eggs or olives, red onions or marinated turnips.

Or garnish it with only a couple of the savories from our list and try others that may appeal to you: perhaps minced hot pickled peppers, sautéed bread crumbs, scallions, capers, sliced radishes, or chopped fresh sage, parsley, or fennel. The mild bean flavor is especially satisfying with slightly bitter tender leaves of endive or sautéed broccoli rabe.

Some of us have gotten hooked on this salad for breakfast, as is common in the Middle East.

SERVES 4
COOKING TIME: 5 MINUTES
TOTAL TIME: 25 MINUTES

PER 15-OUNCE SERVING: 490 CALORIES, 17.9 G PROTEIN, 24.8 G FAT, 54.8 G CAR-BOHYDRATES, 3.5 G SATURATED FATTY ACIDS, 132 MG CHOLESTEROL, 1907 MG SODIUM, 9.3 G TOTAL DIETARY FIBER

BEAN PURÉE

3 cups cooked butter beans (two 16-ounce cans, drained and rinsed)
2 tablespoons extra-virgin olive oil
3 tablespoons fresh lemon juice
¼ teaspoon salt
⅛ teaspoon ground black pepper
1 garlic clove, minced or pressed

SAVORIES

½ cup sliced black olives
2 tomatoes, diced into ½-inch cubes
2 hard-boiled eggs, peeled and minced
½ red onion, peeled and minced
½ turnip, peeled and thinly sliced or shredded (about 1 cup)
1 tablespoon white vinegar
dash of salt and ground black pepper
2 garlic cloves, minced
2 teaspoons olive oil
4 cups loosely packed fresh spinach (about 5 ounces), rinsed, stemmed, and coarsely chopped
2 or 3 pita breads

Combine the butter beans, olive oil, lemon juice, salt, pepper, and garlic in a food processor and purée until smooth. Set aside.

Place the olives, tomatoes, hard-boiled eggs, and red onions in separate small bowls and set them aside. Place the turnips in a small bowl, drizzle on the vinegar, sprinkle with salt and pepper, and set aside.

In a frying pan, sauté the minced garlic in the olive oil on medium heat for just a minute, until it begins to turn golden. Add the spinach with whatever water still clings to the leaves, cover the pan, and cook for about 1 minute, until the spinach wilts. Stir the spinach, sprinkle with salt and pepper, stir again, and remove from the heat.

When ready to serve, cut the pita breads into wedges and arrange them around the edge of a platter. Mound the bean purée in the center and surround with all of the savories. Each diner will take some of the beans and whatever savories they like.

Note This dish can be prepared ahead and refrigerated, but is best eaten at room temperature.

MENU IDEAS Moroccan Root Vegetable Stew (page 45) * **chilled Creamy Yogurt Barley Soup (page 146)** * **Algerian Tomato Soup with Vermicelli (page 66)** * **Tunisian Pumpkin Soup (page 56)** * **Italian Green, White & Red Soup (page 82)**

Broccoli Pine Nut Pasta Salad

This colorful salad features farfalle (pasta butterflies) and is garnished with crunchy toasted pine nuts.

The challenge with any pasta salad containing a green vegetable is how to maintain a sufficiently robust zing while keeping the color bright. So we add the lemon juice just before serving: that way the broccoli looks as vivid as the tomatoes and peppers and the full citrus flavor is not lost. For added zest, splash on a little balsamic vinegar at the table.

SERVES 4 TO 6
PREPARATION TIME: 10 MINUTES
COOKING TIME: 15 TO 20 MINUTES

PER 10-OUNCE SERVING: 311 CALORIES, 8.8 G PROTEIN, 14.4 G FAT, 40.5 G CARBO-HYDRATES, 2 G SATURATED FATTY ACIDS, 0 MG CHOLESTEROL, 92 MG SODIUM, 5.5 G TOTAL DIETARY FIBER

½ pound farfalle (about 3 cups)
5 cups broccoli florets and peeled chopped tender stems (1 large head)
¼ cup extra-virgin olive oil
4 garlic cloves, minced or pressed (about 1 tablespoon)
1½ cups chopped bell peppers, yellow preferred for color
1½ cups chopped tomatoes
1 tablespoon capers
2 tablespoons fresh lemon juice
salt and ground black pepper to taste

¼ cup toasted pine nuts*
chopped fresh parsley
cruet of balsamic vinegar or a few lemon wedges (optional)

Lightly toast the pine nuts in a dry skillet on medium heat until their color deepens. Or bake them in an oven or toaster oven on an unoiled baking sheet at 350° for about 5 minutes, until fragrant and lightly browned.

Bring a large pot of water to a boil. Cover and cook the pasta until al dente, about 10 minutes.

Meanwhile, steam the broccoli for about 5 to 7 minutes, until crisp but still tender and bright green. While the broccoli steams, warm the oil in a saucepan, gently heat the garlic in the oil for about 2 minutes, stirring frequently, and remove from the heat. Drain the broccoli and set aside.

When the pasta is ready, drain it and transfer to a serving bowl. Toss lightly with the garlic and oil. Add the broccoli, bell peppers, tomatoes, and capers to the pasta and toss well. Just before serving, stir in the lemon juice and salt and pepper to taste. Top with the pine nuts and parsley and serve immediately. If desired, pass a cruet of balsamic vinegar or a small bowl of lemon wedges at the table.

Variations Serve with sliced fresh mozzarella cheese or top with grated Parmesan cheese.

MENU IDEAS **Creamy Herbed Carrot Soup (page 121)** ✳ **chilled August Melon Soup (page 140)** ✳ **chilled Fragrant Lemongrass Fruit Soup (page 150)** ✳ **Artichoke Heart Soup (page 27)** ✳ **Autumn Minestrone (page 67)**

Broiled Tofu & Sugar Snap Peas

Spicy tofu gives this artistic salad a flavorful kick. It's easy to prepare the salad ingredients and dressing ahead of time; when you're ready to serve, just pop the tofu in the broiler, arrange the greens, and voilà!

If sugar snap peas are not available, use snow peas instead. If you don't have mirin and rice vinegar on hand, substitute 2 teaspoons of sugar and 1½ tablespoons of white vinegar. If you don't have mirin, add 1 teaspoon of sugar and increase the rice vinegar to 2 tablespoons. If you don't have rice vinegar, increase the mirin to 2 tablespoons and add 1 tablespoon of white vinegar.

SERVES 2
TOTAL TIME: 45 TO 60 MINUTES

PER 20-OUNCE SERVING: 563 CALORIES, 27 G PROTEIN, 42.2 G FAT, 28.3 G CARBOHYDRATES, 5.1 G SATURATED FATTY ACIDS, 0 MG CHOLESTEROL, 591 MG SODIUM, 9.7 G TOTAL DIETARY FIBER

DRESSING

1 tablespoon grated fresh ginger root
¼ teaspoon Chinese chili paste with garlic (page 359)
1 tablespoon soy sauce
2 tablespoons dark sesame oil
1½ teaspoons light miso
1½ tablespoons mirin
1½ tablespoons rice vinegar
3 tablespoons finely ground walnuts (about ½ cup walnut halves)
1 tablespoon water

1 cake of firm tofu, pressed (12 to 16 ounces)*
2 cups sugar snap peas, stem ends and strings removed (about 8 ounces)
6 cups salad greens, such as mesclun, baby lettuce, young spinach, or Asian mustard greens, loosely packed

finely diced red or yellow bell peppers
finely slivered red cabbage

Sandwich the tofu between two plates and rest a weight on the top plate. Press for about 15 minutes while you prepare the dressing; then drain the expressed liquid from the bottom plate.

Whisk together all of the dressing ingredients in a bowl to form a smooth paste and set aside.

Cut the pressed tofu horizontally into ½-inch-thick slices. Stack the slices and then either cut them into ½-inch-wide strips or slice through both diagonals to form bite-sized triangles. Spread ⅓ of the dressing on a nonreactive baking sheet or broiler pan. Arrange the tofu pieces close together in a single layer on top of the dressing and spread ⅓ of the dressing on top of the tofu. Set aside for at least 15 minutes.

Preheat the broiler. Broil the tofu for 5 to 15 minutes, until the tops are firm and browned. Using a metal spatula, carefully turn them over and broil the other side for another 5 to 15 minutes, until browned. Meanwhile, steam or boil the sugar snaps until crisp-tender, 4 to 5 minutes. Drain and let cool.

In a large salad bowl or on individual salad plates, arrange a bed of greens and top with the sugar snaps, the warm tofu, and the remaining dressing. Sprinkle on the peppers and red cabbage and serve at once.

MENU IDEAS Miso Noodle Soup (page 89) ✳ **Chinese Velvet Corn Soup (page 116)** ✳ **Ozoni (page 48)** ✳ **Faux Pho (page 34)** ✳ **Parsnip Pear Soup (page 49)**

Bulghur Grape Salad

The sweetness of grapes, the crunchy bite of walnuts, and the fragrance of cumin and coriander make a wonderfully refreshing salad. It's a great pick-me-up on a hot summer day, and it has a natural place in autumn menus as well. Try serving it on a bed of spring mix or bitter greens, or pair it with one of the salads in our menu suggestions for an enjoyable salad combo plate.

SERVES 6 TO 8
PREPARATION TIME:
 15 TO 20 MINUTES
CHILLING TIME:
 ABOUT 30 MINUTES

PER 8.75-OUNCE SERVING: 436 CALORIES, 10.3 G PROTEIN, 25.6 G FAT, 49.2 G CARBOHYDRATES, 2.7 G SATURATED FATTY ACIDS, 0 MG CHOLESTEROL, 311 MG SODIUM, 10.7 G TOTAL DIETARY FIBER

2 cups raw bulghur
2½ cups boiling water
1 cucumber
1 red bell pepper
1 cup minced red onions
2 cups walnut halves (8 ounces)
2 cups rinsed and stemmed seedless red grapes (12 ounces)

DRESSING
¼ cup extra-virgin olive oil
¼ cup fresh lemon juice
2 teaspoons ground cumin
2 teaspoons ground coriander
1 teaspoon salt
1 teaspoon coarsely ground black pepper

sharp-tasting sprouts, such as radish sprouts
fresh mint leaves

Place the bulghur in a heatproof bowl, pour the boiling water over it, cover, and set aside to soak for 15 to 20 minutes.

While the bulghur soaks, peel the cucumber, cut it lengthwise into halves, and scoop out the seeds with a spoon. Cut each half lengthwise again and then slice all 4 long strips crosswise into thin bite-sized pieces. Stem, seed, and chop the bell pepper. Place the cucumbers, peppers, and minced red onions into a serving bowl and set aside.

Toast the walnuts in a single layer on an unoiled baking tray in a toaster oven at 350° for about 5 minutes, until fragrant. Let them cool slightly and coarsely chop. Cut each grape into halves. Add the walnuts and grapes to the serving bowl. In a small bowl, whisk together all of the dressing ingredients.

When the bulghur has softened, fluff it with a fork and refrigerate it, uncovered, until cooled to at least room temperature. Add the cooled bulghur to the serving bowl, pour on the dressing, and toss well.

Serve topped with sprouts and/or mint.

DAILY SPECIAL

MENU IDEAS **Tunisian Pumpkin Soup (page 56)** ✳ **Egyptian Red Lentil Soup (page 76)** ✳ **Middle Eastern Chickpea Soup (page 88)** ✳ **Indian Roasted Eggplant Soup (page 40)** ✳ **Bean & Radicchio Salad (page 249)** ✳ **North African Roasted Cauliflower (page 279)** ✳ **Greek Chickpea Salad (page 277)**

Chef Salad à la Moosewood

At Moosewood, this big, beautiful, whole-meal salad is an enduring crowd pleaser. You could choose another dressing for it, of course, but our favorite is Best Blue Cheese Dressing.

SERVES 4 TO 6
TOTAL TIME: 35 MINUTES,
  INCLUDING DRESSING

PER 7.75-OUNCE SERVING (WITHOUT DRESSING): 110 CALORIES, 5.3 G PROTEIN, 8.1 G FAT, 5.1 G CARBOHYDRATES, 1.9 G SATURATED FATTY ACIDS, 125 MG CHOLESTEROL, 259 MG SODIUM, 1.6 G TOTAL DIETARY FIBER

1½ cups sliced raw mushrooms
1 tablespoon canola or other vegetable oil
1 tablespoon olive oil
1 tablespoon cider vinegar
½ teaspoon salt
dash of ground black pepper
5 ounces fresh spinach, stemmed, rinsed, and patted dry
1 cucumber
1 large tomato
1 green bell pepper
½ small red onion (optional)
3 hard-boiled eggs

seasoned croutons
crumbled blue cheese (optional)
Best Blue Cheese Dressing (page 318)*

Try with other dressings such as our Versatile Vinaigrette (page 325), Russian dressing, or Zesty Feta Garlic Dressing (page 326). Several of our Moosewood salad dressings may be available in your local markets.

Place the sliced mushrooms in a bowl, sprinkle them with the oils, vinegar, salt, and pepper, and toss well to coat evenly. Set aside.

Place the spinach in a wide salad bowl. Peel and slice the cucumber and cut the tomato into 10 or 12 wedges. Remove the stem and seeds of the bell pepper and slice it crosswise into thin rings.

Arrange the cucumbers, tomatoes, and bell peppers on top of the spinach. If using red onion, peel it, thinly slice it crosswise, separate it into rings, and sprinkle the rings on the salad. Peel and slice the eggs and decorate the edges of the salad with them. Mound the marinated mushrooms in the middle.

Top the salad with seasoned croutons and sprinkle on a little crumbled blue cheese, if you like. Pass the dressing at the table.

MENU IDEAS **Creamy Herbed Potato Soup (page 122)** ✳ **Potage Celeste (page 130)** ✳ **Parsnip Pear Soup (page 49)** ✳ **Creamy Tomato Soup (page 125)** ✳ **Bourride (page 164)** ✳ **chilled Cherry Berry Beet Soup (page 143)** ✳ **chilled Raspberry Soup (page 157)**

Classic Sichuan Noodles

These noodles are perfect for picnics and lunch boxes. (We think of them as an adult version of the unsurpassed peanut butter sandwich for kids.) The peanut dressing is also great on vegetables, grains, and fish.

At Moosewood, we use these noodles for one of our most popular composed salad plates: Sichuan Noodles with Marinated Broccoli & Carrots (page 275) and Baked Seasoned Tofu (page 336). To create this salad plate in just over an hour, prepare the noodles while the tofu is pressing; then steam and marinate the broccoli and carrots while the pressed tofu bakes.

For a simpler presentation, serve the noodles on a bed of lettuce, or pair them with steamed or sautéed spinach dressed with a little soy sauce and sugar.

SERVES 4
TOTAL TIME: 20 MINUTES

PER 10.5-OUNCE SERVING: 469 CALO-
RIES, 18.7 G PROTEIN, 23.8 G FAT, 50.1 G
CARBOHYDRATES, 4.2 G SATURATED
FATTY ACIDS, 49 MG CHOLESTEROL,
780 MG SODIUM, 5.3 G TOTAL DIETARY
FIBER

DRESSING
½ cup natural peanut butter
⅓ cup warm water
3 tablespoons soy sauce
3 tablespoons rice vinegar
1 tablespoon dark sesame oil
1½ teaspoons Chinese chili paste (page 359), or to taste

½ pound linguine
2 cups mung bean sprouts

1 cucumber, peeled, seeded, and julienned
½ cup chopped scallions
2 tablespoons toasted sesame seeds*

Toast a single layer of sesame seeds on an unoiled baking tray in a 350° oven for 2 to 3 minutes, until fragrant and golden brown.

Bring 2 quarts of water to a boil in a pot. Meanwhile, whisk together all of the dressing ingredients in a bowl and set aside.

Break the uncooked linguine in half and gently ease it into the boiling water. Cook the noodles for about 6 minutes, until tender, stirring occasionally. Drain the noodles, return them to the pot, and toss with the sprouts and the dressing. Transfer to a serving bowl or platter.

Decorate with cucumber strips, scallions, and sesame seeds or serve the garnishes separately at the table.

Note If Sichuan Noodles are made in advance, their flavor and sauciness may diminish as the noodles absorb the dressing. To revive creaminess, stir in about 2 tablespoons of water, and add vinegar and Chinese chili paste to taste.

MENU IDEAS **Asian Bean Curd Soup (page 64)** ✳ **Spicy Tofu & Greens Soup (page 92)** ✳ **chilled Gingered Plum Soup (page 152)** ✳ **Tomato Egg Drop Soup (page 133)** ✳ **chilled Fragrant Lemongrass Fruit Soup (page 150)** ✳ **Hot & Sour Shrimp Soup (page 168)**

Curried Rice Salad

Basmati rice is prized for its delightful fragrance and nutty flavor. We've chosen brown basmati rice for this salad because it not only offers the nutritional benefits of a whole grain but also absorbs flavors more readily and stays moister than white basmati. Here it's combined with aromatic spices, crunchy vegetables, and apples to create a very satisfying dish.

Because this salad is complex, match it with a smooth puréed soup for a Daily Special. It is good served at room temperature or chilled.

Finely chopped mango chutney can replace the sugar or honey in the dressing, if desired.

SERVES 4 TO 6
PREPARATION TIME: 20 MINUTES
COOKING TIME: 40 MINUTES
COOLING TIME: 15 MINUTES

PER 9-OUNCE SERVING: 280 CALORIES, 3.9 G PROTEIN, 10.9 G FAT, 44.9 G CARBO-HYDRATES, 2.7 G SATURATED FATTY ACIDS, 0 MG CHOLESTEROL, 326 MG SODIUM, 3.7 G TOTAL DIETARY FIBER

RICE
1 cup raw brown basmati rice
½ teaspoon turmeric
½ teaspoon ground cinnamon
¼ teaspoon salt
2 cups water

VEGETABLES
1⅔ cups diced tomatoes
1 cup diced celery
1 cup diced red or green bell peppers
1 cup diced apples
½ cup currants or raisins

DRESSING
¼ cup canola or other vegetable oil
¼ cup fresh lemon juice
1 tablespoon packed brown sugar or mild honey
1 tablespoon grated fresh ginger root
1½ teaspoons ground cumin
1 teaspoon curry powder
½ teaspoon ground cinnamon
½ teaspoon ground coriander
¼ teaspoon ground cardamom
½ teaspoon salt
pinch of cayenne

plain nonfat yogurt
toasted chopped cashews
peeled and cubed mango (page 367) (optional)

In a small saucepan, combine the rice with the turmeric, cinnamon, salt, and 2 cups of water. Cover, bring to a boil, lower the heat, and simmer very gently for about 40 minutes, until the rice is tender.

Meanwhile, combine the tomatoes, celery, peppers, apples, and currants or raisins in a large bowl. Whisk together all of the dressing ingredients in a small bowl and pour it over the vegetables and fruit.

Cool the cooked rice for 15 minutes; then toss it into the vegetables. Top each serving with yogurt and cashews, and mango, if desired.

DAILY SPECIAL

MENU IDEAS **Indian Roasted Eggplant Soup (page 40)** ✳ **Jamaican Tomato Soup (page 41)** ✳ **Parsnip Pear Soup (page 49)** ✳ **Tomato Rasam (page 96)** ✳ **Cream of Spinach Soup (page 120)** ✳ **Pineapple Passion (page 265)**

Eastern European Kasha & Mushrooms

Kasha, a staple of Eastern Europe, is actually the protein-packed seed of the buckwheat plant. The seed is roasted and possesses a nutty flavor. You will find kasha in health food stores or with other Jewish foods in supermarkets. Be sure to purchase roasted kasha in a medium or coarse grain.

This substantial salad with its mustardy dressing pairs nicely with a light soup with some sweetness or with a beet salad for a very pretty combo plate.

SERVES 6
TOTAL TIME: 40 MINUTES

PER 13.5-OUNCE SERVING: 413 CALORIES, 11.7 G PROTEIN, 17.8 G FAT, 54.7 G CARBOHYDRATES, 4.5 G SATURATED FATTY ACIDS, 44 MG CHOLESTEROL, 426 MG SODIUM, 6.8 G TOTAL DIETARY FIBER

2 tablespoons canola or other vegetable oil
1 large onion, chopped (about 2 cups)
2 cups water or vegetable stock*
1 egg, lightly beaten
1 cup medium- or coarse-grained raw kasha (buckwheat groats)
4 quarts water
4 cups sliced mushrooms (¾ pound)
3 tablespoons chopped fresh dill (1 tablespoon dried)
½ teaspoon salt
½ to 1 teaspoon freshly ground black pepper
4 cups cauliflower florets (about ½ large cauliflower)
8 ounces farfalle (butterfly pasta)

DRESSING
¼ cup canola or other vegetable oil
¼ cup cider vinegar
1 tablespoon Dijon mustard
1 tablespoon chopped fresh marjoram (1 teaspoon dried)
¼ teaspoon salt

chopped fresh parsley, minced chives, or fresh dill sprigs
plain nonfat yogurt or sour cream (optional)

* Dark Vegetable Stock (page 18) is particularly nice in this dish.

Warm 1 tablespoon of the oil in a medium skillet. Add the onions and sauté on medium heat for about 5 minutes, until they begin to soften. In a separate pot, bring the water or stock to a boil. In a small bowl, combine the egg and kasha. When the onions are soft, add the kasha mixture to the skillet and mix well. Continue to stir until the egg-coated kasha becomes dry. Carefully pour the boiling water or stock into the skillet, cover, and simmer for about 15 minutes, until all of the water is absorbed.

While the kasha cooks, bring 4 quarts of water to a boil in a large covered pot. Meanwhile, warm the remaining tablespoon of oil in a separate skillet, add the mushrooms, dill, salt, and pepper, and sauté until tender, about 5 minutes. Remove the skillet from the heat and set aside.

When the water boils, add the cauliflower florets, cover, and simmer for about 5 minutes, until tender. Remove the florets with a slotted spoon or skimmer and place in a large serving bowl. Return the water to a boil, add the pasta, and cook for 8 to 10 minutes, until al dente. Drain well. Add the pasta and the sautéed mushrooms to the cauliflower in the serving bowl. When the kasha is cooked, stir it in and mix well.

Whisk together all of the dressing ingredients, pour over the salad, and toss lightly. Garnish with parsley, chives, or dill sprigs. Serve hot or at room temperature topped with a dollop of yogurt or sour cream, if desired.

MENU IDEAS **Shchi (page 53)** ✳ **Composed Beet Salad (page 254)** ✳ **Lobio (page 274)** ✳ **Cherries Royale (page 265)** ✳ **Parsnip Pear Soup (page 49)** ✳ **chilled Cherry Almond Soup (page 142)** ✳ **chilled Gingered Plum Soup (page 152)**

Farfalle e Fagiole Salad

The pairing of beans and pasta has its origins in the simple home cooking of southern Europe. For a more complex flavor, we have added fresh oregano, sliced artichokes, and savory bits of sun-dried tomatoes to this salad.

SERVES 4 TO 6
TOTAL TIME: 40 MINUTES
CHILLING TIME (OPTIONAL):
  30 MINUTES

PER 13-OUNCE SERVING: 427 CALORIES, 16.2 G PROTEIN, 11.9 G FAT, 71.5 G CAR-BOHYDRATES, 1.6 G SATURATED FATTY ACIDS, 0 MG CHOLESTEROL, 1105 MG SODIUM, 14.1 G TOTAL DIETARY FIBER

3 cups chunky pasta, such as farfalle (butterfly), shells, or spirals (about 8 ounces)
16 sun-dried tomatoes (not oil-packed)
1 cup boiling water
2 cups julienned zucchini
¼ cup extra-virgin olive oil
¼ cup fresh lemon juice
1 tablespoon chopped fresh oregano (½ teaspoon dried)
⅓ cup minced fresh parsley
4 garlic cloves, minced or pressed
1½ cups halved small cherry tomatoes
1½ cups quartered artichoke hearts (9-ounce frozen package or 15-ounce can, drained)
1½ cups cooked cannellini or other white beans (15-ounce can, drained and lightly rinsed)
salt and ground black pepper to taste

Bring a large pot of water to a boil and cook the pasta until al dente.

Meanwhile, place the sun-dried tomatoes in a nonreactive heat-proof bowl, pour on the boiling water, cover, and set aside. Steam the zucchini until tender but still crisp, about 2 minutes. Drain it thoroughly and set it aside.

In a large serving bowl, whisk together the olive oil, lemon juice, oregano, parsley, and garlic to make a dressing. When the pasta is ready, drain it, briefly rinse with cool water, and drain again. Transfer the pasta to the serving bowl and toss it with the dressing. Drain and finely chop the softened sun-dried tomatoes and gently stir them into the pasta. Add the steamed zucchini, cherry tomatoes, artichoke hearts, and cannellini and toss well. Add salt and pepper to taste.

Serve at room temperature or chill for at least 30 minutes and serve cold.

Variation   This salad can be made more substantial by adding a topping of grated feta or Parmesan cheese.

MENU IDEAS Cream of Spinach Soup (page 120) ✳ **chilled Peach Soup (page 156)** ✳ **Creamy Herbed Carrot Soup (page 121)** ✳ **Classic Tomato Garlic Soup (page 30)**

Fattoush

All throughout the Mediterranean, simple bread salads are popular summer staples: Fattoush is one from Syria and Lebanon that's made with pita bread. In this recipe you can use fresh or dried pita since it is toasted until crisp.

Fattoush is characteristically flavored with tangy crushed sumac, which can be found in Middle Eastern groceries and in the spice section of well-stocked supermarkets. If you can't find sumac, increase the tartness with more lemon juice. Be sure to use tomatoes that are ripe and juicy, and olive oil that is green and fragrant. As the salad sits, the pita will swell as it soaks up the dressing, which traditionalists adore; we think Fattoush is best while the bread is crisp.

SERVES 6
TOTAL TIME: 20 MINUTES

PER 6.5-OUNCE SERVING: 175 CALORIES, 3.7 G PROTEIN, 10.5 G FAT, 19.5 G CARBOHYDRATES, 1.3 G SATURATED FATTY ACIDS, 0 MG CHOLESTEROL, 145 MG SODIUM, 2.3 G TOTAL DIETARY FIBER

2 whole wheat pita breads (about 6 inches across)
3 medium tomatoes, cut into ½-inch cubes (about 3 cups)
1 large cucumber, peeled, seeded, and cut into ½-inch cubes
6 to 8 scallions, thinly sliced
1 green, red, or yellow bell pepper, seeded and cut into ½-inch cubes
½ cup chopped fresh parsley
2 tablespoons chopped fresh mint (2 teaspoons dried) (optional)
2 garlic cloves, minced or pressed
¼ cup extra-virgin olive oil
¼ cup fresh lemon juice
1 tablespoon ground powdered or crushed sumac (optional)
salt and freshly ground black pepper to taste

Preheat the oven or toaster oven to 375°. Tear the pita into 1-inch pieces, place on a tray in a single layer, and bake for 5 to 10 minutes, until dry and crisp. Set aside to cool.

In a large bowl, combine the tomatoes, cucumbers, scallions, bell peppers, parsley, and, if using, the mint. Whisk together the garlic, olive oil, lemon juice, and sumac, if desired, and pour over the vegetables. Season to taste with salt and pepper. Add the pita bread, toss the salad, and serve immediately.

Variations   There are many versions of Fattoush. The proportions of ingredients can be freely adjusted to make the salad a little different each time. Possible additions are torn romaine leaves, sliced radishes, toasted sesame seeds, chopped fresh cilantro, the seeds and juice of a pomegranate, chickpeas, thyme or cumin, and crumbled feta cheese.

MENU IDEAS **Tunisian Pumpkin Soup (page 56)** ✳ **Middle Eastern Chickpea Soup (page 88)** ✳ **Cream of Spinach Soup (page 120)** ✳ **Syrian Beet Salad (page 291)** ✳ **Bean & Radicchio Salad (page 249)** ✳ **Mediterranean Orange & Olive Salad (page 276)**

French Barley Salad

Barley is the perfect grain for a hearty salad because it's chewy and readily absorbs flavors. It takes about 40 minutes to become tender, so there's plenty of time to prepare the rest of the ingredients while it cooks.

Here we combine the barley with marinated mushrooms, sweet peppers, carrots, and crunchy green beans. Buttery walnuts round out the flavors and textures. For beautiful, bright green beans, mix them into the salad just before serving.

You might want to double the recipe, keeping the walnuts and green beans separate, since this colorful salad holds up well for 2 or 3 days. It matches quite pleasantly with any number of dishes.

SERVES 4
PREPARATION TIME: 50 MINUTES
SITTING TIME: 30 MINUTES

PER 10.5-OUNCE SERVING: 463 CALORIES, 8 G PROTEIN, 28.7 G FAT, 49.2 G CARBOHYDRATES, 4.3 G SATURATED FATTY ACIDS, 5 MG CHOLESTEROL, 655 MG SODIUM, 8.8 G TOTAL DIETARY FIBER

½ cup raw pearled barley
2 cups water

DRESSING
¼ cup fresh lemon juice
¼ cup olive oil
2 garlic cloves, minced or pressed
½ teaspoon Dijon mustard
1 tablespoon chopped fresh dill (1½ teaspoons dried)
1 teaspoon salt
freshly ground black pepper to taste

1 cup halved or quartered mushrooms
1 cup peeled and diced carrots
1 cup cut green beans, trimmed and halved
1 cup thinly sliced red or yellow bell peppers
½ cup chopped fresh parsley
2 teaspoons butter
⅔ cup coarsely chopped walnuts

Using a strainer, rinse the barley and drain. In a small heavy skillet on low heat, roast the barley until fragrant and beginning to brown. Place the barley and water in a small saucepan, cover, and bring to a simmer. Cook on low heat until most of the water has been absorbed and the barley is soft, about 40 minutes.

While the barley cooks, whisk together all of the dressing ingredients. In a separate bowl, pour half of the dressing over the mushrooms and set aside. Blanch the carrots in boiling water for about 1 minute. Transfer with a slotted spoon to a large serving bowl. Blanch the green beans for 3 to 4 minutes. Drain and set aside to cool. Stir the bell peppers and parsley and marinated mushrooms into the bowl of carrots.

In a skillet, heat the butter. When it sizzles, sauté the walnuts until they are coated and the butter begins to brown. Remove from the heat.

When the barley is tender, drain it in a colander. Add the drained barley and the remaining dressing to the serving bowl and mix well. Allow the salad to sit for at least 30 minutes before serving. Just before serving, gently toss the green beans and walnuts into the salad.

MENU IDEAS **Parsnip Pear Soup (page 49)** * **Back to Your Roots Soup (page 113)** * **Cream of Spinach Soup (page 120)** * **Creamy Tomato Soup (page 125)** * **Tomato Flowers (page 236)** * **Asparagus Vinaigrette (page 248)**

French Pasta Salad

The rich flavors of toasted hazelnuts and chèvre are in heady contrast to the robust Dijon vinaigrette. This is a simple yet elegant salad of pasta studded with bright green beans or asparagus, roasted red peppers, and aromatic herbs. Crumbled feta, Roquefort, freshly grated Parmesan, or Jarlsberg can be used in place of the chèvre, although goat cheese is especially nice with the hazelnuts.

If you're in a hurry, try replacing the vinaigrette with one of our bottled Moosewood dressings. We think our Versatile Vinaigrette would be great.

SERVES 6
TOTAL TIME: 30 MINUTES

PER 13-OUNCE SERVING: 509 CALORIES, 14.8 G PROTEIN, 18.6 G FAT, 72.6 G CARBOHYDRATES, 3.3 G SATURATED FATTY ACIDS, 8 MG CHOLESTEROL, 541 MG SODIUM, 6.1 G TOTAL DIETARY FIBER

1 pound penne or ziti
3 cups green beans, stemmed and cut in half crosswise

VINAIGRETTE DRESSING
2 teaspoons minced fresh tarragon
2 teaspoons minced fresh basil
1 large shallot, minced
¼ cup extra-virgin olive oil or other vegetable oil
¼ cup red wine vinegar
1 tablespoon Dijon mustard
1 teaspoon salt
¼ teaspoon coarsely ground black pepper

⅔ cup chopped pimientos or roasted red peppers
2 tablespoons finely chopped fresh parsley
⅓ cup toasted hazelnuts, finely chopped*
1 tablespoon drained capers (optional)
½ cup chèvre or feta cheese, crumbled (about ¼ pound)**

* *Toast the nuts for about 10 minutes in a 325° oven, then rub them briskly with a towel to remove the skins.*
** *Chèvre is a flavorful white goat cheese found in the cheese section of most well-stocked supermarkets.*

In a large pot of boiling water, cook the pasta for about 8 minutes, until al dente. Drain the pasta in a colander, rinse well with cool water, and set aside to drain again.

Meanwhile, blanch the green beans in boiling water to cover for about 3 minutes, or until just tender. Drain them and set aside. Whisk together the vinaigrette ingredients in a small bowl.

Combine the pasta, green beans, and pimientos or roasted red peppers in a large serving bowl and toss with the dressing. Sprinkle on the parsley, hazelnuts, and, if using, the capers and arrange the crumbled cheese around the outer edge of the salad.

Serve at room temperature or slightly chilled (see Note).

Note Olive oil congeals when refrigerated. If preparing this salad ahead of time, let it return nearly to room temperature before serving.

Variation If you prefer, use 3 cups of asparagus cut into 1½-inch pieces in place of the green beans.

MENU IDEAS **Everyday Split Pea Soup (page 77)** ✳ **Classic Tomato Garlic Soup (page 30)** ✳ **Butternut Squash Soup with Sizzled Sage (page 28)** ✳ **Cream of Mushroom Soup (page 119)** ✳ **chilled Peach Soup (page 156)**

Gado Gado

In Indonesia, the spicy peanut sauce gado gado is often served with a large selection of fresh vegetables, both raw and steamed, and accompanied by seasoned tempeh, baked or marinated tofu, or hard-boiled eggs. We present this dish on fresh spinach, but you can omit the potatoes and serve it on a bed of rice. Pay attention to the color and texture of different vegetable combinations and offer a range of both.

We steam all of the vegetables in one large pot, beginning with those that take longest to cook. This method lets you drain everything all at once at the end. If you don't have a pot large enough to steam all of the vegetables, use two pots. The most important thing is to cook the vegetables just until tender and still brightly colored—so test them as you go.

SERVES 6
TOTAL TIME: 45 MINUTES

PER 18-OUNCE SERVING: 642 CALORIES, 27.5 G PROTEIN, 42.4 G FAT, 49.6 G CARBOHYDRATES, 8.5 G SATURATED FATTY ACIDS, 83 MG CHOLESTEROL, 951 MG SODIUM, 11.2 G TOTAL DIETARY FIBER

SAUCE

2 teaspoons canola or other vegetable oil
2 cups chopped onions
¼ teaspoon cayenne or 1 minced fresh green chile, more to taste
3 garlic cloves, minced or pressed
1 tablespoon grated fresh ginger root
2 cups natural peanut butter*
3 cups water, vegetable stock, or a combination**
¼ cup cider vinegar
1 tablespoon soy sauce
¾ teaspoon salt
1 tablespoon brown sugar, packed (optional)**
2 tablespoons fresh lime juice

VEGETABLES

1 potato, cut into ¼- to ½-inch-thick slices (large ones cut into semicircles)
1 sweet potato, peeled and cut into ¼- to ½-inch-thick slices
½ cup carrots, peeled and sliced on the diagonal
2 cups bite-sized broccoli florets
3 cups bite-sized cauliflower florets
3 or 4 large cabbage leaves, cut into 1 x 3-inch strips
1 green or red bell pepper, sliced into strips
½ cup mung bean sprouts

5 ounces spinach, stemmed, rinsed, and drained
1 tomato, cut into wedges
2 hard-boiled eggs, quartered

* *By natural peanut butter, we mean unhomogenized peanut butter with no sweeteners, preservatives, or stabilizers.*
** *You may wish to replace 1 cup of the water and/or stock with apple juice; since the juice adds more sweetness, omit the brown sugar.*

Combine the oil and onions in a soup pot and sauté on medium-high heat for 5 minutes, stirring frequently, until softened. Add the cayenne or chile, garlic, and ginger root, cover, and continue to cook for about 10 more minutes, stirring occasionally.

In a bowl (see Note), mash and blend the peanut butter with about a cup of the water or stock. Gradually add the rest of the liquid, stirring until smooth. Add the blended mixture to the sautéed onions. Stir in the vinegar, soy sauce, salt, and brown sugar, if using. Cover and simmer the sauce on low heat for about 15 minutes, stirring now and then to prevent sticking.

Meanwhile, bring several inches of water to a boil in a pot with a tight-fitting lid. When the water is boiling, lower the heat to a medium simmer, add the potato and sweet potato slices, and cover. After 7 minutes, add the carrots. Wait about 3 minutes and add the broccoli and cauliflower. After 5 minutes, add the cabbage and peppers and steam for about 5 more minutes, until everything is crisp-tender. Add the mung sprouts and steam for 1 more minute. Drain all of the vegetables thoroughly in a large colander and set aside to cool for several minutes.

Stir the lime juice into the finished sauce and transfer to a serving bowl with a small ladle to pass at the table. On a large platter, make a bed of spinach, arrange the steamed vegetables on it, and finish with alternating tomato and hard-boiled egg wedges placed decoratively around the edge of the platter. Serve at room temperature.

Note If you prefer, combine the peanut butter and the water and/or stock in a blender and purée until smooth.

DAILY SPECIAL ∽

MENU IDEAS **Carambola, Grapes & Apples (page 265)** ✳ **Baked Seasoned Tofu (page 336)** ✳ **Spiced Paneer (page 351)** ✳ **chilled Mango Soup (page 154)** ✳ **chilled Peach Soup (page 156)** ✳ **chilled Fragrant Lemongrass Fruit Soup (page 150)** ✳ **Roasted Red Pepper Coconut Soup (page 52)** ✳ **Pineapple Passion (page 265)**

Greek Pasta Salad

Chickpeas, pasta, and cheese make this a protein-rich salad, as healthful as it is tasty and attractive. The vegetables are gently sautéed with garlic and the chickpeas are lightly marinated before tossing with the cooked pasta. Everything is brightly seasoned with our favorite Greek classics: olive oil, oregano, fennel, lemon, kalamata olives, and feta cheese.

For the prettiest salad, cut the vegetables to match the size of the chickpeas and pasta.

SERVES 6 TO 8
TOTAL TIME: 45 MINUTES
CHILLING TIME (OPTIONAL):
  30 MINUTES

PER 8-OUNCE SERVING: 275 CALORIES, 9.1 G PROTEIN, 10 G FAT, 38.8 G CARBO-HYDRATES, 3 G SATURATED FATTY ACIDS, 13 MG CHOLESTEROL, 569 MG SODIUM, 4.3 G TOTAL DIETARY FIBER

MARINADE
1 tablespoon olive oil
1 tablespoon fresh lemon juice
1 teaspoon ground fennel seeds
1 teaspoon dried oregano
¼ teaspoon salt
dash of ground black pepper

1½ cups cooked chickpeas (15-ounce can, drained)
1 tablespoon olive oil
2 tablespoons minced or pressed garlic
½ cup diced celery
1 red bell pepper, seeded and diced
1½ cups diced tomatoes
½ cup finely chopped scallions
½ pound pasta, such as tubetti, orzo, macaroni, or small shells
12 pitted chopped kalamata olives*
¼ cup chopped fresh parsley
2 tablespoons fresh lemon juice

1 cup grated feta cheese

To pit, slice lengthwise all the way around each olive and twist the halves apart, or place the flat side of a broad-bladed knife on the olive and whack it sharply with the heel of your other hand to break open the olive.

Whisk together all of the marinade ingredients in a medium bowl. Add the chickpeas and set aside. Bring a large, covered pot of water to a boil.

Meanwhile, warm the oil in a nonreactive saucepan and gently sauté the garlic until just golden, a minute or two. Add the celery, bell peppers, and tomatoes and continue to cook, stirring occasionally, for about 10 minutes. Stir in the scallions and marinated chickpeas and cook for about 3 minutes.

When the water boils, cook the pasta until al dente. Drain in a colander, rinse under cool water, and drain again. Transfer the pasta to a large serving bowl and add the sautéed vegetables and the olives, parsley, and lemon juice. Toss well.

Serve warm or chilled, topping each serving with feta cheese.

DAILY SPECIAL

MENU IDEAS **Grecian Isle Stew (page 39)** ✻ **Artichoke Avgolemono (page 112)** ✻ **Classic Tomato Garlic Soup (page 30)** ✻ **Tunisian Carrot Salad (page 293)** ✻ **Oranges Exotic (page 265)**

Harvest Rice Salad

Looking for something new to serve for Thanksgiving or at a winter holiday meal? This rice salad combines the fruits and grains from both northern and southern climes into a flavorful dish with the virtues of fibrous, whole-grained goodness and unrefined sweetness.

Dried cranberries, also called craisins, are often *not* in the supermarket's baking section next to the raisins, where you might expect them. Check in the bulk section and in the produce aisle near other dried fruits and vegetables.

At Moosewood, we would choose an earthy salad or a hearty soup to complement this appealing dish.

SERVES 6
PREPARATION TIME: 55 MINUTES
SITTING TIME: 30 MINUTES

PER 10-OUNCE SERVING: 404 CALORIES, 7.1 G PROTEIN, 17.9 G FAT, 58.8 G CARBO-HYDRATES, 2.4 G SATURATED FATTY ACIDS, 0 MG CHOLESTEROL, 408 MG SODIUM, 4.7 G TOTAL DIETARY FIBER

3 cups water
1 cup raw brown basmati rice
½ cup raw wild rice
½ teaspoon salt
1 tablespoon freshly grated orange peel

DRESSING
juice of 1 orange (¼ to ⅓ cup)
2 tablespoons canola or other vegetable oil
3 tablespoons cider vinegar
3 tablespoons orange juice
2 teaspoons chopped fresh rosemary or sage
½ teaspoon salt
⅛ teaspoon ground black pepper, more to taste

1½ cups hot water
1 cup currants, golden raisins, chopped dried pears, or dried cranberries, or a combination
¾ cup pecans
½ cup chopped fresh parsley
½ cup chopped scallions

In a small heavy saucepan with a tight-fitting lid, bring to a boil the water, basmati rice, wild rice, salt, and half of the grated orange peel. When steam escapes, reduce the heat to low, place the pot on a heat diffuser, and simmer until the water is absorbed, about 35 minutes.

Meanwhile, preheat the oven to 325°.

In a small bowl, whisk together the rest of the grated orange peel with all of the dressing ingredients and set aside. In another small bowl, pour the hot water over the dried fruit, cover, and soak for 10 to 15 minutes, until softened. Drain thoroughly.

Spread the pecans on an unoiled baking sheet and toast in the oven for 10 to 15 minutes, until lightly browned. Chop coarsely and set aside.

When the rice is done, place it in a large bowl and cool for 10 minutes. Add the dressing and toss well. Stir in the drained fruit, pecans, parsley, and scallions. Set aside at room temperature for at least 30 minutes to allow the flavors to mingle. Serve at room temperature.

MENU IDEAS **Tunisian Pumpkin Soup (page 56)** ✳ **Autumn Minestrone (page 67)** ✳ **Celery Roquefort Soup (page 115)** ✳ **Creamy Onion & Fontina Soup (page 123)** ✳ **Wilted Spinach & Portabella Mushrooms (page 239)** ✳ **Fennel Salad with Blue Cheese (page 260)**

Hijiki Rice Salad

Hijiki, one of the more popular seaweeds, is available in natural food markets and Asian groceries. It is rather expensive, but just a small amount adds a delicious briny taste, and its slender black strands make a truly handsome presentation. Macrobiotics around here kick up their flip-flops with joy at this healthful, New Age Japanese salad. It's really good.

Warm rice absorbs the flavor of the dressing most readily, so put on a fresh pot of rice before you begin to prepare the ingredients, or reheat leftover rice.

The Carrot Dressing is also great on salad greens or steamed vegetables.

SERVES 8
PREPARATION TIME: 30 MINUTES
COOKING TIME: 25 TO 30 MINUTES

PER 10.5-OUNCE SERVING: 249 CALORIES, 9.2 G PROTEIN, 9.1 G FAT, 35.2 G CARBOHYDRATES, 1.5 G SATURATED FATTY ACIDS, 0 MG CHOLESTEROL, 497 MG SODIUM, 3 G TOTAL DIETARY FIBER

½ cup dry hijiki seaweed soaked in 1½ cups cool water*
1 cake of firm tofu (about 15 ounces)

TOFU MARINADE
2 tablespoons ketchup or tomato paste
1 tablespoon soy sauce
1 teaspoon Dijon mustard
1 tablespoon hijiki-soaking water

4 cups warm cooked short-grain brown rice**
2 cups finely chopped tomatoes
1 cup peeled and shredded carrots
1 cup minced red onions
1 cup peeled, seeded, and minced cucumber
½ cup peeled and shredded daikon radish
2 tablespoons toasted sesame seeds***

CARROT DRESSING
1 small carrot, peeled and shredded
2 tablespoons mirin
2 tablespoons rice vinegar or cider vinegar
2 to 4 tablespoons soy sauce
1 teaspoon dark sesame oil
1 tablespoon grated fresh ginger root
2 tablespoons peanut or canola oil

* Soak the hijiki for 30 minutes while you prepare the rest of the salad ingredients.
** 2 cups of raw brown rice will yield about 4 cups cooked. Put the rice in a saucepan, add 3 cups of water, cover, and bring to a boil; then lower the heat and simmer for about 40 minutes, until the water is absorbed and the rice is tender but firm.
***Toast a single layer of sesame seeds on an unoiled baking tray in a conventional or toaster oven at 350° for 2 to 3 minutes, until fragrant and golden brown.

Drain the hijiki, reserving a tablespoon of the soaking liquid for the tofu marinade.

Preheat the oven to 400°. Prepare a 9 × 12-inch baking pan with cooking spray or oil.

Cut the tofu into 4 even slices. Stack the slices and cut down through them 3 times in each direction to yield 64 small cubes. In a bowl large enough to hold the tofu, mix together all of the tofu marinade ingredients. Add the tofu cubes to the bowl and toss lightly to coat evenly with the marinade. Transfer the tofu to the prepared baking dish and bake for 25 to 30 minutes, stirring once or twice, until golden but still juicy.

Meanwhile, in a large serving bowl, combine the warm rice with the tomatoes, carrots, red onions, cucumbers, daikon radish, and sesame seeds. Roughly chop the hijiki into shorter strands, add it to the bowl, and set aside.

Combine all of the Carrot Dressing ingredients in a blender, purée until smooth, and set aside.

When the tofu is baked, remove it from the oven and allow it to cool slightly. Add it to the salad with the Carrot Dressing and toss well.

 MENU IDEAS **Potage Celeste (page 130)** ✳ **Cream of Spinach Soup (page 120)** ✳ **chilled Gingered Plum Soup (page 152)** ✳ **chilled Creamy Orange Soup (page 145)** ✳ **Azuki Bean Soup (page 68)**

Indonesian Tahu Goreng

Raw tofu has the marvelous capacity to soak up seasoning. So we marinate it in a light sweet-and-sour sauce with garlic and star anise before frying—and later we incorporate the marinade into the spicy peanut dressing! Fried tofu, dark brown and crisp on the outside and creamy on the inside, is often a favorite even of those who don't consider themselves tofu fans.

Mung sprouts and a bed of lettuce perfectly complement the fried tofu. The lettuce provides a pleasant contrast in texture, and ruby lettuce can add a colorful, bright red accent. The cool, crunchy mung sprouts readily soak up the "hot" peanut dressing. Covered and refrigerated, the dressing will keep for up to 10 days, but it's best served at room temperature.

SERVES 4 TO 6
TOTAL TIME: 45 MINUTES

PER 8.75-OUNCE SERVING: 327 CALORIES, 13.2 G PROTEIN, 24.6 G FAT, 18.4 G CARBOHYDRATES, 5.4 G SATURATED FATTY ACIDS, 0 MG CHOLESTEROL, 469 MG SODIUM, 3.2 G TOTAL DIETARY FIBER

2 cakes of tofu, pressed* and cut into ½-inch cubes (12 ounces each)

MARINADE
3 tablespoons soy sauce
¼ cup fresh lemon or lime juice
¼ cup brown sugar, packed
3 garlic cloves, minced or pressed
¾ teaspoon ground star anise**

3 cups mung bean sprouts (¼ pound)
4 cups shredded lettuce
¼ cup plus 2 tablespoons canola or other vegetable oil
3 tablespoons cider vinegar
2 tablespoons water
¼ cup peanut butter
1 fresh green chile (about 3 inches long), seeded for a milder "hot"
1 teaspoon ground cumin

* *Sandwich the tofu between two plates and rest a weight (a heavy can or book) on the top plate. Press for at least 15 minutes.*
** *Freshly ground star anise adds the brightest flavor, but it is very difficult to grind by hand in a mortar and pestle. If you have a spice grinder (or an electric coffee grinder reserved for spice grinding), it will do the job nicely. If star anise is unavailable, freshly ground anise seeds are also an option, but we prefer the slightly more complex flavor of the star anise.*

In a nonreactive pan or large shallow bowl, spread out the tofu cubes in a single layer. In a blender, whirl the marinade ingredients until smooth. Pour the marinade over the tofu and with a spatula gently turn the cubes in the marinade to coat evenly. Set aside.

Blanch the mung sprouts for about a minute to remove their raw edge—they should still retain some crunchiness. Transfer the sprouts to a colander, run under a gentle stream of cold water, and drain well. Arrange the lettuce in a large serving bowl, top with the mung sprouts, and refrigerate.

Heat ¼ cup of the oil in a 10-inch skillet until very hot but not smoking. With a slotted spoon or spatula, carefully transfer the tofu to the skillet—it may splatter a little at first. Reserve the leftover marinade. Fry the tofu on high heat, uncovered, for about 15 minutes, turning once or twice during the first 10 minutes and stirring almost constantly during the final 5 minutes.

While the tofu fries, make the dressing. In a blender, combine the reserved marinade, the remaining 2 tablespoons of oil, and the vinegar, water, peanut butter, chile, and cumin and purée until smooth. Set aside.

When the tofu is dark brown and crisp on the outside, remove it from the skillet and drain on a double thickness of paper towels. Add the tofu to the bowl of mung sprouts and lettuce. If you don't expect to have any left over, dress the salad just before serving. Otherwise, offer the peanut dressing on the side, since undressed salad will stay crisper when stored.

Variation Replace half or all of the mung bean sprouts with julienned or coarsely shredded cucumbers.

MENU IDEAS **Potage Celeste (page 130)** * **chilled Fragrant Lemongrass Fruit Soup (page 150)** * **chilled Mango Soup (page 154)** * **Indian Green Beans & Red Peppers (page 270)** * **Persian Yogurt Rice Soup (page 129)**

Lentil, Rice & Fruit Salad

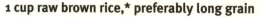

Apples, grapes, and peppers lend their sweet, cool crunchiness to the complementary proteins in this hearty salad. This dish can be prepared quickly with leftover rice and lentils and carried off to a picnic or dish-to-pass. It is best served at room temperature and is delicious topped with crumbled chèvre or grated Fontina or Gruyère cheese and fresh tarragon or parsley sprigs.

SERVES 6 TO 8
TOTAL TIME: 1 HOUR

PER 7-OUNCE SERVING: 288 CALORIES, 5.9 G PROTEIN, 15.2 G FAT, 33.8 G CARBO-HYDRATES, 2.1 G SATURATED FATTY ACIDS, 0 MG CHOLESTEROL, 329 MG SODIUM, 4.6 G TOTAL DIETARY FIBER

1 cup raw brown rice,* preferably long grain
4⅔ cups water
2 bay leaves
2 garlic cloves, minced or pressed
scant ½ teaspoon dried thyme
½ cup dried brown lentils*
1 crisp apple, such as Crispin or Ida Red
2 tablespoons fresh lemon juice
1 cup seedless grapes
1 large red, green, or yellow bell pepper
1 celery stalk (optional)

DRESSING
½ cup olive oil
⅓ cup white balsamic vinegar
4 teaspoons Dijon mustard
4 garlic cloves, minced or pressed
2 tablespoons minced fresh tarragon (2 teaspoons dried)
1 teaspoon salt
½ teaspoon ground black pepper

* To make this salad with leftover rice and/or lentils, use 4 cups of cooked rice, 1½ cups of cooked lentils, and add ½ teaspoon of thyme to the dressing.

In a small, heavy pot with a tight-fitting lid, combine the rice, 1⅔ cups of the water, 1 bay leaf, 1 garlic clove, and ¼ teaspoon of the thyme. Bring to a boil, reduce the heat, cover, and simmer until the rice is tender, about 45 minutes.

Meanwhile, in another pot, cook the lentils in 3 cups of water with the remaining bay leaf, garlic, and thyme. Simmer until just tender, 20 to 30 minutes, adding water if needed. Drain any excess liquid.

While the rice and lentils cook, core and dice the apple, and toss it with lemon juice to prevent discoloration. Cut the grapes into halves. Stem, seed, and dice the bell pepper. Dice the celery, if using.

Whisk together all of the dressing ingredients. Combine the cooked rice and lentils in a serving bowl, remove the bay leaves, and toss with half of the dressing. Set aside to cool for about 10 minutes, and then stir in the fruit and vegetables. Offer the rest of the dressing at the table in a cruet.

MENU IDEAS **Tunisian Carrot Salad (page 293)** ✳ **Honey Mustard Green Beans Vinaigrette (page 269)** ✳ **Chilled Cucumber Yogurt Soup (page 147)** ✳ **Cream of Spinach Soup (page 120)** ✳ **Creamy Onion & Fontina Soup (page 123)** ✳ **Popovers (page 334)**

Louisiana Black-eyed Pea Salad

Make this colorful, spicy, and nutritious salad with the end-of-summer peppers and tomatoes from your garden. Serve it with freshly baked Southern Wheat-free Cornbread (page 335) and sautéed greens such as collards or kale for a Southern combo plate.

SERVES 4 TO 6
PREPARATION TIME: 20 MINUTES
COOKING TIME: 25 MINUTES
MARINATING TIME: 20 MINUTES

PER 8-OUNCE SERVING: 328 CALORIES, 8.9 G PROTEIN, 19.8 G FAT, 31.4 G CARBO-HYDRATES, 2.8 G SATURATED FATTY ACIDS, 0 MG CHOLESTEROL, 451 MG SODIUM, 1.7 G TOTAL DIETARY FIBER

2 cups water
2 ten-ounce packages frozen black-eyed peas

DRESSING
3 tablespoons fresh lemon juice
½ teaspoon Tabasco or other hot pepper sauce, more to taste
1 tablespoon honey or sugar
¼ to ½ teaspoon ground cloves
1 teaspoon salt
½ teaspoon ground black pepper
½ cup olive oil

1 cup diced celery
1 cup diced red bell peppers
½ cup diced red onions
1 cup quartered cherry tomatoes
salt and ground black pepper to taste

sliced scallions (optional)
smoked Cheddar cheese (optional)

In a saucepan, bring the water to a boil and add the black-eyed peas. Cover, return to a boil, reduce the heat, and simmer gently for about 25 minutes, until the peas are tender. Drain and set aside to cool.

Combine all of the dressing ingredients except the oil in a small bowl. In a steady stream, whisk in the olive oil. In a large bowl, combine the black-eyed peas, celery, bell peppers, red onions, and tomatoes. Add the dressing and toss well. Add Tabasco, salt, and black pepper to taste.

Set aside to allow the flavors to marry for at least 20 minutes or preferably for a few hours or overnight. Garnish with scallions and/or smoked Cheddar, if you wish. Serve cold or at room temperature.

DAILY SPECIAL

MENU IDEAS **Jamaican Tomato Soup (page 41)** ✳ **Butternut Squash Soup with Sizzled Sage (page 28)** ✳ **Curried Zucchini Soup (page 126)** ✳ **Catfish Gumbo (page 166)**

North African Couscous Salad

Couscous has a naturally mild taste and the capacity to maintain its light, fluffy texture even when combined with this exotic assortment of colorful delicacies that offer a surprise in every bite. The salad is seasoned with the complex, aromatic spices of North Africa and the zest and juice of orange and lemon—it's almost as intriguing as visiting an old bazaar.

SERVES 4 TO 6
TOTAL TIME: 30 MINUTES

PER 6.5-OUNCE SERVING: 246 CALORIES, 6.6 G PROTEIN, 7.9 G FAT, 39.5 G CARBO-HYDRATES, 1.3 G SATURATED FATTY ACIDS, 0 MG CHOLESTEROL, 543 MG SODIUM, 3.7 G TOTAL DIETARY FIBER

1 cup peeled and diced carrots
¼ cup minced dried apricots
½ teaspoon grated fresh ginger root
1 teaspoon freshly grated lemon peel
1 teaspoon freshly grated orange peel
pinch of saffron
¼ teaspoon ground cumin
¼ teaspoon ground coriander
¼ teaspoon ground cinnamon
½ teaspoon salt
½ cup orange juice
1 tablespoon fresh lemon juice
1 tablespoon canola or other vegetable oil
1½ cups water
½ cup diced red bell peppers
½ cup fresh or frozen green peas
1 cup quick-cooking couscous
¼ cup pitted and chopped kalamata olives (about 8 olives)*

2 tablespoons toasted pine nuts**
1 tablespoon dried currants
fresh mint sprigs

* To pit, slice lengthwise all the way around each olive and twist the halves apart, or place the flat side of a broad-bladed knife on the olive and whack it sharply with the heel of your other hand to break open the olive.

** Toast a single layer of pine nuts on an unoiled baking sheet in an oven or toaster oven at 350° for about 5 minutes, or until they're fragrant and lightly browned.

In a nonreactive saucepan, combine the carrots, apricots, ginger root, lemon peel, orange peel, saffron, cumin, coriander, cinnamon, salt, orange juice, lemon juice, oil, and water. Cover, bring to a boil, reduce the heat, and simmer for about 5 minutes, until the carrots are just tender. Add the bell peppers and continue to cook for 2 minutes.

Remove the saucepan from the heat and add the peas. Stir in the couscous, cover, and set aside for 10 to 15 minutes. Add the chopped olives and fluff the couscous with a fork to break up any lumps.

Serve in a large bowl or on a platter, topped with toasted pine nuts, currants, and mint sprigs.

DAILY SPECIAL

MENU IDEAS Egyptian Red Lentil Soup (page 76) ✳ **chilled August Melon Soup (page 140)** ✳ **Yellow Pepper Purée (page 58)** ✳ **tossed green salad with Luscious Lemon Tahini Dressing (page 322)**

Orzo & Pesto Stuffed Tomatoes

Serve stuffed tomatoes as an easy, yet elegant main dish or side dish. Here they are filled with orzo, a small rice-shaped pasta, that we season with a classic Pesto Genovese. For regal flair, crown them with grated cheese, chopped olives, and fresh herbs.

SERVES 6
TOTAL TIME: 35 MINUTES

PER 11-OUNCE SERVING: 433 CALORIES, 15.8 G PROTEIN, 19.8 G FAT, 50.1 G CAR-BOHYDRATES, 5.2 G SATURATED FATTY ACIDS, 14 MG CHOLESTEROL, 352 MG SODIUM, 3.6 G TOTAL DIETARY FIBER

2 quarts water
1½ cups raw orzo

PESTO GENOVESE
1½ cups fresh basil leaves, packed
2 garlic cloves, minced or pressed
¼ cup pine nuts
½ cup grated Parmesan cheese
¼ cup olive oil
salt and ground black pepper to taste

1 teaspoon olive oil
6 large ripe tomatoes
dash of salt and ground black pepper
⅓ cup tiny cubes of feta or other sharp cheese (optional)

chopped California black olives and/or chopped fresh basil

Bring the water to a boil in a large pot. Add the orzo, stir, lower the heat, cover, and simmer for about 7 minutes, stirring as needed.

While the orzo cooks, combine the basil leaves, garlic, pine nuts, and Parmesan in a food processor (see Note) and whirl until well chopped. Add the oil in a thin stream to make a smooth paste, scraping down the sides a couple of times as needed. Add salt and pepper to taste.

Drain the orzo. Toss it lightly with the teaspoon of olive oil and allow it to cool to room temperature, about 10 minutes.

Meanwhile, cut a hole about 2 inches across in the top of each tomato and remove the core. Scoop out the pulp with a small spoon to leave a ½-inch-thick shell. Lightly sprinkle the inside of each tomato with salt and pepper. When the orzo is at room temperature, mix it with the Pesto Genovese and, if using, the cheese cubes. Stuff each tomato with about a cup of filling.

Decorate with olives and/or basil and serve at room temperature.

Note If using a blender, it may be necessary to chop the basil and pine nuts first and to add the oil all at once before blending.

Variation Use cooked brown rice instead of orzo and season it with Cilantro Lime Pesto (page 337) or Cilantro Peanut Pesto (page 338). Garnish with peas, chopped scallions, slivers of red bell pepper, and/or toasted peanuts.

MENU IDEAS **Bean & Radicchio Salad (page 249)** ✳ **Marinated Mushrooms (page 347)** ✳ **Asparagus Vinaigrette (page 248)** ✳ **Tuscan Bean Soup (page 100)** ✳ **Corn Chowder (page 117)** ✳ **French Roasted Onion Soup (page 37)**

Persian Rice & Pistachio Salad

The cuisine of Persia is alluring and timeless. Aromatic basmati rice is a perfect vehicle for the enticing scents of cinnamon, cardamom, and orange. Sweet currants and the crunch of pistachios and celery make this versatile pilaf a delight for the senses.

Offer it warm as a winter side dish. Or, in summer, serve it chilled or at room temperature, mounded in the hollow of a generous wedge of cool, ripe melon or on a bed of fresh greens garnished with slices of seasonal fruit.

SERVES 4 TO 6
PREPARATION TIME: 15 MINUTES
COOKING TIME: 25 TO 30 MINUTES
COOLING TIME: 20 MINUTES
CHILLING TIME (OPTIONAL):
  30 MINUTES

PER 7.5-OUNCE SERVING: 258 CALORIES, 5.2 G PROTEIN, 10.8 G FAT, 36.7 G CARBO-HYDRATES, 2 G SATURATED FATTY ACIDS, 0 MG CHOLESTEROL, 212 MG SODIUM, 2.8 G TOTAL DIETARY FIBER

1 cup raw white basmati rice*
2 tablespoons canola or other vegetable oil
½ teaspoon ground cinnamon
generous pinch of ground cardamom
pinch of ground black pepper
½ teaspoon salt
1 teaspoon freshly grated orange peel
2 cups water
½ cup currants, chopped raisins, dates, or dried apricots
½ cup coarsely chopped pistachios, toasted**
½ cup minced celery
juice of 1 orange (about ⅓ cup)

 * If you prefer, use brown basmati rice. Just increase the cooking time to 45 minutes; then let stand for 10 minutes with the cover on. The finished salad will have a nuttier flavor and a chewier texture.

** The pistachios can be replaced by toasted chopped almonds. To toast nuts, spread them in a single layer on an unoiled baking sheet and bake in a 350° oven for 10 to 15 minutes, stirring once or twice, until lightly browned.

Rinse the rice in a sieve and set aside to drain. In a saucepan on medium heat, warm 1 tablespoon of the oil. Add the rice and sauté, stirring constantly, for 3 minutes. Stir in the cinnamon, cardamom, black pepper, salt, and grated orange peel and continue to sauté for 1 minute. Stir in the water, cover, and gently simmer for 25 to 30 minutes, until the rice is tender and the water absorbed.

In a serving bowl, mix together the hot rice and the dried fruit. Allow to cool for 20 minutes. Add the pistachios, celery, orange juice, and the remaining tablespoon of oil. Stir well.

Serve at room temperature or chill for at least 30 minutes and serve cold.

Variations Add 1 tablespoon of minced fresh mint. If a little more tang is desired, 1 teaspoon of fresh lemon juice will make all of the flavors sparkle.

MENU IDEAS **Potage Celeste (page 130)** ∗ **Indian Roasted Eggplant Soup (page 40)** ∗ **Choklay's Tibetan Lentil Soup (page 73)** ∗ **chilled August Melon Soup (page 140)** ∗ **Spiced Paneer (page 351)**

Roasted Garlic Aioli Salad

For garlic lovers, this is a variation on aioli, the classic Provençal sauce, served with a colorful variety of steamed vegetables. You have a choice of roasting or sautéing the garlic; both methods produce a mellow, slightly sweet flavor. We like the convenience of using prepared mayonnaise with its safe, pasteurized eggs, and we often use canola mayonnaise for its nutritional value.

Leftover aioli, stored in a sealed container, will keep in the refrigerator for about 7 to 10 days. It's excellent in salads, on sandwiches, brushed on broiled fish, or however else you like to use mayonnaise.

SERVES 6 TO 8
YIELDS 2 CUPS OF AIOLI AND
12 CUPS OF VEGETABLES
TOTAL TIME: 50 MINUTES, PLUS
ABOUT 1 HOUR TO ROAST THE
GARLIC

PER 11.5-OUNCE SERVING: 338 CALORIES, 5.4 G PROTEIN, 19.7 G FAT, 39.3 G CARBOHYDRATES, 2.9 G SATURATED FATTY ACIDS, 15 MG CHOLESTEROL, 440 MG SODIUM, 3.4 G TOTAL DIETARY FIBER

ROASTED GARLIC AIOLI SAUCE

2 whole garlic heads
2 cups prepared mayonnaise
1 tablespoon fresh lemon juice
2 tablespoons chopped fresh dill or tarragon
salt and ground black pepper to taste

COOKED VEGETABLES (SEE NOTE)

4 cups potatoes cut into bite-sized chunks
4 cups halved mushrooms (about 1 pound)
3 cups red bell pepper strips
1 pound asparagus, tough stem ends removed

RAW VEGETABLES

rinsed and chopped lettuce or other fresh greens
2 tomatoes, cut into wedges
2 scallions, sliced on a severe diagonal

hard-boiled eggs, cut into quarters
pitted California black olives

Roast the garlic (page 363). Cool, then squeeze the soft garlic out of the skins into a food processor or bowl. Add the mayonnaise, lemon juice, and dill or tarragon. Whirl or whisk into a smooth sauce and add salt and pepper to taste. Set aside in the refrigerator.

Steam or boil the potatoes, mushrooms, bell peppers, and asparagus, one vegetable at a time, until just tender. Drain and set aside at room temperature.

On a large serving platter, make a bed with the greens. Arrange the cooked vegetables in the center and the tomato wedges around the edges. Sprinkle with the scallions and garnish with the hard-boiled eggs and olives. Offer the Roasted Garlic Aioli Sauce in a small serving bowl to pass at the table or in individual cups.

Note Carrots, broccoli, green beans, and zucchini also work well in this recipe. Use 10 to 12 cups of vegetables, but be sure to include some potatoes in the mix—we especially like aioli with potatoes.

Variation For a Sautéed Garlic Aioli, replace the roasted garlic with 3 minced large garlic cloves sautéed in 1½ tablespoons of olive oil until golden.

DAILY SPECIAL

MENU IDEAS **chilled Fast & Fresh Tomato Soup (page 148)** ✳ **chilled Minted Pea Soup (page 155)** ✳ **Algerian Tomato Soup with Vermicelli (page 66)** ✳ **Tuscan Bean Soup (page 100)**

Roasted Red Pepper & Cauliflower Salad

Cauliflower is a vegetable with a strong character and it doesn't often appear in salads as the featured ingredient. Sometimes crunchy raw florets are nestled next to carrots, celery, and peppers on a relish plate, or perhaps steamed cauliflower is combined with other vegetables in a marinated salad.

But this composed salad is strikingly and invitingly different. The cauliflower, bell peppers, and potatoes are roasted and then tossed in a lemony fennel vinaigrette to make a terrific dish for brunch or supper. A mix of red and green lettuce makes a nice presentation. If you wish, offer grated feta at the table for a finishing touch.

SERVES 4
TOTAL TIME: 45 MINUTES

PER 9-OUNCE SERVING: 289 CALORIES, 3.8 G PROTEIN, 24.1 G FAT, 18 G CARBO-HYDRATES, 4.1 G SATURATED FATTY ACIDS, 0 MG CHOLESTEROL, 554 MG SODIUM, 4 G TOTAL DIETARY FIBER

1 red bell pepper
½ head cauliflower, cut into small florets (about 4 cups)
1 large russet potato, sliced into ¼-inch-thick rounds
2 tablespoons olive oil
dash of salt

DRESSING

2 tablespoons canola or other vegetable oil
2 tablespoons olive oil
1 tablespoon fresh lemon juice
1 tablespoon cider vinegar
2 garlic cloves, minced or pressed
2 teaspoons ground fennel seeds
½ teaspoon salt, or more to taste
pinch of ground black pepper

4 cups mesclun (page 367) or torn leaf lettuce
2 tablespoons chopped fresh parsley
8 kalamata olives

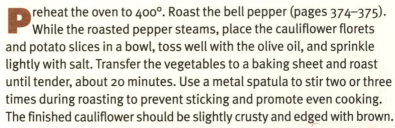

Preheat the oven to 400°. Roast the bell pepper (pages 374–375). While the roasted pepper steams, place the cauliflower florets and potato slices in a bowl, toss well with the olive oil, and sprinkle lightly with salt. Transfer the vegetables to a baking sheet and roast until tender, about 20 minutes. Use a metal spatula to stir two or three times during roasting to prevent sticking and promote even cooking. The finished cauliflower should be slightly crusty and edged with brown.

Meanwhile, peel off the loosened skin of the cooled roasted pepper. If some of the charred skin doesn't slip off easily, rinse it with cool running water and gently rub it off. Cut the pepper in half, remove its seeds and stem, slice it lengthwise into thin strips, and set aside.

Whisk together all of the dressing ingredients. When the cauliflower and potatoes are ready, remove them from the oven and set aside.

Rinse and drain the mesclun or lettuce. On a large platter, prepare a bed of the greens. Arrange the roasted vegetables on the greens and decorate with the strips of red pepper. Drizzle on the dressing, sprinkle with parsley, and dot with the olives.

DAILY SPECIAL

MENU IDEAS **Cream of Spinach Soup (page 120)** ✳ **Classic Tomato Garlic Soup (page 30)** ✳ **Celery Roquefort Soup (page 115)** ✳ **chilled Creamy Yogurt Barley Soup (page 146)** ✳ **chilled Cucumber Yogurt Soup (page 147)** ✳ **Pepperpot (page 50)**

Solstice Salad

This special salad was inspired by a cooking class given in Ithaca by famed chef Joyce Goldstein, who emphasizes a balance of flavors. With beets, raisins, marsala, and oranges, sweetness dominates, but lemony crisp jicama, toasty pine nuts, and faintly bitter greens all add different notes for an interesting and showy salad, especially suited to fall and winter.

The salad components can be prepped ahead but should be assembled just before serving. Arrange this attractive salad on a platter rather than in a deep salad bowl to highlight the colorful toppings. If jicama is not available, mung sprouts or julienned cucumber can provide the crisp element.

SERVES 3 TO 4
TOTAL TIME: 45 MINUTES

PER 15-OUNCE SERVING: 376 CALORIES, 6.4 G PROTEIN, 20.2 G FAT, 49 G CARBO-HYDRATES, 2.8 G SATURATED FATTY ACIDS, 0 MG CHOLESTEROL, 196 MG SODIUM, 7.8 G TOTAL DIETARY FIBER

6 cups lightly packed mixed baby greens, such as mesclun or spring mix (about 6 ounces)
3 beets (about ½ pound)
1 tablespoon cider vinegar
salt and ground black pepper to taste
½ cup regular or golden raisins
¼ cup marsala, apple juice, or orange juice
¼ cup pine nuts
2 oranges
2 cups jicama, cut into matchsticks (about ¾ pound)*
2 tablespoons fresh lemon juice
½ small red onion (optional)

DRESSING
¼ cup red wine vinegar
¼ cup extra-virgin olive oil
salt to taste (about ⅛ teaspoon)
freshly ground black pepper

*Jicama is a light brown root vegetable from Mexico. The crisp, succulent white interior has a mild flavor. Jicama readily absorbs flavors and is usually served raw.

Rinse and dry the salad greens and refrigerate. Cook the beets in boiling water until easily pierced with a knife, 20 to 30 minutes. When they are cool enough to handle, cut off the stem ends and rub off the peels. Cut the beets into thin wedges. In a bowl, toss them with the vinegar, salt, and pepper and set aside.

Meanwhile, in a small saucepan, bring the raisins and marsala or fruit juice to a boil. Remove from the heat and set aside. Toast the pine nuts (page 374). Peel and section the oranges (page 373) and set aside. In a small bowl, combine the julienned jicama and the lemon juice, add salt and pepper to taste, toss well, and set aside. Thinly slice the red onion, if using. Whisk together all of the dressing ingredients in a bowl.

To assemble the salad, arrange the mixed greens on a large platter. Remove the beets and jicama from their marinades and spread them over the greens. Scatter on the orange sections and red onions and sprinkle on the raisins and pine nuts. Drizzle a few tablespoons of the dressing over all and serve the rest of the dressing on the side.

DAILY SPECIAL

MENU IDEAS French Roasted Onion Soup (page 37) ✳ **Tuscan Bean Soup (page 100)** ✳ **Butternut Squash Soup with Sizzled Sage (page 28)** ✳ **Classic Tomato Garlic Soup (page 30)** ✳ **Chinese Velvet Corn Soup (page 116)**

Southern Red Rice & Pecan Salad

Aromatic wehani rice is a reddish-brown hybrid crossed with basmati. Along with much of the rice in this country, it grows in the rich farmland of southern Louisiana. The Creole flavors in this attractive salad spring from the same fertile soil. Garnished with red kidney beans lightly marinated in a vinaigrette and topped with avocado, you have a hearty, colorful main dish salad.

Southern Red Rice & Pecan Salad also makes an exceptional filling for avocado halves or scooped-out tomatoes.

SERVES 6 TO 8
PREPARATION TIME: 1 HOUR
CHILLING TIME:
  AT LEAST 15 TO 30 MINUTES

PER 9.5-OUNCE SERVING: 371 CALORIES, 6 G PROTEIN, 18.3 G FAT, 49 G CARBOHYDRATES, 1.9 G SATURATED FATTY ACIDS, 0 MG CHOLESTEROL, 467 MG SODIUM, 3.9 G TOTAL DIETARY FIBER

1 cup raw wehani rice
1 cup raw long-grain brown rice
½ teaspoon salt
3½ cups water
½ teaspoon dried thyme
½ teaspoon dried oregano
1 red bell pepper
2 tomatoes
2 celery stalks
1 cup minced scallions
½ cup currants
½ cup chopped fresh parsley
3 tablespoons red wine vinegar
3 tablespoons olive oil
½ teaspoon salt
ground black or white pepper to taste
pinch of cayenne or splash of Tabasco or other hot pepper sauce
1 cup toasted and finely chopped pecans*

avocado slices
marinated red kidney beans (optional)**

* Toast the pecans in a single layer on an unoiled baking tray at 350° for about 5 minutes, until fragrant and golden brown.
** See our Marinated Chickpeas or White Beans (page 346) for a nice marinade.

Rinse the wehani rice and brown rice in a sieve and drain. In a saucepan, combine the rice, salt, water, thyme, and oregano. Cover and bring to a boil; then reduce the heat and cook for 45 minutes, until all of the water is absorbed.

While the rice cooks, finely chop the bell pepper, tomatoes, and celery and place them in a large serving bowl. Add the scallions, currants, and parsley and mix well. Whisk together the vinegar, oil, salt, black pepper, and cayenne or Tabasco. Toss with the vegetable mixture and set aside in the refrigerator.

When the rice is tender, remove it from the heat. After 5 minutes, fluff it with a fork and stir into the vegetables. Chill for at least 15 to 30 minutes. Just before serving, stir in the pecans.

Serve with avocado slices and, if you wish, marinated kidney beans.

DAILY SPECIAL

MENU IDEAS Jamaican Tomato Soup (page 41) ✳ **Black Bean & Chipotle Soup (page 70)** ✳ **Texas Two-Bean Soup (page 95)** ✳ **Liberian Black-eyed Pea Soup (page 84)** ✳ **Celery Roquefort Soup (page 115)** ✳ **Herbed Cheese Quick Bread (page 332)**

Speltberry & Fruit Salad

Spelt is a hardy, ancient member of the wheat family, grown mostly in Europe. Speltberries are chewy little grains packed with vitamins and minerals, and they have a wonderful, nutty flavor. Some of us prefer them to wheatberries, which can be used in place of the spelt in this recipe. People sensitive to wheat can often tolerate a moderate amount of spelt without ill effect. Nearby Cresset Farms bakes a spelt bread that is very popular with Ithacans.

This fortifying yet refreshing salad has no oil added and is therefore lower in fat. It's nice for winter holiday meals or spring lunches.

SERVES 3 TO 4
PREPARATION TIME: 15 MINUTES
COOKING TIME: 40 MINUTES
  WITH SOAKED SPELTBERRIES,
  1½ HOURS WITH UNSOAKED
COOLING TIME: 20 TO 30 MINUTES

PER 10.5-OUNCE SERVING: 306 CALORIES, 5 G PROTEIN, 12.8 G FAT, 49.6 G CARBOHYDRATES, 1 G SATURATED FATTY ACIDS, 0 MG CHOLESTEROL, 170 MG SODIUM, 6.8 G TOTAL DIETARY FIBER

1 cup speltberries*
8 cups warm water
⅓ cup fresh orange juice
¼ cup fresh lemon juice
¼ teaspoon salt, more to taste
2 ripe flavorful pears
½ cup chopped toasted pecans or walnuts**
½ cup minced celery
10 unsulphured dried apricots, finely chopped***

* *Speltberries are available in natural food stores and in the bulk food or natural food sections of larger supermarkets. A cup of raw speltberries yields 2½ cups cooked.*
** *Toast nuts in a single layer on an unoiled baking tray in a 350° oven for about 5 minutes, until fragrant and golden brown.*
*** *Many dried apricots are dense, soft, and easily chopped. But if yours are tough, soak them until softened: submerge in apple juice for about 30 minutes or in hot water for about 20 minutes. Then drain and chop.*

In a saucepan on high heat, bring the speltberries and water to a boil. Reduce the heat, cover, and simmer for about 1½ hours, until the speltberries are soft but chewy and have a nutty rather than starchy flavor (see Note).

Drain the speltberries. Combine the orange juice, lemon juice, and salt in a serving bowl. Add the hot speltberries and mix well. Set aside to cool to room temperature, stirring occasionally. Core the pears and cut them into ¼-inch cubes.

When the speltberries have cooled, stir in the nuts, celery, apricots, and pears. Add salt to taste. Store in the refrigerator, but serve at room temperature for the best flavor.

Note For a shorter cooking time, soak the speltberries in 4 cups cool water for 8 to 24 hours at room temperature. Drain well. Simmer in 4 cups fresh water for about 40 minutes.

DAILY SPECIAL

MENU IDEAS Everyday Split Pea Soup (page 77) ✳ **Baked Bean Soup (page 69)** ✳ **Creamy Tomato Soup (page 125)** ✳ **Cream of Spinach Soup (page 120)** ✳ **Back to Your Roots Soup (page 113)** ✳ **chilled Gingered Plum Soup (page 152)**

Spicy Pineapple Tofu Salad

Crisp lettuce and vegetables, luscious pineapple, chewy tofu, crunchy peanuts, and a sweet, salty, and spicy hot dressing—this attractive salad has it all, Pacific Rim style.

SERVES 2 TO 3
TOTAL TIME: 40 MINUTES

PER 19-OUNCE SERVING: 476 CALORIES, 18 G PROTEIN, 26.8 G FAT, 47.6 G CARBO-HYDRATES, 5.4 G SATURATED FATTY ACIDS, 0 MG CHOLESTEROL, 1656 MG SODIUM, 6.4 G TOTAL DIETARY FIBER

1 cake of firm tofu, pressed (14 to 16 ounces)*

MARINADE
¼ cup soy sauce
2 tablespoons rice vinegar or cider vinegar
1 tablespoon canola or other vegetable oil
1 tablespoon brown sugar, packed
2 teaspoons grated fresh ginger root
½ fresh chile, minced, seeded for a milder "hot"

DRESSING
2 tablespoons canola or other vegetable oil
¼ cup rice vinegar or cider vinegar
2 tablespoons soy sauce
2 teaspoons brown sugar, packed
2 large garlic cloves, minced or pressed
3 tablespoons chopped fresh cilantro
1 fresh chile, minced, seeded for a milder "hot"

2 cups fresh or unsweetened canned pineapple chunks
½ head of leaf or iceberg lettuce
1 carrot
1 cucumber

¼ cup chopped peanuts
fresh mung bean sprouts (optional)

Sandwich the tofu between two plates and rest a weight (a heavy can or book) on the top plate. Press for about 15 minutes while you assemble the rest of the ingredients, prepare the marinade, and preheat the oven; then drain the expressed liquid from the bottom plate.

Preheat the oven to 375°.
Whisk together all of the marinade ingredients in a small bowl and set aside. Cut the tofu into 1-inch cubes and arrange in a single layer in a 7 × 11-inch or 8-inch square nonreactive baking pan. Pour the marinade over the tofu cubes and toss to coat. Bake until the marinade is absorbed and the tofu is lightly browned, 25 to 30 minutes, carefully turning the tofu once about halfway through baking. Remove from the oven and transfer to a large platter to cool.

While the tofu is baking, combine all of the dressing ingredients in a bowl and whisk until the sugar dissolves. Add the pineapple chunks and toss to coat. Pour off and reserve the extra dressing and set the pineapple aside.

Cut the lettuce into thin shreds; there should be about 5 cups. Peel and grate the carrot. Peel the cucumber, cut it in half lengthwise, scoop out the seeds with a spoon, and then cut into ½-inch strips on the diagonal. You should have about 1½ cups each of carrots and cucumbers.

Spread the lettuce on a serving platter, leaving a 2-inch border around the rim. Top with the grated carrots. Arrange the cucumber strips around the edge of the platter. Drizzle the reserved dressing over the lettuce and carrots and top with the pineapple chunks. When the tofu is cool, add it to the platter and sprinkle on the peanuts.

Top with a few mung sprouts, if desired, and serve at once.

Note Canned pineapple works well in this salad, but fresh, perfectly ripe pineapple can be just short of divine. Many supermarkets carry precut fresh pineapple. If a store near you has it, give it a try; then it's as easy to use fresh as canned.

MENU IDEAS Chilled Mango Soup (page 154) ✶ **Creamless Broccoli Soup (page 31)** ✶ **Chilled Fragrant Lemongrass Fruit Soup (page 150)** ✶ **Tomato Egg Drop Soup (page 133)**

Three-Bean Pasta Salad

Here are three colorful beans—green, burgundy, and light tan—bolstered by tiny spelt pasta shells, crisp vegetables, and a tangy dressing that is slightly sweet-and-sour. And it's a "perfect protein" salad! Because this salad has it all, choose a simple vegetable soup for a Daily Special.

You may want to cook kidney beans and chickpeas especially for the salad, but drained canned beans or leftover cooked beans will work fine too.

You could also stir the orange marmalade into a bottled Honey-Dijon dressing—look for Moosewood brand dressing in your area.

SERVE 6 TO 8
TOTAL TIME: 30 MINUTES
CHILLING TIME (OPTIONAL):
    AT LEAST 20 MINUTES

PER 9.5-OUNCE SERVING: 345 CALORIES, 12.4 G PROTEIN, 8.6 G FAT, 56 G CARBOHYDRATES, 2 G SATURATED FATTY ACIDS, 0 MG CHOLESTEROL, 809 MG SODIUM, 5.6 G TOTAL DIETARY FIBER

SALAD

10 ounces small spelt pasta shells (page 373) or other small pasta
¾ pound green beans (about 2 cups)
1½ cups cooked drained chickpeas (15-ounce can)
1½ cups cooked drained kidney beans (15-ounce can)
½ cup minced celery
½ cup chopped dill pickles
½ cup scallions, sliced on the diagonal
2 tablespoons grated radishes (4 or 6 whole)

DRESSING

¼ cup canola or other vegetable oil
2 tablespoons cider vinegar
1½ tablespoons Dijon mustard
2 tablespoons orange marmalade
¼ teaspoon dried oregano (½ teaspoon fresh)*
2 teaspoons dried dill (1½ tablespoons fresh)*
1½ teaspoons salt
ground black pepper to taste (optional)

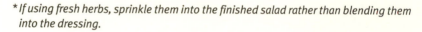

If using fresh herbs, sprinkle them into the finished salad rather than blending them into the dressing.

Bring a large pot of water to a boil, add the pasta, cover, and cook until al dente, about 7 minutes. Drain in a colander, gently rinse with cold water, and set aside to drain again.

Meanwhile, bring a saucepan of water to a boil. While the water heats, stem the green beans and cut them into 1-inch pieces. Ease the green beans into the boiling water, cover, and simmer just until tender and still brightly colored, 5 to 10 minutes. Drain the beans, rinse with cold water, and drain again.

Combine the chickpeas, kidney beans, and green beans in a large serving bowl. Add the celery, dill pickles, scallions, and radishes and toss gently. In a blender, combine the oil, vinegar, mustard, orange marmalade, oregano, dill, salt, and, if you wish, pepper to taste. Whirl until smooth. Add the pasta to the serving bowl, pour on the dressing, and mix well.

Serve immediately or chill for at least 20 minutes and serve cold.

MENU IDEAS **Creamy Tomato Soup (page 125)** ✳ **Yellow Pepper Purée (page 58)** ✳ **Creamy Herbed Carrot Soup (page 121)** ✳ **chilled Fennel Vichyssoise (page 149)** ✳ **Oaxacan Potato Soup (page 128)**

Thai Noodle Salad

Over time, Thai Noodle Salad has evolved at Moosewood and now we prepare it with the unlikely selection of a short sculpted Italian pasta. We find the pasta's shape admirably catches both the dressing and the vegetables —which are apt to slip off longer noodle strands and end up at the bottom of the bowl. The multicolored pasta is also very pretty with the colorful vegetables.

When thoroughly chilled, the coconut milk will solidify and may make the salad somewhat dry and sticky. So for the best flavor and creamiest texture, serve at room temperature or only slightly cooler. If desired, garnish with toasted peanuts and/or slices of tofu-kan or Baked Seasoned Tofu (page 336).

SERVES 3 TO 4
PREPARATION TIME: 40 MINUTES
SITTING TIME: 20 MINUTES

PER 14.25-OUNCE SERVING: 356 CALORIES, 11 G PROTEIN, 6.5 G FAT, 67 G CARBOHYDRATES, 2 G SATURATED FATTY ACIDS, 0 MG CHOLESTEROL, 1290 MG SODIUM, 4.8 G TOTAL DIETARY FIBER

½ **pound** *fusilli tricolore* **(tricolored pasta spirals)**
1 **cup drained canned straw mushrooms (15-ounce can)**
1 **cup drained canned baby corn (10-ounce can)**
1 **cup julienned red bell pepper, cut into 1½-inch-long matchsticks**
1½ **cups julienned zucchini, cut into 2-inch-long matchsticks**

DRESSING
2 **tablespoons chopped fresh cilantro, Thai basil, or basil**
1 **scallion, chopped**
1 **small fresh green chile, coarsely chopped**
2 **large garlic cloves, minced or pressed**
1 **teaspoon ground coriander**
1½ **teaspoons salt**
1 **tablespoon brown sugar, packed**
1 **tablespoon canola or other vegetable oil**
2 **to 3 teaspoons freshly grated lime peel**
¼ **cup fresh lime juice, more to taste**
1½ **tablespoons rice vinegar**
¼ **cup coconut milk (page 360)**

Bring a large covered pot of water to a boil. Add the pasta and cook on medium heat until al dente, about 15 minutes.

While the pasta cooks, place the straw mushrooms and baby corn in a large serving bowl. Bring a small pot of water to a boil. Blanch the bell peppers for 30 seconds, add the zucchini, and continue to simmer for another 30 seconds, until both vegetables are tender-crisp and brightly colored. Drain. Submerge in very cold water for about 15 seconds to help set the color and stop further cooking. Drain well again and add to the serving bowl.

Reserve 1 tablespoon of the chopped cilantro or basil, and then combine all of the remaining dressing ingredients in a blender or food processor and purée until smooth.

When the pasta is ready, drain it and rinse well with cold water. Transfer it to the serving bowl and gently toss it with the vegetables and dressing. Sprinkle on the reserved tablespoon of cilantro or basil. Set aside at room temperature for at least 20 minutes to allow the flavors to meld.

DAILY SPECIAL

MENU IDEAS Asian Bean Curd Soup (page 64) ✳ **Chinese Velvet Corn Soup (page 116)** ✳ **Southeast Asian Rice & Tofu Soup (page 91)** ✳ **chilled Fragrant Lemongrass Fruit Soup (page 150)** ✳ **chilled Gingered Plum Soup (page 152)** ✳ **Choklay's Tibetan Lentil Soup (page 73)** ✳ **Wonton Soup (page 104)**

Thai Rice & Mushroom Salad

This is a subtly flavored salad that paradoxically packs a wallop—which is probably why food writer Elizabeth Schneider describes one of this salad's main seasonings, lemongrass, as "both remarkably potent and soft-spoken."

The peanuts or cashews, although optional, are a really nice touch.

SERVES 4 TO 6
TOTAL TIME: 1 HOUR

PER 7-OUNCE SERVING: 228 CALORIES, 5.2 G PROTEIN, 6.1 G FAT, 38.8 G CARBO-HYDRATES, 2.7 G SATURATED FATTY ACIDS, 0 MG CHOLESTEROL, 336 MG SODIUM, 1.8 G TOTAL DIETARY FIBER

RICE

1⅓ cups raw jasmine rice, rinsed
1 fresh lemongrass stalk, cut into 3 or 4 pieces*
½ fresh chile, seeded and minced
1 teaspoon canola or other vegetable oil
1¼ cups boiling water
¾ cup reduced-fat or regular coconut milk**
¼ teaspoon salt

DRESSING

¼ cup reduced-fat or regular coconut milk
3 tablespoons fresh lime juice
1 teaspoon sugar
½ teaspoon salt
2 tablespoons chopped fresh basil, preferably Thai basil
2 tablespoons chopped fresh cilantro or mint (optional)

1 medium red or orange bell pepper
8 ounces asparagus
12 ounces mushrooms, such as oyster, cremini, shiitake, moonlight, or a combination
2 teaspoons minced or pressed garlic
2 teaspoons grated fresh ginger root
1 teaspoon freshly grated lime peel
½ fresh chile, minced, seeded for a milder "hot"
2 teaspoons canola or other vegetable oil
dash of salt

chopped fresh basil
roasted peanuts or cashews (optional)

* *Using a mallet or hammer, gently pound the stalk of lemongrass before cooking to help release its full flavor. If fresh lemongrass is unavailable, dried shredded lemongrass can be used: place about 1 tablespoon in a bouquet garni or tea ball and add it to the rice pot; remove immediately when the rice is cooked. Or use 1½ teaspoons of freshly grated lemon peel: the flavor will be different but acceptable.*
** *Leftover coconut milk will keep for several days refrigerated and indefinitely frozen.*

In a small, heavy pot with a tight-fitting lid, sauté the rice, lemongrass, and chile in the oil for 1 to 2 minutes, stirring constantly. Add the boiling water, coconut milk, and salt and bring to a boil; then stir, reduce the heat to very low, cover, and cook until all of the liquid has been absorbed, about 15 minutes.

Meanwhile, whisk together all of the dressing ingredients in a small bowl and set aside. Seed the pepper and cut it into thin strips about 1½ inches long. Blanch the pepper strips in boiling water for 1 to 2 minutes, until just tender, and set aside in a serving bowl. Rinse the asparagus, snap off and discard the tough stem ends, and cut the spears on the diagonal into 1½-inch pieces. Blanch in boiling water until just tender, about 3 minutes, and add to the serving bowl.

When the rice is tender, remove the lemongrass pieces, fluff the rice with a fork, and set it aside to cool.

Remove and discard any tough stems from the mushrooms, then rinse and slice the caps into bite-sized pieces. In a skillet, combine the garlic, ginger root, lime peel, chile, and oil and sauté on medium heat for 1 minute, stirring constantly. Add the mushrooms and salt and toss well. Cover the skillet, reduce the heat, and cook until the mushrooms are softened and begin to release their juices, 3 to 5 minutes.

Add the sautéed mushrooms and cooled rice to the serving bowl, pour on the dressing, and toss well. Serve at room temperature, garnished with basil and, if desired, with peanuts or cashews.

MENU IDEAS **Spicy Tofu & Greens Soup (page 92)** ✳ **chilled August Melon Soup (page 140)** ✳ **Chinese Velvet Corn Soup (page 116)** ✳ **Spicy Carrot Peanut Soup (page 55)** ✳ **Baked Seasoned Tofu (page 336)** ✳ **serve beside grilled shrimp on a skewer** ✳ **Asian Pear & Grapefruit on Greens (page 264)**

Tomato Flowers

Ripe, juicy tomatoes are essential for these "flowers," which make very pretty seasonal showpieces. The alchemy between the kiwi dressing and the fresh mozzarella yields an intriguing smoky taste. Whether served with a hearty soup or a substantial salad, striking-looking Tomato Flowers will steal the show.

SERVES 4
TOTAL TIME: 30 MINUTES

PER 12-OUNCE SERVING: 473 CALORIES, 10.2 G PROTEIN, 41.8 G FAT, 19.6 G CAR-BOHYDRATES, 11.6 G SATURATED FATTY ACIDS, 16 MG CHOLESTEROL, 364 MG SODIUM, 5.3 G TOTAL DIETARY FIBER

KIWI DRESSING
2 ripe kiwis, peeled and chopped
1 garlic clove, minced or pressed
1 teaspoon grated fresh ginger root
⅛ teaspoon cayenne
1 teaspoon Dijon mustard
2 tablespoons cider vinegar
½ cup canola or other vegetable oil
¼ teaspoon salt
ground black pepper to taste

4 medium ripe tomatoes
4 ounces fresh mozzarella, diced (page 368)
1 Hass avocado, pitted, peeled, and diced*
5 ounces mesclun or other salad greens
dash of salt

* To dice an avocado, slice around its center lengthwise, gently twist the halves apart, and remove the pit. With a paring knife, cut the flesh into cubes right in the skins and scoop them out with a serving spoon.

In a blender, purée all of the dressing ingredients. Either set the dressing aside or, if the tomato flowers are to be assembled later, refrigerate it.

With a sharp paring knife, slice a thin cap from the top stem end of each tomato. Cut each tomato into 4 to 6 partial wedges by cutting each wedge almost to the bottom of the tomato but not all the way through. Fan the wedges open into a flower. In a bowl, gently mix together the mozzarella and avocado cubes for the filling.

Arrange the mesclun on individual plates; place a tomato flower in the center of each. Sprinkle the tomatoes with salt, mound them with filling, and drizzle 2 or 3 tablespoons of the dressing on each one.

Serve immediately and pass the remaining dressing at the table.

Note The avocado/mozzarella filling, if sprinkled with lemon juice to slow discoloration, will keep well for a few hours—so you can prepare it in advance. If the dressing is made ahead of time, whisk or briefly blend again just before assembling and serving the tomato flowers.

MENU IDEAS **North African Couscous Salad (page 222)** ✳ **Caribbean Sweet Potato Coconut Soup (page 29)** ✳ **Black Bean & Chipotle Soup (page 70)** ✳ **Ybor City Garbanzo Soup (page 107)** ✳ **Mole de Olla Rodriguez (page 42)** ✳ **Oaxacan Potato Soup (page 128)** ✳ **Popovers (page 334)** ✳ **Avocado Melon Mélange (page 264)**

Tostada Salad

This salad can be quite simple or piled high with colorful ingredients. Present it one of three ways: Make one large decorative platter, create individual composed salads, or serve it buffet style with each ingredient in its own bowl (and let the diners do the assembling).

We prefer to marinate the beans in the Cilantro Lime Dressing and then top the salad with the Chipotle Sour Cream. For a lighter salad, omit the Chipotle Sour Cream and top with the Cilantro Lime Dressing.

Extras to pile on could include thinly sliced scallions or red onions, corn kernels, grated cheese, peeled and diced jicama, chopped hard-boiled eggs, and seeded, diced cucumbers.

SERVES 4
PREPARATION TIME: 20 MINUTES
FOR BASIC SALAD, 40 MINUTES
WITH LOTS OF EXTRAS
CHILLING TIME: 1 HOUR

PER 15-OUNCE SERVING (WITH BOTH DRESSINGS): 654 CALORIES, 10.8 G PROTEIN, 57.7 G FAT, 30.7 G CARBOHYDRATES, 11.1 G SATURATED FATTY ACIDS, 22 MG CHOLESTEROL, 1354 MG SODIUM, 6.2 G TOTAL DIETARY FIBER

CHIPOTLE SOUR CREAM

1 cup sour cream
1 tablespoon olive oil
2 teaspoons finely chopped canned chipotles in adobo sauce*
½ teaspoon salt
1 tablespoon water
pinch of sugar

CILANTRO LIME DRESSING

1 cup chopped fresh cilantro, loosely packed
½ cup fresh lime juice
½ cup olive oil or other vegetable oil
1 small garlic clove, pressed
salt to taste

1½ cups cooked black beans or pinto beans (15-ounce can, drained)
1 head of romaine, green leaf, or iceberg lettuce, shredded or torn into bite-sized pieces
1 ripe tomato, chopped
1 ripe avocado, diced into ½-inch cubes**
½ cup sliced California black olives
crumbled tortilla chips or fried tortilla strips

* Canned chipotles in adobo sauce are available in small cans or jars in Latin American groceries and the ethnic section of many supermarkets. The peppers add a smoky flavor and the adobo adds body. Adobo sauce contains tomatoes, vinegar, onions, sugar, and spices. We recommend La Torre brand of Mexico, distributed by Intermex Products, PO Box 170062, Arlington, Texas 76003 (214-660-2071).
** To dice, slice around the center lengthwise, twist the halves apart, and remove the pit. Score the flesh into cubes right in the skins and scoop them out with a spoon.

In a small bowl, stir together all of the Chipotle Sour Cream ingredients and set aside in the refrigerator.

Whirl all of the Cilantro Lime Dressing ingredients in a blender until smooth. In a bowl, combine the dressing with the beans and chill for at least 1 hour. Drain the beans, reserving the dressing.

On a large platter, in separate bowls, or on individual salad plates, arrange the lettuce, beans, tomatoes, avocado cubes, and olives. Top with tortilla pieces and serve either or both dressings on the side.

Variations Try refried beans in place of the marinated beans.

MENU IDEAS Oaxacan Potato Soup (page 128) ✳ **chilled Mango Soup (page 154)** ✳ **chilled Creamy Orange Soup (page 145)** ✳ **Cauliflower, Cheese & Tomato Soup (page 114)** ✳ **finish with Pineapple Passion (page 265)**

Vietnamese Cellophane Noodle Salad

This salad has wonderfully contrasting textures: slippery noodles, crisp vegetables, and crunchy nuts in a refreshing Southeast Asian dressing. The baked tofu, if you choose to make it, adds succulence and a rich sesame flavor. For a lighter salad, omit the tofu and use sesame seeds rather than the peanuts.

SERVES 2 TO 3
TOTAL TIME: 40 MINUTES

PER 8-OUNCE SERVING: 278 CALORIES, 7.8 G PROTEIN, 7.4 G FAT, 46.4 G CARBO-HYDRATES, 1 G SATURATED FATTY ACIDS, 0 MG CHOLESTEROL, 824 MG SODIUM, 4.6 G TOTAL DIETARY FIBER

3¾ ounces cellophane noodles (page 357)
1 tablespoon dried tree ears (page 370)
Baked Seasoned Tofu (page 336) (optional)

DRESSING

3 tablespoons rice vinegar
2 tablespoons dry sherry
3 tablespoons soy sauce or 2 tablespoons fish sauce (page 363)
4 garlic cloves, minced or pressed
1 tablespoon minced fresh chiles, seeded for a milder "hot"
2 tablespoons coarsely chopped fresh mint leaves
1 teaspoon sugar

2 cups snow peas, strings removed
1½ cups mung bean sprouts
⅓ cup chopped scallions

⅓ cup chopped roasted peanuts or 2 tablespoons toasted sesame seeds*

Toast a single layer of peanuts on an unoiled baking tray in a 350° oven for about 15 minutes, until fragrant and golden brown—or toast sesame seeds for only 2 to 3 minutes.

Place the cellophane noodles in a heatproof bowl, cover with boiling water, and cover the bowl. Put the tree ears in a separate bowl and cover with boiling water. Set both aside for 30 minutes. If preparing the Baked Seasoned Tofu, start that now.

In a large serving bowl, whisk together all of the dressing ingredients and set aside. Bring a large pot of water to a boil. Add the snow peas and blanch for about 1 minute, and then stir in the sprouts and blanch for 30 seconds more, until both are just tender. Drain and add to the serving bowl.

When the noodles are soft, thoroughly drain them, arrange on a cutting board, and cut into 4- to 6-inch lengths. Drain, rinse, and coarsely chop the tree ears. Transfer the noodles, chopped tree ears, and scallions to the serving bowl and toss with the dressing. Sprinkle each serving with the peanuts or sesame seeds and top with baked tofu, if desired.

DAILY SPECIAL

MENU IDEAS **Korean Pine Nut Porridge (page 83)** ✳ **chilled Fragrant Lemongrass Fruit Soup (page 150)** ✳ **chilled Gingered Carrot Soup (page 151)** ✳ **Faux Pho (page 34)** ✳ **chilled Gingered Plum Soup (page 152)**

Wilted Spinach & Portabella Mushrooms

This substantial salad or side dish brings us down to earth any time of year. Succulent, meaty, warm portabella mushrooms complement delicate, sweet spinach leaves in a tangy, garlicky sauce. This dish can stand on its own as a light meal, especially when accompanied by good bread to sop up the juices.

SERVES 3 TO 4
PREPARATION TIME: 15 MINUTES
COOKING TIME: 5 MINUTES

PER 6.75-OUNCE SERVING: 171 CALO-RIES, 4.2 G PROTEIN, 14.9 G FAT, 8.6 G CARBOHYDRATES, 2 G SATURATED FATTY ACIDS, 0 MG CHOLESTEROL, 102 MG SODIUM, 4.2 G TOTAL DIETARY FIBER

10 ounces fresh spinach
3 large portabella mushrooms (about 1¼ pounds)
¼ cup olive oil
3 garlic cloves, minced or pressed
3 tablespoons fresh lemon juice or cider vinegar
salt and ground black pepper to taste
½ cup thinly sliced small red onion rings (optional)

Rinse and stem the spinach. Drain it well or spin it dry in a salad spinner and place it in a serving bowl. Rinse the portabella mushrooms and trim the stem ends. Chop the caps and the stems into ½- to 1-inch cubes.

In a saucepan or skillet on medium-high heat, warm the olive oil until it is hot but not smoking. Sauté the garlic for just 30 seconds, until golden, and quickly stir in the portabellas. Sauté for 3 to 5 minutes, stirring often, until the mushrooms are softened.

Stir in the lemon juice or vinegar. Immediately pour the hot mushrooms over the spinach and toss well. Sprinkle on salt and pepper to taste and continue to toss until the spinach has darkened in color and wilted. If you wish, top the salad with thinly sliced red onion rings. Serve.

MENU IDEAS **Tuscan Bean Soup (page 100)** ✳ **chilled Fennel Vichyssoise (page 149)** ✳ **Artichoke Avgolemono (page 112)** ✳ **Creamy Herbed Carrot Soup (page 121)** ✳ **chilled Scandinavian Dried Fruit Soup (page 158)** ✳ **Farfalle e Fagiole Salad (page 208)** ✳ **Fattoush (page 209)** ✳ **Goat Cheese Toasts (page 344)** ✳ **Focaccia (page 330)**

SIMPLE VEGETABLE & SIDE DISH SALADS

We are often asked what it's like to be part of Moosewood. There is no uniform answer, especially since most of us have been at Moosewood for between ten and twenty-five years. But there is one experience that may be almost universal among us: the joy we feel at the sight of seasonal vegetables. Tender spring asparagus, frilly-edged kale, and sugar snap peas, and later, locally grown tomatoes and beets with their dark green tops inspire the same feeling of gratitude as the first shoot emerging from newly thawed earth. They affirm our faith in nature. A single seasonal vegetable can inspire our culinary creativity and hold a place of honor on our tables. Simple salads and side dishes add to your meal, bringing balance, variety, interest, and color to the menu. In tasteful combinations, they are a meal in themselves, and satisfy our yen to mix and match. ✳ As a first course, a stimulating but light salad softens the edge of hunger and whets the appetite in anticipation of good things to come. **A simple salad can make everything that comes afterward taste better.** A decorative side dish salad can provide refreshment, contrast, and relief from the richer textures and savory or spicy flavors of a main dish. A bowl of soup and one of these salads can make a meal. On our Daily Salad Combo Plates, simple vegetable salads either accompany a main dish salad or are combined with one or two other small salads. People love the variety on these combination plates — the fun of sampling a little of this and a little of that. ✳ This section is devoted to simple salads. We've included an array of Fresh Fruit Combinations as well as Simple Tomato Salads. See also the special sidebar (pages 180–183) called Greens Galore, which provides information about various greens and how to select them, and suggests a few good combinations for simple greens and dressings. ✳ There is no simpler way to make salad than to prepare one excellent vegetable carefully and serve it unheated with a vibrant dressing. When it's difficult for one of our customers to choose between entrées, the deciding factor is often the irresistible Honey Mustard Green Beans Vinaigrette being served beside one of the main dishes. Several recipes in this section feature single vegetables, such as Tunisian Carrot Salad and Celeriac Remoulade, or perfect partnerships like Asparagus & Snow Pea Salad. ✳ Some of these recipes are for composed salads, that is, salads whose elements are deliberately arranged for aesthetic appeal rather than tossed together. Composed Beet Salad is one good example: its striking, magenta-colored beets glistening with marinade are arranged on red and white radicchio and topped with blue cheese or chèvre. Fabulous contrasts in its flavors as well as in its visual presentation make it a very nice first course. Florida Salad with Ginger Dressing is our version of a popular spa creation, with a pretty pinwheel of tropical fruits radiating sunshine from a bed of tender greens. ✳ We've included some unusual fruit salads that are lovely served for brunch, snacks, or dessert. One way to enjoy the sheer lusciousness of seedless grapes, big red strawberries, and chunks of pineapple and melon is to spear them on wooden skewers and brush them with our delectable Light Syrup for Fruit. ✳ When we want to create a Salad Combo Plate, we often follow an ethnic theme and serve, for instance, Curried Potato Salad with spicy East Indian Fruit Salad and Indian Green Beans & Red Peppers. For a Daily Special, we might add to this a cup of warm Curried Zucchini Soup or chilled Gingered Plum Soup. When Italian food is featured on our Sunday ethnic night menu, we might serve Fresh Pear & Blue Cheese Salad with Classic Tomato Garlic Soup. ✳ We think of many of these small salads as quintessential side dishes that complete a main dish presentation. Their slightly crisp textures and bright colors complement casseroles and savory strudels and pies, while the piquancy of their herbed vinaigrettes offsets the entrée's mild or rich flavors. Marinated Broccoli & Carrots is a good example. Unusual dishes that make versatile accompaniments include zesty Seaweed Salad and a delightful Bean Sprout Salad, either of which is refreshing alongside fish or with brown rice. Golden Tomato Avocado Salad is perfect with refried black beans. ❋ At home, most people may not want to take the time to prepare several different salads at once. But in just a few days, most of us can accumulate quite an interesting collection of leftovers — and so the fun begins. With a little ingenuity, you can concoct your own Daily Specials with little or no cooking and plenty of good eating. ❋ It may be stating the obvious, but when cooking a vegetable to use in a salad, it is essential to pay close attention to the cooking time. The taste, texture, and color of the freshest, most glorious vegetables can be ruined if overcooked even two or three minutes; then, not even the best dressing will disguise the problem. So **please prepare and cook your vegetables with care, and make salad a showcase for them.** ❋

Alabama Hot Slaw

The "hot" in the name of this delicious slaw refers not to pepper but to the cooking technique. Dressed with a simple heated dressing, which softens and mellows the flavor of the onions and bell peppers, this is a colorful, festive-looking slaw. For a "hot" hot slaw, increase the Tabasco or other hot sauce in the dressing to make it as spicy as you wish.

Unlike many other slaws, Alabama Hot Slaw is great served right away; it doesn't need sitting time for the flavors to develop. Leftover slaw can be reinvigorated by adding just a splash of vinegar, if needed.

SERVES 8 TO 10
TOTAL TIME: 30 MINUTES

PER 4-OUNCE SERVING: 97 CALORIES, 1.3 G PROTEIN, 7.3 G FAT, 8 G CARBOHYDRATES, 1.9 G SATURATED FATTY ACIDS, 0 MG CHOLESTEROL, 333 MG SODIUM, 2.5 G TOTAL DIETARY FIBER

1 **small head of cabbage (about 1 pound)**
2 **celery stalks**
1½ **cups peeled and shredded carrots**
½ **red bell pepper, seeded and diced**
1 **heaping tablespoon minced red onions**
¼ **cup white or cider vinegar**
1 to 2 **teaspoons sugar**
1 **teaspoon salt**
¼ **teaspoon ground black pepper**
1 **teaspoon prepared mustard, such as yellow, brown, or hot**
Tabasco or other hot pepper sauce to taste
¼ **cup canola or other vegetable oil**

Finely shred the cabbage to make about 4 cups and place it in a large bowl. Halve the celery stalks lengthwise and thinly slice them crosswise. Without mixing together, pile the celery on top of the cabbage and follow with the carrots, bell peppers, and red onions.

In a small bowl or a cup, whisk together the vinegar, sugar, and salt until clear. Stir in the black pepper, mustard, and Tabasco to taste and pour on the vegetables. In a small pan, heat the oil to just smoking: you should see a few ripples in the oil and some heat waves. Pour the hot oil over the vegetables, aiming especially for the onions and peppers. Let sit for 3 or 4 minutes.

Toss and serve or refrigerate for later.

MENU IDEAS **Southern Red Rice & Pecan Salad (page 228)** ✳ **Florida Salad with Ginger Dressing (page 263)** ✳ **chilled Peach Soup (page 156)** ✳ **Catfish Gumbo (page 166)** ✳ **Corn Chowder (page 117)** ✳ **Welsh Rarebit Soup (page 135)**

Asian Spinach & Orange Salad

Few of us at Moosewood grew up eating salads that combined greens and fruit, although in other parts of the world, especially in hot-weather countries, preparing fresh fruit with vegetables is quite common. Serve it immediately, because fresh young greens wilt quickly.

This dish, with its bright, delicate, sweet, and savory qualities, can be a great introduction to this genre of salads. It can serve as a refreshing contrast to a spicy soup in an Asian-style Daily Special. But don't confine yourself to Asian cuisine — it would also be great with our Summer Millet Salad.

SERVES 4 TO 6
TOTAL TIME: 45 MINUTES

PER 5.5-OUNCE SERVING: 89 CALORIES, 1.8 G PROTEIN, 4.3 G FAT, 12.3 G CARBO-HYDRATES, 0.9 G SATURATED FATTY ACIDS, 0 MG CHOLESTEROL, 149 MG SODIUM, 3.1 G TOTAL DIETARY FIBER

3 cups spinach, rinsed, stemmed, and dried
3 cups mixed baby greens, rinsed
3 navel oranges*
1 small red onion, thinly sliced crosswise into rounds
dash of rice vinegar

DRESSING
2 tablespoons rice vinegar
3 tablespoons orange juice
1 tablespoon soy sauce
1 tablespoon grated fresh ginger root
1 tablespoon freshly grated orange peel
2 teaspoons dark sesame oil
1 tablespoon canola or other vegetable oil
pinch of cayenne

2 tablespoons minced fresh chives

Grate the peel of 1 orange before peeling and sectioning it; the grated peel will be used in the dressing.

Arrange the spinach and greens in a large serving bowl and set aside. Peel and section the oranges (page 373) and set aside in another bowl. Separate the thinly sliced red onion into rings and place them in a nonreactive dish. Sprinkle with a little rice vinegar and set aside to soften for 5 to 10 minutes.

Place all of the dressing ingredients in a small bowl and mix well with a fork or small wire whisk. Toss the greens with the dressing. In the serving bowl or on individual plates, arrange the orange segments and onion rings on a bed of the greens and top with chives.

DAILY SPECIAL

MENU IDEAS **Korean Pine Nut Porridge (page 83)** ✳ **Faux Pho (page 34)** ✳ **Spicy Carrot Peanut Soup (page 55)** ✳ **Azuki Bean Soup (page 68)** ✳ **Choklay's Tibetan Lentil Soup (page 73)** ✳ **Southeast Asian Rice & Tofu Soup (page 91)**

Asparagus & Snow Pea Salad

We get excited when fresh asparagus and snow peas become abundant in our local markets. The lovely presentation of these wonderful, bright green vegetables makes this a delightful spring and early summer salad. We use both asparagus and snow peas, but if you prefer to make the salad with only one or the other, use 1½ pounds of asparagus or 1 pound of snow peas.

SERVES 4 TO 6
TOTAL TIME: 20 MINUTES

PER 4.5-OUNCE SERVING: 97 CALORIES, 4.5 G PROTEIN, 5.1 G FAT, 10.8 G CARBO-HYDRATES, 0.9 G SATURATED FATTY ACIDS, 0 MG CHOLESTEROL, 299 MG SODIUM, 1.2 G TOTAL DIETARY FIBER

1 pound fresh asparagus
¼ pound snow peas

PEANUT DRESSING

2 tablespoons fresh lemon juice
2 tablespoons peanut butter
2 tablespoons soy sauce
1 tablespoon dark sesame oil
1 tablespoon mild honey, or more to taste

sliced scallions
mung bean sprouts
quartered cherry tomatoes

Rinse the asparagus and remove the tough stem ends. Steam or boil the spears until tender but still crisp, about 5 minutes. Drain, rinse under a gentle stream of cold running water or plunge into a pot of cold water to cool them quickly, and drain again. Set aside in a serving bowl.

Remove any tough stem ends from the snow peas. Blanch for just a minute or two, until the color brightens and they are crisp-tender. Drain, rinse with cold water, and drain again. Add the snow peas to the serving bowl and refrigerate.

When ready to serve, whisk together all of the dressing ingredients in a small bowl until smooth. Drizzle the asparagus and snow peas with the dressing, top with some scallions and mung sprouts, and garnish with a few cherry tomato quarters.

MENU IDEAS **Hot & Sour Shrimp Soup (page 168)** ✳ **Faux Pho (page 34)** ✳ **Roasted Red Pepper Coconut Soup (page 52)** ✳ **Thai Noodle Salad (page 233)** ✳ **Balinese Rice Salad (page 195)** ✳ **Baked Seasoned Tofu (page 336)**

Asparagus Vinaigrette

Like a basic black dress, vinaigrette serves as a classic foundation for many accessories. Here, it is done up with cracked peppercorns, fresh tarragon, and thyme. On another occasion, it might be adorned with chopped dill, chives, basil, chervil, or garlic scapes.

Asparagus Vinaigrette is the kind of salad you can slip in on the side to enhance a meal. Think of a French bistro meal; think of a New England farm supper. Or serve it next to an omelet for an elegant brunch.

Vinaigrette dressing tends to bleach the vegetables it touches, so toss the asparagus in the dressing just before serving. If you choose to steam the asparagus, use the smaller quantity of water; if you boil them, use the larger quantity.

SERVES 4 TO 6
TOTAL TIME: 15 TO 20 MINUTES

PER 3-OUNCE SERVING: 60 CALORIES, 2.2 G PROTEIN, 4.7 G FAT, 3.9 G CARBO-HYDRATES, 0.7 G SATURATED FATTY ACIDS, 0 MG CHOLESTEROL, 29 MG SODIUM, 0.1 G TOTAL DIETARY FIBER

1 pound asparagus spears, rinsed and trimmed
1 to 4 cups water

VINAIGRETTE
2 tablespoons fresh lemon juice
2 to 3 tablespoons olive oil
1 garlic clove, minced or pressed
½ teaspoon Dijon mustard
¼ teaspoon coarsely cracked black pepper
salt to taste
1 to 2 teaspoons minced fresh tarragon (1 teaspoon dried)
1 teaspoon minced fresh thyme (¼ teaspoon dried)

Steam or boil the asparagus in the water for 3 to 5 minutes, until tender but still crisp. Drain well and transfer to a serving bowl. Chill, if desired.

Just before serving, place all of the vinaigrette ingredients in a jar and shake vigorously to blend. Pour the dressing over the asparagus and toss to coat.

Variation Omit the mustard and stir in 1 tablespoon of nonfat or low-fat yogurt cheese (page 387).

MENU IDEAS **Wild Rice & Mushroom Soup (page 103)** ✳ **Creamy Herbed Potato Soup (page 122)** ✳ **Flemish Farm Soup (page 36)** ✳ **Farfalle e Fagiole Salad (page 208)** ✳ **Creamy Onion & Fontina Soup (page 123)** ✳ **French Roasted Onion Soup (page 37)**

Bean & Radicchio Salad

In just a few minutes you can toss together these simple ingredients for an attractive red and white salad with a sophisticated combination of flavors. The bitterness of the radicchio complements the mildness of the beans.

At Moosewood, we use this salad over and over again in the supporting role on combo plates.

SERVES 6
TOTAL TIME: 10 MINUTES

PER 5-OUNCE SERVING: 155 CALORIES, 6.9 G PROTEIN, 5.2 G FAT, 21.5 G CARBO-HYDRATES, 0.7 G SATURATED FATTY ACIDS, 0 MG CHOLESTEROL, 266 MG SODIUM, 7.2 G TOTAL DIETARY FIBER

1½ cups cooked small red beans (15-ounce can, rinsed and drained)
1½ cups cooked butter beans (15-ounce can, rinsed and drained)
1 small head of radicchio (about ½ pound)
1 tablespoon minced red onion (optional)
3 tablespoons fresh lemon juice
2 tablespoons extra-virgin olive oil
¼ teaspoon salt
freshly ground black pepper

Combine the beans in a serving bowl. Cut the radicchio into fine shreds about 1½ inches long. Mix them into the beans along with the minced red onion, if using. Add the lemon juice, olive oil, salt, and pepper to taste.

Gently toss and serve immediately.

DAILY SPECIAL

MENU IDEAS **Wilted Spinach & Portabella Mushrooms (page 239)** ∗ **Fattoush (page 209)** ∗ **Butternut Squash Soup with Sizzled Sage (page 28)** ∗ **Tomato & Kale Soup with Barley (page 98)** ∗ **a good dark bread**

Bean Sprout Salad

Not much of a sprouts fan? If any dish can get you to change your mind, this one will. The spicy pan-Asian flavors of chiles, garlic, and shallots mingle in a dressing that is sweet, hot, and tart. To be authentically Asian style, use shallots and rice vinegar — but red onions and cider vinegar work well too.

The vinegar dressing is poured hot over the sprouts. Served right away, the sprouts will retain a crisp raw crunch. Allowed to marinate, the sprouts will absorb more dressing and be more like pickled sprouts, a traditional Chinese condiment.

SERVES 4 TO 6
TOTAL TIME: 25 MINUTES

PER 3.25-OUNCE SERVING: 90 CALORIES, 1.7 G PROTEIN, 4.9 G FAT, 11.5 G CARBOHYDRATES, 1.3 G SATURATED FATTY ACIDS, 0 MG CHOLESTEROL, 401 MG SODIUM, 1.3 G TOTAL DIETARY FIBER

2 tablespoons canola or other vegetable oil
2 tablespoons minced or pressed garlic
2 shallots, minced (about ¼ cup)
1 fresh chile, seeded for a milder "hot" (see Note), or ½ teaspoon dried red pepper flakes
1 red or green bell pepper, seeded and cut into 1-inch matchsticks
2 scallions, cut into 1-inch matchsticks
4 cups fresh mung bean sprouts
¼ cup rice or cider vinegar
2 tablespoons sugar
1 teaspoon salt

In a saucepan on medium heat, warm the oil, add the garlic, shallots, and chile or red pepper flakes and sauté until fragrant, stirring continuously, for about 2 minutes. Add the bell peppers and scallions and continue to sauté, stirring frequently, for about 5 minutes, until the vegetables have softened.

Meanwhile, place the bean sprouts in a serving bowl. Cover the sprouts with the hot vegetables. In the same saucepan, combine the vinegar, sugar, and salt and cook on low heat just until the salt and sugar have dissolved, 1 to 2 minutes. Pour immediately over the salad and toss well.

Note For an aesthetic touch, make an elegant "chile flower" for a garnish. Keep the chile intact at the stem end and slice through both sides of the chile from just below the stem and through the tip. Reposition the chile and make 1 or 2 more slices to create 4 or 6 equal sections still connected at the stem end. Carefully separate the "petals" and scrape out the seeds.

Or simply cut the chile crosswise into rings that are large enough for the timid to avoid and the heat seekers to find.

MENU IDEAS **Spicy Carrot Peanut Soup** (page 55) ✳ **Miso Noodle Soup** (page 89) ✳ **Southeast Asian Rice & Tofu Soup** (page 91) ✳ **Classic Sichuan Noodles** (page 204) ✳ **Thai Noodle Salad** (page 233)

Brussels Sprouts & Carrot Salad

You'll wonder why you thought you didn't like Brussels sprouts after tasting this surprisingly appealing and easily prepared dish. With the bracing bite of horseradish and the sweet succulence of carrots, it makes an attractive side dish for a Thanksgiving dinner . . . or anytime. It fits into a Scandinavian- or Russian-style meal quite well. Try it next to any mild, creamy soup for a Daily Special.

We couldn't choose between the vinaigrette and the creamy dressing, so we thought we'd let you try them both and decide which you like best.

SERVES 4 TO 6
TOTAL TIME: 30 MINUTES
CHILLING TIME (OPTIONAL):
  30 MINUTES

PER 5-OUNCE SERVING: 134 CALORIES, 2.5 G PROTEIN, 9.9 G FAT, 11.6 G CARBO-HYDRATES, 2.5 G SATURATED FATTY ACIDS, 0 MG CHOLESTEROL, 429 MG SODIUM, 0 G TOTAL DIETARY FIBER

3 cups water
½ teaspoon salt
3 large carrots, peeled and cut into 1-inch chunks
1 pound Brussels sprouts

Choose one of the following dressings:

VINAIGRETTE DRESSING

¼ cup canola or other vegetable oil
4 teaspoons cider vinegar
4 teaspoons prepared horseradish
1 tablespoon chopped fresh dill (1 teaspoon dried)
¼ teaspoon salt

MAYONNAISE DRESSING

¼ cup prepared mayonnaise
4 teaspoons prepared horseradish
1 tablespoon chopped fresh dill (1 teaspoon dried)
1 to 2 teaspoons fresh lemon juice

freshly ground black pepper
fresh dill or parsley sprigs
diced red onions (optional)

Combine the water and salt in a saucepan, cover, and bring to a boil. Add the carrots and cook until just tender, 6 to 8 minutes. Meanwhile, wash the Brussels sprouts, cut off the stems, remove any loose outer leaves, and halve any that are larger than 1 inch across. When the carrots are tender, remove them with a slotted spoon and set aside in a large bowl. Ease the Brussels sprouts into the boiling water and cook until just tender, 6 to 8 minutes.

While the Brussels sprouts cook, choose a dressing and whisk together all of the ingredients in a small bowl. When the Brussels sprouts are tender, drain well and add them to the carrots. Pour the dressing over the vegetables and toss gently.

Serve immediately or chill for about 30 minutes. Garnish with a sprinkling of freshly ground pepper and a few dill or parsley sprigs. If desired, some diced red onions will add color and spark.

DAILY SPECIAL

MENU IDEAS **Creamy Onion & Fontina Soup (page 123)** ✳ **Welsh Rarebit Soup (page 135)** ✳ **Scandinavian Salmon Soup (page 171)** ✳ **Creamy Herbed Potato Soup (page 122)** ✳ **Ybor City Garbanzo Soup (page 107)** ✳ **Lobio (page 274)** ✳ **Lentil, Rice & Fruit Salad (page 220)**

Butternut Squash with Spicy Cranberry Sauce

This very pretty salad is tangy and sweet with a hint of hotness. The roasted squash provides a substantial bass note beneath the high notes of the fruit and celery and the accents of the walnuts and chiles.

We like this salad best chilled, but it is also good served warm as a side dish or eaten at room temperature. If serving warm, stir the apples, celery, and walnuts directly into the hot squash and cranberry sauce. Otherwise, let the squash and sauce cool first so that the other ingredients will stay crunchy.

In season, fresh cranberries are usually sold in 12-ounce bags, so it's easy to double the Spicy Cranberry Dressing ingredients and make extra cranberry sauce.

SERVES 8
PREPARATION TIME: 1 HOUR
CHILLING TIME: ABOUT 20 MINUTES

PER 8-OUNCE SERVING: 170 CALORIES, 2.6 G PROTEIN, 6.4 G FAT, 29.5 G CARBO-HYDRATES, 0.9 G SATURATED FATTY ACIDS, 0 MG CHOLESTEROL, 37 MG SODIUM, 1.9 G TOTAL DIETARY FIBER

1 large butternut squash ($2\frac{1}{2}$ to 3 pounds)
1 tablespoon canola or other vegetable oil
dash of salt and ground black pepper
$\frac{1}{2}$ cup coarsely chopped walnuts

SPICY CRANBERRY DRESSING

6 ounces fresh cranberries (see Note)
$\frac{1}{2}$ teaspoon freshly grated orange peel
juice of 1 orange plus water to make 1 cup
$\frac{1}{4}$ to $\frac{1}{3}$ cup sugar, to taste
1 fresh jalapeño or other chile, stemmed, seeded, and minced

2 celery stalks
1 crisp green apple

Preheat the oven to 400°.
Peel and seed the butternut squash and cut it into 1-inch cubes. Place the cubes in a bowl, drizzle them with the oil, sprinkle with salt and pepper, and toss well to coat evenly. Spread the squash on an unoiled baking sheet and roast for about 45 minutes, stirring twice during roasting. Spread the chopped walnuts on an end of the baking sheet for the last 5 minutes of roasting. The finished squash should be soft and lightly browned and the walnuts fragrant. Reserve the walnuts.

While the squash roasts, rinse the cranberries and discard any that are soft or discolored. Combine all of the dressing ingredients in a partially covered nonreactive saucepan and bring to a boil. Reduce the heat and cook at a low boil for 5 minutes. Stir well, mashing any unpopped cranberries. Remove from the heat and set aside.

In a large bowl, stir together the roasted squash and the Spicy Cranberry Dressing. Refrigerate until cooled to room temperature. Mince the celery, core and dice the apple, and stir them into the salad. Add the reserved walnuts and chill for about 20 minutes before serving.

Note If fresh cranberries are unavailable, frozen ones will work fine. Just add the still-frozen cranberries to the saucepan and stir several times until the dressing comes to a boil. Or use canned whole cranberries and their juice: omit the sugar and water in the recipe, and simmer, uncovered.

DAILY SPECIAL

MENU IDEAS **Very Creamy Vegetable Chowder (page 134)** ✳ **Baked Bean Soup (page 69)** ✳ **Wild Rice & Asparagus Soup (page 102)** ✳ **Celery Roquefort Soup (page 115)** ✳ **Creamy Potato Cabbage Soup (page 124)**

Celeriac Remoulade

Traditionally, remoulade is a French mayonnaise-based sauce with gherkins, capers, mustard, scallions, chervil, tarragon, and anchovies that is usually served on chilled fish or meat.

These days, a similar tangy mayonnaise is served on celeriac salad in most French bistros, its refreshing crunch a reliable sidekick for richer fare. While a familiar taste in many European countries, celeriac has yet to gain a popular following in the States, but that may change. While the matchstick version gives the look of a traditional remoulade, our grated option is also quite nice.

Try the Apple Pear Remoulade variation for a sweeter, juicier version.

SERVES 4 TO 6
TOTAL TIME: 15 MINUTES

PER 3.25-OUNCE SERVING: 58 CALORIES, 1.6 G PROTEIN, 2.2 G FAT, 9.3 G CARBO-HYDRATES, 0.3 G SATURATED FATTY ACIDS, 2 MG CHOLESTEROL, 331 MG SODIUM, 1.4 G TOTAL DIETARY FIBER

1 pound celeriac (celery root)*
½ teaspoon salt
1 tablespoon fresh lemon juice

DRESSING
2½ tablespoons prepared mayonnaise
2½ tablespoons plain nonfat yogurt
1 tablespoon fresh lemon juice
1 teaspoon Dijon mustard
¼ teaspoon ground black pepper

Celeriac is a variety of celery, Apium graveolens rapaceum, which has a large, edible, brown, knobby, turnip-like root. It can be found in the produce section of many well-stocked supermarkets.

Peel the celeriac with a sharp knife or vegetable peeler. Either julienne (see Note) or coarsely grate the celeriac. To julienne, slice the celeriac in half through the stem end. Place each half flat side down on the counter and cut into ⅛-inch-thick slices. Stack the slices and cut them into ⅛-inch-thick matchsticks. Place the julienned or grated celeriac in a large bowl, sprinkle it with the salt, and toss with the lemon juice.

In a small bowl, whisk together all of the dressing ingredients. Pour over the celeriac and toss well. Serve immediately or chill.

Note Don't attempt to julienne the celeriac unless you have a very sharp knife. A dull knife just won't do the job (and may cause undue frustration). If you are having difficulty cutting the celeriac, simply grate it instead.

Variation For a lovely Apple Pear Remoulade, replace the celeriac with 1 pound of firm apples and pears (Crispin and Bosc are ideal) and, if you like, add about ¼ pound of jicama. Peel, quarter, and core the apples and pears. Peel and halve the jicama. Cut everything into ⅛-inch slices, stack the slices, and cut them into ⅛-inch-thick matchsticks. Sprinkle with the salt and lemon juice and toss with the dressing.

DAILY SPECIAL

MENU IDEAS **French Roasted Onion Soup (page 37)** ✳ **Everyday Split Pea Soup (page 77)** ✳ **Tuscan Bean Soup (page 100)** ✳ **Vegetable Pistou (page 101)** ✳ **Mushroom Noodle Goulash (page 46)**

Composed Beet Salad

Both the robust flavor and white color of the blue cheese provide a provocative counterpoint to the lemony sweetness and dark crimson of the beets. The crumbled cheese turns pink upon contact with the beets, so add it just before serving if you want to preserve its contrasting color. Spicy, assertive greens complete the salad, which looks especially stunning on radicchio.

These beets are very appealing even without the greens and cheese and can make a great side accompaniment to a sandwich. The marinated beets will keep well for 3 or 4 days, if any are left over.

SERVES 4 TO 6
TOTAL TIME: 35 TO 45 MINUTES

PER 6-OUNCE SERVING: 170 CALORIES, 6 G PROTEIN, 12.1 G FAT, 11.4 G CARBO-HYDRATES, 5 G SATURATED FATTY ACIDS, 12 MG CHOLESTEROL, 696 MG SODIUM, 2.8 G TOTAL DIETARY FIBER

2 quarts water
3 large beets, scrubbed
5 tablespoons fresh lemon juice
3 tablespoons canola, olive, or other vegetable oil
1 tablespoon minced fresh parsley
8 scallions, sliced
1 teaspoon salt
2 cups mesclun, radicchio, watercress, spinach, or arugula
3 to 4 ounces crumbled blue cheese or sliced fresh goat cheese

Bring the water to a boil in a soup pot and, meanwhile, trim the leaf stems of the beets to about an inch. Ease the whole beets into the boiling water, partially cover, and simmer on medium-high heat until tender and easily pierced with a knife, 30 to 40 minutes.

Meanwhile, whisk together the lemon juice, oil, parsley, scallions, and salt in a medium bowl and set aside. Rinse and dry the greens and transfer to a serving platter.

Drain the cooked beets and rinse them with cold water. When the beets have cooled enough to handle, squeeze and slip them out of their skins. Slice off the stem ends and cut into 1-inch cubes (see Note). Add the beets to the dressing and toss well. Arrange the beets on the bed of greens and top with the cheese.

Note Cooking beets whole will preserve more sweetness than cutting them before cooking, but cut beets will cook faster if you're short on time. Just peel the raw beets, cut off the stem ends, and cut into cubes. Cook in boiling water until tender, about 15 minutes

MENU IDEAS **Butternut Squash Soup with Sizzled Sage (page 28)** ✳ **French Roasted Onion Soup (page 37)** ✳ **Matzo Ball Soup (page 86)** ✳ **Wild Rice & Mushroom Soup (page 103)** ✳ **Loblo (page 274)** ✳ **Eastern European Kasha & Mushrooms (page 206)**

Curried Potato Salad

Potatoes are great curried and creamy. This salad is good picnic or side dish fare. Or serve it on mixed greens with hard-boiled eggs and a light soup, and you have a complete meal.

Optional pretty garnishes for this spicy, hearty salad include chopped tomatoes, fresh cilantro sprigs, and/or toasted sesame seeds.

SERVES 4 TO 6
PREPARATION TIME: 20 MINUTES
STANDING TIME: 30 MINUTES

PER 9-OUNCE SERVING: 251 CALORIES, 6.5 G PROTEIN, 9.6 G FAT, 36.6 G CARBO-HYDRATES, 4.9 G SATURATED FATTY ACIDS, 21 MG CHOLESTEROL, 538 MG SODIUM, 5.3 G TOTAL DIETARY FIBER

6 cups cubed potatoes
1 teaspoon salt
½ teaspoon turmeric
1 cup peeled and diced carrots
1 cup diced red or green bell peppers
1 cup fresh or frozen green peas

DRESSING

1 tablespoon canola or other vegetable oil
2 teaspoons grated fresh ginger root
1 tablespoon ground coriander
1 teaspoon ground cumin
¼ teaspoon ground cloves
½ teaspoon turmeric
⅛ teaspoon cayenne, or to taste
4 ounces Neufchâtel or cream cheese, at room temperature*
¼ cup plain yogurt
2 to 3 teaspoons fresh lemon juice
salt to taste

* Cream cheese or Neufchâtel can be heated briefly in a microwave or toaster oven if it isn't soft enough to mix easily.

Put the cubed potatoes in a saucepan with water to cover. Add the salt and turmeric, cover, and bring to a boil; then reduce the heat and simmer until just tender, about 10 minutes. Drain and set aside.

Meanwhile, in a separate pot of boiling water, blanch or steam the carrots, peppers, and peas, one vegetable at a time, until just tender. Remove with a sieve and transfer to a large serving bowl.

In a small skillet, warm the oil for the dressing. Add the ginger root, coriander, cumin, cloves, turmeric, and cayenne and cook for about a minute, stirring constantly to prevent burning; then remove from the heat. In a small bowl, whisk together the Neufchâtel or cream cheese, the yogurt, 2 teaspoons of the lemon juice, and the sautéed spices.

Add the cooled potatoes to the bowl of blanched vegetables, pour on the dressing, and toss gently to coat. Let the salad sit at room temperature for at least 30 minutes for the flavors to blend.

Add salt and more lemon juice to taste and serve.

MENU IDEAS **Tomato Rasam (page 96)** ✳ **chilled Mango Soup (page 154)** ✳ **Jamaican Tomato Soup (page 41)** ✳ **Potage Celeste (page 130)** ✳ **Honey Mustard Green Beans Vinaigrette (page 269) with Spicy Border-style Tomato Salad (page 287)**

Curried Tofu Salad

Tofu salads are showing up everywhere now—not only in natural food stores and gourmet delis, but in groceries, supermarkets, and some mainstream restaurants as well. This is our favorite version of a simple tofu salad to serve on greens, as a filling for sandwiches, or to spread on crackers as an appetizer or snack. It's tasty and good for you.

SERVES 6
PREPARATION TIME: 30 MINUTES
CHILLING TIME: AT LEAST 1 HOUR

PER 5-OUNCE SERVING: 164 CALORIES, 6.5 G PROTEIN, 11.6 G FAT, 11.3 G CARBOHYDRATES, 1.6 G SATURATED FATTY ACIDS, 5 MG CHOLESTEROL, 279 MG SODIUM, 2.7 G TOTAL DIETARY FIBER

3 cups water
1 teaspoon salt
1 cake of tofu, cut into ½-inch cubes (12 ounces)
1 large carrot, peeled and shredded
1 small red bell pepper, seeded and minced
1 small green bell pepper, seeded and minced
1 celery stalk, minced
1 tablespoon minced fresh chives
¼ cup pumpkin or sunflower seeds
½ cup mayonnaise
1 to 2 teaspoons of your favorite curry powder, to taste
1 tablespoon fresh lemon juice
salt and ground black pepper to taste

fresh salad greens (optional)

Bring the water to a boil in a saucepan. Add the salt, ease in the tofu cubes, and blanch for 3 minutes. Drain well and refrigerate.

In a serving bowl, toss together the carrots, bell peppers, celery, chives, and pumpkin or sunflower seeds. In a small bowl, mix together the mayonnaise, curry powder, and lemon juice. Stir the dressing into the vegetables and set aside in the refrigerator.

When the tofu has cooled, mix it into the vegetables and add salt and pepper to taste. Chill for at least an hour, to allow the flavors to emerge.

Serve on salad greens, if desired.

Variations   Replace the chives with an equal amount of minced red onions or scallions.

MENU IDEAS **East African Groundnut Soup (page 74)** ✳ **Indian Tomato Rice Soup (page 81)** ✳ **Jamaican Tomato Soup (page 41)** ✳ **Roasted Red Pepper Coconut Soup (page 52)** ✳ **Asian Spinach & Orange Salad (page 246)** ✳ **Wilted Spinach & Portabella Mushrooms (page 239)**

Dave's Mom's Best Slaw

In the Dietrich clan, no family meal is complete without Dave's mom's slaw. You'll need a blender to produce this pretty cabbage-carrot-parsley confetti. It holds its dressing beautifully and doesn't become watery as it sits. The trick is to drain all of the ingredients well.

SERVES 4 TO 6
TOTAL TIME: 30 MINUTES

PER 6-OUNCE SERVING: 156 CALORIES, 2.6 G PROTEIN, 7.4 G FAT, 22.1 G CARBO-HYDRATES, 1.4 G SATURATED FATTY ACIDS, 8 MG CHOLESTEROL, 272 MG SODIUM, 3.1 G TOTAL DIETARY FIBER

6½ cups coarsely chopped cabbage, loosely packed (1 small head)
1 carrot, peeled and cut into chunks (about 1 cup)
½ cup prepared mayonnaise
¼ cup sugar
2½ tablespoons cider vinegar
¼ teaspoon salt
¼ cup evaporated milk
½ cup minced fresh parsley, well packed*

2 tablespoons chopped fresh chives or scallions (optional)

*Be sure the parsley is not wet from rinsing. Pat it dry before adding it to the slaw.

Working in batches, fill a blender to the top with chopped cabbage and add cool water until ¾ full. Whirl on low speed for about 4 seconds, just until the cabbage is evenly chopped—but not too fine—and transfer to a large colander. Repeat with the remaining cabbage. Occasionally stir the cabbage in the colander up from the bottom to help it drain until the water completely stops dripping.

Place the carrot chunks in the blender and cover them with cool water. Whirl for about 8 seconds. Drain the carrots very well. In a small bowl, whisk together the mayonnaise, sugar, vinegar, salt, and evaporated milk and set the dressing aside.

In a serving bowl, mix together the well-drained cabbage, carrots, and the parsley. Toss with the dressing and add more sugar, vinegar, and/or salt to taste. If you like, serve topped with chives or scallions.

Tightly covered and refrigerated, this slaw will keep for a week.

MENU IDEAS **Baked Bean Soup (page 69)** ✳ **Texas Two-Bean Soup (page 95)** ✳ **Catfish Gumbo (page 166)** ✳ **Green & White Gumbo (page 80)** ✳ **Avocado Seitan Salad (page 194)** ✳ **Louisiana Black-eyed Pea Salad (page 221)** ✳ **Seafood Paella Salad (page 308)**

East Indian Fruit Salad

The essential superiority of fresh fruit in season is the key to this marvelous fruit salad. Fresh coconut is fantastic and extracting the coconut meat from its shell is well worth the effort. Mineolas are larger and sweeter than mandarin oranges or tangerines and we recommend using them if you can find them. Although fresh fruit needs no adornment, the spices add a clean freshness and exotic fragrance to the salad.

The sweet succulence of East Indian Fruit Salad is the perfect counterpoint to a thick soup or a curried salad. Or it can be served as dessert.

SERVES 6 TO 8
TO PREPARE FRESH COCONUT:
40 MINUTES
TOTAL TIME: 20 MINUTES WITH PREPARED COCONUT

PER 5-OUNCE SERVING: 105 CALORIES, 1.4 G PROTEIN, 3.6 G FAT, 19.2 G CARBOHYDRATES, 2.9 G SATURATED FATTY ACIDS, 0 MG CHOLESTEROL, 26 MG SODIUM, 3.5 G TOTAL DIETARY FIBER

¼ **teaspoon black peppercorns**
⅛ **teaspoon cardamom seeds**
½ **teaspoon coriander seeds**
¼ **teaspoon cumin seeds**
⅛ **teaspoon ground cinnamon**
pinch of freshly grated nutmeg
dash of salt
4 oranges, preferably Mineola*
2 kiwis, peeled and sliced into ½-inch-thick circles
1 cup fresh coconut chips (see Note)
1 teaspoon grated fresh ginger root
2 bananas, sliced into rounds
1 cup sliced fresh strawberries

Mineolas look like "outie" navel oranges. They have large, exceptionally juicy sections, few seeds, and a bright sweet flavor.

In a small dry skillet, toast the peppercorns, cardamom, coriander, and cumin on low heat until fragrant. Combine the toasted spices with the cinnamon, nutmeg, and salt in an electric spice grinder and whirl until fine and powdery. Set aside.

Section each orange (page 373). Squeeze the juice from the membrane into a serving bowl. Cut the kiwi slices into quarter circles. Add the orange sections, kiwi, coconut, ginger root, bananas, and strawberries to the bowl. Toss the salad with half of the ground spice mixture, then add more to taste.

Serve at room temperature.

Note Pierce the eyes of a fresh coconut and drain out the mildly sweet liquid. To shrink the meat from the shell, bake the whole drained coconut at 350° for 15 to 30 minutes. Crack open the coconut with a hammer. Separate the meat from the husk and peel off the brown papery skin. (See page 360 for more details.) For the prettiest salad, cut the meat into ½-inch strips and thinly slice crosswise to make chips.

If you prefer shredded coconut, use either ⅔ cup fresh or ½ cup dried. Using dried coconut will make a sweeter salad.

Unused fresh coconut can be wrapped in plastic and frozen for future use.

MENU IDEAS **Curried Cauliflower Soup (page 32)** ✳ **Choklay's Tibetan Lentil Soup (page 73)** ✳ **Cream of Spinach Soup (page 120)** ✳ **Gado Gado (page 212)** ✳ **chilled Strawberry Soup (page 159)** ✳ **Curried Scallop & Noodle Salad (page 300)** ✳ **Curried Tofu Salad (page 256)**

Fennel & Arugula Salad with Grapefruit

If you want to tantalize guests with a tossed salad that departs from the norm, try this crisp, juicy, aromatic alternative. The secret is in the dressing, a mix of odd bedfellows that come together in a remarkable way. In a Daily Special, you'll want a distinctive soup to underscore the high-flying flavor of this salad. We especially like it with Spanish-style soups.

With our quick method, there's time to drain and thicken the yogurt while you prepare the rest of the salad and dressing.

SERVES 6
TOTAL TIME: 35 MINUTES

PER 6.5-OUNCE SERVING: 130 CALORIES, 4.4 G PROTEIN, 6 G FAT, 16.5 G CARBOHY-DRATES, 1.8 G SATURATED FATTY ACIDS, 3 MG CHOLESTEROL, 116 MG SODIUM, 1.1 G TOTAL DIETARY FIBER

1 fennel bulb
2 to 3 cups arugula leaves or mesclun
½ red onion, very thinly sliced
2 grapefruits, peeled and sectioned*

LIGHT CITRUS DRESSING

2 tablespoons canola or other vegetable oil
¼ cup fresh grapefruit juice*
¾ cup drained plain nonfat yogurt (see Note)
½ teaspoon ground fennel seeds
½ teaspoon ground black pepper
2 tablespoons grated Parmesan cheese
1 to 2 tablespoons honey
salt to taste

* To section a grapefruit, remove the peel and white pith with a knife. Holding the grapefruit over a bowl, slip a paring knife between the membrane and one of the sides of a section, cutting in toward the center and back out the other side with a single V-like motion to release the section into the bowl. Repeat the process around the grapefruit.

The 2 sectioned grapefruits for this recipe should yield at least ¼ cup of fresh grapefruit juice. The bowl will catch any dripping juices as you work and squeezing the pulp after sectioning will provide more juice. Strain before using.

Trim and rinse the fennel bulb. Cut it in half lengthwise, thinly slice each half into semicircles, and transfer to a serving bowl. Rinse the arugula or mesclun and dry it in a salad spinner or with a towel. Tear the leaves into bite-sized pieces, add them to the bowl, and top with the red onion slices and grapefruit sections. Cover the bowl with a damp towel and chill until ready to serve.

In a small bowl, whisk together all of the dressing ingredients until creamy. Refrigerate the dressing in a glass jar until ready to serve.

Just before serving, pour the dressing over the salad and toss gently to distribute well.

Note Quick Yogurt Draining Method: Spoon 1½ cups of yogurt into a colander lined with coffee filters or several layers of cheesecloth. Place the colander in a large bowl. Cover the yogurt with plastic wrap and weight the top with a plate and heavy can or other object. Drain for 30 minutes in the refrigerator. This will yield about ¾ cup of drained yogurt.

MENU IDEAS Albondigas Soup (page 26) ✳ **Classic Tomato Garlic Soup (page 30)** ✳ **Yellow Pepper Purée (page 58)** ✳ **Liberian Black-eyed Pea Soup (page 84)** ✳ **Ybor City Garbanzo Soup (page 107)**

Fennel Salad with Blue Cheese

Popular with lovers of French or Italian cuisine, fennel bulbs (sometimes mistakenly labeled anise) are now available in many large supermarkets. With a licorice flavor and a celery-like crunchiness, fennel bulb is delicious raw or cooked, and its lacy fronds have a delicate flavor and make an elegant garnish. In this recipe, the bulbs are sliced or grated into a slaw and tossed with a creamy blue cheese vinaigrette, then garnished with chopped fronds.

Fennel seeds, used ground in the dressing, are a richly aromatic spice that sweeten the palate. The seeds are harvested from yet another fennel plant that is a member of the parsley family and doesn't form bulbs. The salad can be refrigerated overnight and will remain crisp and tasty.

SERVES 4 TO 6
TOTAL TIME: 30 MINUTES

PER 3.25-OUNCE SERVING: 77 CALORIES, 1.9 G PROTEIN, 4.8 G FAT, 7.8 G CARBO-HYDRATES, 1.7 G SATURATED FATTY ACIDS, 8 MG CHOLESTEROL, 152 MG SODIUM, 0.1 G TOTAL DIETARY FIBER

4 cups thinly sliced or coarsely grated fennel bulb (about 2 small bulbs, with fronds)
1 tablespoon fresh lemon juice
⅓ cup chopped fresh parsley
chopped fennel fronds

DRESSING

⅓ cup sour cream
3 tablespoons prepared mayonnaise
1 tablespoon cider vinegar
2 teaspoons ground fennel seeds
¼ teaspoon coarsely ground black pepper
2 to 3 tablespoons chopped fresh tarragon (1 to 2 teaspoons dried)
2 tablespoons crumbled blue cheese
salt to taste
2 to 3 tablespoons milk (optional)

In a large colorful serving bowl, toss the sliced or grated fennel bulb with the lemon juice, parsley, and fennel fronds until evenly distributed. Set aside.

In a blender or food processor, whirl all of the dressing ingredients for a few seconds until blended but not perfectly smooth. Add a little milk if the dressing is too thick. Stir the dressing into the salad and mix well.

Serve immediately or chill until ready to serve.

MENU IDEAS **Classic Tomato Garlic Soup (page 30)** ✳ **French Roasted Onion Soup (page 37)** ✳ **Potato & Escarole Soup (page 51)** ✳ **chilled Scandinavian Dried Fruit Soup (page 158)** ✳ **Curried Zucchini Soup (page 126)** ✳ **Liberian Black-eyed Pea Soup (page 84)**

Fig & Endive Salad

The Calimyrna is a fairly recent addition to the ancient fig family. It was derived from the Turkish Smyrna, which was introduced to California in the late nineteenth century. Here the natural sweetness and moistness of its flesh is heightened by the natural sweetness of the orange juice. Chèvre and endive contribute the perfect top and bottom notes to this elegant salad trio.

SERVES 4
TOTAL TIME: 20 MINUTES

PER 8.5-OUNCE SERVING: 359 CALORIES, 8.3 G PROTEIN, 20.9 G FAT, 42.9 CARBOHYDRATES, 5.7 G SATURATED FATTY ACIDS, 11 MG CHOLESTEROL, 257 MG SODIUM, 8.9 G TOTAL DIETARY FIBER

10 dried Calimyrna figs (page 363)
½ cup orange juice

DRESSING

½ teaspoon freshly grated orange peel
2 tablespoons orange juice
2 tablespoons canola or other vegetable oil
1 tablespoon cider vinegar
¼ teaspoon salt
¼ teaspoon ground black pepper

3 heads of Belgian endive, rinsed and drained
2 ounces chèvre or other mild goat cheese, crumbled
½ cup coarsely chopped toasted walnuts*

Toast the walnuts in a single layer on an unoiled baking tray in a conventional or toaster oven at 350° for about 5 minutes, until fragrant and golden brown.

In a small saucepan, bring the figs and orange juice to a boil and cook on high heat for 1 minute. Cover with a tight-fitting lid, remove from the heat, and set aside.

In a small bowl, whisk together all of the dressing ingredients and set aside. Cut the heads of endive lengthwise into halves and remove the cores. Chop the leaves into 1-inch pieces to yield about 3 cups, loosely packed. When the figs are soft and plump (see Note), cut them into quarters.

Arrange the endive on a large platter and top it with the figs, chèvre, and walnuts. Drizzle the dressing over the salad and serve.

Note The amount of "plumping" time varies with different figs but is usually 10 to 20 minutes.

Variation Try a vegan version of the salad and omit the chèvre. It's still sweet, delicious, and interesting. It could even pass as dessert in some circles.

MENU IDEAS **French Roasted Onion Soup (page 37)** ✳ **Baked Bean Soup (page 69)** ✳ **Black Bean & Chipotle Soup (page 70)** ✳ **chilled Fennel Vichyssoise (page 149)** ✳ **Tunisian Pumpkin Soup (page 56)**

Five-Herb Salad

This is a vibrant salad with a vitamin jolt that should make you feel healthy and virtuous. The clean, strong flavors of herbs and greens lightly dressed make it an interesting counterpoint to a richer, milder dish.

SERVES 6
TOTAL TIME: 20 MINUTES

PER 4.25-OUNCE SERVING: 43 CALORIES, 1.6 G PROTEIN, 2.6 G FAT, 4.2 G CARBO-HYDRATES, 0.4 G SATURATED FATTY ACIDS, 0 MG CHOLESTEROL, 64 MG SODIUM, 2.4 G TOTAL DIETARY FIBER

6 cups mixed salad greens*
1 to 2 cups celery leaves
2 or 3 scallions, sliced on the diagonal
1 tablespoon chopped fresh basil
¼ cup chopped fresh parsley
1 tablespoon chopped fresh dill
1 tablespoon sliced or chopped fresh mint
1 tablespoon fresh lemon juice or balsamic vinegar
1 tablespoon extra-virgin olive oil
1 or 2 garlic cloves, very finely minced or pressed
salt and ground black pepper to taste

For convenience and a good mix of greens, we recommend ready-to-serve bulk mixed baby greens, which in the produce market might be called spring mix, field mix, or mesclun.

If you prefer, prepare 2 cups of stemmed whole or halved spinach leaves, 2 cups of arugula torn in half, and 2 cups of whole or halved mizuna. The greens ought to be bite-sized, so tear or chop accordingly.

Combine the greens, celery leaves, scallions, basil, parsley, dill, and mint in a large serving bowl. Sprinkle on the lemon juice or balsamic vinegar and the olive oil and garlic. Toss well, add salt and pepper to taste, and serve.

MENU IDEAS **Creamy Onion & Fontina Soup (page 123)** ✳ **Bourride (page 164)** ✳ **Welsh Rarebit Soup (page 135)** ✳ **Flemish Farm Soup (page 36)** ✳ **Green & White Gumbo (page 80)** ✳ **Parsnip Pear Soup (page 49)**

Florida Salad with Ginger Dressing

This fabulous-looking salad is a tiny tropical holiday on a plate. Pair Florida Salad with dishes from the Caribbean, and also with those from Mexico, Southeast Asia, West Africa, and India.

SERVES 4 TO 6
TOTAL TIME: 35 MINUTES

PER 9.5-OUNCE SERVING: 208 CALORIES, 2.3 G PROTEIN, 12.9 G FAT, 24.9 G CARBO-HYDRATES, 1.9 G SATURATED FATTY ACIDS, 0 MG CHOLESTEROL, 207 MG SODIUM, 4.8 G TOTAL DIETARY FIBER

1 ripe mango
1 ripe Hass avocado*
2 ruby grapefruits
1 papaya
5 ounces mixed baby greens, such as mesclun or field mix

DRESSING

1 tablespoon grated fresh ginger root
1 teaspoon freshly grated orange peel
6 tablespoons orange juice (3/8 cup)
1/3 cup fresh lime juice
3 tablespoons olive oil or vegetable oil
1/2 teaspoon salt

1 kiwi, sliced
1/2 cup walnut pieces (optional)

A ripe avocado yields slightly to pressure, has no extremely soft spots, and is still shapely. To hasten ripening, place in a paper bag at room temperature.

Peel the mango and slice it lengthwise into slender wedges. Cut the avocado in half lengthwise, twist to separate the halves, and remove the pit. Score each half into slender wedges and, with a spoon or your thumb, separate the wedges from the peel. Peel and section the grapefruits (page 259). Cut the papaya in half lengthwise and remove the seeds. Score it down to the peel into small cubes and scoop the cubes away from the peel with a spoon (see Note). Rinse and drain the greens and set them aside in a bowl.

Combine all of the dressing ingredients in a blender and purée until smooth. Toss the greens with half of the dressing. On individual plates, make a bed of greens and mound the papaya cubes in the very center. Arrange the mango, avocado, and grapefruit pieces around the papaya like spokes of a wheel: group each color together like three fans or alternate colors like a pinwheel. Have fun creating designer plates. Drizzle the remaining dressing over the fruit.

Garnish with slices of kiwi and, if you like, a few walnut pieces. Serve immediately.

Note If the papaya is not very ripe, it will be easier to separate the cubes of flesh from the peel by using a scooping motion with a small sharp knife.

DAILY SPECIAL

MENU IDEAS Caribbean Sweet Potato Coconut Soup (page 29) * **Chinese Velvet Corn Soup (page 116)** * **Indian Roasted Eggplant Soup (page 40)** * **Spiced Mexican Squash Stew (page 54)** * **Catfish Gumbo (page 166)**

Fresh Fruit Combinations

If poets have license with words, then cooks should have license with ingredients — and fruit is the perfect medium for taking culinary artistic liberties. With a dazzling palette of common and uncommon fruits and vegetables, you can create refreshing seasonal salads, intriguing combo plates, and delicious accompaniments. * Fruits from over the border and over the seas appear regularly in supermarkets across the United States. Fruits with names like blood orange, Australian orange, passion fruit, Asian pear, pomegranate, carambola, prickly pear, and persimmon catch our attention and pique our curiosity. Other "fruits" that have long been grouped with vegetables make tasty companions for their long-lost relatives: cucumbers, avocados, tomatoes, and chiles add crunch, lusciousness, color, and spice to fruit salads. * Fruits such as pears, apples, and peaches stay bright and fresh when sprinkled with vinegar or citrus juice or when dipped in a light syrup. Here's our simple syrup recipe.

LIGHT SYRUP FOR FRUIT

Combine 1 cup of water and 2 to 4 tablespoons of sugar in a saucepan. Add one or more of the following, if you wish: vanilla bean, cinnamon stick, slices of fresh ginger root, rosemary leaves, thyme leaves, freshly grated lemon, orange, or lime peel, a few raspberries, pomegranate seeds, or fresh mint leaves. Simmer for about 10 minutes. Cool slightly and add 2 teaspoons of fresh lemon juice. Strain. Dip sliced fruit into the syrup and then add to salads.

We hope the following ideas will stimulate your imagination and add to your repertoire of appealing, beautiful salads:

Apricot Berry Sweet Talk   Steep sliced apricots, sliced peaches, and berries in vanilla-, cinnamon-, thyme-, orange-, or raspberry-flavored syrup. Serve over mesclun.

Asian Pear & Grapefruit on Greens   Prepare a bed of arugula on a serving platter. Arrange pear slices and grapefruit sections (page 259) on it and top with sliced scallions. Peel a pomegranate, remove the seeds from the membrane, and add them to the salad. Serve plain or drizzled with a light vinaigrette.

Avocado Melon Mélange   Peel, pit, and slice an avocado. Peel and seed a honeydew melon and 2 cucumbers and chop into bite-sized pieces. Peel and section a grapefruit (page 259). Gently combine everything in a serving bowl and stir in chopped fresh mint and cilantro. Serve immediately.

Carambola, Grapes & Apples Dip sliced carambola and apple slices in light syrup and gently toss with grapes. Serve chilled or at room temperature.

Cherries Royale Prepare our light syrup with fresh lemon juice and no other flavoring. Dip cherries and mango or peach slices into the syrup. Arrange the fruit on a platter or in a bowl and serve immediately.

Mango Salsa Salad Peel, pit, and slice a mango. Peel, seed, and slice a cucumber. Halve some cherry tomatoes and seed and dice a red bell pepper. Sprinkle with fresh lime juice, chopped fresh cilantro, and minced jalapeños.

Melba Vinaigrette Peel, pit, and slice peaches into a bowl. Sprinkle raspberries and vinaigrette over the peaches. Gently toss. Set aside for 1/2 hour before serving.

Melon & Mint Sprinkle slices or chunks of honeydew, crenshaw, watermelon, or cantaloupe with freshly squeezed lime juice and chopped fresh mint.

Oranges, Hot & Sweet Peel oranges and section into a bowl (page 373). Stir in a few tablespoons of honey and minced jalapeños. Allow the oranges to macerate at room temperature for 30 to 45 minutes before serving, or chill and then bring to room temperature before serving.

Oranges Exotic Toast walnuts in a 350° oven for about 10 minutes. Combine peeled and sectioned oranges (page 373), a few pomegranate seeds, and a few thin slices of sweet red onion in a bowl. Place the remaining pomegranate seeds in a sieve and press with the back of a spoon to drizzle their juice over the fruit. Top with walnuts and serve.

Pears Parmesan Thinly slice pears (and/or apples) and place them in light syrup. Toast walnuts at 350° for 10 minutes, cool, and coarsely chop. Remove the fruit from the syrup and arrange with the nuts on a platter. Top with slivers of Parmesan cheese.

Pineapple Passion Choose a ripe, mostly yellow pineapple with a sweet aroma. Peel the fruit and cut it into bite-sized chunks. Sprinkle the pineapple with fresh lime juice. Cut a wrinkled brown passion fruit in half and scoop out the seeds and juice into a small cup or bowl. Strain and discard the seeds and stir the juice into the pineapple. Serve at room temperature or chill until needed.

Strawberries with a Touch of Tart Hull the strawberries, sprinkle them with a little sugar and balsamic vinegar or fresh lemon juice, and stir gently. Set aside at room temperature for at least 1/2 hour before serving.

Summer Fruit Fest Place peeled kiwi, hulled strawberries, and a little sugar in a blender and purée to a sauce. Drizzle the kiwi-strawberry sauce over summer fruits, such as peaches, nectarines, apricots, and berries.

Fresh Pear & Blue Cheese Salad

What an understated, elegant green salad, featuring the perfect pairing of crumbled creamy blue cheese, aged and musky, and crisp slivers of pear, dewy and sweet. It is an impressive first or last course, and it's the perfect partner for a hearty fall or winter soup in a simple Daily Special.

SERVES 4
TOTAL TIME: 15 MINUTES

PER 5-OUNCE SERVING: 158 CALORIES, 5.1 G PROTEIN, 10.5 G FAT, 13.3 G CARBOHYDRATES, 2.7 G SATURATED FATTY ACIDS, 7 MG CHOLESTEROL, 452 MG SODIUM, 1 G TOTAL DIETARY FIBER

4 cups arugula or other salad greens
1 large firm Bosc, Bartlett, or red D'Anjou pear

DRESSING
3 tablespoons orange juice
2 tablespoons fresh lemon juice
2 tablespoons olive oil
2 garlic cloves, minced or pressed
½ teaspoon salt

⅓ cup crumbled blue cheese

Thoroughly rinse and dry the greens and spread them on a serving platter. Peel and core the pear and cut it into thin slices. Arrange the pear slices (decoratively, if you're so inclined) on top of the greens. In a small bowl, whisk together the dressing ingredients until well blended.

To serve, pour the dressing over the pears and greens and sprinkle the blue cheese on top.

DAILY SPECIAL

MENU IDEAS **Vegetable Pistou (page 101)** ✳ **Everyday Split Pea Soup (page 77)** ✳ **Butternut Squash Soup with Sizzled Sage (page 28)** ✳ **Scandinavian Salmon Soup (page 171)** ✳ **Autumn Minestrone (page 67)**

Fruit with Cranberry Currant Dressing

Crisp fresh fruit is so welcome in midwinter. The tart-sweet dressing gives a pleasant jolt and a gorgeous ruby-red color to this easily made salad. It's refreshing unadorned, or you can transform it into a luscious dessert with a dollop of yogurt or scoop of your favorite vanilla ice cream.

SERVES 6
PREPARATION TIME: 10 MINUTES
COOKING TIME: ABOUT 15 MINUTES
TOTAL TIME: 25 MINUTES

PER 7-OUNCE SERVING: 161 CALORIES, 1.1 G PROTEIN, 0.5 G FAT, 41.7 G CARBO-HYDRATES, 0 G SATURATED FATTY ACIDS, 0 MG CHOLESTEROL, 2 MG SODIUM, 5.4 G TOTAL DIETARY FIBER

WARM CRANBERRY CURRANT DRESSING

1 teaspoon freshly grated orange peel
juice of 1 orange, plus water to make 1 cup
⅓ cup sugar
1 teaspoon grated fresh ginger root (optional)
12 ounces fresh cranberries
½ cup currants

2 firm, tart apples, such as Granny Smith or Crispin
2 firm, ripe pears, such as Bartlett or D'Anjou
1 tablespoon fresh lemon juice
1 tablespoon water

toasted walnuts or pecans*
sliced bananas

* Toast the nuts in a single layer on an unoiled baking tray in a conventional or toaster oven at 350° for about 5 minutes, until fragrant and golden brown.

In a nonreactive saucepan on medium heat, bring the orange peel, diluted orange juice, sugar, and ginger, if using, to a simmer. Meanwhile, rinse the cranberries and discard any that are discolored or soft. Stir the simmering liquid until the sugar dissolves. Add the cranberries and bring to a low boil. Cook, stirring occasionally, for about 5 minutes. Add the currants and continue to simmer for about 5 minutes, until the cranberries begin to pop. Remove from the heat.

Rinse the apples and pears. Peel them, if you wish, cut into bite-sized pieces, and place in a bowl. Combine the lemon juice and water, sprinkle it over the fruit, and toss well to prevent discoloration. Stir the cranberry dressing, and if it has thickened too much, add a little water.

Spoon the apples and pears into individual serving bowls, ladle on the dressing, and top with toasted nuts and sliced bananas.

DAILY SPECIAL

MENU IDEAS **Welsh Rarebit Soup (page 135)** ✳ **Wild Rice & Mushroom Soup (page 103)** ✳ **Creamy Onion & Fontina Soup (page 123)** ✳ **French Roasted Onion Soup (page 37)** ✳ **Green & White Gumbo (page 80)** ✳ **Baked Bean Soup (page 69)**

Golden Tomato Avocado Salad

Very pretty in a full spectrum of greens and golds, this tangy, refreshing salad is quite versatile. Use it as a delightful accompaniment to a Mexican or Caribbean entrée or serve it as a salsa topping. Try it on chilled seasoned black beans atop a bed of fresh greens, or use a few spoonfuls of it to dress up a hot bean dish served on rice or quinoa.

Create an almost instant chilled gazpacho soup by the simple addition of 1½ to 2 cups of chilled Basic Light Vegetable Stock (page 16) and serve with a crusty bread or tortilla chips.

SERVES 4 TO 6
PREPARATION TIME: 15 MINUTES
CHILLING TIME: 30 MINUTES

PER 6.5-OUNCE SERVING: 135 CALORIES, 2.1 G PROTEIN, 10.5 G FAT, 11.3 G CARBO-HYDRATES, 1.6 G SATURATED FATTY ACIDS, 0 MG CHOLESTEROL, 42 MG SODIUM, 3.9 G TOTAL DIETARY FIBER

2 cups chopped yellow and/or orange tomatoes*
1 yellow bell pepper, seeded and chopped into bite-sized pieces
1 large cucumber, peeled, seeded, and chopped
1 large avocado, diced into ½-inch cubes (see Note)
½ cup finely sliced scallions
⅓ to ½ cup fresh lime juice
¼ cup orange juice
2 tablespoons extra-virgin olive oil
2 tablespoons minced fresh basil
1 large garlic clove, minced or pressed
1 teaspoon minced fresh cilantro (optional)
salt and ground black pepper to taste

*Yellow and orange tomatoes are only available seasonally in many climates and we recommend you take advantage of this recipe when they're around. Ripe, tasty red tomatoes can also be used, however.

Combine all of the ingredients in a serving bowl, toss well, and serve or refrigerate.

Note To dice an avocado, slice around its center lengthwise, gently twist the halves apart, and remove the pit. With a paring knife, cut the flesh into cubes right in the skins and scoop them out with a serving spoon. This is amazingly quick and easy when an avocado is perfectly ripe and more troublesome (and less tasty) when it's under- or overripe. A ripe avocado will be a little fragrant and yield slightly to thumb pressure.

DAILY SPECIAL

MENU IDEAS **Caribbean Sweet Potato Coconut Soup (page 29)** ✳ **Black Bean & Chipotle Soup (page 70)** ✳ **San Juan Shrimp & Rice Soup (page 170)** ✳ **Mexican Butter Bean Soup (page 85)** ✳ **Andean Quinoa & Corn Salad (page 189)** ✳ **Southern Wheat-free Cornbread (page 335)**

Honey Mustard Green Beans Vinaigrette

The combination of honey and mustard is common—a popular favorite—and yet whenever we serve this easy-to-make salad, people always ask, "What *is* the intriguing and delicious dressing on the beans?"

SERVES 4
TOTAL TIME: 25 MINUTES

PER 5-OUNCE SERVING: 105 CALORIES, 2.4 G PROTEIN, 5.8 G FAT, 13.5 G CARBO-HYDRATES, 1.5 G SATURATED FATTY ACIDS, 0 MG CHOLESTEROL, 377 MG SODIUM, 0.1 G TOTAL DIETARY FIBER

8 cups water
1 teaspoon salt
1 pound green beans
¼ cup fresh lemon juice
2 tablespoons canola or other vegetable oil
1 tablespoon honey
2 tablespoons Dijon mustard
salt and ground black pepper to taste

a few thin strips of pimiento, red bell pepper, or red onion

Combine the water and salt in a saucepan and bring to a rolling boil. Meanwhile, stem and rinse the green beans, then cut them in half crosswise to yield about 4 cups. Blanch or steam the green beans in the boiling water for about 5 minutes, or just until soft.

While the beans cook, whisk together the lemon juice, oil, honey, and mustard in a small bowl until smooth. Drain the green beans and place them in a serving bowl. Pour the dressing over them and toss well. Add salt and black pepper to taste.

The salad can be served hot, cold, or at room temperature, but the bright, deep green of the beans is most vibrant when served immediately. Regardless of the temperature of the dish, however, a few thin strips of pimiento, red bell pepper, or red onion make a nice taste and color contrast.

DAILY SPECIAL

MENU IDEAS **Corn Chowder (page 117)** ✳ **Creamy Herbed Potato Soup (page 122)** ✳ **Creamy Tomato Soup (page 125)** ✳ **Roasted Potato & Tomato Salad (page 284)** ✳ **Harvest Rice Salad (page 215)**

Indian Green Beans & Red Peppers

This quick, colorful side salad will look its best if the lime and/or yogurt is added at the table. Yogurt adds both creamy texture and tang, and we love that finishing squirt of lime juice — giving a bright touch to this excellent salad.

Use Indian Green Beans & Red Peppers to perk up an Indian-style meal. It is also an appropriate side dish in other cuisines that use complex spice mixtures, such as those of Southeast Asia and North Africa.

SERVES 4
TOTAL TIME: 25 MINUTES
CHILLING TIME (OPTIONAL):
  20 MINUTES

PER 8-OUNCE SERVING: 144 CALORIES, 3.9 G PROTEIN, 8 G FAT, 18 G CARBOHY-DRATES, 2 G SATURATED FATTY ACIDS, 0 MG CHOLESTEROL, 350 MG SODIUM, 6 G TOTAL DIETARY FIBER

1 quart lightly salted water
2 tablespoons canola or other vegetable oil
1 teaspoon whole cumin seeds
1 teaspoon whole black mustard seeds
1 teaspoon curry powder
2 teaspoons seeded and minced fresh green chiles
2 garlic cloves, minced or pressed
4 cups stemmed and cut green beans, 1-inch lengths (about 1 pound)
2 cups red bell peppers, cut into thin lengthwise strips, then
    crosswise into 1-inch pieces
½ teaspoon salt
¼ cup unsweetened dried shredded coconut (optional)

1 lime, cut into 4 wedges
½ cup plain nonfat yogurt (optional)

Bring the salted water to a boil for blanching the vegetables. Meanwhile, warm the oil in a small skillet. Add the cumin and mustard seeds and maintain medium heat for about a minute, until the mustard seeds begin to pop. Add the curry powder, chiles, and garlic and sauté on medium-low heat for about 4 minutes, stirring constantly to avoid scorching the spices. Remove from the heat and set aside.

Boil the green beans in the salted water for 3 to 5 minutes, until crisp but tender. Remove them with a strainer or slotted spoon and submerge in very cold water for about 1 minute. Drain well and transfer to a serving bowl. Repeat this process with the bell peppers, boiling for just 3 minutes. Add the spice mixture to the vegetables, being sure to scrape all of the fragrant spices and oil into the bowl. Stir in the salt.

If using, toast the coconut in a 350° oven or toaster oven for 5 minutes, until lightly golden. Stir the coconut into the salad. Garnish with lime wedges.

Serve at room temperature or chill for about 20 minutes. At the table, top each serving with some yogurt, if desired.

MENU IDEAS **Spinach with Cilantro Cashew Dressing (page 289) and Spiced Paneer (page 351)** * **Indian Roasted Eggplant Soup (page 40)** * **Tunisian Pumpkin Soup (page 56)** * **Indian Tomato Rice Soup (page 81)** * **Curried Scallop & Noodle Salad (page 300)** * **Broiled Tofu & Sugar Snap Peas (page 199)**

"Japanese" Tofu Salad

Probably no one else has ever made a salad exactly like this Moosewood original. The dressing is sort of a cross between Japanese *sunomono* (but we've added peanut butter and soy sauce) and *goma-ae,* a nut paste dressing (made with walnuts, not peanuts). Whatever its kinship to various Asian dishes, this is one good-tasting salad with an appealing smooth and crunchy texture. It also makes an innovative and yummy filling for pita sandwiches.

SERVES 6
PREPARATION TIME: 30 MINUTES
CHILLING TIME: AT LEAST 1 HOUR

PER 6-OUNCE SERVING: 130 CALORIES, 7.6 G PROTEIN, 6.4 G FAT, 13.3 G CARBO-HYDRATES, 1.1 G SATURATED FATTY ACIDS, 0 MG CHOLESTEROL, 618 MG SODIUM, 2.7 G TOTAL DIETARY FIBER

1 quart water
1 teaspoon salt
1 cake of tofu (12 ounces), cut into ½-inch cubes
2 carrots, peeled and cut into matchsticks* (about 1 cup)
1 red or green bell pepper, seeded and cut into thin 1-inch-long strips
¼ pound mung bean sprouts

DRESSING
¼ cup white, cider, or rice vinegar
1 tablespoon soy sauce
2 tablespoons sugar**
3 tablespoons natural peanut butter**

1 cucumber, peeled, seeded, and diced
1 tablespoon minced scallions, chives, or red onions
salt to taste

fresh spinach or lettuce leaves (optional)

* *By matchsticks, we mean 1½ × ¼-inch pieces. It's worth the effort—they make the look, harmony, and "mouth feel" of the salad just right.*
** *By natural peanut butter, we mean unhomogenized peanut butter with no sweeteners, preservatives, or stabilizers. If you use commercial sweetened peanut butter, reduce the sugar to 1 tablespoon.*

Bring the water and salt to a boil in a large pot. Carefully ease the tofu cubes into the boiling water, cook for 1 minute, and add the carrots. After another minute, add the bell pepper strips. Wait 1 minute, add the mung sprouts, and cook for just 30 seconds. Thoroughly drain everything in a colander or large sieve.

Purée the dressing ingredients in a blender or whisk together in a small bowl until smooth. Transfer the still warm tofu and vegetables to a serving bowl, add the dressing, and toss lightly. Chill for at least 1 hour, tossing every 15 to 20 minutes to redistribute the dressing.

About 10 minutes before serving, place the cucumbers in a colander, sprinkle some salt on them, and allow to drain. This will prevent their watery juices from diluting the salad dressing.

Just before serving, stir in the cucumbers and scallions, chives, or red onions. Add salt to taste. If you like, serve on a bed of spinach or lettuce.

DAILY SPECIAL

MENU IDEAS **Scallion Pancakes (page 350)** * **Ozoni (page 48)** * **Miso Noodle Soup (page 89)** * **chilled Gingered Plum Soup (page 152)** * **chilled Cherry Berry Beet Soup (page 143)** * **Seaweed Salad (page 285)**

Kale Salad

Like greens? This salad has lively flavor and is loaded with vitamins, iron, and other minerals—all good news for us aging baby boomers and everyone else. Look for young, tender kale; Red Russian is a flat-leafed variety that is exceptionally tender with a mild flavor.

This is a very pretty salad that can be an accompaniment to almost any main course fish dish. Or create a vegetable combo plate garnished with creamy avocado slices and/or juicy cantaloupe wedges. Make it even more festive by garnishing with the blossoms of a few edible flowers.

SERVES 6 TO 8
TOTAL TIME: 40 MINUTES

PER 6.5-OUNCE SERVING: 132 CALORIES, 4.2 G PROTEIN, 6.4 G FAT, 18.4 G CARBOHYDRATES, 0.9 G SATURATED FATTY ACIDS, 0 MG CHOLESTEROL, 205 MG SODIUM, 3.4 G TOTAL DIETARY FIBER

2 large bunches of kale, stemmed and well rinsed
3 tablespoons olive oil
1 cup diced red bell peppers
1 cup finely chopped red onions
1 cup diced celery
4 garlic cloves, minced or pressed
1 teaspoon paprika
⅛ teaspoon cayenne
¼ teaspoon ground black pepper
½ teaspoon salt
1 cup fresh, frozen, or canned corn kernels (15-ounce can, drained)*
2 tablespoons fresh lemon juice
1 tablespoon cider vinegar
1 cup chopped tomatoes

* Canned white corn is tender, crunchy, and sweet and especially nice in this salad, but yellow corn is fine, too. If using fresh or frozen corn, blanch in boiling water for 2 to 5 minutes, until just tender, and then drain.

In a covered pot, bring about 2 inches of water to a boil. Chop the kale leaves into bite-sized pieces to yield about 12 lightly packed cups. Cook the kale for 2 to 3 minutes, until bright green and tender but not soggy. Be careful not to overcook. Drain well.

In a skillet on medium heat, warm the olive oil. Add the bell peppers, onions, celery, garlic, paprika, cayenne, black pepper, and salt and sauté for 2 minutes, stirring often.

In a serving bowl, stir together the kale, sautéed vegetables, and spices. Add the corn, lemon juice, vinegar, and tomatoes and toss well. Serve at room temperature or chilled.

DAILY SPECIAL

MENU IDEAS **Southern Red Rice & Pecan Salad (page 228)** ✳ **Butternut Squash with Spicy Cranberry Sauce (page 252)** ✳ **Caribbean Sweet Potato Coconut Soup (page 29)** ✳ **chilled Avocado Tomatillo Soup (page 141)** ✳ **Creamy Herbed Potato Soup (page 122)** ✳ **Herbed Cheese Quick Bread (page 332)**

Kiwi, Orange & Baby Greens

This salad is lovely, luscious, easy to make, *and* it's "nutritionally correct"! The flavors and hues of the fruits and greens complement each other superbly and the vitamin C in the fruit helps the body absorb the iron in the greens. Most navel oranges separate into segments without having to remove the membrane, making preparation even simpler.

SERVES 4 TO 6
TOTAL TIME: 20 MINUTES

PER 4.5-OUNCE SERVING: 56 CALORIES, 1.1 G PROTEIN, 0.4 G FAT, 13.6 G CARBOHYDRATES, 0 G SATURATED FATTY ACIDS, 0 MG CHOLESTEROL, 103 MG SODIUM, 1.4 G TOTAL DIETARY FIBER

6 ounces mesclun (also called field mix, baby greens, or field greens)
2 navel oranges
3 kiwis
4 fresh strawberries

CITRUS DRESSING
2 tablespoons fresh orange juice
1 teaspoon fresh lime juice
1 tablespoon cider vinegar
1 teaspoon mild honey
¼ teaspoon salt
¼ teaspoon ground black pepper

Rinse and drain the greens. Wrap them loosely in a damp towel and refrigerate. Peel the oranges with a sharp paring knife and separate them into sections. Peel the kiwis and slice them into ¼-inch-thick rounds. Hull and slice the strawberries.

In a small bowl, whisk together all of the dressing ingredients.

In a serving bowl, gently toss the greens with half of the citrus dressing. Arrange the orange segments, kiwi slices, and strawberry slices on top and drizzle with the remaining dressing. Serve right away.

MENU IDEAS **Creamy Herbed Carrot Soup (page 121)** ✳ **Cream of Mushroom Soup (page 119)** ✳ **Everyday Split Pea Soup (page 77)** ✳ **Cauliflower, Cheese & Tomato Soup (page 114)** ✳ **Potage Celeste (page 130)**

Lobio

Lobio is the word for "bean" in the Georgian Republic, and this handsome and savory mixture of kidney beans and walnuts is a classic there. It goes especially well with root vegetables, cabbage, and mushrooms and other foods that we associate with Eastern European cuisines.

If you use canned beans, it's a breeze to make.

SERVES 4 TO 6
PREPARATION TIME: 25 MINUTES
SITTING TIME: 30 MINUTES

PER 6-OUNCE SERVING: 289 CALORIES, 13.5 G PROTEIN, 13.8 G FAT, 31 G CARBO-HYDRATES, 1.5 G SATURATED FATTY ACIDS, 0 MG CHOLESTEROL, 40 MG SODIUM, 1.3 G TOTAL DIETARY FIBER

3 cups cooked red kidney beans (two 14-ounce cans)
1 cup minced red onions
3 large garlic cloves, minced or pressed
3 tablespoons red wine vinegar
2 tablespoons olive oil
¾ cup toasted chopped walnuts*
¼ cup chopped fresh cilantro
¼ cup chopped fresh parsley
1 teaspoon ground coriander
salt and ground black pepper to taste

romaine or leaf lettuce
fresh cilantro or parsley sprigs
sliced radishes
tomato slices
pita bread wedges

* *Walnuts can be toasted in a dry skillet on medium heat or on an unoiled baking sheet in an oven or toaster oven at 350° for about 5 minutes. Toast until fragrant and lightly browned.*

If using dried kidney beans, sort and rinse them, cover with a generous amount of cold water, and let them soak for several hours or overnight. Discard the soaking water and simmer the beans in 2 quarts of fresh water until just tender, about 1 hour.

Drain the cooked beans and place them in a bowl (if using canned beans, rinse and then drain them). Toss with the onions, garlic, vinegar, olive oil, walnuts, cilantro, parsley, and coriander. Add salt and pepper to taste. Let the Lobio sit for at least 30 minutes to allow the flavors to meld.

Serve on a bed of greens, garnished with cilantro or parsley sprigs, sliced radishes, tomato slices, and wedges of toasted pita bread.

MENU IDEAS **Shchi (page 53)** ✳ **chilled Cucumber Yogurt Soup (page 147)** ✳ **Creamy Herbed Potato Soup (page 122)** ✳ **Simple Tomato Salads (page 286)** ✳ **Marinated Mushrooms (page 347)**

Marinated Broccoli & Carrots

This is a refreshing side salad with bright flavor and color. It's packed with vitamins and other essential nutrients: both broccoli and carrots have recently been hailed in nutrition reports as two of the most health-fortifying vegetables you can eat. This salad makes the perfect tangy side dish for baked fish, a creamy casserole, or a savory tart.

The Asian-style marinade is ready in minutes and the salad can marinate while you prepare other accompaniments or a main dish.

At Moosewood, one of our all-time favorite salad plates is Marinated Broccoli & Carrots with Classic Sichuan Noodles and Baked Seasoned Tofu.

SERVES 4
PREPARATION TIME: 20 MINUTES
CHILLING TIME: 20 MINUTES

PER 5-OUNCE SERVING: 111 CALORIES, 3.5 G PROTEIN, 7.5 G FAT, 9.6 G CARBO-HYDRATES, 1.9 G SATURATED FATTY ACIDS, 0 MG CHOLESTEROL, 187 MG SODIUM, 4.2 G TOTAL DIETARY FIBER

MARINADE
1 large garlic clove, minced or pressed
1 teaspoon grated fresh ginger root
2 tablespoons canola or other vegetable oil
2 tablespoons rice vinegar
2 teaspoons soy sauce

1 large broccoli stalk, peeled and cut into spears
2 medium carrots, peeled and cut into 2½ x ¼-inch sticks

Whisk together all of the marinade ingredients and set aside. In a large saucepan, blanch (see Note) the broccoli spears in boiling water for about 2 minutes. Stir in the carrots and continue to simmer for 5 minutes or less, until both vegetables are just tender and still brightly colored. Drain them and transfer to a serving bowl.

Pour the marinade on the vegetables and toss well. Refrigerate or set aside at room temperature for about 20 minutes to allow the flavors to mingle and permeate.

Note If you prefer, blanch or steam each vegetable separately. Steaming may take a few minutes longer.

DAILY SPECIAL

MENU IDEAS **Classic Sichuan Noodles (page 204)** ✳ **Baked Seasoned Tofu (page 336)** ✳ **Green & White Gumbo (page 80)** ✳ **Spicy Carrot Peanut Soup (page 55)** ✳ **Asian Bean Curd Soup (page 64)** ✳ **Liberian Black-eyed Pea Soup (page 84)** ✳ **Spicy Tofu & Greens Soup (page 92)** ✳ **Wonton Soup (page 104)** ✳ **Chilled Fennel Vichyssoise (page 149)** ✳ **Asian Beet & Tofu Salad (page 192)** ✳ **Indonesian Tahu Goreng (page 218)**

Mediterranean Orange & Olive Salad

This attractive salad shows up all around the Mediterranean Sea: in Morocco, Algeria, and Sicily. Here in upstate New York, we enjoy it with foods from the cuisines of North Africa, Italy, Greece, Spain, and the Middle East. The ingredients are plain and simple, but in combination they are a refreshing surprise.

SERVES 4
TOTAL TIME: 15 MINUTES

4 oranges, peeled and sectioned (page 373)
8 kalamata olives, pitted and sliced*
2 tablespoons very thinly sliced red onions, cut into 1-inch lengths
1 tablespoon extra-virgin olive oil
salt and ground black pepper to taste

* To pit, slice lengthwise all the way around each olive and twist the halves apart, or place the flat side of a broad-bladed knife on the olive and whack it sharply with the heel of your other hand to break open the olive.

Toss all of the ingredients together in a bowl and serve. Or, if you prefer, arrange the orange sections, sliced olives, and onions on a plate, drizzle with the oil, and sprinkle with salt and pepper.

Variations Add 3 artichoke hearts cut into quarters to the salad. Try it topped with freshly grated or shaved Parmesan cheese.

MENU IDEAS **Albondigas Soup (page 26)** ✴ **Tunisian Pumpkin Soup (page 56)** ✴ **Broccoli & Pasta Soup (page 71)** ✴ **Bean & Radicchio Salad (page 249)** ✴ **Focaccia (page 330)**

Mexican Chickpea Salad

This nutritious and tasty salad is very easy to make. The chiles and garlic are gently sautéed in olive oil, a nice touch that rounds out and softens their flavor. The fresh lime juice and red onions add a bright sharpness complemented by the tomatoes and cilantro. These spicy chickpeas are also delicious served over greens and topped with sour cream.

SERVES 4
TOTAL TIME: 20 MINUTES

PER 8-OUNCE SERVING: 225 CALORIES, 5.4 G PROTEIN, 11.9 G FAT, 26.1 G CARBO-HYDRATES, 1.6 G SATURATED FATTY ACIDS, 0 MG CHOLESTEROL, 1160 MG SODIUM, 5.1 G TOTAL DIETARY FIBER

1 or 2 jalapeños or other fresh chiles, stemmed, seeded, and finely chopped
3 tablespoons olive oil
1 garlic clove, minced or pressed
1½ cups cooked chickpeas (16-ounce can, drained)
2 tomatoes, chopped
2 tablespoons chopped red onions
2 tablespoons chopped fresh cilantro
2 to 3 tablespoons fresh lime juice
½ tablespoon salt
ground black pepper to taste

In a small skillet or saucepan on low heat, sauté the chiles in the olive oil for about 4 minutes. Add the garlic and cook for another minute, stirring constantly, until the chiles are soft and the garlic just golden. Remove from the heat and set aside.

Combine the chickpeas, tomatoes, red onions, cilantro, lime juice, salt, and pepper in a serving bowl. Add the chiles and garlic with their sautéing oil and toss well. Serve immediately or chill to allow the flavors to develop.

Variation For a Greek Chickpea Salad, omit the chiles and the fresh tomatoes and forget about sautéing. Instead, use 1 tablespoon of chopped kalamata olives and 12 to 14 sun-dried tomatoes (not oil-packed). Replace the cilantro with 2 tablespoons each of chopped fresh mint and parsley and use lemon juice instead of lime juice.

To assemble this Greek version, place the sun-dried tomatoes in a heat-proof bowl with 2 cups of boiling water and soak for about 15 minutes, until softened. Drain well, chop, and set aside. In a large serving bowl, toss together the olive oil, garlic, chickpeas, olives, softened sun-dried tomatoes, red onions, mint, parsley, lemon juice, salt, and pepper. Serve on a bed of fresh lettuce garnished with ½ cup grated feta cheese and a few fresh tomato wedges.

MENU IDEAS Mexican Shrimp & Spinach Salad (page 301) ✳ **chilled Avocado Tomatillo Soup (page 141)** ✳ **Spiced Mexican Squash Stew (page 54)** ✳ **Mole de Olla Rodriguez (page 42)**

Nepalese Egg Salad

This is an interesting and unusual egg salad. It's quite spicy and very pretty to look at, speckled with red tomatoes and black mustard seeds. Be sure to ventilate the kitchen well while toasting the spices: they can smoke a bit.

Try the egg salad as a spread on a slice of chewy sourdough bread or whole grain crackers or as a filling in pita pockets. Or serve it on lettuce with sprouts and shredded carrots.

SERVES 4
PREPARATION TIME: 30 MINUTES
CHILLING TIME: 30 MINUTES

PER 5-OUNCE SERVING: 216 CALORIES, 8.6 G PROTEIN, 16.8 G FAT, 8.2 G CARBO-HYDRATES, 3.9 G SATURATED FATTY ACIDS, 269 MG CHOLESTEROL, 365 MG SODIUM, 0.7 G TOTAL DIETARY FIBER

4 large eggs
1 tablespoon canola or other vegetable oil
1 teaspoon black mustard seeds
1/8 to 1/4 teaspoon cayenne
1/2 teaspoon cumin seeds
1/3 cup prepared mayonnaise
1 tablespoon fresh lemon juice
1 cup chopped tomatoes
1/4 teaspoon salt, or to taste

Place the eggs in a saucepan with cold water to cover and bring to a boil; then lower the heat, cover, and simmer for about 5 minutes. Remove the saucepan from the heat, keep covered, and allow to sit for about 15 minutes.

Meanwhile, warm the oil in a very small skillet or saucepan. Add the mustard seeds, cayenne, and cumin seeds, cover, and cook on medium-low heat until the mustard seeds begin to pop. Shake the pan occasionally to prevent burning. Transfer the spice mixture to a serving bowl, stir in the mayonnaise and lemon juice, and set aside.

When the eggs are cooked, drain them and place in very cold water. Peel and chop them (see Note). Add the eggs, tomatoes, and salt to the serving bowl and mix well.

Serve chilled.

Note Rapidly cooling hot eggs in cold water can sometimes make them easier to peel. Crack each egg lightly all around, then gently roll it between the palms of your hands to loosen the shell.

DAILY SPECIAL

MENU IDEAS **Persian Yogurt Rice Soup (page 129)** ✻ **chilled Mango Soup (page 154)** ✻ **chilled Raspberry Soup (page 157)** ✻ **Curried Cauliflower Soup (page 32)** ✻ **Anadama Bread (page 328)** ✻ **Our Special Gluten-free Bread (page 333)**

North African Roasted Cauliflower

On occasion it's nice to honor just one vegetable. This salad pays special homage to the cauliflower. It is a quick salad to prepare, beautiful in its simplicity. The spices used are often found in Tunisian cuisine, making this salad suitable for a North African dinner.

SERVES 4
PREPARATION TIME:
  ABOUT 10 MINUTES
COOKING TIME: 20 TO 30 MINUTES
COOLING TIME: 10 MINUTES

PER 5.5-OUNCE SERVING: 129 CALORIES, 2.4 G PROTEIN, 11.3 G FAT, 6.7 G CARBO-HYDRATES, 1.5 G SATURATED FATTY ACIDS, 0 MG CHOLESTEROL, 319 MG SODIUM, 3.4 G TOTAL DIETARY FIBER

4 cups large cauliflower florets
  (about 1½ inches wide)
3 tablespoons olive oil
1 garlic clove, minced or pressed
½ teaspoon ground caraway seeds*
½ teaspoon ground coriander
½ teaspoon salt
1 cup chopped tomatoes
1 to 2 tablespoons chopped fresh parsley

lemon wedges

Preground caraway seeds are not always available. Freshly grinding the seeds in an electric spice grinder is very easy and produces the fullest flavor.

Preheat the oven to 450°.
  Toss the cauliflower florets with the oil, garlic, caraway, coriander, and salt until well mixed and evenly coated. Place in a single layer on an unoiled baking tray and bake until the cauliflower is tender and begins to turn a golden brown, 20 to 30 minutes. Carefully stir a few times during baking.

Remove the roasted cauliflower from the oven and transfer it to a platter or shallow serving bowl. Allow to cool to room temperature; then top with the tomatoes and parsley.

Decorate with lemon wedges and serve.

MENU IDEAS **Moroccan Root Vegetable Stew (page 45)** * **Tunisian Pumpkin Soup (page 56)** * **Middle Eastern Chickpea Soup (page 88)** * **Tunisian Carrot Salad (page 293)** * **Bean Purée with Seven Savories (page 197)** * **Spinach with Cilantro Cashew Dressing (page 289)** * **Curried Croutons (page 339)**

Pinzimonio

Pinzimonio (from the Italian for "pincers") is served in Italy in December as a celebration of newly pressed extra-virgin olive oil. This is a convivial way to begin a meal; finger food at its simplest and best.

Make your assortment of vegetables as colorful as possible, with a variety of textures and tastes: some hard and crisp, others tender and leafy, some sweet and mild, others sharp. A dense peasant bread is just the thing to capture the last delicious drops of fragrant oil.

SERVES 4
TOTAL TIME: 15 TO 20 MINUTES

PER 4.75-OUNCE SERVING: 279 CALO-RIES, 1.7 G PROTEIN, 28.6 G FAT, 6 G CAR-BOHYDRATES, 3.9 G SATURATED FATTY ACIDS, 0 MG CHOLESTEROL, 72 MG SODIUM, 2.2 G TOTAL DIETARY FIBER

CHOOSE JUST A FEW OR A LOT OF THESE VEGETABLES

celery, the tender inner stalks with leaves
fennel, cut into large but manageable pieces
carrots, peeled and left whole if small or cut into sticks
radishes, trimmed and halved
radicchio, separated into whole leaves
romaine, whole tiny inner leaves
small cucumbers, peeled and cut into wedges
bell peppers, stemmed, seeded, and cut into thick slices
Belgian endive, whole leaves
scallions, trimmed
cherry tomatoes
sugar snap peas or snow pea pods
lightly blanched asparagus
lightly blanched tiny artichokes
lightly blanched broccoli or cauliflower florets

½ cup best-quality extra-virgin olive oil
salt and freshly ground black pepper to taste

Arrange the vegetables of your choice attractively on a large platter or in a large deep bowl with ice.

Either fill a common dipping bowl with the olive oil or evenly divide the oil into small individual bowls or ramekins and center each bowl on a plate. Season the oil with salt and pepper.

Be seated, dig in, and dip away.

MENU IDEAS **Cauliflower, Cheese & Tomato Soup (page 114)** ✳ **Zucchini & Rice Soup (page 59)** ✳ **Classic Tomato Garlic Soup (page 30)** ✳ **Potato & Escarole Soup (page 51)** ✳ **Summer Minestrone (page 94)**

Olive Oil

Like fine wines, olive oils differ depending on climate, soil, weather conditions, location, and the type of olive. Even oils made from the same trees can vary in different years. European olive oil labels must designate one of the three basic grades: extra-virgin, virgin, and pure; no similar oil labeling regulation exists in the United States. Good news about olive oil—it's a healthful, monounsaturated fat. * Extra-virgin olive oil is made from the highest-quality hand-picked olives and pressed only once by purely physical or mechanical means. It has a potent, fruity flavor and aroma and a greenish, viscous, sometimes cloudy appearance. It has the lowest acidity and a low smoking point, making it best suited to using raw on salads or pasta. Although often made on private estates and rather expensive, a little can go a long way and is well worth the price. * Virgin olive oil is made with lower-grade riper olives but is produced by a single pressing just like extra-virgin oil. Its color is somewhat more yellow than green and its taste less full-bodied. Its higher smoking point makes it better for cooking; it can be up to four times as acidic as extra-virgin oil. Virgin olive oil is quite a bit less expensive as well. * Pure olive oil is most common. Made from lower-grade olives and successive heated pressings of the residual pulp from other oils, it is produced in factories in mass quantities. Often it is refined by chemicals to make it paler, blander, and less aromatic. It can be heated to 400° and is quite practical for everyday cooking use. * We do not recommend refrigerating olive oil. It can be stored for up to a year in a sealed glass container in a cool, dark place. * Many fine artisanal oils are now available, ranging from spicy, assertive Tuscan oil to mild and fruity southern Italian. Excellent olive oils made in Greece, Spain, France, and California are also lining the shelves of food shops. We recommend Colavita, Berio, and Bertolli commercial brands.

Pilwun's Daikon Salad

Daikon is a kind of hefty white radish with an intense, peppery taste. However, the liberal use of salt helps to tame the intensity of its bite while leaving a nice crunchy texture.

Jenny Wang's mother has made this dish for years and, quite frankly, it couldn't be improved. Sometimes it's best to leave a good thing alone. Jenny has faithfully reproduced her mother's recipe, and we think you'll love it. Be sure to use the traditional Chinese method of pouring hot oil over the mound of scallions to release their fragrant and slightly sweet essence, absent in their raw form.

SERVES 6 TO 8
PREPARATION TIME: 10 MINUTES
DRAINING TIME: 30 MINUTES

PER 4-OUNCE SERVING: 61 CALORIES, 0.9 G PROTEIN, 3.8 G FAT, 6.6 G CARBO-HYDRATES, 1 G SATURATED FATTY ACIDS, 0 MG CHOLESTEROL, 463 MG SODIUM, 2 G TOTAL DIETARY FIBER

2 pounds daikon
1½ teaspoons salt
1 carrot
1 tablespoon sugar
1 tablespoon white vinegar
dash of dark sesame oil
3 scallions
2 tablespoons canola or other vegetable oil

Trim the ends of the daikon, peel, and coarsely grate it (see Note). In a colander set into a larger bowl, toss the grated daikon with the salt. Set aside to drain for 20 to 30 minutes, until about a cup of liquid has collected in the bowl. (Squeezing some of the liquid out of the daikon from time to time will speed up the process.)

Meanwhile, peel and coarsely grate the carrot and place it in a serving bowl. In a small bowl, mix together the sugar, vinegar, and sesame oil and set aside. When the daikon is well drained, stir it into the carrots. Add the vinegar mixture and toss well.

Slice the scallions thinly on the diagonal and mound them on top of the salad. Heat the vegetable oil until smoking and immediately pour it over the scallions—this will make a sizzling sound. Toss well.

Serve at room temperature or chilled.

Note A food processor makes short work of grating the daikon.

MENU IDEAS **Chinese Velvet Corn Soup (page 116) with Broiled Tofu & Sugar Snap Peas (page 199)** ✳ **Classic Sichuan Noodles (page 204)** ✳ **Thai Noodle Salad (page 233)**

Roasted Green Tomato & Feta Salad

As soon as tomatoes appear on the vine, the impulse to pick them takes hold. By autumn, harvesting here in the Northeast can feel like a race against time: Will all those green tomatoes ripen before the first hard frost? Little green tomatoes can be pickled and larger ones can be put to good use in this adaptation of a Turkish recipe.

Roasting green tomatoes and onions tenderizes them and draws out their natural sugars, mellowing them. The vegetables can be roasted in a very hot oven or wrapped in aluminum foil and roasted on a grill. Crusty bread or warm pita wedges are a good contrast for the salad's intense flavors.

SERVES 4 TO 6
PREPARATION TIME:
 20 TO 25 MINUTES
ROASTING TIME: 15 TO 30 MINUTES

PER 4.5-OUNCE SERVING: 171 CALORIES, 4.3 G PROTEIN, 14.8 G FAT, 6.7 G CARBO-HYDRATES, 4.8 G SATURATED FATTY ACIDS, 21 MG CHOLESTEROL, 330 MG SODIUM, 1.1 G TOTAL DIETARY FIBER

3 large green tomatoes, cut into wedges
1 medium onion, sliced into thin rounds
3 large garlic cloves, minced or pressed
dash of salt
¼ cup chopped fresh basil, lightly packed
3 tablespoons extra-virgin olive oil
1¼ cups crumbled feta cheese
1 tablespoon minced fresh mint (1 teaspoon dried)
2 tablespoons fresh lemon juice
1 tablespoon olive oil
salt and ground black pepper to taste

pimiento or roasted red bell pepper strips
fresh basil leaves
a few kalamata olives

Preheat the oven to 500°. On a nonstick or lightly oiled baking sheet, spread out the tomatoes and onions. Sprinkle on the garlic, salt, and 1 tablespoon of the basil. Drizzle on the extra-virgin olive oil and turn the vegetables to coat evenly. Bake for 15 to 30 minutes, turning once or twice, until tender and quite browned at the edges. Ovens vary, so you may need to brown the vegetables directly under the broiler, but be careful not to burn them.

Meanwhile, combine the feta, mint, lemon juice, olive oil, and the remaining 3 tablespoons of basil in a small bowl and set aside.

When the vegetables are browned, remove them from the oven, add salt and pepper to taste, mound them in the center of a platter or shallow serving bowl, and surround them with a ring of the feta mixture. Top with sliced pimiento or roasted red pepper strips and scatter on a few basil leaves and olives.

Serve warm or at room temperature.

DAILY SPECIAL

MENU IDEAS **Zucchini & Rice Soup (page 59)** ✳ **Spring Minestrone (page 93)** ✳ **Summer Minestrone (page 94)** ✳ **Autumn Minestrone (page 67)** ✳ **Tuscan Bean Soup (page 100)**

Roasted Potato & Tomato Salad

This dish offers a tasty and exotic alternative to classic potato salads made with mayonnaise dressings and can easily be multiplied for dinner parties or large summer picnics.

Although any variety of potato can be used, we have a fondness for the creamy texture of red-skinned potatoes. If the potato skins are taut and unblemished, we just scrub them rather than peeling. The potatoes can be cut in a cube size of your choosing, keeping in mind that the smaller the cubes, the shorter the baking time. Boiling the potatoes is also a possibility, but roasting adds a golden hue to their appearance and a richer flavor to the dish.

SERVES 4
PREPARATION TIME: 20 MINUTES
BAKING TIME: 20 TO 30 MINUTES

PER 6-OUNCE SERVING: 471 CALORIES, 5.6 G PROTEIN, 25.7 G FAT, 58 G CARBO-HYDRATES, 6.5 G SATURATED FATTY ACIDS, 0 MG CHOLESTEROL, 616 MG SODIUM, 6 G TOTAL DIETARY FIBER

6 cups cubed potatoes
3 tablespoons plus ¼ cup canola or other vegetable oil
3 garlic cloves, minced or pressed
1 teaspoon salt
2 fresh green chiles, minced, seeds removed for a milder "hot"
2 teaspoons ground cumin
2 tablespoons fresh lime or lemon juice
1 tablespoon red wine vinegar
1½ cups chopped tomatoes
2 tablespoons minced fresh cilantro, more to taste

Preheat the oven to 400°.

In a bowl, toss the potatoes with 3 tablespoons of the oil, half of the garlic, and all of the salt. Spread them evenly on a large baking sheet—or use two, if needed—and roast until tender, 20 to 30 minutes, depending on the variety of potato and the size of the cubes. Carefully stir once or twice during baking to prevent sticking.

Meanwhile, warm the remaining ¼ cup of oil in a small skillet or saucepan. Sauté the rest of the garlic, the chiles, and cumin, on medium-high heat, stirring constantly, just until the oil begins to foam but before the garlic browns. Remove from the heat immediately. Transfer to a nonreactive bowl, add the lime or lemon juice and the vinegar, and set aside.

When the potatoes are tender, place them in a serving bowl and toss with the spicy vinaigrette. Gently stir in the tomatoes and cilantro.

Serve at room temperature or chill, if you prefer.

MENU IDEAS **Tortilla Soup (page 99)** ✳ **Kiwi, Orange & Baby Greens (page 273)** ✳ **Spiced Mexican Squash Stew (page 54)** ✳ **Flemish Farm Soup (page 36)** ✳ **Creamless Broccoli Soup (page 31)** ✳ **Indian Roasted Eggplant Soup (page 40)**

Seaweed Salad

Salads of shocking emerald-green seaweed are becoming popular in many big cities. No longer limited to Japanese sushi bars, seaweed salads are appearing in other Asian restaurants, take-out counters, and fish markets. Anyone who tries one is rewarded with a piquant, crunchy salad and a briny shot of minerals.

Those of us who aren't in an urban cultural center probably can't buy it fresh, but we can use the dried seaweed now available in many supermarkets. Dried seaweed has the same spicy sweet flavor and clear sharp taste as its fresh counterpart, and is just as rich in calcium and low in both fat and calories.

SERVES 4
PREPARATION TIME: 25 MINUTES
CHILLING TIME: 20 MINUTES

PER 2.5-OUNCE SERVING: 67 CALORIES, 6.9 G PROTEIN, 2.5 G FAT, 7.9 G CARBO-HYDRATES, 0.5 G SATURATED FATTY ACIDS, 0 MG CHOLESTEROL, 315 MG SODIUM, 0.8 G TOTAL DIETARY FIBER

1 ounce dried wakame (about 2 cups)
½ ounce dried arame or hijiki (about 1 cup)

DRESSING
1 tablespoon sugar
⅓ cup rice vinegar or ¼ cup white vinegar
1 tablespoon soy sauce
1 to 2 tablespoons toasted sesame seeds*
½ to 1 fresh red chile, seeded and minced (optional)**
1 teaspoon dark sesame oil (optional)**

* *Toast a single layer of sesame seeds on an unoiled baking tray in a conventional or toaster oven at 350° for 2 to 3 minutes, until fragrant and golden brown.*
** *If you add chiles, be sure to also add the sesame oil, because the oil carries and spreads the hot flavor. We've specified a red chile because it looks so nice against the seaweed, but tastewise any chile will do.*

Place the 2 dried seaweeds in separate heatproof bowls, add boiling water to cover, and set aside to soak. Wakame and hijiki usually soften in about 10 minutes, although it can take longer. Arame softens in about 5 minutes.

In a small bowl, whisk together all of the dressing ingredients.

When softened, drain each seaweed well. Remove any tough center ribs of the wakame, cut it into thin strips, and place it in a serving bowl. Add the arame or hijiki, pour on the dressing, and toss well. Cover and refrigerate for at least 20 minutes.

Serve chilled.

MENU IDEAS **Miso Noodle Soup (page 89)** ✳ **Asian Bean Curd Soup (page 64)** ✳ **Hot & Sour Shrimp Soup (page 168)** ✳ **Scandinavian Salmon Soup (page 171)** ✳ **Teriyaki Fish & Soba Noodle Salad (page 310)** ✳ **Ozoni (page 48)** ✳ **Classic Sichuan Noodles (page 204)**

Simple Tomato Salads

In its season, a luscious, ripe, locally grown tomato requires little in the way of culinary effort. But the natural glories of a perfect tomato can be enhanced and a less-than-perfect tomato can be much improved with just a little embellishment, as in these quickly-put-together salads. An easy little tomato salad can add the bright note needed to turn a soup or another salad into a complete meal.

These recipes work equally well with yellow and/or red tomatoes as long as they are ripe. If you stumble across them at a farmers' market or green-grocer, try some of the beautiful heirloom varieties of tomatoes, with their interestingly diverse shapes, sizes, colors, and flavors.

Store tomatoes at room temperature, out of direct sunlight. Refrigerated tomatoes lose flavor and firmness. If you must refrigerate a tomato salad, be sure it is tightly covered, and bring it back to room temperature before serving.

EACH SALAD SERVES 2 TO 4
TOTAL TIME: 10 MINUTES

Tomatoes Capriccio

1 large tomato, sliced into thin rounds or half rounds
2 to 3 teaspoons extra-virgin olive oil
salt and ground black pepper to taste
1 or 2 large fresh basil leaves, minced

Arrange the tomato slices on a plate, drizzle with the olive oil, and sprinkle with salt, pepper, and minced fresh basil.

Variation Intersperse the tomato slices with slices of fresh mozzarella. A mozzarella ball about the same size as the tomato works best.

PER 1.5-OUNCE SERVING: 35 CALORIES, 0.3 G PROTEIN, 3.1 G FAT, 1.9 G CARBOHYDRATES, 0 G SATURATED FATTY ACIDS, 0 MG CHOLESTEROL, 47 MG SODIUM, 0 G TOTAL DIETARY FIBER

Farm-style Tomato Salad

1 large tomato, chopped into bite-sized pieces
2 tablespoons minced red onions, or more to taste
1 tablespoon red wine vinegar
1 teaspoon sugar
¼ teaspoon salt

Stir everything together in a bowl and serve.

PER 1.75-OUNCE SERVING: 14 CALORIES, 0.4 G PROTEIN, 0.1 G FAT, 3.4 G CARBOHYDRATES, 0 G SATURATED FATTY ACIDS, 0 MG CHOLESTEROL, 153 MG SODIUM, 1 G TOTAL DIETARY FIBER

Spicy Border-style Tomato Salad

1 large tomato, chopped
2 tablespoons minced onions
¼ to ½ fresh chile, seeded and minced
1 teaspoon minced fresh cilantro, or more to taste
1 tablespoon olive, corn, or other vegetable oil
1 to 1½ tablespoons fresh lemon juice
salt and ground black pepper to taste

Stir everything together in a serving bowl.

Variation   Add 1 peeled, seeded, halved, and sliced cucumber

PER 1.75-OUNCE SERVING: 43 CALORIES, 0.5 G PROTEIN, 3.7 G FAT, 2.8 G CARBOHYDRATES, 0 G SATU-
RATED FATTY ACIDS, 0 MG CHOLESTEROL, 48 MG SODIUM, 1 G TOTAL DIETARY FIBER

Garlicky Tomato Salad

2 large tomatoes, chopped
2 garlic cloves, minced or pressed
1 tablespoon olive oil
salt and ground black pepper to taste

Put the tomatoes in a serving bowl. In a small saucepan, sauté the
garlic in the oil on low heat for 1 to 2 minutes, until the garlic is beginning to turn golden. Drizzle the garlic and oil over the tomatoes and
add salt and pepper.

Note   If you have the time, this salad tastes best made 20 or 30 minutes
before serving.

PER 2.75-OUNCE SERVING: 48 CALORIES, 0.7 G PROTEIN, 3.8 G FAT, 3.7 G CARBOHYDRATES, 0 G SATU-
RATED FATTY ACIDS, 0 MG CHOLESTEROL, 51 MG SODIUM, 2 G TOTAL DIETARY FIBER

DAILY SPECIAL

MENU IDEAS   **Zucchini & Rice Soup (page 59)** ✳ **Risi e Bisi (page 90)** ✳ **Broccoli & Pasta Soup
(page 71)** ✳ **Creamy Onion & Fontina Soup (page 123)** ✳ **Focaccia (page 330)** ✳ **Three-Bean
Pasta Salad (page 232)**

Spicy Cucumber Salad

Crisp and chilly but spicy hot, this is a very zingy, refreshing salad that adds relish and interest to many of our Moosewood combo plates. Without the optional roasted peanuts there is virtually no fat in this salad, but we think the peanuts are really nice on top.

SERVES 6
TOTAL TIME: 15 MINUTES

PER 2.75-OUNCE SERVING: 24 CALORIES, 0.6 G PROTEIN, 0.1 G FAT, 5.1 G CARBO-HYDRATES, 0 G SATURATED FATTY ACIDS, 0 MG CHOLESTEROL, 138 MG SODIUM, 0.6 G TOTAL DIETARY FIBER

DRESSING
½ cup rice vinegar
1 tablespoon soy sauce
1 tablespoon sugar
½ fresh green chile, seeded and minced
¼ teaspoon ground black pepper
2 teaspoons minced fresh ginger root

2 medium cucumbers
½ red onion, very thinly sliced

coarsely chopped roasted peanuts (optional)

Stir together the rice vinegar, soy sauce, sugar, chile, black pepper, and ginger root in a serving bowl.

Peel the cucumbers, halve them lengthwise, and scoop out the seeds with a spoon. Slice the cucumbers crosswise into ¼-inch-thick crescents. Add the cucumbers and the onions to the dressing and refrigerate.

Serve cold, garnished with chopped roasted peanuts, if desired.

DAILY SPECIAL

MENU IDEAS **Thai Noodle Salad (page 233)** ∗ **Indonesian Tahu Goreng (page 218)** ∗ **Balinese Rice Salad (page 195)** ∗ **Chinese Velvet Corn Soup (page 116)** ∗ **Tamarind Pineapple Fish Soup (page 173)** ∗ **Korean Pine Nut Porridge (page 83)**

Spinach with Cilantro Cashew Dressing

Fresh spinach and ripe tomatoes are a classic duo, topped here with a delightful, almost addictive dressing. Toasted cashews both thicken the dressing and add a distinctive sweetness and body. Toss in Spiced Paneer or Baked Seasoned Tofu for a glorious, high-protein salad that makes a stimulating, healthful lunch.

SERVES 4
TOTAL TIME: 15 MINUTES

PER 6.5-OUNCE SERVING: 275 CALORIES, 7.9 G PROTEIN, 22.1 G FAT, 14.4 G CARBO-HYDRATES, 6.3 G SATURATED FATTY ACIDS, 9 MG CHOLESTEROL, 451 MG SODIUM, 2.2 G TOTAL DIETARY FIBER

8 cups fresh spinach, loosely packed (about 5 ounces)
1 large tomato, cut into wedges
¼ cup canola or other vegetable oil
3 tablespoons fresh lime juice
2 small garlic cloves, minced or pressed
2 tablespoons chopped fresh cilantro
¼ teaspoon salt, more to taste
2 tablespoons toasted coarsely chopped cashews*
Spiced Paneer (page 351)

Toast the cashews in a single layer on an unoiled baking tray at 350° for about 5 minutes, until fragrant and golden brown. ¼ cup of whole cashews will yield about 2 tablespoons chopped.

Stem and rinse the spinach. Spin or gently pat it dry. Tear the large leaves into smaller pieces and leave the small leaves whole. Arrange the spinach in a serving bowl and top it with the tomato wedges. Combine the oil, lime juice, garlic, cilantro, salt, and cashews in a blender and purée until smooth.

Just before serving, add the Spiced Paneer cubes to the salad, pour on the dressing, and toss well.

Variation If paneer is unavailable or if you prefer, serve with Baked Seasoned Tofu (page 336).

MENU IDEAS **Curried Cauliflower Soup (page 32)** ✳ **Indian Roasted Eggplant Soup (page 40)** ✳ **Roasted Red Pepper Coconut Soup (page 52)** ✳ **Faux Pho (page 34)** ✳ **Tamarind Pineapple Fish Soup (page 173)**

Summer Millet Salad

Millet is not just for the birds! It's a delicious grain with a distinctive, nutty flavor. This tiny, round, golden grain is available in most natural food stores and often in the bulk or specialty food sections of larger supermarkets. One of the most nutritious and easily digested grains, millet is very rich in amino acids, protein, iron, phosphorus, and B vitamins and is an integral part of most African diets.

If you're unfamiliar with it, give it a try. We think you'll be tempted to go back for seconds. For a millet salad with a surprisingly unique flavor, replace the basil with chopped fresh cilantro and use either ripe or green olives. This salad becomes even more flavorful as it sits.

SERVES 6
TOTAL TIME: 35 MINUTES

PER 6-OUNCE SERVING: 182 CALORIES, 4.7 G PROTEIN, 7.5 G FAT, 25.3 G CARBO-HYDRATES, 1 G SATURATED FATTY ACIDS, 0 MG CHOLESTEROL, 264 MG SODIUM, 4 G TOTAL DIETARY FIBER

1 cup raw hulled whole millet (see Note)
2 cups water
¼ teaspoon salt
¼ cup finely chopped fresh basil
¼ cup minced chives, scallions, or red onions
1 cup green peas, snap peas, or snow peas
¼ cup fresh lemon juice
2 tablespoons olive oil
2 ripe tomatoes, diced
6 kalamata or other ripe olives, pitted and chopped*
salt and ground black pepper to taste

To pit, slice lengthwise all the way around each olive and twist the halves apart, or place the flat side of a broad-bladed knife on the olive and whack it sharply with the heel of your other hand to break open the olive.

In a heavy saucepan, stir together the millet, water, and salt. Cover and bring to a boil; then reduce the heat and gently simmer for 20 minutes, stirring occasionally during the final 10 minutes. Remove from the heat and stir well with a fork to fluff and break up any clumps. Set aside, uncovered, for 10 minutes. The millet should be tender but chewy.

Meanwhile, place the basil and the chives, scallions, or red onions in a serving bowl and set aside. No preparation is needed for green peas. For snap peas, stem them, removing the fibrous strings, and cut crosswise into ½-inch pieces. For snow peas, slice them crosswise into ¼-inch strips. Blanch your choice of peas in boiling water until bright green and tender-crisp, about 3 minutes. Drain.

Add the warm millet to the serving bowl and mix well. Pour on the lemon juice and olive oil and stir in the peas, tomatoes, and olives. Add salt and black pepper to taste.

Serve warm or at room temperature.

Note Different batches of millet may require different cooking times and amounts of water. The size and heaviness of the pan, how well the lid fits, and the intensity of the heat all contribute to how the millet cooks. If the millet is a little crunchy, stir in ¼ cup of boiling water before setting it aside. If the millet is soft and wet, remove the lid and continue to cook so the water will evaporate.

We do not dry-roast millet or sauté it with oil or butter before cooking.

DAILY SPECIAL

MENU IDEAS **Chilled Fast & Fresh Tomato Soup (page 148)** ✳ **Golden Summer Soup (page 38)** ✳ **Kiwi, Orange & Baby Greens (page 273)** ✳ **Wilted Spinach & Portabella Mushrooms (page 239)** ✳ **Yemiser Salata (page 295)** ✳ **Marinated Chickpeas or White Beans (page 346)** ✳ **Spicy Carrot Peanut Soup (page 55)** ✳ **Liberian Black-eyed Pea Soup (page 84)**

Syrian Beet Salad

This versatile salad can easily harmonize with Middle Eastern, Indian, or Mexican meals. It is also simple and fast to prepare. Peeling and cubing the beets first makes quick work of a vegetable that requires long cooking when left whole, and while the beets cook, you can prepare the rest of the ingredients for the dish.

SERVES 4 TO 6
PREPARATION TIME: 30 MINUTES
CHILLING TIME: 30 MINUTES

PER 3-OUNCE SERVING: 95 CALORIES, 1.3 G PROTEIN, 7.3 G FAT, 7.3 G CARBO-HYDRATES, 1 G SATURATED FATTY ACIDS, 0 MG CHOLESTEROL, 446 MG SODIUM, 1.3 G TOTAL DIETARY FIBER

2 quarts water
3 large beets
1 tablespoon chopped fresh chives
2 tablespoon chopped fresh cilantro
2 garlic cloves, minced or pressed
½ fresh chile, seeded for a milder "hot" and minced
     (about 1 tablespoon)
1 teaspooon ground cumin
2 tablespoons fresh lemon juice
3 tablespoons olive or other vegetable oil
1 teaspoon salt, or to taste

In a large pot, bring the water to a boil. Meanwhile, peel the beets and cut them into ½-inch cubes. Ease them into the boiling water, cover, lower to a simmer, and cook until tender and easily pierced with a knife, about 10 minutes.

When the beets are ready, drain well and transfer to a serving bowl. Add the chives, cilantro, garlic, chile, cumin, lemon juice, oil, and salt and toss well. Chill for at least 30 minutes before serving.

DAILY SPECIAL

MENU IDEAS **Mexican Butter Bean Soup (page 85)** ✴ **Persian Yogurt Rice Soup (page 129)** ✴ **Choklay's Tibetan Lentil Soup (page 73)** ✴ **chilled Creamy Yogurt Barley Soup (page 146)** ✴ **Artichoke Avgolemono (page 112)**

Thai Tossed Salad

This recipe was inspired by the house salad served at our favorite local Thai restaurant. It has a nice mix of colors, flavors, and textures that will make you dream you are in Bangkok.

SERVES 4
TOTAL TIME: 30 MINUTES

PER 13-OUNCE SERVING: 214 CALORIES, 9.4 G PROTEIN, 11.2 G FAT, 23 G CARBO-HYDRATES, 3.1 G SATURATED FATTY ACIDS, 0 MG CHOLESTEROL, 600 MG SODIUM, 5.3 G TOTAL DIETARY FIBER

DRESSING

½ cup reduced-fat or regular canned coconut milk (page 360)
¼ cup smooth peanut butter
1 tablespoon soy sauce
3 tablespoons fresh lemon or lime juice
1 teaspoon grated fresh ginger root
1 teaspoon brown sugar, packed
1 rounded tablespoon chopped fresh cilantro
½ fresh chile, seeded and minced (optional)
salt to taste

SALAD

6 to 8 cups mixed salad greens
2 tomatoes, cut into wedges
1 small red or yellow bell pepper, seeded and cut into thin strips
8 ounces tofu-kan or other spiced tofu (page 386) or
    Baked Seasoned Tofu (page 336), cut into ½-inch cubes or
    thin bite-sized slices
4 thinly sliced red onion rings
¼ cup fresh basil chiffonade (page 358)
1 cup fresh mung bean sprouts
2 hard-boiled eggs, cut into quarters (optional)

Combine all of the dressing ingredients in a blender and whirl until smooth and creamy. Add a little salt, if needed. Serve at room temperature, but store in the refrigerator if making ahead and return to room temperature before serving.

Arrange the salad greens on individual plates. Alternate the tomato wedges and the bell pepper strips on the bed of greens and scatter the tofu on top. Drizzle 2 tablespoons of the dressing over each salad and offer the rest of the dressing at the table. Finish garnishing each salad plate with the red onion rings, basil, mung sprouts, and the egg wedges, if using.

Serve immediately.

DAILY SPECIAL

MENU IDEAS **Hot & Sour Shrimp Soup (page 168)** ✳ **Spicy Carrot Peanut Soup (page 55)** ✳ **chilled Mango Soup (page 154)** ✳ **chilled Creamy Orange Soup (page 145)**

Tunisian Carrot Salad

This colorful little salad takes only minutes to prepare and at Moosewood it embellishes a wide variety of our combo plates. Ground coriander, caraway, and cayenne sautéed in olive oil give an intriguingly spicy contrast to the chewy sweetness of carrots and currants.

If you don't find ground caraway in the spice section of your supermarket, look for it in German or Hungarian specialty shops. Or freshly grind the whole seeds with an electric spice grinder just before use to produce the best flavor.

SERVES 4
PREPARATION TIME: 15 MINUTES
MARINATING TIME: 30 MINUTES

PER 3.25-OUNCE SERVING: 83 CALORIES, 1.2 G PROTEIN, 3.8 G FAT, 12.3 G CARBO-HYDRATES, 0.5 G SATURATED FATTY ACIDS, 0 MG CHOLESTEROL, 176 MG SODIUM, 2.7 G TOTAL DIETARY FIBER

2 cups peeled and grated carrots
2 tablespoons currants
1 tablespoon olive oil
1 garlic clove, minced and pressed
1½ teaspoons ground coriander
½ teaspoon ground caraway seeds
pinch of cayenne, more to taste
¼ teaspoon salt
3 tablespoons orange juice

Place the carrots and currants in a serving bowl. Warm the oil in a very small saucepan or skillet. Add the garlic, coriander, caraway, and cayenne and cook on low heat, stirring constantly, for about 2 minutes, just long enough to cook the garlic and spices.

Remove from the heat and add the salt and orange juice. Spoon the dressing over the carrots and currants and toss well. Set aside at room temperature to marinate for about 30 minutes before serving.

MENU IDEAS **Fattoush (page 209)** ✳ **Persian Yogurt Rice Soup (page 129)** ✳ **chilled Creamy Yogurt Barley Soup (page 146)** ✳ **Algerian Tomato Soup with Vermicelli (page 66)** ✳ **Cream of Spinach Soup (page 120)**

Turkish Roasted Eggplant Salad

Each forkful of this multilay-ered salad offers a sensation that is savory, sweet, and tart as well as crusty, saucy, and creamy.

The traditional method of preparing this dish is to fry the vegetables; here's a lighter roasted version. We like to use bell peppers, egg-plant, and zucchini, but you can omit one or even two of the vegetables; just use a similar total quantity.

SERVES 6
PREPARATION TIME: 15 MINUTES, PLUS 30 MINUTES DRAINING
ROASTING TIME: 1 HOUR

PER 11-OUNCE SERVING: 188 CALORIES, 4 G PROTEIN, 12.9 G FAT, 16.7 G CARBO-HYDRATES, 2.1 G SATURATED FATTY ACIDS, 2 MG CHOLESTEROL, 633 MG SODIUM, 4.1 G TOTAL DIETARY FIBER

1 medium eggplant, peeled, trimmed, and cut into ¾-inch cubes
1½ teaspoons salt
2 red bell peppers
2 small zucchini
¼ cup plus 1 tablespoon olive oil
¼ teaspoon ground black pepper
3 tomatoes
2 garlic cloves, minced or pressed
2 tablespoons water
½ teaspoon sugar
1 teaspoon cider vinegar
1 cup plain yogurt

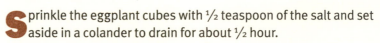

Sprinkle the eggplant cubes with ½ teaspoon of the salt and set aside in a colander to drain for about ½ hour.

Preheat the oven to 450°.

Cut the bell peppers and zucchini into ¾-inch pieces. Rinse the egg-plant and drain well. In a large roasting pan, combine the drained egg-plant, the bell peppers, zucchini, ¼ cup of the olive oil, ½ teaspoon of salt, and the black pepper and toss to coat well. Spread the vegetables evenly and roast for 1 hour, stirring every 15 minutes.

Meanwhile, cut the tomatoes into ½-inch pieces and set aside. In a nonreactive saucepan, heat the remaining tablespoon of olive oil, stir in the garlic, and sauté on medium heat until fragrant, about 30 sec-onds. Add the tomatoes and cook until softened, 1 or 2 minutes. Stir in the water, sugar, and vinegar and the remaining ½ teaspoon of salt. Remove the tomato sauce from the heat.

When the roasted vegetables are done, layer them in the bottom of an unoiled, shallow 2-quart baking dish. Cover the vegetables with a layer of yogurt and top with the tomato sauce.

Serve at room temperature or cold.

Variation If you are not opposed to frying (or cleaning up afterward), you should try the traditional method just to experience the glory of the original dish. Instead of cubing the vegetables, cut them into ¾-inch slices, salt them lightly, and be sure to pat them dry. Fry them in an inch of hot, almost smoking oil until tender and lightly browned. Drain them on paper towels, transfer to a serving bowl, and layer with the yogurt and sauce.

MENU IDEAS Egyptian Red Lentil Soup (page 76) ✳ **Middle Eastern Chickpea Soup (page 88)** ✳ **Lentil, Rice & Fruit Salad (page 220)** ✳ **Eastern European Vegetable Stew (page 33)** ✳ **Melon & Mint (page 265)**

Yemiser Salata

The strict dietary laws of the Coptic Christian Church in Ethiopia and Eritrea decree that its followers abstain from meat for almost 200 days of the year, so lentils are one of many vegetarian staples. This salad was inspired by the plentiful barrels of beautiful red lentils in the bustling markets in Addis Ababa and Asmara. Brown lentils will work in this dish, but we prefer the red ones for their color, smaller size, and secret surprise—turning gold when cooked.

SERVES 4 TO 6
TOTAL TIME: 40 MINUTES
CHILLING TIME (OPTIONAL):
  ABOUT 1 HOUR

PER 5.5-OUNCE SERVING: 221 CALORIES, 10.3 G PROTEIN, 9.9 G FAT, 24.7 G CARBO-HYDRATES, 1.3 G SATURATED FATTY ACIDS, 0 MG CHOLESTEROL, 303 MG SODIUM, 9.4 G TOTAL DIETARY FIBER

1½ cups dried red lentils
4 cups water
¼ cup olive oil
2 large garlic cloves, minced or pressed
1 large minced fresh chile, seeded for a milder "hot"
3 tablespoons red wine vinegar
¾ teaspoon salt
1 cup minced red bell peppers
¼ cup chopped fresh cilantro
1 large celery stalk, minced (optional)

Wash the lentils and place them in a saucepan with the water. Cover and bring to a boil on high heat. Reduce the heat and simmer for 10 to 15 minutes, or until the lentils are just tender. Be vigilant when using red lentils; they cook much faster than brown lentils and it's easy to overcook them. Drain and set aside in a serving bowl.

While the lentils are cooking, heat the oil in a small skillet or saucepan. Add the garlic and chiles and sauté on medium heat, stirring constantly, for about 2 minutes. Place in a cup or small bowl, stir in the vinegar and salt, and set aside.

To the bowl of lentils, add the bell peppers, cilantro, and the celery, if using. Add the dressing and toss gently. If you like, refrigerate for about an hour or until cold.

Yemiser Salata can be served very cold or at room temperature.

DAILY SPECIAL

MENU IDEAS **Moroccan Root Vegetable Stew (page 45)** ✳ **Tunisian Pumpkin Soup (page 56)** ✳ **Persian Rice & Pistachio Salad (page 224)** ✳ **Tunisian Carrot Salad (page 293)** ✳ **chilled Minted Pea Soup (page 155)** ✳ **Spiced Paneer (page 351)**

SEAFOOD SALADS

Seafood is perfectly suited to salads. It tastes just as wonderful chilled or at room temperature as it does when served hot. Seafood cooks and then cools off quickly —a real advantage for assembling a light, main dish salad with ease. Even plain steamed or baked fish served cold with a wedge of lemon and a little salt and pepper can be very tasty and refreshing, but seafood is beautifully enhanced by tart, tangy, and spicy dressings. We've gone all out with our dressings, sauces, and spices, so if you love seafood and fish, get ready for some great eating. ❋ Fish and other seafoods are combined with colorful vegetables or luscious fruits and maybe noodles or rice, and then really sparked up with a few select seasonings such as mustard, capers, paprika, garlic, rice vinegar, chiles, curry spices, lime, scallions, ginger, or fresh herbs. Experience what happens when the subtle, briny flavors of seafoods meet up with aromatic saffron and citrus, a fiery cilantro pesto, or deep, rich sesame oil and soy sauce in these gorgeous salads. ❋ **You can pair seafood salads with almost any kind of soup:** light brothy soups, creamy soups, and even hearty bean and vegetable soups. At Moosewood, we often combine a spicy salad with a mild soup, a rich salad with a thin piquant soup. Avoid redundancy like noodles with noodles or beans with beans. ❋ Read the introduction to the Seafood Soups section (pages 162–163) for tips on buying and storing fish and other seafood. All of our recipes give directions for cooking fresh raw seafood. The only exception is when we give you the option of using cooked peeled and deveined shrimp: The shrimp that is cleaned, cooked, and refrigerated at fish markets seems to be fairly reliable and is a convenient time-saver. But the taste and texture of packaged frozen cooked seafood are a far cry from fresh, and we don't recommend it. Never overcook fish or other seafood, or it will become leathery and dry right before your eyes. Fish is already tender, and the less cooking, the better. When the flesh loses its translucence and can be easily flaked with a fork, it's ready. ✳ Most of our seafood salads are also good made with other kinds of seafood than that called for, so when a particular salad appeals to you, try it with whichever seafood you like most or with whatever looks best at the market. You can make good salads using leftover cooked fish or seafood as long as it's moist and holds its shape and when it hasn't been breaded or seasoned with flavors that conflict with the salad recipe. But be sure to use up leftover fish within a day or two. ✳

Curried Scallop & Noodle Salad

If you want to wow them, this is the salad for you. It's slightly spicy, bright with citrus flavors and vivid colors, and makes a fantastic presentation. The linguine absorbs the spiciness and hue of the curry powder—a beautiful marked contrast to the broccoli, tomatoes, and garlicky scallops.

The salad is at its best when served warm or at room temperature.

SERVES 4 TO 6
TOTAL TIME: 70 MINUTES

PER 12-OUNCE SERVING: 311 CALORIES, 16.8 G PROTEIN, 9.9 G FAT, 43.1 G CARBO-HYDRATES, 2.3 G SATURATED FATTY ACIDS, 48 MG CHOLESTEROL, 519 MG SODIUM, 6.6 G TOTAL DIETARY FIBER

1 large onion, sliced lengthwise into strips (about 2 cups)
2 tablespoons minced garlic
3 tablespoons canola or other vegetable oil
1 tablespoon grated fresh ginger root
1½ teaspoons freshly grated orange peel
1 teaspoon ground cumin
1 teaspoon ground coriander
1 teaspoon turmeric
¼ teaspoon ground cinnamon
pinch of cayenne
1 teaspoon salt
¼ cup orange juice
¼ cup fresh lemon juice
2 broccoli stalks, cut into florets, stems removed
1 tablespoon curry powder
8 ounces linguine
12 ounces sea scallops, sliced in half horizontally, or whole bay scallops
1 tomato, cut into wedges
chopped scallions

In a nonreactive skillet, sauté the onions and 1 tablespoon of the garlic in 2 tablespoons of the oil for 4 minutes. Stir in the ginger root, orange peel, cumin, coriander, turmeric, cinnamon, cayenne, and salt. Add the orange and lemon juices. Reduce the heat and simmer for 10 minutes, stirring frequently; then cover and remove from the heat.

Meanwhile, bring a large pot of water to a boil. Add the broccoli florets and cook until just tender, 2 to 3 minutes. With a slotted spoon, remove the broccoli and set it aside. Add the curry powder and linguine to the pot and cook until al dente, 8 to 10 minutes. Drain the pasta, toss it gently with the sautéed onions, and set aside.

In a medium skillet on medium heat, cook the rest of the garlic in the remaining tablespoon of oil until just softened. Add the scallops to the skillet and sauté on high heat until firm but tender and just becoming opaque, 3 to 4 minutes.

On a platter, surround the linguine with the broccoli and the tomato wedges. Top with the scallops and the scallions.

DAILY SPECIAL

MENU IDEAS **Kiwi, Orange & Baby Greens (page 273)** * **chilled Mango Soup (page 154)** * **Tomato Rasam (page 96)** * **Caribbean Sweet Potato Coconut Soup (page 29)** * **chilled Creamy Orange Soup (page 145)** * **Apricot Berry Sweet Talk (page 264)**

Mexican Shrimp & Spinach Salad

This colorful salad looks especially nice on a brightly colored, glazed ceramic platter. We recommend a Hass avocado because of its dense, creamy texture and rich flavor. If possible, use large fresh shrimp, not previously frozen, for their sweetness and tender, succulent consistency.

The dressing is very piquant and is served on the side. Since jalapeños can differ wildly in hotness, you may want to start with a smaller amount and add more to taste.

SERVES 4 TO 6
TOTAL TIME: 40 MINUTES

PER 6.5-OUNCE SERVING: 251 CALORIES, 15.9 G PROTEIN, 18.8 G FAT, 6.3 G CARBO-HYDRATES, 2.8 G SATURATED FATTY ACIDS, 130 MG CHOLESTEROL, 205 MG SODIUM, 3.5 G TOTAL DIETARY FIBER

1 pound shrimp, rinsed, shelled, and deveined
1 ripe Hass avocado*
1 large tomato
½ cucumber
5 ounces fresh spinach, rinsed and stemmed
⅓ cup thinly sliced scallions

DRESSING
⅓ cup olive oil
juice of 2 limes
2 tablespoons chopped fresh cilantro
1 garlic clove
½ jalapeño, seeds removed
1 teaspoon minced fresh thyme (optional)
salt and ground black pepper to taste

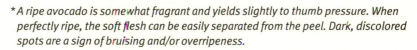

A ripe avocado is somewhat fragrant and yields slightly to thumb pressure. When perfectly ripe, the soft flesh can be easily separated from the peel. Dark, discolored spots are a sign of bruising and/or overripeness.

In a pot of boiling water, cook the shrimp just until pink, about 3 minutes. Drain and set aside.

Slice the avocado lengthwise around its center, gently twist the halves apart, and remove the pit. Without cutting through the peel, slice through the flesh of each avocado half, first crosswise into ¼-inch slices and then lengthwise in half. Scoop the avocado slices away from the peel with a large spoon.

Cut the tomato through the stem end into quarters and then cut each quarter into ¼-inch slices. Peel the ½ cucumber, slice it in half lengthwise, and remove the seeds with a spoon. Cut each section lengthwise into quarters and then crosswise into ¼-inch slices.

Arrange the spinach on a serving platter. Arrange the avocado, tomato, and cucumber slices on top of the bed of spinach. Top the salad with the shrimp and scallions.

Combine the oil, lime juice, cilantro, garlic, jalapeño, and thyme, if using, in a blender and mix for 30 seconds. Add salt and pepper to taste and transfer to a cruet or small bowl. Serve the dressing on the side of the salad.

MENU IDEAS **Oaxacan Potato Soup (page 128)** ✳ **chilled Mango Soup (page 154)** ✳ **chilled Creamy Orange Soup (page 145)** ✳ **Herbed Cheese Quick Bread (page 332)** ✳ **Oranges, Hot & Sweet (page 265)**

Lemon Rice & Seafood Salad

Gremolata, an Italian seasoning mixture of citrus, garlic, and parsley, adds an alluring, bright accent to this flavorful and elegant salad. Two good lemons will yield enough juice for this recipe and the zest of one will be enough for both the rice and the gremolata.

SERVES 4
TOTAL TIME: ABOUT 1 HOUR

PER 14-OUNCE SERVING: 558 CALORIES, 24.6 G PROTEIN, 24.8 G FAT, 60.8 G CARBOHYDRATES, 7.8 G SATURATED FATTY ACIDS, 169 MG CHOLESTEROL, 730 MG SODIUM, 2.2 G TOTAL DIETARY FIBER

GREMOLATA
3 tablespoons chopped fresh parsley
3 garlic cloves, peeled
¾ teaspoon freshly grated lemon peel

SEASONED RICE
2¼ cups water
1½ cups raw white basmati rice
3 tablespoons butter
¼ teaspoon salt
¾ teaspoon freshly grated lemon peel
1½ teaspoons fresh lemon juice

CITRUS DRESSING
⅓ cup fresh lemon juice
¼ cup olive oil
2 teaspoons cider vinegar or wine vinegar
½ teaspoon salt
½ teaspoon ground black pepper

2 garlic cloves, peeled
1 celery stalk, cut into 2 or 3 pieces
1 bay leaf
4 to 6 whole black peppercorns
4 cups water
12 ounces raw shrimp
1 pound asparagus, tough stem ends removed
1 cup chopped watercress, spinach, arugula, or baby greens
1 tomato, cut into bite-sized wedges

fresh watercress sprigs

Thoroughly mince together the gremolata ingredients and set aside.

In a saucepan with a tight-fitting lid, bring the water for the rice to a boil. Add the rice, butter, salt, lemon peel, and lemon juice. Cover and return to a boil; then simmer on low heat for 15 minutes.

Meanwhile, whisk together the citrus dressing ingredients and set aside.

In a soup pot, combine the garlic, celery, bay leaf, peppercorns, and 4 cups of water and bring to a boil. Lower the heat and simmer for about 15 minutes to make a light stock. Meanwhile, peel and devein the shrimp. With a strainer or slotted spoon, remove and discard the garlic, celery, bay leaf, and any floating peppercorns from the stock. Boil the asparagus in the stock for 3 to 4 minutes, until just tender and still bright green; then remove and set aside. Add the shrimp to the stock and simmer for 30 to 60 seconds, until the shrimp are pink and firm. Remove the shrimp, rinse them with cold water, and set aside.

With a fork, fluff the rice and mix in the chopped watercress or other greens. Spread the rice mixture evenly on a large serving platter. Arrange the asparagus, shrimp, and tomato wedges artfully on the rice. Stir the dressing and drizzle half of it on the salad. Sprinkle with the gremolata and garnish with watercress sprigs.

Serve immediately and pass the rest of the dressing at the table.

MENU IDEAS **Creamy Herbed Carrot Soup (page 121)** ✳ **chilled Peach Soup (page 156)** ✳ **chilled Raspberry Soup (page 157)** ✳ **Caribbean Sweet Potato Coconut Soup (page 29)** ✳ **Potage Celeste (page 130)** ✳ **Cream of Asparagus Soup (page 118)**

Mussel Salad

Freshly steamed mussels, potatoes, and vegetables combined with a robust dressing make a hearty and delectable salad, perfect for warm-weather entertaining. This is a great meal to prepare with friends on a sociable weekend evening. It takes awhile, but each step is easy to do. Serve, preferably at room temperature with lemon wedges, accompanied by a good red wine or frosty glass of beer.

Most supermarket seafood sections carry prepackaged 2-pound bags of rinsed and cleaned mussels that are convenient and easier to sort than loose mussels. Discard any that are open or broken and rinse the rest with cold water.

SERVES 6 TO 8
TOTAL TIME: 1¼ HOURS

PER 11-OUNCE SERVING: 299 CALORIES, 8.5 G PROTEIN, 12.6 G FAT, 41 G CARBOHYDRATES, 1.9 G SATURATED FATTY ACIDS, 17 MG CHOLESTEROL, 405 MG SODIUM, 3.2 G TOTAL DIETARY FIBER

2 pounds mussels
2 pounds small red potatoes, cut into quarters
1 bunch of asparagus or 2 cups green beans, cut into 1-inch pieces
1 cup thinly sliced celery

DRESSING
1 tablespoon olive oil
3 garlic cloves, minced or pressed
3 large shallots, minced, or ⅓ cup minced red onions
1 cup mayonnaise
1 tablespoon German-style or Dijon mustard
3 tablespoons fresh lemon juice or cider vinegar
3 tablespoons drained capers
2 roasted red peppers, chopped (page 374)
dash of cayenne or Tabasco sauce or other hot sauce to taste
salt and ground black pepper to taste

1 or 2 large ripe tomatoes, cut into wedges
½ cup minced fresh parsley

Scrub the mussels and remove their beards. Bring ½ cup of water to a boil in a large pot with a tight lid. Add the mussels, cover, and steam for about 5 minutes. Remove the mussels with a slotted spoon, discard any that haven't opened, and set the rest aside. Unless it's very sandy, strain the broth through cheesecloth and reserve.

In a large pot, cover the potatoes with water, bring to a boil, and cook for about 10 minutes until tender. Drain. Meanwhile, in a separate pot, blanch the asparagus or green beans until crisp-tender; then drain well. Transfer the cooked vegetables to a serving bowl and add the celery.

Heat the olive oil in a small saucepan and sauté the garlic and the shallots or red onions for 2 minutes. Transfer to a bowl and mix with the mayonnaise, mustard, lemon juice, capers, roasted peppers, and cayenne or Tabasco sauce. For added flavor, stir in a few tablespoons of the strained mussel broth. Add salt and pepper to taste.

Select the 6 most attractive mussels in their shells and set them aside for garnishes. Shell the rest of the mussels, add them to the serving bowl, and toss everything with the dressing. Decorate with tomato wedges, parsley, and the unshelled mussels.

MENU IDEAS **French Roasted Onion Soup (page 37)** ∗ **Yellow Pepper Purée (page 58)** ∗ **Celery Roquefort Soup (page 115)** ∗ **chilled Strawberry Soup (page 159)** ∗ **Cream of Spinach Soup (page 120)** ∗ **Popovers (page 334)**

Seafood Salad with Salsa Verde

This salad for seafood lovers makes a colorful and elegant presentation for a special luncheon or summer dinner. Fish and vegetables poached to perfection are topped with a classic, tangy herb and anchovy green sauce— delicious. For an added touch, present it on a bed of mixed baby greens such as mesclun and garnish with lemon or lime wedges.

The poaching broth makes an excellent fish stock for soup or stew. Strain it, put it in a plastic container, and refrigerate or freeze it for later use.

SERVES 4 GENEROUSLY
PREPARATION TIME: 25 MINUTES
COOKING TIME: 20 MINUTES
CHILLING TIME: 15 MINUTES

PER 13.5-OUNCE SERVING: 590 CALO-RIES, 50.6 G PROTEIN, 33.7 G FAT, 19.4 G CARBOHYDRATES, 5.4 G SATURATED FATTY ACIDS, 153 MG CHOLESTEROL, 450 MG SODIUM, 3 G TOTAL DIETARY FIBER

4 salmon, mahimahi, or monkfish fillets, cut in half (about 7 ounces each), or 1 pound scallops

POACHING BROTH
1 garlic clove, sliced
parsley stems (reserved from 1 cup chopped parsley)
1 celery stalk, sliced
3 cups water

SALSA VERDE
¼ cup olive oil
4 garlic cloves, minced or pressed
4 anchovy fillets
1 tablespoon fresh lemon juice
2 to 3 tablespoons water
1 cup firmly packed chopped parsley, stems reserved
⅓ cup chopped fresh basil
¼ cup chopped scallions

2 red potatoes, cut into ¼-inch slices (about 2 cups)
1 carrot, peeled and cut on the diagonal into ½-inch slices
1 tomato, cut into wedges

Rinse the fish well and refrigerate. Combine all of the poaching broth ingredients in a nonreactive soup pot; cover and bring to a simmer. Meanwhile, in a food processor or blender, purée all of the Salsa Verde ingredients to make a thick sauce; chill.

Strain the poaching broth and return it to the pot. Add the potatoes, cover, and simmer for about 5 minutes. Add the carrots and cook for 5 to 10 more minutes, until both vegetables are just tender. Remove with a slotted spoon to a platter and refrigerate.

Return the broth to a simmer. Add the seafood, cover, and poach until opaque and tender: fish for about 5 minutes per ½-inch thickness or scallops for 2 to 5 minutes. Transfer the seafood to the platter and chill for at least 15 minutes.

To serve, artfully arrange the potatoes, carrots, tomatoes, and seafood on a serving platter or on individual serving plates. Drizzle on some of the Salsa Verde and offer the rest at the table.

DAILY SPECIAL

MENU IDEAS **chilled Mango Soup (page 154)** ＊ **chilled Creamy Orange Soup (page 145)** ＊ **chilled Peach Soup (page 156)** ＊ **Focaccia (page 330)** ＊ **Pears Parmesan (page 265)**

Seafood & Chermoulla Couscous Salad

As a first course, lunch, or light dinner, this festive and colorful salad offers an irresistible combination of textures and tastes. Fresh seafood, marinated and sautéed in the powerful flavors of the Chermoulla sauce, is served with light and aromatic couscous and cool, refreshing garnishes.

Chermoulla Dressing is very hot and spicy. We recommend starting with one chile, tasting the dressing, and adding another if you like (or dare).

SERVES 4 TO 6
TOTAL TIME: 1½ HOURS

PER 11-OUNCE SERVING: 357 CALORIES, 23 G PROTEIN, 13.4 G FAT, 38.5 G CARBO-HYDRATES, 2 G SATURATED FATTY ACIDS, 37 MG CHOLESTEROL, 563 MG SODIUM, 6.4 G TOTAL DIETARY FIBER

1 pound firm fresh fish fillets, such as cod, haddock, or salmon, or peeled and deveined shrimp, or sea scallops — or any combination

CHERMOULLA DRESSING
2 garlic cloves, minced or pressed
1 tablespoon paprika
1 tablespoon ground cumin
2 teaspoons ground coriander
½ teaspoon red pepper flakes
1 to 2 fresh chiles, chopped with seeds
¼ cup chopped fresh cilantro
¼ cup fresh lemon juice
¼ cup olive oil
salt to taste

1 cup quick-cooking couscous
½ teaspoon salt
pinch of saffron
1⅓ cups boiling water
4 to 6 artichoke hearts, drained and cut into quarters (14-ounce can)
1 cucumber, peeled and sliced
1 tomato, cut into bite-sized wedges
1 orange, peeled and sliced crosswise into rounds
8 to 12 kalamata olives

a few lemon wedges
several fresh cilantro sprigs

Rinse and drain the seafood and set it aside. Combine all of the dressing ingredients in a blender or food processor and whirl until smooth. Place the drained seafood in a bowl, cover with the dressing, and marinate in the refrigerator for about 1 hour.

Place the couscous, salt, and saffron in a heatproof bowl. Pour in the boiling water, cover tightly, and set aside for about 5 minutes. Uncover and fluff with a fork to break up any lumps, then set aside (see Note).

Transfer the seafood and its marinade to a lightly oiled skillet. Sauté fish fillets on medium heat for about 10 minutes, turning once, until the flesh is firm and opaque; then remove the skin and flake with a fork. Sauté shrimp until it just turns pink, 2 to 3 minutes. Sauté scallops for 2 to 5 minutes, until opaque and firm to the touch.

To serve, spread the couscous on a large serving platter. Arrange the seafood in the middle surrounded by the artichoke hearts, cucumber slices, tomato wedges, orange rounds, and olives. Drizzle the marinade over the top and garnish with lemon wedges and cilantro.

Serve the salad warm or at room temperature.

Note If you plan to serve the dish warm rather than at room temperature, cover the couscous when you set it aside so it will retain heat.

MENU IDEAS **Classic Tomato Garlic Soup (page 30)** ∗ **Tunisian Pumpkin Soup (page 56)** ∗ **Egyptian Red Lentil Soup (page 76)** ∗ **chilled Cucumber Yogurt Soup (page 147)** ∗ **Melon & Mint (page 265)**

Seafood Paella Salad

All the elements of a classic paella are here: fragrant, golden saffron rice and an array of seafood — with the advantage that the salad can be composed ahead of time so that you can enjoy it as much as your guests. It is delicious either chilled or slightly cooled from cooking.

Serve paella salad with a recording of the Romero brothers playing in the background (or Bizet's *Carmen,* if you prefer), put a rose between your teeth, and get those heels clicking.

SERVES 4 TO 6
PREPARATION TIME:
 70 MINUTES
CHILLING TIME: AT LEAST
 20 MINUTES

PER 8.75-OUNCE SERVING: 264 CALORIES, 17.6 G PROTEIN, 8.5 G FAT, 29 G CARBOHYDRATES, 1 G SATURATED FATTY ACIDS, 83 MG CHOLESTEROL, 615 MG SODIUM, 1.2 G TOTAL DIETARY FIBER

2 teaspoons olive oil
1 cup raw long-grain brown rice
¼ teaspoon crumbled saffron threads
2 cups water

POACHING LIQUID
1 cup water
1 cup dry white wine
2 garlic cloves, minced or pressed
2 bay leaves
pinch of salt

½ pound shrimp, shelled and deveined or unshelled*
½ pound sea scallops or firm fish fillets, such as monkfish
    or mahimahi
1¼ pounds mussels, scrubbed and debearded**

DRESSING
1 teaspoon freshly grated orange peel
¼ cup fresh orange juice
2 tablespoons fresh lemon juice
1 teaspoon salt
2 tablespoons olive oil
pinch of cayenne

1 cup diced tomatoes
1 cup diced red or green bell peppers
3 tablespoons minced red onions
2 tablespoons minced fresh parsley
1 tablespoon capers (optional)
salt to taste

a few lemon wedges

  * *Unshelled shrimp will add extra flavor to the poaching liquid.*
** *For convenience, many supermarkets carry prepackaged bags of rinsed and cleaned mussels. Do not use any mussels that have opened or have cracked shells.*

Warm the olive oil in a saucepan and sauté the rice for 1 to 2 minutes. Add the saffron and water, cover, and bring to a boil. Reduce the heat to very low and cook until the rice is tender and all of the liquid is absorbed, about 40 minutes.

Meanwhile, in a nonreactive saucepan, combine all of the poaching liquid ingredients and bring to a boil. Ease in the shrimp and simmer for 2 to 4 minutes, until they just turn pink and are still tender. Remove immediately with a large slotted spoon or mesh strainer and set aside. If using scallops, simmer in the poaching liquid for about 5 minutes, stirring often, until tender and opaque. Remove as before and set aside. If using fish fillets, simmer until firm and opaque, about 4 minutes for each ½ inch of thickness, and remove. Add the mussels to the poaching liquid, cover, and cook until they open, about 2 minutes; then remove and set aside. Discard any mussels that do not open. Reserve a tablespoon of the poaching liquid for the dressing.

Peel and devein the shrimp, if necessary. Cut the scallops or fish into bite-sized pieces. Remove about ⅔ of the mussels from their shells and set aside the remaining mussels to use as a garnish. Refrigerate all of the seafood.

Whisk together the dressing ingredients in a small bowl, add the reserved poaching liquid, and set aside. When the rice is cooked, transfer it to a large bowl and refrigerate or cool at room temperature for at least 20 minutes.

When cool, stir in the tomatoes, bell peppers, red onions, parsley, and, if using, the capers. Add the chilled seafood and dressing and mix thoroughly. Add salt to taste. Garnish with the reserved mussels in their shells and lemon wedges.

MENU IDEAS **Creamy Herbed Potato Soup (page 122)** ✳ **Creamy Onion & Fontina Soup (page 123)** ✳ **chilled Fennel Vichyssoise (page 149)** ✳ **chilled Cherry Almond Soup (page 142)** ✳ **chilled Minted Pea Soup (page 155)** ✳ **Oranges Exotic (page 265)**

Teriyaki Fish & Soba Noodle Salad

The centerpiece of this hearty main dish salad is broiled or grilled fish that has been marinated in teriyaki sauce. Fresh spinach topped with cool orange-and-sesame-dressed soba noodles provides a lovely bed for the fish.

The teriyaki marinade is a delicious, low-fat, salty-sweet concoction—and there will be enough extra to pass around the table. Use any leftover sauce to dress steamed vegetables and grains, season stir-fries, or marinate tofu, grilled fish, and vegetables. Unused marinade will keep for several weeks in a sealed container in the refrigerator.

SERVES 4
TOTAL TIME: 50 MINUTES

PER 14-OUNCE SERVING: 483 CALORIES, 37.1 G PROTEIN, 13.4 G FAT, 52.8 G CARBOHYDRATES, 2.3 G SATURATED FATTY ACIDS, 84 MG CHOLESTEROL, 1563 MG SODIUM, 2.5 G TOTAL DIETARY FIBER

TERIYAKI MARINADE
½ cup soy sauce
½ cup sake (page 376) or dry sherry
2 garlic cloves, minced or pressed
1-inch piece of ginger root, cut into thin rounds
3 tablespoons brown sugar, packed

1 pound firm fish fillets or steaks, such as salmon, mahimahi, or sea bass, rinsed and patted dry
3 quarts water
¼ teaspoon salt
4 ounces fresh spinach, rinsed and drained
2 carrots
2 scallions
2 garlic cloves
8 ounces soba noodles*
2 tablespoons rice vinegar
½ cup orange juice
2 teaspoons dark sesame oil

* Different brands of soba noodles come in packages of different weights. If your package weighs more than 8 ounces (½ pound), just estimate the amount needed for the recipe.

In a small nonreactive saucepan, combine all of the teriyaki marinade ingredients. Bring them to a boil; then lower the heat and simmer for 5 minutes. Transfer the marinade to a nonreactive baking pan and refrigerate to cool quickly. Strain the cooled marinade into a measuring cup and discard any solids.

Place the fish in the same baking pan, pour on ⅓ cup of the marinade, and refrigerate it while you prepare the remaining ingredients or up to 2 hours (see Note). In a large covered pot, bring the water and salt to a boil. Meanwhile, remove any large stems from the spinach, cut or tear it into bite-sized pieces, and set it aside in a large serving dish. Peel and grate the carrots, thinly slice the scallions on the severe diagonal, and mince the garlic.

Preheat the broiler or prepare a grill.

When the water boils, ease in the soba noodles and cook for about 5 minutes, until al dente. Drain in a colander, rinse with cold water, drain again, and set aside in a shallow bowl. Whisk together the minced garlic, the rice vinegar, orange juice, sesame oil, and 2 tablespoons of the remaining marinade. Pour over the cooked soba noodles and gently toss.

Remove the fish from the marinade. Broil or grill each side for 4 to 5 minutes per inch of thickness. When turning the fish, brush on additional marinade (see Note). The fish is cooked when it flakes easily with a fork and its color changes from translucent to opaque.

Mound the soba noodles on the bed of spinach. Sprinkle the grated carrots around the outside edge of the bowl and place the cooked fish in the center. Top with the chopped scallions and serve at once.

Notes You could marinate the fish longer (even overnight), but the longer it marinates, the saltier and darker it becomes.

If the fish has skin, remove it when it's cooked enough to peel off easily. Then brush the fish with marinade and broil or grill a few more minutes.

MENU IDEAS **Scallion Pancakes (page 350)** ✳ **Pilwun's Daikon Salad (page 282)** ✳ **Seaweed Salad (page 285)** ✳ **tossed green salad with Moosewood Ginger Miso Dressing (page 323)** ✳ **chilled Peach Soup (page 156)** ✳ **chilled Cherry Almond Soup (page 142)** ✳ **Pineapple Passion (page 265)**

Tropical Fruit & Shrimp Salad

Spending a few productive minutes in the produce section of the supermarket can be the start of this stunning Caribbean-style salad. An additional stop for a pound of shrimp and a can of coconut milk completes the shopping list.

At home, make the dressing, choose a beautiful platter, and arrange it with the bounty of fruits from the sea and shore. If you like, serve it on light fragrant jasmine rice.

SERVES 4
TOTAL TIME: 30 MINUTES

PER 12.5-OUNCE SERVING: 251 CALORIES, 23.7 G PROTEIN, 6.7 G FAT, 25.9 G CARBOHYDRATES, 3.4 G SATURATED FATTY ACIDS, 195 MG CHOLESTEROL, 538 MG SODIUM, 3.2 G TOTAL DIETARY FIBER

1 pound shrimp, peeled and deveined
1 cup reduced-fat or regular coconut milk
½ teaspoon salt
½ fresh chile, seeded and finely minced
2 tablespoons fresh lime juice
2 teaspoons brown sugar, packed
2 teaspoons chopped fresh cilantro
½ jicama (page 365)
1 red bell pepper
1 ripe mango
2 star fruits or peeled kiwis
½ head of shredded red or green leaf lettuce or romaine,
** or 2 handfuls of mesclun**

Rinse the shrimp and set it aside.
In a small saucepan, bring the coconut milk and salt to a boil and then reduce the heat. Stir in half of the shrimp and cook just until pink, 3 to 5 minutes; then with a slotted spoon transfer the shrimp to a bowl. Cook the remaining raw shrimp the same way and add them to the bowl. Cover and refrigerate.

Add the chiles, lime juice, and brown sugar to the saucepan and simmer for 10 minutes. Stir the cilantro into the sauce and set aside to cool.

Peel the jicama, slice it into ½-inch-thick rounds, and then cut into 1 × ½-inch strips. Core and seed the bell pepper and slice it lengthwise into strips. Peel, pit, and cube the mango (page 367). Slice the star fruits or kiwis. Rinse the lettuce and pat or spin dry.

On a large platter, arrange a bed of the lettuce. Artfully place the jicama, bell peppers, shrimp, and fruit on the greens and drizzle with the coconut sauce. Serve immediately.

DAILY SPECIAL

MENU IDEAS **Chilled Avocado Tomatillo Soup (page 141)** ✳ **Caribbean Rice Salad (page 202)** ✳ **Golden Tomato Avocado Salad (page 268)** ✳ **Roasted Red Pepper Coconut Soup (page 52)** ✳ **Caribbean Sweet Potato Coconut Soup (page 29)** ✳ **Jamaican Tomato Soup (page 41)**

Vietnamese Shrimp & Noodle Salad

In Ithaca, New York, far away from the trendy Vietnamese restaurants in large cities, we are lucky to have a local eatery owned by a wonderful woman from Vietnam named Liêú-Thu-Pham. Her delectable salads, like this one, are light and refreshing, with the flavors of lime, cilantro, and a hint of peanut.

The shrimp should be marinated for at least 2 hours (and up to 24 hours), so plan ahead when making this dish. Prepare the rest of the ingredients just before serving the salad.

For a delicious Vietnamese Vegan Noodle Salad, include the mixed baby greens, omit the shrimp, and reserve ½ cup of the dressing to pass at the table.

SERVES 6 TO 8
MARINATING TIME:
  AT LEAST 2 HOURS
PREPARATION TIME:
  1 HOUR

PER 12-OUNCE SERVING: 451 CALORIES, 19.1 G PROTEIN, 18.9 G FAT, 53.6 G CARBOHYDRATES, 4.3 G SATURATED FATTY ACIDS, 111 MG CHOLESTEROL, 358 MG SODIUM, 2.3 G TOTAL DIETARY FIBER

DRESSING
½ cup peanut or canola oil
½ cup rice vinegar
1 tablespoon dark sesame oil
1 tablespoon sugar
¼ cup fresh lime juice
2 tablespoons soy sauce
1 teaspoon red pepper flakes, more to taste
1 tablespoon freshly grated lime peel

1 pound cooked jumbo shrimp, peeled and deveined*
1 pound flat rice noodles or linguine
4 cups shredded green cabbage
1 cup chopped fresh herbs: cilantro, basil, scallions
1 large red bell pepper, seeded and cut into thin strips (about 1 cup)
1 cup mung bean sprouts
3 tablespoons chopped toasted peanuts**

4 cups mixed baby greens (optional)
2 limes, quartered into wedges

* *Purchasing cooked shrimp is easiest, but it's fine to marinate raw shrimp and then grill them for 2 minutes on each side while brushing on more marinade.*
** *Toast peanuts in a single layer on an unoiled baking tray in a conventional or toaster oven at 350° for about 5 minutes, until fragrant and golden.*

Whisk together the dressing ingredients. Place the shrimp in a bowl, toss with ½ cup of the dressing, cover, and refrigerate for at least 2 hours. In a separate container, refrigerate the rest of the dressing.

Just before serving, bring 4½ quarts of water to a boil. Stir in the rice noodles and simmer for about 2 minutes, then remove from the heat and test for doneness every minute, until the noodles are soft but not mushy. If using linguine, cook until al dente, 8 to 10 minutes. In a colander, drain the noodles, rinse with cold water, and drain again.

In a serving bowl, toss well the shrimp, drained noodles, and reserved dressing. Mix in the shredded cabbage and chopped herbs. Sprinkle on the bell peppers, mung sprouts, and toasted peanuts.

Mound the salad on a bed of baby greens, if you wish. Serve at room temperature, decorated with lime wedges.

DAILY SPECIAL

MENU IDEAS **Chinese Velvet Corn Soup (page 116) * Asian Bean Curd Soup (page 64) * Azuki Bean Soup (page 68) * Tomato Egg Drop Soup (page 133) * chilled August Melon Soup (page 140) * chilled Mango Soup (page 154) * Spicy Carrot Peanut Soup (page 55)**

Accompaniments

Dressings

Breads & Biscuits

Tempting Extras

Here are some of our favorite toppings and garnishes for soups and salads, plus dressings and a few easy breads. **These tasty additions are what can make a soup distinctive or a salad complete**. Because they can be used in a variety of ways to enhance many different dishes, you'll find frequent references to the items in this section scattered throughout the book. Here are the dressings that are long-standing customer favorites. There are also recipes for some great garnishes with crunchy textures, such as Fried Shallots, Filo Croutons, and Curried Croutons. Herbed Croutons, found on page 30 (Classic Tomato Garlic Soup), are also simple and versatile and hit the spot on either soup or salad. Toppings like Spiced Paneer and Baked Seasoned Tofu add protein and pizzazz, as do the Marinated Chickpeas or White Beans we serve daily at Moosewood on our Mediterranean salads. Try one of our special and unusual condiments, such as Cilantro Lime Pesto or Jalapeño Cream. They don't take long to make, and they add lots of flavor.

And then there's bread. At Moosewood, there isn't one person among us who doesn't *love* good bread. Bread is the perfect medium for soaking up the last drop of soup and that final little bit of dressing. At the restaurant, oven space is limited. So, although we do bake our own cakes, pastries, biscuits, cornbread, and muffins, we rely on several great local bakeries to provide the light, tender, whole grain and European-style breads we serve every day. Because the texture of good French and Italian breads is not easy to reproduce in conventional home ovens, we recommend you find local sources of good, preservative-free, crusty breads.

But at home, we bake. And here, some of our avid bread bakers have shared a few of their special recipes — ones that are simple, out of the ordinary, and wonderful with soups and salads. Good bread adds substance and the satisfaction that rounds out a meal of soup and salad.

See pages 340–341 for our advice and fanciful notions about edible flowers. Beautiful, delicate blooms, one of nature's most exquisite pieces of handiwork, are disarming, charming, and nourishing as decorative nibbles — what could be better?

ACCOMPANIMENTS

DRESSINGS

BREADS & BISCUITS

TEMPTING EXTRAS

Dressings

Best Blue Cheese Dressing

The flavors of blue cheese vary widely in strength and saltiness. Experiment with different kinds to find your favorites. This dressing thickens beautifully when well chilled and will keep for several days if tightly covered and refrigerated.

YIELDS 2 CUPS
TOTAL TIME: 10 MINUTES

PER 1-OUNCE SERVING: 126 CALORIES, 1.9 G PROTEIN, 12.9 G FAT, 1.4 G CARBO-HYDRATES, 4.2 G SATURATED FATTY ACIDS, 6 MG CHOLESTEROL, 178 MG SODIUM, 0 G TOTAL DIETARY FIBER

¾ cup canola or other vegetable oil
1 cup crumbled Danish, Maytag, or your
favorite blue cheese
2 tablespoons cider vinegar
3 tablespoons fresh lemon juice
½ teaspoon salt
½ teaspoon ground black pepper
1 to 2 teaspoons sugar
⅔ cup 2% milk

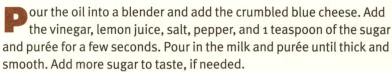

Pour the oil into a blender and add the crumbled blue cheese. Add the vinegar, lemon juice, salt, pepper, and 1 teaspoon of the sugar and purée for a few seconds. Pour in the milk and purée until thick and smooth. Add more sugar to taste, if needed.

Pour the dressing into a serving container, cover tightly, and refrigerate.

Variation For a Chunky Blue Cheese Dressing, just stir up to ¾ cup of additional crumbled cheese into the blended dressing.

MENU IDEAS **Chef Salad à la Moosewood (page 203)** ✳ **dip for raw vegetables** ✳ **Bean & Radic-chio Salad (page 249)** ✳ **Five-Herb Salad (page 262)** ✳ **Simple Tomato Salads (page 286)** ✳ **Wilted Spinach & Portabella Mushrooms (page 239)** ✳ **Marinated Mushrooms (page 347)**

"Creamy" Fresh Herbed Tofu Dressing

Using firm silken tofu makes this oil-free dressing rich in protein, full of body, and velvety smooth. The spinach blends so well with the bright accent of the fresh herbs that no one ever suspects its presence, but we like the way it intensifies the lovely, rich green color of the dressing. A small clove of garlic adds quite a pleasant bite, but if you're a garlic lover, try a medium or large clove. If you prefer to use a whole standard cake of silken tofu, just double the recipe exactly.

YIELDS ¾ TO 1 CUP
TOTAL TIME: 10 MINUTES

PER 1-OUNCE SERVING: 26 CALORIES, 2.2 G PROTEIN, 1.2 G FAT, 2.4 G CARBOHYDRATES, 0.2 G SATURATED FATTY ACIDS, 0 MG CHOLESTEROL, 158 MG SODIUM, 0.4 G TOTAL DIETARY FIBER

6 to 7 ounces firm silken tofu (½ cake)
2 tablespoons cider vinegar
2 tablespoons unsweetened apple juice or orange juice
½ teaspoon Dijon mustard
1 small garlic clove, minced or pressed
1 tablespoon chopped fresh basil
1 tablespoon chopped fresh dill
1 tablespoon chopped fresh tarragon
5 spinach leaves, rinsed and large stems removed
½ teaspoon salt
dash of freshly ground black pepper to taste (optional)

Combine all of the dressing ingredients in a blender or food processor and purée until smooth. You may need to stop once or twice to scrape down the sides of the blender with a rubber spatula. Covered and refrigerated, this dressing will keep for about 5 days.

Variation For a simpler and slightly milder dressing, omit the tarragon, garlic, and spinach and use a generous, packed tablespoon each of fresh basil and dill.

For a tarragon-accented dressing (nice with a French-style meal), replace the dill with an additional tablespoon of fresh tarragon.

MENU IDEAS **This sparky dressing is nice on mild greens, such as ruby lettuce or mixed baby greens, topped with a few golden cherry tomato halves. Try it as a dip for crudités or as a topping on steamed or roasted vegetables. It's especially good on a simple tomato salad or with roasted new potatoes.**

Low-fat Honey Dijon Vinaigrette

The tangy sweet flavor of this dressing artfully disguises the fact that it is low in fat, and the mixture of roasted garlic paste, honey, and mustard thickens the dressing without the use of any oil at all. We like the flavor that just a tablespoon or two of oil imparts, but we leave it to you to decide. This recipe can be easily doubled.

Serve this dressing on any fresh greens or tossed salad, on black beans or white beans with sautéed onions, or on steamed green beans and/or cauliflower garnished with chopped pimientos for a lovely side salad.

YIELDS ABOUT 2 CUPS
TOTAL TIME: 10 MINUTES
  (USING PREROASTED GARLIC)

PER 1-OUNCE SERVING: 30 CALORIES, 0.6 G PROTEIN, 0.2 G FAT, 7.3 G CARBO-HYDRATES, 0 G SATURATED FATTY ACIDS, 0 MG CHOLESTEROL, 121 MG SODIUM, 0.2 G TOTAL DIETARY FIBER

2 heads of roasted garlic (page 363)
2 tablespoons mild honey
2 tablespoons Dijon mustard
3 tablespoons cider vinegar
¼ cup water or unsweetened apple juice
¼ teaspoon salt
pinch of ground black pepper
1 to 2 tablespoons olive oil (optional)

Squeeze the paste from the heads of roasted garlic into a blender, taking care not to let any skins slip in. Add the honey, mustard, vinegar, water or apple juice, salt, pepper, and, if using, the oil. Whirl until the dressing is smooth and creamy. Add more salt to taste.

Low-fat Honey Dijon Vinaigrette keeps in the refrigerator for 2 to 3 weeks.

MENU IDEAS Dress a generous salad and pair it with one of our low-fat soups, such as Choklay's Tibetan Lentil Soup (page 73) ∗ Azuki Bean Soup (page 68) ∗ Faux Pho (page 34) ∗ or chilled Cherry Berry Beet Soup (page 143) for a lean-and-mean meal.

Low-fat Tomato Basil Dressing

Originally developed for *Moosewood Restaurant Low-Fat Favorites,* this dressing has become one of our customers' favorites. Although it can be made without any oil, we usually add just a little olive oil to the original recipe for a pleasing richness. Some of us use extra-virgin olive oil for a more intense and fruity flavor.

YIELDS 1½ CUPS
TOTAL TIME: 15 MINUTES

PER 1-OUNCE SERVING: 44 CALORIES, 1.2 G PROTEIN, 2.6 G FAT, 4.9 G CARBO-HYDRATES, 0.4 G SATURATED FATTY ACIDS, 0 MG CHOLESTEROL, 258 MG SODIUM, 1.1 G TOTAL DIETARY FIBER

6 sun-dried tomatoes (not packed in oil)
1 large tomato, coarsely chopped (about 1½ cups)
1 garlic clove, minced or pressed
¼ cup water
2 tablespoons olive oil
2 tablespoons balsamic vinegar
¼ cup coarsely chopped fresh basil, loosely packed
½ teaspoon salt

Place the sun-dried tomatoes in a small bowl, cover them with boiling water, and set aside for about 15 minutes.

In a blender, combine the chopped fresh tomato and the garlic, water, oil, vinegar, basil, and salt. Drain the softened sun-dried tomatoes. Add them to the blender and purée until smooth.

This dressing will keep in a closed container in the refrigerator for about a week.

MENU IDEAS This is a good dressing for steamed cauliflower, fennel slices, or cooked beans. We don't use it as a marinade for green vegetables because it will spoil the color, but it's a fine artichoke dipping sauce. Its lightness and bright taste make it a good choice for a substantial Chef Salad à la Moosewood (page 203). This recipe makes a good topping for fresh hot pasta, and, if lightly puréed with a dash of Tabasco or a pinch of cayenne, it makes a wonderful Italian salsa for chips or Focaccia (page 330).

Luscious Lemon Tahini Dressing

This is one of the dressings always available at Moose-wood Restaurant. Unlike our previous recipes for this dressing, several of us now make it without any oil at all and like it better that way. A little red wine vinegar seems to sweeten the dressing and round out the sharpness of the lemon and tahini. Although the cumin is optional, it really adds a touch of the Middle East.

YIELDS 1¼ CUPS
TOTAL TIME: 5 TO 10 MINUTES

PER 1-OUNCE SERVING: 43 CALORIES, 1.3 G PROTEIN, 3.5 G FAT, 2.4 G CARBO-HYDRATES, 0.5 G SATURATED FATTY ACIDS, 0 MG CHOLESTEROL, 125 MG SODIUM, 0.7 G TOTAL DIETARY FIBER

½ cup tahini
½ cup water
3 tablespoons fresh lemon juice
1 tablespoon red wine vinegar
1 to 2 garlic cloves, minced or pressed
½ teaspoon salt
⅛ teaspoon ground black pepper
1 teaspoon ground cumin (optional)

In a small bowl, whisk together all of the ingredients until smooth. For the best flavor, let the dressing sit for at least 15 minutes before serving.

Covered and refrigerated, this dressing will keep for at least a month. If needed, shake or whisk to reblend.

Note Occasionally tahini has a bitter flavor. If yours does, replace the ½ cup of water with ¼ cup of olive oil and ¼ cup of water.

MENU IDEAS **This is the dressing of choice for a tossed green salad to accompany Moroccan Root Vegetable Stew (page 45)** ✳ **Middle Eastern Chickpea Soup (page 88)** ✳ **Tunisian Pumpkin Soup (page 56)** ✳ **Egyptian Red Lentil Soup (page 76). Or try it on greens with cucumbers, black olives, pimientos, and feta cheese or make it a topping for falafels, stuffed grape leaves, tofu-kan, or a vegetable pita sandwich.**

Moosewood Ginger Miso Dressing

A favorite of vegans, this sleek, smooth dressing with its refreshing ginger flavor and almost fluffy consistency is made by carefully blending water into the oil, vinegar, and miso. The miso lends a rich, salty taste and contains highly beneficial digestive and antibacterial enzymes.

Leftover rice or pasta, seafood, and vegetables can be transformed into a salad the next day with this versatile dressing.

YIELDS ABOUT 2 CUPS
TOTAL TIME: 15 MINUTES

PER 1-OUNCE SERVING: 119 CALORIES, 0.5 G PROTEIN, 12.6 G FAT, 1.5 G CARBO-HYDRATES, 3 G SATURATED FATTY ACIDS, 0 MG CHOLESTEROL, 130 MG SODIUM, 0.2 G TOTAL DIETARY FIBER

¾ cup canola or other vegetable oil
2 tablespoons dark sesame oil
¼ cup cider vinegar or rice vinegar
¼ cup light miso (page 368)
3 tablespoons grated fresh ginger root
½ cup water

Combine the canola oil, sesame oil, vinegar, miso, and ginger in a blender and whirl until smooth. With the blender still running, add the water in a thin, steady stream; the dressing will become thick and creamy.

This dressing will keep for several weeks covered and refrigerated. If it separates, just shake well, whisk, or repurée in the blender.

MENU IDEAS **This dressing is excellent with salads or pita sandwiches of fresh spinach, grated carrots, sliced cucumbers, and Baked Seasoned Tofu (page 336). It can give an Asian twist to lightly steamed broccoli and makes a tasty salad of grated jicama or turnip. This is the dressing for a tossed salad to serve with Chinese Velvet Corn Soup (page 116) ✳ Wonton Soup (page 104) ✳ Ozoni (page 48) ✳ Everyday Split Pea Soup (page 77).**

Moosewood House Dressing

Here's our house classic — creamy green, slightly sweet, filled with the flavors of fresh spinach and basil. This is, by a landslide, the recipe most often requested by customers. It can be varied by adding garlic, a scallion, or other herbs, such as dill, tarragon, or marjoram. Use fresh herbs, if possible; otherwise, a mixture of dried herbs equal to 1 teaspoon will do. Up to $\frac{1}{3}$ of the oil can be olive oil, but it should not be the dominant flavor.

YIELDS 2¼ CUPS
TOTAL TIME: 5 TO 10 MINUTES

PER 1-OUNCE SERVING: 123 CALORIES, 0.5 G PROTEIN, 13.1 G FAT, 1.5 G CARBO-HYDRATES, 3.6 G SATURATED FATTY ACIDS, 2 MG CHOLESTEROL, 46 MG SODIUM, 0 G TOTAL DIETARY FIBER

1 cup canola or other vegetable oil
3 tablespoons cider vinegar or fresh lemon juice
2 teaspoons mild honey
¼ cup rinsed spinach leaves, packed
¼ cup fresh basil leaves, loosely packed
2 teaspoons Dijon mustard
¼ teaspoon salt, or to taste
pinch of ground black pepper
1 cup milk or buttermilk

In a blender, combine the oil, vinegar or lemon juice, honey, spinach, basil, mustard, salt, and pepper and purée until smooth. With the blender still running, gradually add the milk or buttermilk in a thin stream — the dressing will become thick and creamy. As soon as the dressing thickens, stop the blender or the oil may separate, causing the dressing to become thin.

Moosewood House Dressing will keep for about a week in the refrigerator. If it separates, shake well before serving.

MENU IDEAS *This is such a versatile dressing, we feel confident telling you to try it on anything that needs a dressing. Experiment to your heart's content.*

Versatile Vinaigrette

Simple and zesty, this favorite everyday dressing with its basic olive oil and fresh lemon juice underpinning is highlighted by garlic, thyme, and black pepper. The mustard adds just the right amount of pungency. Vary the fresh green herb to suit your fancy and to complement most favorably the dish you're making.

YIELDS ABOUT 1¼ CUPS
TOTAL TIME: 10 TO 15 MINUTES

PER 1-OUNCE SERVING: 139 CALORIES, 0.1 G PROTEIN, 15.2 G FAT, 1.2 G CARBO-HYDRATES, 2.1 G SATURATED FATTY ACIDS, 0 MG CHOLESTEROL, 129 MG SODIUM, 0.1 G TOTAL DIETARY FIBER

½ **cup fresh lemon juice**
⅔ **cup olive oil**
3 **garlic cloves, minced or pressed**
1½ **teaspoons Dijon mustard**
1 **teaspoon minced fresh thyme (¼ teaspoon dried)**
1 **tablespoon minced fresh tarragon, basil, or dill (1 teaspoon dried)**
½ **teaspoon salt, or to taste**
½ **teaspoon coarsely cracked black pepper**

Place all of the vinaigrette ingredients in a jar with a tight-fitting lid and shake vigorously to blend. Serve immediately or refrigerate for later use.

Our vinaigrette will keep in a closed container in the refrigerator for about 1 month. Shake well before using.

 MENU IDEAS **This will enhance green salads, cooked vegetables, and grain or bean salads without overwhelming their flavors. Try it on pasta topped with Marinated Chickpeas or White Beans (page 346) and grated feta, or enliven leftover cooked pasta with this dressing and a dollop of either Parsley Pesto (page 348) or Rich Dairyless Hazelnut Pesto (page 101).**

Zesty Feta Garlic Dressing

Very popular at Moosewood, this is a robust, garlicky dressing with the clean, briny taste of feta and the redolence of dill.

YIELDS 1⅔ CUPS
TOTAL TIME: 5 TO 10 MINUTES

PER 1-OUNCE SERVING: 95 CALORIES, 1.2 G PROTEIN, 9.8 G FAT, 0.9 G CARBOHYDRATES, 2.2 G SATURATED FATTY ACIDS, 7 MG CHOLESTEROL, 73 MG SODIUM, 0 G TOTAL DIETARY FIBER

½ cup olive oil
2 tablespoons cider vinegar or white wine vinegar
2 garlic cloves, minced or pressed
2 teaspoons chopped fresh dill (¾ teaspoon dried)
¾ cup crumbled feta cheese
⅔ cup milk or buttermilk
ground black pepper to taste

In a blender, combine the oil, vinegar, garlic, dill, and feta and purée until smooth. With the blender running, gradually pour in the milk or buttermilk and whirl until creamy. Add pepper to taste.

This dressing will keep in a covered container for about a week in the refrigerator. If it separates, whisk or shake well before serving.

MENU IDEAS **Try as a delicious alternative dressing for Caesar Salad (page 201) or on Chef Salad à la Moosewood (page 203). It is thick enough to be used as a dip for raw or steamed vegetables or cooked shrimp, or as a topping for stuffed grape leaves or baked potatoes.**

Breads & Biscuits

Featherlight Blue Mountain Biscuits

These easy, quick biscuits are the perfect accompaniment to almost any soup. Their baking time is so short that it's easy to have them ready to serve just as family or guests sit down to eat. Fresh from the oven, flaky aromatic biscuits can help create a warm, congenial atmosphere.

Lisa Wichman developed this recipe for biscuits using oil rather than other types of shortening, and we promise you won't miss that saturated fat a bit.

YIELDS 10 TO 12 BISCUITS
PREPARATION TIME: 10 MINUTES
BAKING TIME: 10 TO 12 MINUTES

PER 1.5-OUNCE SERVING: 138 CALORIES, 2.2 G PROTEIN, 6.5 G FAT, 17.5 G CARBO-HYDRATES, 1.7 G SATURATED FATTY ACIDS, 0 MG CHOLESTEROL, 217 MG SODIUM, 0.4 G TOTAL DIETARY FIBER

2¼ cups unbleached white pastry flour*
1 tablespoon baking powder
¼ teaspoon baking soda
½ teaspoon salt
⅓ cup canola or other vegetable oil
¾ cup buttermilk

* We prefer pastry flour for biscuits, but if it's not available, use 2 cups of all-purpose flour instead.

Preheat the oven to 450°.

In a mixing bowl, sift together the flour, baking powder, baking soda, and salt. Make a well in the center of the dry ingredients and pour in the oil and buttermilk. Using a fork, stir just until mixed—over-mixing will make the biscuits tough.

Turn the dough onto a lightly floured surface and gently knead 5 or 6 times, adding more flour if necessary. Pat or roll out the dough to a ½-inch thickness. Cut out 10 to 12 rounds with a biscuit cutter or a glass and arrange them on an unoiled baking sheet. When you place the biscuits touching one another, they seem to rise better.

Bake for 10 to 12 minutes, preferably on the top shelf of the oven, until golden brown. Serve immediately.

Variation Replace 1 cup of the white flour with whole wheat pastry flour.

MENU IDEAS **Very Creamy Vegetable Chowder (page 134)** ✳ **Corn Chowder (page 117)** ✳ **Green & White Gumbo (page 80)** ✳ **Texas Two-Bean Soup (page 95)** ✳ **Pepperpot (page 50)** ✳ **Westphalian Vegetable Stew (page 57)**

Anadama Bread

In 1973, when Sara Robbins arrived for her job interview at Moosewood, she cleverly brought along a fresh-baked loaf of Anadama Bread as a sample of her considerable skills. The bread is made with a cornmeal porridge sweetened with brown sugar and molasses. Sara was hired on the spot after just one bite.

We've doubled the original recipe; that way, you get 2 loaves in the time it takes to make one. They are absolutely magnificent loaves: light, sweet, and tender with golden brown crusts—the kind of bread people with kids will make again and again. It freezes well and makes excellent toast and croutons.

YIELDS TWO 9-INCH LOAVES
PREPARATION TIME: 3½ HOURS
BAKING TIME: 40 MINUTES

PER 2.75-OUNCE SERVING: 200 CALO-RIES, 4.6 G PROTEIN, 4.1 G FAT, 35.7 G CARBOHYDRATES, 1.2 G SATURATED FATTY ACIDS, 2 MG CHOLESTEROL, 406 MG SODIUM, 1.8 G TOTAL DIETARY FIBER

BREAD

2 cups water
2 cups milk or soy milk
2 cups yellow cornmeal
½ cup brown sugar, packed
1 cup warm water
¼ cup unsulphured molasses
2 packages dry yeast (about 2 tablespoons)
12 to 13 cups unbleached white flour
½ cup canola or other vegetable oil
2 tablespoons salt

a little oil for hands, the rising bowl, and the loaf pans
2 tablespoons melted butter for glazing (optional)

Bring the water and milk or soy milk to a boil in a saucepan; stir in the cornmeal and brown sugar and set aside to cool a bit. In a small bowl, stir together the warm water and molasses and dissolve the yeast in it. When the cornmeal mush has cooled to 105° to 115°, transfer it to a large bowl and stir in the yeast mixture.

Stir in 2 cups of the flour and beat 100 strokes. Cover the bowl with a damp cloth and set it aside in a warm place to rise (see Note) until the mixture bubbles, about 45 minutes. This batter is called a "sponge."

Stir the oil, salt, and 7 to 8 cups of the remaining flour into the sponge to make a stiff dough, mixing well. Generously dust a board with the remaining flour. Turn the dough onto the board and knead it until elastic, about 10 minutes. The dough may be sticky; lightly oiling your hands will be helpful.

Oil the bowl, return the kneaded dough to the bowl, and flip it over to lightly coat with oil. Cover the bowl with a damp cloth and set aside in a warm place until the dough has doubled in size, 45 to 60 minutes.

Punch down the dough and turn it out onto a lightly floured board. Slice it into halves and shape each half to fit a 5 × 9 × 3-inch loaf pan. Lightly oil the two loaf pans, place the dough in them, cover, and let rise in a warm place until doubled, 30 to 45 minutes.

Preheat the oven to 350°.

When the dough has risen, bake for about 40 minutes, or until golden and hollow sounding when tapped on the bottom. Cool on a wire rack. Brush the tops of the loaves with a little melted butter, if desired.

Note To create a warm, draft-free place for the bread to rise, boil two pots of water and place them in the oven with the bowl of dough. The oven is insulated and will retain the warmth produced by the pots of hot water. Or turn on the oven for just a few minutes, turn it off, and put the bowl of dough inside. The residual oven heat should help the dough to rise.

MENU IDEAS **Baked Bean Soup (page 69)** ✳ **Autumn Minestrone (page 67)** ✳ **Creamy Tomato Soup (page 125)** ✳ **Pepperpot (page 50)** ✳ **Very Creamy Vegetable Chowder (page 134)** ✳ **Solstice Salad (page 227)** ✳ **Louisiana Black-eyed Pea Salad (page 221)** ✳ **Roasted Garlic Aioli Salad (page 225)**

Focaccia

Focaccia is a name given to a puzzling array of Italian flatbreads: some round, thick, and dense; some rectangular and light; yet others, thin, chewy, and crusty, like this one—which is similar to pizza crust without the sauce and cheese. A small amount of yeast, a slow cool rising, and a quick hot baking at 500° make this bread crisp and chewy, and nothing like most store-bought breads. If you have a baking stone or a large cast-iron skillet, be sure to read the tip at the end of the recipe.

Our focaccia can be shaped into two 9-inch rounds, one large flatbread, or breadsticks. With a liberal sprinkling of good olive oil and rosemary (and the addition of garlic or grated Parmesan cheese, if you like), it's a terrific accompaniment for light salads and hearty soups.

SERVES 4 TO 6
PREPARATION TIME: 10 MINUTES
RISING TIME: 3 HOURS
BAKING TIME: 10 TO 15 MINUTES

PER 4-OUNCE SERVING: 241 CALORIES, 6 G PROTEIN, 4.2 G FAT, 44 G CARBOHYDRATES, 0.6 G SATURATED FATTY ACIDS, 0 MG CHOLESTEROL, 400 MG SODIUM, 1.9 G TOTAL DIETARY FIBER

DOUGH

1¼ cups warm water
3 cups all-purpose white flour*
scant ½ teaspoon dry yeast
½ teaspoon salt
½ teaspoon sugar
1 tablespoon olive oil

EXTRAS

1 to 2 teaspoons olive oil
1 tablespoon minced fresh rosemary
½ teaspoon coarse sea salt
1 to 2 minced garlic cloves (optional)
2 tablespoons freshly grated Parmesan cheese (optional)

FOR BREADSTICKS ONLY

1 egg white, lightly beaten
2 to 3 tablespoons sesame seeds

Or try replacing 1 cup of the white flour with whole wheat bread flour.

Using a heavy-duty mixer, a food processor powerful enough to handle bread dough, or a strong arm, beat together all of the dough ingredients for about a minute. The dough will be very wet and sticky, but resist the urge to add more flour. When the dough has become elastic—you will notice a certain stringiness—scrape it into an oiled bowl. Cover the bowl with plastic wrap and set it aside in a draft-free area until doubled in volume, 2 to 3 hours depending on the temperature. The slower the rise, the more flavorful and chewy the focaccia will be.

When the dough has doubled, preheat the oven to 500°.

Turn the dough onto a well-floured surface and make two rounds, one larger rectangle, or breadsticks. To make two rounds, divide the dough into two equal parts. Flatten each piece of dough into an 8- to 9-inch round. Dip your fingers into flour and dimple the top of the dough. Brush on some good-quality olive oil and sprinkle with the rosemary, salt, and, if using, the garlic and Parmesan cheese. Transfer the rounds to a baking sheet sprinkled with cornmeal and let rise for 10 to 15 minutes. Bake for 10 to 12 minutes, until lightly browned.

For one larger focaccia, press all of the dough into a 9 × 13-inch baking sheet dusted with cornmeal. Brush the top with oil and sprinkle with the rosemary, salt, and, if using, the garlic and Parmesan cheese.

Let the focaccia rise for 10 minutes; then bake it until lightly browned, about 10 minutes.

For breadsticks, press out the dough to a thickness of about ½ inch. Cut it into ¾-inch-wide strips and twist, pull, stretch, roll, or otherwise shape it into breadsticks. Brush the breadsticks with a beaten egg white and sprinkle with sesame seeds or grated Parmesan cheese. Transfer the breadsticks to a baking sheet sprinkled with cornmeal and bake until browned, about 8 minutes.

Note A baking stone will make the focaccia lighter and crisper. A 12-inch cast-iron skillet (or larger one) that will easily hold the focaccia rounds can likewise be used.

Baking stone method: Place the baking stone or cast-iron skillet in the oven during preheating. Dust a baker's peel or an inverted baking pan with cornmeal. Prepare one of the focaccia rounds and place it on the baker's peel or inverted baking pan. Let it rise for 10 to 15 minutes. When the oven reaches 500°, slide the focaccia from the baker's peel onto the baking stone or into the cast-iron skillet. Bake it for 10 to 12 minutes, until lightly browned. Meanwhile, prepare the second round of focaccia and let it rise. Bake the second focaccia when the first one comes out of the oven.

Focaccia is best eaten the day it is made, but day-old focaccia can be revived by warming it in a hot oven for about 5 minutes. Freezing leftovers immediately works even better. Defrost in a microwave oven and/or lightly toast in a toaster oven, and we think you'll declare it still fabulous!

Create a focaccia platter with a small bowl of flavorful olive oil for dipping, an assortment of olives, some Gorgonzola, aged Provolone, or herbed chèvre, and roasted red peppers and/or portabella mushrooms.

DAILY SPECIAL MENU IDEAS **Portuguese Mussel Stew (page 169)** ✳ **Broccoli Rabe & Rice Soup (page 72)** ✳ **Potato & Escarole Soup (page 51)** ✳ **Tomato & Kale Soup with Barley (page 98)** ✳ **Tuscan Bean Soup (page 100)** ✳ **Artichoke Heart Soup (page 27)** ✳ **Arugula & Warm Mozzarella Salad (page 191)** ✳ **Balkan Roasted Vegetable Salad (page 196)** ✳ **Pinzimonio (page 280)**

Herbed Cheese Quick Bread

Cheddar and chives or scallions are an excellent savory match. They combine here to season an easily prepared bread that is delicious warm from the oven. It complements an extensive range of salads and soups. This recipe is adapted from one that appeared in *Harrowsmith* magazine a number of years ago and has proven to be a favorite of ours.

YIELDS ONE 9 x 5-INCH LOAF
PREPARATION TIME: 15 MINUTES
BAKING TIME: 40 TO 45 MINUTES

PER 2.5-OUNCE SERVING: 199 CALORIES, 9.2 G PROTEIN, 8 G FAT, 22.8 G CARBOHYDRATES, 4.7 G SATURATED FATTY ACIDS, 52 MG CHOLESTEROL, 388 MG SODIUM, 1.4 G TOTAL DIETARY FIBER

1½ cups unbleached white flour
½ cup whole wheat pastry flour*
1 tablespoon baking powder
½ teaspoon salt
1 tablespoon brown sugar, packed
⅓ cup chopped fresh chives or scallions
2 tablespoons chopped fresh parsley
½ teaspoon chopped fresh thyme (¼ teaspoon dried)
1½ cups crumbled sharp Cheddar cheese**
1 egg
¾ cup milk

* Or use 2 cups total of white flour.
** Crumble the cheese by hand rather than grating it; it's okay if the pieces are uneven.

Preheat the oven to 375°. Lightly oil a 9 × 5-inch loaf pan. Sift the flours, baking powder, salt, and brown sugar into a large bowl. Stir in the chives or scallions, parsley, thyme, and cheese. In a smaller bowl, beat together the egg and milk. Add the wet ingredients to the dry ingredients and stir until just combined; the batter will be stiff. Transfer it with a rubber spatula to the loaf pan and smooth the top.

Bake for 40 to 45 minutes, until the top is firm and a knife inserted in the center comes out clean. Cool on a rack for 5 minutes before removing the bread from the pan.

Serve warm or at room temperature.

DAILY SPECIAL

MENU IDEAS **Five-Herb Salad (page 262)** ✳ **Kale Salad (page 272)** ✳ **Louisiana Black-eyed Pea Salad (page 221)** ✳ **Baked Bean Soup (page 69)** ✳ **chilled Golden Gazpacho (page 153)** ✳ **Texas Two-Bean Soup (page 95)** ✳ **Italian Green, White & Red Soup (page 82)** ✳ **Creamy Potato Cabbage Soup (page 124)**

Our Special Gluten-free Bread

There is a growing awareness of wheat sensitivity and gluten allergies. Some people are not only allergic to wheat, but they also can't tolerate gluten, the spongy, elastic substance that gives wheat bread its chewiness. For such people, spelt, oats, barley, and many other grains are not options.

This recipe uses rice and tapioca flours and was inspired by information from Bette Hagman's book, *More from the Gluten-free Gourmet*. We think it's better than anything we've been able to buy from a bakery and it's a third the cost besides. Use it to make jerk croutons for our Jamaican Tomato Soup (page 41).

YIELDS ONE 9 X 5-INCH LOAF
PREPARATION TIME: 15 MINUTES
RISING TIME: 1½ HOURS
BAKING TIME: 45 TO 50 MINUTES
COOLING TIME: 30 MINUTES

PER 1.75-OUNCE SERVING: 121 CALORIES, 1.8 G PROTEIN, 4 G FAT, 19.4 G CARBOHYDRATES, 1.1 G SATURATED FATTY ACIDS, 29 MG CHOLESTEROL, 88 MG SODIUM, 1.3 G TOTAL DIETARY FIBER

2 cups rice flour (page 376)
1 cup tapioca flour* or cornstarch
1 tablespoon xanthan gum**
½ teaspoon salt
1 tablespoon sugar
1¼ cups water
1 package dry yeast (about 1 tablespoon)
2 eggs
¼ cup canola or other vegetable oil or melted butter
1 teaspoon cider vinegar

* *Available at natural food stores and at Asian and Hispanic markets.*
** *A natural food fiber available at some health food stores.*

Using an electric mixer (a wooden spoon works okay, but not as well), combine all of the ingredients. The dough will resemble a thick batter. Scoop it into an oiled 9 × 5-inch loaf pan and smooth the top. Spray or brush the top of the dough with a light coating of vegetable oil. Loosely cover the pan with plastic wrap and set aside to rise until the dough is even with the top of the pan, about 1½ hours.

After the dough has risen for 1¼ hours, preheat the oven to 375°.

Remove the plastic and bake the bread until golden brown, 45 to 50 minutes. Remove from the oven, invert onto a rack, and let cool for 30 minutes before slicing.

Once sliced, this bread freezes well; just toast it before eating.

DAILY SPECIAL

MENU IDEAS **Shchi (page 53)** ✳ **Mole de Olla Rodriguez (page 42)** ✳ **Choklay's Tibetan Lentil Soup (page 73)** ✳ **Azuki Bean Soup (page 68)** ✳ **Fattoush (page 209)** ✳ **Balkan Roasted Vegetable Salad (page 196)** ✳ **Bourride (page 164)**

Popovers

Golden brown and flecked with fresh green herbs, these savory pastries rise impressively without any leavening and have a fascinating "poofy" shape with slightly hollow, custardy centers. Popovers are very easy to make and take only a few moments to prepare. We prefer the ease of making them in the blender, but the ingredients can also be whisked together by hand.

For the first course of a dinner party or when friends arrive unexpectedly, you can whip these together in 10 minutes and serve fresh hot "bread." Vary the herb mixture to suit your soup. For breakfast, slather them with Neufchâtel or cream cheese or prepare them without herbs and enjoy them with jam. They're at their best when served hot.

YIELDS 12 POPOVERS
PREPARATION TIME: 10 MINUTES
BAKING TIME: 30 MINUTES

PER 2-OUNCE SERVING: 115 CALORIES, 4.4 G PROTEIN, 5.1 G FAT, 12.5 G CARBO-HYDRATES, 1.8 G SATURATED FATTY ACIDS, 70 MG CHOLESTEROL, 157 MG SODIUM, 0.5 G TOTAL DIETARY FIBER

1½ cups unbleached white flour*
1½ cups milk
3 large eggs
2 tablespoons canola or other vegetable oil
½ teaspoon salt
3 to 4 tablespoons minced fresh herbs**

* Whole wheat pastry flour can be substituted.
** A mixture of chives, basil, and oregano is nice, or try parsley, dill, and chives.

Preheat the oven to 450°. Generously butter a standard 12-cup muffin tin.

When the oven reaches 450°, heat the empty muffin tin for 5 minutes. It should be smoking hot; a very hot pan is the key to successful, high-rising popovers.

While the muffin tin is getting hot, place the flour, milk, eggs, oil, and salt in a blender and purée until smooth. Use a spatula to scrape down any flour that clings to the sides of the blender. Stir in the herbs by hand.

When the pan is hot, immediately fill each muffin tin ¾ full and bake for 15 minutes. Reduce the temperature to 350° and bake for another 15 minutes. Serve hot.

MENU IDEAS Louisiana Black-eyed Pea Salad (page 221) ✳ **Seafood Paella Salad (page 308)** ✳ **Classic Clam Chowder (page 167)** ✳ **Vegetable Pistou (page 101)** ✳ **Green & White Gumbo (page 80)** ✳ **Cream of Asparagus Soup (page 118)**

Southern Wheat-free Cornbread

This is the kind of no-nonsense cornbread, using cornmeal and buttermilk as its basic ingredients, that is popular in southern and mid-Atlantic states. It is moist, muffin-light, slightly sweet, and completely wheat-free and gluten-free —a real plus for people with wheat sensitivity and gluten allergies.

Use freshly ground fine cornmeal for the best results. Quaker brand yellow cornmeal also works fine. Avoid the coarsely ground cornmeal sometimes sold in bulk in health food stores. For an interesting low-gluten, wheat-free variation, replace ½ cup of the cornmeal with the equivalent amount of rye flour.

SERVES 6 TO 8
YIELDS 12 TO 16 PIECES
PREPARATION TIME: 15 MINUTES
BAKING TIME: 25 TO 40 MINUTES
COOLING TIME: 20 MINUTES

PER 4-OUNCE SERVING: 229 CALORIES, 6.1 G PROTEIN, 6 G FAT, 37.2 G CARBOHYDRATES, 1.6 G SATURATED FATTY ACIDS, 39 MG CHOLESTEROL, 650 MG SODIUM, 3.2 G TOTAL DIETARY FIBER

2 cups yellow or white cornmeal
½ cup boiling water
1 tablespoon sugar
1 teaspoon salt
2 teaspoons baking powder
1 teaspoon baking soda
1 large egg
2 tablespoons canola or other vegetable oil
1¼ cups buttermilk

Preheat the oven to 375°. Oil a baking pan (see Note) and set aside. In a medium bowl, stir together ½ cup of the cornmeal and the boiling water. The cornmeal will become mushy and then stiff. Set aside.

In a large bowl, sift together the remaining 1½ cups of cornmeal, the sugar, salt, baking powder, and baking soda.

Beat the egg into the cornmeal mush and stir in the oil. Whisk in the buttermilk to make a thin batter. Add the liquid ingredients to the dry ingredients, whisk just until the batter is smooth, and immediately pour it into the prepared pan.

Bake until the center of the cornbread is slightly rounded and firm and the edges are golden brown (see Note). Cool for 20 minutes or more before serving.

Note Bake in a square or round baking pan or in a cast-iron skillet: for an 8-inch square or 9-inch round pan, bake for 35 to 40 minutes; for a 9-inch square or 10-inch round pan, bake for 25 to 30 minutes.

MENU IDEAS **Green & White Gumbo (page 80)** ✳ **Spiced Mexican Squash Stew (page 54)** ✳ **Baked Bean Soup (page 69)** ✳ **Black Bean & Chipotle Soup (page 70)** ✳ **Santa Fe Chowder (page 132)** ✳ **Golden Tomato Avocado Salad (page 268)** ✳ **Roasted Red Pepper & Cauliflower Salad (page 226)** ✳ **Louisiana Black-eyed Pea Salad (page 221)**

Tempting Extras

Baked Seasoned Tofu

Tofu has an amazing capacity to absorb the flavors of any sauce or broth it marinates or cooks in — it's a veritable sponge. Here it is cut into easy-to-eat triangles and baked with an Asian-style sauce made with soy sauce, sesame oil, and rice vinegar. Our addition of honey and tomato paste adds a subtle sweetness and depth to an already wonderful combination.

SERVES 4
YIELDS 12 PIECES
PREPARATION TIME: 10 MINUTES
BAKING TIME: 35 MINUTES

PER 3-OUNCE SERVING: 105 CALORIES, 7.2 G PROTEIN, 7.7 G FAT, 3.7 G CARBO-HYDRATES, 1.1 G SATURATED FATTY ACIDS, 0 MG CHOLESTEROL, 344 MG SODIUM, 1.1 G TOTAL DIETARY FIBER

1 cake of tofu (12 ounces), pressed*

SAUCE
1 tablespoon plus 2 teaspoons soy sauce
1 tablespoon water
1 tablespoon dark sesame oil
1 teaspoon tomato paste (optional)
1 teaspoon rice vinegar
1 teaspoon mild honey or sugar
½ teaspoon ground anise**

 * *Sandwich the tofu between two plates and rest a weight (a heavy can or book) on the top plate. Press for about 20 minutes and drain the expressed liquid.*
** *Grinding ¾ to 1 teaspoon of whole anise seeds with a mortar and pestle or small electric grinder will yield about ½ teaspoon ground.*

Preheat the oven to 375°.
Cut the pressed tofu horizontally into 3 slices. Stack the slices and then cut through all three layers on the two diagonals, making an X. This will yield 12 triangles of tofu. Combine all of the sauce ingredients in a bowl and stir until well blended.

Arrange the triangles in a baking dish and cover with the sauce. Bake, uncovered, for about 35 minutes, carefully turning the tofu with a spatula every 10 minutes. When the tofu has a taut, seared appearance and the sauce has mostly evaporated, it is ready to serve.

MENU IDEAS **Classic Sichuan Noodles (page 204)** ✳ **Marinated Broccoli & Carrots (page 275)** ✳ **Balkan Roasted Vegetable Salad (page 196)** ✳ **Caribbean Rice Salad (page 202)** ✳ **Gado Gado (page 212)** ✳ **Thai Noodle Salad (page 233)** ✳ **Vietnamese Cellophane Noodle Salad (page 238)** ✳ **Asian Spinach & Orange Salad (page 246)** ✳ **Spinach with Cilantro Cashew Dressing (page 289)**

Cilantro Lime Pesto

Here's another wonderful condiment to add to puréed potato or squash soups. It can also wake up steamed vegetables, seafood, and hard-boiled eggs. Or, for an interesting and unusual side dish, serve it with ripe tropical fruits such as avocado, mango, or pineapple.

YIELDS ¾ CUP
TOTAL TIME: 10 MINUTES

PER 1.5-OUNCE SERVING: 175 CALORIES, 0.5 G PROTEIN, 19 G FAT, 2 G CARBOHY-DRATES, 2.6 G SATURATED FATTY ACIDS, 0 MG CHOLESTEROL, 104 MG SODIUM, 0.6 G TOTAL DIETARY FIBER

½ cup chopped fresh cilantro
3 scallions, chopped
½ fresh green chile, seeded and chopped
1 tablespoon chopped fresh dill
¼ teaspoon salt, more to taste
½ cup olive oil
1½ tablespoons fresh lime juice

Place all of the ingredients in a blender or food processor. Purée on low speed until everything is moving, then increase to high speed until reaching the consistency of a smooth paste. Or, if you prefer, pulse the mixture, stopping to scrape down the sides with a rubber spatula when necessary.

DAILY SPECIAL ∾ **MENU IDEAS** Spiced Mexican Squash Stew (page 54) ✳ Santa Fe Chowder (page 132) ✳ Butternut Squash Soup with*out* Sizzled Sage (page 28) ✳ Jamaican Tomato Soup (page 41) ✳ Florida Salad with*out* Ginger Dressing (page 263)

Cilantro Peanut Pesto

Here is an unusual Thai- or Indonesian-style topping. Stir it into a brothy soup to spark it with flavor. Toss it together with linguine, brown rice, or rice noodles, add a few sliced water chestnuts and scallions, and you instantly have a rice or pasta salad with a difference.

You can also use it to coat sliced vegetables or shrimp before broiling or grilling them; then serve them at room temperature with more pesto on the side. At Moosewood, we also like it with steamed red bell peppers, potatoes, broccoli, and hard-boiled eggs.

Make sure that the lemongrass and shallots are cooked until soft but not browned—so that the pesto blends smoothly.

YIELDS 3 CUPS
TOTAL TIME: 20 MINUTES

PER 0.75-OUNCE SERVING: 26 CALORIES, 0.9 G PROTEIN, 2 G FAT, 1.6 G CARBOHYDRATES, 0.3 G SATURATED FATTY ACIDS, 0 MG CHOLESTEROL, 77 MG SODIUM, 0.3 G TOTAL DIETARY FIBER

1 tablespoon canola or other vegetable oil
3 garlic cloves, chopped
½ cup chopped shallots
2 tablespoons chopped fresh lemongrass (page 366)
½ cup unsalted roasted peanuts*
¾ teaspoon salt
2 tablespoons grated fresh ginger root
½ to ¾ cup water
1 tablespoon fresh lime juice
1 cup fresh basil leaves, loosely packed
1 cup fresh cilantro leaves, loosely packed
½ teaspoon crushed red pepper flakes, or less to taste

Toast raw peanuts in a single layer on an unoiled baking tray in a 350° oven for 10 to 15 minutes, until fragrant.

In a small saucepan on medium heat, warm the oil. Add the garlic, shallots, and lemongrass and sauté on medium-high heat until soft, 8 to 10 minutes.

Remove from the heat and transfer to a blender. Add the peanuts, salt, and ginger root, turn on the blender, and gradually add ½ cup of the water in a steady stream while puréeing. Add the lime juice, basil, cilantro, and red pepper flakes. Continue to purée until smooth and uniform, stopping as needed to scrape down the sides of the blender with a rubber spatula. If necessary, add all or part of the remaining ¼ cup of water to produce the consistency you prefer.

Serve at room temperature or chilled. This pesto will keep tightly sealed and refrigerated for up to 2 weeks.

MENU IDEAS **Faux Pho (page 34)** ✳ **Indian Tomato Rice Soup (page 81)** ✳ **Hot & Sour Shrimp Soup (page 168)** ✳ **chilled Avocado Tomatillo Soup (page 141)** ✳ **Spicy Tofu & Greens Soup (page 92)**

Curried Croutons

These croutons are an excellent garnish for soups, salads, and stews where a crisp and spicy topping is desirable.

SERVES 6
TOTAL TIME: 20 MINUTES

PER 1-OUNCE SERVING: 116 CALORIES, 1.7 G PROTEIN, 7.9 G FAT, 9.9 G CARBO-HYDRATES, 1.1 G SATURATED FATTY ACIDS, 0 MG CHOLESTEROL, 132 MG SODIUM, 0.7 G TOTAL DIETARY FIBER

2 cups cubed bread (¹/₂- to ³/₄-inch cubes)
3 tablespoons olive oil
1 teaspoon pressed garlic
(about 2 large cloves)
2 teaspoons curry powder
¹/₂ teaspoon ground cumin
generous pinch of salt

Preheat the oven to 350°.

Bake the bread cubes in a single layer on an unoiled baking sheet for about 10 minutes, until dry, crisp, and lightly toasted.

Meanwhile, warm the oil in a small, heavy skillet (see Note). Add the garlic and cook on medium heat, stirring constantly, until just golden and sizzling. Remove from the heat and immediately stir in the curry powder, cumin, and salt. Set aside.

When the croutons are ready, remove them from the oven, drizzle the seasoned oil evenly over them, and toss to coat well. Spread the seasoned croutons apart on the baking sheet and allow them to cool completely. Store unused croutons in a closed container at room temperature.

Note If the garlic and spices are scorched or burned, the mixture will be unattractive and bitter tasting (in other words, ruined). So be sure to use a heavy skillet, pay close attention, and keep stirring.

MENU IDEAS Jamaican Tomato Soup (page 41) ✳ **Butternut Squash Soup with Sizzled Sage (page 28)** ✳ **Creamless Broccoli Soup (page 31)** ✳ **Roasted Red Pepper Coconut Soup (page 52)**

Edible Flowers

Many edible flowers provide dazzling, vivid splashes of color in both soups and salads. Most are chosen for their visual appeal; however, a few do contribute flavor as well. Generally, blossoms are sprinkled or arranged on a dish as a final, festive garnish. We tend to use smaller blooms whole; with large flowers, we arrange a bed beneath a salad or cut the petals to the desired size. Taste and color combinations are many: a simple green salad is disarmingly dressed up with a smattering of vibrant nasturtium blossoms; a humble potato soup is made exquisite with floating chive florets. ✳ Because some flowers are poisonous, always be certain of the identity of the plants used. If the flowers are growing in a mixed border, mark the edibles clearly with tags or stakes until you become familiar with them. (For growing information, check *The Moosewood Restaurant Kitchen Garden*.) ✳ Be sure the flowers have not been sprayed with pesticides or herbicides, avoid picking at roadsides or in unfamiliar locations, and do not use blooms purchased at a florist shop. Check carefully for insects or dirt, but avoid rinsing the blooms since they bruise and tear easily. Instead, soak gently in cold water, then invert on paper towels to drain. ✳ Here is a list of our favorite flowers for culinary and ornamental use. Most are not hard to find as seeds and young plants, and many are available at farmers' markets or specialty groceries.

Beans Scarlet runner beans are the showiest, but any bean flower is edible with a sweet but "beany" flavor. Serve with their more mature relations in bean salads or with marinated vegetables.

Bee Balm or Bergamot Bright shades of red, pink, lavender, or purple with a minty-oregano flavor. Individual florets have an elegant trumpet shape that is best displayed when floated on a light-colored soup or sprinkled on green salads.

Calendula Warm shades of yellow, orange, and red with subtle flavor. Petals will impart a golden hue to delicate soups or broths.

Chives Lavender-pink with oniony flavor. Whole blossoms can be pungent, so separate them into individual florets for garnishing.

Chrysanthemums Available in all shades of warm and cool colors, late-blooming fragrant mums should be used sparingly as a garnish since the flavor is somewhat bitter.

Daylilies Hundreds of varieties with colors predominantly in warm shades of cream, yellow, peach, orange, red, and maroon, as well as pink, lavender, and purple. The large flowers can be cut into a chiffonade (once the stamens and pistil are removed) or used whole. For a snazzy presentation, fill a blossom with a diced fruit salad and place it in an appropriate dish for support. You will have to taste to determine petal flavor, which can range from bland, to sweet, to spicy. Large, unopened flower buds can be steamed until tender for an asparagus-like treat.

Dianthus (carnations and pinks) White, pink, and red shades; some varieties have a delicious cinnamon-clove fragrance. Good with curried or spicy dishes as well as fruit salads or soups.

Hollyhocks Mostly pink and red shades with a mild, lettuce-like flavor. The large individual petals can be used to line or edge a plate for individual salads.

Marigolds (use only Lemon or Tangerine Gem types) These yellow and orange petite blooms have a citrus flavor nice for savory or sweet dishes.

Nasturtiums Pastel to hot shades of cream, yellow, orange, and red with a decidedly peppery, watercress-like flavor. Nasturtiums have a pleasant assertiveness, adding a spicy touch to foods.

Pansies and Violas A wide array of colors, some with a light but sweetly fragrant flavor. Pansy "faces" add an amusing, cheery touch when garnishing dishes.

Roses Innumerable shades and forms with varying degrees of fragrance: some heavily perfumed, others light and fruity, a few with no scent at all. Rose petals should be cut away from the bitter white heel at the junction of the petal and flower center. Scatter petals over mixed greens, toss into grain or vegetable salads, or make an elegant, brilliant bed for finely cut fruit.

Sunflowers Familiar golden flowers also available in deeper shades through red to burgundy. They have a mild flavor. The large petals make a showy bed for grain or rice salads or can be cut into strips and added to leafy salads.

Violets Small white, lavender, and blue blossoms with delicate flavor. Their diminutive size makes them candidates for garnishing cups of soup or fruit.

Filo Croutons

Interesting, uncommon, and ultrachic, these croutons are quick, pop-in-the-oven, melt-in-your-mouth affairs that dress up a salad to the nines. They bake fine in a toaster oven, so you can make them without heating up the whole kitchen. This is a convenient way to use up leftover filo when you have defrosted an entire package and used only a portion.

SERVES 4
YIELDS 12 SMALL CROUTONS
PREPARATION TIME: 5 MINUTES
BAKING TIME: 10 TO 15 MINUTES

PER 0.25-OUNCE SERVING: 45 CALORIES, 0.2 G PROTEIN, 4.4 G FAT, 1.4 G CARBO-HYDRATES, 2.7 G SATURATED FATTY ACIDS, 12 MG CHOLESTEROL, 56 MG SODIUM, 0 G TOTAL DIETARY FIBER

1 to 2 tablespoons butter
1 sheet of filo pastry

Preheat the oven to 400°.
Melt the butter in a small saucepan or in a microwave oven. Have a pastry brush or small new paintbrush and a lightly floured, flat surface ready for laying out the filo sheet. Once you take the filo out of the package, work quickly so that the filo doesn't dry out and crack.

Unfold the sheet of filo and evenly brush it with some of the melted butter. Starting with a short end, carefully fold over 1 inch of the sheet and then continue folding in the same direction to create a long 1-inch tube.

Flatten the tube by pressing it with your fingers and brush both sides with butter. Slice the flattened filo tube crosswise into little cubes with a sharp knife and place the cubes on an unoiled baking tray. Bake the croutons for 10 to 15 minutes, or until golden brown.

Variations   Sprinkle the unfolded filo sheet with 1 tablespoon of freshly grated Parmesan cheese or with an herb that complements your salad.

Top the buttered tube with a smattering of sesame, poppy, fennel, dill, or caraway seeds; then slice and bake.

MENU IDEAS Balkan Roasted Vegetable Salad (page 196) ✳ **Composed Beet Salad (page 254)** ✳ **Fresh Pear & Blue Cheese Salad (page 266)** ✳ **Roasted Green Tomato & Feta Salad (page 283)** ✳ **Chef Salad à la Moosewood (page 203)**

Fried Shallots

This is *the* smell and taste of Southeast Asian cooking. Shallots become sweet and crispy and turn burnished red when fried. They are intensely flavored, so a light sprinkling on a soup or salad is plenty. In a tightly sealed jar, they will keep at room temperature for 2 weeks.

SERVES 8
TOTAL TIME: 25 MINUTES

PER 0.5-OUNCE SERVING: 43 CALORIES, 0.4 G PROTEIN, 3.6 G FAT, 2.8 G CARBO-HYDRATES, 0.9 G SATURATED FATTY ACIDS, 0 MG CHOLESTEROL, 24 MG SODIUM, 0 G TOTAL DIETARY FIBER

4 or 5 shallots, peeled and finely chopped (about 1 cup)
a few pinches of salt
½ cup canola or other vegetable oil

Spread the chopped shallots on a paper towel, sprinkle with the salt, and cover with another paper towel. Let stand for about 10 minutes. Blot the excess moisture from the shallots.

Heat the oil in a small saucepan on medium heat. When the oil is hot but not smoking, add the shallots and stir constantly to fry them evenly. Pay close attention—if even only a few get too dark too fast, all of them will taste burned!

When most of the shallots have turned dark golden brown, pour the shallots and oil through a fine-mesh strainer. Reserve the oil for another use. Spread the shallots on a paper towel to drain. When cool, store in a jar with a tight-fitting lid.

MENU IDEAS **Thai Noodle Salad (page 233)** ✳ **Vietnamese Cellophane Noodle Salad (page 238)** ✳ **Gado Gado (page 212)** ✳ **Indonesian Tahu Goreng (page 218)** ✳ **Caribbean Sweet Potato Coconut Soup (page 29)** ✳ **Roasted Red Pepper Coconut Soup (page 52)** ✳ **Middle Eastern Chickpea Soup (page 88)** ✳ **Potage Celeste (page 130)**

Goat Cheese Toasts

We are lucky to have a number of goat farms nearby that produce excellent varieties of chèvre. Our favorite goat farm belongs to our friend, veterinarian David Deutsch, and our own David Hirsch, who periodically reports on the arrival of brand-new baby goats.

These toasted slices of baguette spread with herbed chèvre are a good accompaniment for a light soup, or add them to your favorite simple green salad for a certain *savoir faire*.

SERVES 6
TOTAL TIME: 10 MINUTES

PER 3-OUNCE SERVING: 251 CALORIES, 9.3 G PROTEIN, 5.8 G FAT, 39.6 G CARBOHYDRATES, 2.9 G SATURATED FATTY ACIDS, 9 MG CHOLESTEROL, 522 MG SODIUM, 2.1 G TOTAL DIETARY FIBER

2½ ounces goat cheese (chèvre)
1 tablespoon chopped fresh chives or parsley
½ to 1 tablespoon milk or buttermilk
1 thin baguette, cut into about 12 slices
1 garlic clove (optional)

In a small bowl with a fork, mash together the goat cheese and chives or parsley with enough milk or buttermilk to make a spreadable consistency and set aside.

Toast the baguette slices in a toaster or toaster oven, or on an unoiled baking sheet in the oven, until crisp and lightly browned. If desired, slice the garlic clove in half and gently rub the cut sides on one side of each of the "toasts." Top each with the chèvre spread and serve immediately.

MENU IDEAS **Navarin of Spring Vegetables (page 47)** ✳ **Wilted Spinach & Portabella Mushrooms (page 239)** ✳ **Five-Herb Salad (page 262)** ✳ **Asparagus Vinaigrette (page 248) with Marinated Mushrooms (page 347)**

Jalapeño Cream

Yogurt cheese and Neufchâtel smooth out the sharp heat of the jalapeño in this savory condiment that makes a mouthwatering spread for bread and crackers, a great topping for soups, or a base for a spirited salad dressing.

If you have a toaster oven, roast the foil-wrapped jalapeño for 20 minutes before blending it into the cheeses. If you don't, we recommend using the stove-top method of roasting the hot pepper (see Note) rather than heating a conventional oven.

SERVES 4 TO 6
YIELDS 1 CUP
TOTAL TIME: 35 MINUTES

PER 1.5-OUNCE SERVING: 80 CALORIES, 2.7 G PROTEIN, 6.6 G FAT, 2.8 G CARBOHYDRATES, 4.2 G SATURATED FATTY ACIDS, 21 MG CHOLESTEROL, 100 MG SODIUM, 0.1 G TOTAL DIETARY FIBER

1 medium to large fresh jalapeño
¾ cup yogurt cheese (page 387)
2 ounces Neufchâtel or cream cheese
salt to taste

Preheat a toaster oven or conventional oven to 400°.
Wrap the jalapeño in aluminum foil and roast for 20 minutes, or until tender. Unwrap and allow to cool for a few minutes before slipping off the skin and removing the stem end (see Note). If you wish, remove the seeds for milder heat. In a food processor or blender, combine all of the ingredients and purée until smooth. Add salt to taste.

Note For a quicker preparation, place the jalapeño directly on a stove burner and center it to maximize contact with the flames. Adjust the flames to medium-high heat and, using long tongs, turn the jalapeño every 1 to 2 minutes to char and blister the skin evenly. Roast for 5 to 7 minutes. Place it in a covered bowl, allow to steam for 5 minutes, and remove the blackened skin with a paring knife.

Variations If you don't have time to prepare the yogurt cheese, replace it with ½ cup of plain nonfat yogurt, increase the Neufchâtel to 4 ounces, and blend in 1 tablespoon of fresh lemon juice.
For variety, add 1 tablespoon of roasted garlic (page 363) or 2 tablespoons of chopped fresh cilantro. Or try using 1 or 2 chopped canned chipotle peppers (page 359) in place of the jalapeño.

MENU IDEAS **Jamaican Tomato Soup (page 41)** ✳ **Spiced Mexican Squash Stew (page 54)** ✳ **Black Bean & Chipotle Soup (page 70)** ✳ **Texas Two-Bean Soup (page 95)** ✳ **chilled Avocado Tomatillo Soup (page 141)** ✳ **Andean Quinoa & Corn Salad (page 189)** ✳ **Tostada Salad (page 237)** ✳ **Roasted Potato & Tomato Salad (page 284)**

Marinated Chickpeas or White Beans

At Moosewood, we cook a big pot of dried chickpeas or white beans just about every night. At home, you can cook enough to keep on hand or stock some good-quality canned legumes. Marinated, these beans make a great salad topping and are one of our standard menu selections for garnishing tossed salads.

They can also be added to a pita sandwich or used as part of a buffet. Maureen Vivino's favorite quick, light, protein-filled snack is a bowl of brown rice topped with grated carrots, some feta cheese, a few sliced scallions, and a big spoonful or two of marinated beans.

YIELDS A GENEROUS 1½ CUPS
PREPARATION TIME: 10 MINUTES
MARINATING TIME: 15 TO 20
  MINUTES

PER 1-OUNCE SERVING: 42 CALORIES, 1.4 G PROTEIN, 1.2 G FAT, 6.6 G CARBOHYDRATES, 0.2 G SATURATED FATTY ACIDS, 0 MG CHOLESTEROL, 86 MG SODIUM, 1.3 G TOTAL DIETARY FIBER

1½ cups cooked chickpeas or white beans
  (15-ounce can)
1 tablespoon olive oil
1 tablespoon cider vinegar or 4 teaspoons
  fresh lemon juice
1 garlic clove, minced or pressed
1½ teaspoons minced fresh dill (½ teaspoon dried)
rounded ¼ teaspoon fennel seeds*
pinch of ground black pepper

* *The fennel seeds may be whole or ground, depending on whether you prefer an intense burst as you bite into a seed or a milder, more pervasive flavor.*

Drain the chickpeas or white beans, reserving 2 tablespoons of the liquid. Rinse the beans and set aside to drain.

In a bowl, whisk together the reserved bean liquid, oil, vinegar or lemon juice, garlic, dill, fennel, and pepper. Stir in the beans and set aside to marinate for at least 15 to 20 minutes before serving.

Marinated chickpeas will keep for several days in the refrigerator.

Variations Try cannellini, pea beans, red kidneys, pintos, or butter beans. Replace the dill with fresh thyme, sage, rosemary, or chervil. Experiment with red wine vinegar or balsamic vinegar — if you don't mind slightly pink or brownish beans.

MENU IDEAS **Artichoke Heart & Bulghur Salat (page 190)** ✳ **Balkan Roasted Vegetable Salad (page 196)** ✳ **Broccoli Pine Nut Pasta Salad (page 198)** ✳ **Roasted Red Pepper & Cauliflower Salad (page 226)** ✳ **Simple Tomato Salads (page 286)** ✳ **Spinach with Cilantro Cashew Dressing (page 289)**

Marinated Mushrooms

These zesty little bite-sized morsels add a chewy texture and snappy sharpness to any tossed fresh greens, chef's salad, or grain salad. They couldn't be simpler and can definitely provide that just-right finishing touch.

SERVES 4
PREPARATION TIME: 5 MINUTES
MARINATING TIME: AT LEAST
 15 MINUTES

PER 1-OUNCE SERVING: 38 CALORIES, 0.5 G PROTEIN, 3.7 G FAT, 1.3 G CARBO-HYDRATES, 0.7 G SATURATED FATTY ACIDS, 0 MG CHOLESTEROL, 150 MG SODIUM, 0.3 G TOTAL DIETARY FIBER

1½ cups sliced mushrooms
1 tablespoon canola or other vegetable oil
1 tablespoon olive oil
1 tablespoon cider vinegar
1 teaspoon minced fresh tarragon or dill
½ teaspoon salt
dash of ground black pepper

Place the sliced mushrooms in a bowl, sprinkle them with the oils, vinegar, tarragon or dill, salt, and pepper, and stir well to coat evenly. Set aside for about 15 minutes to marinate, then cover and chill until serving time.

MENU IDEAS **chilled Chlodnik (page 144)** ✳ **Creamy Potato Cabbage Soup (page 124)** ✳ **Hungarian Green Bean Soup (page 127)** ✳ **Caesar Salad (page 201)** ✳ **Composed Beet Salad (page 254)** ✳ **Lobio (page 274)**

Parsley Pesto

Vivid green with a bright, sharp taste, this pesto is a simple and versatile accompaniment. We like it spread on crisp-toasted rounds of bread that can float atop a mild potato, carrot, onion, or squash soup.

Try this pesto with sliced tomatoes and fresh mozzarella or with steamed vegetables, especially bland or sweet ones like potatoes or carrots. Or boost the flavor of salad dressings and spreads: a dollop added to mayonnaise or yogurt gives a dressing or sandwich spread pizzazz. Make extra pesto and freeze it in an ice cube tray for handy use later on.

YIELDS ABOUT 1 CUP
TOTAL TIME: 10 MINUTES

PER 1-OUNCE SERVING: 21 CALORIES, 0.4 G PROTEIN, 1.9 G FAT, 1.1 G CARBOHYDRATES, 0.3 G SATURATED FATTY ACIDS, 0 MG CHOLESTEROL, 303 MG SODIUM, 0.4 G TOTAL DIETARY FIBER

½ **large tomato, roughly chopped**
1 **tablespoon extra-virgin olive oil**
2 **cups chopped fresh parsley, packed (1 bunch)**
2 **garlic cloves, minced or pressed**
1 **teaspoon salt**

Combine the tomatoes and oil in a blender or food processor and purée briefly. Add the parsley, garlic, and salt and continue to blend, stopping to scrape down the sides with a rubber spatula if necessary, until smooth and thick.

MENU IDEAS **Yellow Pepper Purée (page 58)** ∗ **Autumn Minestrone (page 67)** ∗ **Winter Minestrone (page 106)** ∗ **Spring Minestrone (page 93)** ∗ **Summer Minestrone (page 94)** ∗ **Cauliflower, Cheese & Tomato Soup (page 114)** ∗ **Creamy Herbed Carrot Soup (page 121)** ∗ **Creamy Herbed Potato Soup (page 122)** ∗ **Cream of Mushroom Soup (page 119)**

Pumpernickel Croutons

Dark-colored, coarse, and slightly sour, pumpernickel bread gets its distinctive character from unbolted rye. It makes superb croutons that are especially suited to savory dishes with assertive flavors.

YIELDS ABOUT 2 CUPS
TOTAL TIME: 20 MINUTES

PER 0.15-OUNCE SERVING: 15 CALORIES, 0.3 G PROTEIN, 0.8 G FAT, 1.7 G CARBO-HYDRATES, 0.5 G SATURATED FATTY ACIDS, 2 MG CHOLESTEROL, 31 MG SODIUM, 0.2 G TOTAL DIETARY FIBER

2 cups pumpernickel bread cubes
2 tablespoons butter, melted
¼ teaspoon ground black pepper

Preheat the oven to 350°.
Toss the bread cubes with the melted butter and pepper until evenly coated. Spread in a single layer on an unoiled baking pan and bake for 10 to 15 minutes until crisp. Stir once or twice during baking to ensure even cooking.

Store croutons in a closed container at room temperature.

DAILY SPECIAL

MENU IDEAS **Welsh Rarebit Soup (page 135)** ✳ **Parsnip Pear Soup (page 49)** ✳ **Creamy Onion & Fontina Soup (page 123)** ✳ **Butternut Squash Soup with Sizzled Sage (page 28)** ✳ **Everyday Split Pea Soup (page 77)** ✳ **Westphalian Vegetable Stew (page 57)** ✳ **Cauliflower, Cheese & Tomato Soup (page 114)** ✳ **Caesar Salad (page 201)** ✳ **tossed green salad with Best Blue Cheese Dressing (page 318) or Low-fat Honey Dijon Vinaigrette (page 320)**

Scallion Pancakes

Moosewood chef Jenny Wang's family made these all the time when she was growing up. Often they just used the dough left over from making dumplings: when the dumpling filling ran out . . . time for pancakes. Sometimes they make dessert-style sweet peanut butter pancakes based on the same technique.

This recipe makes somewhat more refined scallion pancakes than the waste-not, want-not ones from Jenny's childhood, and it includes a little baking powder and oil to lighten up the dough.

YIELDS FOUR 8-INCH PANCAKES
PREPARATION TIME: 20 MINUTES
COOKING TIME: 5 MINUTES EACH

PER 6.5-OUNCE SERVING: 375 CALORIES, 8.7 G PROTEIN, 9.8 G FAT, 62.3 G CARBO-HYDRATES, 2.4 G SATURATED FATTY ACIDS, 0 MG CHOLESTEROL, 390 MG SODIUM, 3.5 G TOTAL DIETARY FIBER

½ teaspoon dark sesame oil
7 teaspoons canola or other vegetable oil
2¾ cups unbleached white flour
1 cup hot water
½ teaspoon salt
½ teaspoon baking powder
4 to 8 scallions, chopped (about ½ cup)
sprinkling of salt
vegetable oil for frying

In a small bowl, mix together the dark sesame oil and 4 teaspoons of the canola or other vegetable oil. Set aside.

In a mixing bowl, combine 2¼ cups of the flour, the hot water, salt, baking powder, and 2 teaspoons of the canola oil. Stir until the dough comes together. Lightly dust a working surface with some of the remaining flour and knead for about 2 minutes, adding flour if the dough is too sticky. Cover the dough with the mixing bowl and allow it to rest for about 5 minutes.

Divide the dough into 4 balls. With a rolling pin, roll out each ball into a circle about 10 inches across. Brush each circle with ¼ of the sesame oil mixture, top with ¼ of the chopped scallions, and sprinkle with salt. Roll each circle into a tight cylindrical rope, then coil the rope to form a flat spiral about 5 inches across. Flatten each spiral by hand, and then roll it into a thin 8-inch pancake with a rolling pin, dusting with flour to prevent sticking. It's okay if a few scallions escape from the dough.

Heat a skillet on medium heat, add the remaining teaspoon of canola oil, and swirl to coat the pan. Fry each of the 4 pancakes until brown and cooked through, 3 to 4 minutes per side, turning down the heat if the outside gets too brown too fast. Add a little more oil to the pan, if necessary, for frying.

Cut each pancake into wedges and serve immediately. Leftover pancakes may be refrigerated for 3 or 4 days and then reheated in the toaster.

MENU IDEAS **Miso Noodle Soup (page 89)** ✳ **Spicy Tofu & Greens Soup (page 92)** ✳ **Broiled Tofu & Sugar Snap Peas (page 199)** ✳ **Chinese Velvet Corn Soup (page 116)** ✳ **Asian Bean Curd Soup (page 64)** ✳ **Southeast Asian Rice & Tofu Soup (page 91)**

Spiced Paneer

Paneer is a smooth, firm Indian cheese that looks like Monterey Jack. It has a very mild flavor—a little too bland to eat by itself—but it readily absorbs flavors and doesn't melt like other cheeses. Here it is cooked with aromatic spices, which transform it into the perfect addition for salads and soups.

SERVES 4 TO 6
YIELDS 1½ CUPS
TOTAL TIME: 15 MINUTES

PER 1.75-OUNCE SERVING: 83 CALORIES, 4.5 G PROTEIN, 5.7 G FAT, 3.6 G CARBO-HYDRATES, 2.2 G SATURATED FATTY ACIDS, 9 MG CHOLESTEROL, 251 MG SODIUM, 0.2 G TOTAL DIETARY FIBER

4 teaspoons canola or other vegetable oil
2 teaspoons ground cumin
⅛ teaspoon cayenne, or to taste
¼ teaspoon ground cardamom
1 teaspoon turmeric
½ teaspoon salt
½ cup plain nonfat yogurt
1½ cups paneer, cut into small cubes*

* Paneer can be found in well-stocked supermarkets or Indian and specialty grocery stores. One 227-gram package works for this recipe. Or, to make your own, see Sundays at Moosewood Restaurant, *page 297.*

Warm the oil in a small skillet or saucepan. Add the cumin, cayenne, cardamom, turmeric, and salt and cook on low heat for 1 to 2 minutes, stirring constantly. Add the yogurt and paneer cubes, increase the heat to medium-high, and cook for about 10 minutes, stirring often. As it cooks, the yogurt will separate, the whey (liquid) will evaporate, and the curd will coat the paneer cubes.

Remove from the heat and set aside to cool.

MENU IDEAS **Spinach with Cilantro Cashew Dressing (page 289)** ✳ **Indian Tomato Rice Soup (page 81)** ✳ **Curried Cauliflower Soup (page 32)** ✳ **Tomato Rasam (page 96)** ✳ **Curried Rice Salad (page 205)** ✳ **Indian Green Beans & Red Peppers (page 270)** ✳ **Persian Rice & Pistachio Salad (page 224)** ✳ **Yemiser Salata (page 295)**

Glossary of Ingredients & Techniques

Annatto seeds (*achiote*) are small, triangular-shaped, brick-red seeds that grow on a tropical evergreen and are most widely used in the cuisines of the Caribbean. Annatto has an ultra-mild, nutty taste, reminiscent of pistachio. It is prized not only for its flavor but also for its coloring and dyeing properties, known and appreciated from the time of the Aztecs.

Commercially, it is used as a safe, natural food coloring in butter, margarine, cheese, and smoked fish. At home, it will give rice, potatoes, pasta, and soup or stew broths a vibrant yellow-orange hue.

> To use **annatto seeds**, simmer 1 tablespoon of whole seeds in 1/4 cup of oil for 3 to 5 minutes, until the oil turns a deep orange. Strain the seeds and use the oil. Refrigerated in a tightly closed jar, annatto oil will keep for a week or more.

Annatto can be found in Hispanic markets, in the ethnic section of many supermarkets, and in natural food stores with an extensive herb and spice section.

Apple apricot juice As its name implies, apple apricot juice is a blend of the two juices, sometimes with white grape juice concentrate added for sweetening. It is available in many natural food stores and supermarkets. If you can't find it, try combining apricot nectar with unsweetened apple juice.

Apples, Crispin and Granny Smith These two varieties of green apples are very crisp and more tart than sweet. Crispin and Mutsu are two names for the same apple. Both Crispins and Granny Smiths are good choices for salads because they maintain their texture and their subtle sweetness is a fine complement to vinaigrettes. Immediately after slicing apples, sprinkle them with a little citrus juice to prevent discoloration.

Artichoke hearts The most delicate and delectable part of this ancient thistle is known as the heart, bottom, or fond. It has a buttery, succulent, and mild taste. We favor the salty, tangy quality of canned artichoke hearts packed in simple brine over both the hearts packed in seasoned oil and the blander frozen ones. If you are cooking whole artichokes, be aware that the stem is an extension of the heart and, once peeled, can be cooked and sliced or puréed. Artichoke hearts packed in brine can be found in most supermarkets with the canned vegetables or in the Hispanic or ethnic section.

Arugula (*rocket*) is a dark emerald-hued green with a unique, haunting, slightly bitter, peppery taste that is satisfying and warm. Arugula's flavor has been described as a cross between spinach, mustard greens, and watercress; it shares the bitterness, sweetness, piquancy, and tanginess of all three. It is a nutritious leaf with more calcium per cup than kale or collards.

Arugula's small, prettily toothed leaves require rinsing and drying, but no tearing. It is delightful in mixed salads, balances cool, sweet fruit salads, and can act as a subtle flavoring minced into soups or dressings. Originally, arugula was picked wild in Italy. Eventually, it was cultivated there and then the seeds were brought to the United States by immigrants. Far from its humble beginnings, arugula is now often considered a boutique or gourmet green.

At the market, choose bunches that have pert green leaves and stems; avoid wilted, yellow leaves and soggy stems. Tiny holes in the leaves are the result of arugula's vulnerability to flea beetles but they will not affect the flavor.

> Before using **arugula**, float it in cold water, allowing the sand and grit to settle to the bottom, then lift out into a colander. Repeat until clean.

Arugula spoils quickly: it will keep for a day or two in the refrigerator with the stems immersed in water and the leaves loosely covered with a plastic bag.

Asiago cheese is an imported Italian hard cheese with a sweet-salty taste. It's good for grating. Its flavor tends to be stronger than Parmesan but milder than Romano and the flavor and aroma strengthen with age. Originally, Asiago was made from ewe's milk, but like many farmhouse cheeses that once used sheep's or goat's milk, it is now cultured from cow's milk.

When buying Asiago, choose a wedge that is hard but not crumbly, with a smooth, uncracked rind. Look for it in the imported cheese section of the supermarket, in Italian delicatessens, or in specialty cheese shops. Tightly wrapped and refrigerated, Asiago will keep for up to 4 weeks.

Asparagus It is thrilling when the first spears of asparagus appear in the spring. For those of us with long winters, it is a sure and welcome affirmation of the seasonal cycle, and perhaps for that reason, nothing tastes fresher or more delicious. The best asparagus are available during April and May.

Select bunches with uniformly sized spears to ensure equal cooking time. Look for spears that are bright green, straight, and crisp, with tightly closed buds. Avoid dry, wrinkled, and dull-looking spears. Produce vendors often display asparagus with the stem ends immersed in water; soggy stems indicate old asparagus. Asparagus spears keep best in the refrigerator, either standing in ½ inch of water or wrapped in a damp towel and sealed in a plastic bag.

Because **asparagus** grows well in sandy soil, careful cleaning is necessary. Submerge the stalks in a pan of warm water for a minute or two, and then lift them out and into a colander allowing any sand or dirt to settle on the bottom of the pan. Rinse the pan and repeat the process until the soaking water is clear. To prepare for cooking, snap off the woody bottom of each spear at its natural breaking point.

Avocados For decades avocados were deemed nutritional no-no's because of their high fat content. Currently, nutritionists are giving a stronger voice to the positive role fats play in the diet and to the kinds of fats that best meet nutritional and physiological needs. The fat in avocados is largely mono-unsaturated, the type of fat considered the most healthful. Avocados are also rich in B vitamins and minerals and are a creamy, satisfying food.

Over the years at Moosewood, we've been happiest with Hass avocados, a buttery variety that has a dark green, pebbly skin and a smooth, yellowish-green interior. The leaves of avocado trees contain an enzyme that inhibits ripening, so all avocados ripen off the tree. A hard avocado will ripen at room temperature in 3 to 4 days and in the refrigerator in about a week. One that is firm but resilient is perfect for slicing; a softer one can be used right away for guacamoles or puréeing. A very soft avocado with no resilience is probably brown inside and bitter tasting. The peak season for avocados is December through early spring.

Azuki beans (adzuki, aduki) The azuki bean is small and reddish brown with a thin white strip called a "keel." It originated in China and Japan and holds an esteemed place in Japanese culture as an ingredient in foods prepared to honor the emperor. Although azukis can be eaten fresh, dried beans are most available in the United States. They are about 25 percent protein and are a good source of iron, calcium, and thiamine. Dried or canned, azukis are available at natural food stores.

Baby corn These tiny ears of corn, sometimes labeled "young corn," are available in the Asian section of the supermarket or in Asian grocery stores, often in 15-ounce cans (8 ounces, drained weight) . After opening, store baby corn in a closed container in the refrigerator and use within 3 to 5 days.

Balsamic vinegar Loosely translated, *balsamico* means "that which is good for your health." Without taking a medical stance, we can safely say that this highly aromatic, sweet vinegar is certainly "good for your salad."

Balsamic vinegar is expensive, always imported, and always from Modena, Italy. It is made from the very sweet juice of Italian white grapes in a complicated process that involves aging in open wooden barrels of diminishing sizes and different woods. By Italian law, it must be aged for a minimum of 3 years, although the primo balsamics have aged from 50 to 100 years. (Kegs of vinegars have been included in bequests.) The result is a low-acid vinegar smooth and sweet enough to pour over fresh fruit. A small amount goes a long way. Use balsamic as your sole vinegar in a dressing or for tempering more assertive vinegars. It is available in most supermarkets and in Italian grocery stores.

Barley is the grandmother of grains: evidence shows that it was cultivated during the Stone Age. For eons it was ground to make bread, until wheat was developed to be more cold- and disease-resistant. Barley has a lower protein and gluten content than wheat, but it also has its virtues. It is low-fat and highly digestible, may inhibit cholesterol production, and has a mild, sweet, chewy texture that is terrific in soup. There are 3 or 4 forms of barley on the market; the following is a quick guide:

Hulled barley is the most nutritious barley available. The outermost protective husk has been removed but the vitamin-rich endosperm and germ remain intact. It takes about 1¼ hours to cook using a 4:1 ratio of water to barley.

Pearled barley has had the protective husk, the endosperm, and the germ removed. It cooks in 50 minutes using a 2:1 ratio of water to barley.

Partially pearled barley has only part of the endosperm removed, so it is nutritionally richer than the completely pearled variety. It usually cooks in about an hour.

Instant barley is pearled barley that has been steamed and dried. It cooks in 15 minutes.

Beans, cooking dried   Whenever possible, we cook dried beans from scratch to avoid the added salt and preservatives often found in canned beans. When pressed for time, however, try Eden, Westbrae, Goya, Sahadi, or Randall brands. All of them make some canned beans

variety	water-bean ratio	cooking time after soaking	cooked quantity of 1 cup dried
Azuki beans	3:1	¾ to 1 hour	3 cups
Black beans (turtle)	3:1	1½ hours	3 cups
Black-eyed peas	3:1	½ hour	2½ cups
Chickpeas (garbanzos)	4:1	1½ hours	3 cups
Fava beans	3:1	¾ to 1 hour	3 cups
Kidney beans (red or white)	3:1	1 to 1½ hours	2¾ cups
Lentils, brown	2:1	½ hour	3 cups
Lentils, red	2:1	15 to 20 minutes	3 cups
Lima beans	3:1	1 hour	3 cups
Mung beans	3:1	¾ hour	3 cups
Pinto beans	3:1	¾ hour	3¼ cups
Soybeans	4:1	2 hours	2¾ cups
Split peas, green	3:1	¾ to 1 hour	1¾ cups
Split peas, yellow	3:1	½ hour	2¼ cups
White beans (navy, pea, cannellini)	3:1	¾ to 1 hour	2¾ cups

with no preservatives, and much of the salt can be removed by draining and rinsing.

Sort **dried beans** on a flat tray, discarding stones and shriveled beans; then rinse well to remove dust and debris. With the exception of soft beans such as lentils, split peas, and black-eyed peas, most dried beans should be softened by soaking them in plenty of water before cooking. Either soak for 6 to 8 hours in a cool place or bring to a boil, immediately remove from the heat, cover, and soak for about an hour. Drain. To cook, bring to a boil in fresh water; then lower the heat and simmer until tender, adding water if needed. See our chart for helpful bean specifics.

Beet greens

With more vitamin C, calcium, and iron than beets themselves, beet greens taste mild and earthy and can be used in many recipes that call for greens. The red veins bleed when cooked, so be prepared for creamy sauces, soups, and casseroles to turn faintly pink.

Beet greens are sometimes bunched separately and sometimes attached to beets. The choicest greens are those on small- to medium-sized beets. Select those that are crisp and dark green, not wilted or yellow. Stored in a loosely closed plastic bag in the refrigerator, the greens will keep for 3 to 4 days.

Belgian endive is an odd-looking lettuce with tightly packed, silvery white leaves edged in the palest yellow and with a shape resembling a small ear of unhusked corn. Cultivation in the dark results in their unique color, form, and flavor. It is succulent and crisp with a clean, refreshing taste that suggests a hint of bittersweet (it's in the chicory family). The larger outer leaves are canoe shaped and firm enough to be filled or used as crudités. In mixed salads, it combines well with the sharper, more peppery greens like arugula, radicchio, and watercress.

Choose heads that have crisp, smooth, unspotted, light-colored outer leaves. Belgian endive needs only a quick rinse before using. It will keep for 1 to 2 days in a perforated plastic bag in the refrigerator.

Bell peppers, red see **Red bell peppers**.

Black-eyed peas (*cow peas*) Black-eyed peas originated in Africa, where wild varieties can still be found. They grow well in the South, where they are a staple legume and an ingredient in many classic dishes.

We call most often for dried black-eyed peas in our recipes, but they are also available frozen, canned, and sometimes fresh. Presoaking dried black-eyed peas is unnecessary, but unsoaked beans will need to simmer for 45 to 60 minutes rather than the ½ hour it takes soaked beans to cook. Store dried black-eyed peas for up to a year in an airtight container.

Blue cheese encompasses five types of blue- or green-veined cheeses. The veins are molds that have been incorporated during the cheesemaking process.

Danish blue cheese is made from cow's milk and can be mild, tangy, or sharp depending upon how long it's been aged. It can be soft and creamy or firm and crumbly.

Domestic blue cheese is made in the United States and Canada from cow's milk. It has a piquant, pleasantly sharp taste.

Gorgonzola is an Italian blue with a mild, salty taste and a creamy consistency. It is delicious with wild greens and a tangy vinaigrette.

Roquefort is made only in Roquefort, France, always from ewe's milk, and is aged in limestone caves. It tastes rich, sharp, and salty. Other blue cheeses produced in the Roquefort region are made in the style of Roquefort but with cow's milk.

Stilton is produced solely in England. It is a crumbly cheese that is milder than Roquefort and is made from cow's milk.

Bok choy This is one of the super vegetables—a rich source of calcium and vitamins A and C, and a member of the health-promoting cabbage family. The leaves and stalks are complementary and equally tasty: the stalks, crisp, sweet, and refreshing; the leaves, tangy and a shade bitter. The stalks grow from a base, like celery, but are wide and bright white, topped with wide, deep green leaves similar to Swiss chard.

Bok choy is available throughout the year at Asian markets and in many supermarkets, where it is sometimes labeled Chinese cabbage or grouped with an array of other greens subsumed under that name. Stored in a perforated plastic bag in the refrigerator vegetable crisper, bok choy will keep for 3 or 4 days.

Boston lettuce is a light green, extremely tender lettuce that grows in small- to medium-sized heads. It has soft, silky leaves that have an almost creamy texture. It's a treat to add these sweet, soft leaves to salads and sandwiches. Boston lettuce is highly perishable; use as soon as possible.

Bourride   This classic fish stew from Provence is a delicious, economical kin of bouillabaisse. It does not include shellfish and allows for a wider choice of fish. Another distinctive element of bourride is the inclusion of aioli (freshly made garlic mayonnaise), a luscious Provençal invention that is either blended into the broth, spread on the toast over which the stew is ladled, or swirled on the surface of each serving.

Broccoli rabe *(rapini, rappi, broccoli de rape)*   Despite its name, this

leafy green is in the turnip family, not the broccoli family. However, the name does have its logic: broccoli rabe looks like a leafy, undernourished stalk of broccoli. It has very thin, dark green stalks with loosely budded heads that often sport yellow blossoms.

As for taste, broccoli rabe is a bitter green, but its flavor delights many palates. To mellow the bitterness, blanch the stems, leaves, and buds in boiling water for 3 to 4 minutes. Sautéed in olive oil with garlic, it is good with pasta, potatoes, and sweet root vegetables. When buying broccoli rabe, look for tightly closed buds with few flowers and avoid stems that are brown or slimy. It will keep for 2 to 3 days in a perforated plastic bag in the refrigerator.

Buckwheat groats see **Kasha**.

Bulghur   An alternative to rice, pasta, or potatoes, bulghur is a quick side dish and a flavorful grain for salads and pilafs. A form of wheat, this Middle Eastern staple is perhaps best known to us as the grain in tabouli. By the time bulghur reaches your grocer's shelf, the whole grain wheatberry has been cracked, steamed or parboiled, and dried. Bulghur is available in four grades: fine, medium, coarse, and extra coarse (also known as half-cut bulghur).

To cook **bulghur**, add an equal amount of water to the bulghur, cover, steep, and then fluff with a fork. If the grains are still slightly crunchy, sprinkle with additional hot water, cover, and steep for 10 minutes more. Steep fine-grade bulghur in cold water for 30 minutes. Steep medium-grade bulghur in boiling water for 20 minutes. Steep coarse and extra-coarse bulghur in boiling water for 30 minutes. Stock can be used in place of water and bay leaves, mint, and other herbs can be added to the steeping bulghur to vary its flavor.

Bulghur is sometimes confused with or incorrectly labeled cracked wheat, which is wheatberries that have been cracked but not precooked and which must be boiled and simmered for 20 minutes. Bulghur can be found in natural food stores, Middle Eastern food stores, and the ethnic section of many supermarkets.

Butter beans   Any lima beans might be called butter beans south of the Mason-Dixon line, but when we use the term, we are referring to large yellowish-white canned limas. They have a mild, pleasant flavor and a creamy consistency, which makes them especially good puréed for soups, spreads, and dips. Many people who don't like lima beans *love* our dishes made with "butter beans." Look for butter beans in the canned vegetable section of the supermarket.

Cannellini They sound Italian and you'll find them in a host of Italian dishes, but these mild-flavored white, kidney-shaped beans originated in Mexico or Peru two or three thousand years ago. Once they made it to Italy, they took off, especially in Tuscany, the home of *pasta e fagioli*. Cannellini vary from pea bean size to kidney bean size. They are mostly available canned, but dried beans can be acquired from Italian food purveyors.

Capers How did anyone ever develop the process that brought the buds of this wild Mediterranean flower to their exalted position in gourmet cookery? The tiny buds are harvested just before blooming, sun dried, and then marinated in open barrels of salt water to extract bitterness and acidity. Next, the capers are washed and aged for 2 months, after which they are washed again, marinated in fresh brine, fermented, and packaged for shipping.

Capers are salty, tangy, green "pearls" that can be a unique addition to many sauces, seafoods, and salads. Capers are most readily available packed in a vinegar-based brine but can also be found packed in sea salt. Once opened, brine-packed capers can be stored for up to 3 months in the refrigerator.

To use, drain brine-packed **capers** and give them a quick rinse unless you want the extra tartness of the vinegar. Wash salt-packed capers in several changes of water to reduce the saltiness. Add capers toward the end of cooking; long cooking diminishes their tang and texture.

Catfish This firm, white, fresh-water fish is flavorful and substantial. At Moosewood, we've become partial to it: it doesn't shrink with baking, it's delicious with hot, aromatic spices, and our customers ask for it often. The majority of commercially available catfish are farm raised and feed on floating grain pellets. And here's a hoot — another name for catfish is "tenderloin trout."

Celeriac Food writer and epicure Elizabeth Schneider perfectly describes celeriac as something from a Grimm's fairy tale: a misshapen orb that is brown, gnarled, and warty with tendril roots growing chaotically all over its surface. But like another of Grimm's tales, there's beauty within the beast. Beneath the skin, celeriac roots have a smooth, crisp texture and taste clean and sweet like hearts of celery (a related plant), but with a decided bite.

Because of its sharp flavor, it's good in creamy dressings and sauces and with sweet root vegetables such as potatoes, beets, and carrots. It is a good accent in puréed potato or sweet potato soups and in borscht. Try adding some celeriac to Celery Roquefort Soup (page 115) for added depth and zest.

To prepare **celeriac**, slice off the ends of the spherical root, pare as you would a potato, and rinse well.

Celeriac is available throughout the year but peaks from October through April. Choose roots that are under a pound and have relatively smooth peels. To avoid a spongy core, check that the stalk end is firm. Wrapped in plastic and refrigerated, celeriac will keep for about a week.

Cellophane noodles (*bean threads*) Don't be dismayed — the name for this versatile Asian noodle describes its appearance, not its taste or texture. Cellophane noodles are very thin, clear, mild-tasting noodles made from mung bean starch. Their slippery texture adds interest to savory dishes and they are sponges for flavor. To prepare, soak the noodles in hot water until soft. Cellophane noodles are available at Asian markets and in the Asian section of many supermarkets.

Chanterelles see **Mushrooms**.

Chard has a pleasant earthy taste that has been enjoyed in France since the fifteenth century. Its leaves are tender enough to be wilted, briefly sautéed, or added raw to a soup or stew toward the end of cooking. Young chard is often included in mesclun or baby greens mixes. Both the stalks and leaves of chard can be used, but large stalks may require 3 to 4 minutes extra cooking time.

Chard comes in two varieties. Swiss chard is distinguished by large, wavy-edged green leaves with light green to white midribs. Red chard, also called ruby or rhubarb chard, has green leaves with bright red veins and stems and red stippling. Look for fresh, perky leaves with tender stems. Chard will keep in a plastic bag in the refrigerator crisper for at least 2 to 3 days.

Chayote One of our Moosewood cooks recently spent a month in Mexico and returned with news of a squash that we hadn't tried but that, to our delight, was available at our local market. Chayote is an old, old vegetable. It fed the Aztecs and the Mayans and is still popular in Mexico and Central America. In New Orleans cuisine, it is called mirliton.

Chayote is a very firm, somewhat oval-shaped summer squash with either a lightly pebbled or smooth skin, the green of an unripened pear. Its taste lies somewhere between a cucumber and a zucchini, with a hint of radish and the perfume of freshly mown grass. Chayote is prized more for its aroma and texture than for its flavor, but it readily absorbs other flavors. Unpeeled chayote can be used like any summer squash, raw or cooked or scooped out and stuffed. It is a crisp, fresh-tasting addition to salads, sautés, and stews. Jamaicans use it like apples in pies. Because it is much firmer

than other squash, the cooking time is longer. In selecting chayote, look for an unblemished peel. Refrigerated and loosely wrapped, it keeps for up to 7 days.

Cheese, smoked Cheddar and other cheeses can be infused with a smoky flavor using one of several techniques. The cut cheese can be exposed to smoke from a wood fire, usually hickory. Or the cheese may be salted with smoked salt, giving it a streaked appearance and the desired flavor. A third method calls for "liquid smoke," a chemical that is added to the milk from which the cheese is made or to the curd soon after it is cut. The most readily available smoked cheeses are Cheddar, Gouda, and mozzarella, which may be purchased in the cheese section of well-stocked supermarkets.

Chermoulla A fragrant Moroccan condiment composed most often of garlic, cumin, cayenne, cilantro, olive oil, and lemon juice. Some recipes include cinnamon, allspice, fresh mint, or saffron. We use chermoulla as a topping for fish, a swirl in soups, and a marinade for vegetable kebabs. Almost every Moroccan household has its own special recipe for chermoulla; ours is on page 306.

Chèvre The French name for any cheese made from goat's milk. Sharp and aromatic, chèvre is usually available in small logs or cones, either plain or rolled in herbs.

Herbed and spiced chèvre spreads are also available.

This soft cheese is a good topping for crackers, a novel choice for crudités, and a fine match for cold sweet fruit. Nutritionally, goat's milk is higher in both protein and fat than cow's milk. Some people who are lactose intolerant can tolerate chèvre.

Chiffonade Garnishing, be it soups, salads, main dishes, or desserts, is a fun and creative part of cooking. Eye appeal is an important aspect in the enjoyment of a meal. Chiffonade is a cutting technique for making thin, decorative ribbons from herbs or salad greens.

To **chiffonade**, stack several leaves of herbs or lettuce on top of one another with the stems aligned. Roll up the stack of leaves from leaf tip to stem end and slice across the roll to make thin ribbons.

Chiles Hot peppers not only add pizzazz, they enliven other seasonings and can balance rich or sweet dishes. Chiles, members of the *Capsicum* family, come hot, medium, or mild and hybrid chiles are continually being developed and cross-pollinating on their own. In our experience, the intensity can vary wildly even among chiles of the same type. The only method we've found to test for hotness is tasting a tiny piece. Tasting will give you a clearer sense of how many peppers (or what fraction of one) to use.

The membranes and seeds are the hottest parts of the chile;

removing these in whole or part reduces the heat.

Fresh chiles contain an oil that can burn the skin, so the safest method for working with them is with latex or plastic gloves. If you remove the seeds and membranes, use a small spoon. If you handle chiles bare-handed, rub your hands afterward with vegetable oil and wash them with soapy water. Avoid touching eyes, lips, and other sensitive parts of the body before washing.

Here is a short synopsis of some of the more popular and useful fresh chiles:

Banana: pale yellow, short, fat, oval; very hot

Green or anaheim: bright green, long, slender; mild

Jalapeño: green to red, short, oval; varies from not-so-hot to very hot

Thai peppers: green to red, tiny, oblong; very hot to fiery hot

Habañero or scotch bonnets: crown-shaped yellow, red, or green; mercilessly hot

To prepare **dried chiles**, remove the stems and seeds and soak the chiles in hot water for 30 minutes. Mince or slice as you would a fresh chile.

When buying fresh chiles, look for brightly colored peppers with taut, smooth skins. Avoid bruised, soft, withered, or split skins. Fresh chiles can be stored in a plastic bag in the refrigerator for about 5 days. Sliced or chopped fresh chiles can be frozen for up to 6 months. Dried chiles can be kept in a cool, dry, dark place for up to a year.

Chinese chili paste with garlic
We use this condiment, a blend of chiles, salt, soybean oil, and garlic, for seasoning many of our Asian and Southeast Asian noodle salads, soups, and stir-fries. We recommend Lan-Chi brand chili paste: it's flavorful and doesn't contain additives or preservatives. Chili paste with garlic is available at Asian markets and in the Asian section of many supermarkets. Tightly lidded and refrigerated, it will last a year or more.

Chipotles, which are jalapeños that have been smoked, are available dried or canned in adobo sauce.

Chives Long and thin, with hollow stems and tubular leaves, chives are the mildest relatives in the onion family. Snip them into salads and dressings and sprinkle them as an attractive garnish on soups. They are available fresh, frozen, and freeze-dried.

Cilantro *(fresh coriander leaves, green coriander, Spanish or Chinese parsley)* This green herb looks somewhat like flat-leaf parsley and has a strong, heady, perfumed aroma and flavor. At Moosewood, we only use it fresh, never dried. It is sometimes sold with its roots, which in Thai cuisine are often ground for curry pastes and sauces. Cilantro can be gritty, so repeated rinsings of the leaves and stems, which are edible as well, may be necessary before using.

We think it might have been Craig Claiborne who once said something like, "The presence of cilantro contributes to my peace of mind." For those of us who take to cilantro, that's how it is — deeply satisfying in a way that's hard to explain. And we're not alone. Originally this hardy annual was native to southern Europe and the Middle East, but now cilantro is grown on almost every continent. Most Asians consider it a staple ingredient and it's the most widely consumed culinary herb in the world. Many consider cilantro to have medicinal properties as well. In China, cilantro is thought to prolong life and promote overall well-being. It is used to treat indigestion, migraines, and arthritis. In the Indian Ayurvedic tradition, increased consumption of cilantro is prescribed during the summer months to counteract the effects of scorching heat.

Back in the kitchen, we've found that cilantro heightens flavors and balances rich ingredients and the heat of chiles. This leafy, green herb is now familiar to North Americans in curries, chutneys, and salsas, and in the cuisines of Southeast Asia, Central and South America, Africa, the Caribbean, and East India. It will keep for at least 3 or 4 days in the refrigerator with the stems (or better yet, the roots) immersed in water and a plastic bag loosely covering the leaves. Look for cilantro in the fresh herb section of the produce department and in many ethnic groceries.

Clams We use the hard-shelled round clams indigenous to our East Coast, also known by their Narragansett Bay name, "quahogs." They range in size from 2 to 4 inches. The smallest clams are called "littlenecks," medium-sized are "cherrystones," and the largest are "chowder clams." The smaller the clam, the sweeter and more tender. Littlenecks and cherrystones are good in light soups, stews, and sauces. Chowder clams are best for — you guessed it — chowders.

Clams live buried in the sand or mud, so clean them carefully by rinsing with cold water and then soaking in cold salted water. Repeat until no sand settles to the bottom.

Choose clams that have tightly closed, smooth, moist shells with no cracks or chips. Clams can be opened by poaching, steaming, or shucking. Nine medium shucked clams yield about 1 cup (equivalent to a 7½-ounce can of minced clams). Live clams can be stored in the refrigerator, covered with a moist cloth, for up to 5 days. Shucked clams will keep for 3 days if refrigerated and stored in a saltwater brine with a 2:1 ratio of water to salt. Shucked clams can also be frozen in brine for up to 6 months.

Coconut Good fresh coconut meat is moist, sweet, and delicious. Choose a deep brown- or white-shelled coconut that feels heavy for its size — you should be able to hear liquid splash when you shake it. If it's dry, the coconut is old and its meat may be tough and shriveled. A coconut that is 4 inches in diameter can yield about 2 cups of liquid and 2 cups of chopped coconut meat.

To drain the **coconut**, place it in a small pot that will just hold it or put it in a nonbreakable bowl and wrap a wet towel around its base to keep it from moving. Pierce the three eyes by hammering in a Phillips head screwdriver; pierce the stem end as well for quicker draining. Drain the slightly sweet, mild-tasting, watery liquid at its center. This is not coconut milk and cannot serve as a substitute, but the liquid can make a nice addition to a smoothie, soup, stew, or stock. Sour or bad-smelling liquid means the meat is spoiled; you've bought a lemon, so to speak.

To open the coconut and remove the meat, here are two methods:

Stove Burner Method: Place the coconut in a large stainless steel bowl and whack it hard with a hammer 10 to 15 times in different places until it cracks into large chunks, then heat the chunks to make it easier to pry the meat away from the shell. Rest each chunk of coconut, shell side against the burner, on a gas or electric burner on medium-high heat for about 2 minutes. Remove from the burner with tongs. Score the meat in the shell into several pieces, pry the pieces loose with a regular screwdriver, and peel the brown skin with a paring knife.

Oven Method: Bake the coconut at 350° for 15 to 30 minutes, just until it begins to crack; check at regular intervals after the initial 15 minutes. The meat will shrink away from the shell with the brown skin still adhering to it. Remove the coconut from the oven and whack it into chunks with a hammer (this is easier than with a raw one); then score, pry, and peel the meat as described in the burner method.

Coconut milk This thick, sweet, silky liquid is a puréed and strained combination of water and either fresh or dried grated coconut. With the growing popularity of Southeast Asian, Caribbean, and Pacific cuisines, canned coconut milk is available here as it has never been before. There are a number of brands to choose from, it comes in reduced-fat or light versions, and there are brands that are free of additives and preservatives. Note that coconut milk is a different product than "coconut cream," which is manufactured as an ingredient for mixed drinks.

Coconut milk can be made at home by cutting fresh coconut meat into small pieces and puréeing it with an equal amount of hot water in a blender at high speed for 2 to 3 minutes. Steep for 30 minutes, then pour the purée through a strainer into a bowl, pressing the pulp to extract the maximum amount of milk. Finish by pouring the milk through a fine-mesh strainer. One cup of coconut meat and 1 cup of hot water will yield close to a cup of coconut milk. If using dried coconut, mix 1 cup of unsweetened dried shredded coconut with 1½ cups of hot water. Steep for 5 minutes, then purée for 1 minute. Strain as directed above.

Tightly covered and refrigerated, coconut milk will keep for about 3 days. Frozen, it will keep indefinitely.

Cointreau A strong, moderately sweet, orange liqueur with a bright, fresh, tangy quality. We've always used liqueurs in some of our desserts and recently we have begun using these intensely flavorful infusions in savory dishes such as soups and sauces. Grand Marnier and Triple Sec, other orange liqueurs, are sweeter and syrupy and better suited to flavoring desserts, frostings, and glazes.

Court bouillon is a poaching liquid composed of water, wine, vinegar or lemon juice, bay leaf, onions, carrots, salt, whole black peppercorns, and other herbs and spices. In the United States, court bouillon is used for poaching fish. It is also used to parboil vegetables before marinating them and to cook meats. Court is from the Latin *curtus,* which means "cut short" or "made hastily"; bouillon is from the French "to boil."

Couscous In North Africa, couscous is the name for any dish made in a couscousière, a specialized clay or two-tiered ceramic pot in which couscous is steamed in a perforated pan set over a simmering aromatic stew. In this book, couscous refers to the grain itself, which is a precooked product made from finely milled semolina wheat. Couscous is available in the pasta or rice section of many supermarkets and in Middle Eastern food stores. Whole wheat couscous can be found at some natural food stores.

Couscous can be very quickly and simply prepared. Combine equal amounts of couscous and boiling water, cover, and let sit for 5 to 10 minutes. When the liquid is absorbed, fluff with a fork.

Cranberries, dried *(craisins)* This relatively new sweet-tart dried fruit can be used like raisins or currants in baking, salads, sauces, stews, chutneys, and relishes. Look for them in the bulk section and baking aisle of your supermarket.

Dried **cranberries** can be used as is or softened. To plump, either soak in water, fruit juice, or a liqueur at room temperature for 20 to 30 minutes, or boil them in the liquid, remove from the heat, and steep for 5 minutes.

Cremini see **Mushrooms**.

Croutons Over time, different methods, such as frying, baking, and grilling, have been employed to create this crunchy, flavorful garnish for soups and salads.

At Moosewood, we cube whole wheat bread and bake it at 350° on an unoiled pan for 5 to 10 minutes. Then we toss the bread cubes with garlic butter and return them to the oven to crisp for another 7 to 10 minutes. Sometimes we add fresh or dried herbs to the butter; sometimes we use olive oil instead of butter. We like to toast **croutons** with jerk and cajun seasonings for Caribbean and Creole soups and salads.

Curly endive is a bitter green that grows in bunches with thin, frilly individual leaves. To prepare, remove thicker stems before coarsely chopping the leaves. Try sautéed curly endive on top of mashed or baked potatoes or with creamy cannellini or butter beans. It will keep unwashed in a loosely closed plastic bag in the refrigerator for 3 to 4 days.

Currants Currants are a dried ancient variety of black grape grown in Greece and native to Corinth. The name "currant" is an anglicized adaptation of the French *raisin de Corinthe*. Unlike standard raisins, tiny black currants have a glistening, jeweled appearance that won't fade even when simmered. In our recipes, currants refers to these little dried grapes, *not* the red, white, and black currants in the gooseberry family used for making jellies and preserves. Look for currants with other dried fruit in the supermarket, gourmet food stores, Greek groceries, and in specialty fruit and nut shops.

Daikon It is an understatement to say that radishes don't hold a central place in the American eating experience. Most of us are familiar only with the little red ones and tend to think of them as decorations— barely food. The Japanese radish, daikon, however, has been called "Japan's most fundamental vegetable," considered important in daily nutrition and also useful medicinally.

Daikon is an aid to digestion and a tenderizer of other foods. It usually accompanies oily dishes, either grated or pickled. It is crisp, mildly spicy, and refreshing, and it absorbs strong flavors, adding lift without being intrusive. Grated daikon is a perfect accent for creamy purées and salty broths and ideal for seafood salads and Asian, Pacific, or Caribbean salads.

When shopping, look for 1- to 1$\frac{1}{2}$-foot-long smooth, white daikon that resembles a giant carrot. It should be firm and have an unblemished peel. It will keep for up to 2 weeks in the refrigerator in a plastic bag.

Dried fruit, unsulphured Any dried fruit that is not treated with sulfites to preserve its color and soft texture. Untreated apricots, peaches, and pineapples will be darker and browner in color than those treated with sulfites. Unsulphured dried fruit is available in some supermarkets, most natural food stores, and many specialty stores.

Edam cheese This mild, buttery, semifirm Dutch cheese with a smooth, not sharp, flavor is an interesting alternative to Cheddar or Swiss in soups and salads. When buying Edam, check for resilience, an absence of holes in both the wax coating and the cheese, and a stamp saying THE NETHERLANDS or HOLLAND.

Escarole A mildly bitter, juicy green in the chicory family, escarole is delicious sautéed with olive oil and a bit of garlic or chopped raw and added to soups. It has loosely bunched, wavy-edged, dark green leaves with broad, white, sweet-tasting midribs. Its roots are roasted and ground for the chicory used in coffee blends. When selecting escarole, look for a robust

bunch; avoid wilted, yellow, spotted, or brown-edged bunches. Stored in perforated plastic in the salad bin of the refrigerator, it will keep for 4 to 5 days.

Extracts are strong flavorings used in both sweet and savory dishes. Although vanilla extract is probably most common, you can also find other pure extracts or flavorings, such as maple, chocolate, orange, lemon, almond, and coconut.

Extracts are made by cooking the most flavorful part of the plant in alcohol for a long time to produce a thick syrup. The syrup is then diluted with alcohol in a ratio of 1:4. Pure flavorings, as distinguished from extracts, use glycerin as a medium instead of alcohol.

Pure extracts and flavorings taste so much better than artificial ones that we feel it is worth the extra expense: usually only a small amount is called for. Pure extracts and flavorings can be found in the spice or baking aisle of the supermarket.

Fennel bulb Fresh fennel is a stunning vegetable with a sweet, mild, licorice taste. Its flavor has led to its alternate name, anise, a source of some confusion, since fennel is not the plant that produces the spice anise. Dramatic looking, fennel has a large round bulb with white stalks that culminate in a mantle of feathery green foliage.

The bulb can be eaten raw or cooked. Sliced into a salad, fennel is crunchy, refreshing, and refreshingly different. When cooked, its licorice flavor mellows. We like to roast or sauté fennel bulb before adding it to soups, salads, stews, and seafood dishes. The feathery tops can be minced for a subtle seasoning, but they shine when used whole as a garnish.

Fresh fennel, available year-round, peaks from autumn through early spring. Select smooth bulbs that are free of brown spots. Fennel will keep in a plastic bag in the refrigerator for up to 4 days.

Feta cheese A Moosewood favorite, this creamy, salty, tangy cheese from the Balkans, Greece, and the Middle East is made from goat's, cow's, or sheep's milk. One of feta's chief virtues is that a sprinkling of feta on a salad, stew, or soup is completely satisfying. As an added plus, most domestic feta is lower in fat than harder cheeses such as Cheddar, Swiss, and Provolone.

Feta is available in tins, jars, and plastic or, best of all, loose in a salty brine. Look for feta in the cheese, deli, or ethnic section of the supermarket.

Figs, Calimyrna This variety of fig is golden colored, large, sweet, and moist. Its antecedent is the Smyrna fig of Smyrna, Greece, transplanted and adapted to California soil. Dried Calimyrnas are available in natural food stores, gourmet food shops, and some supermarkets. Avoid figs that appear to be overly dry, hard, split, or moldy.

Fish sauce (*nuoc mam, nam pla, tuk trey*) A staple Southeast Asian condiment made from fermented, salted fish, such as anchovies or mackerel, and one that is both a potent flavorer and conduit of protein and B vitamins. It is salty and pungent. For many Westerners, fish sauce is an acquired taste that, once cultivated, can become habit-forming. Its strong odor dissipates during cooking. Fish sauce is available in Asian food stores.

Flour, unbleached white
When wheat is ground into unbleached white flour, the bran and wheat germ are separated and removed from the endosperm before grinding. When ground between old-fashioned millstones, the flour is called stone-ground and still retains some of the bran and wheat germ. Bleached flour, which we do not recommend, is treated with chlorine dioxide and is often fortified with nutrients that were lost during the milling process.

Flours vary in gluten and fineness according to the type of wheat from which they are made. Bread and pasta flours, milled from hard wheat, contain the most gluten and produce the most elastic doughs. Pastry flour, which has a softer, finer texture and the least gluten, is milled from soft wheat. It is ideal for making crumbly cookies and tender pie and tart crusts. All-purpose flour is made from both hard and soft wheats, and is generally useful for quick breads, biscuits, cakes, and cookies.

White flour will keep for 6 months or longer in an airtight container stored in a cool, dry, well-ventilated place. Be sure to use all of the old flour before adding new, fresh flour to the bin. We recommend King Arthur brand unbleached white flour, which is available in many supermarkets. Or look for a locally milled stone-ground white flour.

Garlic In the countries of East Asia (except Japan) where the most garlic is eaten per capita, this variety of *allium* is integral to both food and medicine. Garlic is a perennial bulb that yields about a dozen cloves per head. Choose heads that are firm and smooth with unbroken skin. Elephant garlic, a relative of leeks, is about twice as large as ordinary garlic and has a much milder flavor. At Moosewood, we never use dried garlic powder or garlic salt.

It is simple to roast **garlic** and the results are glorious. Roasted garlic is creamy and sweet. It thickens dressings nicely, reducing the amount of oil needed, and mashed potatoes need less butter when it's added. Rub the unpeeled garlic bulb with olive oil, place it in a shallow pan, cover with foil, and bake at 350° for 35 to 45 minutes. Allow the bulb to cool, then grasp the root end and squeeze the softened garlic out of its papery skin: the process is something like squeezing frosting through a pastry tube.

Garlic scapes *(garlic shoots, rochambole)* The green tops of garlic that uncurl in the spring. Garlic shoots grow only from "thick-necked" garlic, a variety suited to rugged winters and late springs. Garlic scapes look like a cross between chives and scallions with edible, light green, pointed buds at their tips. They have a garlicky flavor and can be sliced into salads, sprinkled on soups, and stir-fried. Best of all, they make a wicked garnish. They are available at farmers' markets in the spring and again in the late summer.

Ginger, crystallized A confection made of spicy ginger root pieces coated with granulated sugar or sugar syrup: sweet and hot is a compelling combination. Some chefs prefer crystallized ginger prepared with young ginger while others think the young plant has less heat, bite, and texture. Look for crystallized ginger in the spice or baking aisle or in the ethnic food section of supermarkets, or in Asian food stores.

Ginger root Fresh ginger root is in fact not a root at all but a light bronze, knobby, and branching perennial rhizome, or underground stem, resembling the underground stem of an iris. The main stem is sometimes called a hand because its projecting stems suggest fingers. Healthy ginger has smooth, taut, tan skin and golden, juicy flesh. Fresh ginger root is spicy hot (although its heat is milder and markedly different from that of hot peppers) and it has a sweet undertone. It is frequently used in Asian, African, and Caribbean cuisines.

> To use **ginger root,** finely grate it or thinly slice it into rounds. If its skin is smooth, no peeling is necessary, but if the skin is blemished or doesn't grate easily, peel it with a paring knife first.

Ginger root is available year-round, although its peak season is from late winter through early spring. If ginger is fresh and firm, it will keep for a week at room temperature. Wrapped in a paper towel to absorb moisture and prevent mold, sealed in a plastic bag, and stored in the vegetable bin of the refrigerator, it will keep for several weeks. Stored in the freezer, it will keep for several months. Look for fresh ginger in the produce section of the supermarket.

Gouda cheese is a semisoft, mild-tasting cheese from Holland. It can be easily sliced and has nearly universal appeal, much like Cheddar in this country. Good-quality gouda is smooth and elastic. Look for the import imprint HOLLAND or THE NETHERLANDS and avoid rounds or wedges that crumble or have holes.

Grapefruits, peeling and sectioning see Oranges.

Greens A term that refers both to raw salad greens, such as lettuce and spinach, and to leafy greens that are usually cooked, such as kale and chard. Many greens are good both raw and cooked.

Some greens are best cooked, though a good many, when young and tender, make tasty, nutritious, and interesting salad greens as well. For specifics, see beet greens, bok choy, broccoli rabe, chard, curly endive, escarole, kale, mustard greens, turnip greens, and watercress.

Other greens are popular salad bowl greens, but not exclusively so: Belgian endive is delicious sautéed, romaine is in many a lettuce soup, and radicchio is sturdy enough to be grilled. For specifics, see arugula, Belgian endive, Boston lettuce, looseleaf lettuces, mesclun, radicchio, romaine, and spinach.

A word about storage: Do not store salad greens or any vegetable near fruit. Fruit releases ethylene gas, which facilitates ripening and will speed the spoiling of foods in its proximity.

Hijiki see **Seaweed**.

Hominy Corn kernels that have been dried and then soaked in lye wood ash, a process that removes the germ layer and turns the kernel creamy white. The texture of hominy is smooth and chewy, and its taste is distinctive. We enjoy including it in southern and southwestern United States stews and soups.

Although vitamins and minerals are lost with the removal of the germ, the lye-soaking process enhances the availability of the protein and niacin in corn, nutrients that are otherwise bound by its cellular structure. Niacin deficiency contributes to the debilitating bone disease rickets. In indigenous cultures where corn was a staple food, the use of lye in making hominy and tortillas may indicate a centuries-old wisdom that realized this food preparation was linked with having healthy bones.

Horseradish, prepared   This mixture of grated horseradish root, vinegar, and salt is available both plain and sweetened and colored with beet juice. Hot and sharp, it is a natural foil for sour cream, creamy sauces, purées, and fish and seafood chowders. Look for it in or near the dairy area in the supermarket.

Hot pepper sauce   When our recipes call for hot pepper sauce, we probably used Tabasco brand — a combination of vinegar, red peppers, and salt — but the choice is yours. There are a legion of hot pepper sauces on the market and local and regional sauces abound.

Ingredients can range from the mere addition of garlic to the inclusion of tropical fruit. Some sauces are sweet; some are tomatoey. Formulas varying the types of hot peppers, the kinds of vinegar, and the spices used, and the ratio of ingredients account for the differences among brands. The type and quantity of hot peppers used determines whether a sauce is hot, medium, or mild. Store hot pepper sauce at room temperature; it will outlive us all.

Jicama (*hee´–kuh-muh*) is a clean-tasting root vegetable from Mexico and the Amazon, with a translucent white flesh and a taste and texture like a crisp, juicy, early-autumn apple. Because jicama is essen-

tially more texture than flavor, a taste for it need not be acquired. It can weigh anywhere from 8 ounces to a hefty 6 pounds and has a somewhat spherical shape with thin, coarse, potato-brown skin.

> To prepare **jicama**, peel the skin and fibrous undercoat with a paring knife, and then slice, julienne, or cut as directed.

Jicama does not discolor or lose its crispness once cut or cooked, and it's at home with fruit, vegetable, and seafood salads. Select one with smooth, unblemished, thin skin. Thicker-skinned jicamas can be tough, fibrous, and tasteless. Scratch the skin to test for quality. Store in the refrigerator unwrapped and away from moisture. Once cut, wrap in plastic. It will keep for about a week.

Julienne   A slicing technique that produces short, slender, matchstick-sized strips of vegetables, fruit, cheese, or any food that can be sliced. The word *julienne* was originally the name of a traditional French consommé with a mixture of finely shredded vegetables.

Kale is one of our favorite greens. Tender kale has a sweet, very mild, cabbagey taste and curly blue-green leaves and stems with a silvery patina. Nutritionally, kale is a winner: It's very high in calcium and vitamins A and C and is a good source of fiber. Edible varieties include tender, sweet Red Russian and Italian kales and young ornamental kale. For a bed of greens, use only young or very tender kale.

> To prepare cooked **kale**, hold each leaf by the stem and run your other hand down the rib to strip off the leaf, and then chop into ribbons (see Chiffonade, page 358) or bite-sized pieces. One pound of raw kale yields 4 cups cooked.

At the market, avoid wilted bunches with leaves edged in yellow. Kale is a rugged, cold-tolerant plant that yields the sweetest crop after the first frost. Unrinsed kale, wrapped loosely in plastic or paper towels and stored in the vegetable crisper of the refrigerator, will keep for about a week.

Kasha (*roasted buckwheat, buckwheat groats*)   Although botanically a fruit, kasha in the world of food is considered a grain. Its hearty, nutty taste and chewy consistency make it good cold-weather fare. It can be a flavorful pilaf when prepared with caramelized or browned onions.

Kasha is native to Asia and was long a staple in northern provinces until cold-resistant rice varieties were developed. Introduced to Europe during the Middle Ages, kasha gained widespread popularity because it grows in the poorest soils and matures quickly.

Kasha comes whole, coarse, medium, and fine. The least refined variety, whole kasha, can be prepared in 15 minutes; the more refined grades are even quicker. Kasha can be found in the grain or kosher sections of many supermarkets and in most natural food stores.

Kasseri A Greek cheese available as a smooth, firm, white table cheese or as a semihard grating cheese. Kasseri is often a mild-tasting cheese, but the table cheese made with sheep's milk can have a stonger taste and aroma. The grating kasseri at our Ithaca, New York, market is made with cow's milk and, though salty, has a very pleasant taste that makes it a delicious topping for sautéed greens, especially the bitter ones. Kasseri can be found in the specialty cheese section of many supermarkets.

Kelp see **Seaweed: Konbu**.

Kidney beans, red In Hindi, these are *rajma dal*, and in Spanish, *habichuelas*. Red kidney beans are native to South America, where they have long been a staple food. They were eaten by the conquistadores and became popular with American cowboys. We use them in soups, salads, and a myriad of other bean dishes. Dried kidney beans are large, kidney-shaped, maroon-colored beans that become reddish tan when cooked. If dried kidney beans are soaked first, they take about an hour to cook. They are available in most supermarkets, Indian groceries, and natural food stores.

Kiwi A kiwi has brown, fuzzy skin, is about the size of a lime, and grows on climbing vines. It has a brilliant emerald-green interior with central star markings and tiny, edible, jet-black seeds. Its taste is sweet and tart, reminiscent of apples and citrus. One of our local supermarkets has a top-ten list of nutrition-packed fruits and vegetables, and kiwi ranks number one. It has the highest amount of vitamin C of all fruits and vegetables and considerable quantities of vitamin E, potassium, and fiber. Kiwis were originally called Chinese gooseberries, but during the cold war of the late '50s, marketers changed the name for fear that many Americans would be alienated by any moniker that they associated with communism. Because it was first cultivated in New Zealand, the fuzzy kiwi was named after that country's quirky, hairy bird.

Kiwis flatter seafood platters, look great in fruit salads, and are a smashing garnish, especially with strawberries. They are nice in dressings and fruit sauces, but they must be puréed briefly because extended blending crushes the bitter seeds. Another cautionary note: Kiwis contain an enzyme that inhibits gelatin from setting and another one that curdles milk.

California kiwis are available from October through May and New Zealand kiwis from June to October. To choose a good kiwi, select a firm fruit that is free of soft spots or mold. Ripe kiwis will keep in the refrigerator for 2 to 3 days.

Konbu see **Seaweed**.

Leeks grow as thick stalks with wide overlapping leaves and resemble giant scallions. Their subtle flavor makes them a renowned delicacy of the onion family, and they have quite an august history. They were cultivated by the Greeks and Romans, are the basis of French cuisine across classes, and are the national vegetable of Wales.

The most tender leeks are those on the small side: Choose stalks that are under 1¾ inches in diameter. Both the white bulb and the tender parts of the green, blade-like leaves can be used. Look for leeks in the produce section of supermarkets.

> To prepare **leeks**, cut off the root end and the tough part of the leaves and discard (or save for stock). Immerse the stalks in water to remove sand and grit. Slice vertically down the center of the bulb, separate its layers, and submerge again. Transfer the leeks to a colander and rinse well until there is no more sand.

Lemongrass These grass-family stalks are round reeds that have a lemony flavor and are so aromatic that they provide atmosphere almost more than flavor. It has a *je ne sais quois* that some of us can't get enough of. Lemongrass can grow as tall as 2 feet and ranges in color from a light yellow-green to the green-gray of sage.

To use **lemongrass**, cut off the tough root end, peel the thick outside layers, and slice or mince the tender, scallion-like core. Lemongrass can be eaten raw, but we usually sauté or simmer it. The tough exterior layers can be used to flavor either stock or the water used for steaming or parboiling. One stalk of outer leaves and tough stems will flavor about a quart of liquid.

Lemongrass is sold in Asian markets and some supermarkets, but you can also grow it yourself. Unlike other tropical staples, it grows in moderate climates: we have successfully grown it in our short upstate New York summers.

Lentils, red and brown Red lentils are salmon-pink, high-protein, quick-cooking legumes that can be sprouted. Once cooked, they usually turn a surprising gorgeous shade of gold. Red lentils may be purchased whole or split, and the cooking time varies accordingly. Cook split lentils only 10 to 15 minutes or they become too soft. We like to use red lentils in Indian recipes, especially soups. The more familiar brown lentils maintain their original color and take 30 to 40 minutes to cook. Lentils can be found in supermarkets, Indian groceries, and natural food stores.

Looseleaf lettuces include green leaf and red leaf (or ruby lettuce). They have frilly leaves, loosely joined at the stalk, and taste sweet and tender. To store, do not detach leaves from the base until ready for use; wrapped loosely in plastic and refrigerated in the vegetable crisper, these lettuces will keep for up to 4 days.

Mangoes originated in Southeast Asia close to 6,000 years ago and were brought to the Americas in the 1800s. Luscious, delectable, dreamy . . . no wonder they are second only to bananas as the most commonly eaten fruit in the world. Mangoes are round, oval, or kidney shaped and about the size of grapefruits. The leathery skins can range from green to yellow, orange, and red. A ripe mango can be any of these colors or mottled with many of them. The flesh of the best mangoes is apricot colored, sweet, and smooth, resembling a cross of peaches, melons, and oranges.

Mangoes are good in chilled fruit soups, dressings, fruit sauces, shakes, and smoothies. They are a treat in fruit cups, parfaits, upside-down cakes, and ice cream. Look for a mango that is slightly soft, has a taut skin, and exhibits the resilience of a ripe avocado. Avoid those that have soft spots or look deflated. Most important, check the stem end: A distinct floral aroma signals a ripe mango.

Cutting a **mango** can be tricky. There is a large, flat central pit that can occupy almost ⅓ of the fruit. Cut the mango lengthwise into two halves, as close to the pit as possible. Score the fruit of each mango half in a crosshatch pattern, but don't cut through the peel. Bend each mango half backward (turn it inside out) and slice off the cubes.

Mesclun, from the French *mesclumo* or "mixture," is a combination of bitter, sweet, and peppery young tender greens. Mesclun can refer to any number of baby lettuce combinations: A good blend is arugula, red mustard, frisée, mâche (corn salad), baby spinach, tatsoi, and mizuna. The beauty of these mixes is that they are ready to use, easy to clean, and diverse in color, shape, and flavor. Mesclun is expensive; at Moosewood, we mix it with leaf lettuces and romaine.

Millet This small, round, hard yellow grain has the highest percentage of protein of all the grains. Hulled millet is nutritious and quickly prepared. It has a buttery flavor and, when properly prepared, a texture that is both light and chewy. Overcooking, however, can reduce millet to mush.

This ancient grain, cultivated for 6,000 years, enjoyed global popularity before the development of hardy strains of wheat, corn, and rice. It is still a food staple in parts of Africa and Asia, but in the United States, it is primarily farmed as a feed crop. Hulled millet is available in natural food stores and many supermarkets.

Mirin A sweet Japanese rice cooking wine used to flavor salad dressings, marinades, glazes, and sauces. Two types of mirin, hon-Mirin and aji-Mirin, are generally available. Hon-Mirin is brewed from sake, sweet rice, and rice malt; aji-Mirin is a wine flavored with salt, fructose, and corn syrup. According to Bruce Cost, weekly Asian food columnist for the *San Francisco*

Chronicle and the *Washington Post,* Kikkoman brand produces a good hon-Mirin.

If you cannot find mirin, a good substitute is a mixture of ⅔ cup of dry sherry and ⅓ cup of sugar, or ¾ cup of dry sherry and ¼ cup of honey. Mirin is available in Asian markets and in the ethnic section of many supermarkets. Store in a cool, dry place.

Miso   A paste made from fermented soybeans, miso originated in China over 2,000 years ago. Later in Japan, many varieties of miso were developed by adding grains such as rice and barley to the soybeans. Now there are three basic kinds of miso: sweet, amber-colored rice miso; savory, dark red barley miso; and strong, thick soybean miso. Miso is made by adding sea salt and a barley, rice, or wheat culture to crushed cooked soybeans. The miso is then fermented in wooden barrels for a period of 3 months to 3 years. Lighter varieties are aged for only a few months, while the darker, richer varieties are aged much longer.

Miso has twice the protein of tofu, is low in saturated fat, is free of cholesterol, and contains beneficial digestive enzymes. Use miso for seasoning soups, spreads, salad dressings, and marinades.

> Because its enzymes are destroyed by high heat, add **miso** to soups or sauces at the end of cooking, and do not let it boil.

Miso, with its high salt content, can be stored in the refrigerator for several months. Be sure to remove miso paste from the container with a clean spoon to prevent the introduction of any destructive bacteria.

Some brands may contain preservatives, so read the label carefully.

Miso is available in Asian groceries, health food stores, and the ethnic section of many supermarkets.

Molasses, unsulphured
Molasses that is not treated with sulphites is darker in color and does not have the unpleasant after-taste of sulphured molasses. Look for unsulphured molasses in many supermarkets and natural food stores. Blackstrap molasses (high in iron) is very strongly flavored and less sweet, so reduce the amount used in a recipe calling for regular molasses and consider adding a little honey.

Mozzarella, fresh   A soft, creamy, delicate-tasting cheese that excels with more assertive companions like tomatoes, Mediterranean olives, capers, rosemary, and marinated or roasted vegetables. Most fresh mozzarella is locally made from cow's milk and is sold in small balls packed in water or light brine. Fresh mozzarella imported from Italy and made from buffalo's milk is often vacuum packed and has a particularly satiny texture worth seeking out. Look for fresh mozzarella in the specialty cheese section of the supermarket, in Italian food stores, and in gourmet food shops. Stored in water or light brine in the refrigerator, it will keep for 3 to 4 days.

Mung bean sprouts   Sprouts are shoots that have just emerged from seeds. They are delicate and very perishable and are eaten at that moment before they become full-fledged plants. Plump, crunchy, cream-colored mung sprouts are higher in vitamin C and lower in calories than most unsprouted seeds, and higher in protein, B vitamins, and iron than most vegetables. Choose sprightly, fresh-looking sprouts whose tips are not withered and store them in a plastic bag punched with holes for up to 4 days in the refrigerator. Mung bean sprouts are available in the produce section of many supermarkets and in Asian groceries.

Mushrooms   The word *mushroom* comes from the French *mousseron,* meaning "field mushroom." Some supermarkets carry many types of these fungi in an intriguing variety of shapes, colors, and names. At Moosewood, we are constantly adding the textures and flavors of new varieties to our repertoire of soups, sauces, stuffings, and casseroles.

Good air circulation allows fresh mushrooms to remain firm longer. Consequently, they should never be stored in plastic. They will keep in the refrigerator, unwashed, in a paper bag or damp towel for up to

5 or 6 days. Store dried mushrooms in a glass jar with a tight-fitting lid. Remove them with very dry hands, as any moisture may cause molding or spoilage.

> To clean fresh **mushrooms**, rinse briefly in a colander under cool water and pat dry with a towel. Or clean with a soft brush. When you grill large mushrooms, brush them with olive oil to prevent the tops from wrinkling. Use stems and trimmings in stocks, soups, stews, sauces, and stuffings.
>
> Rinse **dried mushrooms** under running water. Place them in a heatproof bowl, pour boiling water over them, and soak until softened, 10 to 30 minutes. Drain, and if the mushrooms weren't sandy, reserve the liquid for stock; otherwise, discard the soaking liquid and rinse the mushrooms again. Remove any tough, woody stems.

Recipes in this book use the following varieties of mushrooms:

Button mushrooms (*moonlight, domestic, common*) Varying in color from white to shades of brown and measuring from 1 to 2 inches in diameter, button mushrooms are the most common commercial variety available in both small groceries and supermarkets. You will easily recognize button mushrooms in their plastic-wrapped 8- or 12-ounce containers or among the bulk vegetables. Button mushrooms can be eaten raw or cooked, plain or marinated, in salads, soups, stews, and casseroles.

Chanterelles During cool, damp weather in the New York State Finger Lakes region, mushroom aficionados steal away into the local forests in search of elusive chanterelles. These delicately flavored, trumpet-shaped mushrooms range in color from shades of golden yellow to orange to (in rare instances) black. Because they are a firm mushroom, they may take longer to cook than the common button. Fresh and dried chanterelles are occasionally available in supermarkets.

Cremini (*brown, Italian brown*) In Italian, *crimini* means "crimes," and it is indeed a crime to pass up these cute brown and tan cousins of button mushrooms. Small, mild ones hold their shape when cooked whole. Larger, more mature ones produce a fuller flavor and darker juice. Cremini are grown year-round and are available in the produce section in many supermarkets.

Oyster mushrooms (*abalone*) With caps shaped like shells or flowers, these mushrooms come in shades of cream, gray, or light brown. They grow in clusters on tree stumps and fallen branches. Oyster mushrooms are bland and chewy with a flavor that is slightly reminiscent of the sea. Try them grilled or stir-fried, served in appetizers, soups, salads, main

dishes, sauces, and pasta. Look for them in the produce section of supermarkets that carry a variety of fresh mushrooms.

Porcini (*cepes*) These large, light brown, fleshy mushrooms grow on dense forest floors, which contribute to their rich, woodsy flavor. They are usually available dried, although you can occasionally find fresh ones.

Portabella These giant open parasols measure up to 6 inches in diameter and range in color from taupe to brown, with dark brownish-black gills. Choose ones that are dry and smooth. Older portabellas tend to be heavier and more fibrous. These popular mushrooms make great grillers and are a delicious addition to roasted vegetables. They are found packaged or loose in the produce section of many supermarkets.

Shiitake (*Chinese black mushrooms, winter mushrooms, fragrant mushrooms*) Large brown fleshy shiitake grow on fallen chestnut and oak logs and, in Japan, on a type of beech tree called *shii*. They may lower cholesterol and are valued in China and Japan as a health stimulant. Because the stems are tough and woody, eat only the caps, which have a chewy texture and a smoky flavor. Dried shiitake are available in Asian groceries and most supermarkets; fresh shiitake can occasionally be found in the produce section of some supermarkets.

Straw mushrooms The name of these beige or brown conical-shaped mushrooms comes from the beds of rice straw or husks in which they grow. They thrive in the warm climates of southern China, Southeast Asia, Malaysia, and the Philippines. Straw mushrooms have a mild flavor and a meaty texture. They are available dried or in 15-ounce cans in well-stocked supermarkets and Asian groceries.

Tree ears (wood ears, black fungus) There is a traditional belief in China that eating these brown-capped, smooth-textured mushrooms assures a long, happy life. Tree ears are mild and crunchy and are often used in sweet-and-sour soups as well as many cold dishes. About 3 heaping tablespoons of dried tree ear mushrooms will yield 1 cup of softened mushrooms. They are available dried in 8-ounce packages in Chinese and Southeast Asian markets.

Mussels These edible mollusks are a low-fat, high-mineral, high-protein food found worldwide. Although broadly appreciated in Europe, mussels are not as popular in the United States. Because mussels grow quickly and reproduce readily, they are easy to cultivate. The shells of these saltwater bivalves commonly range in color from black to dark blue. The blue mussel, which is found in large colonies off the coast of Europe and on the northeastern shores of North America from the Arctic to North Carolina, can be easily recognized by its smooth, dark blue shell, which reveals a pearly inner lining when opened.

Mussels anchor themselves on almost any available surface with strong, stiff threads called byssus, which they secrete from their shells. According to A. J. McClane, internationally known fishing expert, author, and consultant, the ancient Greeks collected byssus and wove them into gloves for the hands of fishermen. These virtually indestructible gloves, stored in buckets of sea water to maintain their durability, remained in use generation after generation.

When purchasing mussels, be sure they are fresh and from an unpolluted source. Farm-grown mussels, sometimes called "cultured," generally do not require cleaning.

To prepare **mussels**, place them in clean, salted water for a few hours. Discard any shells that are open. Scrub the tightly closed shells with steel wool to remove deposits and sand. If your mussels are not already cleaned, pull off the white byssus from the outside of the shells. Fresh, live mussels are either closed or will clamp shut when handled. Once they are cooked, discard any mussels that have not opened.

Mustard, prepared Made from mustard powder, water, vinegar, salt, and spices. Prepared mustard's pungency and hotness come from a reaction of its essential oil when the crushed seed or powder is mixed with water. To preserve this pungency, add mustard near the end of cooking.

Prepared mustard comes in a range of colors and flavors. American or yellow (ballpark) mustard is bright yellow and mildly flavored. Dijon mustard is a duller yellowish-brown flecked with brown or black mustard seeds and flavored with white wine. German mustard is spicy and sweet-and-sour with a smooth or rough texture, and Chinese mustard is smooth and pale yellow with a sinus-clearing hotness.

Mustard greens are a mustardy-tasting, spicy green packed with calcium and vitamins A and C. At Moosewood, we consider mustard greens a terrific flavoring and spicing green, good combined with milder greens such as kale, collards, spinach, or beet greens. They can add zest without the use of hot spices. Mustard greens have long been used in the South, as well as in parts of India, China, and Africa. Young red mustard greens are sometimes included in mesclun or baby greens mixes.

When choosing mustard greens, select bright green bunches and avoid any that are wilted, spotted, or yellowed. To store, rinse in cold water, wrap in paper or cotton towels, enclose in a plastic bag, and refrigerate. Mustard greens will keep for about 3 days.

Neufchâtel In the American marketplace, Neufchâtel refers to low-fat cream cheese. It can be substituted for cream cheese in most recipes and is available in 8-ounce packages in most supermarkets. It is not the original French Neufchâtel.

Nori see **Seaweed**.

Oils The English word *oil* comes from *oliva,* the Latin word for "olive." Various oils add characteristic flavorings to regional and national cuisines. Store oils away from light and refrigerate ones that are used infrequently to prevent rancidity. The following are the varieties we use most often:

    Canola oil *(rapeseed)* An excellent all-purpose oil that has about 7 percent saturated fat, 60 percent monounsaturated fat, and 27 percent polyunsaturated fat. Canola's mild flavor will not interfere with other flavors.

    Olive oil Olives, one of the oldest known fruits, are native to the Mediterranean coast. They are mentioned in Greek and Roman writings and the Bible, and have been cultivated in Egypt for at least 5,000 years.

    Olive trees have been transplanted to many parts of the world. Each variety of this evergreen tree produces fruit of a different color, size, flavor, and oil content. Some are light and delicate, while others are heavy and fruity. Harvesting olives is time-consuming and labor-intensive, hence the high price of olive oil.

    The finest extra-virgin olive oil, cold-pressed from fresh, ripe olives, is pale yellow or green with a distinctive flavor. Because it has a low smoking point and scorches easily, it is most often used in dressings and marinades. "Pure" olive oil is a mix of first and second pressings. Very good oil, suitable for cooking, is made from a second pressing using heat. An avid lover of olive oil is able to judge its quality by rubbing a little in the palms of the hands or dabbing a few drops on the back of a hand and inhaling the aroma as if it were perfume.

    Olive oil has about 15 percent saturated fat and 10 percent polyunsaturated fat. It is high in monounsaturated fat (about 70 percent), a factor which may contribute to the lower rate of cardiovascular disease among people from Mediterranean countries. Most supermarkets carry a range of olive oils, from pricey extra-virgin to less expensive "pure" olive oil.

Peanut oil is valued for sautéing and deep-frying because it will not burn unless the temperature is very high (about 500° F.). Because it does not absorb odors and flavors readily, it can be strained and reused. The most flavorful is "virgin" cold-pressed peanut oil. Peanut oil has about 15 percent saturated fat, 45 percent monounsaturated fat, and 35 percent polyunsaturated fat.

Sesame oil Dark sesame oil, with its burnt-amber color, is a rich, smoky-tasting, aromatic flavoring used in Chinese, Korean, and Japanese cuisines. This oil, pressed from roasted sesame seeds, is seldom used for cooking because it has a low burning point and loses flavor as it cooks. It is used almost exclusively in dressings and dipping sauces or sprinkled at the last minute into broths. At Moosewood, we use it to flavor eggs, salads, rice and noodle dishes, soups, and marinated vegetables.

    Light sesame oil, made from unroasted sesame seeds, is good for salad dressings and sautéing. It has a much milder flavor than its roasted counterpart and cannot substitute for dark sesame oil in our recipes.

    Look in the Asian section of supermarkets and in Asian markets for dark sesame oil packaged in glass or tin. (In plastic, it tends to become rancid more quickly.) Light sesame oil is often sold in natural food stores. If used often, store sesame oil in a cool, dark place. If used less frequently, store in the refrigerator to help prevent rancidity.

Okra Native to tropical Africa or Asia, okra came to the Western Hemisphere in the seventeenth century during the slave trade. When cooked, the fuzzy, tapered, green or purple edible pods become slippery and can thicken liquids, such as soups or stews. Fresh okra is available in the southern United States throughout the year and in the North from July through September. Fortunately, it is available year-round frozen or canned, whole or cut, in most supermarkets.

Olives Cultivated since 3000 B.C., olives were brought to North America in the fifteenth century by the Spanish. A curing process, involving treatment with lye, is necessary to remove the natural bitterness found in olives. They are then allowed to ferment in salt or brine. Although by no means exhaustive, here is a list of those we use most:

California ripe olives are canned in brine immediately after the curing process with lye, and as a result, their flavor is mild and less tangy than olives that are allowed to ferment in salt or brine.

Green Spanish olives are picked before ripening, cured, and preserved in brine.

Kalamata *(calamata)* are purplish-black olives marinated in wine vinegar and then packed in olive oil and vinegar.

California ripe olives and green Spanish olives are found in jars or cans in most supermarkets, while kalamata olives are available in specialty shops, Greek groceries, and the delicatessen section of supermarkets.

Onions The onion family's wild ancestors have been natives of Southeast Asia for 4,000 years. There are hundreds of varieties of the genus *allium,* a relative of the lily. Onions were considered a health food by the Greeks and were included in the diets of athletes and slaves. In Babylonia, onions were considered a sacred symbol of perfection because, when cut, they reveal layers of circles.

Globe-shaped onions grown in warm climates tend to have a mild flavor and are easily perishable. Those grown in colder climates are stronger, firmer, and better keepers. Choose firm, bright, dry, papery-skinned onions that do not have a spongy feeling when pressed around the stem, and store them in a cool, dark place with good air circulation.

Pearl onions *(boiling onions)* These tiny white onion marbles are many layered like pearls. They are harvested in the late summer and fall. Some cooks

call large pearl onions (more than 1½ inches in diameter) "boiling onions." Most often, you can find them in the frozen vegetable section of supermarkets. When pearl onions are occasionally available fresh, choose hard ones with white, papery skin.

To peel fresh **pearl onions,** drop them into boiling water for 15 to 20 seconds, then cut off the root end and slip off the skin.

Red Italian onions Sweet and mild, these onions are most often used raw in salads where they add color, flavor, and crunch. When cooked, they release water, and have a milder flavor than Spanish or Bermuda onions. The freshest red onions are available from late summer to early winter.

Spanish onions *(Valencias)* These large round or oval onions with light amber, papery skin are juicy and sweet and delicious raw or cooked. They are available most of the year, but the best ones arrive in the supermarkets in fall and winter.

For other relatives of onions, see **chives, garlic, leeks,** and **shallots.**

Oranges, peeling and sectioning The best oranges for sectioning are firm navel oranges.

> To peel and section, use a sharp knife to slice off the peel, including the white pith underneath. Then, working over a bowl to catch the juices, slice into a section along one side just inside the membrane and then flick the knife up the other side of the membrane to release a juicy section.
>
> If you don't mind eating the membrane, slice off the peel and then cut the orange through the stem end into halves. Place the halves flat side down on the cutting board and slice into sections.
>
> Or peel and separate the orange in the usual way for eating out of hand: into neat, membrane-enclosed sections.

Parsnips have been cultivated for centuries for both human and animal consumption. This winter root vegetable was used in Europe during medieval times as a cure-all for toothaches and to prevent dysentery. Most parsnips are similar in shape to carrots, although round or "turnip" parsnips also exist. Under their earthy beige skin is a creamy white interior that is sweet and mild with a slightly fibrous texture. The peak season for parsnips is December through March. Choice parsnips are firm and smooth.

Pasta Most dried pasta was imported from Naples, Italy, until 1914 when large-scale production began in the United States. Now, there are many imported and domestic brands of pasta, and for every shape and size there is a delightfully descriptive name. Some familiar shapes and names are fettuccine (small ribbons), spaghetti (strings), vermicelli (little worms), linguine (small tongues), tubetti (small tubes), tubettini (even smaller tubes), and rotini (corkscrews). You may also find farfalle (butterfly), manicotti (small muffs), orecchiette (little ears), ruote (wagon wheels), and conchiglie (conch shells).

Traditionally, how the pasta is used is dictated by its shape and size. Italian cooks use the following rules of thumb: Use small pastas for soups and larger ones for main dishes and salads; with chunky sauces, use spirals, shells, tubes, and other shapes that can hold the sauce; with smooth sauces, use long, thin pasta.

At Moosewood, we use imported pasta made from semolina (hard durum wheat), but wheat-free pastas (spelt, corn, rice, and quinoa) may be substituted in almost any recipe by cooking as directed on the box. Wheat-free pastas are available in natural food stores. Dried pasta can be stored indefinitely in a closed package in a cool, dry place.

> To properly cook dried semolina **pasta**, bring several quarts of water to a rolling boil, add the pasta, and stir until the strands or pieces float freely and the water returns to a boil. Boil, uncovered, until the pasta has softened to *al dente* (tender but firm). Drain the pasta and serve immediately.

Peanut butter Natural peanut butter made from roasted peanuts and a little salt contains no hydrogenated oil, emulsifiers, or sugar. Look for it on the shelves of both supermarkets and natural food stores. In some health food stores, you can grind peanuts on the spot into a smooth, creamy butter that can be even better than the excellent natural peanut butters that come in jars. Peanut butter is an important ingredient in Chinese, Southeast Asian, and West African cooking, adding flavor and richness to sauces, soups, and stews.

Pears Finding a ripe, juicy pear in the produce section of the supermarket is a rare occasion, and one to celebrate. The texture, sweetness, and juiciness of a ripe pear will differ according to its variety. A few of the common types available in most supermarkets are:

Bartlett A red or yellow, bell-shaped summer and autumn pear that is firm enough for cooking and good for eating out of hand.

Bosc A russet winter pear with a long neck and creamy texture, firm enough for cooking and good for eating fresh.

Comice A rotund green or greenish-yellow winter pear that is creamy, sweet, and juicy, and delicious with cheese.

D'Anjou A pale green or red-skinned, egg-shaped winter pear that is good for salads and snacks.

Pine nuts (*Indian nuts, pignolas, piñons*) Pine nuts are the edible seeds of certain varieties of pine trees that grow in the southwestern United States, Central America, and the Mediterranean. These small, creamy, sweet nuts impart a faint pine flavor to pilafs, cakes, cookies, and tortes in the cuisines of Spain, Italy, Eastern Europe, and North Africa. They are also a significant ingredient in southwestern Native American cuisines.

Because they are highly perishable, pine nuts should be stored in an airtight container and will keep in the refrigerator for up to 2 months or in the freezer for up to 6 months. Pine nuts are available in many supermarkets, specialty stores, and natural food stores.

To bring out the flavor of **pine nuts**, lightly roast them in a dry heavy skillet on low heat, or spread them on an unoiled tray in the toaster oven at 350° for 3 to 5 minutes, until golden and fragrant.

Pita bread (*pocket bread*)
A round, flat, Middle Eastern flatbread that, when cut in half, reveals an opening or "pocket" for stuffing with vegetables, cheese, and other sandwich fillings. Pita bread is most often made of whole wheat flour or unbleached white flour. It is available in most well-stocked supermarkets and natural food stores.

Porcini see **Mushrooms**.

Quinoa This ancient grain, indigenous to South America, was first cultivated by the Incas. A miracle food, quinoa is mild, nutty, and slightly crunchy, and easy to digest. It is rich in vitamins and minerals, high in protein, calcium, and iron, and contains all eight essential amino acids. And it takes just 15 minutes to prepare!

Ground quinoa has begun to show up in cereals and pastas. Whole quinoa is great in pilafs, grain salads, and stuffings. It is available in some supermarkets and many natural food stores.

To cook **quinoa**, first rinse it well with plenty of cold water to remove any residue of saponin, a soapy, bitter substance in the grain's natural coating. Add the grain to boiling water, cover, and simmer for 15 minutes.

Radicchio is an Italian red chicory on the decidedly bitter end of the greens spectrum, and its slightly peppery taste is very agreeable juxtaposed with sweeter greens. Its deep cranberry-red leaves swirled with white veins are most often used as colorful accents in tossed salads, but left whole, the bowl-shaped leaves are sturdy enough to hold dips or make beautiful beds for composed salads.

Radicchio is sold in Italian groceries and many supermarkets. In the United States, the small cabbage-like heads of radicchio di Verona or "Red Verona" are most common. Radicchio de Treviso, a nonheading variety loosely bunched at the base like leaf lettuce, is also available. When selecting radicchio, look for a base and leaves that are firm, smooth, and blemish-free. Wrapped in plastic and refrigerated, radicchio will keep for up to a week.

To use **radicchio**, discard the core or base, rinse and dry the leaves, and tear into bite-sized pieces or use whole.

Raisins, golden These light raisins are made from seedless green grapes. Their taste is somewhat different from that of black seedless raisins, and their color offers other aesthetic possibilities. Golden raisins are often treated with sulphur dioxide to preserve their color. Look for golden raisins in the baking aisle or bulk dried fruit section of the supermarket.

Red bell peppers (*sweet or red peppers*) are vine-ripened green bell peppers. They provide a colorful accent in salads, soups, pilafs, and stuffings. They are especially delicious when roasted. While methods of roasting vary from cook to cook, we have used the following ones with excellent results.

Stove-top method: Place a pepper directly on the stove burner and center it to maximize contact with the flame. Turn it with long tongs as it begins to char. Remove the pepper from the flame when it is blackened, about 10 minutes, and place it in a paper bag to steam for about 20 to 30 minutes. When cool, rinse under cold water and peel off the skin.

Broiler method: Set the peppers on a foil-lined tray under the broiler. Turn them so that they char evenly, and follow the steaming and peeling directions described in the stove-top method.

Grilling over wood or charcoal: Follow the directions for the stove-top method.

Roasted red peppers will keep in the refrigerator for 3 to 4 days. Covered with olive oil and vinegar and stored in a glass jar in the refrigerator, they will keep for up to 1 month. They will keep in the freezer for several months. Canned roasted red peppers are also available in the Italian section of the supermarket.

Rice Grown in China at least 3,000 years ago, rice is now cultivated in both the tropical and temperate zones across the continents. Many types of rice are sold in three sizes: short-, medium-, and long-grain. Short-grain is almost round in shape, needs less water during cooking than longer grains, and

clings together when cooked. It is the most widely grown rice in Japan, and good varieties are produced in California. Use short-grain rice for Japanese dishes. Medium-grain is plumper, moister, and more tender than long-grain. Long-grain, or "water rice," is dry, light, and fluffy and is grown in the Carolinas and Texas. It is used in Indian, Chinese, Southeast Asian, and Middle Eastern cuisines.

Arborio rice is an Italian, short-grain white rice that is high in starch and capable of absorbing large quantities of water. Its smooth, creamy texture is perfect for risottos and rice puddings. Look for arborio rice in Italian specialty shops or the Italian section of the supermarket.

Basmati rice is a slender-grain rice that grows in the foothills of the Himalayas. Basmati's sweet fragrance and smooth texture are highly prized by Indians and Pakistanis. Basmati is aged before it is sold and can be quite expensive. Both brown and white basmati rice are sold in natural food stores and in the Indian section of supermarkets.

Brown rice is the least processed form of rice. With

only the hull removed, the bran remains intact to give it a light brown color, nutty flavor, and chewy texture.

Jasmine rice (*Thai basmati rice*) is a creamy, lightly aromatic long-grain rice that comes from Thailand. We use it in Caribbean and Indian cooking. Jasmine rice can be found in Asian markets or among the international foods in well-stocked supermarkets.

Wehani rice was developed by Harlan Lundberg of the Lundberg Brothers, who are organic rice growers in northern California. This beautiful, brownish-red long-grain rice with a chewy texture complements robust stews and hearty salads.

White or "polished" rice has neither hull nor bran because both have been removed. "Enriched" rice has been dusted with thiamine, niacin, and iron.

Wild rice is not a rice at all, but the long, slim, black seeds of an aquatic grass related to the rice plant. It is indigenous to North America where Chippewas and Ojibways harvested large natural fields from their birch bark canoes. Ojibways still manage waterways in which they harvest wild rice by hand. Because the season for growing wild rice is limited and harvesting is labor-intensive, wild rice can be expensive. Larger, cultivated wild rice paddies are often treated with fertilizers and pesticides and harvested by machine, resulting in a less flavorful product. We use wild rice mixed with white or brown rice for side dishes, salads, stuffings, and pilafs.

Rice flour *(rice powder)*   In the West, finely ground white or brown rice flour is often used as a replacement for wheat flour in cakes and breads for those who are allergic to wheat. In Southeast Asia and China, white rice flour is an important ingredient in noodles and wrappings. Glutinous rice flour is used in Japan for sweets and as a thickener. Rice flour is available in Southeast Asian and Chinese groceries as well as supermarkets that carry international foods.

Rice noodles *(rice sticks)*
Varying in width from thin threads to fettuccine-sized flats, these translucent off-white noodles are the staple of many Asian dishes. Find them in Asian markets or in the Asian section of supermarkets.

> To use **rice noodles**, either boil them very briefly or simply immerse them in hot water and soak for several minutes before adding to soups, salads, or other dishes.

Rice vinegar *(rice wine vinegar)*
Originally made in China, rice wine vinegar ranges in color from clear to golden to red to black. In Japan, rice wine vinegar that is clear or slightly golden is made from the pulp that remains after drawing off the liquid that becomes rice wine or sake. Clear is the most delicate and mild, but all rice vinegars are less sharp and acidic than conventional

cider or white vinegars. Rice vinegar is the perfect condiment for Asian salads and cold dishes. Choose a Chinese or Japanese clear or golden variety that does not contain sugar, salt, or monosodium glutamate (MSG). Find rice vinegar in Asian groceries or in the Asian section of many supermarkets.

Rice wine *(sake)*   Sake is to Japan what wine is to France. According to legend, this fermented rice drink is believed to have been brewed by the gods from the first rice of the new year. The earliest known reference to sake is in the early eighth century. Sake was traditionally drunk chilled and served with fish dishes and stews. In the eighteenth century, the custom of drinking warmed sake began, probably to remove impurities.

There are many types and qualities of this celebratory brew, as well as many degrees of sweetness and dryness. California wine producers make sake for cooking as well as more full-bodied, complex, and flavorful sake for drinking. Dry sake has a lemony, mineral flavor while sweet sake imparts a honeyed quality. Sake is served either chilled or warmed, depending upon personal preference. Look for it in well-stocked wine or liquor stores.

Ricotta salata   A hard, salty, dry cheese made from ewe's milk. Ricotta salata is not related to

ricotta, but rather is a cheese that is grated, similar to Pecorino Romano. Use ricotta salata in salads, soups, and pasta dishes.

Romaine, also known as Cos lettuce, was first grown on the Aegean island of Cos. It has large, rounded deep green leaves with wide, crunchy midribs. A rich source of folate and vitamins A and C, it holds the distinction of being the most nutritious of all the lettuces. Because of its full-bodied flavor and crunchy texture, romaine is a good lettuce for heavy, sharp dressings like blue cheese, feta garlic, and lemon tahini and for toppings such as croutons and grated cheese.

Select romaine with crisp, firm, dark green outer leaves that lighten to pale green at the base. Do not separate leaves until ready to use. Stored in a plastic bag in the vegetable bin of the refrigerator, it will keep for up to a week.

Rum, dark   All rum is a distillation of fermented sugarcane juice or molasses. Caramel, also a sugar product, gives dark rum its color.

Sake see **Rice wine**.

Santa Rosa plums   These small to medium plums have a deep reddish-purple skin and juicy yellow pulp with a dark red halo around the pit. Their tart flavor and firm texture make them good for canning, freezing, jellies, and jams. The freshest Santa Rosas are available in supermarkets from June to September.

Look for firm, plump, ripe, shapely fruit that gives slightly when pressed. The light gray cast on the skin is a natural protection and does not affect the quality of the fruit. Off-season, hard Santa Rosas ripen best at room temperature.

Scallops   Because of Aphrodite's scallop shell chariot, the scallop became the symbol of sexual love and beauty, and because of the apostle St. James' personal scallop shell emblem, we call the classic appetizer *coquille St. Jacques.*

While 400 species of scallops are found throughout the world, only a dozen or so are sold commercially. Some scallops have smooth shells; others have ribs that radiate from their hinges. According to genus, they may be red, orange, yellow, black, or white.

Because scallops cannot hold their shells tightly closed, fishermen open them immediately, and with a sharp knife extract only the pure white muscle, which is immediately stored on ice. Some commercial fishing companies store scallops in fresh water: The scallops absorb water, increasing their size and weight by about one third, and although this may result in an attractively plump product, the flavor suffers considerably.

The most abundant scallop is the North Atlantic deep-sea scallop, which measures up to 5 inches in diameter. Most sea scallops are fished by dredging or trawling the deep waters off the coast of Maine;

some gourmets prefer those that are hand-harvested by divers.

Bay scallops, often preferred by fine chefs, are found in shallow waters around Florida, the Gulf of Mexico, and occasionally along the Atlantic coast as far north as Long Island. In its eighteen-month life span, this scallop grows from a microscopic speck to about 2 inches in width.

Scallops are soft, smooth, mild, and adaptable to many dishes and flavors. Buy only the freshest ones.

Seaweed *(sea vegetable)*   There are many kinds of seaweed, and here is a list of the ones we use in the Japanese- and Korean-inspired recipes in this book. Seaweeds are available in well-stocked supermarkets, Asian shops, and natural food stores.

Hijiki *(hiziki)*   The thin, black strands of a brown algae family, *Phaeophyta.* Hijiki expands to up to five times its original size after soaking and cooking. Hijiki is high in protein and minerals, especially iron, phosphorus, and calcium. Hijiki adds an assertive sea flavor to salads, soups, stews, and noodle and rice dishes.

Konbu *(kombu, kelp)* Long, thick, olive-brown leaves, about 5 or 6 inches wide, gathered off the coast of the Japanese island of Hokkaido. There, they are dried in the sun, folded, and packaged for commercial use. Konbu is dusted with a harmless white coating that can be wiped off with a damp cloth. It is a vital flavor enhancer in *dashi,* an all-

purpose stock used in Japanese cooking. Soaked and sautéed, threads of konbu are served as a vegetable side dish or a garnish for salads. Thin sheets of konbu are used as wrappings for meat, fish, and vegetable rolls, sometimes served in Japanese soups.

Nori *(laver)* A marine algae that is harvested and processed in Japan, Korea, and in the northwestern United States. Nori is a familiar wrapping for nori rolls and sushi rolls and is used as a garnish in salads and rice dishes.

To bring out **nori**'s flavor and prevent it from becoming tough, hold a sheet with tongs and pass it briefly over a gas flame just until the color deepens and the sheen brightens. If you have an electric stove, use a candle flame or look for pretoasted nori.

Wakame   A member of the *Alaria* family of sea kelp. Wakame that is harvested in the spring in Japan is eaten fresh. In the United States, we use dried wakame. To preserve its flavor and nutritional value, rehydrate by soaking in tepid water for 20 minutes. When soaked, its green leaves unfurl and can be chopped and served in soups and salads.

Seitan is wheat gluten, a natural substance that is extracted by removing the starch from wheat and leaving behind the concentrated gluten. In China and Japan, it is used as a meat substitute. Seitan is low-fat, protein-rich, highly textured, and flavor absorbing. It comes in sealed packages, which, after opening, will keep for about a week in the refrigerator. Use seitan much as you would use meat in stews, soups, and fillings. Sliced, marinated, and baked seitan is delicious in sandwiches. Look for seitan, both plain and seasoned, in natural food stores and supermarkets that carry vegetarian alternatives.

Sesame seeds *(benne seeds),* from the native East Indian plant *benne,* have been widely cultivated in both India and China for thousands of years. The seeds vary in color from white to gray-black and also orange.

Whole and ground sesame seeds are popular in Asian, African, Balkan, and Middle Eastern cuisines. In the United States, we most often use sesame seeds in breads and pastries in the European tradition. At Moosewood, we mostly use toasted unhulled seeds as a topping or garnish. Look for sesame seeds in natural food stores and supermarkets.

Shallots *(Welsh onions)*   Like garlic, shallots grow with a head made up of cloves wrapped in thin, papery reddish-brown skin. They have a mild, delicate flavor, tender texture, and can be eaten raw or cooked. Shallots are important in the cuisines of Southeast Asia and Europe. Store them in a cool, dark, well-ventilated space. Look for shallots in the produce section of large, well-stocked supermarkets.

Shiitake see **Mushrooms**.

Snow peas *(sugar peas, pea pods)* These flat, edible pea pods were developed from the garden pea to withstand the warm climate of southern China. Snow peas are best when just picked off the vine.

> Remove the strings of **snow peas** by pinching one of the tips and pulling the string down one side, and then repeat for the other side of the pod. Cook snow peas in boiling water for 15 to 20 seconds and remove promptly with a strainer.

Snow peas are available in the produce section of many supermarkets and in most Asian groceries.

Soba noodles   The favorite noodle of the northern Japanese, these hearty noodles are made from buckwheat or more usually from a combination of buckwheat and wheat flours. Soba noodles are traditionally served in *dashi,* a broth made from soy sauce and seaweed or fish. Soba noodles may also be served in hot or cold salads and pasta dishes. Look for these noodles in Asian groceries, natural food stores, and in the Asian section of many supermarkets.

Sour cream   This high-fat product originally made from cream is now available in low-fat and nonfat versions, which provide a significant savings in calories, fat, and cholesterol. One tablespoon of full-fat sour cream contains 30 calories, 3 grams of fat, and 5 milligrams of

cholesterol, while the nonfat version contains only 9 calories, no fat, and no cholesterol. Because thickeners and additives are often used in nonfat sour cream, you may want to consider yogurt cheese (page 387), a delicious, healthy substitute. Low-fat and nonfat sour cream are found in the dairy section of most supermarkets.

Spelt is a nonhybridized form of wheat that has been cultivated for —hold onto your hat—9,000 years. Organic and heritage farmers as well as allergy researchers have all recently rediscovered spelt—and it's experiencing a renaissance. Here's why.

Spelt grows exceptionally well without the assistance of chemical fertilizers, pesticides, or insecticides, which makes it a perfect candidate for organic farming. As a

heritage grain, there are few that are older or purer. Many wheat-sensitive people who suffer digestive or other health problems from eating wheat can tolerate spelt. To quote Arrowhead Mills, an organic grain distributor, "Spelt has a unique type of gluten with high water solubility that is easier to digest than gluten in common wheats."

Spelt is available as whole berries, which can be used much like wheatberries, as whole wheat or white flour, and in breads and pastas at many natural food stores.

Spices

Allspice (Jamaica pepper) Jamaica produces most of the world's supply of all-spice, which grows on a pimiento tree native to the West Indies and to Central and South America. The berries are picked green and then dried in the sun until brown. Allspice is used in both savory and sweet dishes from the Caribbean to Scandinavia to the Middle East. For the best flavor, buy whole berries and grind them just before using. Find whole allspice in the spice section of most supermarkets.

Black mustard seeds Widely used in Indian cuisine, black mustard seeds have a nutty aroma and mild flavor when heated. To use, either dry-roast and grind them, or heat them whole in oil until they pop. Heat develops the flavor and inhibits the enzyme responsible for pungency. Black mustard seeds are available in spice shops, Indian food stores, and many supermarkets.

Black pepper Once an obsession of European explorers and probably the prime motivation for finding a sea route to Asia, black pepper originated in India and the Spice Islands (Indonesia). It is now grown commercially in the warm climates of India, Indonesia, Burma, Madagascar, and Brazil. Black pepper varies in aroma, pungency, and size depending upon where it is grown.

Perhaps black pepper has become basic to most cuisines because it contains a stimulant called piperine, which triggers the flow of saliva and gastric juices that aid digestion. Because black pepper loses flavor after it is ground, it is best to grind whole peppercorns just before using.

Caraway seeds Caraway is a biennial that grows wild in Europe, Asia, and North Africa. Both the seeds and the leaves have a mild flavor similar to parsley and dill and are used for culinary purposes. In Germany and Austria, the seeds are used in breads, cakes, cheeses, sauerkraut, fresh cabbage dishes, and salads. Find caraway seeds in the spice racks of most supermarkets. As for the leaves, you will probably have to grow your own.

Cardamom is a perennial of the ginger family that grows wild in South India, where it was obtained by European caravans on the spice route and then taken to Europe. Today, cardamom is not only an essential spice used in curries and pilafs in India and Pakistan but also has been adopted by cooks in northern Europe, Scandinavia, and Russia, where it appears in breads, pastries, custards, pickled herring, punches, and hot spiced wine. Always buy whole cardamom because it loses its essential oils and flavor quickly once it is ground. Whole cardamom is available in the spice section of most supermarkets.

Spices

Cayenne These tiny, narrow red chile peppers originated on Cayenne Island, the capital of French Guiana. Now cayenne has become the generic name for finely ground red pepper made from chiles grown in many places. As a result, cayenne varies in hotness. In many dishes, a pinch of cayenne is used to "wake up" other flavors. When adding cayenne to a dish, a rule of thumb is to use $\frac{1}{8}$ teaspoon or less per 4 servings along with the other spices. Cayenne's raw taste may be mitigated by dry-roasting a little of the powder or sautéing it in a little oil. Look for cayenne in the spice section of most supermarkets.

Cinnamon Indigenous to Burma, cinnamon bark is peeled from the branches of a small evergreen shrub and dried in the sun. Cinnamon is used in a myriad of savory and sweet dishes in many cuisines. Its essential oil contains phenols, which reduce the growth of bacteria.

The best-quality cinnamon sticks are pale brown and look like small rolls of dried paper. Whole sticks of cinnamon can be used to flavor soups, stews, hot drinks, and syrups. Use ground cinnamon in baked goods, puddings, and savory dishes. Cinnamon sticks are found in the spice section of supermarkets, specialty shops, and natural food stores. Ground cinnamon is universally available.

Cloves are cultivated on the islands of Southeast Asia, Zanzibar, Madagascar, and the West Indies. The thirty-foot-high evergreen tree that produces cloves flourishes best near the sea. The pink buds of these trees are picked and dried on palm leaf mats over gentle heat until they turn reddish brown.

Cloves vary in appearance and pungency according to their source and age. They are used frequently in soup stocks, desserts, spiced wine, liqueurs, and many types of curries and pickles. The freshest cloves are round, plump, and oily. Oil of clove is a powerful antiseptic. When possible, grind whole cloves just before using and use discreetly to avoid overpowering other flavors. Whole and ground cloves are available in most grocery stores and supermarkets.

Coriander Even though coriander is the seed of the cilantro plant, it has a very different flavor and character than fresh cilantro. While cilantro adds a fresh, clean fragrance and burst of flavor to food, coriander adds a subtle foundation of flavor that underscores other, sharper spices.

Coriander is popular in dishes throughout the Middle East and Near East, North Africa, the Balkans, Spain, Portugal, Mexico, and South America. It is the basic spice in Indian, Indonesian, and Malaysian curries. Coriander's seeds and oil are

Spices

used in baked goods, liqueurs, and condiments. Roast whole coriander before using to bring out its aroma and flavor. Coriander may be purchased in Indian shops and in the spice section of most supermarkets.

Cumin This annual plant grows primarily in Malta, Sicily, India, the Middle East, and the North African coast. In Mediterranean countries, cumin was used both medicinally and as a substitute for pepper. Many North Americans now know cumin through Mexican, Indian, and North African dishes.

Cumin is available whole or ground, but the whole seeds retain their flavor longer. Briefly roast whole seeds in a dry skillet on low heat before grinding. Whole and ground cumin are available in the spice section of most supermarkets.

Curry powder The word *curry* may be derived from the Tamil word *kari,* which means "a sauce." Over time it has come to mean hot, spicy dishes containing curry spices and originating in the East. Commercial curry powders are a staple in the spice section of almost any grocery store or supermarket, although these premixed powders are rarely used in India's highly refined and distinctive cuisine.

You can easily make a flavorful curry powder to suit your own taste and the dishes you enjoy preparing. Curry powder most often includes black pepper, red chiles, cloves, cinnamon, cardamom, cumin, dried curry leaves, fenugreek, dried ginger, mustard seed, mace, nutmeg, and allspice. Toast cumin, fenugreek, and mustard seeds in a heavy skillet on low heat to bring out their flavor and aroma before grinding.

Fennel seeds These licorice-flavored seeds are similar to anise seeds, but are milder, sweeter flavored, and plumper. They are harvested from the common fennel plant, a perennial in the parsley family with umbelliferous flowers and feathery fern-like leaves. Use whole fennel seeds in biscuits, marinades, and strudels, and add ground fennel to soups, stews, curries, and sauces. Fennel seeds add a complex depth that can fool people's taste buds, making them think there's meat in the dish. To elicit the most flavor, toast the seeds and grind them just before using.

Ginger Whole, dried ginger, available in Asian, Middle Eastern, and Indian markets, may be pounded or ground to release essential oils, and then sifted to remove the fibers. Ground ginger, which doesn't have the heat and bright flavor of fresh, is available in the spice section of most grocery stores and supermarkets. Do not substitute ground ginger for freshly grated ginger in our recipes. (See page 364 for fresh ginger root.)

Spices

Nutmeg is the seed of a fruit that looks like a plum, which grows on an evergreen tree native to the Philippines and some of the Indonesian Islands. After the Portuguese sailed to the Spice Islands (Indonesia) in 1512, nutmeg became more widely used, and it is now grown in the West Indies.

The color of nutmeg ranges from light to dark brown. Grate the whole spice for the strongest, most aromatic flavor. Nutmeg is used sparingly in both sweet and savory dishes, including baked goods, puddings, cheese dishes, punches, spicy stews, and casseroles. It is poisonous in large quantities and may cause sleepiness. Whole and ground nutmeg are available in most supermarkets.

Paprika, Hungarian or Spanish Paprika is made from the dried flesh of mild, sweet peppers; however, the Hungarian version is more pungent and may be either mild or hot. This sweet or slightly hot bright red powder is essential for Hungarian goulash, paprikash, and many Spanish and Hungarian dishes and can add a decorative dash of color as a garnish. Mild paprika is found in many corner grocery stores and supermarkets; look for Hungarian paprika in specialty food shops and supermarkets with an extensive spice selection.

Red pepper flakes These crushed, dried red chiles are available in the spice section of most supermarkets and Asian markets. Brands of red pepper flakes vary greatly in size, hotness, and the number of seeds. Thai red pepper flakes tend to be the hottest. Test each batch for hotness before using.

Saffron These reddish-orange, thread-like filaments are the dried stigmas of the saffron crocus. Saffron, which may have originated in Greece and Asia Minor, was used by Persians and Phoenicians before it was brought to Spain by Arabs in about A.D. 900. In Spain, where most saffron is presently cultivated, the stigmas are painstakingly gathered by hand. One pound of whole saffron or saffron powder requires 75,000 to 250,000 filaments!

Saffron imparts a bright yellow color and an intriguing flavor to Spanish, Portuguese, and Provençal rice dishes, sauces, stews, and soups, in particular, bouillabaisse and other fish soups. To get the most flavor, pinch and rub a few threads between your fingers and add them to the broth at the last minute, or let the saffron soak for 5 minutes in a little of the hot liquid before adding it to the pot.

Good saffron is less than a year old, with a brilliant orange color and strong perfume. It is very expensive, so beware of bargains — you may not be getting a high-quality saffron. Do not use tumeric as a substitute for saffron. Look for saffron in specialty shops and in the gourmet section of the supermarket.

Spices

Sichuan peppercorns (Szechuan peppercorns) Unrelated to black peppercorns or chiles, Sichuan peppercorns are reddish brown with a mild flavor and spicy, woodsy fragrance. They are native to the province of Sichuan, in China. Look for whole Sichuan peppercorns in Chinese markets and supermarkets with an extensive spice section. Keep peppercorns in a tightly covered jar.

Star anise (Chinese anise) The star-shaped fruit of a small evergreen tree related to the magnolia family, star anise grows in southern China and Southeast Asia. Its seeds are smooth and oval shaped. Most often used whole in cooking, star anise pods impart a more earthy, pungent, cinnamon-like flavor than anise seeds (from an herbaceous plant) with their stronger licorice-like flavor. A substitute can be Chinese five-spice powder, which contains star anise and is sold in Asian groceries. Whole star anise pods may be purchased in Asian markets and in supermarkets with a well-stocked spice section.

To use star anise, break off one or two of the star-shaped points, enclose in cheesecloth or a tea ball, and immerse in the hot liquid of your soup or stew.

Turmeric (Indian saffron) This bright yellowish-orange powder comes from a perennial rhizome (underground stem) native to Southeast Asia. A relative of ginger, it now grows in tropical places throughout the world. In India and Southeast Asia, it is sometimes used fresh. To obtain the commercial spice, the rhizomes are boiled and dried in the sun, the skin is removed, and it is then ground into a powder.

Turmeric is used to dye cloth and to add color to food, such as mustard, pickles, and relishes. It is used liberally in the cuisine of India, where it is considered an aid to digestion. Do not substitute turmeric for saffron, which looks similar but has a very different flavor. Turmeric is widely available in supermarkets and Indian stores.

Spinach A delectable, tangy green that pairs well with feta, Cheddar, and other salty cheeses. Its deep green color provides a welcome contrast to lighter-hued lettuces. Spinach is a good source of beta carotene and vitamins A, C, and E. Choose crisp, unspotted, dark green leaves.

> To prepare **spinach,** remove tough stems, rinse thoroughly to remove sand, and drain.

Wrapped in paper or cotton towels to absorb moisture, enclosed in a plastic bag, and refrigerated in the crisper, it will keep for up to a week.

Star fruit (*carambola*) This ribbed, yellow, oblong fruit becomes a perfect five-pointed star when sliced. It requires no peeling or seeding. Its tangy, citrusy flavor, which ranges from sweet to tart according to variety, has been compared to lemons, pineapples, grapes, and plums.

A delicious addition to desserts and salads, star fruit is high in fiber, potassium, and vitamins A and C. Although it is available year-round in supermarkets with an extensive produce section, the peak season for star fruit is from August to mid-February. Choose firm fruit and allow it to ripen to a golden yellow with thin brown edges along the ribs. Ripe star fruit lasts for about 2 weeks in the refrigerator.

Sumac This unusual ingredient is as integral to Middle Eastern dishes as lemon is to Mediterranean cuisine. Milder than lemon,

with a sour, fruity, pleasantly astringent taste, sumac's extracted juice or powder is used to flavor drinks, salads, and spicy fish stews.

Sun-dried tomatoes Originally an Italian specialty, primarily from the region of Emilia-Romagna, sun-dried tomatoes now appear on this side of the Atlantic on menus in restaurants, in supermarkets, and even in prepared foods. The finest sun-dried tomatoes are split in half, the bitter-tasting seeds removed, and the fruit spread on grates to dry in a well-ventilated area shaded from the sun.

At Moosewood, we enjoy the chewy texture and mild, slightly sweet flavor of sun-dried tomatoes in soups, sauces, salad dressings, and stuffings. Sun-dried tomatoes are usually found in the Italian section of well-stocked supermarkets. We recommend the plain dried tomatoes, not those packed in oil, which have both a higher price and a higher fat content.

> To use **sun-dried tomatoes**, either soak the tomatoes in very hot water for 15 to 30 minutes or place them in a heatproof bowl, cover with boiling water, and steep for about 10 minutes. Drain well.

Sweet potatoes (*yams*) In the United States, these tubers are almost always *Ipomoea batatas,* a genus of the morning glory family native to South America. Most tan, red, and dark brown "yams" found in North American markets are really

sweet potatoes. Two varieties of "batatas" or sweet potatoes are sold commercially: pale yellow ones with a dry, fluffy interior and reddish-orange ones that are moist and juicy. At Moosewood, we use sweet potatoes in dishes from the cuisines of Africa, India, the Caribbean, southern United States, South America, and Southeast Asia. They can be found in most groceries or supermarkets.

True yams belong to *Dioscorea,* of the amaryllis/lily family and are native to West Africa. They have white flesh and a rough brown exterior, and they only grow in tropical countries. In fact, 90 percent of the world's true yams are still cultivated in Africa. A few are grown in the Deep South of the United States, but are rarely shipped north, although you will occasionally find them in urban Spanish or Asian markets. True yams have a quite different texture and flavor and cannot be substituted for sweet potatoes in our recipes.

Tabasco sauce see **hot pepper sauce**.

Tahini This thick, smooth, creamy tan paste is made from unroasted hulled sesame seeds. It is widely used in Mediterranean, Middle Eastern, Asian, and North African cuisines, and especially in Greek, Turkish, and Chinese dishes. At Moosewood, we use tahini in soups, sauces, salad dressings, and desserts. A little bit can add a wealth of richness.

Do not confuse tahini with sesame paste or sesame butter,

a product made from roasted unhulled sesame seeds that is a thicker, darker, stronger-flavored paste. Look for tahini in Middle Eastern and Greek grocery stores and in the ethnic section of supermarkets.

Tamarind This highly acidic, tart fruit is the pod of a tree in the bean family that is cultivated in India, Burma, East Africa, and the West Indies. The acid in the soft pulp is sometimes used as a laxative and for reducing fevers. In Indian cooking, tamarind is used to flavor soups, curries, chutneys, sauces, and beverages.

> **Tamarind** is available in many forms: concentrate, paste, pulp, and fresh pods. The concentrate can be added to a simmering dish or dissolved first in water. The pulp should be soaked and mashed, and its soaking liquid added to cooking or beverages.

In a pinch, fresh lime juice or white vinegar may be substituted. Look for tamarind in the Indian or produce section of supermarkets or in Indian and Asian groceries.

Tempeh Originally from Indonesia, this cultured soybean product is used as a high-protein substitute for meat. Valued for its chewy texture, it also absorbs flavors well. Tempeh usually comes frozen and is most easily cut into bite-sized pieces when partially thawed. At Moosewood, we use tempeh in chilis, sandwiches, stuffings, and sautés. Ready-to-use commercially prepared tempeh is available in natural food stores and sometimes in supermarkets with a natural food section.

Thai basil Also called holy basil or *ocimum sanctum,* this herb is a member of the mint family. It has small, serrated, dark green or reddish-green leaves and small, dark purple flower stalks. Its flavor is slightly sharper than ordinary basil. Thai basil is frequently used in Southeast Asian dishes. If unavailable, a good substitute is a combination of basil and mint leaves. Look for this herb in the produce section of supermarkets that carry fresh herbs, or look for seeds and cultivate it in your garden.

Tofu *(bean curd)* We can trace the origin of this high-protein staple, which is low in saturated fat, back to China. The technique was passed on to Japan in the tenth or eleventh century. It has since become the main source of protein for the people of China, Japan, and Korea and is an important staple in India and Southeast Asia and in vegetarian diets throughout the world.

Tofu is made from soy milk (extracted from soybeans) to which a coagulant has been added. The curds that form are separated from the whey and molded into cakes of varying firmness. Tofu is usually sold in blocks that can vary in weight, but usually range from 10 to 16 ounces. It is often packed in water and found in the refrigerated dairy section of the supermarket. Tofu may also be purchased in vacuum-packed containers that have an indefinite shelf life at room temperature if unopened. Once opened, this highly perishable food should be stored in the refrigerator in a container of water that is changed daily to maintain freshness.

> **Frozen tofu** To change the character of tofu, place it on a tray, cover it with plastic wrap, and freeze it for 6 to 8 hours; then defrost it and squeeze out the water to make a crumbly, dense, chewy product good for fillings, soups, and stews. At Moosewood, we grate it in a food processor for fillings and stuffings. Be sure to use defrosted tofu immediately; it will remain fresh for only a short time.

Silken tofu is sometimes referred to as "Japanese-style tofu." It is made with a higher ratio of soybeans to water than regular tofu, which means it also has a higher protein and fat content. Rich and mild, with a delicate, silky texture, silken tofu can be easily puréed for dairyless drinks and dressings. Firm, soft, and "lite" silken tofu is available in vacuum-packed boxes in the produce or Asian section of many supermarkets and in Asian groceries and natural food stores.

Tofu-kan is the brand name of our locally made, baked seasoned tofu which is similar to Chinese five-spice bean curd found in Asian markets. Another similar product is made by "Smoke and Fire." These ready-to-use products may be sliced and added to soups, salads, sandwiches, and sautés, or shredded for use in fillings. Look for these convenient tofu products in supermarkets and natural food stores on the East Coast.

Tomatillos *(tomatitos verdes, Mexican green tomatoes, tomatoes verdes)*   A close kin of ground cherries, Cape gooseberries, and Chinese lanterns, these plum-sized fruits resemble small, firm, green tomatoes. Under their tissue-thin, papery husks is a sticky, smooth skin. They have a tart, lemony flavor and are high in vitamins C and K.

Tomatillos are used in many Mexican and southwestern United States dishes. Look for them year-round in the produce section of well-stocked supermarkets. Choose firm, dry fruit with clean, tight husks. Tomatillos will keep in the refrigerator for 2 to 4 weeks.

> Husk, stem, and chop raw **tomatillos** for salads, sandwiches, dressings, or gazpacho and other cold soups. To use in sauces and salsas, remove the husks and stems, cover with water, and simmer until soft. Drain, allow to cool, and use immediately or freeze for later use.

Tree ears see **Mushrooms**.

Turnips   This hardy vegetable, the "potato" of ancient European cuisines, has been cultivated for about 5,000 years. High in potassium, both the root and leaves are edible. The common white and purple variety is most tender, crisp, and sweet in the spring and fall. Winter turnips are larger, with a woody texture and stronger flavor.

Choose small, smooth, heavy, firm vegetables with unsprouted tops. Turnips will winter over when kept in a root cellar, or will keep for a week or two in a plastic bag in the refrigerator. They may be more readily available in supermarkets in cooler climates.

Turnip greens are a rich source of vitamins A and C, iron, potassium, folic acid, and fiber. They are the best source of calcium among the leafy greens.

> **Turnip greens** are not ones to solo; they are bitter greens that do best in the company of milder, sweeter greens. To reduce their bitterness, parboil them in water for about 3 minutes before using them.

Peak availability is from November through March. Look for small, tender, moist leaves bunched as greens. You won't find them attached to turnips — they're an altogether different plant! Warmth dries and toughens these highly perishable greens and increases their bitterness, so avoid bunches displayed in warm conditions and use as soon as possible. To store,

rinse in cool water, wrap in a cotton towel, enclose in a plastic bag, and refrigerate for up to 2 or 3 days.

Udon noodles   These round, square, or flat hearty Japanese noodles are made of wheat flour, salt, and water. Traditionally used in broth and delicious in salads, udon noodles may be interchanged with soba noodles (page 378), which are made with buckwheat flour. Udon noodles are usually available in 12-ounce or 1-pound packages in the Asian section of supermarkets and in natural food stores and Japanese groceries.

Wakame see **Seaweed**.

Water chestnuts   These fleshy underwater stems from which a type of grass sprouts are cultivated throughout China and Southeast Asia. They are so named because they are grown in water and their outer skin is chestnut colored. Their flesh is mild, crisp, sweet, and crunchy.

Anyone lucky enough to try fresh water chestnuts will discover a rare delicacy, but, alas, most of us are only able to obtain the canned variety. Water chestnuts contribute a fresh, crisp texture to Asian soups, salads, and sautés. They are available in 8-ounce cans in Asian food stores or in the Asian section of many supermarkets; rinse well before using.

Watercress   This perennial aquatic plant is high in vitamins and minerals and is a member of the *cruciferous* family. It roots readily in clean, flowing water. Both the stems and the pungent, peppery leaves are edible. Watercress is mildest early in the spring; after it blossoms, it tends to become more bitter and pungent. Like arugula and parsley, it adds a spicy note to mixed salad greens.

> To reduce the strong, bitter flavor that **watercress** may impart to cooked dishes, first plunge it into boiling salted water for a minute.

Select watercress with perky, dark green leaves and avoid any that has wilted, yellowing leaves with dark, bruised spots. Because it is extremely perishable, store watercress in the refrigerator wrapped in a damp towel or immerse the stems in a glass of water and cover the tops loosely with plastic. Watercress can be found in specialty markets and in the produce section of most supermarkets.

Wheatberries are whole grains of wheat with only the hull removed. Most wheatberries are ground into flour or processed to make cereals, bread, pasta, cracked wheat, and bulghur, but they can also be purchased whole and cooked like rice and barley for use in hearty grain salads, pilafs, and fillings. Wheatberries are carried in natural food stores and in the natural food section of some supermarkets.

> To prepare **wheatberries**, keep in mind that 1/2 cup of raw wheatberries will yield about 1 1/4 cups cooked. In a covered saucepan, first soak the raw

wheatberries at room temperature in ample water to cover for 8 to 24 hours. (We experimented with cooking without presoaking, but it didn't work.) Drain, rinse, and return to the saucepan. Add fresh water to cover the wheatberries by 2 inches. Bring to a boil, lower the heat, cover, and simmer until tender, about 1 to 1 1/2 hours. Drain well. Chill for about 20 minutes before using or store for later use. Drained, cooked wheatberries can be stored in a sealed container in the refrigerator for up to 1 week and in the freezer for several months.

Wonton wrappers Invented before noodles, wontons are the earliest recorded stuffed food. The use of wontons in soup was first recorded in the Tang period (A.D. 618–907). For hundreds of years, these wheat and egg dough wrappings have been made at home and stuffed with vegetables, meat, or fish.

Now commercial wonton wrappers, round or square with varying thicknesses, are available both fresh and frozen in Asian markets and in many supermarkets. Stuffed wontons are also available in the freezer section of some supermarkets, but most contain meat or seafood, so vegetarians should read the labels. Add them frozen to simmering soups or thaw them first before frying.

Worcestershire sauce, vegetarian This zesty, savory condiment adds a lively flavor to soups,

sandwiches, sauces, dressings, and grilled vegetables and fish. Edward and Sons Trading Company, Inc., in California produces a delicious sauce called The Wizard's Vegetarian Worcestershire Sauce that almost duplicates the original classic version, which contains sardines. Try a natural food store for this or some other vegetarian Worcestershire sauce.

Yogurt cheese (drained yogurt, yogurt cream) Any yogurt without gelatin can be made into yogurt cheese, which is a thickened yogurt from which most of the water has been drained. It resembles sour cream in texture and can often be used as its lower-fat or nonfat substitute. Use it in soups and salad dressings, as a topping on fruit, or as a filling in tarts or cheesecakes. One quart of nonfat yogurt will yield about 2 cups of yogurt cheese; higher-fat yogurts will yield slightly more.

> To make **yogurt cheese**, line a colander with two or three layers of cheesecloth or one layer of overlapping coffee filters and set it in a large bowl. Spoon the yogurt into the colander and cover it with a plate or plastic wrap. Refrigerate for 3 to 6 hours or overnight, depending on how thick you want the yogurt cheese to be. For quicker results, weight the plate with a pound or two: The yogurt cheese will be ready in a couple of hours. Store yogurt cheese in a closed container in the refrigerator for up to 1 week.

Special Lists

CHILDREN'S FAVORITES   Children can have food preferences as definite and quirky as any adult's, but they can also be adventurous explorers — and they tend to know a good thing when they see it. The items on this list have interesting textures, are not too spicy, catch the attention, go down easy, and/or are fun to make. Check the Quick & Easy list to see which dishes are a double bonus: Kids love them *and* they're a cinch to make.

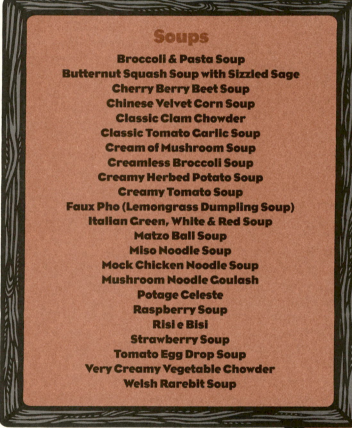

Soups

Broccoli & Pasta Soup
Butternut Squash Soup with Sizzled Sage
Cherry Berry Beet Soup
Chinese Velvet Corn Soup
Classic Clam Chowder
Classic Tomato Garlic Soup
Cream of Mushroom Soup
Creamless Broccoli Soup
Creamy Herbed Potato Soup
Creamy Tomato Soup
Faux Pho (Lemongrass Dumpling Soup)
Italian Green, White & Red Soup
Matzo Ball Soup
Miso Noodle Soup
Mock Chicken Noodle Soup
Mushroom Noodle Goulash
Potage Celeste
Raspberry Soup
Risi e Bisi
Strawberry Soup
Tomato Egg Drop Soup
Very Creamy Vegetable Chowder
Welsh Rarebit Soup

Salads

Balinese Rice Salad
Chef Salad à la Moosewood
Dave's Mom's Best Slaw
Fruit with Cranberry Currant Dressing
Honey Mustard Green Beans Vinaigrette
Marinated Broccoli & Carrots
Tunisian Carrot Salad

Accompaniments

Anadama Bread
Featherlight Blue Mountain Biscuits
Herbed Cheese Quick Bread
Moosewood Ginger Miso Dressing
Moosewood House Dressing
Popovers

FESTIVE BRUNCHES & BUFFETS   These light and attractive dishes are ones we like to prepare and share at special get-togethers. All of them are lovely to look at, some make perfect centerpieces, and most sit well, an attribute that keeps a buffet spread looking its best throughout the entire event.

Soups

Bourride
(Provençal Soup with Aioli)

Butternut Squash Soup
with Sizzled Sage

Creamy Onion & Fontina Soup

Faux Pho (Lemongrass
Dumpling Soup)

Korean Pine Nut Porridge

Mango Soup

Matzo Ball Soup

Navarin of Spring Vegetables

Scandinavian Dried
Fruit Soup

Strawberry Soup

Venetian Seafood Stew

Salads

Asparagus & Fennel Pasta Salad
Balinese Rice Salad
Balkan Roasted Vegetable Salad
Bean Purée with Seven Savories
Caesar Salad
Chef Salad à la Moosewood
Curried Potato Salad
Fig & Endive Salad
Florida Salad with Ginger Dressing
French Barley Salad
Fruit with Cranberry Currant Dressing
Gado Gado
Greek Pasta Salad
Harvest Rice Salad
Lemon Rice & Seafood Salad
Lentil, Rice & Fruit Salad
Mussel Salad
Persian Rice & Pistachio Salad
Roasted Garlic Aioli Salad
Seafood & Chermoulia Couscous Salad
Seafood Paella Salad
Seafood Salad with Salsa Verde
Simple Tomato Salads
Speltberry & Fruit Salad
Teriyaki Fish & Soba Noodle Salad
Thai Rice & Mushroom Salad
Tostada Salad
Tropical Fruit & Shrimp Salad
Vietnamese Shrimp & Noodle Salad

Accompaniments

Anadama Bread
Featherlight Blue Mountain Biscuits
Focaccia
Marinated Chickpeas or White Beans
Marinated Mushrooms
Popovers
Scallion Pancakes
Southern Wheat-free Cornbread

HEALTHY LOW-FAT FAVORITES At Moosewood, one of our goals is to create really good-tasting food that's good for you too, so there's no struggle to eat right—just more and more delightful options. All of the items on this list contain less than 7 grams of fat per serving. In fact, more than three quarters of them contain less than 5.5 grams of fat per serving. Those highlighted in color derive only 20 percent or less of their calories from fat and fall well within the recommended guidelines for a healthy diet. * Combining a soup, salad, and bread from this list or making a combo plate of half-sized servings of two or three complementary salads will create a satisfying low-fat meal. Or pair one low-fat choice with a higher-fat choice: The result still can be a reasonably moderate overall daily fat intake.

Salads

Asian Beet & Tofu Salad

Asian Spinach & Orange Salad

Asparagus & Snow Pea Salad

Asparagus Vinaigrette

Bean & Radicchio Salad

Bean Sprout Salad

Brussels Sprouts & Carrot Salad
(with mayonnaise dressing)

Butternut Squash with Spicy Cranberry Sauce

Celeriac Remoulade

East Indian Fruit Salad

Fennel & Arugula Salad with Grapefruit

Fennel Salad with Blue Cheese

Five-Herb Salad

Fruit with Cranberry Currant Dressing

Honey Mustard Green Beans Vinaigrette

"Japanese" Tofu Salad

Kale Salad

Kiwi, Orange & Baby Greens

Marinated Broccoli & Carrots

Mediterranean Orange & Olive Salad

Pilwun's Daikon Salad

Seaweed Salad

Simple Tomato Salads (Farm-style)

Spicy Cucumber Salad

Thai Noodle Salad

Thai Rice & Mushroom Salad

Tropical Fruit & Shrimp Salad

Tunisian Carrot Salad

Vietnamese Cellophane Noodle Salad

Accompaniments

Anadama Bread

Cilantro Peanut Pesto

"Creamy" Fresh Herbed Tofu Dressing

Featherlight Blue Mountain Biscuits

Filo Croutons

Focaccia

Fried Shallots

Goat Cheese Toasts

Jalapeño Cream

Low-fat Honey Dijon Vinaigrette

Low-fat Tomato Basil Dressing

Luscious Lemon Tahini Dressing

Marinated Chickpeas or White Beans

Marinated Mushrooms

Our Special Gluten-free Bread

Parsley Pesto

Popovers

Pumpernickel Croutons

Southern Wheat-free Cornbread

Spiced Paneer

Soups

Albondigas Soup
Algerian Tomato Soup with Vermicelli
Artichoke Avgolemono
Artichoke Heart Soup
Asian Bean Curd Soup
Asian Soup Stock
August Melon Soup
Autumn Minestrone
Azuki Bean Soup
Back to Your Roots Soup
Baked Bean Soup
Basic Light Vegetable Stock
Broccoli Rabe & Rice Soup
Caribbean Shrimp & Vegetable Soup
Cherry Almond Soup
Cherry Berry Beet Soup
Chinese Velvet Corn Soup
Chlodnik
Choklay's Tibetan Lentil Soup
Corn Chowder
Creamless Broccoli Soup
Creamy Herbed Carrot Soup
Creamy Herbed Potato Soup
Creamy Orange Soup
Cucumber Yogurt Soup
Curried Cauliflower Soup
Curried Zucchini Soup
Dark Vegetable Stock
Eastern European Vegetable Stew
Ecuadorian Quinoa & Vegetable Soup
Egyptian Red Lentil Soup
Everyday Split Pea Soup
Farinata
Fassoulada
Faux Pho
Fennel Vichyssoise
Fragrant Lemongrass Fruit Soup
Garlic Stock
Gingered Carrot Soup
Gingered Plum Soup
Golden Gazpacho
Golden Summer Soup
Hot & Sour Shrimp Soup
Hungarian Green Bean Soup

Jamaican Tomato Soup
Liberian Black-eyed Pea Soup
Mango Soup
Middle Eastern Chickpea Soup
Minted Pea Soup
Miso Noodle Soup
Mock Chicken Stock
Mole de Olla Rodriguez
Moroccan Root Vegetable Stew
Mushroom Noodle Goulash
Navarin of Spring Vegetables
Ozoni
Parsnip Pear Soup
Peach Soup
Pepperpot
Persian Yogurt Rice Soup
Potage Celeste
Raspberry Soup
Roasted Vegetable Stock
San Juan Shrimp & Rice Soup
Scandinavian Dried Fruit Soup
Southeast Asian Rice & Tofu Soup
Spiced Mexican Squash Stew
Spicy Carrot Peanut Soup
Spicy Tofu & Greens Soup
Spring Minestrone
Strawberry Soup
Summer Minestrone
Tamarind Pineapple Fish Soup
Texas Two-Bean Soup
Tomato Egg Drop Soup
Tomato & Kale Soup with Barley
Tomato Rasam
Tortilla Soup
Tuscan Bean Soup
Venetian Seafood Stew
Westphalian Vegetable Stew
Wild Rice & Asparagus Soup
Wild Rice & Mushroom Soup
Winter Minestrone
Ybor City Garbanzo Soup
Yellow Pepper Purée
Zucchini & Rice Soup

LOW-CARBOHYDRATE LIST   Since many people have started counting their carbs (or at least considering their carbohydrate intake in the big picture), we thought this list of recipes containing just 10 grams of carbohydrates per serving or fewer could be helpful.

Salads

Alabama Hot Slaw
Asian Beet & Tofu Salad
Asparagus & Snow Pea Salad
Asparagus Vinaigrette
Celeriac Remoulade
Chef Salad à la Moosewood
Fennel Salad with Blue Cheese
Five-Herb Salad
Marinated Broccoli & Carrots
Mexican Shrimp & Spinach Salad
Nepalese Egg Salad
North African Roasted Cauliflower
Pilwun's Daikon Salad
Pinzimonio
Roasted Green Tomato & Feta Salad
Seaweed Salad
Simple Tomato Salads
Spicy Cucumber Salad
Syrian Beet Salad
Wilted Spinach & Portabella Mushrooms

Soups

Asian Soup Stock
Basic Light Vegetable Stock
Celery Roquefort Soup
Dark Vegetable Stock
Garlic Stock
Mock Chicken Stock
Roasted Vegetable Stock
Sopa de Camarones

Accompaniments

Baked Seasoned Tofu
Best Blue Cheese Dressing
Cilantro Lime Pesto
Cilantro Peanut Pesto
Curried Croutons
Filo Croutons
Fried Shallots
Jalapeño Cream
Low-fat Honey Dijon Vinaigrette
Low-fat Tomato Basil Dressing
Luscious Lemon Tahini Dressing
Marinated Chickpeas or White Beans
Marinated Mushrooms
Moosewood Ginger Miso Dressing
Moosewood House Dressing
Parsley Pesto
Pumpernickel Croutons
Spiced Paneer
Versatile Vinaigrette
Zesty Feta Garlic Dressing

QUICK & EASY All of these recipes can be prepared in 30 minutes or less! Bear in mind that many of the other recipes in this book take less than 30 minutes to assemble and then cook unattended.

Soups

Artichoke Heart Soup
Caribbean Shrimp & Vegetable Soup
Cherry Almond Soup
Classic Tomato Garlic Soup
Cream of Spinach Soup
Creamy Orange Soup
Cucumber Yogurt Soup
Gingered Plum Soup
Italian Green, White & Red Soup
Korean Pine Nut Porridge
Ozoni
Peach Soup
Raspberry Soup
Sopa de Camarones
Strawberry Soup
Tomato Egg Drop Soup
Zucchini & Rice Soup

Salads

Alabama Hot Slaw
Arugula & Warm Mozzarella Salad
Asparagus & Snow Pea Salad
Asparagus Vinaigrette
Avocado Seitan Salad
Bean Purée with Seven Savories
Bean & Radicchio Salad
Bean Sprout Salad
Broccoli Pine Nut Pasta Salad
Caesar Salad
Celeriac Remoulade
Classic Sichuan Noodles
Dave's Mom's Best Slaw
Fattoush (Savory Bread Salad)
Fennel Salad with Blue Cheese
Fig & Endive Salad
Five-Herb Salad
Fresh Pear & Blue Cheese Salad
Fruit with Cranberry Currant Dressing
Honey Mustard Green Beans Vinaigrette
Indian Green Beans & Red Peppers
Kiwi, Orange & Baby Greens
Mediterranean Orange & Olive Salad
Mexican Chickpea Salad
North African Couscous Salad
Pinzimonio
Simple Tomato Salads
Spicy Cucumber Salad
Spinach with Cilantro Cashew Dressing
Thai Tossed Salad
Tomato Flowers
Tropical Fruit & Shrimp Salad
Wilted Spinach & Portabella Mushrooms

Accompaniments

Best Blue Cheese Dressing
Cilantro Lime Pesto
Curried Croutons
Featherlight Blue Mountain Biscuits
Filo Croutons
Fried Shallots
Low-fat Honey Dijon Vinaigrette
Low-fat Tomato Basil Dressing
Luscious Lemon Tahini Dressing
Marinated Chickpeas or White Beans
Marinated Mushrooms
Moosewood Ginger Miso Dressing
Moosewood House Dressing
Parsley Pesto
Popovers
Pumpernickel Croutons
Scallion Pancakes
Spiced Paneer
Versatile Vinaigrette
Zesty Feta Garlic Dressing

VEGAN LIST A vegan diet is based solely on plant foods. All of the following recipes adhere to vegan guidelines and contain no animal products, dairy products, or honey.

Salads

Alabama Hot Slaw

Andean Quinoa & Corn Salad

Asian Beet & Tofu Salad

Asian Spinach & Orange Salad

Avocado Seitan Salad

Bean & Radicchio Salad

Bean Sprout Salad

Broccoli Pine Nut Pasta Salad

Broiled Tofu & Sugar Snap Peas

Bulghur Grape Salad

Caribbean Rice Salad

Classic Sichuan Noodles

Curried Rice Salad

Curried Tofu Salad

Farfalle e Fagiole Salad

Fattoush (Savory Bread Salad)

Five-Herb Salad

Florida Salad with Ginger Dressing

Fruit with Cranberry Currant Dressing

Cado Cado

Golden Tomato Avocado Salad

Harvest Rice Salad

Hijiki Rice Salad

Indian Green Beans & Red Peppers

Indonesian Tahu Goreng

"Japanese" Tofu Salad

Kale Salad

Lentil, Rice & Fruit Salad

Lobio (Georgian Red Bean Salad)

Louisiana Black-eyed Pea Salad

Mediterranean Orange & Olive Salad

Mexican Chickpea Salad

North African Couscous Salad

North African Roasted Cauliflower

Persian Rice & Pistachio Salad

Pilwun's Daikon Salad

Pinzimonio

Roasted Potato & Tomato Salad

Roasted Red Pepper & Cauliflower Salad

Seaweed Salad

Solstice Salad

Southern Red Rice & Pecan Salad

Speltberry & Fruit Salad

Spicy Cucumber Salad

Spicy Pineapple Tofu Salad

Summer Millet Salad

Syrian Beet Salad

Thai Noodle Salad

Thai Rice & Mushroom Salad

Thai Tossed Salad

Tunisian Carrot Salad

Vietnamese Cellophane Noodle Salad

Wilted Spinach & Portabella Mushrooms

Yemiser Salata (Ethiopian Lentil Salad)

Accompaniments

Baked Seasoned Tofu
Cilantro Lime Pesto
Cilantro Peanut Pesto
Curried Croutons
Focaccia
Fried Shallots
Low-fat Honey Dijon Vinaigrette
Low-fat Tomato Basil Dressing
Luscious Lemon Tahini Dressing
Marinated Chickpeas or White Beans
Marinated Mushrooms
Moosewood Ginger Miso Dressing
Scallion Pancakes
Versatile Vinaigrette

Soups

Algerian Tomato Soup with Vermicelli
Artichoke Heart Soup
Asian Bean Curd Soup
August Melon Soup
Autumn Minestrone
Avocado Tomatillo Soup
Azuki Bean Soup
Baked Bean Soup
Black Bean & Chipotle Soup
Butternut Squash Soup with Sizzled Sage
Caribbean Sweet Potato Coconut Soup
Cherry Almond Soup
Cherry Berry Beet Soup
Choklay's Tibetan Lentil Soup
Creamless Broccoli Soup
Curried Cauliflower Soup
East African Groundnut Soup
Eastern European Vegetable Stew
Ecuadorian Quinoa & Vegetable Soup
Egyptian Red Lentil Soup
Everyday Split Pea Soup
Farinata
Fassoulada
Fast & Fresh Tomato Soup
Faux Pho (Lemongrass Dumpling Soup)
Golden Gazpacho

Grecian Isle Stew
Green & White Gumbo
Indian Roasted Eggplant Soup
Jamaican Tomato Soup
Korean Pine Nut Porridge
Liberian Black-eyed Pea Soup
Middle Eastern Chickpea Soup
Miso Noodle Soup
Mock Chicken Noodle Soup
Moroccan Root Vegetable Stew
Ozoni
Parsnip Pear Soup
Pepperpot
Roasted Red Pepper Coconut Soup
Southeast Asian Rice & Tofu Soup
Spicy Carrot Peanut Soup
Spicy Tofu & Greens Soup
Spring Minestrone
Summer Minestrone
Texas Two-Bean Soup
Tomato & Kale Soup with Barley
Tomato Rasam
Tortilla Soup
Tunisian Pumpkin Soup
Tuscan Bean Soup
Vegetable Pistou
Wild Rice & Mushroom Soup
Wonton Soup
Ybor City Garbanzo Soup

Index

Conversion Chart
EQUIVALENT IMPERIAL AND METRIC MEASUREMENTS

American cooks use standard containers, the 8-ounce cup and a tablespoon that takes exactly 16 level fillings to fill that cup level. Measuring by cup makes it very difficult to give weight equivalents, as a cup of densely packed butter will weigh considerably more than a cup of flour. The easiest way therefore to deal with cup measurements in recipes is to take the amount by volume rather than by weight. Thus the equation reads:

1 cup = 240 ml = 8 fl. oz.   ½ cup = 120 ml = 4 fl. oz.

It is possible to buy a set of American cup measures in major stores around the world.

Liquid Measures

FLUID OUNCES	U.S.	IMPERIAL	MILLILITERS
	1 teaspoon	1 teaspoon	5
¼	2 teaspoons	1 dessertspoon	10
½	1 tablespoon	1 tablespoon	14
2	¼ cup	4 tablespoons	56
4	½ cup		110
5		¼ pint or 1 gill	140
6	¾ cup		170
8	1 cup		225
10	1¼ cups	½ pint	280
15		¾ pint	420
16	2 cups		450
20	2½ cups	1 pint	560
24	3 cups		675
32	4 cups		900
36	4½ cups		1000, 1 liter
40	5 cups	2 pints or 1 quart	1120

Oven Temperature Equivalents

FAHRENHEIT	CELSIUS	GAS MARK	DESCRIPTION
225	110	¼	cool
250	130	½	
275	140	1	very slow
300	150	2	
325	170	3	slow
350	180	4	moderate
375	190	5	
400	200	6	moderately hot
425	220	7	fairly hot
450	230	8	hot
475	240	9	very hot
500	250	10	extremely hot

Equivalency Chart

Dash/pinch = less than ⅛ teaspoon

3 teaspoons = 1 tablespoon (½ fluid ounce)

2 tablespoons = ⅛ cup (1 fluid ounce)

4 tablespoons = ¼ cup (2 fluid ounces)

8 tablespoons = ½ cup (4 fluid ounces)

16 tablespoons = 1 cup (8 fluid ounces)

2 cups = 1 pint

4 cups = 1 quart

2 pints = 1 quart

4 quarts = 1 gallon

1 gram = 0.035 ounces

1 ounce = 28.35 grams

16 ounces = 1 pound (453.59 grams)

1 kilogram = 2.21 pounds

Solid Measures

U.S. AND IMPERIAL MEASURES		METRIC MEASURES	
Ounces	Pounds	Grams	Kilos
1		28	
2		56	
3½		100	
4	¼	112	
8	½	225	
9		250	¼
12	¾	340	
16	1	450	
18		500	½
27		750	¾
54		1500	1½

Equivalents for Ingredients

all-purpose flour – plain flour
coarse salt – kitchen salt
cornstarch – cornflour

eggplant – aubergine
half and half – 12% fat milk
heavy cream – double cream

light cream – single cream
lima beans – broad beans
scallion – spring onion

unbleached flour – strong, white flour
zest or peel – rind
zucchini – courgettes or marrow

About the Authors

As 1998 draws to a close, we are dotting the *i*'s and crossing the *t*'s on this cookbook, readying it for delivery to our trusty publisher. It's a landmark year for us — Moosewood celebrated its twenty-fifth anniversary. A quick look back shows we have grown bigger in every way. Although still in our original location, we've had the good fortune to be able to expand by degrees into an adjoining space. Now we have a cafe/bar with extended hours, the capacity for appetizers, morning muffins, fresh juices, espresso drinks, and mixed drinks (instead of just beer, wine, and regular coffee), almost twice as much seating for customers, twice as many entrances, three times as many restrooms, double the art walls, and a lovely space for acoustic music performances. We also have a bigger group of energetic employees, more committee meetings, increased business, more to do, more to juggle, and bigger hearts, softened by time and experience.

Seventeen of the nineteen members of the Moosewood Collective collaborated to develop these recipes and write this book. For the sake of history, we'll list ourselves in order of longevity in the ranks. Linda Dickinson, Joan Adler, and Susan Harville get royal mention for twenty-five years of service far beyond table service. In the twenty-plus-and-still-trying tier are David Hirsch, Lisa Wichman, Sara Wade Robbins, Nancy Lazarus, and Maureen Vivino. The fifteen- to nineteen-year veterans include Laura Branca, Eliana Parra, Ned Asta, Tony Del Plato, and Wynelle Stein. The under-fifteen-years "new" bloods are Kip Wilcox, Penny Goldin, Jenny Wang, and Neil Minnis.

It's been a long haul for most of us, but we'd probably do it again if we got the chance. When we rally together, we recognize our individual and collective strengths and weaknesses and sporadic moments of completely harmonious decision making. These moments feed a kind of deep respect that grows slowly, organically. The dual sense of the slow and laborious and the quick and immediate is constantly churning at Moosewood. Who knows what's next?

And maybe the real Daily Special is just those simple, unremarkable, everyday exchanges that eventually add up to the road once traveled: a quarter of a century of footsteps, hard work, sharp knives, thinking, no thinking, dishes, dirty sinks, unbelievable food, laughter, tears, spoons, camradarie, disagreements, forks, love affairs, parking tickets, excruciatingly long meetings, surprisingly brief meetings, fun-filled parties, and meaningful moments that no one can quite put a finger on. Happy birthday, Moosewood.

Look for Moosewood bottled dressings at your local market or contact us at our website
www.moosewoodrestaurant.com